Project Management

Eighth Edition

Project Management

EIGHTH EDITION

Dennis Lock

First published in 1968
Second edition 1977
Third edition 1984
Fourth edition 1988
Fifth edition 1992
Sixth edition 1996
Seventh edition 2000

This edition published by
Gower Publishing Limited
Gower House
Croft Road
Aldershot
Hampshire GU11 3HR
England

Gower
Suite 420
101 Cherry Street
Burlington
Vermont 05401-4405
USA

British Library Cataloguing in Publication Data
Lock, Dennis, 1929–
   Project management. – 8th ed.
   1. Project management
   I. Title
   658.4'04

ISBN 0–566–08578–X Hardback
     0–566–08551–8 Paperback

Library of Congress Cataloging-in-Publication Data
Lock, Dennis.
   Project management/ Dennis Lock.–8th ed.
      p. cm.
   ISBN 0–566–08578–X   ISBN 0–566–08551–8
   1. Project management. I. Title.

   T56.8 .L6 2003
   658.5—dc21   2002035443

Typeset in Times by Bournemouth Colour Press, Poole and printed in Great Britain by MPG Books Ltd., Bodmin.

Contents

Figures

Preface to the eighth edition

Once, some time ago, my fellow day-release management students and I were invited to write a 5000-word assignment as part of our first-year course work. Most of my colleagues spent many hours and late nights diligently researching this or that aspect of industry, marketing or economics for their material. Always keen to save time and effort, however, I chose to describe my own job. I think the result received an 'A-minus' but, more importantly, it seeded the first (1968) edition of this book. Now, after many subsequent years as a manager, I teach project management to MBA and MSc students. So a book originally written by a management student has been developed and improved through my management years and is now written very much with the needs of students in mind.

Project management is well supported in the literature. Excellent texts appear regularly in new editions that combine comprehensive theory with practical advice and case studies. Sometimes one or more of these admirable works are used alongside this book as recommended course texts. I am always pleased when students tell me that they prefer my book because they find it particularly approachable and easy to read. Of course, when the warm glow of satisfaction has subsided, I try to analyse the reasons and build on them. My abhorrence of unnecessary jargon and 'management speak' must be one reason. A writer must always seek to inform using plain language rather than set out to impress with words that compel the reader to have the book in one hand and a dictionary in other. So writing style is obviously important. But the text must also be easy to navigate. Readers, especially time-starved students on intensive courses, must be able to find or revisit any topic quickly. Some otherwise excellent books fall down in this respect. The chapters have to be organized in a logical sequence and, most important, everything must be comprehensively indexed.

My sequence of chapters has always been intended to track the logical progression of a project through its active life cycle from concept to closedown. There might be one or two anomalies in this respect because I have generally held back from significant restructuring that could cause inconvenience and rework for universities and other academic establishments where this book forms part of the recommended reading and where their course notes refer to particular chapters. It was necessary, however, to rearrange the chapters in Part VI to some extent to accommodate a new chapter on risk management. The total number of chapters has increased from 24 to 25.

Reproduction of very complex illustrations (large network diagrams, for instance) is not very practicable on a book page so, once again, I have reviewed every figure to ensure that it is designed and drawn for optimum clarity. The seventh edition introduced a few images captured from my computer screen that lost some definition in the printing process. All computer screen images have therefore been replaced in this edition by faithful simulations, prepared using a drawing program.

Text revisions are too numerous to list in detail, so I shall outline just a few of the more significant changes. These begin in Chapter 1, which has been extended to give more emphasis to the views of stakeholders beyond the project owner and project manager. The more mature view recognizes that the perceived success or failure of a project often depends on more than the three primary factors of time, money and quality.

Chapter 3 has been restructured to present its material in a more logical sequence.

The section on insurance that was previously placed in Chapter 6 has been updated (for which I am indebted once again to Robert Pow) and transferred to become part of Chapter 24, the completely new chapter dealing with project risk management. A new financial appraisal example, improved treatment of feasibility analysis and a short section on sensitivity analysis now strengthen the remainder of Chapter 6.

Some manual procedures, especially in the planning and resource scheduling chapters, have been removed because they are now well out of date and almost always performed using computers. While arrow networks can still play a valuable part in preliminary planning sessions and are therefore retained in Part III, the last computer program known to me that could process these networks has recently been changed to a precedence-only capability. I have therefore updated all the examples in Part IV accordingly.

Following the format of previous editions, each part of this book ends with a short list of references and further reading. These have all been checked and, where appropriate, revised. For this eighth edition I have decided to add a general bibliography of books on project management.

Although an author might write with a particular readership in mind, he or she has no control over who buys and uses their work. Early editions of this book were intended for students and fellow industrial managers who might appreciate a practical and holistic guide to project management. Experience has since revealed a readership that extends to professional people with no apparent connection to industry or projects, demonstrating that project management has grown into a core management skill, to be practised in any organization and by any professional person undertaking a programme of change.

Dennis Lock
St Albans
2002

Acknowledgements

I am grateful to the following people and organizations who have helped in different but valuable ways in the preparation of this edition.

4c Systems Limited
Association for Project Management
Microsoft Corporation
Primavera
Robert Pow
Martin Stevens
Welcom Software

Artemis Views is a registered trademark.
Microsoft Project, Microsoft Project 98, Microsoft Project 2000 and Microsoft Project 2002 are registered trademarks and Windows is a trademark of Microsoft Corporation.
Open Plan, Open Plan Professional, COBRA and *OPERA* are registered trademarks of Welcom Software Corporation.
PMI and the PMI logo are service and trademarks registered in the United States and other nations.
PMBOK, PM Network and *PMI Today* are trademarks registered in the United States and other nations.
Project Management Journal and 'Building professionalism in project management' are trademarks of the Project Management Institute, Inc.
Primavera Project Planner is a registered trademark.
4c is a trademark of 4c Systems Limited.

Part I

The nature and organization of project management

Chapter 1

The nature and purpose of project management

Project management as we know it today has evolved in order to plan, coordinate and control the complex and diverse activities of modern industrial, commercial and management change projects.

Clearly, man-made projects are not new; monuments surviving from the earliest civilizations testify to the incredible achievements of our forebears and still evoke our wonder and admiration. Modern projects, for all their technological sophistication, are not necessarily greater in scale than some of those early mammoth works. But economic pressures of the industrialized world, military defence needs, competition between rival companies, and greater regard for the value and well-being (and hence the employment costs) of working people have all led to the development of new ideas and techniques for managing projects.

All projects share one common characteristic – the projection of ideas and activities into new endeavours. The ever-present element of risk and uncertainty means that the events and tasks leading to completion can never be foretold with absolute accuracy. For some very complex or advanced projects even the possibility of successful completion might be in serious doubt.

The purpose of project management is to foresee or predict as many of the dangers and problems as possible and to plan, organize and control activities so that projects are completed as successfully as possible in spite of all the risks. This process starts before any resource is committed, and must continue until all work is finished. The primary aim of the project manager is for the final result to satisfy the project sponsor or purchaser, within the promised timescale and without using more money and other resources than those that were originally set aside or budgeted.

Much of the development in project management methods took place in the second half of the twentieth century, spurred by impatient project purchasers (who wanted their projects finished quickly so that their investments could be put to profitable use as soon as possible). Competition between nations for supremacy in weapons and defence systems played a significant role in the development of project management techniques, and the process has been accelerated by the widespread availability of powerful, reliable and cheap computers. Project management is more effective when it makes appropriate use of these sophisticated techniques and facilities and, in this sense, is a highly *specialized* branch of management.

Planning and control must, of course, be exercised over all the activities and resources involved in a project. The project manager therefore needs to understand how all the various participants operate, and to appreciate (at least in outline) their particular skills, working methods, problems and weaknesses. This demands a fairly wide degree of general experience so that, in this practical sense, project management is akin to *general* management.

A software house once advertised its wares with the claim: 'If you can move a mouse you can manage a project'. Most people realize, however, that there is far more to project management than the application of a few computer programs, no matter how sophisticated those programs might be. Successful project management involves a whole framework of logical and progressive planning and decisions, perceptiveness, the liberal application of common sense, proper organization, effective commercial and financial management, painstaking attention to documentation, good communication skills and a clear grasp of proven and long-established principles of management and leadership.

Projects

The principal identifying characteristic of a project is its novelty. It is a step into the unknown, fraught with risk and uncertainty. No two projects are ever exactly alike: even a repeated project will differ from its predecessor in one or more commercial, administrative or physical aspects.

I find it convenient to classify projects under four main headings.

1 Civil engineering, construction, petrochemical, mining and quarrying

Projects in this category are those which spring to mind most readily whenever industrial projects are mentioned. One common feature is that the fulfilment phase must be conducted on a site that is exposed to the elements, and usually remote from the contractor's head office.

These projects incur special risks and problems of organization. They often require massive capital investment, and they deserve (but do not always get) rigorous management of progress, finance and quality.

For very large industrial projects the funding and resources needed are often too great for one contractor to risk or even find. The organization and communications are therefore likely to be complicated by the participation of many different specialists and contractors, with the main players possibly acting together as a consortium or joint venture company.

2 Manufacturing projects

Manufacturing projects aim to produce a piece of equipment or machinery, ship, aircraft, land vehicle or some other item of specially designed hardware. The finished product might be purpose-built for a single customer, or the project could be generated and funded from within a company for the design and development of a new product intended for subsequent manufacture and sale in quantity.

Manufacturing projects are usually conducted in a factory or other home-based environment, where the company should be able to exercise on-the-spot management and provide an optimum environment.

Of course, these ideal conditions do not always apply. Some manufacturing projects can involve work away from the home base, for example in installation, commissioning and start-up, initial customer training and subsequent service and maintenance. More difficult is the case of a complex product (such as an aircraft) that is developed and manufactured by a consortium of companies, very possibly overlapping international borders, with all the consequent problems of risk, contractual difficulties, communication, coordination and control.

3 Management projects

This class of projects proves the point that every company, whatever its size, can expect to need project management expertise at least once in its lifetime. These are the projects that arise when companies relocate their headquarters, develop and introduce a new computer system, launch a marketing campaign, prepare for a trade exhibition, produce a feasibility or other study report, restructure the organization, mount a stage show, or generally engage in any operation that involves the management and coordination of activities to produce an end result that is not identifiable principally as an item of hardware or construction.

Not all projects are conducted commercially or for profit. Most not-for-profit organizations – including national and local government departments, professional associations, charities and disaster relief agencies – conduct projects that fall into this category of management projects.

Although management projects might not result in a visible, tangible creation, much often depends on their successful outcome. There are well-known cases, for instance, where failure to implement a new computer system correctly has caused serious operational breakdown and has exposed the managers responsible to public discredit. Effective project management is at least as important for these projects as it is for the largest construction or manufacturing project.

4 Research projects

Pure research projects sometimes result in dramatically profitable discoveries. They can, on the other hand, consume vast amounts of money and last for many years, but yield no practical result. Research projects carry the highest risk because they are attempting to extend the boundaries of current knowledge. The project objectives are usually difficult or impossible to define. Research projects might not, therefore, be amenable to the project management methods that can be applied to industrial, manufacturing or management projects.

Some form of control over research projects must, however, be attempted. Budgets have to be set in line with available funding. Expenditure can be controlled to some extent by conducting regular management reviews and reassessments, and by authorizing and releasing funds in periodic, controlled and carefully considered steps (a process known as stage-gate controlling).

Although the research activities might themselves lie outside the scope of project management methods, providing the necessary accommodation, communications, equipment and research materials might well constitute capital investment projects to which proper project management can and must be applied.

The primary project objectives

The evaluation of any completed project as a success or a failure depends very much on who is asked to make the assessment. The environmentalist's views of a new highway project might differ greatly from those of the highways authority, the contractor, the project manager and the road user. This introduces the issue of project stakeholders, which means considering the views of all those who have some interest, direct or indirect, in the outcome of a project. This subject will be pursued later in this chapter, but first the primary objectives of the project owner and the project contractor must be considered. These are the outcomes ('deliverables' is the buzzword) that the project owner expects and which the project manager is usually employed principally to achieve.

The primary objectives of any project can be grouped under three headings: *specification, budget* and *time to completion.*

1 Specification, performance and quality

The end result of any project must be fit for the purpose for which it was intended. The project owner and all the other principal stakeholders must be satisfied with the results of the finished project.

A copper refinery that was intended and designed to process 200 000 tonnes of cathode copper per annum must be able to do so, and it must produce that copper at the specified level of purity. The plant must function reliably, efficiently and safely. There will be trouble for all concerned if the plant causes environmental pollution.

Development projects for consumer goods must produce articles that satisfy the market requirements and conform to relevant legislation. The design concept and manufacture have to result in a product that is safe, reliable and appealing to the customer.

At one time quality was seen primarily as the responsibility of a quality control department, relying heavily on inspection and testing to discover faults, and then arranging for their rectification. In more recent years many organizations have embraced the concept of total quality management, where a 'quality culture' is created throughout the organization, with quality built in to design and work processes, and with responsibility for quality shared by all the staff and workforce from top management downwards.

Most of this book is about achieving the time and cost objectives. Achieving the quality, performance and reliability objectives obviously requires competence in engineering and design. This, however, must be complemented by adequate quality management (for which the ISO 9000 series of standards is widely accepted as the base from which to design, implement and operate an effective quality management system).

2 Budget

The project must be completed without exceeding the authorized expenditure. Failure to complete work within the authorized budget will reduce profits and the return on the capital invested, with risk of a more serious (and terminal) financial outcome in extreme cases.

There are many projects, of course, where there is no direct profit motive. Examples include internal management projects, pure scientific research programmes, charitable works and projects carried out by local authorities using public funds. For these projects too, even in the absence of a profit motive, proper attention to cost budgets and financial management is vital. A project might have to be abandoned altogether if funds run out before completion, in which case the money and effort already invested become forfeit and must be written off. In extreme cases, the project contractor could face ruin.

3 Time to completion

Actual progress has to match or beat planned progress. All significant stages of the project must take place no later than their specified dates, to result in total completion on or before the planned finish date.

Late completion of a project will not please the project purchaser or sponsor, to say the least. Consistently failing to keep delivery promises cannot enhance the contractor's market reputation. Further, any project that continues to use resources beyond its planned finish date can have a knock-on effect and disrupt other projects that are either in progress or waiting to follow.

A common risk to projects is failure to start work on time. Very long delays can be caused by procrastination, legal or planning difficulties, shortage of information, lack of funds or other resources, and a host of other reasons. All of these factors can place a project manager in a difficult or impossible position.

> If a project is not allowed to start on time, it can hardly be expected to finish on time.

Balancing the primary objectives

Of course, the aim of a good project manager must be to achieve success in all aspects of the project. But it is occasionally necessary to identify one of the three primary objectives as being of special importance. This emphasis can affect the priority given to the allocation of scarce resources and the way in which management attention is concentrated. It might also influence the choice of project organization structure (which is discussed in Chapter 2).

A project for a charitable organization with very limited funds would, for example, have to be controlled very much with costs in mind. Some companies stake all on their reputation for quality, and pay relatively less attention to time and costs. In some industries (nuclear energy, for example) safety and reliability are paramount. A project to set up a trade exhibition, for which the dates have been announced and the venue booked, is so dependent on meeting the time objective that it might be necessary to take expensive measures and accept overspent budgets if that is the only way to avoid missing the dates.

Triangle of objectives: Version 1

The apparent conflict between the three primary objectives (time, cost and quality) has been illustrated as a triangle (Figure 1.1). The purpose of this triangle is to help the person or management team responsible to concentrate their minds on the priorities: they are expected to ask and answer the question 'In which order of priority should we rank these objectives for our project?' Although it is usually possible to produce this list, the approach can sometimes be too simplistic because all three objectives are interrelated. Change one objective, and the others are almost certain to be affected.

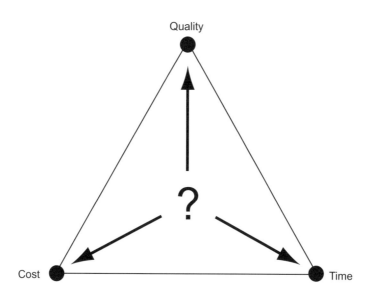

Figure 1.1   Triangle of objectives: Version 1
The three primary objectives of quality, cost and time are interrelated.

The time/cost relationship

Remember that TIME IS MONEY!
(Benjamin Franklin, in *Advice to a Young Tradesman*, 1748)

There is usually a direct and very important relationship between time and money. If the planned timescale is exceeded, the original cost estimates are almost certain to be overspent. A project costs money during every day of its existence, working or non-working, weekday or weekend, from day one of the programme right through until the last payment has exchanged hands. These costs arise for a variety of reasons, some of which will now be explained.

The effect of project delays on direct costs

The *variable* or *direct* project costs of materials and workforce man-hours are time-related in several ways. Cost inflation is one factor, so that a job started and finished later than planned can be expected to cost more because of intervening materials price rises and increases in wages, salaries and other costs.

There are other less easily quantifiable causes where late working implies inefficient working, perhaps through lost time or waiting time (often the result of materials shortages, missing information, or poor planning, communications and organization). If any project task takes longer to perform than its planned duration, it is probable that the budgeted man-hours will also be exceeded. This is true not only for a single task, but also for the project as a whole.

The effect of project delays on indirect (overhead) costs

The *fixed* or *overhead* costs of management, administration, accommodation, services and general facilities will be incurred day by day, every day, regardless of work done, until the project is finished. If the project runs late, then these costs will have to be borne for a longer period than planned. They will then exceed their budget.

The effect of project delays on the costs of financing

Another important time-related cost is *financing*. Where the contractor has an overdraft at the bank or relies on other loan financing, interest has to be paid on the loan. Even if the contractor can finance the project from internal funds, there is still a notional cost of financing, equivalent to the interest or dividends that the same funds could have earned had the contractor invested the money elsewhere (such as in a bank deposit account). If a project runs late, the financing period is extended, and the total amount of interest or notional interest payable must increase correspondingly.

Much of the finance raised for a large project is likely to be invested in work in progress. This work in progress includes not only work carried out in a factory or at a construction site, but also all the costs of engineering and design that have yet to be recovered from the customer. In many cases the contractor is only able to charge for work actually finished and delivered to the customer, or for amounts of work done and supported by certified invoices. Such invoices are validated by certificates from an independent professional third party (such as a quantity surveyor or an engineer) which agree the amount of work done and claimed for. Certified invoices are often linked to planned events. If an event is late, or if a measurable progress stage has not been reached, a certified invoice cannot be issued. The contractor's revenue is then delayed, which means that the contractor must continue to finance the mounting costs of the project. The contractor could suffer severe cash flow problems as a result, perhaps leading to bankruptcy in the worst case.

Cost penalties

Late completion can invoke the ignominy of contract cost penalties. Some contracts contain a penalty clause which provides the customer with the sanction of a cost penalty against the contractor for each day or week by which the contractor fails to meet the contracted delivery obligation.

The total cost effect of project delays

All these time/cost considerations mean that delays on a large project can easily cause additional costs amounting to thousands of pounds per day. It is clear, therefore, that if work can be monitored and managed carefully so that it proceeds without disruption against a sensible, achievable plan, much of the battle to control costs will already have been won.

The quality/cost relationship

The relationship between quality and project costs is not straightforward. It is a fundamental error to believe that there is a simple and acceptable trade-off between quality and cost. Downgrading quality is not an option. Quality means fitness for purpose, and includes the contractor's commitment to provide a product or service that is safe and reliable. Further, those who promote total quality management argue (rightly) that quality can be achieved without extra cost (see, for example, Crosby, 1979). So, if quality is not an option, why include it in the triangle of objectives?

Consider a property development company that wants to build a new office block. Suppose that the initial estimates are too high and that construction costs must be reduced. One option might be to build on relatively simple foundations instead of using deep sunk piles, which could save thousands of pounds. But if the ground conditions demand piling for the building to be safe, that cost-saving option is ruled out on the grounds of reliability and safety. It would compromise quality, and is not a true option.

Now suppose that the same developer reviews the specification for interior finishes and finds that marble-finished floors could be replaced with carpeted floors at a substantial cost saving. The floors would still be serviceable, safe, reliable and fit for purpose. Carpeting would therefore be an option that would not compromise quality.

The developer might also review the performance specifications for services such as lighting and air conditioning. It is possible that the performance parameters could be downgraded slightly for a further substantial saving in costs. Again, this should not affect the safety and reliability of the building and, provided that lighting and ventilation are legal and adequate, would not render the building unfit for its intended purpose.

The triangle of objectives shown in Figure 1.1 will therefore become a more useful basis for argument if the word 'quality' is replaced by 'specification', 'specified standard', 'specified performance' or something equivalent.

The triangle of objectives: Version 2

Don't forget the people!

When considering the project objectives it is easy but dangerous to forget that no objective can be achieved without people. The proper management, organization and motivation of all who contribute to a project cannot be taken for granted, and this must be acknowledged from the start. With this in mind, Kliem and Ludin (1992) set out a modified triangle of objectives with 'People' shown at its centre. Thus consideration of all the points made in this section suggests that the most appropriate triangle of objectives is that shown in Figure 1.2.

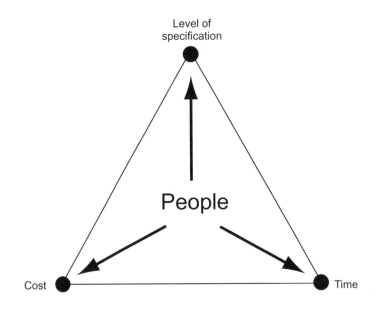

Figure 1.2   Triangle of objectives: Version 2
Compare this version of the triangle with Figure 1.1. There are two differences:
1.   Kliem and Ludin (1992) argue that people cannot be ignored.
2.   'Level of specification' replaces 'quality', because quality is not a negotiable option to be set against time and cost. But cost and time might be saved by downgrading the specification.

Perceptions of project success or failure beyond the three primary objectives

Most project managers are motivated towards completing their projects so that they satisfy the three primary objectives of time, cost and performance. These are usually the most important factors that drive the project contractor, and they should align with the foremost expectations of the project owner. Most project management procedures (and this book) are directed at achieving these goals, which could be summarized as delighting the customer while creating a commercial success for the contractor. In this context the contracting organization and the customer are both primary stakeholders in the project.

It must be recognized, however, that many projects have to satisfy more than two primary stakeholders. For example, a bank which has provided loan finance for a project will have a keen interest in whether the project succeeds or fails.

There will always be people and organizations who, while not being principal stakeholders, nevertheless have an interest in how the outcome of a project might affect them. Subcontractors and suppliers are an obvious example. Staff working on a project have a stake in the outcome because, apart from contributing to job satisfaction, success or failure can have profound implications for their future employment and careers.

Perceptions of success or failure will differ between the various stakeholders. The residents of houses lying in the path of a proposed new motorway would take a different view from that of the potential motorway users. A project to build a transport system that runs out of cash and ruins its main contractor would be an undoubted failure from the point of view of the shareholders, project staff and unpaid creditors. But the travelling public would not see that project as a failure if a replacement contractor and new cash injections allowed the project to be finished as planned.

Some environmental groups might be dismayed by new project proposals: many project managers have learned to their cost that work can be seriously delayed by determined protesters, who may be able to publicize a good case and attract a great deal of public support.

It is clear, then, that the true gauge of project success or failure depends on how the project outcome is perceived by all the stakeholders. Hartman (2000) declares that a 'project is successful if all the stakeholders are happy'. Although that ideal may not always be achievable, it is best project management practice to try to identify all the stakeholders and satisfy their aspirations as far as possible.

The stakeholders

Identifying and ranking the stakeholders

The range and nature of stakeholders will vary very greatly from one project to another, but the principle of stakeholder identification can be illustrated by an example. Suppose that a project has been proposed to redevelop a derelict urban area. This ambitious project will provide a shopping mall, offices, cinema and live entertainments, other leisure facilities, new connecting roads and so on. The project might have a contract matrix organization similar to that described in Chapter 2, and illustrated in Figure 2.9. The primary stakeholders for this project will certainly include the main project contractor and the project owner. The banks or other organizations financing the project will also have a considerable primary interest in the project's success or failure.

Not least of the stakeholders are all those who hold shares or have otherwise invested in participating companies that, by accepting an element of risk, stand to make a profit or loss as a result of the project.

Subcontractors, suppliers, staff, artisans and labourers can all be considered stakeholders too, although perhaps these could be placed in the second rank. Intended occupiers of the shops, offices and other premises also have a large stake in the project.

There are others who will be dependent on the secondary stakeholders. These are the wholesale suppliers of merchandise to be sold in the new shops, service staff such as car park attendants, shop and office workers, companies expecting to provide security, cleaning and maintenance services, and so on.

Public transport organizations must consider how the development will affect passenger numbers: some of their existing services might need to be changed to suit the new travel patterns (and take advantage of the new business generated).

Then there are the various regulatory authorities, such as the local building inspectors, planning office and many other official organizations. These are all stakeholders whose decisions can affect the project.

People living near the proposed development will benefit from the new shopping and leisure facilities but might resent the inconvenience of construction works and the prospect of increased traffic and noise when the new premises start to function. Parents might be concerned that their schoolchildren will have to cross busier streets. Motorists and other road users will be interested in how the new road layouts will affect their journeys. The new entertainments facilities will provide wider opportunities for live artistes.

This discussion could be carried on at length to identify still more stakeholders. Some will have the power to influence the project, while others will be able only to voice opinions. All stakeholders might be ranked (primary, secondary, tertiary, and so on) according to the power they can wield and the impact the project will have on them.

Consideration of all the stakeholders' interests

Once all the stakeholders have been identified, the means of communicating and dealing with them will have to be considered. Regulations and local byelaws will determine how local government and other official bodies must be consulted. There might have to be meetings with some stakeholders' groups or associations. Publicity can include, for example, announcements in the local press and advance public display of architects' plans and models. Consultation is always better than confrontation.

When the preliminary investigation of stakeholders' interests is finished, the triangle of objectives could, in theory at least, be supplemented by a more complex matrix of stakeholders' perceptions. Figure 1.3 shows a theoretical format.

Stakeholders	Objectives		
	Time	Cost	Specification
Project owner			
Project manager			
Bank			
Guarantor			
Statutory bodies			
Main contractor			
Subcontractors			
Suppliers			
Project workers			
General public			
Local residents			
Environmental groups			
and so on ↓	↓	↓	↓

Figure 1.3   Example of a stakeholders' objectives matrix
A method for setting out priorities for project objectives as viewed by different stakeholders.

Customers, clients, contractors and end-users

Throughout this book I have used the following expressions to represent the two principal parties in a project contract:

● **Customer** – the person or organization for which the project is being conducted. I have also used the terms *client* and *owner* in this context, while recognizing that these are not always true synonyms. Although the common perception of a customer is a person or organization that pays money in return for a project, the customer in many management projects is represented by the board or management of the company that itself carries out the project.

● **Contractor** – the organization that is principally responsible for executing the project work to the customer's requirements. I have not restricted this term to its more common use (in the contracting industry for construction projects). So, again purely for convenience, I use the term *contractor* in my text to describe any organization or group that carries out a project, whether or not the project is carried out against a formal sales contract. I use this term, for example, in the context of manufacturing projects and for projects in the not-for-profit sector.

Projects are very diverse in their natures, and the common notion that every project is carried out by one organization or contractor for one customer is really too simplistic. Figure 1.4 gives a taste of this diversity, with examples given for each of the four project categories introduced at the beginning of this chapter. This figure introduces the end-user, who is often an important third party in projects. For convenience and simplicity, however, I have confined most of the illustrations and case studies throughout this book to the simple customer–contractor relationship.

Project category	Project example	Project customer	Principal 'contractor'	End-user	Operated and maintained by:
1 Civil engineering, construction, petrochemical, mining and quarrying	Local authority housing development	Local authority	Wimply	Housing tenants	Local authority
	Private toll road	Landowner	Tarpack	Road users	Landowner
	Copper mine	Cupric Ltd	Cupric Ltd (head office)	Cupric (Zambia) Ltd	Cupric (Zambia) Ltd
2 Manufacturing	New passenger aircraft	Going Ltd	Going Ltd	Various airlines	Various airlines
	Automatic rifle	Ministry of Defence	Small Arms Ltd	Military units	Military units
	Washing machine development	Hotwash Ltd	Hotwash R&D dept	Domestic users	Domestic users
3 Management	Design and implement new sales procedures	ABC Ltd	ABC Ltd (+ external consultant)	ABC staff	ABC Ltd
	Office relocation	Greens of London	Greens' (internal task force)	Greens of Exeter	Greens of Exeter
4 Research	Speculative research for new plastic materials	Chemikl Ltd	Chemikl Ltd (laboratory)	Unknown	Not applicable

Figure 1.4   Examples of project relationships
A few examples to illustrate that many project relationships are more complex than one supplier–one contractor. 'Contractor' is here intended to mean any organization or group that is primarily responsible for managing and executing the project.

Project life cycle

When writers describe the life cycle of a typical project, they usually refer to the period that starts with design and planning and ends with handover of the project to its customer. Whilst it is true that this is the period of activity most likely to fall within the interest and influence of the project manager, the true nature of a project life cycle is often misunderstood. To start with, there is really no such thing as a *typical* life cycle, because all projects differ enormously.

Figure 2.2 gives an example of a project life cycle, which is cyclical in the sense that the activities begin and end with the customer. But that cycle really only depicts the project as seen through the eyes of the project manager. The total life of a typical project is rarely a true cycle, because there is often no return to the start or regeneration. So, strictly, we should talk about the project *life history*. The principal phases are depicted in Figure 1.5, which is greatly simplified and cannot apply to all projects.

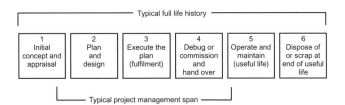

Figure 1.5   Typical project life history

Associations representing the profession of project management

The International Association of Project Management (IPMA)

The profession of project management is represented by the International Association of Project Management. Once known as INTERNET, the abbreviation, for obvious reasons, was changed to IPMA.

The UK Association for Project Management (APM)

The corporate member of the IPMA in the UK is The Association for Project Management (APM), and further information is available from their secretariat at:

The Association for Project Management
Thornton House
150 West Wycombe Road
High Wycombe
Buckinghamshire
HP12 3AE
E-mail: <secretariat@apm-uk.demon.co.uk>
Website: <www.apm.org.uk>

The association arranges seminars and meetings through a network of local branches and publishes the monthly journal *Project*. Membership of the association is a good way for project managers and all others involved in project management to meet and to maintain current awareness of modern techniques, practices and computer systems.

The following explanation is a summary of the APM's comprehensive membership and qualification structure, condensed from information provided by the association.

Membership starts at student level and rises through various grades to full member (MAPM) and fellow (FAPM). The association's basic qualification, which depends on suitable experience and two written examinations, is APMP. This is a professional qualification that recognizes an individual's baseline knowledge and experience in project management. It is regarded by the association as the benchmark qualification in the project management profession, and is the first step towards certification.

The APM has a well-established certification procedure for project managers, who must already be full members. To quote from the association's own literature: 'the certificated project manager is at the pinnacle of the profession, possessing extensive knowledge and having carried responsibility for the delivery of at least one significant project'. As evidence of competence, certification has obvious advantages for the project manager, and will increasingly be demanded as mandatory by some project purchasers. Certification provides employers with a useful measure when recruiting or assessing staff, and a company that can claim to employ certificated project managers will benefit from an enhanced professional image. Certification also has relevance for project clients. It helps them to assess a project manager's competence by providing clear proof that the individual concerned has gained peer recognition of his or her ability to manage projects.

The Project Management Institute (PMI)

Founded in the USA in 1969, the PMI is the world's leading not-for-profit organization of choice for individuals around the globe who work or are interested in project management. PMI develops recognized standards, not least of which is the widely respected project management body of knowledge guide, commonly known by its abbreviated title, the *PMBOK Guide*.

PMI publications include the monthly professional magazine *PM Network*, the monthly newsletter *PMI Today* and the quarterly *Project Management Journal*.

In addition to its many research and education activities, PMI has (since 1984) been dedicated to developing and maintaining a rigorous, examination-based professional certification program to advance the project management profession and recognize the achievements of individual professionals. PMI claims that its Project Management Professional (PMP) certification is the world's most widely recognized professional credential for project management practitioners and others in the profession.

For more information, contact PMI at:

PMI Headquarters
Four Campus Boulevard
Newtown Square
PA 19073-3299
USA
Telephone: +610-356-4600
E-mail: <pmihq@pmi.org>
Website: <www.pmi.org>

Chapter 2

Project management organization

It should be obvious that if all the project objectives are to be achieved, the people, communications, jobs and resources must be properly organized. But the form which that organization should take might not be so obvious.

Every company has its own ideas about how to organize itself and its work. It is highly probable that if three companies doing similar work could be compared, three different organization structures would be found. Further, all three companies might be equally successful (or equally unsuccessful), implying that it is not always possible to say with any degree of confidence that there is one best organization solution.

This chapter cannot therefore declare exactly how every project should have its organization structured. Instead, it starts by setting out some of the properties that are essential for efficient organization. It then describes possible organization options, together with their advantages and disadvantages.

Effective organization and communications

An effective organization will have clear lines of authority, and every member of the project will know what he or she is expected to do to make the project a success. This is part of the management communication framework needed to motivate all the staff employed. A well-motivated group can be a joy to work with. A badly informed group, with vague responsibilities and ambiguous levels of status and authority, is likely to be poorly motivated, slow to achieve results, costly to run and extremely frustrating to work with.

The complement of good management communications is the provision of adequate feedback paths through and across the organization. These facilitate cooperation and coordination. They allow progress to be monitored and difficulties to be reported back to executive management. They should also give all participants access to the relevant experts for advice or instruction on technical and commercial difficulties.

The emergence of project management in a developing company

The subject of project management organization can be introduced conveniently by considering the historical development of a small company. The organization invented for this example happens to be a manufacturing company, but many of the principles and arguments apply equally to all kinds of other projects.

Case study: Street Components Ltd

The company

Street Components Ltd had its origins many years ago as a manufacturer of street lamps and other associated items of 'street furniture'. Later, the company's expertise and activities were developed to include components for automatic traffic signals (traffic lights). In more recent times, the company's expertise and range of products have been extended to many other aspects of traffic control equipment and systems, which it sells to local government authorities, developers and other large companies.

Routine manufacture

The time is sixty years ago.

Street Components Ltd employs 200 people, and is making and selling small street lamps and other associated products. Manufacture takes place in batches or in continuous assembly lines, depending on the product. All operations are managed by a production manager, who relies on a production controller to schedule all the work.

In normal conditions the backlog of work awaiting issue to the workshops might run, at most, into a few weeks. Loading of production departments and their machines must be arranged to ensure a reasonably smooth flow of work without bottlenecks and without too much idle time, but planning methods are straightforward and within the capability of the competent production controller. Exceptional work peaks or bottlenecks are resolved by rearranging the existing schedules, overtime working, or by the short-term employment of subcontractors.

Estimators, job planners and production engineers analyse all new manufacturing drawings and specifications. The time required for every manufacturing operation can therefore be assessed with reasonable accuracy, based on past experience of similar or identical operations. There is no need for any specialized planning or scheduling technique other than the application of well-proven production control methods, such as daily loading wall charts.

Job costing is carried out in arrears by recording man-hours and materials used. The time cycle from start to finish of each operation is fairly short, and the total cost of each unit produced usually becomes evident fairly soon after the work has been done, using normal cost accounting procedures.

Transition from high-volume/low-cost to low-volume/high-cost manufacture

The time is thirty years ago.

Street Components Ltd has grown, and has extended its product range. It now offers a standard range of traffic control products, which include relatively simple sets of traffic lights (comprising a standard controller, three or more signal lamp assemblies, vehicle sensors and cabling). Most of the manufacture is still in batches, or as continuous production for stock. Routine production management and production control procedures still apply, now assisted in some areas by computer systems.

One complication is that customers occasionally ask for non-standard items which do not form part of the customary catalogued range. Many of these special items are trivial variations on the normal production theme, but other requested changes are more radical and complex. These special requests are regarded by the production management team as a nuisance, and they also create difficulties and additional work for the company's engineering design department.

As the company's expertise and size expand, the increased level of sales includes more orders for sets of traffic signals that differ in some respect from the standard catalogue description and have to be specially custom-built. Some of these products have become so specialized that no market could be found for them outside the needs of the customers who have ordered them. The company that once mass-produced simple street lights as standard catalogue items is now supplying some of its customers with sets of road traffic signals that are becoming more complex and more costly. Street Components Ltd is experiencing a change from high-volume/low-cost to high-cost/low-volume production.

Some of the equipment included on the customers' orders is becoming so specialized that usual production control and work scheduling methods are proving difficult to apply, with risk of late delivery or worse. There are now many more components to be designed, manufactured or specially purchased and assembled into each new customer order. The company's cost estimators are having difficulty in evaluating new work, for which there is often no precedent and (at the cost estimating stage) no detailed drawings. The time from receipt of order to delivery has grown from one or two weeks to several months.

In these circumstances, Street Components Ltd is experiencing some difficulty in coordinating all the requirements. The company must start to question whether or not special management methods are needed to handle these special orders.

Transition from product manufacturer to project contractor

The time is the present.

As road traffic demands have become heavier, many traffic control systems must be planned on a larger scale. Instead of considering just one crossroads or junction individually, whole road systems have to be taken into account. For each of these systems, traffic volumes must be recorded and analysed at key points throughout the area before a control system can be designed. Then the sequence and timing of signals at all the road junctions have to be calculated and coordinated to ensure optimum traffic flow. Street Components Ltd has been forced to expand its design, engineering and manufacturing capabilities accordingly.

Now, when an order is placed for a town traffic control system, Street Components Ltd is likely to be involved in much more than the supply and installation of a single set of traffic lights. The company might be called upon to provide automatic diversion signs, remote-controlled television cameras, automatic car park routeing and status signs, several sets of traffic lights and other highly sophisticated paraphernalia, all linked to one or more controlling computers.

The company is no longer concerned with the sale of equipment or 'hardware' alone. It now has to support its sales with a high proportion of customer consultation, systems engineering and other services or 'software'. Instead of being able to satisfy each customer order by supplying direct from a finished stocks warehouse, it has to design, manufacture, install and commission complex systems to highly specialized customer requirements. Customer orders that could once be delivered within a few days or weeks have been supplanted by orders for projects that can take many months, if not years, to complete.

Work scheduling and control must take into account all the activities needed to bring the project to a successful conclusion (including all the software tasks, such as writing computer programs and preparing operating and maintenance instructions). Some of the items purchased by the company as part of the project must themselves be considered as special, and they too will have to be brought into the control function. Some of those purchased items might be sufficiently complex for their suppliers to manage their design and manufacture as projects in their own right.

Cost control (a basic factor in achieving profitability) has become more complex. Cost and management accountants are not the only contributors to this process; they must be helped by specialists who can define the total work content in detail and then report on achievement and cost implications as the project proceeds.

When this stage has been reached, where simple jobs have given way to complex projects, the answer to the question of whether or not new management methods are needed becomes very clear. Customary procedures for work planning and control will no longer be just difficult to apply: they will fail altogether if they are not brought into a wider framework of management. A total project management system is required.

Work management in a conventional manufacturing organization

A clearer picture of some of the problems encountered in project handling can be seen by studying the management organization structure of a manufacturing company. In its earlier days, a small engineering company like Street Components might have been organized as outlined in Figure 2.1.

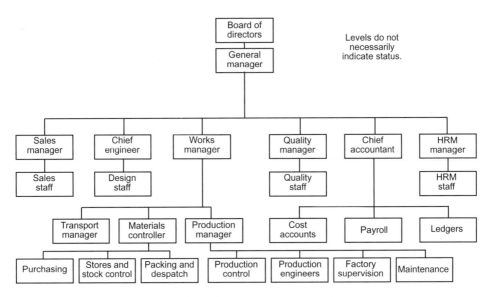

Figure 2.1   Example of a manufacturing company organization
This is a line and function organization. It may be ideal for the continuous or batch manufacture of standard products, but no provision is made for the holistic coordination of activities necessary for the fulfilment of special projects.

Line organizations of this type are set up to manage work within departmental (functional) boundaries or specialist disciplines. Thus the chief engineer is responsible for design and development, but very little else. The works manager concentrates on the production aspects of the business. Managers concentrate on those reporting directly to them in the line, and they generally have no direct responsibilities outside their own functions. Of course, no company could ever exist on such a rigid basis, and there must be some cooperation and interaction between different managers. Nevertheless, any cross-functional relationships that do exist are regarded as secondary to the main line structure. They are not defined, no special provision is made for them, and they are not brought under any form of control. Such communication weaknesses are potentially damaging to any company, but they become particularly serious when a firm undertakes a multidisciplinary project.

One might ask whether general managers should not play a significant part in coordinating all the various project functions. To some extent they might, of course, but they cannot be expected to deal efficiently or effectively with the level of detail involved in the day-to-day running of projects. The company's general management should be left free to make higher-level decisions about the business, implement policies decided by the board of directors, and carry out administration at high level.

Even if the general manager or other senior executive is held to be ultimately responsible for the success of projects, he or she must be able to delegate the tasks of planning, coordination and day-to-day management. But delegate to whom? In the organization structure depicted in Figure 2.1 there is no obvious person who can logically be charged with the direct responsibility for following any complex project through all its stages. The positions of line responsibility are clearly shown for each function, but the coordination between them, necessary for effective project control, is missing.

Communications in the project cycle and the need for a project manager

Engineering projects, in common with most other customer-funded projects, are partly cyclical in nature. This is illustrated in Figure 2.2, which shows some of the key stages for a typical project. Each project is conceived when the customer and the contractor's sales engineering department first make contact. The project is given life when the customer issues a purchase order or when some other contract document is signed. Thereafter, many other stages must be passed through in turn, until the work finally arrives back at the customer as a completed project. Clockwise rotation around the cycle only reveals the main stream. Within this flow, many small tributaries, cross-currents and even whirlpools are generated before the project is finished.

As instructions are issued within departments and from one department to another, information must be fed back along the communication channels to signal the results obtained as each instruction is carried out. These feedback data are used to correct any errors discovered in the design drawings and for the essential task of controlling the general progress of the project.

Much project information will not flow along the defined lines of authority, but will cross them in complex and changing patterns. In fact, when a manufacturing project is compared with routine production, the emphasis has shifted from looking principally at the line relationships to consideration of the functional

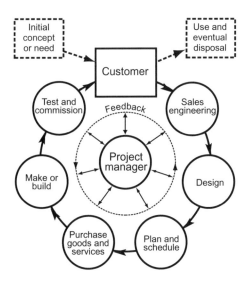

Figure 2.2   Project life cycle
The role of the project manager as a coordinator and communicator is emphasized in this summary of the key stages in a project.

connections. This has to be reflected in the formal organization structure if the project is to be coordinated and managed satisfactorily. Someone must be made responsible for managing the project as an entity, rather than having this responsibility spread vaguely over a number of managers in the line structure. What is needed is a kind of project champion, a person who can ensure that all the activities are planned, coordinated and directed towards the clear aim of achieving the project objectives. Thus, at the hub of the project cycle, a new figure has emerged – the project manager.

Project matrix organizations

Functional matrix for a single project

Figure 2.3 shows how a project manager might be introduced into a company that is undertaking a special, complex project alongside its more routine manufacturing activities. This arrangement is fairly common. It allows the general line organization of the company and its departmental management structure to continue normally, but the project manager is asked to give undivided attention to the 'intruding' project. The project manager here acts principally as a coordinator, and has no direct line authority over any other manager or their staff. The name

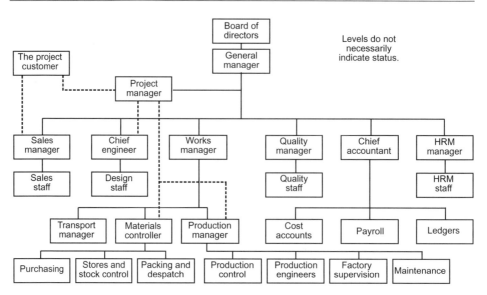

Figure 2.3   A functional matrix for a single project in a manufacturing company
In addition to its standard production range, the company depicted in Figure 2.1 has now undertaken a special project for a customer. A project manager has been introduced to plan and progress the special project work through the organization. The project manager has no direct line authority, and acts as a coordinator. This arrangement is also known as a *coordination matrix*.

often given to this organizational arrangement is a *functional matrix*.

When conflict arises or when people refuse to cooperate with the project manager or with each other, lack of authority can make the project manager's job very difficult, causing great demands on his or her skills in dealing with people. If all else fails, the project manager must be able to call on the support of the company's senior management so that they can exert their authority or take other action to resolve the problem.

Matrix for multiple projects

The case described above for the functional matrix becomes a little more complicated when a company is handling several projects at the same time.

Figure 2.4 is an organization chart for a manufacturing company which customarily handles several projects simultaneously. In this example, each project is either big enough to justify its own full-time project manager or it can be coupled with one or more other suitable projects to allow sharing (so that one project manager looks after two or more projects). This matrix is the multiple-project variant of the single-project functional matrix described in the previous section and illustrated in Figure 2.3. Street Components Ltd, the company

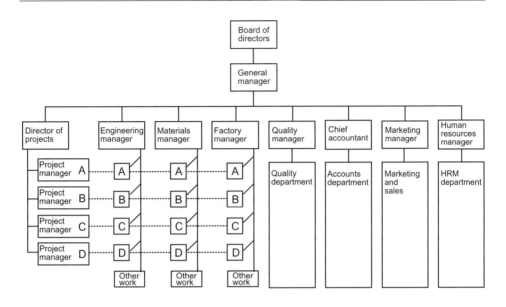

Figure 2.4   Matrix organization for several simultaneous manufacturing projects
Several projects are being handled by this manufacturing company (Projects A, B, C and D are shown here). All projects share the company's design and manufacturing resources, but each has its own project manager. The degree of authority given to these project managers by comparison with the departmental managers varies between companies.

described earlier, might benefit from this kind of structure. Figure 2.5 shows a similar organization structure, but suitable for the head office of a company that specializes in capital design and construction projects such as mines or chemical plants.

Both of these examples are matrix organizations. Permanently established groups of people are organized according to their special skills or functional disciplines. The people in these functional groups are responsible to their own departmental line managers, but also have to take account of the project managers' directions to a lesser or greater degree.

Different matrix strengths

The degree of authority given to the project managers in a matrix can be varied (at the discretion of higher management) in relation to that enjoyed by the departmental or functional managers. Matrix charts such as those shown in Figures 2.4 and 2.5 cannot usually indicate the balance of authority between project and departmental managers. They remain valid even when the project

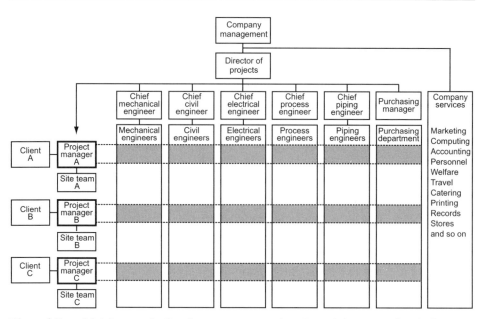

Figure 2.5   Matrix organization for a company engineering mining, petrochemical or large construction projects
This chart shows a company that is organized functionally for engineering several simultaneous projects. There are dual lines of command, so that a person in a functional group might have to take instruction from both their own departmental manager and a project manager. Note that general company services are not included within the matrix. Many companies will also exclude the purchasing department from the matrix.

managers are given far more authority. It is therefore unnecessary to show new organization charts for the matrix variants described below.

Weak matrix

In a *weak matrix*, each project manager's degree of authority and control is less than that enjoyed by the managers of the functional departments. Each project manager is able to plan and coordinate, but not able to issue direct commands through the line organization. Each project manager is entirely dependent on the departmental managers for the provision of people and equipment for project tasks. The project managers, although key people, have to be content with a coordinating role.

The weak matrix can encourage conflicts. For example, different project managers might compete with each other in claiming attention and resources for their own projects, and they can also come into conflict with the departmental managers over the allocation of people, machines and other facilities to project tasks. An additional complication is that functional departments usually have work, both routine and occasional, that is not connected with any current project. The departmental managers might decide, without agreement from the project managers, to give non-project work priority over project tasks.

These arguments are not intended to condemn the weak matrix. But, as with the case of the single-project functional matrix, the project managers must depend on their motivational and persuasive skills to achieve their aims, and they must be able to call upon higher-level management support to resolve any dispute that cannot be settled at the project and departmental management level.

Balanced matrix

The *balanced matrix* (or overlay matrix) is very similar to a weak matrix, and is sometimes described as such. In the balanced matrix, there is a declared balance of power and authority between the project managers and the functional department managers. Project and functional managers are expected to collaborate constructively and allocate personnel and other resources to tasks according to genuine priorities to ensure the successful outcome of all projects. This is perhaps the most common form of matrix. It is elegant in theory, and has many advantages over other forms of organization. It is not, however, as some have claimed, a universal solution for all projects. All organization forms have their advantages and disadvantages (discussed later in this chapter).

Like the weak matrix, the balanced matrix can also give rise to conflict between project managers and departmental managers. There can also be motivational difficulties for people working within functional groups, who find themselves with a dual reporting line that violates the principle of unity of command. When given conflicting instructions, who should they obey – the project manager or their departmental manager?

Stronger forms of the matrix

In a *project matrix* the authority of each project manager takes precedence over the authority of the functional managers, at least as far as the allocation and progressing of work is concerned.

In a *secondment matrix*, which is the strongest form of the matrix, the functional managers must nominate and assign members of their departments to work full-time for the project managers. The people assigned report principally to their respective project managers for as long as each project manager needs them (although they might have to remain physically located in their home departments).

Project teams and task forces

Pure project team organization

It is, of course, possible to arrange things differently from the matrix options described above. A complete work group or team can be created for each project as a self-contained unit with the project manager placed at its head. The project manager is given direct line authority over the team, and is responsible not only for planning, progress and work allocation, but also for all technical aspects of the project.

The example shown in Figure 2.6 is a project team organization that might be set up for a petrochemical or mining project. Such a team should be able to devise the processes and reagent flows, specify and purchase the plant and equipment, design, build and commission all the buildings and other facilities for a chemical processing plant or a mining complex. The project manager is in direct command, with complete authority for directing the participants so that the project meets all the objectives.

Communications across the various technical and professional disciplines are made easier when the project manager is in total command. All members of the team identify with the project and can (at least in the short term) be strongly

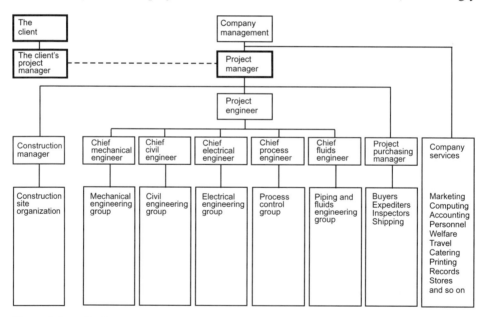

Figure 2.6   Project team organization

This example shows the organization of a temporary project team brought together for the design, procurement, construction and commissioning of a chemical processing plant. The project manager has complete responsibility for all aspects of the project, backed by the clear authority of direct command.

motivated towards achieving the project goals. It is best if the key members of the team can be located near each other in the same building, but this is not always practicable. If possible, an office should be set aside for use as a 'project war room', where some or all of the team's senior members can meet formally or informally whenever they wish, and where drawings, charts and plans can be displayed on tables and walls. War rooms for larger projects should include computers and other electronic communications equipment.

Task forces in manufacturing projects

A complete, all-embracing, self-contained project team can be impracticable to organize in a manufacturing company owing to the nature of the facilities and machinery required. Many of those facilities represent considerable capital investment and, together with their human operators, cannot be allocated full-time to a single project, no matter how urgent the demands of that project might be. These facilities must be shared among all the projects and other work being undertaken by the company. Project managers cannot therefore be given direct line authority over any of those shared manufacturing functions, and a matrix organization of some sort might be indicated rather than a pure team.

There are occasions, however, when the strong project focus and fast internal communications of a team are preferable to a matrix. To take just one case, suppose that an important project is running extremely late and is in dire need of a rescue operation: in other words, there is an existing or impending crisis. In those circumstances, the company's management would be well advised to consider setting up a task force to finish the remainder of the project in the shortest possible time. But the problem remains of how to deal with common manufacturing facilities that must continue to carry out other work.

A task force solution is possible. It depends on seconding managers (or their senior deputies) from all the relevant departments to form a task force dedicated to executing the project. A leader for this task force must be found, preferably from within the company. This person must possess determination and a positive outlook. He or she should also be experienced in the project management arts: if not, it might be prudent to engage an external consultant to provide urgent on-the-job training and guidance.

The task force members will communicate more effectively and make better and faster decisions if they can be located together, away from their usual offices or workplaces. Better still, they should be provided with a dedicated office that can be used as their project 'war room'. The result should be a powerful and effective management team with the expertise and authority needed to give the project the best chance of success.

Although the project might still depend on the use of resources and facilities shared with other work, the seniority of the task force members should ensure that all critical project tasks get top priority. Suppose, for instance, that a machine shop is represented on the task force by its manager or a deputy. Then, when a critical project task requires the use of a machine that is used heavily for other work, the project task force leader is provided with a direct line of authority over the use of that machine through the senior machine shop delegate who is serving on the task force.

Task forces for management change projects

A task force arrangement can be most effective in projects set up to create management changes, or to design and implement changed management procedures. Such projects, especially in their formative stages, can give rise to undesirable rumours among staff, sometimes causing unfounded apprehension and dismay. A task force, because it is a contained team, stands a good chance of maintaining confidentiality. Announcements concerning the change can be made at a time to suit management, when the project details have become facts, not speculation.

An example of a management project where a task force approach can be beneficial is a company relocation project. Consider, for instance, an insurance company that wishes to relocate its central city offices to a provincial town. Apart from the obvious questions of where or whether to relocate, there will be all kinds of problems to solve, such as predicting how many staff will decide to move and how to support them, how to compensate staff who decide not to remain in employment, ensuring continuity of service to clients, and so on. A task force that includes managers or senior delegates from the human resources, information systems, claims, sales and other company departments should be able to work collectively and privately to arrive at a project solution, arrange for communication of the intentions to staff, and then implement the project.

Site construction teams

Team organization is the customary arrangement where the project construction site manager and all those working to build the project have been assembled at a site that is some distance away from the company's home office. It is then usually more sensible to place all site staff under the direct command of the most senior manager who is actually at the site, rather than depend on multiple lines of command back to the home office. Unless the project is so large that the company must set up local semi-permanent design and administration offices, the site team will probably operate as a sub-organization within a matrix or larger project team. Figures 2.5 and 2.6 both indicate site teams set up in this way, with the site team managers reporting to the overall project managers back at the home office (for more on site teams, see Chapter 20).

Organization of central administration functions

A mistake sometimes made is to describe as typical an organization chart that shows all company functions as part of the project team or lying within the project boundaries in a matrix. This error is seen even in well-respected textbooks. Functions such as accounting, marketing, human resources, facilities management and general administration, although they might provide essential support to projects, are not usually involved directly in performing scheduled project tasks. It is true that there are exceptions, especially for management projects. For example, the human resources department would be directly involved in a project set up to recruit staff or relocate a company. Marketing staff would be the principal players in a market research or new product promotion campaign. But for most industrial projects the project manager must regard these other company functions as general supporting services rather than resources under his or her control. So it is important to draw the boundaries of the project manager's authority with care.

Which type of organization is best?

Consider a company which is about to embark upon a project for the first time. A competent project manager is available, but this firm has never had to handle a complex project before, and now has to set up the most suitable organization. If asked to advise, the project manager might immediately be faced with the question that often causes much controversy:

● Should the company take all the key people destined to work on the project and place them under the direct management of the project manager, so that a purpose-built team will carry out the project?

Or, at the other extreme:

● Would it be better to have a weak or balanced functional matrix in which the project manager, although held responsible for the whole project, has no direct line authority over the workforce. The project manager must then rely on the goodwill and cooperation of all the line managers for the success of the project.

It must be said that project managers do not always enjoy the luxury of being able to organize their own workforce. They are more likely to be appointed to an organization that either exists already or has been set up specially by more senior managers. In both cases the project manager has to accept the organization as a *fait accompli.* However, someone will have the ultimate authority to choose or change the organization structure so, if only for their benefit, the arguments for and against the principal options are presented below.

The first point to note is that the most successful organization will make the best use of the people working within it. Those faced with the task of designing a new or changed project organization would do well to imagine themselves working as an average person within the proposed organization and ask the following questions:

- Would they have a clear sense of purpose and direction?
- How strongly motivated would they feel towards contributing to the project objectives?
- How easy would it be to communicate with other members of the organization?
- Would they have ready access to expert help or advice on technical matters within their own professional discipline?
- How would they perceive their short- and long-term career prospects?

The case for a dedicated project team

Project teams have the advantage that they can each be directed to a single purpose: the successful completion of one project. A team can be completely autonomous. It is provided with and relies upon its own resources. There is no clash of priorities resulting from a clamour of different projects in competition for common (shared) resources.

Short-term leadership and motivation

Much is rightly said and written about the importance of motivating people who work on projects. An important aspect of motivation is the generation of a team spirit, in which everyone feels themselves to be part of the team and strives to meet the common team goals. It is clearly easier to establish a team spirit when a project team actually exists, as opposed to the case where the people are dispersed over a matrix organization which is handling more than one project.

A person working within a project team is made responsible to one manager (who is either the project manager or a manager who reports directly to the project manager). The line of authority is unambiguous. There is unity of command. A team member knows exactly where he or she stands, and there should be little chance of that person being given conflicting instructions from more than one superior.

Good cross-functional communications

Most projects require people from many different skills or professional disciplines to work together. In a project team organization, the project manager can ensure that strong and fast communication links exist up, down and across the project organization. There should be no delays while information has to cross departmental boundaries. Decisions can be made more easily and with greater speed. Action can follow decisions with little or no delay.

Security and confidentiality

If work is being conducted for a government defence contract, or for any commercial project that requires a secret or confidential environment, the establishment of a project team greatly helps the organizers to contain all the work and its information within closed, secure boundaries.

The case against the team

Inflexibility and inefficient use of resources

Unless a project is very big, the individual specialist subgroups set up to perform all the varied activities within the project team will be too small to allow sufficient flexibility of labour and other resources.

Where, for example, a design department of 100 people is coping with several projects in a matrix organization, the absence of a few people through sickness would cause temporary difficulties, but these could probably be overcome to a great extent by rescheduling work within the department. If, on the other hand, a project team had been set up to include its own small independent design group, perhaps needing only five people, the absence of two or three of these for any reason could pose a more serious problem.

An item of manufacturing plant purchased specially for use by a project team will undoubtedly spend much of its time idle. The same item of plant installed in a common production facility would, on the other hand, be available for general work and it could probably be used far more efficiently, with less idle time for the machine and its operator. Then, the return on the capital invested in that plant should be greater. The same argument might be applied to any expensive facility set up for the sole use of a project team.

Now consider the example of a chemical plant construction project whose team organization is like that shown in Figure 2.6. Suppose that the team includes four electrical engineers. The project manager might face one or more of the following problems:

● difficulty in finding enough tasks to keep all four electrical engineers gainfully occupied all the time.
● severe problems if two or more of the engineers fell ill at the same time or were otherwise unavailable for work at times of peak project activity.

If, instead of a project team, the company operated a matrix organization (like that shown in Figure 2.5), those same engineers would be part of a larger electrical engineering group. They would be found working alongside engineers allocated to all the other projects. The larger group would offer far more flexibility, and the chief electrical engineer should be able to reallocate work among the remaining engineers to minimize the effect of a temporarily depleted workforce or the peak demands of a single project.

Inflexibility associated with small groups can also be expected in some of the specialist administrative functions, where it is often more difficult, if not impossible, to rectify matters at short notice using temporary employees. In the manufacturing case, for example, it is quite possible that only one or two people would be responsible for all project purchasing, or for project production control. Indeed, it is not unknown for one person to be responsible for both of these activities on a small project team. In such circumstances, the fate of the project may depend on the capabilities and health of just one individual, who becomes virtually indispensable and almost impossible to replace at short notice.

Isolation of specialists

Specialist engineers located in small project teams are deprived of the benefits of working in a department with colleagues of their own specialist discipline. They are less able to discuss technical problems with their peers or to have access to the valuable fund of general historic technical and professional data plus current awareness that permanently organized specialist departments accumulate.

Administrative difficulties

Even if a project is of sufficient size to justify its own exclusive team, not all the problems of project coordination will necessarily be overcome. Very often it might be found impossible to house all the participants under one roof, or even in the same locality. Although team organization might be logical and ideal for the project, it could be physically impossible to achieve in practice.

Life after the project

When the project is completed, the team and its project manager have no further purpose. As various aspects of the project are finished, so the team will gradually be reduced in size until it is finally disbanded. Think of Haydn's 'Farewell Symphony' where, as the work draws to its conclusion, the orchestral players depart one by one, extinguishing the candles on their desks as they go, so that the stage is finally left in darkness and silence. People working on a project team know that something similar will happen to them. That knowledge can be a powerful demotivator.

Another possible danger is that something could go seriously wrong with the project after its supposed completion, with expert attention required from the team's engineers to satisfy the client and put matters right. If the team no longer exists, and the engineers who designed the project have been dispersed, events could take an embarrassing, even ugly, turn for the company.

The project customer or client will expect the provision of post-project services from the project contractor. These services can include advice on difficulties experienced by the customer in operating plant and equipment, recommendations for routine care and maintenance, and prompt action to rectify any hardware or software malfunction. The project contractor should also be able to carry out possible future orders from the customer to adapt, modify, expand, augment or replace plant or equipment supplied with the original project. Temporary project teams do not survive for long enough to provide continuity of service to the customer, and the company must make alternative, more permanent arrangements.

The case for the matrix

The matrix option allows the establishment of specialist functional groups which, in theory, have 'eternal life' independent of the duration of individual projects. Each member of every specialist group should be able to enjoy a reasonably stable basis for employment (provided that the order book remains full). An environment is created that facilitates the building of long-term trust and loyalty. Pooling specialist skills gives greater flexibility in allocating resources to projects. Concentration of specialist skills enhances the organization's collective technical ability and quality. Organizational continuity promotes the accumulation of knowledge, expertise and experience with time, both for individuals and for the group as a whole. There is a clear promotion path within each group, and any person with sufficient drive and ambition should be able to compete fairly against his or her colleagues for more senior positions as vacancies arise, with chief engineer or department manager and beyond being seen as achievable longer-term goals.

Performance assessment of each individual, and any recommendation for promotion, improved salary or other benefits, is carried out by a manager of the same professional skill within the stable group. This is more likely to result in a fair assessment and employee satisfaction. These possibilities are not readily available to the specialist engineer or other professional person working alone in a multi-disciplined project team.

The case against the matrix

The matrix organization has its own characteristic disadvantages. Not least of these is the split responsibility which each group member faces between his or her line manager and the project manager.

Too much reliance can be placed on the supposed 'eternal life' of the matrix organization in modern times, when many businesses face sudden devastating changes as a result of mergers, takeovers, corporate re-engineering, downsizing or even failure.

Most of the advantages connected with a project team (listed above) are denied to the project manager in a weak matrix, but this situation is improved when the matrix is made stronger (with more authority given to the project manager).

Characteristic	Organization indicated	
	Team	Matrix
Maximum authority for the project manager	√	
Freedom from duplicated or ambiguous lines of command	√	
Maximum motivation of staff to meet difficult targets	√	
High security of information: by enclosing work in secure areas	√	
High security of information: by restricting the number of staff who need to know about the work	√	
Most flexible deployment of resources		√
Most effective use across the company of those with rare specialist skills or knowledge		√
Large project, employing many people for a long duration	√	
Several small simultaneous projects, each needing a few people for a short time		√
Career motivation of individuals: opportunities for promotion within a person s specialist discipline		√
Career motivation of individuals: through long-term continuity and relative stability of the organization		√
Post-design support to construction or commissioning staff		√
Efficient post-project services to the customer		√
Establishment of 'retained engineering' information banks from which future projects can benefit		√

Figure 2.7   Project team versus a balanced matrix

Comparison of team and matrix

The arguments will no doubt continue as to which is the better of the two organizations. Some of the pros and cons are summarized in Figure 2.7. As a general rule (although it is dangerous to generalize in this subject), large projects of long duration will probably benefit from the formation of project teams. The same applies to projects that are, by their nature, self-contained, such as work on a remote construction site. Matrix organizations are indicated for companies which handle a number of relatively small simultaneous projects in the same premises.

The hybrid option

Sometimes companies adopt the solution of a hybrid organization: operating a matrix organization in general, but with teams set up for certain projects when the need arises. An example of such an organization is shown in Figure 2.8. It is arranged principally as a matrix, with specialist groups under their respective highly qualified and experienced chief engineers. The project management group

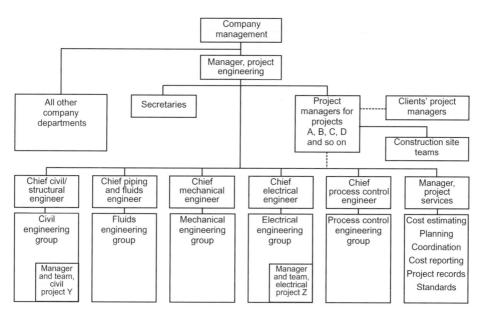

Figure 2.8   A hybrid organization
An international mining company is organized as a matrix, but a team will be set up within the relevant department for any single-function project. Here, project Y is wholly confined to civil engineering tasks, and project Z is for the replacement of a large electrical transformer.

contains project managers and project engineers who draw on the resources of the specialist groups for the skilled engineering and expert advice needed for most projects.

If, however, a project should arise which is predominantly within one of the specialist skills, the company might decide to appoint a project manager from within the relevant specialist group, managing a team contained within the group. For example, a project to install a large new electrical transformer in an existing plant might be regarded as a project that could be handled entirely by a team within the electrical department. Similarly, a land reclamation project might be assigned solely to the civil engineering group, who would set up their own internal team to deal with it under a civil engineer as project manager.

Another type of hybrid organization occurs when a company operates generally as a project matrix organization but sets up a separate, autonomous team whenever the size and scope of a project justifies that arrangement.

The project manager

The project manager's job title and role in the organization

When a company organization is searched to find a project manager, the first results may be fruitless because no one with that job title can be found. The project manager's identity is often hidden behind some other organizational role. This is particularly true for specialized in-house projects where, for example, a person with the title 'facilities manager' might act as project manager during a major reorganization of accommodation. Another example is where a person styled 'senior engineer' is made responsible for managing a costly new product design and development project.

Even where project management is accredited with the importance of a full-time appointment, the situation can be made less clear by the variety of titles used to describe the job. Contract manager, scheduling and estimating manager, project coordinator, project coordination engineer, programme engineer, project leader and project manager are but a few of the titles which have been used. Previous editions of this book have recommended the adoption of 'project manager' as a standard title (which has long been the usual practice in the construction industry). The trend in recent years has been encouraging, and project management is now widely recognized as a profession that deserves reasonable status and rewards, with its own professional associations (The Association for Project Management in the UK) and with far less confusion over the job title.

The forms of organization described earlier in this chapter demonstrate that the levels of responsibility and authority given to project managers vary considerably from one organization to another. In some cases they act simply as planners and coordinators. In other businesses the project manager will have complete authority over all those responsible for achieving the project objectives.

The career of a project manager might have started as an information technologist, as a specialist in one of the operational research disciplines, a contracts manager or a qualified engineer. One of the more common routes to project management lies through the engineering design department. Frequently the engineer in command of a particular project design is charged with some degree of overall responsibility for seeing the entire project through to completion. When this happens, the engineer has a dual organizational position, exercising direct line authority and supervision over the engineering design staff, while acting only in a functional role when trying to influence all the other departments engaged on the project.

The project management function in a small company might be conducted entirely on a part-time basis by one of the existing department heads, or by some other individual as in the case of the engineer just described. Other companies could be forced to recognize the need for a full-time project manager, the incumbent being held responsible for either one individual project or for several projects which are being handled simultaneously.

Seniority of the project manager

The questions 'How senior is the project manager?' and 'To whom should the project manager report?' now arise.

The person appointed will be expected to provide the company's general management with relevant facts whenever it becomes necessary for them to exert their senior authority or take other executive action to maintain the project on its specified financial, technical and delivery course. The project manager should therefore have reasonable access to general management.

Much of the project manager's time will be spent in coordination – steering and integrating the activities of some departments and relying on others for information or supporting services. This demands cooperation with and from the managers of most departments in the company, whether these departments are directly engaged in project fulfilment (such as engineering and production) or are service departments (like accounts and personnel). Ideally, therefore, the project manager should not be handicapped by being placed in an organizationally inferior position to any departmental manager in particular or to departmental managers in general.

Thus the desirable organizational status for the project manager appears to be indicated on a level at least equivalent to the company's departmental managers. This view is reinforced when it is realized that the person appointed will probably be called upon to supervise subcontractors and (once the marketing people have finished taking the order) to represent the company to the customer. The project manager is often a significant part of the corporate image which the company presents to the outside world.

Personality

What is the ideal personality specification for a project manager? If the objectives of project management could be condensed into responsibility for ensuring work completion within time and cost restrictions, then these goals could be achieved by a variety of approaches. One project manager might operate successfully by inducing fear and trepidation in his or her subordinates, so that every word is seen as a command to be instantly obeyed. Another might achieve the same results through gentle but firm persuasion. The essential element here is the ability to motivate people, by whatever means: the seasoned expert will be able to vary his or her management style according to the response of the individual being managed.

The average project participant will appreciate being led by a project manager who displays competence, makes clear decisions, gives precise, achievable instructions, delegates well, listens to and accepts sound advice, is enthusiastic and confident, and thus generally commands respect by example and qualities of leadership.

Perceptiveness and the use of project information

Other essential characteristics of the project manager can be grouped under the heading of 'perceptiveness'. Project managers must be able to select the salient facts from a set of data or a particular arrangement of circumstances. They must then be able to use these facts to best effect by taking action or reporting important exceptions to executive management, whilst filtering out the unimportant and irrelevant material.

Most project managers will become accustomed to being presented with information that is incomplete, unduly optimistic, inaccurate or deliberately misleading. Therefore, it is important that project managers should not be gullible. They will learn to check much of the information which they receive, particularly by knowing what questions to ask in order to probe its validity. As they gain experience of a particular organization they should become capable of assessing the reliability of individuals or departments, so that they can apply 'confidence factors' to the data supplied by those individuals or departments and the stories that they tell.

Project managers of any merit will know the frustration caused not simply by receiving inaccurate information, but also through receiving no information at all. Data deficiencies can take the form of delayed instructions or approvals from the customer, late information from subcontractors and vendors, and tardy release of design and other information within the project manager's own company. It can be difficult to obtain reliable and regular reports of cost and progress from far-flung project outposts, particularly where the individuals responsible feel themselves to be remote and out of range from the project manager's authority or are educated to standards below those of the more developed nations.

The ability to gather and assess relevant data is therefore another essential property for project managers. It is no good expecting to obtain the complete picture and manage a project simply by sitting behind a desk for the duration of the project. The project manager must take (and be seen to take) an active interest. He or she should visit personally and regularly those parts of the organization on which the project is dependent (a process sometimes known as 'management by walking about'). It might be necessary for the project manager to visit vendors, subcontractors, the customer and a remote construction site at suitable intervals to gather facts, resolve local disputes, generate enthusiasm, or simply to witness progress at first hand.

General knowledge and current awareness

Project managers in the age of technology could be described as specialists. Their background may be in one of the specialist engineering or other professional disciplines and they will certainly need to be trained in one or more of the current special project management techniques if they are to operate effectively. Nevertheless, the term 'specialist' can be misleading, since much of the project manager's time will be taken up with coordinating the activities of project participants from a wide variety of administrative, professional, technical and craft backgrounds. This work, far from requiring specialization, demands a sufficient general understanding of the work carried out by those participants for the project manager to be able to discuss the work sensibly, understand all the commercial and technical data received, and appreciate (or question) any reported problem.

The project manager should have a general understanding of administrative procedures as they will be applied throughout the project organization. If a person is asked to handle a flow of project data between different departments, he or she should be able to use their understanding of the administration and its procedures to arrange for the information to be presented in the form most likely to be helpful to the various recipients. In the jargon of computer technology, the project manager may be asked to solve interface problems, the solutions to which need some understanding of how the peripheral units operate.

There is little doubt that project management tools, techniques and philosophy will continue to undergo development and change. The project manager must be prepared to keep abreast of this development, undergoing training or retraining whenever necessary, and passing this training on to other members of the organization where appropriate. Some new developments will advance the practice of project management in general, and others will not. Some practices and techniques will be more useful to a particular project than others, and the project manager must be able to choose, use or adapt the most appropriate management methods for the particular project. The temptation to impose unsuitable methods on an organization for the sole reason that they represent the height of current fashion must be resisted.

Support, cooperation and training for the project manager

No matter how experienced, competent, enthusiastic and intelligent the person chosen for the job of project manager, he or she cannot expect to operate effectively alone, without adequate support and cooperation. This includes the willing cooperation of all staff engaged on the project, whether or not they report to the project manager in the line organization. It also includes support from higher management in the organization, who must at least ensure the provision of finance, accommodation, facilities, equipment, manpower and other resources when they are needed, and the availability of suitable clerical or other supporting staff. Just as those working on the project need to be properly motivated, so does the project manager, and supportive higher management who show constructive and helpful interest in the project can go a long way to achieve this. They can also help in the longer term by providing opportunities for training as new techniques or management systems are developed.

A person who is responsible for the overall allocation and progressing of project tasks will inevitably be called upon to decide priorities or criticize progress. The project manager must often arrange for the issue of work instructions in the full knowledge that he or she has no direct authority over all the departments involved. In a line and function organization, departmental managers alone are responsible for the performance, day-to-day management and work allocation within their own departments. I have even known cases where departmental managers have told project managers to keep out of their departments. In such circumstances the project manager's influence can only be exerted as reflected authority from higher management, without whose full backing the project manager must be ineffective.

The main show of authority which the project manager can wield stems from his or her own personality and ability to persuade or motivate others. In these enlightened times discipline no longer implies the imposition of rigid authoritarian regimes or management by fear through the constant threat of dismissal or other punitive action. Mutual cooperation and established job satisfaction are the more likely elements of an effective approach, especially in the long term. There will, however, be occasions when firm discipline has to be exercised – when, in the last resort, the full backing and support of higher management must be available as a reserve force which the project manager can call upon in any hour of need.

Sometimes it would be apt to include project managers in that group of individuals described as 'human dynamos'. There will be times when the apathy or inertia of some project participants has to be overcome by an electrifying injection of enthusiasm. The output of any dynamo, however, may be weakened if it is switched into an inefficient or wrongly connected circuit. The astute project manager will soon recognize any wasteful shortcomings in the project organization. If this happens, and an alteration in the organization can be proven necessary, the project manager should be able to rely on senior management to authorize and implement the change. Higher management, after installing the project manager, must provide continuous support and encouragement and work with him or her to create an ideal project management environment.

To maintain the company's competitive edge, the project manager should keep abreast of new developments in project control and management techniques and thinking. Senior management must recognize that much training is a continuous process and not simply a question of sending a person away for a one- or two-day course. Various training authorities arrange project management seminars where, in addition to the formal training given, delegates from different companies are able to meet and discuss mutual problems and solutions, and exchange views and experiences generally. The effectiveness of these individuals and of the profession as a whole must benefit from this type of exchange. It should also be remembered that the most effective form of learning is achieved from on-the-job training, which might need help from an external training consultant so that the training can be purpose-designed.

Just as important as the project manager's own training is the creation of an enlightened and informed attitude to modern project management methods among all those in the project organization. Ideally, when the objectives of a particular project are outlined, the project manager should ensure that participating managers, engineers and line supervisors have at least been given an elementary grounding in the appreciation of network analysis, scheduling, principles of cost and progress control, and the interpretation of associated computer reports. This should all be with specific relevance to the procedures chosen for use on the actual project. Training or instructions should be given in the use of the various forms and other documents to be used, and (where appropriate) in the active use of relevant computer systems. There is a serious danger that people who are suddenly asked to work with unfamiliar techniques and procedures, without sufficient training or explanation, will fail to cooperate. People neglected in this respect cannot be expected to provide the necessary feedback and other responses. If participating staff understand the procedures and the reasons for them, their cooperation is far more likely to be forthcoming and effective.

Project services groups

Unless the organization is too small to support the additional expense, it makes sense to support the project management function by setting up a central project management services group. This group, often known as the 'project office', is staffed with people (not too many!) who are capable of taking on the day-to-day chores of planning, resource scheduling, cost estimating, cost reporting, cost control, work progressing, progress reporting and general supervision of the company's project management computer systems. A project services group can be used in most kinds of project organization. The group can be a functional department within a pure project team, where it will serve and report directly to the project manager. If the organization is a multi-project matrix or a hybrid organization, the services group can be established as one of the departmental functions (an arrangement which is shown in Figure 2.8).

For a company that handles a relatively large number of small projects, none of which is big enough to justify its own full-time project manager, the project services group can take the place of project managers, at least as far as the cost and time objectives are concerned. When the project services group has this coordinating role, its leader must be given sufficient seniority in the organization for the coordination and control to be effective.

A project services group concentrates a company's expertise in the techniques of project management just as any other functional grouping can enhance a particular professional discipline. Centralization helps to standardize project administration procedures across all projects in a company. A project services group can be the logical place in the organization from which to coordinate all parts of the project cycle, from authorization to closedown. It can administer procedures such as project registration and change control. A well-motivated and expertly staffed services group can also spearhead the development and effective implementation of some advanced methods, so that the organization will be able to save time and money by exploiting methods such as templating and standard networks (described in Chapter 14).

Some powerful project management computer systems, especially those handling multi-project scheduling, are best placed under the supervision of specially trained experts. Those experts must have a good working knowledge of all the organization's projects, and combine that with special training in using the system and safeguarding the integrity of its database and backup files. A central project services group is an excellent choice to bear the burden of that responsibility.

Organizations with more than one project manager

Any project of significant size will probably have more than one project manager. These can usually be found spread throughout the overall project organization on the staffs of the customer, important subcontractors, and the manufacturers of some specially purchased goods and equipment.

Customer's project manager

Whenever a company sells a project to a customer, that customer will probably wish to monitor progress in order to be assured that there is every chance of the work being completed in accordance with the contract. For simple manufacturing contracts this role might be performed by the customer's purchasing department, using its own expediting and inspecting personnel. But, except in this very simple case, the customer might want to appoint an internal project manager to oversee the contract and manage the customer's own activities for accepting and taking over the completed project. The appointment of a customer's project manager would be expected, for example, where the customer is involved in planning to accommodate, install and start up plant supplied under the project.

Sometimes the customer will seek the services of an independent professional project manager, to oversee the project in return for a management fee. This role is often undertaken by specialist companies or by professional partnerships and individuals (such as consulting engineers or architects).

Project managers in customer/supplier chains

There is often more than one project contractor, especially in projects involving construction work. In multi-contractor projects it is probable that one contractor would be nominated by the project customer (the project owner) as the main or the managing contractor, with overall project responsibility to the owner for managing or coordinating all the other contractors and subcontractors.

The managing contractor, in addition to serving the project customer, will itself be a significant purchaser (that is, customer) for all the expensive equipment and other goods or services to be provided by suppliers and subcontractors. For large projects some of these subcontracts could amount to significant projects in their own right, each needing planning and project management procedures similar to those used by the managing contractor. Some equipment manufacturers and construction subcontractors would therefore need to assign project managers to manage their own internal sub-projects. Indeed, the managing contractor might even insist that such project managers are appointed, and could wish to question and approve the project management methods to be used, possibly as a precondition to awarding the purchase orders or contracts.

There is thus a chain of suppliers and customers in the project organization hierarchy. Such chains can be complex, extending to several levels, with project managers found scattered all over the organization in the offices of key participating companies. Those project managers are important not only for the purposes of planning and control; they also provide unambiguous and safe points of contact in the network of project communications.

Contract matrix

In large projects the customer–supplier chains are found in a type of organization which is sometimes called a contract matrix. A contract matrix is illustrated in Figure 2.9. In the example shown, the project owner (the customer or client) has engaged a managing contractor to design the project, carry out purchasing, hire subcontractors and generally manage all the activities at a construction site.

The organization chart shows that many of the companies involved in the

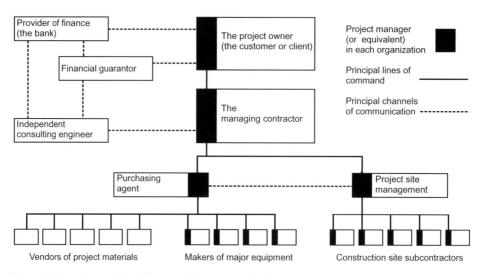

Figure 2.9   A project with more than one project manager
Most big projects will have at least two project managers: one employed by the organization with principal responsibility for carrying out the work, and the other representing the client or project owner. The construction project organization shown here is sometimes called a *contract matrix*. It includes several people who must practise project management skills. Every special-equipment manufacturer, for example, needs a project manager to plan and control its share of the project. Many of the practices and principles described in this book apply to all these 'satellite' project managers as well as to the principals.

project will have their own project managers, in addition to the principal project manager employed by the main contractor.

This project is being funded initially by a bank. The bank in this case has lent the funds on condition that the project owner finds a guarantor who is willing to underwrite a substantial part of the lending risk. In the UK, for example, the Export Credits Guarantee Department (ECGD) acts as guarantor for some projects carried out for overseas clients. Visit <http://www.ecgd.gov.uk> for more information about ECGD.

Both the bank and the guarantor are in need of expert independent advice. This has been provided in the example of Figure 2.9 by a professional engineering organization. This organization, sometimes known simply as 'the engineer', can inspect progress and certify all significant claims for payments so that monies are only paid against work that has actually been performed correctly and in the quantities listed on the contractor's invoices.

Joint ventures and other large projects

For very large projects several companies might agree to combine their resources and share the technical problems, expense and risk by forming a consortium or joint venture company. This approach will add yet another complication to the organization, and at least one more project manager.

It is not unusual to find projects where the participants are separated by international borders and thousands of miles. The volume of information for a large project, whether in the form of drawings, other technical documents, commercial correspondence, queries or even hotel and travel arrangements can be mind-boggling. For any complex project, apart from the obvious need to define responsibilities and all the contractual details, it is vital that the lines of communication between all the parties are clearly established and specified.

In any project organization which is complicated by the number of different participating companies, it makes sense to nominate one individual in each sub-organization (including the customer) as the principal local information and communications coordinator. These coordinators can ensure that all incoming correspondence is properly directed to the responsible recipients for action, followed up where necessary, and filed for safe keeping and subsequent retrieval. E-mail and other electronic messages are a little more difficult to control, but provision should be made in procedures for all material with contractual or significant technical content to be seen by the coordinator. Each sub-organization within the overall project organization is likely to have its own project manager, and he or she will often be able to nominate and supervise an appropriate information coordinator.

References and further reading for Part I

Atkinson, J. (2001), *Developing Teams Through Project-Based Learning,* Aldershot, Gower

Belbin, R.M. (1996), *How to Build Successful Teams ... The Belbin Way* (CD-ROM),Oxford, Butterworth-Heinemann

Belbin, R.M. (1996), *Management Teams: Why They Succeed or Fail,* Oxford, Butterworth-Heinemann

Briner, W. Hastings, C. and Geddes, M. (1996), *Poject Leadership,* 2nd edn, Aldershot, Gower

Crosby, P.B. (1979), *Quality is Free: The Art of Making Quality Certain,* New York, McGraw-Hill

Hartman, F.T. (2000), *Don't Park Your Brain Outside,* Philadelphia, PA, Project Management Institute

Huczynski, A. and Buchanan, D.A. (2001), *Organizational Behaviour: An Introductory Text,* 4th edn, Hemel Hempstead, Prentice-Hall

International Journal of Project Management (bi-monthly), Exeter, Elsevier Science Ltd. (This journal is available to IPMA members and affiliates. Members should contact their national association for details.)

Kliem, R.L. and Ludin, I.S. (1992), *The People Side of Project Management,* Aldershot, Gower

Morris, P.W.G. (1997), *The Management of Projects,* London, Thomas Telford (a detailed chronological history of project management)

Project, (10 issues per year), High Wycombe the Association for Project Management

Project Management Journal (quarterly journal), PMI

Project Manager Today (11 issues per year), Hook (Hampshire), Larchdrift Projects Ltd.

Randolph, W.A. (1991) *Getting the Job Done: Managing Project Teams and Task Forces for Success,* Hemel Hempstead, Prentice-Hall

Stewart. R. (1999), *Gower Handbook of Teamworking,* Aldershot, Gower

Wearne, S. (1993), *Principles of Engineering Organization,* 2nd edn, London, Thomas Telford

Part II

The financial and commercial framework

Chapter 3

Defining the project

Project definition is a process that starts when the idea of a project is first conceived, and does not end until the last piece of information has been filed to describe the project in its finished 'as-built' condition. Figure 3.1 illustrates how information from various sources is gathered with the passage of time, so that the definition becomes more comprehensive and accurate as the project life cycle proceeds from concept to completion. Figure 3.1 lists documents and information flows that might apply to a construction or manufacturing project, but the same general principle of definition growth throughout the life cycle applies to any project capable of being planned and pursued to a successful conclusion.

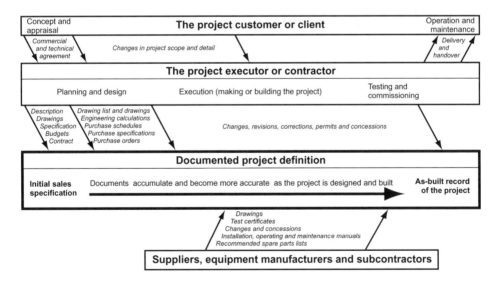

Figure 3.1   The project definition process
Project definition continues throughout the project life cycle until as-built records are archived.

This chapter deals with that part of project definition which should take place before a project is authorized to proceed from its conceptual stage to the use of valuable resources in executing the project. This is the part most relevant to setting the project on its proper course and which (for commercial projects) plays a vital role in helping to establish the initial contractual commitments. Subsequent aspects of project definition are discussed later in this book, particularly in Chapter 25.

When any company receives a customer's enquiry for new work – and certainly before any tender preparation can be authorized – the customer's requirements must be clearly established and understood. The project must be defined as accurately as possible right at the start. The contracting company must know what it is bidding for and what its commitments would be in the event of winning the contract.

Adequate project definition is equally important for the customer, who must be clear on what outcomes (deliverables) to expect in return for the money paid out. This point also applies to any company considering an in-house project, in which case that company can be regarded as both customer and contractor.

Projects which are difficult or impossible to define

This book generally takes a deterministic approach, in which it is expected that firm project objectives can be agreed at the beginning with the customer or client. Naturally, customer-requested modifications are bound to occur during the course of most projects, and these can change the original objectives. But the essence of successful project management is a positive and determined attitude towards setting, maintaining and eventually achieving firmly set objectives, with action taken wherever necessary to keep the project on its planned course.

Most of the procedures and project cases described in this book are written from the point of view of the contractor's project manager. They assume that the customer's project objectives and the contractor's commitments have been well defined and documented in advance, enabling all stages of the project and its expenditure to be managed effectively against clear benchmarks.

Of course there are times when a proposed project is so complex, or is fraught with so much uncertainty and risk that its progress and outcome cannot be foretold at the beginning. In other words, it might simply be impossible for the customer or investor to define the project.

Some safeguards for ill-defined projects

When a project cannot be adequately defined, if the project is not to be abandoned altogether, special measures must be taken to limit the risks. One approach, dealt with more fully in Chapter 24, is to adopt a step-by-step approach to authorization.

Avoidance of fixed-price contracts

A contractor asked to embark upon a project in which their expected role is not adequately defined can of course accept the order, provided that the payment arrangements guarantee reimbursement of all the contractor's costs plus reasonable fees or profit mark-ups. The contractor should ensure that the customer or investor bears the risk in these cases. Such arrangements can still be inconvenient or potentially difficult because it might be awkward for the contractor to arrange and commit resources for a project whose duration is unknown and which is liable to be cancelled at short notice.

Provisional items in fixed-price projects

It is common practice, especially in quotations for construction projects, to list separately any parts of the project that cannot adequately be defined and which are beyond the contractor's control. Those items will be named as provisional items, outside the scope of work covered by firm pricing.

An example of a provisional item can be envisaged in a proposed project to refurbish a building where part of the structure is hidden from view by wall cladding and is in uncertain condition. The proposal might assume the structure to be sound, and be priced accordingly. The list of provisional items would include a separate estimate of the costs likely to be charged to the customer should additional work be necessary when the cladding is eventually removed and the true state of the structure is revealed.

Feasibility studies to improve early project definition

The investor faced with a very uncertain prognosis for an industrial project might start by commissioning a feasibility study from a consultant or professionally orientated contracting company to obtain more facts and expert advice. This approach is frequently used to examine and appraise the technical, logistical, environmental, commercial and financial aspects of all kinds of projects requiring a high level of investment. Banks and other institutions asked to finance or otherwise sponsor ill-defined projects may require a satisfactory feasibility study report before committing funds. Government departments often demand or commission study reports for projects which are of significant public or international importance.

A feasibility study for a large capital project can be quite an undertaking in itself, perhaps taking one or more years to prepare and costing many millions of pounds. But a good feasibility study report can do much to point a project in the right direction and define its risks and achievable objectives.

Checklists

Checklists are a useful way to ensure that nothing important is forgotten when a new project is being evaluated. Contractors who have amassed a great deal of experience in their particular field of project operation will learn the type of questions that must be asked to fill most of the information gaps and arrive at a specification that is sufficiently complete.

One very simple application of a project definition checklist is seen when a sales engineer takes a customer's order for equipment that is standard, but which can be ordered with a range of options. The sales engineer might use a pad of pre-printed forms, ticking off the options that the customer requires. People selling replacement windows with double glazing use such pads. So do some automobile salesmen. The forms are convenient and help to ensure that no important detail is omitted when the order is taken and passed back to the factory for action.

A manufacturer of special-purpose machining systems may have a host of questions to ask about details of the products which the machines must eventually produce, and how the customer wants any loading and unloading points, locating lugs, jigs, fixtures and so on arranged. The standard network diagram which appears later in this book as Figure 19.7 was used by a company as a sequenced checklist for such cases.

Companies about to tender for large civil engineering, construction or mining projects can make good use of checklists. One list might be concerned with ensuring that plant performance or building accommodation needs are properly specified. Local climatic and geological data at the intended project site may have to be defined. If the project site is in a foreign country, the contractor may not know about potential physical hazards such as high winds or earth tremors. It is also necessary to check whether or not any special statutory regulations apply in the region. Other data might cover national working practices and the influence of local trade unions, the availability of suitable local labour, facilities to be provided for the contractor's expatriate staff and so on. Many, many questions will have to be asked and answered. Checklists are ideal in these circumstances. The example in Figure 3.2 includes some of the items that might feature in a complete list.

Defining a project for financial appraisal

When a project requiring significant expenditure is contemplated, the proper approach is for the potential investor to use one or more of the accepted processes for project financial appraisal. These help to forecast the likely net savings or profits that the investment will yield, put these into perspective against the company's corporate objectives, and assess any risk that might prevent the expected benefits from being achieved.

All of this demands proper and extended project definition, the full scope of

Project site and other local conditions

Availability of utilities
- Electrical power
- Potable water
- Other water
- Sewerage
- Other services
Transport
- Existing roads: Access difficulties (low bridges, weight limits, etc.)
- Nearest railpoint
- Nearest suitable seaport
- Nearest commercial airport
- Local airstrip
- Local transport and insurance arrangements
Physical conditions
- Seismic situation
- Temperature range
- Rainfall or other precipitation
- Humidity
- Wind force and direction
- Dust
- Barometric pressure
- Site plans and survey
- Soil investigation and foundation requirements
Local workshop and manufacturing facilities
Local sources of bulk materials
Local plant hire
Site safety and security
Local human resources available
- Professional
- Skilled
- Unskilled
Site accommodation arrangements for:
- Offices
- Secure stores
Site living accommodation for:
- Expatriate managers and engineers
- Artisans
- Short stay visitors
- Married quarters (see separate checklist if these are required)

Figure 3.2   Part of a definition checklist for a new project
The first pages of a checklist used by an international mining company for initial project definition. Any experienced company should be able to develop its own list.

Other site facilities
- First aid, medical and hospital facilities
- Catering and messing arrangements
- Hotels or other accommodation for VIPs
- Local banking arrangements

Communications
- General mail and airmail service
- Special mail or courier service
- Telephone over public network
- Telephone over dedicated terrestial or satellite link
- Fax
- E-mail
- Other

Contractual and commercial conditions

How firm are the proposals?
What are the client's relative priorities for:
- Time?
- Cost?
- Quality?

What are the client's delivery requirements?
Do we know the client's budget levels?
Scope of work envisaged:
- Basic design only?
- Fully detailed design?
- Procurement responsibility: (ourselves, the client, or someone else?)
- Construction responsibility: (ourselves, the client or a managing contractor?)
- Commissioning, customer training, operating and maintenance manuals, etc. (these must be specified)

How accurate are the existing cost estimates:
- Ball park?
- Comparative?
- Have all estimates been checked against the estimating manual checklist?

How is the project to be financed?
Is there to be a financial guarantor?
What do we know about the client s financial status and invoice payment record?
Are contract penalty clauses expected?
Is the pricing to be firm, or otherwise?
What are the likely arrangements for stage or progress payments?
What retention payment will be imposed?
What insurances must we arrange?
What guarantees or warranties will the client expect?

Figure 3.2   *Continued*

Project organization

Is the overall project organization known?
Is there an organization chart?
Obtain relevant information for each company or organization involved, as follows:
- Name of organization
- Name of project manager or other person in charge
- Names, job titles and responsibilities of other key personnel
- Name of addressee for all correspondence (if not the project manager)
- Mail address, including zip or post code
- Street address for goods and all other non-postal deliveries
- Telephone number
- Fax number
- E-mail address(es)

Initial design and technical information

Flowsheets
Layouts
Is further information required from the client?
Process parameters
Design parameters
Company design standards
National standards
Drawing sheets
Numbering systems for drawings and other documents
Special local engineering standards or statutory design regulations
Any similar previous projects from which useful design information might be
    retrieved and re-used?

(The checklist continues in similar fashion.)

Figure 3.2   *Concluded*

which would include the evaluation and assessment of some or all of the following parameters:

- outline description of the project, with its expected deliverables quantified in unambiguous terms
- total amount of expenditure estimated for carrying out the project and bringing its resulting product or structure into use
- expected date when the product or structure can be put to its intended use
- forecast of any subsequent operating and maintenance costs for the new product or structure
- operating and maintenance costs of any existing plant or structure that would be rendered unnecessary (saved) when the new project becomes operational
- any scrap or resale value expected from disposal of the superseded plant or structure
- economic operational life expectancy of the new plant or structure
- forecast scrap or resale value expected at the end of the working life of the new plant or structure
- forecast of financing costs over the project life (bank interest rates, inflationary trends, international exchange rate trends and so on, as appropriate)
- fiscal considerations (taxes or financial incentives expected under national or local government legislation)
- a schedule which sets out all items of estimated expenditure (cash outflows) against the calendar
- a schedule which sets out all expected savings or other contributions to profits (cash inflows) against the same calendar
- a net cash flow schedule (the difference between the inflow and outflow schedules, again tabulated against the same calendar).

For short-term commercial projects the financial appraisal may take the form of a simple payback calculation. This sets out the cumulative expenditure and the cumulative benefits (savings or profits) against time. The data can be tabulated on a spreadsheet, or two graphs can be plotted on a common set of axes (money against time). At first expenses will predominate but, as the project moves towards completion and implementation, benefits start to accrue so that the cumulative profits or savings should increase until they eventually overtake the cumulative expenses. The graphical method shows this most clearly, with the point in time where the cost and benefits graphs intersect indicating the project's break-even point. That is the time when the project can be said to have 'paid for itself'. The time taken to reach this break-even point is called the *payback period.*

Any sum of money listed as a saving or cost item in future years will have its significance distorted through the intervening period of time. Spending £1000 today is, for example, effectively more expensive than spending £1000 in a year's time. One way of explaining this is to consider the lost interest that the money might have earned for the investor if it had been placed on deposit in the meantime. Spend the money today and no interest can be earned, so that £1000 spent means exactly that. Place the money in a bank at five per cent simple interest for one year, then spend £1000 at the end of the year, and you will still be left with £50 accrued interest. Such distortions can have a considerable effect on the forecast cash flows of a project lasting more than two or three years if factors are not introduced to correct them. It is therefore best to use a discounting technique for the financial appraisal of long-term projects in place of the simple payback method. This is developed more fully in Chapter 6.

Project managers do not, of course, have to be expert in all or any of the techniques of project financial appraisal. It might, however, help to increase a manager's determination to meet the defined objectives of a project after authorization if he or she realizes that those objectives (time, money, specification) were key factors in an earlier appraisal decision – factors on which the investor and the contractor are both dependent if the completed project is to be a mutual success.

Although extremely important, the outcome of a financial appraisal is not always the deciding factor in choosing whether or not to proceed with a project. There might be overriding legal, ethical or operational reasons for going ahead where there is no hope of recovering the costs or making any profit or savings. One example would be a programme of structural works specified on the grounds of statutory health and safety regulations, where the organization is given the stark choice between carrying out the work or being forced by a court order to close down.

Customer enquiries

Enquiries and subsequent orders for commercial projects generally enter contracting companies through their sales engineering or marketing organization, and it is usually from this source that other departments of the company learn of each new enquiry or firm order. Even when enquiries bypass the sales organization, sensible company rules should operate to ensure referral to the marketing or sales manager, so that all enquiries are 'entered into the system' for effective handling and response. This will ensure that every enquiry received can be subjected to a formal screening process that will assess its potential project scope, risk and value.

Every enquiry must be registered and allocated a reference name or number that identifies it uniquely. There is no point in spending time and money in defining a project at the enquiry stage unless it is going to be possible at all subsequent times to know without ambiguity to which enquiry – and, just as important, to which *version* of that enquiry, a particular definition refers. The procedure can be quite simple; the register can be similar to the project register described in Chapter 19.

A company whose work involves a large number of small projects can receive a proportionately large number of customer enquiries, often as telephone calls. A useful and common practice is to provide the sales engineers or other relevant members of staff in such companies with pre-printed pads, designed with two purposes in mind:

1   The first is to provide a checklist of information requirements, arranged so that the person receiving an enquiry is prompted to ask all the necessary questions. The forms will have space in which the name and address of the potential customer can be written, together with the name and job title of the person calling. They must also have space for a summary of the work required. A company specializing in a particular technology will be able to devise tick-squares or boxes in which commonly used design and performance parameters can be entered.

2   The other purpose of using pre-printed forms is that, if properly designed and used, they can save a great deal of time in taking down the initial enquiry details.

Screening enquiries

The work involved in responding to an enquiry and preparing a tender can easily constitute a small project in itself, needing significant preliminary engineering design work plus sales and office effort that must be properly authorized and budgeted. The potential contractor will want to consider every enquiry received in order to decide the appropriate response. Enquiries from customers with a poor reputation for paying their bills or who are not financially sound are likely to be viewed with some disfavour. Other enquiries might be outside the capability of the receiving company, or be inconvenient and unwanted for a variety of other reasons.

It is customary, therefore, for companies to subject enquiries for new projects to a rigorous screening process to determine the appropriate response and either authorize or refuse to commit the time and costs needed to prepare a formal tender. Screening decisions are usually made at senior management level, often at regular meetings held for the purpose. Some companies record their screening decisions and manage appropriate follow-up action using a form for every enquiry such as that shown in Figure 3.3.

The potential customer will almost certainly set a date by which all competitive tenders for a project must be submitted, so the time available for preparation of a formal project proposal is usually limited. Everything must be properly planned, coordinated and controlled if a tender of adequate quality is to be delivered on time. What often happens is that tender preparation starts at a slack pace, with inadequate control, so that insufficient time is left for the end activities of typing, checking, correcting, printing, binding, signing and despatch. Then there is a frantic last-minute rush, with people working all night to produce the final version and special messengers or couriers given the almost impossible task of delivering the tender by the purchaser's deadline.

ACTION PLAN

Project title:		Enquiry number	Rev or case

Client's name and address:

Client's reference:
Enquiry date:
Telephone:
Fax:
E-mail:

Name and title of contact:

Outline description of proposed project:

Screening committee authorization: Comments

We will bid. Inform client: ☐

We will not bid. Inform client: ☐

Clarify with
customer and screen again: ☐   Signed:

	For action by	Authorized budgets			Date wanted
		Labour	Travel costs	Other costs	
Define the task					
Review task definition with client					
Develop possible solutions					
Evaluate client's operating costs					
Review of solutions with client					
Estimate our project costs					
Write proposal and draw artwork					
Printing and binding					
Time allowed for proposal delivery					
Presentation of proposal					
Total budgets					
Name of engineer in charge					

Figure 3.3   A screening and action plan for new sales enquiries

The customer's project specification

Initial enquiries from customers can take many different forms. Perhaps a set of plans or drawings, or a written description of the project objectives will be provided. Ensuing communications between the customer and contractor, whether written or spoken, can be long and protracted, often resulting in subsequent qualifications, changes or additions to the original request.

All of these elements, when taken together and documented, constitute the 'customer specification', to which all aspects of any tender and subsequent project authorization must relate. As with all other types of specification, the customer's project specification must be identifiable at all times by means of a unique reference number, date, and the issue or revision number.

Defining the project scope

When a project contract is eventually agreed, the contractor will have to ensure that the customer's specification is satisfied in every respect. The contractor's commitments will not be confined to the technical details, but must also encompass the fulfilment of all specified commercial conditions. The terms of the order might lay down specific rules governing methods for invoicing and certification of work done for payment. Inspection and quality standards may be spelled out in the contract and one would certainly expect to find a well-defined statement of delivery requirements. There might even be provision for penalties to be paid by the contractor should the agreed project completion date not be met.

Any failure by the contractor to meet the contractual obligations could obviously be very damaging for the contractor's reputation. Bad news travels fast throughout an industry, and the contractor's competitors will, to put it mildly, not attempt to slow the process. The contractor may suffer financial loss if the programme cannot be met or if they have otherwise miscalculated the size of the task undertaken. It is therefore extremely important for the contractor to determine in advance exactly what the customer expects for the money.

The customer's specification should therefore set out all the requirements in unambiguous terms, so that they can be understood and similarly interpreted by customer and contractor alike. Of particular importance is the way in which responsibility for the work is to be shared between the contractor, the customer and others. In more precise terms, the scope of work required from the contractor, the size of the contractor's contribution to the project, must be made clear.

At its simplest, the scope of work required might be limited to making and delivering a piece of hardware in accordance with drawings supplied by the customer. At the other extreme, the scope of a large construction or process plant project could be defined so that the contractor handles the project entirely, and is responsible for all work until the purchaser is able to accept delivery or handover of a fully completed and proven project (known as a *turnkey operation*).

Whether the scope of work lies at one of these extremes or the other, there is always a range of ancillary items that have to be considered. Will the contractor be responsible for any training of the customer's staff, and if so, how much (if any) training is to be included in the project contract and price? What about commissioning, or support during the first few weeks or months of the project's working life? What sort of warranty or guarantee is going to be expected? Are any operating or maintenance instructions to be provided? If so, how many and in what language?

Answers to all of these questions must be provided as part of the project definition before cost estimates, tenders and binding contracts can be considered.

The contractor's specification and questions of strategy

The contractor's design specification

If, after serious consideration of the customer's enquiry specification, a contractor decides to prepare a tender, the contractor must obviously develop technical and commercial proposals for carrying out the work. These proposals will also provide a basis for the contractor's own provisional design specification. It is usually necessary to translate the requirements defined by the customer's specification into a form compatible with the contractor's own normal practice, quality standards, technical methods and capabilities. The design specification will provide this link.

It is well known that there are often several different design approaches (proposed solutions) by which the desired end results of a project can be achieved. There are therefore likely to be considerable technical differences between the proposals submitted by different companies competing for the same order. Once the contract has been awarded, however, the number of possible design solutions should have been reduced to one: namely, that put forward by the chosen contractor. But within that general solution or concept there might still exist a considerable range of different possibilities for the detailed design and make-up of the project.

Taking just a tiny element of a technical project as an example, suppose that an automated plant is being designed in which there is a requirement to position a lever from time to time by automatic remote control. Any one or combination of a number of drive mechanisms might be chosen to move the lever. Possibilities include hydraulic, mechanical, pneumatic or electromagnetic devices. Each of these possibilities could be subdivided into a further series of techniques. If, for example, an electromagnetic system were chosen, this might be a solenoid, a stepping motor or a servomotor. There are still further possible variations within each of these methods. The device chosen might have to be flameproof or magnetically shielded, or special in some other respect.

Every time the lever has been moved to a new position, several methods can be imagined for measuring and checking the result, including electro-optical, electrical, electronic or mechanical. Very probably the data obtained from this positional measurement would be used in some sort of control or feedback system to correct errors. There would, in fact, exist a very large number of permutations of all the possible ways of providing drive, measurement and positional control. The arrangement eventually chosen might depend not so much on the optimum solution (if such exists) as on the contractor's usual design practice or simply on the personal preference of the engineer responsible.

With the possibility of all these different methods for such a simple operation, the variety of choice could approach infinite proportions when the permutations are considered for all the design decisions for a large project. It is clear that coupled with all these different possibilities will be a correspondingly wide range of different costs, since some methods by their very nature must cost more than others. When a price or budget is quoted for a project, this will obviously depend not only on economic factors (such as the location of the firm and its cost/profit structure), but also on the system concept and the detailed design intentions.

Ways of estimating project costs are considered in Chapters 4 and 5. It can already be seen, however, that owing to its cost implications, the technical strategy must be established before serious attempts at estimating can start. Once the design guidelines have been decided, they must be recorded in a provisional design specification.

Without a detailed design specification, there would be a danger that a project could be costed, priced and sold against one set of design solutions, but actually executed using a different, more costly, approach. This danger is very real. The danger is greater when the period between submitting a quotation and actually receiving the order exceeds a few weeks, allowing time for the original intentions to be forgotten.

Not invented here

It sometimes happens that engineers prefer to make a new design even though a perfectly adequate design already exists. They feel that they could do better themselves, or find fault unreasonably with the designs of others (even though those other engineers might enjoy a good reputation and their designs have been proven in successful earlier projects). This state of affairs is sometimes called the 'not invented here' syndrome. The results can be ugly. Two (of many) examples from my own experience follow; names have been omitted to avoid any risk of subsequent unpleasantness.

In one case, a British company won an important export order to design, supply and install expensive electronic equipment to a famous European university. Owing to an internal reorganization, the chief engineer resigned. His successor had different ideas and caused all design work completed or in progress to be scrapped and restarted. The design costs of that project eventually reached the same figure as the fixed price for which the whole project had originally been sold.

That meant that the company had to bear all the considerable manufacturing and installation costs of the project itself. The university professor was, quite understandably, making regular use of the telephone to ask, with commendable politeness, what were these 'unforeseen circumstances' that were preventing him from receiving his desperately needed equipment. Not only did the British contractor make a huge loss, but also the university had to wait for more than a year past the originally promised delivery date.

In another case, an American company with a very high reputation for product excellence shipped a set of engineering and manufacturing drawings to its new British subsidiary. This was a complete, finished design package for a large heavy engineering project. The intention was that it would provide the brand new machine and assembly shops with work during the period when the local British design team was becoming established and capable of designing subsequent projects. However, the drawings produced in America needed to be 'Anglicized'. The intention was that the British engineers should check through all the drawings and, with help from the purchasing department, ensure that the standards specifications and lists of bought-out components would be suitable for purchase from British suppliers. What actually happened was that the UK team poured scorn on the American design, and the whole project was re-engineered from scratch at a cost of more than a million pounds.

A specification is intended to do what its name implies: to specify that which shall be done. Managers who allow those reporting to them to depart from a design specification without good cause are guilty of incompetence, or weakness, or both.

Production methods

Similar arguments to those discussed above for engineering design apply to the need to associate the production methods actually used in manufacturing projects with those assumed in the cost estimates and subsequent budgets.

It can happen that certain rather bright individuals come up with suggestions during the proposal stage for cutting corners and saving expected costs – all aimed at securing a lower and more competitive tender price. That is, of course, laudable. Provided that these ideas are recorded with the estimates, all should be well and the cost savings can be achieved when the project goes ahead.

Now imagine what could happen if, for instance, a project proposal were to be submitted by one branch of the organization, but for strategic reasons the company's managers decided to switch the work to a production facility at another, far-away location in the organization. If all the original ideas for saving production costs had not been recorded, the cost consequences could prove to be disastrous.

Unfortunately, it is not necessary to transfer work between different locations for mistakes of this kind to arise. Even the resignation of one production engineer from a manufacturing company could produce such consequences if his or her intentions had not been adequately recorded.

The golden rule, once again, is to define and document the project in all essential respects before the estimates are made and translated into budgets and price.

Construction specification

Construction projects offer another example of work which has to be defined by specification. All building contractors of any repute work from detailed specifications. The requirement to satisfy the statutory authorities is just one reason for documenting specifications of building location, layout, intended use, means of escape in case of fire, appearance, and many other factors.

There are, of course, many design aspects of a building which can greatly affect its costs, including, for instance, the style of interior decoration, the quality of the fittings and installed equipment, lighting and air conditioning standards.

Disputes can be minimized, if not prevented altogether, if a contractor produces a detailed project specification and asks the customer to accept it before the contract is signed. Any changes subsequently requested by the customer can then be identified easily as changes from the agreed specification, and charged as variations to the original order.

Specifications for product development projects

Development programmes aimed at introducing additions or changes to a company's product range are prone to overspending on cost budgets and late completion. One possible cause of this phenomenon is that chronic engineer's disease which I call 'creeping improvement sickness'. Many will recognize the type of situation illustrated in the following example.

Case study

The project

A company producing electronic and audio equipment for domestic users has carried out a market survey. From the results of this study the company plans to introduce a new 'fun' model stereo tape cassette player. The aim is a device with attractive styling, dual mains or battery operation, reasonable performance, but at a low price and calculated to appeal to the tastes of children against the competition of foreign imports.

By any standards this can be regarded as a simple, small project. It requires only simple budgeting and a modest degree of programme control: it is certainly not dependent for its success on state-of-the-art project management techniques. Everything should be straightforward. Nothing can go wrong.

The kick-off meeting

The launch of the new product design can be visualized, starting with a meeting in the chief engineer's office in the company's development laboratories. In addition to the chief engineer, the meeting would probably include representatives from other interested departments, such as sales and production. The other member needed to establish the necessary quorum is, of course, the design engineer (George) assigned to carry out the actual development work. Discussion would undoubtedly be aimed at setting George on the right track to create the unit envisaged by the company's directors on the basis of the recent market survey. Thus George will be given a set of objectives. However, let us assume, that, as often happens, these objectives are fairly broadly based and not written into a formal product specification.

George can be imagined emerging from the meeting, full of ideas arising from the discussion and carrying his own rough notes of the proceedings and perhaps a few sketches. He will undoubtedly have been given some idea of target production costs, styling, performance, the preferred selling price and an approximate date for stocks to be available for distribution and release to the market.

Initial design stage

We can safely assume that George will be fairly bubbling over with enthusiasm. Most competent engineers become keen when suddenly given responsibility for a new project on which their creative abilities can be unleashed. After a week or two of activity behind the closed doors of his laboratory, George can be expected to emerge with the first experimental model of the new cassette player. This model must then be subjected to the critical attention of various experts, among whom may be marketing staff, an industrial designer and production engineers or other suitable representatives of the department that will eventually have to manufacture the product.

Pre-production stage

Following successful evaluation of the prototype, and incorporation of recommendations from the experts, the next stage in the project will be the preparation of production drawings, bills of materials and specifications from which a small pilot production batch can be manufactured. From experience, one might reasonably expect that this pre-production phase of the project would take considerably longer than the original design of the laboratory model. The production department may decide to go ahead with some limited tooling, and the production engineers and others will want to set up trial manufacturing procedures, check on tolerances, test-program any automatic operations, and think generally about methods for assembly and testing.

Second thoughts

A period of waiting must be endured by George, during which, apart from having to check drawings or answer occasional production or purchasing queries, he is free to reflect upon his design. This leads him to have second thoughts. On thumbing through his component catalogues, he has discovered that he could have specified a different amplifier, giving improved performance at a slightly reduced component cost.

Early modifications

George decides to implement the change, which, incidentally, requires a redesign of the printed circuit boards at a stage when they have already been drawn and ordered in production prototype quantities. George puts the redesign in hand and cancels the first order for prototype boards.

Modified drawings and parts lists are issued to the production and purchasing departments. The production cost estimators find that the cost saving expected from changing to the new amplifier will amount to less than 1 per cent of the total estimated production cost per unit. So far, the change has caused a three-week hold-up in the programme and preparatory work in several departments has had to be scrapped and restarted.

George, in the mean time, has received a visit from a representative of the company which he chose to supply the loudspeakers. The representative is delighted with the potential business but, taking a technical brochure from her briefcase, wishes George to know that she can offer, at modest cost, new loudspeakers that would suit the size and shape of the cabinet, extend the bass response by a whole octave, and be better able to withstand the increased power of the new amplifier. The slightly increased size of the replacement loudspeakers will result in further drawing modifications and the scrapping of some work already carried out on the pilot batch. George considers this a small price to pay for the significant increase in performance, and decides to make the change.

Unforeseen problems

At length, and in spite of the delays and additional expense, the prototype batch is completed and passed back to the laboratory for evaluation. George is dismayed to find that every single one of the prototype batch exhibits two faults which were not apparent on the first laboratory-built experimental model. There is a significant amount of rumble from the tape cassette drive motor, now shown up as a result of the improvement in bass response. For the same reason, mains hum is audible.

Three possible choices are now open to George. He could revert to the initial design, using the original amplifier and loudspeakers. However, George has high ideals, and the idea of degrading the performance does not appeal to him. The second option would be to introduce a simple filter circuit to cut the bass response to attenuate the rumble and hum. But this, again, would degrade the performance.

George decides that the third option is the only acceptable one. He modifies the mains power unit to remove the mains hum and specifies a higher-quality tape drive motor to reduce the rumble. These changes, although they cause additional delay and costs, result in a prototype that finally passes all its tests.

It is time to evaluate the result.

A good result?

The eventual result is outstandingly good. The performance of the modified prototype finally measures up to George's most critical requirements. George is well pleased with the results of his labours, and congratulates himself on a job well done.

The company's management is not so well pleased. The oft-repeated phrase 'time is money' is as true in project management as anywhere, and it is usually fairly safe to assume that if the planned timescale has been exceeded, so have the budgeted costs. It is apparent that development costs have rocketed over budget in this case.

The manufacturing cost per unit has become so high that it will no longer be possible to sell the unit economically at the intended price. In any case, the new model has been produced so late that the gap in market where the demand originally lay has since been filled by a competitor's product.

All of this could have been prevented if George had carried out his original instructions. But what exactly were those original instructions? Where is the documentary proof? George was given only vague guidelines at the start of this project, and it was easy for him to choose and change his own course. This simple example serves to show some of the pitfalls that can happen in a product development project that is not controlled from an adequate project specification.

George has, in fact, designed a very good product, but not the product which management expected. He has allowed his own ideas to intrude, and he has lost sight of the original objectives. George has fallen into a common trap by allowing the 'best' to become the enemy of the 'good'.

Case study revisited: How should it have been done?

It might be as well to take a second look at this imaginary project and see how the course of events would have run under a regime employing some of the essential elements of project control.

Written specification

The first noticeable difference would be the provision of a written project specification. The main part of this specification would be a technical product specification, intended to define clearly all the design objectives from the start. Such product specifications should include an account of the expected performance, with quantified data, quality and reliability standards, styling guidelines, size and weight limits, and so on.

Commercial objectives for the product development project must also be specified. In order to assess the probable rate of return on capital investment (as part of initial project appraisal) the management must start with a fair idea of what this investment will be.

Budgets for development expenditure, production tooling and other costs should therefore be compiled and agreed at the beginning and recorded in the commercial part of the specification. The maximum permissible unit production cost and the target selling price must also be determined, both of these figures being related to sales forecasts giving the expected quantities to be produced for the first two or three years.

Finally, there is the question of timescale. The target date for market release has to be decided carefully. It must be an objective that can be achieved. Product release target dates are often chosen to allow the product launch announcement to be made at an important trade exhibition.

Planning and control

A more effective check could have been kept on progress in our example if a simple programme schedule (such as a bar chart) had been included as part of the project specification. Provided that this identified all the important project events ('milestones'), regular management checks would have indicated the danger of late running soon enough for corrective action to be taken.

Change control

Now suppose that George has reached the stage in the project where previously he was allowed to introduce his first design change (the amplifier). Under conditions of effective control, he would not have been allowed to introduce any change after the issue of production drawings without prior discussion with other departments likely to be affected.

It is usual for changes of this nature to be brought up for approval before a representative 'change committee'. The committee will assess all the possible effects of any proposed change on stocks and work in progress, reliability, costs, timescale and so on before giving their consent or other instructions. We can be sure that at least some of the adverse effects of George's first change proposal would have been foreseen by a change committee. Apart from any technical reasons, this change would have been nipped in the bud because of the threat it posed to the timescale.

Detailed procedures for controlling modifications are given in Chapter 23. It is enough at this stage to note that the other modifications introduced in the cassette player project would also have met with an early demise under a sound administration. George would have been kept on the right lines by the provision of a formal product specification and development programme, by the sensible control of modifications and, of course, by the-day-to day supervision of his superiors.

Developing and documenting the project specification

Given the importance of specifying project requirements as accurately as possible, it is appropriate to end this chapter with some thoughts on the preparation of a specification document.

Project specification development (solution engineering)

Although customers might be clear from the very first about their needs, it is usual for dialogue to take place between the customer and one or more potential contractors before a contract for any project of significant size is signed. During this process each competing contractor can be expected to make various preliminary proposals to the customer for executing the project. Some of those proposals might suggest changes to the customer's initial enquiry specification – changes intended to improve the project deliverables or otherwise work to the mutual benefit of customer and contractor.

In some companies this pre-project phase is aptly known as *solution engineering*. Each contractor's sales engineering group works to produce and recommend an engineering solution which they consider would best suit the customer (and win the order). Solution engineering might last a few days, several months, or even years. It can be an expensive undertaking, especially when the resulting tender fails to win the contract.

Although it is tempting to imagine the chosen contractor's sales engineers settling down contentedly to write a single, definitive project specification, the practice is likely to be quite different. The first draft descriptive text, written fairly early in the proceedings, will probably undergo various additions and amendments as the solution develops. It is likely to be revised and reissued more than once. The text will typically be associated with a pile of drawings, artists' impressions, flowsheets, schedules or other documents appropriate to the type of project. Those documents, too, might suffer several changes and re-issues before the agreed solution is reached.

A fundamental requirement when a contract is eventually signed is to be able to identify positively which of these specification versions, which revision of the text and which issues of the attached documents record the actual contract commitment. Remember that the *latest* issue of any document might not be the *correct* issue.

The only safe way to identify any document is to label it with a unique serial or identifying number, and augment that with a revision number every time the document is re-issued with changes.

Format and content

The format described here is typical for a well-prepared project specification:

1. **Binder** – The specification for a large project is going to be around for some time and receive considerable handling. It deserves the protection of an adequate binder. The binder should be loose-leaf, or otherwise allow the addition or substitution of amended pages.

2. **Specification identifier** – The binder should carry the specification serial (identification) number, the project number (if different), and the project title. All of these should be prominently displayed.

3. **Control schedule of specification documents** – This vital part of the specification complements the specification identifier by denoting the revision status of the complete document. Ideally, it should be bound in the folder along with the main text (either in the front or at the back). The control schedule must list every document which forms part of the complete specification. This includes drawings too large to be conveniently bound with the main text, and other external documents that are relevant to adequate project definition (for example, engineering standards specifications or statutory regulations).

    Minimum data required for each document are its title, serial number and correct revision number. Should any of the associated documents itself be complex, it too should have its own inbuilt control schedule.

    The control schedule should be given the same serial and amendment number as the document that it controls. If the specification is numbered XYZ123 and is at revision 6, then the control schedule itself should also be numbered XYZ123, revision 6. Thus the amendment state of the entire project specification (including all its attachments and associated documents) can always be identified accurately simply by giving one amendment number.

    There is more information of general relevance to the administration of multi-page documents and their amendments in Chapter 18 (see page 419).

4. **Descriptive text** – The narrative describing the project should be written clearly and concisely. The text should be preceded by a contents list, and be divided logically into sections, with all pages numbered.

    Every amendment must be given an identifying serial number or letter, and the overall amendment (or revision) number for the entire specification must be raised each time the text is changed. Amended paragraphs or additional pages should be highlighted, for example by placing the relevant amendment number alongside the change (possibly within an inverted triangle in the manner often used for engineering drawings).

5. **Supporting documents** – Most project specifications need a number of supporting engineering and other documents that cannot conveniently be contained within the binder. These effectively form part of the specification, and they must all be listed in the control schedule.

6. **Distribution list** – A responsible person must keep a list of all those who received the initial issue of the specification. This can be used as a control document to ensure that all holders of the specification receive subsequent amendments. The safest form of control is to bind the distribution list in with all copies of the specification, although this can occasionally be politically undesirable.

Chapter 4

Cost estimates, Part 1: Definitions and principles

A good estimate of project costs is necessary for subsequent management decisions and control. The most obvious reason for producing cost estimates is to assist in pricing decisions, but that is by no means the whole story. Cost estimates are usually needed for all projects, including in-house management projects and those sold without fixed prices. Timescale planning, pre-allocation of project resources, the establishment of budgets for funding, manpower and cost control, and the measurement of achievement against expected performance all demand the provision of sound estimates.

Cost definitions and principles

It is generally understood in accounting circles that the word 'cost' should never be used alone, without a qualifying adjective. It must always be made clear exactly what kinds of costs are meant. There are many ways in which costs can be described, but within the space of this chapter it is necessary to outline some of the terms with which cost estimators and project managers should be acquainted. There is no need to clarify self-explanatory terms (such as labour costs, material costs and so on), and the following list has been limited to a few terms that may not be familiar to all readers. The list is in alphabetical order.

Absorption costing

See *Overhead recovery*.

Below-the-line costs

A collective name for the various allowances that are added once a total basic cost estimate has been made. These can include allowances for cost escalation, exchange rate fluctuation and other contingencies.

Cost escalation

Cost escalation is the increase in any element of project costs when the cost of that element is compared between two different dates (for example, now and two years hence). Caused by wage and salary awards and inflationary pressures on prices paid for materials and purchased components, cost escalation is usually expressed at an annual rate per cent.

Direct costs

Costs which can be attributed directly to a job or project task are termed direct costs. Thus if a person spends two hours in the manufacture of a component which is identifiable as being required for a particular project, then that time can be classed as direct labour and its cost can be recorded as a direct cost to be charged direct to the project. Similarly, materials, components and expenses directly attributable to a particular project can be classed as direct.

Factory cost

Applicable to manufacturing projects, the factory cost is the total cost of a job or project before the addition of mark-up for profit. It comprises all direct and indirect costs for labour, materials and expenses. A very simple example which shows the relationship of factory cost in the pricing structure is given in Figure 4.1.

Design costs are often treated as indirect in routine manufacturing, to be recovered as overheads against bulk sales of the resulting product. The example in Figure 4.1, however, is for a special project. Although this is a very simple project, it can rank as a project none the less because it is for the design and one-off manufacture of a component to satisfy a customer's special purchase order. All the design costs in this case can be recorded and attributed directly to the project, and they have therefore been treated as direct costs.

Fixed costs

Costs are said to be fixed when they remain virtually unchanged and must continue to be incurred even though the workload might fluctuate between zero and the maximum capacity. These costs typically include management and administrative salaries, rent, business rates, heating, insurance, buildings maintenance and so on. Fixed costs usually form by far the biggest component of a company's indirect or overhead costs (see *Indirect Costs*).

Item	£ per hour	£	£
Direct materials			
Brass sheet		1000.00	
Brass rod		1500.00	
Other		1250.00	
Total cost of direct materials			3750.00
Direct labour (standard cost rates)			
Design			
10 hours senior engineer	25.00	250.00	
15 hours design engineer	15.00	225.00	
1 hour checker	17.00	17.00	
Manufacture			
200 hours sheet metal	13.00	2600.00	
30 hours turner	13.00	390.00	
10 hour assembly	13.00	130.00	
1 hour inspection	16.00	16.00	
Total direct labour cost			820.00
Prime cost			4570.00
Overheads at 130% of direct labour			1066.00
Factory cost			5636.00
Mark-up at 50%			2818.00
Indicated selling price			8454.00

Figure 4.1   **Cost and price structure for a simple manufacturing project**

Indirect costs (overhead costs or overheads)

The provision of facilities and services such as factory and office accommodation, management, personnel and welfare services, training, cost and management accounting, general administration, heating, lighting and maintenance gives rise to costs that must generally be incurred in running a business. These costs can include salaries and wages, materials and other expenses, but (except in the unusual case of an entire organization set up specially to fulfil only one project) these general costs cannot be allocated directly to one job or project. They are therefore termed indirect costs, often called 'overhead costs', or simply 'overheads'.

Note that the provision of facilities at the site of a construction project, although these might include accommodation and services that would be classed as indirect back at the main or home office, can be classed as direct costs. This is because they are provided specifically for the project in question, and can therefore be identified solely with that project and charged directly to it.

There are considerable differences between companies in the interpretation of direct and indirect costs. Some firms charge to projects the costs of printing drawings, for example, and recover those costs directly by billing them to the client or customer. Other firms would regard such costs as indirect, and charge them to overheads. Sometimes the classification of costs as direct or indirect can vary even from project to project within the same company, depending on what each customer has agreed and contracted to pay for as a direct charge. Cost estimators and project managers must be clear on what constitutes direct and indirect costs in their particular company, and must also pay attention to any special provisions contained in the proposal or contract for each project.

Indirect costs, although they are predominantly fixed costs, can sometimes include an element of variable costs. Maintaining a permanent headquarters would be a fixed indirect cost, since it must be incurred irrespective of normal workload fluctuations. Hiring temporary office staff to work in administrative departments would be a variable cost, because the rate of expenditure (the number and type of temporary staff hired) will vary according to factors such as workload and availability of permanent staff. Management can decide to increase or reduce the number of temporary staff (and hence their cost) at will. Classification of overheads into fixed and variable costs is not relevant to much of the argument in this book, but it is important in the manufacturing and process industries as a control in relating prices, profitability and the volume of production.

Whatever the industry, management must always strive to keep the overhead expenses as low as possible in relation to the direct costs, because high overheads can kill a company's chances of being competitive in the marketplace. It is in the variable overhead costs where the easiest and quickest savings can be made (short of relocating the company or dismissing some of the permanent administrative and management staff).

Labour burden

The labour burden is an amount, usually expressed as a percentage of wages or salaries, that is added to the basic hourly or weekly rate for employees to allow for non-working time and various additional expenses. The constituents of a typical labour burden might be the cost of paid holidays, illness or other absence, and *per capita* amounts payable by the employer as employee benefits, either voluntarily or as a requirement of the national legislation. In the UK, for example, these would include employers' National Insurance contributions.

Materials burden

Materials purchased for a project, which are themselves chargeable as a direct cost, are typically marked up by contractors in order to recover their administrative and handling costs. These mark-ups generally range from 15 per cent (or less) for very large, costly items shipped directly to site to 25 per cent or even more on small, low-cost items that have high handling and administration costs relative to their value. A common all-round rate used for the materials burden is 15 per cent.

Overhead costs

See *Indirect costs*.

Overhead recovery

Most project costing systems work on the basis of charging direct labour costs (including the labour burden) as time recorded on the job multiplied by the standard hourly cost applicable to the grade. An amount can then be added to this labour cost (usually as a rate per cent) to recover a part of the company's indirect, overhead costs. The simple example in Figure 4.1 illustrates this principle.

The same overhead rate (130 per cent in Figure 4.1) would normally be applied over all similar projects carried out by the company. In some industries the overhead rate can rise to 200 per cent or even higher (as, for example, in companies with a very high level of research and development to fund). In labour-intensive industries, with little research and development and no high-grade premises, the overhead rate might be 50 per cent or even less. It is not possible to indicate norms, since the circumstances of companies vary considerably from one to another (even where they are carrying out similar work). Obviously, a company which manages to keep its indirect costs (and overhead rate) to a minimum enjoys a competitive cost and pricing advantage.

This method of recovering overheads as a 'levy' on direct labour costs is called *absorption costing*. Setting the percentage overhead rate is an accounting task demanding perception and skill. Getting the answer right depends on accurate workload forecasts and effective overhead cost estimating and control.

If the planned direct workload should fail to materialize for any reason (perhaps through cancelled orders or over-optimistic sales forecasts), the amount of direct labour costs that can be allocated to jobs and charged out in invoices will be less than the forecast. Because overheads have been estimated as a fixed percentage of the direct labour costs, the amount of revenue received to pay for the overheads will also fall below plan. This condition is called *overhead under-recovery*. The principal remedies to consider include the following:

● Increase sales revenue by putting up the overhead rate, thus increasing prices (which might, however, reduce the quantity of products or project work sold).

● Increase sales revenue by a marketing drive to sell more products or project work.

- Persuade each new project client to agree to pay for some jobs previously regarded as indirect. This will depend on being able to identify those jobs and record their costs in a way that would satisfy subsequent audit. Examples of such costs are special printing and copying of project drawings and other documents, telephone calls, travel expenses and so on.

- Make economies to reduce the overhead costs.

Clients for large capital projects can be very critical of proposed overhead rates chargeable to their projects. They often ask for detailed explanations of what the overhead costs are intended to include. In fact, the overhead rate used for a large project might have to be negotiated with the client before an order can be won.

Overhead over-recovery will occur if workload and direct labour billings exceed expectations, so that the percentage rate set proves to be too high. Although this can increase profitability in the short term, it may not be desirable because it can imply that the company's pricing is not sufficiently competitive, with damaging consequences for future order prospects.

Prime cost

The sum of all direct costs needed to fulfil a particular job or project (direct labour plus direct materials plus direct expenses) is sometimes called the prime cost.

Standard costing

Standard costing is a system in which cost estimates and budgets are composed using *standard costs* (derived from average costs) for labour and materials.

In project costing, these standards are used both in cost estimating and in subsequent routine job cost collection (from timesheets and material requisitions). A measure of performance can be obtained by comparing the expenditure against the corresponding budget, provided that the same standard cost rates are used throughout. The differences (variances) between expenditure and budget can be analysed to provide management control information.

From time to time (preferably at regular intervals) the current cost rates are calculated by accountants and compared against the standard rates in use. Any differences give rise to another set of variances, indicating that the standard cost rates in use have become outdated. When the variances become significant (usually as a result of cost inflation), the standards must be reviewed and corrected as necessary.

Standard costing methods extend to other production quantities and measurements in manufacturing companies, but these are not relevant here in the context of project management. See also *Variance*.

Standard labour costs

When estimating, budgeting, accounting and cost reporting for any job or project, it would be tedious and impracticable to attempt to use all the different rates of pay earned by individuals. For example, two engineers with similar capabilities and identical job titles might be earning quite different salaries. Such differences can obviously occur for valid reasons at any level in the management or workforce. The cost estimator cannot possibly name the individuals who will be engaged on jobs that might not be started for months, even years after the estimates are made. Even if names could be pencilled in, there would be no guarantee that those same people would actually do the work. There is also the need to keep confidential the actual salaries earned by individual members of staff. Standard costing solves this problem.

For labour costs, the first step is to classify people according to some convenient rules (usually based on a combination of the work that they do and their general level in the salary structure). Categories which one international company found suitable for its home office staff are given in Figure 4.2. These few grades were found to be sufficient even for large capital projects involving engineering, purchasing and construction management.

It is best if the number of standard grades can be kept to a minimum (not more than ten, if possible). The accountants work out an average salary cost (the standard cost) for those in each grade. All estimates and actual jobs are then costed using these grades and standard rates.

Because the standards are calculated within the confines of the accounts department, the method has the advantage of preserving the confidentiality of individuals' earnings: cost estimators and project administration staff need only be told the current standard rates. However, these standard rates should still be treated as confidential proprietary information, because they might be of use to competitors.

Standard materials costs

Standard cost rates can be devised for commonly stocked materials and purchased components, but these apply more commonly to routine manufacturing operations than to projects where all materials are specially purchased. The standards are calculated as averages based on unit costs in suppliers' invoices.

Variable costs

Variable costs are those costs which are incurred at a rate that depends on the level of work activity. They are typically confined to the direct costs, but may have a small indirect content.

Grade	Those included	Notes
1	Company directors Divisional managers	Grade 1 also includes professional staff of consultant rank
2	Project managers Departmental managers	Grade 2 also includes chief engineers of the specialist engineering groups
3	Project engineers Senior engineers	Grades 3 and 4 include staff in all engineering groups, covering all the specialist engineering disciplines
4	Engineers	
5	Drawing office group leaders Checkers	
6	Draughtsmen and women	
7	General administrative staff	Grade 7 is used for clerks, secretaries, commercial officers, buyers and all others classed as indirect staff except managers, regardless of seniority or salary

Figure 4.2   Example of labour grades for standard costing in a project engineering company

Variance

A variance is any measured deviation between a planned or budgeted quantity and the quantity actually used on the project. Variances usually apply to cost differences, although they can also describe differences between scheduled and achieved times. These variances are particularly useful in project management because they highlight errors and satisfy the principle of management by exception.

Variances are also used by accountants to describe the errors (usually small) that result from using standard cost rates in budgets and project costing. These variances are revealed when payroll and purchase ledger costs are reconciled periodically with their corresponding standard rates. These variances are usually concerns for the accountants rather than for the project manager.

Estimating accuracy

Estimating must start from some form of project specification. It is clear that the more precisely the project can be defined at the outset, the less chance there should be of making estimating errors. However, the possibility of error can never be reduced to zero. No sensible person could ever declare the initial cost estimates for a total project to be entirely free from error and completely accurate. Estimating always involves an element of personal judgement. A project, because it is a new venture, must contain some surprises. If the final project costs did happen to equal the initial estimates, that would be a matter for some congratulation and celebration, but it would also be a matter of chance. In some cases it might not even be possible to declare with confidence what the true costs actually are at the end of a project, owing to the complexities of cost collection, cost apportionment and accounting methods.

There are clearly many reasons beyond the estimator's control why the final project costs might differ from the best possible estimates. It is therefore strictly inappropriate to label early estimates as 'accurate' or 'inaccurate' because the outcome can never be foretold with certainty and one can only determine the true accuracy of any estimate after the work has been done and the true costs become known. Perhaps 'reliability' or 'degree of confidence' would be better measures of an estimate's quality.

Steps can, of course, be taken to remove some sources of estimating errors. Several of these methods are discussed in this chapter and elsewhere in this book. Cost estimators should be aware of the problems, but must not allow these to deflect them from their primary task, which must always be to use all the data and time available to produce the best estimate possible – in other words a calculated judgement of what the project *should* cost if all goes according to plan.

Estimates made with a high degree of confidence will greatly assist those responsible for any competitive pricing decision, and good estimates improve the effectiveness of cost budgets and resource schedules.

Classification of estimates according to confidence

Some companies in the construction, petrochemical, civil engineering and other industries find it convenient to classify project cost estimates according to the degree of confidence that the estimators can express in their ultimate accuracy. These classifications depend on the quality of information available to the estimators, the time allowed for preparing the estimates, and the stage in the project life cycle when the estimates are made. Different organizations have their own ideas, but here is one example of a classification set:

1 **Ballpark estimates** are those made before a project starts, when only vague outline information exists and when practically all details of the work have yet to be decided. Ballpark estimates are also made in emergencies, when all the

detailed information necessary for a more detailed estimate is available but there is insufficient time available for its proper consideration. An example of such a ballpark estimate is seen when a manager is presented with a set of detailed manufacturing drawings and, when asked to answer the question, 'What will this lot cost to make?', weighs the pile of drawings thoughtfully in his or her hand and declares: 'There's about fifty thousand pounds' worth of work here.'

Ballpark estimates are widely used in many industries. They are particularly valuable for carrying out preliminary checks on possible resource requirements, for screening enquiries for tenders, and for other early planning decisions. Ballpark estimates are not likely to provide sufficient accuracy for other purposes, and should clearly not be used as a basis for fixed-price tendering. A well-reasoned ballpark estimate might achieve an accuracy of ± 25 per cent, given a very generous amount of luck and good judgement, but far wider divergence is to be expected.

2   **Comparative estimates,** as their name implies, are made by comparing work to be done on the new project with similar work done on previous projects. They can be attempted before detailed design work takes place, when there are no reliable materials lists or work schedules. They depend on a good outline project definition, which must enable the estimator to identify all the principal elements and assess their degree of size and complexity. The other main requirement is access to cost and technical archives of past projects which contain comparable (they need not be identical) elements. Apart from commercial risks outside the estimator's control (foreign exchange rate fluctuations, for example), accuracy will depend very much on the degree of confidence that can be placed in the proposed design solutions, on the working methods eventually chosen and on the closeness with which the new project elements can be matched with those of previous projects. It might not be possible to achieve better than ± 15 per cent accuracy.

Comparative estimates are commonly used as the basis for tenders in manufacturing and other engineering projects. When the time available for tendering is very short, contractors for construction projects may also be obliged to rely on comparative estimates, but they should then build in as many allowances for contingencies as competitive pricing will permit.

3   **Feasibility estimates** can be derived only after a significant amount of preliminary project design has been carried out. In construction projects, for example, the building specification, site data, provisional layouts and outline drawings for services are all necessary. Quotations must be obtained from potential suppliers of expensive project equipment or subcontracts, and material take-offs or other schedules should be available to assist with estimating the costs of materials. The accuracy 'confidence factor' for feasibility estimates should be better than ± 10 per cent. This class of estimate is often used for construction tenders.

4   **Definitive estimates** cannot be made until most design work has been finished, all significant purchase orders have been placed at known prices, and work on the project construction or assembly is well advanced or nearing completion. Definitive estimates can be produced from scratch, but the best practice is to arrive at them by updating the original comparative or feasibility estimates routinely as part of the project cost reporting and control procedure. The accuracy of any project estimate should obviously improve with time as known actual costs replace their corresponding original estimates in the total project cost estimate. Estimates can be labelled as 'definitive' when the time is reached where confidence is such that their accuracy is regarded as ± 5 per cent or better. Unless the accounting and cost control systems are flawed the figures for actual project costs and the definitive project estimate should converge when the project ends.

The degrees of accuracy quoted in these examples are about as good as could ever be expected. It is very likely that many organizations will assign wider limits. It is also common to find asymmetric limits, slewed about zero. A company might, for example, work on the assumption that its ballpark estimates are accurate to within +50 or +10 per cent.

All those using estimates for pricing decisions, setting budgets, financial planning, or any other purpose need to be aware of how much confidence can be placed in the figures put before them. If the organization's estimating procedures recognize and define different categories, such as ballpark, comparative, feasibility, definitive or whatever, then managers can make their decisions accordingly, and to better effect.

Estimating accuracy in relation to prices and profits

It is difficult to lay down rules on what should be a reasonable accuracy in estimates intended for pricing and control. For pricing purposes much depends on the size of the intended profit margin, since a large margin will cushion the effects of small estimating errors. Margins vary greatly, depending on market conditions and, particularly, on accepted practice in the relevant industry. Reliable estimates are a valuable asset to managers faced with the difficult task of trying to price a project in the teeth of keen competition, where there is no scope for the luxury of safety factors such as a high mark-up on costs or significant contingency allowances.

Profit vulnerability

The vulnerability of profits to erosion from costs which exceed budgets is not always appreciated. A simple example will illustrate this point.

Consider a project which was sold for a fixed price of £1 million against a total cost estimate of £900 000. The budgeted gross profit was therefore £100 000, which is 10 per cent of the selling price.

Now suppose that the project actually cost £950 000 instead of the estimated £900 000. This £50 000 cost variance represents an estimating error of just over 5.5 per cent. Some might think that 5.5 per cent is a small error, given the difficult nature of cost estimating. But the effect on the gross profit would not be small. It has been slashed from a planned £100 000 to only £50 000, a reduction of not 5.5 per cent but 50 per cent. The expected profit has been halved. That is how the outcome would be viewed by this company's management and shareholders.

Planned profits may fall victim to many risks. Some of these can be predicted, but others often come as unpleasant surprises. The aim must be to reduce the number of unknown variables or risks as far as possible, and then provide a sensible allowance to cover those that remain.

Profits are vulnerable and deserve the protection of good estimates and budgets. Managing a project which has been underestimated can be a soul-destroying experience, with everything running late, everyone demoralized, and all remaining cost predictions made only for the purpose of assessing the size of the impending loss. Project managers who have presided over this depressing state of affairs would not wish to repeat the experience. If they were in any way responsible, they may not be given the chance.

Version control of project cost estimates

It is not unusual, especially for large capital projects, for protracted technical and feasibility discussions to take place between the contractor and the potential client before agreement and authorization of a final version of the project specification and its associated cost estimate. The client's ideas on project scope might change during these discussions, and some versions could envisage different roles for the contractor. Proposed engineering solutions often change, particularly when the contractor's engineers are able to suggest alternative technical solutions that would bring mutual benefit to both the client and the contractor.

Project feasibility studies are another case where several versions of a project might be specified. Quite often a number of different project strategies are thoroughly investigated, each with its own project specification, cost estimate and financial appraisal report.

Each different version of a proposed project is certain to require its own, unique, cost estimate. It is therefore important to be able to relate every one of these different cost estimates to the relevant version of the project. Failure to do so would carry enormous risk for the contractor should a fixed-price proposal be made and accepted on the basis of the wrong version of the cost estimate.

The solution is usually straightforward. Every different version of the project specification must be given a unique identifier. This could be a separate proposal number, but it is often only necessary (and preferable) to use the same proposal number for all the versions and simply give each version a distinguishing case number. Then every cost estimate can carry the proposal and case numbers so that it can be related without ambiguity to the correct version of the project.

Work breakdown structure

Consider a project aimed at developing a mining complex or other plant for on-the-spot extraction and processing of mineral resources in an area that was previously uninhabited and which is many miles from the nearest railhead, port or airport. The project for building the plant might cost well over £100 million but that would represent only one aspect of the total work. It might be necessary to build roads, possibly a railway, an airstrip, housing, schools, churches, hospital, shops, and indeed a whole township (all of which would constitute the project infrastructure).

Now imagine trying to estimate the cost of such a large project, and attempting to establish budgets and plans against which to manage the work. Most projects, even if they are not on this grand scale, are too complex to be estimated, planned and controlled effectively unless they are first divided into smaller portions of more manageable size. If the project is very big, it might have to be split into smaller projects or sub-projects. Each project or sub-project must then itself be further divided into smaller work packages and tasks.

Developing the work breakdown structure (WBS) for a project is therefore a necessary step in the chain of project management activities. Devaux (1999) emphasizes the importance of the WBS very well when he writes:

> If I could wish but one thing for every project, it would be a comprehensive and detailed WBS. The lack of a good WBS probably results in more inefficiency, schedule slippage, and cost overruns on projects than any other single cause.

Family tree hierarchy

Work breakdowns must be made and analysed in a systematic fashion, so that there is a logical, hierarchical pattern to the breakdown (in the fashion of a family tree).

An example of the higher levels of a work breakdown structure is given in Figure 4.3. This is for a large mining project, such as the example mentioned above. The breakdown starts from the project itself, represented by the box at the top of the illustration. The first large box shows the work packages identified at the first level of the breakdown. These are the major work packages that together constitute the whole project.

Each first-level work package can be broken down into smaller work packages

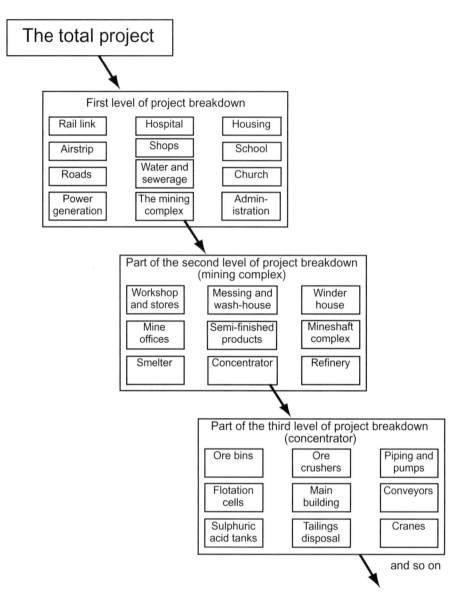

Figure 4.3   Part of the work breakdown for a large mining project
This chart, based on actual projects, shows how, starting from the total project, the work breakdown is undertaken in steps of steadily increasing detail. The complete breakdown would continue down to the level of all the individual tasks and small purchases.

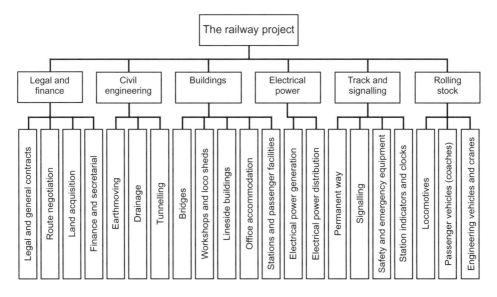

Figure 4.4   Work breakdown for a project to build a new railway

This logical work breakdown of the total project is very closely related to the management structure needed to execute the work.

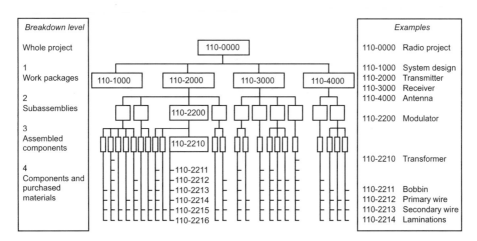

Figure 4.5   Work breakdown and cost-coding structure for a small radiocommunications project

that lie in the second level of breakdown. For simplicity, only one of the first-level packages (the mining complex) has been broken down into its second level in Figure 4.3.

For the third level of breakdown, only the concentrator plant from the mining complex is shown (again, for simplicity). In practice, the work breakdown process would continue downwards for all work packages until, at the lowest level, the many individual tasks and small purchases needed for the entire project are reached. It can readily be appreciated that the complete work breakdown structure for a project of this size is a very detailed, large and complex document.

Figure 4.4 is a notional work breakdown for a project to build a completely new railway. For clarity, only the first and second breakdown levels are shown, and there would be many more work packages at these and lower levels in practice. However, the diagram shows the general concept. This example not only breaks down the physical components, but it also suggests the organizational structure, indicating where managers should be appointed to take charge of specific parts of the project.

Figure 4.5 gives another example of a work breakdown structure, this time showing most breakdown levels for a fairly small radio engineering and manufacturing project. It can be seen that the first level of breakdown for this venture comprises four work packages. One of these is for the whole system design concept, and the three others each relate to one of the main system components (transmitter, receiver and the transmitting antenna).

Logical interfacing and completeness

In addition to regarding the work breakdown as a family tree, it is also possible to visualize it as a jigsaw puzzle, with every piece put in its right place and with no piece missing. This concept is useful on two counts:

1   A method must be found that clearly and simply identifies each piece of the puzzle and denotes its position in relation to all the other pieces. This objective can be achieved by giving each piece an identification number which, through the use of a carefully devised, logical system, acts as a locator or address (discussed in the following section of this chapter).

2   It is important that when the work breakdown is produced, every piece of the puzzle is included, with no piece missing to spoil the total picture. This objective is more difficult, but the risks of omission can be reduced by the use of suitable checklists. Brainstorming can be useful for projects with no similar predecessors.

Cost-coding systems

Although this section is headed 'cost-coding systems', those responsible for designing a coding system must always bear in mind that it should not be treated in isolation from other management and engineering information systems in the same organization. There are many advantages to applying a common coding system across all of a company's projects and across other areas of the company's activities in addition to cost estimating, accounting and budgetary control. Some of these benefits are listed later in this section.

Functions of code

A code is a shorthand and precise method for conveying essential data about an item. For project management purposes, an item might be anything from the whole project to the smallest part of it, physical or abstract. It could be a component, a drawing, a job, a manufacturing operation, a piece of construction work, an engineering design activity, part of a computer program – anything, in fact, which is necessary for the project. One thing that most of these items have in common is that they are associated with cost. Each item (either by itself or grouped with others) has costs that must be estimated, budgeted, spent, measured, reported, assessed and (where appropriate) recovered.

There are many reasons for allocating codes to items, rather than simply describing them in words. For example, codes can be designed to be precise and unambiguous. They also have the advantage, essential in computer systems, of facilitating filing, analysis, editing and sorting for reporting and control.

The code for a particular item will perform the first or both of the following functions:

1   A code must act as a unique name that *identifies* the item to which it refers.
2   The identifying code, either by itself or by the addition of subcodes, can be arranged so that it categorizes, qualifies, or in some other way *describes* the item to which it relates.

The best coding systems are those which manage to combine both these functions as simply as possible in numbers that can be used throughout a company's management information systems.

Typical examples of coding systems

Listed below is the kind of information that can be contained within the code for any item. The systems used as examples here and illustrated in Figures 4.5, 4.6, 4.7 and 4.8 are taken from light and heavy engineering and from mining, but the general principles are interchangeable between these and all other types of projects.

1   **Project identifier** – The project identification number for the breakdown shown in Figure 4.5 is 110-000. This number is sufficient to identify the project for all accounting, engineering and manufacturing purposes. Such project numbers are typically allocated from a register (see Chapter 19). Some

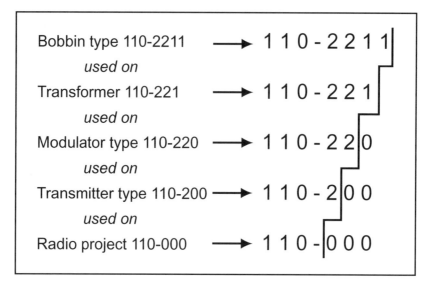

Figure 4.6   Detail from the work breakdown for the radiocommunications project
This small extract, chosen from the work breakdown at random, shows how the coding system can be used to denote the position of any component within a project. This arrangement works well for individual parts, but needs to be adapted when parts are used on more than one part of the project.

companies might call them 'contract numbers' or 'works order numbers' instead. It is possible to design the project numbering method in a way that allows each number to signify certain key information about its project, in addition to acting as a simple identifier. Examples of this occur in Figures 4.7 and 4.8.

2   **Item identifier** – Each number, provided it is unique within the system, is an unambiguous way of naming any item. It is easy, however, to transpose digits or make other errors when entering numbers on forms or keyboards. It is wise, therefore, to bracket a concise description with the number whenever possible as a simple precaution against undiscovered numerical errors. Thus it is usually better to refer to an item as 'Transformer 110-221' in documents such as purchase requisitions, rather than just '110-221'.

3   **Relationship within the project** – Further examination of Figure 4.5 shows that the code numbers have been designed to correspond with the work breakdown (or family tree) hierarchy. Examples are given for components of the Transformer 110-221 and set out more clearly in Figure 4.6. The numbers denote that all numbers starting with the string 110 are used on Project 110-000 and, further that numbers starting 110-221 are used on Transformer 110-221.

4   **Operation identifier** – The task of winding the purpose-built transformer 110-221 might be given a related cost code, such as 110-221C, where the C suffix denotes the coil winding operation. A two-digit suffix is more likely to be used than a single letter, allowing greater scope for detailed breakdown into several individual operations.

5   **Identifiers for department, discipline or trade and labour grade** – A one- or two-digit subcode is often incorporated to show which department is responsible for a particular task or cost item. More digits can be added to denote the trade or engineering discipline involved. Consider, for instance, the activity of designing Transformer 110-221. The cost code might be 110-221-153, with the three-digit subcode 153 in this case showing that the engineering department (1) is responsible for the task, the engineering discipline is electrical (coded (5)), and the last digit (3) indicates the standard cost grade of person (for example senior engineer, engineer or designer) normally expected to carry out the task of designing this transformer.

6   **Family identifier** – Many items to be considered for coding can be classified into families. Such families extend across all projects and can apply to huge capital projects or to the smallest engineering and manufacturing projects. The convenience of grouping items into families of items with common or similar characteristics is important for many comparative purposes. Family grouping and identification can be built into item codes using suitable digits as subcodes.

A family might comprise, for example, all pumps specified by a mining or petrochemical company. Another example might be that the subcode digits 01 appearing in a particular place in the item code for a piece of manufactured equipment would always indicate the mainframe assembly. Another type of family is encountered in machined objects that have similar shapes or other physical characteristics which call for similar machining operations; an application of family coding which is vital to the manufacture of components in group technology cells.

Benefits of a logical coding system

Although the primary purpose of a coding system might be to identify parts or to allocate costs, there are many benefits available to the company which is able to maintain a logical coding system in which all the codes and subcodes have common significance throughout the company's management information systems. These benefits increase with time and the accrual of records, provided that the system is used consistently without unauthorized adaptations or additions.

The benefits depend on being able to retrieve and process the data effectively, which invariably requires the use of a computer system. If a coding system is designed logically (taking account of hierarchical structure and families) and is well managed, some or all of the following benefits can be expected:

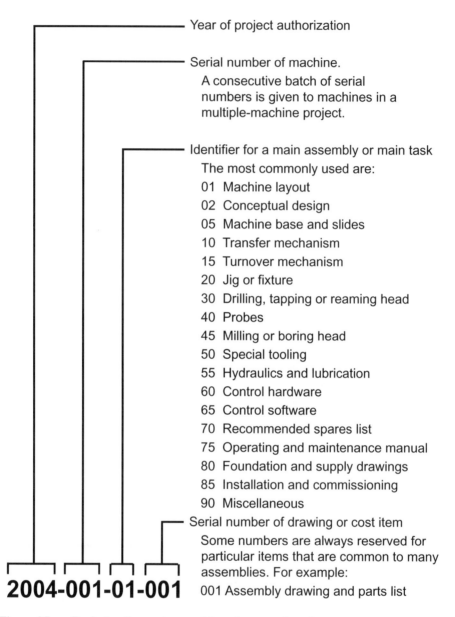

Year of project authorization

Serial number of machine.
A consecutive batch of serial
numbers is given to machines in a
multiple-machine project.

Identifier for a main assembly or main task
The most commonly used are:

01 Machine layout
02 Conceptual design
05 Machine base and slides
10 Transfer mechanism
15 Turnover mechanism
20 Jig or fixture
30 Drilling, tapping or reaming head
40 Probes
45 Milling or boring head
50 Special tooling
55 Hydraulics and lubrication
60 Control hardware
65 Control software
70 Recommended spares list
75 Operating and maintenance manual
80 Foundation and supply drawings
85 Installation and commissioning
90 Miscellaneous

Serial number of drawing or cost item
Some numbers are always reserved for
particular items that are common to many
assemblies. For example:

2004-001-01-001   001 Assembly drawing and parts list

Figure 4.7   Project coding system used by a heavy engineering company
This company designs and manufactures heavy special-purpose machine tool systems.

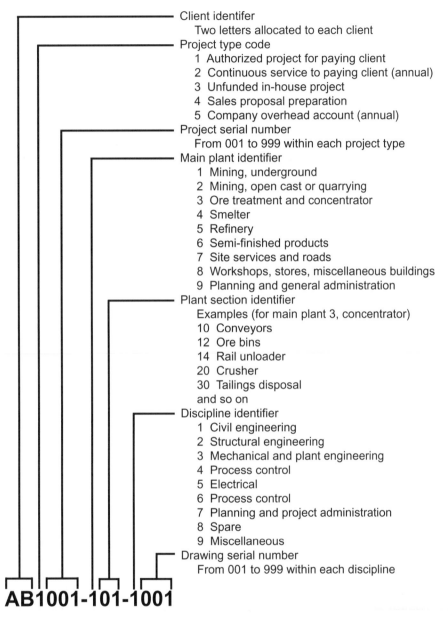

Client identifer
    Two letters allocated to each client
Project type code
    1 Authorized project for paying client
    2 Continuous service to paying client (annual)
    3 Unfunded in-house project
    4 Sales proposal preparation
    5 Company overhead account (annual)
Project serial number
    From 001 to 999 within each project type
Main plant identifier
    1 Mining, underground
    2 Mining, open cast or quarrying
    3 Ore treatment and concentrator
    4 Smelter
    5 Refinery
    6 Semi-finished products
    7 Site services and roads
    8 Workshops, stores, miscellaneous buildings
    9 Planning and general administration
Plant section identifier
    Examples (for main plant 3, concentrator)
    10 Conveyors
    12 Ore bins
    14 Rail unloader
    20 Crusher
    30 Tailings disposal
    and so on
Discipline identifier
    1 Civil engineering
    2 Structural engineering
    3 Mechanical and plant engineering
    4 Process control
    5 Electrical
    6 Process control
    7 Planning and project administration
    8 Spare
    9 Miscellaneous
Drawing serial number
    From 001 to 999 within each discipline

AB1001-101-1001

Figure 4.8   Project coding system used by a mining engineering company

- Easy retrieval of items from records of past projects which correspond to or are similar to items expected in new projects, essential as a basis for making comparative cost estimates.

- Easy search and retrieval of design information (especially flowsheets, calculations and drawings) for processes, assemblies or components used on past projects which are relevant to a current project. This 'retained engineering' can result in a saving of considerable engineering design work, time and costs if all or part of the previous design can be re-used or adapted. Not only does such design retrieval avoid the unnecessary costs of designing everything afresh, but it also allows the new project to incorporate designs that have already been proven or debugged, so that the scope for errors is reduced. With computer-aided design, or in any other system where the drawings are stored digitally, the scope and possibilities for such retrieval become even more practicable and attractive.

- Rapid identification of purchase requisitions and specifications from previous projects for equipment which corresponds to new equipment requirements. One application of this is to speed the preparation of new purchase specifications, particularly when much or all of the previous text can be used again.

- Grouping of components into families according to their basic shapes and sizes. This is particularly necessary for manufacturing operations where the plant is arranged in cells for group technology.

- If it is possible to use a common system, cost estimates, budgets, recorded costs, drawing schedules, many other documents, and tasks on the project plan can all be related in a database for project administration, management reports and control.

- The ability to carry out statistical analyses on cost records and other documents from past projects for a variety of reasons, including monitoring performance trends.

The following examples from my experience had great practical use in a heavy engineering company, and illustrate only two of the many possibilities for exploiting properly coded records:

1   The averaging of recorded costs for commonly recurring work packages in a range of categories from many past projects. This led to the preparation of project estimating tables (expressed in man-hours and updated materials costs). These tables proved very useful for planning and resource scheduling new projects and for making global checks on detailed estimates for new project proposals.

2   Analysis in detail of past shipping records enabled a table to be compiled that

listed all the main components commonly produced in the company's very heavy engineering projects. For each item it was possible to forecast the most likely average and the maximum weight of each part of the project after it had been broken down into parts of 20 tonnes or less for shipping. Cost estimates were added with the help of a shipping company. The result was given to the materials control manager as a 'ready reckoner'. With occasional updating, this table was used successfully for estimating future project shipping weights and costs to all parts of the world.

Choosing a coding system

Once a coding system has become well established it is difficult and unwise to make any fundamental change. Any comprehensive system must therefore be designed with a great deal of care. Suppose that a company has been operating for many years with a comprehensive arrangement of codes that are recognized by all its management information systems. Suppose, further, that this arrangement of codes is common to many applications and procedures. As an example, the number for the drawing of a manufactured component would also be used as (or would be a recognizable constituent of) related manufacturing job numbers, job cost records and the stock and part number of the component itself. If this company were to make a change to the numbering system, so that numbers which previously had one meaning would denote something entirely different in the future, some of the following problems might arise:

1   drawings filed under two different systems
2   similar inconvenience caused to long-standing customers who maintain their own files of project drawings
3   no easy way of identifying similar previous jobs for the purpose of comparative cost estimating
4   difficulty in retrieving earlier designs – the opportunity to use retained engineering from past work to reduce future design effort might be lost
5   staff must live with two different systems, instead of one universal set of numbers
6   problems for storekeepers and stock controllers, with more than one part numbering method – parts common to earlier projects may have to be renumbered for newer projects, so that there is a possibility of having identical common parts stored in two places with different part numbers
7   mayhem created in any attempt to use a relational database that relies on code numbering.

The need for simplicity

This is the place to insert another word of warning. It is tempting to be too ambitious and try to make numbers include too much information. The result can be numbers that are 14, 15 or more digits long. It is easy to fall into such a trap, especially when the system is designed by a committee, each of whose members contributes his or her own idea of what the numbers might be expected to denote. Beware of phrases such as 'Wouldn't it be nice if …'

The designer of a system that depends on exceptionally long codes may feel very proud of their system's capability. Computer systems are well able to accept and process huge numbers, but please remember the human element – the 'people interface'. People will have to work with these numbers, entering them in written or electronic records. I remember an attempt to introduce a very complex coding system on a mine development project in a remote area of Australia. The system designer was a highly qualified and well-respected member of the London head office management staff. Supervisors, professional people and artisans at the mine were all expected to read and write 18-digit job codes on documents accurately while exposed to unpleasant and hazardous conditions both above and below ground. The people at the mine never even attempted to use the codes. Even if they had used them, the depth of information that the codes contained was far in excess of that needed for management information. Simple codes use less effort and result in fewer errors. Remember the sensible slogan KISS: 'Keep It Simple, Stupid'.

What happens when the customer says 'You shall use my coding system!'?

Not infrequently, an irritating problem arises when customers insist that their own numbering system is used, rather than the project contractor's own long-established and proven arrangement. This happens, for example, when a customer is to be presented with a complete set of project drawings as part of the contract and wants to be able to file these along with all the other drawings in the customer's head office system. This, unfortunately, is a case where 'the customer is always right'.

This problem of having to use customers' codes is not always restricted to drawings. In some projects it can apply to equipment numbers or part numbers. It also occurs, and is a great nuisance, in the cost codes used for work packages or large purchases for major projects. The customer and contractor sometimes work together to plan, authorize and arrange the release of funds (either from the customer's own resources or from an external financing organization). In such cases the customer might insist that all estimates, budgets and subsequent cost reports for the project are broken down against the customer's own capital appropriation or other cost codes.

Three options

There are three possible options when the customer asks the contractor to use a 'foreign' coding system.

Option 1: Say 'No!' to the customer

The person who adopts this course is either courageous or foolhardy. It might even be impossible under the terms of contract. In any case, it would be a short cut to establishing bad customer relations or losing the customer altogether.

Option 2: Change over completely to the customer's system

In this case the contractor calls the project a 'special case', abandons the in-house system, asks the customer for a set of their own procedures, and uses those for the project. This option cannot be recommended, for the following reasons:

- The information management benefits of the in-house system would be lost for all data for the project.
- It will soon be discovered that every project is a 'special case'. The contractor might soon have to deal with as many coding systems as there are customers.

Option 3: Use both systems simultaneously

This option, the sensible compromise course, offers the only proper solution. Every drawing and other affected item must be numbered twice: once for each system.

Everything must, of course, be diligently cross-referenced between the two systems. This is tedious, time-consuming and means that staff have to learn more than one system. Some time ago it would have caused enough extra work to provide a weak argument for trying to obtain extra reimbursement from the customer. Fortunately, computer systems greatly reduce the effort needed for cross-referencing, sorting and retrieving data numbered under duplicate systems.

Chapter 5

Cost estimates, Part 2: Estimating in practice

The previous chapter concentrated on the principles and some of the ground rules encountered in cost estimating. This chapter takes the subject further by examining the actual estimating process.

Top-down or bottom-up?

A work breakdown structure for a forthcoming project about which little is known cannot be taken down to its lowest levels, and it might not be possible to describe or even identify every first-level package. There are, however, occasions when cost estimates for a new project have to be made with such scarce information. The most practicable approach open to the cost estimator in these circumstances is to start by visualizing the entire project at completion, identify one or more similar projects from the recent past, research the actual costs of those past projects, and use that information as a basis for a comparative estimate for the new project.

Such estimates can contain very little detail, perhaps forecasting only the total project cost and the expected contributing costs of a few principal work packages. These ballpark estimates would be unsuitable for calculating detailed task and departmental budgets to be used in subsequent cost management, but might be very useful to higher management for making strategic decisions. Because estimating at this coarse level must start from consideration of the entire project, the process is called *top-down estimating*.

If, on the other hand, a detailed work breakdown structure and task list is available, the cost of every item can be estimated using comparative methods or (in some cases) tables and suppliers' quotations starting from the lowest level of the breakdown. The total project cost estimate is then made by adding the estimates for all the constituent parts. This is *bottom-up estimating,* the converse of top-down estimating.

This chapter describes bottom-up estimating, and this approach is generally assumed throughout the remainder of this book as the basis for all the control methods described. However, top-down estimating can still be useful when bottom-up estimates are checked or reviewed. This is explained in the final section of this chapter.

Compiling the task list

The first stage in the bottom-up cost estimating process is to compile a complete list of every known item that is going to cost money. This can prove difficult. But any item inadvertently left out of the cost estimates will result in an underestimate for the project as a whole. This can jeopardize planning and scheduling, and (if not realized in time) lead to serious problems and red faces when the time comes to hand the project over to the customer. And, of course, if the project has been sold for a fixed price, the additional work must be paid for not out of the budgeted project funds, but from the contractor's expected profits.

The work breakdown as a starting point

Preparation of a work breakdown (as a family tree or 'goes into chart'), complete with cost codes, is a logical way of considering the total project, and should reduce the risk of errors of omission. Coded work breakdowns were described in the previous chapter, and examples can be seen in Figures 4.3, 4.4 and 4.5. At the outset of a project, however, the work breakdown can usually only be compiled in fairly broad terms. Many of the smaller items will remain unknown or ill-defined until the project has advanced well into its engineering design phase. In many cases a detailed work breakdown will not be possible until long after the contract has been signed and everything has become a firm commitment. A fair degree of judgement is therefore necessary in deciding what should go into the earliest version of a project task list.

Using checklists

One very useful way of helping to prevent forgotten tasks is to use checklists. Every company with sufficient experience can develop these (see Figure 3.3, for instance). A full checklist would include all possible factors – technical, commercial, statutory, environmental, social and so on – that might eventually have a bearing on the work and its costs. Some checklists can be long and detailed documents: typically they list as many possibilities as the compiler can think up, so that they must inevitably include some irrelevancies and seem tedious. However, it is in this very wealth of detail that the importance and strength of checklists lie.

Software tasks

The task list must include not only all the obvious items of project hardware, but also every associated software job. 'Software' is a familiar term in the context of computers and IT projects, but most projects quite remote from computer work have their own software content. Schedules for production inspection and testing, instruction and maintenance manuals, lists of recommended spares and consumable items may have to be specially written. These, together with any other documentation specified in the proposal or contract, are software tasks which must usually be allowed for in the estimated costs.

Forgotten tasks

Activities often forgotten during the estimating phase of manufacturing projects, only to be remembered too late for inclusion in the project budgets (and price), include incidental processes such as paint spraying, heat treatments, inspection and testing. In some firms these may be covered by the general overhead rate, but in many others they will not, and must be listed among the direct cost estimates. Protective plating, silk screen printing, engraving and so on are frequently omitted from estimates.

A more serious victim, sometimes neglected during project cost estimating, is the work entailed in final commissioning, handover and customer acceptance of the completed project.

Contracts often require the project contractor to provide training facilities for some of the customer's staff. The manufacturer of a complex and special machine might be expected, for example, to install the machine and supervise its start-up by training the customer's operatives and maintenance technicians. Training sessions can involve the contractor's senior engineers in much hard work, both in the actual training and in preparing the training manuals beforehand. Incidental expenses may also arise for accommodation and meals, depending on where the training is to be carried out.

Whether the proposal is for a manufacturing project or for a large capital construction project, the business of filling as many gaps as possible in the task list is really a continuing aspect of project definition. Indeed, the project specification might have to be revised and reissued more than once as the task list is developed.

Level of detail in project cost estimating

Some difficulty might be experienced in deciding how much detail to show in the task list. What is a 'task' for this purpose?

Consider the problem of estimating the total cost of a manufacturing project, as part of the process of preparing a fixed-price proposal. The cost estimate must be made before any detailed design has taken place, and therefore without the benefit of any production drawings. It will obviously not be possible to list all the operations needed for each separate piece part. It will not even be known at this early stage what or how many parts are going to be needed. Therefore, this initial cost estimate, even though it might lead to a fixed-price commitment, can only be carried out on a much broader scale than estimates for run-of-the-mill production.

Each task should be selected so that it is small enough to be visualized easily for estimating purposes. On the other hand, the task must be large enough to represent a measurable and significant part of the whole project. The design and manufacture of each subassembly from a main piece of equipment might rank as a task, while the final assembly of all these subassemblies could be regarded as another. Writing, editing and printing an instruction manual together comprise another item that should be set out as a discrete task. Separately identifiable purchases of expensive bought-out components and equipment should also be listed, where these are not already included in other tasks. Any special requirement for packing and despatch might have to be listed as a task, particularly if the project has to be delivered to a customer overseas.

Every one of the examples just given is an identifiable and specific part of the project, chosen at a level intended to make the job of estimating easier and more reliable. Careful identification of all significant tasks at this stage, in addition to its importance for cost estimating, will provide a good basis for budgeting, scheduling and subsequent control.

Estimating formats

Completion of a task list has established the basis for project cost estimating. When the estimates have been collected they will contain a large amount of data. These data should be presented in a format that will allow easy reference, detailed analysis and extension into total amounts – whether for departmental costs or for packages at any level of the project work breakdown structure.

A certain amount of procedural discipline has to be imposed on the estimating function throughout the organization, and from one project to another. Estimates should be tabulated according to a standard company procedure, itemized, where possible, by cost codes within the work breakdown structure. This will help to ensure that comparisons can readily be made between the estimates and the cost accountant's records of the actual costs eventually incurred, on a strict item-for-item basis. This is essential as part of the cost control function. As experience builds up over a few years and more data are collected, it will also contribute to the accuracy of comparative estimates for new projects.

Some contracts, especially those for defence and other national government projects, may become liable to investigation by technical cost officers or other auditors at one or more stages. These investigations can be exhaustive and taken into considerable detail. Starting off on the right foot by paying careful attention to logic and detail in presenting the cost estimates can help to establish the good relations necessary for reaching a fair agreement.

Observance of company policy on cost rates and costing methods, as well as the need to determine working budgets, imposes an obligation on the project manager to ensure that the estimates are set down in a standard and logical manner. Calculations performed in odd corners of notebooks, on scraps of paper, and on the backs (or fronts) of envelopes are prone to error and premature loss. They will be unlikely to fulfil any of the conditions already mentioned. In other words, standardized estimating formats are needed (either as hard copy or as forms on a computer).

Project estimating forms can be arranged to fit in with the kind of work breakdown structures that were shown in Figures 4.3, 4.4 and 4.5. One page can be allocated to each main project work package or group of tasks, while every row on each page would be occupied by one task or activity.

Adding the costs along each row yields the estimated cost of the relevant task. This can, incidentally, sometimes be very convenient for pricing spare parts.

Totalling the relevant columns gives the cost commitment expected from each department, and can also give a broad indication of the labour input needed. These results can help with departmental budgeting and coarse resource scheduling.

Attempts to design estimating forms will fail if they are too ambitious. There is no need to provide a column for every contingency. Instead, one or more columns can be left as spares, with their headings blank, so that these can be filled in as required for any special purposes.

For any project of significant size, the use of a computer for collating and aggregating estimates is assumed. Estimating forms will have to be designed with the computer input format in mind. If the company's procedures have been developed with care and forethought, the estimating data can be fed into a comprehensive management information system that will, as work progresses, be used to compare expenditure and progress against these original estimates. Some project management software can also perform these comparisons.

A project estimating format for manufacturing and general purposes

An example of a general-purpose estimating tabulation is given in Figure 5.1. This design is based on a form used by more than one division of a company for projects ranging from military electronic equipment to prefabricated hospital operating theatres. All these projects, although very different in design and work content, shared the typical manufacturing project characteristic of requiring special engineering design, followed by project purchasing, leading to manufacture and completion in single or small batch quantities.

COST ESTIMATE

Project number
or sales reference:

Estimate number:
Case:
Date:
Page of

Estimate for:

Compiled by:

1	2	3	4		5		6		7		8		9		10	11	12	13	14	15
Code	Item	Qty	Labour times and costs by department or standard grade												Total direct labour cost	Overhead cost %	Materials			Total cost 10+11+12+13
			Hrs	£	Hrs	£	Hrs	£	Hrs	£	Hrs	£	Hrs	£			Standard or net cost	Burden %	Longest delivery (weeks)	

Figure 5.1 A general-purpose cost estimating format

Owing to space limitations in the pages of this book, the general-purpose format in Figure 5.1 allows only six grades of labour to be shown. It assumes that all hours will be costed at the appropriate standard cost rates. Six grades will usually be adequate, provided the standard costing system has been designed sensibly and has not been complicated by interference from the 'wouldn't it be nice if ...' brigade. The standard grade code and cost rate used should be entered in the space at the head of each column to show the rates that were current at the time of estimating.

Generally speaking, whilst wages and their related standard cost rates change from year to year, the time needed to carry out any particular job by a given method should not. Work time is therefore regarded as the fundamental basis for cost estimates. It is always wise to record both man-hours and cost on estimate tabulations. Conversion from man-hours to money can only be regarded as a derivative, secondary process which is dependent on factors and other influences that change costs with the passage of time. Comparative estimates for labour should be made by comparing man-hours or other time units, not costs, from records of past projects.

There is no need to complicate a general-purpose estimating form by adding columns for such things as special tooling. Such items can easily be accommodated by considering them as separate tasks in their own right. Each can be entered on a row, and the costs added up along the row in the same way as any other task.

The inclusion of a column headed 'Longest lead time' in the materials section might appear unusual in a form intended primarily for cost estimating. However, the people who estimate material costs are also the people most probably able to predict delivery times. It is convenient and more efficient to collect both sets of data from them as early as possible and on the same occasion. This extends the usefulness of these forms by enabling their use as a valuable information source for subsequent timescale planning.

Additional columns could be provided on the estimating form to allow mark-ups and selling prices to be shown. These were deliberately omitted from the example in Figure 5.1, partly through lack of space, and also because the relationship between cost estimates and project pricing is often too complex to allow calculation on a simple form. More will be said about project pricing in Chapter 6.

Estimating forms for large construction projects

Many designs of forms are used for tabulating and summing the cost estimates for large projects in the fields of mining, petrochemicals, construction and civil engineering.

In manufacturing projects, the prime costs are likely to comprise mainly labour and materials (often in roughly equal proportions) with a relatively small subcontract element. In large construction contracts, the balance is usually shifted,

COST ESTIMATE FOR MATERIALS
AND PURCHASED EQUIPMENT

Estimate for:

Project number
or sales reference:

Compiled by:

Estimate number:
Case:
Date:
Page   of

Cost code	Description	Spec. No. (if known)	Proposed supplier	Unit	Unit cost FOB	Quoted currency	Exchange rate used	Converted FOB cost	Qty	Project FOB cost	Ship mode	Freight cost	Taxes/ duties	Delivered cost

Total delivered materials and equipment costs this page ⟶

Figure 5.2   Cost estimating format for purchased materials on large projects

with most of the direct labour content found in head office engineering design and the project management and supervision functions. The employment of direct labour for construction trades and plant installation is often entrusted to specialist subcontractors (see, for example, the contract matrix organization shown in Figure 2.9). Therefore, a considerable proportion of the total capital costs is expended on subcontracts. Material costs will probably be divided between bulk supplies (steel, pipework, the constituents of concrete, and so on) plus a considerable investment in specially ordered items of expensive equipment (the provision of some of these constituting significant projects in themselves).

Most of the costs incurred in large construction projects can often be grouped conveniently under a few main headings, for example:

1   Engineering and project management (subdivided between home office and site office)
2   Purchases (subdivided between bulk construction materials and purchases of major items and equipment for installation)
3   Subcontracts and plant hire
4   Other expenses such as legal fees.

Estimates for home office engineering and project management times can be compiled on general-purpose forms similar to the example shown in Figure 5.1.

Estimates for many of the bulk materials are often made on very detailed schedules or material 'take-offs' which are specially designed for each of the particular engineering disciplines involved (such as piping take-offs compiled by fluids engineers, and steel take-offs worked out by the civil and structural engineers).

The form shown in Figure 5.2 can be used for listing the cost estimates for significant items of equipment required for a project. Provision is made on the form for including freight and duty costs, which are, of course, especially relevant when the site is distant or overseas from the source of supply. Totals or convenient subtotals from materials take-offs should be transferred to this form to allow the complete project materials costs to be summarized and totalled.

A general-purpose project cost and price summary format

The format in Figure 5.3 can be used in many cases to summarize project cost estimates and assist in pricing. This has been designed for flexibility, for use over a wide range of different projects and companies. Although spaces for various rates, allowances and mark-ups are provided, the way in which these are used can be chosen to fit in with a particular company's management and accounting requirements. The form allows the actual figures and formula used in the cost–pricing relationship to be recorded, but it does not dictate the pricing mechanism too rigidly, because the price must usually be considered by senior management according to the merits of each case.

Project cost and price summary   Estimate ref:

Project title: Case number:

Client/customer: '   Date:

                                                 £

Labour costs by standard grade

1   _____ hours at £ ____ = £ _____

2   _____ hours at £ ____ = £ _____

3   _____ hours at £ ____ = £ _____

4   _____ hours at £ ____ = £ _____

5   _____ hours at £ ____ = £ _____

6   _____ hours at £ ____ = £ _____

Total labour cost   ⟶

Materials, equipment and bought-out services   ⟶

Other expenses (professional fees, licensing, etc.) ⟶   _____

Prime cost   ⟶

Overhead costs at ____ % of total labour cost   ⟶

Materials burden at ____ % (if any)   ⟶

Overseas costs and handling charges (if any)   ⟶   _____

Basic estimated project cost   ⟶

Allowances

Escalation at ____ % per annum for ____ years   ⟶

Contingency ____ %   ⟶

Other allowances (if any)   ⟶   _____

Total estimated project cost   ⟶

Mark-up ____ %   ⟶

Indicated selling price   ⟶   [   ]

Notes, provisional items, etc.

Figure 5.3   **A format for indicating project price**

Estimating manufacturing costs

Estimates with production drawings

Suppose that a cost estimate has to be made for the routine fabrication of a batch of boxes from sheet metal. A set of manufacturing drawings is needed first. Other important details are the total quantity of boxes required, and the rate at which they are to be produced. Further necessary information would include the type of production facilities likely to be used, and the amount of money available (if any) for spending on special tooling. All these facts would allow the job to be considered as a series of production elements or operations. Every single step necessary to convert the raw material into a finished box could be listed in great detail, and in chronological order, on a schedule or process sheet.

An estimate of the labour time required for each operation – whether for cutting, folding, punching, welding, riveting and so on – could be made by reference to data accumulated from past experience. Tables of standard times for all routine operations might even be available. The depth of detail in some sets of standard timetables is very comprehensive. Times needed to set up jigs or machines might also be well documented.

In the case of this metal box it should be possible to make a very good estimate, obtained by adding all the operation times and certain allowances for non-productive time. If each box had to contain some sort of apparatus or instrumentation, the assembly time could also be forecast with a fair degree of accuracy. The number of screws or rivets to be used, the size, length and number of wires and pipes, and the types of connections could all be counted up from the drawings. Once again the estimates could be based on tables derived from the known characteristics and production performance of the organization and its operators.

It is possible to forecast materials requirements with ease and reasonable certainty for production work. Raw materials usage can be assessed by examining the drawings and by then making allowances for cutting wastage, breakages and losses. Other materials and components are listed by the designers on parts lists or bills of material on which the standard costs can be filled in.

It is now time to admit that this brief account of traditional production cost estimating has little or nothing to do with project management. But it has been included to serve as a contrast for a discussion of the particular difficulties facing project cost estimators. Notice that several common key factors can be identified in the use of routine methods. Work is always broken down into small elements before estimates are applied. The estimates themselves can usually be described as 'standard' or 'known' quantities, and any need for guesswork is either eliminated or reduced to a minimum. Reliance is placed not on personal opinions of how long each job should take, but on the results of long experience, detailed analysis and scientific work measurement.

Estimates without production drawings

Suppose now that an estimate is to be prepared for a control unit. This is a box filled with instrumentation but, unlike the example in the previous section, detailed design has yet to take place and manufacturing drawings do not exist. Only one box of this special type is to be made, for use on a particular project. The only information on which a cost estimate can be based is an engineer's written design specification. This specification includes little or no information about dimensions, materials or the contents of the box. It simply states the functional performance expected of the completed product in terms of its input and output parameters and its planned operating environment. If the estimator is very lucky, there might be a rough outline sketch of the box.

Standard estimating tables will be of little help here. Build-up of time and cost standards depends upon the establishment of production continuity, which demands in turn that a certain minimum volume of production must take place. Such standards cannot be applied to 'one-off' production, where unknown variables dominate the picture. In any case, there are no drawings from which to break the work down into its constituent operations, so there is no hope of using standard estimates.

A stage in the project preparation and planning process has now been reached where many professional estimators, production engineers and work study devotees find themselves floundering well out of their normal depth. Their trusted records of standard times, with which they have worked for many years, and much of their professional training will be virtually useless when they are faced with the problem of estimating for work where no drawings exist. Drawings and parts lists are the customary means of expression and communication for these people. Without such aids, they are rendered helpless. They feel deprived and will be unwilling to commit themselves to forecasts that they might be called upon to justify later.

Project cost estimating is not made any easier by the short time usually available. All too often a tender has to be prepared within a few days if it is to meet the deadline set by a prospective customer. Failure to meet the closing date could mean that the proposal is automatically disqualified, with the order irrevocably lost to a competitor. Within the short time available, cost estimates might have to be made for a large number of items. The project might need, for example, hundreds of control units, all different and all to be manufactured singly. Even if drawings could be found, there would be insufficient time to analyse these for detailed cost estimating.

The job of cost estimating can itself be expensive. It is easy to spend a great deal of time and money in the process, especially where there is no pressure to produce the estimates quickly. Low probability of obtaining a project order might not justify much expenditure on estimating and tender preparation.

Project estimating, as has already been seen, is carried out on a much broader scale than run-of-the-mill production work. In the absence of detailed information, larger work packages must be visualized. The only people capable of taking this broader view are likely to be the more senior members of the organization. Departmental managers often become involved, if not in making the estimates, at least in approving them. For project manufacturing estimates, therefore, input will probably be needed from production management.

There is no simple solution to all these problems, but it is possible to outline an approach that can yield acceptable results. Fortunately, the lack of drawings and the need for making estimates in a short space of time are both conditions that demand a similar estimating technique.

Within the context of our simple example of a control unit (a small metal box filled with instrumentation), the estimating method might proceed along the following lines.

First, a description of the proposed box is needed, with some idea of its likely contents. The design engineers must provide this information, because they are the only people at this early stage who can possibly have any real idea what the final, assembled box will be like.

Once a description of the box has been set down, it is usually possible to scan the archives to find a previous piece of work which bears some resemblance to the new job. Classification and coding of work and cost records can be a great help when it comes to making such a search. Once again it is only the design engineers who can be asked to draw useful comparisons at this early stage. It might well be found that no direct parallel exists, but that a previous similar job was carried out which was somewhat simpler than the present object of concern. 'How much simpler?' is the question that must now be asked. The engineer might say that about 10 per cent more components will be needed this time, giving a basis on which the production department can make a comparative estimate.

When the records of actual expenditure on the previous box have been looked up, the production supervisor or production manager can reasonably be expected to make an estimate for the new work, given the information that about 10 per cent more components will have to be accommodated and assembled. If the old box took one man-week to fabricate, this might be considered a good enough estimate for the new sheet metal operations. Only a couple more holes are going to be needed to fix the extra components. Wiring and piping must take longer, however, since the 10 per cent increase in the number of components must result in a corresponding increase in the number of connections to be made. A previously recorded assembly time of two man-weeks might therefore be extended to give an estimate of two-and-a-half man-weeks for the slightly more complex box.

Of course, these comparative estimates can never be considered or expressed in fine units of time. Man-weeks or man-hours are the usual choices. Using anything less (man-minutes, for example) would expose the cost estimator to the same trap as the scientist who carries out research using data and measurements accurate to no better than 1 or 2 per cent, but then has the temerity to express the final results using long strings of decimal places.

Once the idea has been accepted that production time estimates have to be seen in broad terms, on a scale that equates with packages in the work breakdown, they can be collected and collated in exactly the same way as estimates for design engineering and other non-manufacturing project activities. The estimating system can therefore be standardized, with all cost predictions collected according to the same set of rules and using a common estimating form.

Collecting estimates for labour times

In project work there is a shift of emphasis compared with routine production estimating, where detailed estimates could safely be entrusted to an individual or a group specializing only in cost estimating or production engineering. Wherever possible, estimates for project labour times should be obtained from managers or senior individuals of the departments that are going to be responsible for carrying out the project tasks later. It would be reasonable, for example, to expect a chief engineer to provide the design engineering estimates.

Decentralizing the estimating function in this way reflects the change in scale when progressing from production estimating to project work. It is not done simply to gain a more accurate estimate of project costs, although that is usually the prime reason. When a large project is being planned, the labour time estimates can have a profound influence on the staffing budgets of the departments involved for years to come. Any departmental budget, whatever the type of work involved, should be more realistic and achievable if the departmental manager has either produced or fully agreed the cost estimates on which the budget (and the manager's future commitments) is based.

If the estimating function is to be decentralized, it follows that the set of project estimating forms must be circulated among all the participating departments. This can be done in several ways, with varying degrees of effectiveness.

The first proposition is that one master set of forms could be assembled, attached to a circulation list and sent to the department which is first on the list. That department would be expected to enter its estimates and pass the set of forms on to the next-listed department until, all the estimates having been completed, the bundle should arrive back on the project manager's or proposals manager's desk. Everyone knows how long a library copy of a magazine takes to complete its circulation, and the risks that it faces on its journey – it might never be returned to the library at all. For the same reasons, the circulation method can be dismissed as impracticable for collecting project estimates.

A second possibility is to prepare a set of pre-headed estimating forms for each department and send them all out simultaneously, either as hard copy or over a computer network. This has the advantage of cutting out the serial delays of the first proposition, but it still relies on the wholehearted cooperation of all the departmental heads. Late input can be expected, while it is known from bitter experience that some hard-copy sets might even be lost altogether.

Estimating is often regarded as an unpleasant task, a chore to be avoided at all costs if other priorities can be found as an excuse. Therefore, no one can expect to rely solely upon polite requests for data to be provided on blank estimating forms. A more direct approach is sometimes needed.

Another way in which to collect the estimates would be to ask for them during the network planning session (described in Chapter 8) and complete a set of estimating sheets on the spot. This occasion provides the opportunity, since all key project members should be on hand. This approach might be considered for very small projects, but there are at least four snags:

1   Network estimates are always made principally for activity durations (for total elapsed time) rather than for their work content in man-hours. However, some forms of work content estimates are made at network meetings in addition to the activity duration estimates if the networks are intended for subsequent resource scheduling.

2   Network planning meetings can involve much effort and take considerable time – perhaps needing more than one session of several hours. Protracted meetings do not produce the best results, and it is wise to avoid asking too much of the members. The law of diminishing returns can apply when any meeting exceeds about two hours. Members will start to fidget and want to get back to their departments to sort out more pressing problems or go home.

3   Material costs are not usually considered at network planning meetings. A separate estimate collection exercise for material costs would therefore be needed in most cases.

4   Perhaps the most important problem of all is that the network planning session is likely to take place far later than the time when the cost estimates are needed for the project proposal or tender.

Short of applying legal compulsion or threat of physical violence, personal canvassing is the best way to get quick and dependable results. The process starts by preparing a complete set of estimating sheets for the project, with every known task listed and cost-coded. The sheets should be arranged in logical subsets according to the work breakdown structure. The project manager (or delegate) can then embark on a tour of all the departments involved, arriving purposefully at each manager's desk in turn. This applies equally if the estimating forms have been set up in a computer. The aim is to remain firmly rooted in each department until all the desired data have been entered on the forms or in the computer system. The person performing this task may become unpopular in the process, but becoming well-liked is not the most important aspect of a project manager's job.

Canvassing affords the project manager or proposals manager an opportunity to assess the estimating capabilities of all the individuals concerned. Any estimate which appears unrealistic or outrageous can be questioned on the spot, and many other details can be sorted out with the least possible fuss and delay. One type of question which must frequently be asked of the estimator takes the form: 'Here is a job said to require four man-weeks; can four people do it in one week, or must the job be spread over four weeks of elapsed time with only one person able to work on it?' The answers to such questions are of obvious importance in scheduling time and resources, of which more will be said in later chapters.

Production staff often need help in their project estimating task. If an engineer collects the estimates, he or she can often supply this help by explaining the design specification in terms that production people can understand. Similarities with past projects can be suggested and any artists' impressions or other sketches that might be available can be shown and amplified by verbal description.

Personal estimating characteristics

Project cost estimating is never an exact science. Much of the process, particularly when estimating labour times, has to rely on the subjective judgement of individuals. If any ten people were to be asked separately to judge the time needed for a particular project task, it is hardly conceivable that ten identical answers would be received. Ask these same ten people to estimate the times for a large number of different project tasks, and a pattern should emerge when the results are analysed. Some people will tend always to estimate on the low side. Others might give answers that are consistently high. The person collecting project cost estimates needs to be aware of this problem. In fact, just as it is possible to classify estimates according to confidence in their accuracy (described in Chapter 4), so it is possible to classify the estimators themselves.

Optimistic estimators

As a general rule, it can be taken that estimates for any work will more frequently be understated than overstated. Many people seem to be blessed with an unquenchable spirit of optimism when asked to predict completion times for any specific task. 'I can polish off that little job in three days,' it is often claimed, but three weeks later the only things produced are excuses. Without such optimism the world might be a much duller place in which to live and work, but the project manager's lot would be far easier.

An interesting feature of optimistic estimators is the way in which they allow their Cloud-cuckoo-land dreams to persist, even after seeing several jobs completed in double the times that they originally forecast. They continue to churn out estimates which are every bit as hopeful as the last, and appear quite unable to learn from their previous experience. Fortunately, the 'ill wind' proverb holds good here, with the wind in this case blowing to the good of the project manager. The source of consolation in analysing such estimates lies in the fact that they are at least consistent in their trend. Shrewd project managers will come to learn by experience just how pronounced the trend is in their own particular company. Better still, they will be able to apportion error factors to particular individuals. A typical multiplication factor is 1.5. In other words, it is often necessary to add about 50 per cent to the original estimates.

Pessimistic estimators

Occasionally, another kind of individual is encountered who, unlike the optimist of more customary experience, can be relied upon to overestimate most tasks. This characteristic is not particularly common and, when seen, it might pay to investigate the underlying cause. Possibly the estimator lacks experience or is incompetent. These explanations are unlikely, since the typical symptom of estimating incompetence is random behaviour, not a consistent error trend.

The picture becomes clearer, if more unsavoury, when it is remembered that project estimates play a large part in determining total departmental budgets. Higher project estimates mean (if they are accepted) bigger budgets for costs and manpower, and thus expanding departments. This in turn adds to the power and status of the departmental heads. In these cases, therefore, 'E' stands not only for 'estimator' but also for 'empire builder'. Correction factors are possible, but action is more effective when it is aimed not at the estimates, but at their originators.

Inconsistent estimators

The inconsistent estimator is the universal bane of the project manager's existence. Here we find a person who is seemingly incapable of estimating any job at all, giving answers that range over the whole spectrum from ridiculous pessimism to ludicrous optimism. The only characteristic reliably displayed is inconsistency. Incompetence or inexperience suggest themselves as the most likely causes. Complacency could be another. Older people looking forward to retirement rather than promotion, and staff who were overlooked during the last round of promotions can display these symptoms.

Unfortunately, this category can manifest itself at departmental head level – precisely the people most frequently asked to provide estimates. Only time can solve this problem.

Accurate estimators

It has to be allowed that there is a possibility, however remote, of finding a manager capable of providing estimates that prove to be consistently accurate when the work actually takes place. This contingency is so remote that it can almost be discounted. When this rare phenomenon does occur, it is apt to produce a very unsettling effect on the work-hardened project manager who has, through long experience, learned that it pays always to question every report received and never to take any forecast at its face value.

Making allowances

Why should we not try to educate the estimators? Prevention, after all, is better than cure. But the results of such a re-education programme must be unpredictable, with the effects varying from person to person, upsetting the previous equilibrium. In any case, all of the estimators could be expected to slip back into their old ways eventually and, during the process, their estimating bias could lie anywhere on the scale between extreme optimism and pessimism. Arguing wastes time if nothing is achieved. Accept the situation as it exists, and be grateful that it is at least predictable.

Here, then, is a picture of a project manager or proposals manager obtaining a set of estimates for a project, sitting down with a list of all the estimators who were involved, complete with the correction factor deemed appropriate for each individual, and then factoring the original estimates accordingly. Far-fetched? The value of this procedure has been proved in practice.

Estimates for material and equipment costs

Materials always need two types of estimate. For each purchase, these are as follows:

1   the total expected cost, including all charges and taxes payable in transporting the materials to the project location
2   the total lead time, which is the time expected to elapse between issuing the purchase order and receiving the consignment (failure to obtain materials on time is a common cause of delays and late project completion).

It might also be necessary to make estimates of other factors for operational purposes: for example, the volume or weight of materials (information needed for storage and handling).

If detailed design has yet to be carried out, no parts lists, bills of materials or other schedules will exist from which to start the estimating process. Therefore, the next best approach is to ask the engineers to prepare provisional lists of materials for each task. This may be impossible to carry out in detail, but the problem is not as difficult as it would first seem. In most work, the engineers have a very good idea of the more significant and most expensive items that will have to be purchased. There might be special components, instruments, control gear, bearings, heavy weldments or castings, all depending on the type of project. Items such as these can account for a high proportion of the costs, and are frequently those which take the longest time to obtain. In construction projects, outline assumptions can be made for the types and quantities of bulk materials needed.

Foreknowledge of these main items of expense reduces the unknown area of estimating, and therefore improves the forecasting accuracy. If all the important items can be listed and priced, the remaining miscellaneous purchases can be estimated by intelligent guesswork. Records of past projects can be consulted to help assess the probable magnitude of the unknown element. If, for example, the known main components are going to account for 50 per cent of the total material costs, an error of 10 per cent in estimating the cost of the other materials would amount only to 5 per cent of the total. It is most important, however, to prepare the list of known items very carefully, ensuring that the job is done conscientiously and without serious omissions.

The purchasing department or purchasing agent should be involved, and estimates for prices and delivery times must be obtained through their efforts whenever possible. If the purchasing organization is not allowed to partake in preparing the detailed estimates, a danger exists that when the time eventually comes to order the goods, these will be obtained from the wrong suppliers at the wrong prices. It is far better if the big items of expense can be priced by quotations from the anticipated suppliers. The buyer can file all such quotations away in readiness for the time when the project becomes live. If the purchasing department is to be held down to a project materials budget, then it is only reasonable that they should play the leading role in producing the material estimates.

The responsibility for estimating materials therefore lies in two areas. The engineers or other design representatives must specify what materials are going to be used. The purchasing department should be expected to find out how much those materials will cost and how long they will take to obtain.

Any estimate for materials is not complete unless all the costs of packing, transport, insurance, port duties, taxes and handling have been taken into account (see, for example, the reference to Incoterms in Chapter 16 page 388). The intending purchaser must be clear on what the price includes, and allowances must be made to take care of any services that are needed but not included in the quoted price.

Another cautionary word concerns the period of validity for quotations received from potential suppliers. Project cost estimates are often made many months – even years – before a contract is eventually awarded. Suppliers' quotations are typically valid for only 90 days, or even less, so that there could be a problem with the materials cost budget or the availability of goods when the time eventually arrives for the purchase orders to be placed.

Below-the-line costs

Contingency allowances

A common source of estimating errors is the failure to appreciate that additional costs are bound to arise as the result of design errors, mistakes made by those carrying out work according to the design, material or component failures and the like. The degree to which these contingencies are going to add to the project costs will depend on many factors, including the type of project, the general efficiency performance of the firm, the soundness (or otherwise) of the engineering concepts, and so on.

Performance on previous projects is a reliable pointer that can be used to decide just how much to allow on each new project to cover unforeseen circumstances. For a straightforward project, not entailing an inordinate degree of risk, an allowance set at 5 per cent of the above-the-line costs might be adequate.

The scope for adding an adequate contingency allowance will be restricted if there is high price competition from the market. If the perceived risk suggests the need for a very high contingency allowance, perhaps the company should reconsider whether to tender at all.

Cost escalation

Every year wages and salaries increase, purchased goods and services tend to cost more, transport becomes more expensive and plant and buildings absorb more money. All of these increases correspond to the familiar decrease in the real value of money that is termed 'inflation'. This decay appears to be inevitable, and the rate is usually fairly predictable in the short term. In a country where the rate of inflation is 10 per cent, a project that was accurately estimated in 2003 to cost $5 million (say) might cost an extra million dollars if its start were to be delayed for two years.

Suppose that a project were to be initiated to build a new sea wall along 20 kilometres of coastline at the rate of 2 kilometres per year (a ten-year building programme). The building costs would gradually increase with the passage of time as a result of cost inflation. The effect is compound, so that an annual inflation rate of about 7.5 per cent would result in the last 20 kilometres of wall costing double the amount needed for the first 20 kilometres.

Unfortunately, cost inflation rates are not easy to predict over the long term, because they are subject to a range of political, environmental and economic factors. However, a cost escalation allowance based on the best possible prediction should be made for any project whose duration is expected to exceed one year. The rate chosen for below-the-line cost escalation allowances might have to be negotiated and agreed with the customer, for example in defence or other contracts to be carried out for a national government.

The conditions of contract may allow a price increase claim in the event of specified cost escalation events that are beyond the contractor's control (for example, an industry-wide wage award), but that is a different case from including escalation in quoted rates and prices as a below-the-line allowance.

Using a validity time limit to reduce cost escalation risk

The starting date for a project can often be delayed for a considerable time after the contractor submits a fixed-price proposal. Such delays are common. Factors such as internal committee decisions, internal committee indecision, legal considerations, local authority planning requirements, environmental pressures, political interference, confirmation of final technical details and arranging a financing package can easily add many months or years to the start date and subsequent timescale of a project. The contracting company will usually safeguard itself against this risk to a great extent by placing a time limit on the validity of rates or prices quoted in the tender.

Provisional sums

It often happens, particularly in construction contracts, that the contractor foresees the possibility of additional work that might arise if particular difficulties are encountered when work actually starts. For example, a client might specify that materials salvaged from a building during demolition work are to be re-used in the new construction. The contractor might wish to include a provisional sum, to be added to the project price in the event that the salvaged materials prove unsuitable for re-use. It is not unusual for a project quotation to include more than one provisional sum, covering several quite different eventualities.

Foreign currencies

Most large projects involve transactions in currencies other than their own national currency. This can give rise to uncertainty and risk when the exchange rates vary. Some mitigation of this effect can be achieved if the contract includes safeguards, or if all quotations can be obtained in the home currency. Otherwise, it is a matter of skill, judgement and foresight.

Common practice in project cost estimating is to nominate one currency as the control currency for the project, and then to convert all estimated costs into that currency using carefully chosen exchange rates. Although contractors would normally choose their home currency, projects may have to be quoted in foreign currencies if the terms of tendering so demand, and if the potential client insists.

Whether or not the contractor wishes to disclose the exchange rates used in reaching its final cost estimates, the rates used for all conversions must be shown clearly on the estimating forms.

Reviewing the cost estimates

When all the detailed estimates have been made, it should theoretically be possible to add them all up and produce a bottom-up forecast of the whole project cost. When this stage has been reached, however, it is never a bad plan to stand well back for a while and view the picture from a wider angle. Perhaps a top-down estimate of the project might be made for comparison. Or, as a particularly valuable exercise, try converting the figures for labour times from hours into man-years.

Suppose that the engineering design work needed for a project appears to need 8225 man-hours or 235 man-weeks (according to which units were used). Assume that 1645 man-hours or 47 man-weeks are roughly equivalent to one net man-year (after allowing for holidays and other non-productive absences). Dividing the 8225 man-hours estimate by 1645 shows that five man-years must be spent to complete the project design. Now assume that all the design is scheduled to be finished in the first six months of the programme. This could be viewed (simplistically) as a project requirement of ten engineers for six months.

The manager starting this project might receive a rude awakening if he or she makes a top-down estimate for the project or refers to records of past projects. These might well show that projects of similar size and complexity take not ten engineers for six months, but the equivalent of ten engineers for a whole year. An apparent error of five man-years exists somewhere. This is, in any language, a king-sized problem. Part of its cause could be the failure of estimators to allow for that part of engineering design which is sometimes called 'after-issue' work: making corrections, incorporating unfunded modifications, answering engineering queries from the workforce or the customer, writing reports and putting records to bed.

It goes without saying that cost estimates for a project are extremely important. Any serious error could prove disastrous for a fixed-price contractor – and for the customer if it leads the contractor into financial difficulties. A competent person who is independent of the estimate compiler should therefore always check estimates as far as possible. Comparisons with actual cost totals experienced on past projects (for all materials and labour, not just engineering design) are valuable in checking that the new cost estimate at least appears to be in the right league.

Because the cost estimate will be used for many important commercial and management decisions, it is sensible to arrange for an authorizing signature from a responsible senior person who is satisfied that all reasonable care has been taken.

Chapter 6

Commercial management

Most project managers are appointed after the project's initial commercial environment has been established by others. Thereafter, the project manager's degree of involvement in commercial management must depend on the size and nature of the organization. Many large organizations expect their project managers to refer all matters requiring commercial decisions to their marketing, commercial or legal departments. Other companies will delegate all or most commercial authority to their project managers, so that they would (for example) be solely responsible for negotiating changes to the main contract or setting up subcontracts. Apart from marketing activities, as far as project management is concerned the principal areas of commercial management are:

- financial project appraisal
- funding
- contracts and negotiations (including purchasing)
- accounting, invoicing and credit control
- insurance (see Chapter 24).

Each of these subjects would justify at least one volume in its own right. Many aspects of commercial management are highly specialized and, particularly for legal and insurance matters, these are areas where it can be dangerous for the layperson to venture without rigorous training or professional help. However, it is possible to outline some of the more important points. For study in greater depth, there is a further reading list at the end of this chapter.

Project feasibility analysis

Managers frequently have to make decisions on whether or not to authorize investment in a project, or they might be asked to decide between two or more different project options. Depending on the type of project under consideration, their final decision will depend on many factors, including answers to questions like the following:

- Is the project feasible technically?
- Are we confident that the claims of the engineers, designers, consultants or architects are valid?
- What are the environmental implications?
- What are the implications, if any, for our staff?
- Will the proposed new plant produce as much output as the experts claim?
- For a new consumer product development, can we produce it, will people like it, how many can we sell and at what price?
- Is the project likely to be finished on time?
- How much will it all cost?
- For machinery or process plant, what are the expected operating costs?
- What is the expected operational life of the new machinery?
- Is there no better project strategy than the one proposed?
- What are the technical risks?
- What are the commercial risks?
- How can we raise the money?
- Is the return on our investment going to be adequate?

It is sometimes necessary to commission one or more feasibility studies from independent experts to answer many of these questions. A feasibility study might examine more than one possible project strategy in depth. For example, a project to develop a copper mine in an undeveloped region can be approached from a number of strategic standpoints. Many geological, environmental, political and economic factors must be considered for each of a number of different case options. Should the ore be mined, given some treatment to concentrate the copper, and then be shipped a great distance to an existing smelter and refinery? Or should a smelter and refinery be built at the new mine location? A feasibility study for any new project could therefore examine several different strategic options in considerable depth.

Experts' reports can be open to doubt or give rise to further questions, but a feasibility report will usually be required as part of the business case to be considered by the potential owner or fund provider for any significant project. Whatever the circumstances, a careful appraisal of the expected financial outcome is likely to have great influence on most project authorization decisions.

Financial project appraisal

For many commercial projects, a financial appraisal might be conducted to forecast the return on the capital to be invested. Another case is where a company is considering a project to replace an asset such as machinery or equipment to increase productivity or otherwise save money through more efficient operation.

All project appraisal methods have, in some way, to consider the financial difference, measured over an appropriate number of years, between two or more project options. The simplest of these options is the choice between investing in a new project or not investing at all.

There are two common approaches to financial appraisal. One is the simple payback method, and the other uses one of a range of techniques based on discounting the forecast cash flows. Whichever of these methods is chosen, the appraiser needs to have a good estimate of the amount and timing of each significant item of expenditure (the cash outflows) and of the revenue or savings expected (the cash inflows).

The main cash outflow items include the following:

●   the initial acquisition cost – this might be a single purchase payment, a series of phased payments, or payments scheduled against a leasing or rental plan. The differences between these options are important not only for the timing of payments, but also for the tax implications
●   interest payable on financing loans
●   if the project is for new machinery or plant, the costs of operating and maintaining the plant
●   commissioning, debugging and other implementation costs
●   staff or operator training costs
●   all other expenses and fees payable as a result of the new project.

Against these items of expenditure must be balanced all the savings and revenue that the new project is expected to generate. These items might include the following:

●   savings in operating and maintenance costs achieved by replacing old methods with the new project – for example, although a stainless steel tower bought to replace an existing mild steel tower would be expensive initially, it would have a longer life and would not need regular repainting
●   revenue from the sale of products or services made possible by the new project
●   proceeds from the sale of assets no longer required as a result of the new project
●   proceeds from the sale of the new project hardware in the future, when the new project itself has reached the end of its economic life.

Fiscal measures can have a significant effect on the outcome. Many cash inflows will attract taxes, while some expenditure might be offset by allowances against taxation. Some capital investment projects might generate cash inflows in the form of government grants or special tax incentives and allowances. These circumstances vary considerably from place to place and from one country to another. They can complicate financial appraisal calculations considerably, and are best handled by experts. The examples in this chapter illustrate the general methods, and have been kept relatively simple by excluding these fiscal elements.

The simple payback method

Simple payback is the appraisal method familiar to most managers. It seeks to answer the blunt question: 'How long would this project take to pay for itself?' The method compares the predicted cash outflows and inflows relating to a new investment option against those of an alternative option (which in many cases means comparing the relative merits of proceeding with a project against the option of doing nothing). Costs and income or savings are analysed over consecutive periods (typically years) until a point is reached where the forecast cumulative costs of the new project are balanced (paid back) by the cash inflows that the project is expected to generate.

A simple payback example

A project is under consideration for the installation of new, more efficient central heating boilers for a group of industrial buildings situated in a cold region. Also included in the project would be an electronic optimizer control unit to increase fuel economy and heat insulation for the buildings. Total installed cost of the

Year	2004	2005	2006	2007	2008	2009
Existing system:						
Fuel	90	90	90	90	90	90
Maintenance	10	10	10	10	10	10
Annual cash outflows	100	100	100	100	100	100
Cumulative outflow	100	200	300	400	500	600
New proposal:						
New plant investment	60					
Fuel	85	80	80	80	80	80
Maintenance		6	8	10	10	10
Annual cash outflows	145	86	88	90	90	90
Cumulative outflow	145	231	319	409	499	589
Saving (loss) if new plant starts up on 1 July 2004:						
Annual cash saving (loss)	(45)	14	12	10	10	10
Cumulative cash saving (loss)	(45)	(31)	(19)	(9)	1	11

Note: All figures are £'000s.

Figure 6.1   Boiler replacement project: Payback calculation
This tabulation of cash flow predicts break-even towards the end of 2008. In other words, the payback period is between four and five years.

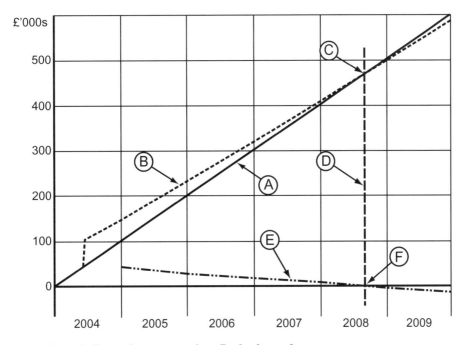

Figure 6.2 **Boiler replacement project: Payback graphs**
There are two different methods combined on these axes. Both predict the payback date
more precisely than the tabulation in Figure 6.1.

project is estimated at £60 000, and the work could be carried out over a week or
so in mid-2004. Benefits claimed for the new system include a reduction in fuel
costs from the current £90 000 to £80 000 in each calendar year, although only
£5000 savings could be expected in the year 2004 because the project would not
come on stream until July. Maintenance of the new plant is free for the remainder
of the year 2004, under the terms of a guarantee. After that, maintenance costs are
expected to be £6000 for the second year, rising to £8000 for the third year as the
plant begins to age, finally reaching £10 000 per annum (which is the same
maintenance rate as the old system).

The forecasts for each calendar year can be tabulated, as shown in Figure 6.1.
In this case, it is seen that the project seems set to break even before the end of
2008, so that the payback period is between four and five years.

The payback period can be pinpointed with greater accuracy by drawing a
graph. There are two ways in which this can be done, and both methods are shown
in Figure 6.2. The curve labelled *A* is the expenditure to be expected if the existing
plant is retained and the proposed new project is not authorized. Curve *B* is the
alternative expenditure pattern expected if the project proposal is accepted and the
new plant is installed during June 2004 for startup on 1 July 2004. Curves *A* and

B intersect at *C*, which is the break-even point, where the additional costs of the new project have just been balanced by the resulting savings. A vertical line *D* has been drawn to highlight the break-even date, which is seen to be about two-thirds through 2008.

Curve *E* shows another way of drawing the graph. In this case only one curve has to be drawn. This is the cumulative net cash flow, plotted with data from Figure 6.1. The point at which this changes from an outflow to an inflow is marked at *F*, the point where the curve crosses zero. This should, and does, give the same break-even result as the two-curve method described above. It would, however, allow more sensitive vertical scaling, giving a greater crossing angle at the intersection and, therefore, a more accurate result.

Discounted cash flow

The simple payback method is adequate provided that the total payback period is one or, at the most, two years. It is less satisfactory when looking ahead for longer periods, especially when high rates of return on investment are required. The reason for this is that any given sum of money earned or spent in the future has less real value than the same amount of money earned or spent today. The main cause lies in the notional earning power of today's money. If £100 is received today and invested for an annual net return of 10 per cent, that £100 should be worth £110 after one year. Put another way, £110 received or spent in one year's time is equivalent to receiving or spending only £100 today. Today's £100 is called the discounted or *net present value* (npv) of the future £110.

Although cost inflation can also have a significant effect, it is usually ignored for the purposes of appraisal calculations (partly because the amounts arising from inflation usually occur on both sides of the inflow/outflow equation, and therefore tend to cancel out).

Tables can be obtained which list discount factors over a wide range of percentage discounting rates and periods. Project life periods are usually broken down into years for discounting, but shorter periods are sometimes chosen, especially where very large sums are involved. A short but useful table of discount factors is given in Figure 6.3.

The discounting rate used for a particular project is a matter for management judgement, probably influenced by prevailing interest rates, certainly related to corporate financial objectives, and preferably assessed with the advice of the company's financial director or accountants.

Net present value of the boiler replacement project

The boiler replacement project can be used to demonstrate the net present value concept. The example has been kept simple, and does not include all possible cash flow items (especially taxation).

Year	1%	2%	3%	4%	5%	6%	7%	8%	9%	10%	11%	12%	13%	14%	15%	16%	17%	18%	19%	20%
0	1.000	1.000	1.000	1.000	1.000	1.000	1.000	1.000	1.000	1.000	1.000	1.000	1.000	1.000	1.000	1.000	1.000	1.000	1.000	1.000
1	0.990	0.980	0.971	0.962	0.952	0.943	0.935	0.926	0.917	0.909	0.901	0.893	0.885	0.877	0.870	0.862	0.855	0.848	0.840	0.833
2	0.980	0.961	0.943	0.925	0.907	0.890	0.873	0.857	0.842	0.826	0.812	0.797	0.783	0.770	0.756	0.743	0.731	0.718	0.706	0.694
3	0.971	0.942	0.915	0.889	0.864	0.840	0.816	0.794	0.772	0.751	0.731	0.712	0.693	0.675	0.658	0.641	0.624	0.609	0.593	0.579
4	0.961	0.924	0.889	0.855	0.823	0.792	0.763	0.735	0.708	0.683	0.659	0.636	0.613	0.592	0.572	0.552	0.534	0.516	0.499	0.482
5	0.952	0.906	0.863	0.822	0.784	0.747	0.713	0.681	0.650	0.621	0.594	0.567	0.543	0.519	0.497	0.476	0.456	0.437	0.419	0.402
6	0.942	0.888	0.838	0.790	0.746	0.705	0.666	0.630	0.596	0.565	0.535	0.507	0.480	0.456	0.432	0.410	0.390	0.370	0.352	0.335
7	0.933	0.871	0.813	0.760	0.711	0.665	0.623	0.584	0.547	0.513	0.482	0.452	0.425	0.400	0.376	0.354	0.333	0.314	0.296	0.279
8	0.923	0.854	0.789	0.731	0.677	0.627	0.582	0.540	0.502	0.467	0.434	0.404	0.376	0.351	0.327	0.305	0.284	0.266	0.249	0.233
9	0.914	0.837	0.766	0.703	0.645	0.592	0.544	0.500	0.460	0.424	0.391	0.361	0.333	0.308	0.284	0.263	0.243	0.226	0.209	0.194
10	0.905	0.820	0.744	0.676	0.614	0.558	0.508	0.463	0.422	0.386	0.352	0.322	0.295	0.270	0.247	0.227	0.208	0.191	0.176	0.162
11	0.896	0.804	0.722	0.650	0.585	0.527	0.475	0.429	0.388	0.351	0.317	0.288	0.261	0.237	0.215	0.195	0.178	0.162	0.148	0.135
12	0.887	0.789	0.701	0.625	0.557	0.497	0.444	0.397	0.356	0.319	0.286	0.257	0.231	0.208	0.187	0.169	0.152	0.137	0.124	0.112
13	0.879	0.773	0.681	0.601	0.530	0.469	0.415	0.368	0.326	0.290	0.258	0.229	0.204	0.182	0.163	0.145	0.130	0.116	0.104	0.094
14	0.870	0.758	0.661	0.578	0.505	0.442	0.388	0.341	0.299	0.263	0.232	0.205	0.181	0.160	0.141	0.125	0.111	0.099	0.088	0.078
15	0.861	0.743	0.642	0.555	0.481	0.417	0.362	0.315	0.275	0.239	0.209	0.183	0.160	0.140	0.123	0.108	0.095	0.084	0.074	0.065
16	0.853	0.728	0.623	0.534	0.458	0.394	0.339	0.292	0.252	0.218	0.188	0.163	0.142	0.123	0.107	0.093	0.082	0.071	0.062	0.054
17	0.844	0.714	0.605	0.513	0.436	0.371	0.317	0.270	0.231	0.198	0.170	0.146	0.125	0.108	0.093	0.080	0.069	0.060	0.052	0.045
18	0.836	0.700	0.587	0.494	0.412	0.350	0.296	0.250	0.212	0.180	0.153	0.130	0.111	0.095	0.081	0.069	0.059	0.051	0.044	0.038
19	0.828	0.686	0.570	0.475	0.396	0.331	0.277	0.232	0.195	0.164	0.138	0.116	0.098	0.083	0.070	0.060	0.051	0.043	0.037	0.031
20	0.820	0.673	0.554	0.456	0.377	0.312	0.258	0.215	0.178	0.149	0.124	0.104	0.087	0.073	0.061	0.051	0.043	0.037	0.030	0.026

Figure 6.3   **Table of discount factors for calculating net present values**

Year	Cash inflow £	Cash outflow £	Net cash flow £	Discount factor at 10% rate	Discounted cash flow £
0 (2004)		45 000	(45 000)	1.000	(45 000)
1 (2005)	14 000		14 000	0.909	12 726
2 (2006)	12 000		12 000	0.826	9 912
3 (2007)	10 000		10 000	0.751	7 510
4 (2008)	10 000		10 000	0.683	6 830
5 (2009)	10 000		10 000	0.621	6 210
Net present value					**(1 812)**

Figure 6.4   Boiler replacement project: Net present value calculation
An annual discounting rate of 10 per cent has been used in this example. The factors were taken from Figure 6.3.

A five-year total period has been chosen in this case, because management has considered this to be a reasonable life expectancy for the new boiler without further change. In many other financial appraisal cases, some event forecast or planned for a fixed date in the future will place a finite limit on the project life and determine the appraisal period. Examples of such events are the expiry of a lease on a building, the planned discontinuance of a product, or the date forecast for a mineral deposit to become exhausted to the point where it is no longer economic for mining.

Net present value calculations can seem a little strange at first, but they are really quite simple if the correct procedure is followed. The secret lies in careful tabulation of all the financial elements, setting each item of cash inflow and outflow in its appropriate time period on a sensibly designed layout.

In the boiler project example, the tabulation and calculation of net flows before discounting has already been performed (Figure 6.1). The discounting calculations are illustrated in Figure 6.4. Using a discount rate of 10 per cent, it is seen that this project has a net present value of minus £1812 after five years. In fact it would not break even (the npv would not become positive) until the year 2010. That result depends on operation of the boiler without major overhaul for more than its expected trouble-free life of five years. This is a more pessimistic (but more realistic) result than that obtained from simple payback analysis. It suggests that the project cannot be justified on purely financial grounds (although there might, of course, be environmental, welfare or other good reasons for going ahead).

Calculating the expected rate of return on investment

Suppose that management want to know the expected rate of return on their company's investment in the boiler project over the five-year period. The rate of return is equivalent to the percentage discounting rate that would give a forecast net present value of zero. This rate can be found by repeating the calculation shown in Figure 6.4 with different percentage discounting rates until one is found that yields the required zero npv. There are three possible ways in which this can be done:

1   One of the test calculations might, with good fortune, yield zero npv, or a value which is sufficiently close to zero to be accepted.

2   It is more likely that no calculation using a whole-number percentage rate will give zero npv. The calculation will probably have to be reiterated using fractional percentages, changing the discounting rate in small steps until zero npv occurs.

3   Instead of reiterations by trial and error, calculations can be made using a few whole-number discounting rates that give a range of fairly small positive and negative npv values. These results can be drawn on a graph, plotting npv against the discounting rates used. The point at which the line crosses zero npv will allow the forecast percentage return on investment to be read off.

Although many computer programs are capable of carrying out discounted cash flow calculations, the process can be followed quickly and easily using an ordinary pocket calculator. It is not even necessary to use tables of discount factors, since the calculator will provide these on demand. If, for example, the discount rate to be tested is 7.5 per cent per annum, it is only necessary to divide 1 by 1.075 to find the discount rate for year 1 (0.9302). On most calculators, repetitive use of the = button will immediately give the discount factors for as many subsequent years as are needed.

Financial appraisal of a tollbridge project

Here is a slightly more complicated case. Mrs Goldbags, a lady of considerable wealth, owns land that includes a long section of a river valley. Two fairly busy highways run alongside both banks of the river for many miles, and Mrs Goldbags wishes to profit by linking these highways with a short road and bridge that would cut road journeys and save road users much time and inconvenience. She plans to recover her initial investment and thenceforth make a profit by charging a toll for each road user who crosses the bridge in either direction. Here are the parameters for the proposed tollbridge project:

* project start, 1 July 2005
* road opening date, 1 July 2007
* total costs of designing and building, £20 million, spread evenly over the two-year construction period; for simplicity, this includes start-up costs of recruiting and training staff just before the road opens
* toll revenues, based on traffic predictions, £3 million per annum, with no allowance made for growth
* maintenance costs free for the first full year of operation (1 July 2007 to 30 June 2008)

- subsequent maintenance costs £1 million per annum, starting 1 July 2008
- management and administration costs (insurances and staff salaries) £100 000 in each full year of operation
- all funding is from existing cash reserves, so that there are no loan interest charges to be incurred
- rate of return on investment required is 7.5 per cent over an appraisal period ending on 31 December 2020.

The discounted cash flow schedule in Figure 6.5 indicates a net present value of minus £3.612 million. So, this project cannot yield the required 7.5 per cent return on capital invested according to the parameters given. Recalculations tested with different discount factors (not illustrated here) show that the net present value becomes positive when the discount factor (and rate of return on capital) is reduced to 5 per cent.

Other ways of viewing this project give different but deceptive results. A full

Year	Item	Cash outflows £'000s	Cash inflows £'000s	Net cash flows £'000s	Discount factor at 7.5%	Discounted cash flows £'000s
0 (2005)	Design and building costs	5000		(5000)	1.0000	(5000)
1 (2006)	Building costs	10000		(10000)	0.9302	(9302)
	Building costs	5000				
2 (2007)	Administration expenses	50		(3550)	0.8653	(3072)
	Revenue from tolls		1500			
	Administration expenses	100				
3 (2008)	Maintenance costs	500		2400	0.8050	1932
	Revenue from tolls		3000			
	Administration expenses	100				
4 (2009)	Maintenance costs	1000		1900	0.7489	1423
	Revenue from tolls		3000			
5 (2010)	As for year 4	1100	3000	1900	0.6966	1324
6 (2011)	As for year 4	1100	3000	1900	0.6480	1231
7 (2012)	As for year 4	1100	3000	1900	0.6028	1145
8 (2013)	As for year 4	1100	3000	1900	0.5607	1065
9 (2014)	As for year 4	1100	3000	1900	0.5216	991
10 (2015)	As for year 4	1100	3000	1900	0.4852	922
11 (2016)	As for year 4	1100	3000	1900	0.4513	857
12 (2017)	As for year 4	1100	3000	1900	0.4199	798
13 (2018)	As for year 4	1100	3000	1900	0.3906	742
14 (2019)	As for year 4	1100	3000	1900	0.3633	690
15 (2020)	As for year 4	1100	3000	1900	0.3380	642
Net present value						**(3612)**

Figure 6.5   Tollbridge project: Net present value calculation
The negative net present value shows that this project is not expected to produce the required 7.5 per cent internal rate of return within the period of appraisal.

year's operating profit and loss account would, before taxation, show total costs of £1.1 million against sales revenue of £3 million, which is a handsome gross annual operating profit of 63.33 per cent. But that ignores the sunk cost of £20 million. Using a simple payback calculation (again not illustrated here), this project would appear to break even during the year 2017 (after about 12 years).

What the discounted cash flow method shows, however, is that Mrs Goldbags would be better off by abandoning the idea of this project (with all its attendant risks) altogether if she placed her £20 million in deposit accounts yielding interest of 5 per cent or more per annum.

Sensitivity analysis

The results of project financial appraisal can be the prime factor in deciding whether or not to commit vast sums of money to launching a new project. Yet quantifying many parameters used in the appraisal can only be matters of judgement, and even the best estimates are often subject to risk. Sensitivity analysis is one way to gain more confidence in the reliability of an appraisal. The process consists of repeating the discounted cash flow calculations with a changed value for one or more of the parameters to test the effect (sensitivity) on the predicted net present value.

Still considering the tollbridge project described in the previous section, the estimated cost of maintenance and repairs might be arrived at with some degree of confidence by obtaining an advance quotation for a service contract to carry out this work. The annual costs of managing the operation should be relatively simple to estimate, because the number of staff needed and the salaries to be paid can be assessed fairly well.

Two factors in the tollbridge project cannot be so reliably predicted, however:

1 Unforeseen problems during construction which, although not affecting the fixed price agreed, could delay the completion date, thus putting back the start of operations and cash inflows. A few examples from similar projects in the past include exceptionally bad weather, actions by environmental groups, discovery of archaeological remains, disturbance of rare fauna or flora, stoppages through industrial action, unexpected geological conditions, and so forth.

2 The forecast for traffic flows and consequent toll revenues might prove to be very inaccurate when the bridge opens, possibly resulting in revenues well below the target levels.

Each or both of these factors could be changed, either independently or in combination, perhaps in steps of ± 5 per cent, in reiterations of the discounted cash flow schedule. The sensitivity of net present value to these changes will help to indicate the reliability of the financial appraisal.

Project funding

Sources of finance

Project funding may not be of direct concern to every project manager – unless shortage of funds puts the future of the project (and its manager) in question. However, here is a list of possible sources from which an organization may be able to find the capital needed for investment in a project:

- cash reserves (money held in the bank or in short-term investments, including profits not distributed as dividends to shareholders)

- sale of assets (for example, the owner of a stately home sells a valuable work of art to raise capital for a building restoration project, or a company realizes cash on its real estate in a sale and leaseback deal)

- mortgaging property

- borrowing from a bank or other financial institution, either as an overdraft or as a fixed-term loan

- borrowing through a lease purchase agreement

- renting or leasing (in which case the project will be owned by the financing institution, and not by the project user)

- issuing debentures or loan stock

- raising share capital, either in a private or public company; the company may be specially set up for the project

- collaborating with other companies to set up a consortium or a joint venture company in which skills, resources and risk are all shared

- government sources at international, national or local level, through direct grants or fiscal incentives; for export projects, it might be possible to borrow from a bank against security provided by a government's export credit guarantee scheme.

A company will be able to reduce its borrowing requirement if it can improve its cash flow. The following are some of the methods that might be considered:

- reducing inventory (stocks and work-in-progress)

- using trade creditors to advantage, negotiating longest possible credit terms for the payment of suppliers' and subcontractors' invoices

- keeping trade debtors to a minimum through prompt and accurate invoicing, asking for progress payments where appropriate, and applying rigorous credit control.

The contractor's viewpoint

Project funding considerations are not the sole concern of the purchaser. Contractors often need to take a serious interest in the financing of projects for several reasons:

- In some cases the contractor might undertake to help or advise the customer to arrange finance. Financing proposals may even feature in the project tender.

- The contractor must be assured that the customer is financially viable, and has access to sufficient funds to meet all project costs. Will the customer be able to pay the bills?

- The contractor may need finance to invest in new plant or to expand other facilities in order to be able to carry out the project.

- If the project size is significant compared to the contractor's other work, cash flow will have to be considered. The contractor may have to fund costly work-in-progress until payment is eventually received from the customer. Invoices may be disputed, delaying revenue receipts. Some customers pay late, not just through innocent tardiness, but because of a deliberate policy to delay payment of every bill for as long as possible. The experienced contractor will attempt to minimize these effects by insisting on a contract that allows for progress payments, and by efficient invoicing and credit control methods.

- Money due from overseas customers can be particularly difficult to collect, with risk of serious delays or non-payment (see the references to export credit insurance on pages 50 and 588). It is easy for an inexperienced contractor to cause delay in payment through any failure (however trivial) to observe the complex documentation formalities imposed by some governments. The big banks are excellent sources of advice for those new to exporting.

Financial viability of participating organizations

A sensible contractor will take steps to try to investigate the financial viability of any important new customer. The contractor might start by asking for copies of the customer's audited annual accounts and reports for recent years. Wary customers often make similar enquiries of potential contractors and suppliers.

Complementary processes can exist, therefore, where on the one hand a contractor wants to be assured that the customer will be able to meet all proper claims for payment, while the customer takes steps to ensure that the contractor is not likely to get into financial difficulties or even go bankrupt before being able to complete the project.

There are several ways in which these investigations can be conducted. Some companies make discreet enquiries themselves, asking other companies who have used the organization under scrutiny to provide references. To preserve anonymity, a professional organization such as Dun and Bradstreet (visit <http://www.dnb.com>) can usually research information on a company's financial performance and status on a confidential basis.

Credit control and cash flow

The contractor's project manager has a substantial role to play in protecting his or her organization's cash flow. Apart from managing the project itself to keep it on plan, the project manager must see that claims for payment are issued promptly. All invoices and other claims for payment from the customer must be correct, supported by contractually agreed certificates or other documentation. For international projects, all invoices and other export/import documentation must be completed properly, to avoid any reason for dispute. Claims for payment must be followed up with polite but prompt credit control action if payment becomes overdue.

Contracts

Essential elements of a contract

Although a legally binding contract can exist between two parties on the basis of a verbal agreement, for project management purposes it is assumed that the contract between the customer and the contractor will be in writing. This applies also to all contracts made between the project contractor and the subcontractors and other suppliers of goods and services. Properly drafted written documents are likely to ensure that all aspects of each agreement are available for subsequent reference, both for routine administration of the contract and as evidence should any dispute require resolution.

The contract documentation might be a purchase order, an exchange of letters, a specially drafted contract or a pre-printed standard form. It is assumed that any subsequent amendments to the contract will also be written on suitable documents.

Several conditions must be satisfied in order for a legally binding contract to exist. The following notes are a summary, and do not list the exceptions:

1 **Intention** – The parties must intend that the contract shall be legally binding. In project contracts this intention will be assumed unless the parties have specifically declared otherwise, in which case the contract becomes only a formal version of a 'gentleman's agreement'. Project managers are not likely to be concerned with this question of intention, except perhaps when problems arise with collective agreements between management and trade unions.

2 **Offer and acceptance** – The contractor must make a definite offer stating willingness to contract on specified terms, and the contract becomes legally binding on both parties when the customer informs the contractor that the

offer is accepted without qualification. The customer must communicate acceptance before the expiry of any offer time limit set by the contractor.

It may happen that the picture becomes blurred as to what has been offered and what has actually been accepted. Therefore, the offer must be defined by a specification that is as complete and up to date as possible, amended as necessary to take account of all changes agreed during negotiations.

Purchase order forms usually have the purchaser's conditions of purchase attached or printed as a standard list on the reverse side. The supplier is asked to acknowledge the order and to accept its conditions as binding on the contract by returning a tear-off acknowledgement slip to the purchaser. Many suppliers never return such slips, but acknowledge receipt of an order instead by returning a form listing the supplier's own standard conditions. The supplier's conditions are unlikely to agree in all respects with those stated by the purchaser. It might then be argued that no contract exists because neither party has accepted the other's offer. However, a great many purchasing contracts are made in such circumstances. If a dispute should arise, it is possible that legal argument would favour the party who made the last offer, provided that the other party has not actually rejected it.

3   **Consideration** – A contract must result in each party promising the other a valuable benefit. In projects, this usually means that one party promises to deliver certain goods, property or services by a specified date, and the other promises to accept the goods, property or services and pay for them. Failure of one party to keep its promise can lead to action by the other for breach of contract.

4   **Capacity** – In general, if the offer made by a company falls outside the scope of its powers as set out in the objects clause of its memorandum of association, then the company has no power to make the offer and the contract is void (said to be *ultra vires*, or 'beyond the power').

Terms describing the parties to a project contract

In general, this book refers to the two main parties in project contracts as the 'customer' and the 'contractor', but many other terms are used in practice.

Terms describing the project purchaser

Some people use the term 'owner' to mean the customer, but this can be misleading because there are several possible circumstances where the customer will not have immediate legal title to the project. One example is where the project is being funded under a lease purchase agreement, so that the finance house will be the initial legal owner. A few contractors adopt the confusing practice of calling their own project managers 'project owners', with the intention of stressing that the project managers 'own' responsibility for their projects until the completed work has been handed over to the purchasers (the real project owners).

When a project passes through a customer to a third party, the expression 'end-user' can be useful to describe the eventual recipient.

The terms in most general use are 'customer', 'client', 'purchaser' or 'buyer', but the terms 'promoter' and 'employer' are occasionally seen. For simplicity, 'customer' is used in most cases throughout this book, but 'client' is commonly preferred in projects involving construction or the supply of professional services.

Terms describing the project supplier

The organization carrying out the project may be described as the 'contractor', 'vendor', 'manufacturer', 'supplier' or 'seller'. The terms 'main contractor', 'managing contractor' and 'management contractor' are used to identify an organization employed by the project purchaser for help in managing and fulfilling a project. These terms are not strictly synonymous, and the generally accepted distinctions between them are as follows:

● A *main contractor* or *managing contractor* is a person or (more likely) organization that accepts commercial risk and responsibility to the customer and directly employs other contractors (subcontractors) to execute some or all of the work. A common arrangement is for the contractor to carry out design work in their own offices, and then engage and supervise subcontractors to perform the work.

● A *management contractor* is a person or organization engaged by the project customer to provide professional assistance in planning, coordinating and supervising the work of other contractors.

Throughout this book I have used the term 'contractor' generally to mean the company or other organization that has entered into a contract to carry out all or most of the work required for a project.

Independent consultants

Independent consultants often figure in large contracts, and may be appointed to safeguard the interests of one party or the other (usually the purchaser). In most cases, the consultant is either a professional organization or a suitably qualified person, often referred to contractually as 'the engineer'. Refer, for example, to the role of the professional consulting engineer in a contract matrix, which is described briefly in Chapter 2 and illustrated in the organization chart of Figure 2.9.

Contract scope

The contract documents should specify, without ambiguity, the exact role that the contractor is required to perform. The purchaser and the contractor must both be clear about what is included in any quoted price or charging rate, and what is excluded. At its lowest level, the contract scope might be limited to minor involvement by a company as a subcontractor. At the other extreme, a contractor could be completely in charge of a large project, with 'turnkey' responsibility for all the works (which means handing the project over to the customer only after full completion and commissioning). Specifying the technical and commercial scope of a contract is part of the project definition process (see Chapter 3).

Abbreviations describing contract scope

Abbreviations are sometimes used as a succinct way to describe the scope expected of a contractor for a building or item of plant. These terms relate specifically to the expected role of the contractor in work such as the following:

- building the initial project
- handing over the project ready for immediate use (turnkey)
- training the customer's staff to operate or use the project
- operating the project for the customer initially
- operating the project for the customer in the longer term
- providing maintenance services.

The following are commonly used abbreviations:

BOOM – Build – Own – Operate – Maintain
BOOT – Build – Own – Operate – Transfer ownership
BOTO – Build – Own – Train – Operate
OMT – Operate – Maintain – Train
TK – Turnkey

Contracts with model or standard terms and conditions

In order to avoid errors and omissions, and to promote the use of contracts that are likely to be most effective in use, many organizations use standard or model forms that either guide the process of drafting new contracts or remove the need altogether. The most common case of a standard form of contract intended to remove any need for drafting is the common purchase order, which has standard terms of contract printed on its reverse.

Professional institutions (especially the engineering institutions), national bodies, trade associations and some large companies have developed model terms of contract that are relevant to their particular industries or specialized disciplines. Model terms of contract recommended by various professional and national institutions are summarized and compared in Wearne (1993). Dates and editions of all model contracts are subject to revision from time to time, and intending users should always ensure that they have the latest edition.

Contract payment structures

There are many ways in which contractors and their customers set up pricing and payment arrangements for project work. The payment terms will typically depend on the following factors:

- Risk, uncertainty, and any other factor affecting the accuracy with which the project can be defined, estimated and budgeted.

- The customer's intention to set the contractor performance incentives – these incentives are usually aimed either at completion on time or at completion below budget, but they can also have a bearing on the standard of workmanship and quality. A penalty clause may be included in the contract as an attempt to limit failure in performance, the most common form being a penalty payment calculated according to the number of days, weeks or other stated periods by which the contractor is late in successfully completing the project.

Pricing considerations

It can be assumed that any company worth its salt will be equipped with a well-defined general pricing policy. Profit targets and the relationship between estimated costs and selling prices might be laid down very firmly. Pricing decisions for any significant project usually fall within the responsibility, not of the project manager, but of the company's higher management. Companies typically have procedures for authorizing quotations, and it is usual for new proposals to be discussed and agreed at senior management – or board-level meetings before the firm allows any commitment to be made to a potential customer.

One might imagine that a fixed selling price could always be obtained by taking a set of project estimates and marking up the cost at the specified level. Life, unfortunately, is seldom quite so straightforward. Even where a project is to be quoted on the basis of a schedule of rates or on some other cost-reimbursable basis, setting the level of charges can be a matter for expert judgement rather than simple accountancy.

Under certain conditions a firm may be forced to submit a tender or accept an order at a price so low that any possibility of making a fair profit is precluded right from the start. Consider, for example, a company that is temporarily short of work, but which can confidently foresee long-term continuity and expansion of its business. It may be that a period of market recession is seen to be coming to an end. Perhaps the start of one or more new projects is being delayed while customers arrange funding, or for other commercial, political or technical reasons (such delays are common with new projects).

The contractor might be faced with a real dilemma: the choice between dismissing idle staff as redundant, or keeping them on the payroll for no return. Specialists and skilled people are difficult and expensive to recruit. Their training and acquired experience in a company's methods is an investment which represents a valuable part of the firm's invisible assets. Disbanding such a team can be compared to cutting down a mature tree. The act of chopping down and dismembering takes only a few hours, but to grow a replacement tree of similar size takes many years. No one can tell whether the new tree will turn out to be such a fine specimen as its predecessor. In addition, of course, trying to ensure the survival of work groups can be argued (usually unsuccessfully) as a moral or social obligation of employers, especially in the larger industries where entire local communities may be dependent on one company for employment and local prosperity.

Contracts taken on to tide a firm over a lean period are sometimes termed 'bridging contracts', for obvious reasons. The profit motive becomes secondary in these circumstances, but there are, of course, risks to be considered and accepted in adopting such a policy. The impact of an estimating error or any other problem that causes a budget to be overspent is always greater without the cushioning effect of a planned profit margin. There is also some danger that customers who return with requests for projects in the future might be disappointed or aggrieved when they discover that prices for the new work are not quoted at comparable, artificially low rates. A more likely risk is that an underpriced project will materialize far later than expected (as many large projects have a way of doing), so that the workload no longer falls in the business trough, but hits the contractor just when more profitable work is materializing. This could put the profitable work at risk: it might even prevent the contractor tendering for or accepting new, profitable work until the underpriced project has been completed.

It might be expedient to submit a tender at an artificially low price in an attempt to gain entry into a market not previously exploited. There are, of course, other proven ways of achieving this end, not least of which is to acquire a firm that is already well established in the chosen market sector. Underpricing (offering 'loss leaders') remains a common, less drastic alternative. It is hardly necessary to stress that any company which decides to adopt a deliberate policy of underpricing will soon suffer from badly burned fingers if it has not first done the essential marketing homework.

Market conditions generally dictate the price which can be charged for any commodity, service or project, although the exact relationship is not straightforward, and can produce surprises. In certain cases sales can actually be increased by pricing high, contrary to normal expectations. Usually, however, the laws of supply and demand operate. Most project tenders stand a better chance of acceptance if they are kept low compared to competition. Even when a firm boasts a market monopoly, with competition entirely absent, the intensity of demand can influence the prices that can be charged; if a price is too high, the potential customer might simply decide to do without the project altogether.

Local government authorities and other public bodies under strict obligations as trustees of public money may be compelled to accept the lowest tender for a given project. If such an organization wishes to place an order at anything other than the very lowest price possible, they must have an overriding reason which they are prepared to defend.

Orders can be unwelcome and possess nuisance value under some circumstances. Suppose, for example, that a firm has been asked to tender for a project at a time when the order book is already full to overflowing. This firm knows that either a very long delivery time must be quoted or, in the event of receiving the order, it will have to divert work to subcontractors that it would prefer to keep in-house. Outsourcing conceptual engineering and design, for instance, might be a particularly unattractive option for a company that wishes to safeguard its hard-earned reputation for quality and reliability. Taking on too much work can give rise to overtrading and cash flow difficulties. Unless the company can foresee a continuing expansion of business, sufficient to justify raising new capital and increasing its permanent capacity, it may simply not want the order. In a case such as this the company can choose between quoting at a very high price, or not quoting at all.

Accurate project definition and reliable cost estimates are essential to the pricing process. They provide the platform from which profits can be predicted relative to the price set. Shaky estimates produce a tendency to increase contingency allowances and mark-up rate to cover the increased risk, possibly destroying any chance of gaining an order in a competitive market. Sound estimates are also vital as a basis for any subsequent price negotiations with the customer: contractors must know as accurately as possible just how far they can be pushed into paring a price before any hope of profit dwindles to useless proportions.

Fixed- (or firm-) price contracts

A fixed-price contract is the result of the familiar situation in which one or more contractors bid for work against a purchaser's clear specification, stating a total price for all the works. The purchaser understands that the contractor cannot, in normal circumstances, increase the price quoted. The offer to carry out a project for a fixed price demonstrates the contractor's confidence in being able to complete the specified project without spending more than its estimated costs.

In practice, there are sometimes clauses, even in so-called fixed-price contracts, which allow limited price renegotiation or additional charges in the event of specified circumstances that may arise outside the contractor's control (national industry wage awards are a common cause).

Cost-reimbursable contracts

There are, of course, many types of contracts which do not start with the inclusion of a known total fixed price. Most of these are 'cost-reimbursable' contracts, where the customer agrees to repay the contractor for work done against a prearranged scale of charges. These charges might be for certified quantities of work completed, or for reimbursing the costs of labour time and materials used.

Fixed prices are usually avoided by contractors in all circumstances where the final scope of a project cannot be predicted with sufficient accuracy when the contract is signed, or where the work is to be carried out under conditions of high risk. Projects for pure scientific research where the amount of work needed and the possible results are completely unpredictable would obviously be unsuitable for fixed-price quotations. Many construction contracts for major capital works or process plants are subject to high risk, owing to site conditions or to political and economic factors outside the contractor's control.

Even in cost-reimbursable contracts, with no fixed prices to bid, managers have to decide the levels at which to set the various charging rates. It cannot be assumed that a contractor will charge all customers the same rates. Some customers will demand details of how the direct and overhead charges are built up, and will expect to negotiate the final rates before agreement can be reached.

In any contract where payment is related to agreed rates of working, the customer will want to be assured of the veracity of the contractor's claims for payment. This might entail access to the contractor's books of account by the customer, or by auditors acting for the customer. In construction contracts based on payment by quantities, independent quantity surveyors can act for the customer by certifying the contractors' claims to verify that the work being billed has in fact been done.

Estimating accuracy might seem less important where there are no fixed prices operating but, practically without exception, tenders for contracts with no fixed prices must contain budgetary estimates. If these are set too high, they can frighten a potential customer away, and the contractor stands to lose the contract to competitors. If the estimates are set too low, all kinds of problems could arise during the execution of the work, not least of which might be the customer running out of funds with which to pay the contractor. Any contractor wishing to retain a reputation for fair dealing will want to avoid the trap of setting budgetary estimates too low, especially where this is done deliberately in pursuit of an order. In any case, avoidable estimating inaccuracies must prejudice subsequent attempts at planning, scheduling and management control.

Summary of contract types

Quoted prices or rates do not always fall entirely into the clear category of fixed-price or cost-reimbursable, often because one of the parties wishes to introduce an element of performance incentive or risk protection. Some contracts (compound contracts) incorporate a mix of these arrangements. Others (convertible contracts) allow for a change to a fixed-price arrangement at some pre-agreed stage in the project when it becomes possible to define adequately the total scope of work and probable final costs.

Some well-known options are summarized below, and Figure 6.6 gives an idea of the relationships between risk and incentives.

Fixed price

A price is quoted and accepted for the work specified in the contract. The price will only be varied if the customer varies the contract, or if the contract conditions allow for a price increase to be negotiated under particular circumstances (for example, a nationwide wage award in the particular industry).

Target price

Target-price contracts are similar to fixed-price contracts, but they are used where there is some justifiable uncertainty about the likely costs for carrying out the project as it has been defined. The contract allows for price adjustment if the audited final project costs either exceed estimates or show a saving, so that the risks and benefits are shared to some extent between the customer and the contractor.

Guaranteed maximum price

A guaranteed maximum-price arrangement is a target-price contract in which, although cost savings can be shared, the contractor is limited in the extent to which excess costs may be added to the target price.

Simple reimbursable

A simple cost-reimbursable arrangement means that the contractor is reimbursed for costs and expenses, but makes no profit. This type of payment sometimes occurs when work is performed by a company for its parent company, or for another company which is wholly owned within the same group of companies. A formal contract might not be used in such cases.

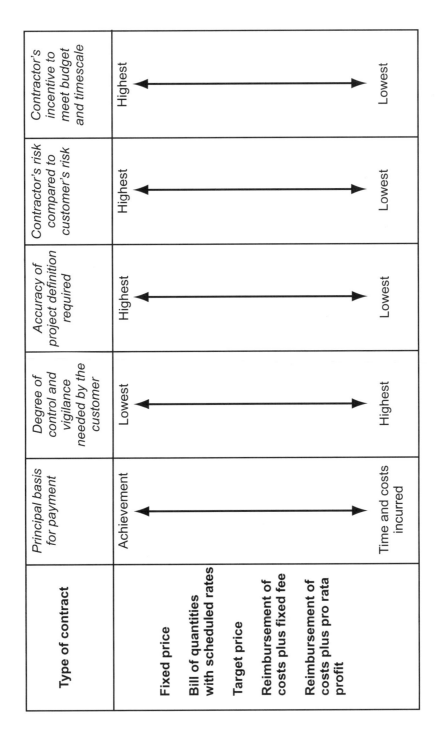

Figure 6.6 Relationship between the basis of payment and project control emphasis

Cost-plus

Cost-plus is a common form of reimbursable contract. As in simple reimbursable contracts, the contractor charges for materials used and for time recorded against the project on timesheets, but the charging rates agreed with the customer are set at levels which are intended not only to recover direct costs and overheads, but are marked up to yield profit.

Schedule of rates

Contracts with scheduled rates are reimbursable contracts (usually cost-plus), charged according to the number of work units performed. A specific work unit charging rate will be agreed with the customer beforehand for each trade or type of work involved.

Reimbursable plus management fee

This is a form of reimbursable contract in which the contractor's profit element is charged as a fixed fee, instead of being built in as a 'plus' element in the agreed rates. Unlike cost-plus, the contractor's profit revenue does not increase with cost, but instead decreases proportionally as total project costs rise, arguably providing an incentive for the contractor to keep costs low.

Bill of quantities with scheduled rates

A bill of quantities contract is reimbursable, operating with an agreed schedule of rates, but the total number of work units expected in each trade or type of work is estimated and quoted beforehand.

The timing of payments

Timing of invoices for fixed-price contracts

Many large projects, spread out over time scales that might extend to several years, could involve the investment of large sums of the contractor's money. By the time the contract is completed and paid for, the resulting profit could be offset or nullified by the cost of capital employed. In other words, the contractor has had to bear the interest costs (real or notional) on all money tied up in stocks and work-in-progress. For these reasons, 'progress' or 'stage' payments are often agreed between the contractor and the customer. This enables the contractor to raise some invoices during the course of the project. The contractor is not called upon to carry the whole cost of the project until completion, when the final invoice can be issued.

The basis for making stage payment claims may be cut and dried contractually, being dependent upon completion of certain stages in the project, or on the deliveries of specified items of equipment to the customer. Standard contract conditions for various trade organizations may define the stage payment requirements. The following example is remembered from a project for the supply and installation of a passenger lift (elevator):

Percentage of the total contract price	*When payable*
10	On signing the contract (before the contractor actually starts work)
20	When the customer has approved the contractor's general design; this marks the point at which manufacture can start
30	Upon delivery of the main consignment of materials and components to the customer's premises
30	On handover of the new lift (elevator) to the customer for normal use
10	a final 'retention payment', to be withheld by the customer until the lift has given six months of satisfactory use or operation
100	

In other cases, no such stages will be defined. Instead, progress payments will be made at regular intervals, the amounts being decided according to a measurement of the actual work done (the amount of progress achieved). The customer will usually want to see evidence for claims, and these are typically provided by certificates signed by an independent professional person. It is obviously important that such work achievement can be accurately measured to ensure that invoicing is kept in step with real progress. The subject of relating achievement to costs is dealt with in Chapter 22.

Timing of invoices for cost-reimbursable projects

Payments for day works or casual work using temporary agency staff may be invoiced at weekly intervals, but most contractors will invoice their customers at regular calendar-monthly intervals, either against certificates of work done or against cost records that are subject to independent audit.

References and further reading for Part II

CIMA, (1996), *Management Accounting Official Terminology*, 3rd edn, London, Chartered Institute of Management Accountants

Devaux, S.A. (1999) *Total Project Control: A Manager's Guide to Integrated Planning, Measuring and Tracking*, New York, Wiley

Drury, Colin (2000), *Management and Cost Accounting*, 5th edn, London, Thomson Learning

Duxbury, R. (2000), *Contract Law*, London, 5th edn, Sweet & Maxwell (a good introduction in the 'Nutshell' series)

Marsh, P.D.V. (1995), *Contracting for Engineering and Construction Projects*, 4th edn, Aldershot, Gower

Marsh, P.D.V. (2001), *Contract Negotiation Handbook*, 3rd edn, Aldershot, Gower

O'Reilly, M. (1999), *Civil Engineering Construction Contracts*, 2nd edn, London, Thomas Telford

Roetzheim, W.H. and Beasley, R.A. (1997), *Software Project Cost and Schedule Estimating: Best Practices*, Hemel Hempstead, Prentice-Hall

Smith, N.J. (1995), *Project Cost Estimating*, London, Thomas Telford

Smith, N.J. and Wearne, S. (1994), *Construction Contract Arrangements in EU Countries: A Review of the Contract Arrangements for the Construction of Buildings, Infrastructure and Industrial Products in France, Germany, Italy, the Netherlands, Spain and the United Kingdom*, Loughborough, European Construction Institute

Spons pricing and estimating guides (2003), a comprehensive range of pricing and estimating books and CD-ROMs, updated annually, London, Spon

Stewart, R.D. (1991), *Cost Estimating*, 2nd edn, Chichester, Wiley

Sweeting, J. (1997), *Project Cost Estimating: Principles and Practice*, London, Institution of Chemical Engineers

Treitel, G.H. (1995), *The Law of Contract*, London, Sweet & Maxwell

Wearne, S.H. (1989), *Civil Engineering Contracts*, London, Thomas Telford

Wearne, S.H. (1989), *Control of Engineering Projects*, London, Thomas Telford

Wearne, S.H. (1993), *'Engineering Contracts'*, Chapter 15 in Lock, D. (ed.), *Handbook of Engineering Management*, 2nd edn, Oxford, Butterworth-Heinemann

Part III

Planning and scheduling

Chapter 7

An introduction to planning and scheduling

Whenever any job has to be accomplished according to a time or date deadline, it is advisable to have at least some idea of the relationship between the time allowed and the time needed. This is true for any project, whether a dinner is being prepared or a motorway constructed. In the first case one would be ill-advised to tell guests: 'Dinner is at seven – but the potatoes will not be ready until 7.30.' Similarly, there would be little point in having an eminent personage arrive to open a new motorway if, by cutting the tape, the eager and unsuspecting traffic stream were to be released towards a bridge that still consisted of a few girders over a yawning chasm (complete with rushing torrent below).

So it is a safe assumption that a plan of some sort is always advisable if a project is to be finished on time. In the culinary example, the planning might be very informal – a mental exercise by the cook. Projects such as motorways are more complicated and have to be planned with more formal techniques.

This is the first of five chapters that explore the principles and techniques of project planning and scheduling. After some brief initial thoughts on planning and scheduling in the wider business environment, this introductory chapter will describe matrix and time-scaled charts.

The planning and scheduling environment

Anyone planning a project of significant size will soon find that there are a number of factors, both inside and outside the project organization, that can have a profound effect on the planner's intentions. Also, the quality of the planning and scheduling will influence the benefits that can be expected for the company or other organization that carries out the project. Figure 7.1 is a simple representation of this idea.

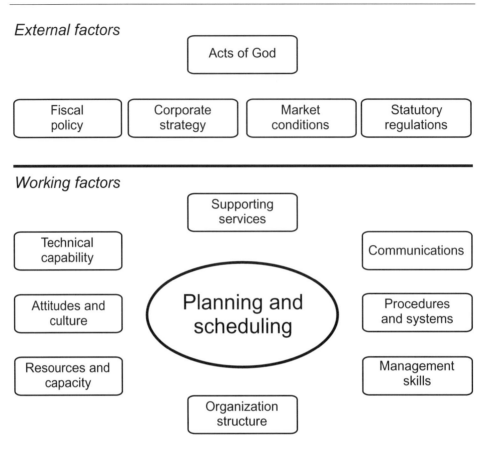

External factors

Acts of God

Fiscal policy | Corporate strategy | Market conditions | Statutory regulations

Working factors

Supporting services

Technical capability

Communications

Planning and scheduling

Attitudes and culture

Procedures and systems

Resources and capacity

Management skills

Organization structure

Contribution to results

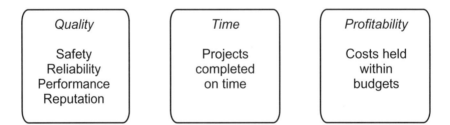

Quality

Safety
Reliability
Performance
Reputation

Time

Projects
completed
on time

Profitability

Costs held
within
budgets

Figure 7.1   The planning and scheduling environment

External factors

External factors are events and conditions that lie outside the control of the project management organization. Some of these factors can affect or completely wreck attempts at project planning. The following paragraphs list a few examples from the many possibilities.

Acts of God

All projects are subject to risk, and many of those risks can have an enormous impact on plans. The following are just four from the long catalogue of happenings that can be classified as Acts of God:

- An earthquake devastates a project organization's headquarters.
- A hurricane and flood put a project site under a metre of water and delay the start or ruin the work in progress.
- An influenza epidemic puts half the project workforce out of action.
- The project manager (a keen golfer) is struck by lightning.

Fiscal policy

Fiscal policy, which is the policy of a national government in respect of taxation and other financial measures, can have a profound effect on projects and their planning. One extreme manifestation of this is seen when a government-funded project is cancelled or abandoned through a political decision (defence projects are a prime example). Less immediate, but of more general concern, are the wider and longer-term economic consequences of government policy. These can lead to project downscaling, delays and cancellations in all sectors of industry.

Corporate strategy

Strategic decisions made by managers outside and above the project organization can affect many aspects of planning. Here are just a few examples:

- A decision is made at the top management level of a group of companies to conduct a project in a different company within the group from that originally intended.
- A decision is made to delay the start of an internal project owing to diversion of funds for other purposes.
- A strategic decision is made to halt all new staff recruitment, so reducing the resources previously expected to be available for projects.
- Directives are sometimes received from senior managers to change previously agreed project priorities. This is often regarded by project managers as unwelcome and unwarranted interference.

Statutory regulations

Legislation by national and regional governments can impose extra burdens on project designers and contractors which have to be taken into account at the planning stage. This can be a particularly important feature of projects carried out in foreign countries, where the project manager would need to research the local employment, welfare, technical and commercial regulations before committing resources to a plan.

Working factors

The items labelled 'working factors' in Figure 7.1 are those most likely to affect the project manager and the project plans on a routine, day-by-day basis. The factors shown in the figure should be self-explanatory. Although responsibility for these items usually lies with managers close to the project organization, they might be outside the control of the project manager, who has to learn to accept them and plan accordingly.

Contribution to results

Effective planning and scheduling, because they provide a proper basis for progress management, should promote efficient working. Project personnel who are not constantly trying to overcome crises caused by bad planning can devote more of their time to achieving the quality standards expected. A well-planned project stands more chance of being completed on time, and this in turn should contribute greatly to cost-effectiveness and higher profitability.

Distinction between planning and scheduling

In project management terminology, the words 'plan' and 'schedule' can have different meanings. I have found it convenient to observe the following distinction.

A *plan* can be considered as the listing or visual display that results when all project activities have been subjected to estimating, logical sequencing, target timing and the determination of priorities. For projects of any significant size, some form of network analysis (see Chapters 8 and 9) is usually the preferred method for preparing a plan. However, some of the charting methods described in this chapter provide better visual aids, can be more effective for communicating plans to project personnel, and are often quite adequate for small projects.

A *schedule* is obtained by doing additional work on the initial plan, so that resources needed to carry out all the project activities are taken into account. In other words, a schedule is the practicable working document that results from matching the organization's available resources to the initial plan.

The planning time frame

Planning (and scheduling) can be considered from two opposite viewpoints:

1   A set of estimates could be obtained and used to produce a plan that predicts a project completion date that is then accepted by everyone as the goal. Suppose we call this the *free planning* approach.

2   The end-date requirement is predetermined, governed by factors outside the planner's control. A delivery promise might already have been given to a customer in a sales proposal, or the project might have to be finished to meet a forthcoming exhibition or public event. This can be called the *target-led planning* approach.

Neither option is wholly good or bad.

The free planning approach

Schedules produced entirely from estimates, with no external pressure to compress the timescale, should allow the planner to develop a working schedule that is capable of being achieved with certainty. There is no need to overstretch any person or resource in the project organization. This might be regarded by some as an ideal state of affairs. However, a new project plan made with no external pressure whatsoever is likely to predict an end date that is ludicrous from the customer's point of view, destroying any possibility of gaining a valuable order.

Completely free planning therefore has its dangers. Pressure to find ways of completing a project reasonably quickly is not such a bad thing, because time is money and projects which are allowed to drag their feet tend to attract higher costs from fixed overheads and other causes. Giving planners complete freedom to dictate the project timescale might, therefore, not be quite so advisable as it at first seems.

Target-led planning

If a plan has to be suited to a predetermined target delivery requirement, all the estimates must be fitted into the available time frame as best they can.

One temptation that must be resisted is for estimates to be shortened for no better reason than that the time available is too short. Another danger is of removing all possible reserves (for example, by planning to work overtime or seven-day weeks) so that the plan is too tight and leaves no room for error. Of course, it is sometimes possible to reduce times by allocating more resources, but the project manager must never be persuaded or coerced into trying to expedite a plan simply by 'marking down' estimates without any justification. Any honest person will admit that projects planned on this artificial basis are unlikely to be finished on time. Such optimistic plans can gain a temporary advantage by serving to pacify higher management or by deceiving a trusting customer into placing an order. Unfortunately, the truth is bound to emerge sooner or later, bringing consequent discredit on the project contractor.

Most planning is, however, time-constrained. If the time available is restricted, practical ways have to be found to compress the project timescale. One way is to examine the sequence of jobs critically, and rearrange or overlap them to shorten the overall time. There is a technique called *fast-tracking*, which uses this approach intensively, but without creating unacceptable risks. Another approach is *cost-time optimization,* which is described in Chapter 8 by means of the Gantry Project case study. For maximum effect, fast-tracking and cost-time optimization can be combined.

What happens if the target time for a new project is set later than strictly necessary, so that the project plan is relaxed and stripped of all urgency? That would be rather unusual, but not impossible. Such extended schedules are an ideal breeding ground for budgetary excesses according to Professor Parkinson's best-known law: 'Work expands so as to fill the time available for its completion' (*Parkinson's Law or the Pursuit of Progress,* John Murray, London, 1958).

Resources in target-led planning

Resource limitations can complicate target-led planning. The usual problems occur because the initial plan is made without reference to available resources. Then, much later, work schedules are produced that are impossible to achieve, because the resources needed are either not there or are being used on other projects in the organization. These important aspects of planning and scheduling are dealt with in Chapters 9, 10, 11 and later chapters.

The ideal approach

In the best plans, the constituent elements are reliably estimated and arranged in their most logical sequence. Careful cooperation between the key participants in the proposed work is required, all striving to meet the needs of the customer, and balancing these with the capabilities and resources of the project organization.

Matrix charts

Matrix charts list one set of factors in a column at the extreme left-hand side of a tabulation, and align factors directly associated with them across columns to the right in a matrix display. There are many possible variations, the simplest of which are not time-scaled. If this explanation seems complicated, a few examples should make things clear. In project work, matrix charts are particularly useful for the managers of small groups who have to allocate tasks to people.

Book project: A very simple matrix chart

Matrix charts have proved useful to me for planning and controlling the compilation of large handbooks. Such books typically rely on contributions from many different authors. The fourth edition of *The Gower Handbook of Management,* for example, contains 72 chapters from 65 contributors. Preparation of a handbook manuscript involves much correspondence, several stages for each chapter, takes about a year, and certainly ranks as a project for which planning is recommended. Once the list of chapters has been established (which is like a project task list), a very simple matrix chart provides adequate planning and control.

Figure 7.2 is a fictitious, shortened example which illustrates the effectiveness of the simple matrix for this type of project. The left-hand column lists all the chapters, and is the first set of data to be entered. The names of possible authors are shown in the next column and, when a person has promised to write a chapter and agreed the terms, the next three columns can be filled for that chapter. As the work proceeds, blank squares in the matrix show tasks not yet accomplished.

When each chapter has been received, accepted and edited, the square in the 'editing done' column can be blacked in. As the work nears completion, that column gradually becomes a solid black strip.

In practice, a typical chart will occupy an A3-sized sheet. Use of a computer is not strictly necessary. Every month, a photocopy is mailed to the publisher to report progress. The whole process is simple, effective, provides a good visual display, and is ideal for progress reporting with very little effort.

Matrix charts for allocating activities to people or other resources

Project resource scheduling is covered more comprehensively in Chapters 10 and 11, but Figure 7.3 shows several ways in which resources and activities can be planned using simple matrix charts. These charts can be displayed using whiteboards, blackboards, proprietary kits, as hand-drawn diagrams, or they can be set up in a computer. Simple charts can be effective, but any chart becomes too

Chapter title	Possible author	Author signed	Fee agreed	Date due	Chapter accepted	Author paid	Editing done	Comments
1 Corporate strategy	C E Yeo	Yes	500	Jan 31	Yes	Yes	■	
2 Company organization	A Ranger	Yes	150	Mar 31				
3 Manpower planning	R E Croot							
4 Employment legislation	T Law	Yes	200	Jan 31	Yes	Yes	■	
5 Financial management	A Count							
6 Cost accounting	I Reckon	Yes	125	Feb 15	Yes	Yes	■	
7 Cost budgets	U Savit	Yes	350	Jul 18				
8 Marketing	I Sellit	Yes	150	Feb 25	Yes	Yes	■	
9 Sales engineering	?							
10 Contracts	G Signup							Author being difficult
11 Risk management	H I Premium							
12 Purchasing	I Byatt							
61 Coding	A Numero	Yes	125					
62 Standards	A Flagstaff							
63 Quality management	I S Goode	Yes	150	May 7				
64 Reliability	A L L Kaput	Yes	150	Mar 31	Yes			
65 Post-design services	C U Later							

Figure 7.2   Simple matrix chart for planning and controlling a book editing project

Machine	Hour 1	Hour 2	Hour 3	Hour 4	Hour 5
Rowing	Smith	Patel	Murphy	Jenkins	MacBeth
Treadmill	MacBeth	Smith	Patel	Murphy	Jenkins
Weights	Jenkins	MacBeth	Smith	Patel	Murphy
Strider	Murphy	Jenkins	MacBeth	Smith	Patel
Bicycle	Patel	Murphy	Jenkins	MacBeth	Smith

Chart B: Assigning facilities to people (alternative to Chart A)

Job number	Week 1	Week 2	Week 3
A 3993	Rossetti		Gomez
A 3994	Gomez	Gomez	
A 4221	MacBeth	MacBeth	
A 4222			MacBeth
A 4223	Patel		
A 4435	Smith	Smith	Smith
B 5000	Stravinski	Stravinski	Stravinski
B 5001	Jenkins		Jenkins
B 5002	Murphy	Murphy	Murphy
B 5003	Goldberg		
B 5004		Goldberg	Goldberg

Chart D: Assigning jobs to people or other resources (alternative to Chart C)

Person	Hour 1	Hour 2	Hour 3	Hour 4	Hour 5
Smith	Rowing	Treadmill	Weights	Strider	Bicycle
MacBeth	Bicycle	Rowing	Treadmill	Weights	Strider
Jenkins	Strider	Bicycle	Rowing	Treadmill	Weights
Murphy	Weights	Strider	Bicycle	Rowing	Treadmill
Patel	Treadmill	Weights	Strider	Bicycle	Rowing

Chart A: Assigning people to facilities

Person	Week 1	Week 2	Week 3
Smith	A 4435	A 4435	A 4435
MacBeth	A 4221	A 4221	A 4222
Jenkins	B 5001	Training	B 5001
Murphy	B 5002	B 5002	B 5002
Patel	A 4223	Holiday	Holiday
Goldberg	B 5003	B 5004	B 5004
Rossetti	A 3993	Left	
Gomez	A 3994	A3994	A 3993
Strauss	Training	Holiday	Holiday
Nielsen	Maternity	Maternity	Maternity
Stravinski	B 5000	B 5000	B 5000

Chart C: Assigning people or other resources to jobs

Figure 7.3   Four possible matrix chart arrangements

complicated to draw, interpret and revise if it attempts to show too much information or if the project is anything other than very small.

Gymnasium project

This gymnasium example is not strictly a project, but it demonstrates two alternative matrix chart arrangements for simple day-to-day planning of facilities in a small group or department. In this example a company engaged in commercial projects provides a small gymnasium for the use of its staff. The gymnasium has one each of five different machines for the use of its members. Charts A and B in Figure 7.3 show two ways in which the gymnasium manager might use a matrix chart for the allocation of these machines to a five-strong company athletics team. Each member of the team needs to use each machine for one hour during a five-hour day that is reserved exclusively for the team's use. In this case there are arguments for and against each of the options shown and, in practice, either Chart A or Chart B would be of equal value.

Matrix charts for planning jobs in a small group or department

The lower half of Figure 7.3 shows ways in which the manager of a small project department might use a simple matrix chart to match tasks and people. As with the gymnasium project, the manager can choose between two basic configurations but, in this case, there is a difference in effectiveness between Charts C and D.

Chart C is useful in small departments where the manager needs to allocate a relatively constant group of people to a set of changing activities. The names of those in the department are listed at the left-hand side, and the planned jobs or other activities for each person are listed in the body of the matrix. The simplest and most common example of this pattern is the familiar staff holiday chart, where the timescale must include all the working days in the calendar year.

Chart D is another way of showing the data given in Chart C. This version is less effective in the use of space and Chart D in our example would need to be considerably taller if it were to include all the information shown in Chart C. The arrangement in Chart D is, however, often convenient for the allocation of project work to people because its left-hand column can be obtained directly from the task list for the entire project. Chart D is also of interest here because its pattern is very similar to the project bar charts that will be introduced later in this chapter.

Simple tabular planning (timetables)

This chapter will now start to consider methods for planning entire projects. The 'timetable' method is the easiest and simplest approach. Although simple planning methods often have merit (and can be ideal for very small projects), the timetable method is really *too* simple. The following case will serve as a good 'how not to do it' example.

Case study: How not to plan a project

A prototype for a small electromechanical device needed to be designed and built. The company's chief engineer was asked to oversee the project, and was given a total of 19 weeks in which to have a completed and tested prototype ready for appraisal.

The plan

When asked to prepare a plan, the chief engineer agreed the following timetable with fellow managers:

	Start	*Finish*
Design and draw	7 Jan 2002	15 Mar 2002
Purchase components	18 Mar 2002	19 Apr 2002
Manufacture prototypes	15 Apr 2002	3 May 2002
Assemble and test	6 May 2002	10 May 2002

Progress meetings

At the end of January, at an informal progress meeting, the chief engineer reported 'good progress' on this project. No difficulties were expected.

After another four weeks, at the end of February, another progress meeting was told that engineering was 'running a little late, owing to unforeseen problems'. When pressed, the chief engineer estimated that the delay would amount to 'about a week'.

A third progress meeting took place in the middle of March. Although the design should have been finished, the chief engineer was forced to admit that the drawings were 'not quite ready', and that three weeks' design work still remained.

Too late

Drawings and purchase requirements were not actually finished and issued until the middle of May. This left the other departments no chance of completing the project on time. So the prototype was finished very late. Furthermore, all the other jobs on to which the design engineers should have moved suffered a serious 'knock-on' delay.

What went wrong?

A project manager must be able to answer two complementary questions at any time in a project:

1   Where *should* we be on the plan now?
2   Where exactly *are* we on the plan now?

There were some serious deficiencies in the supervision of this project, but much of the blame can be laid at the door of the inadequate plan. Timetable plans are seldom ideal, and are often written down with insufficient care and thought. The plan in this example proved ineffective for progress monitoring and control for the following reasons:

- It was prepared with insufficient attention to detail, not allowing objective day-to-day measurement against intermediate events.
- Such detail as the plan did contain was badly presented. Figure 7.4 is a bar chart version of the same plan. It can be seen at once that this displays the programme more effectively.

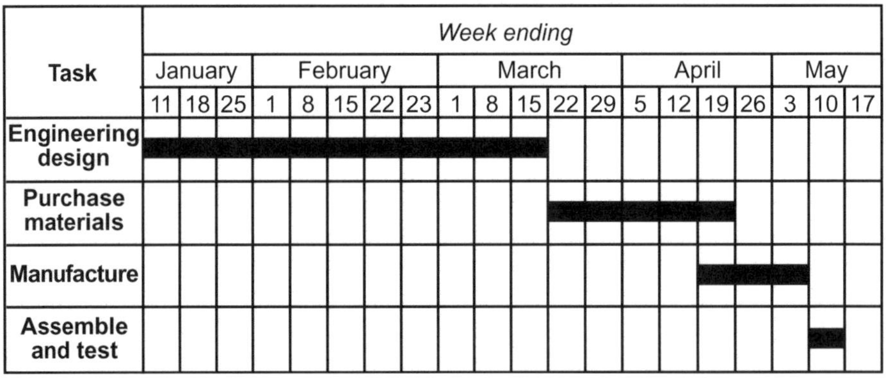

Task	Week ending																			
	January			February					March					April				May		
	11	18	25	1	8	15	22	23	1	8	15	22	29	5	12	19	26	3	10	17
Engineering design																				
Purchase materials																				
Manufacture																				
Assemble and test																				

Figure 7.4   A simple bar chart

Bar charts (Gantt charts)

Bar charts derive from and are often called Gantt charts, after the American industrial engineer Henry Gantt (1861–1919). Gantt worked for Frederic Winslow Taylor, and was one of the pioneer band of 'scientific managers' that flourished in the late nineteenth and early twentieth centuries. These charts have been in widespread use since those earlier times and they continue to be very valuable planning aids. Bar charts are easy to draw or construct and interpret, and can be used for a great variety of planning requirements.

The visual impact of a well-displayed schedule can be a powerful aid to controlling a simple project. Bar charts are still preferred to other methods in many executives' offices, on project sites and in factories. All levels of supervision and management find them convenient as day-to-day control tools. Even when projects have been planned with advanced computer techniques, the same computer systems are often used to plot the schedule data as bar charts for day-to-day use.

Representation of time

Bar charts are drawn or constructed on a scale where the horizontal axis is directly proportional to time. Calendar weeks were used in Figure 7.4, but days, months, years or other units are often used instead, chosen to suit the overall duration of the project. Each horizontal bar represents a project task, its length scaled according to its expected duration. The name or description of each job is written on the same row, usually at the left-hand edge of the chart.

Time-now cursor

A bar chart's effectiveness can be improved by ruling a vertical line or by placing a cursor on the chart to coincide with the 'time-now date', highlighting the jobs (or proportions of jobs) that should have been done (to the left of the cursor), and those jobs which remain to be done (to the right of the time-now line).

Coding

Bars can be given distinctive shading or filled with a colour to denote the department, trade or individual responsible for the relevant job. Red is sometimes used, especially in charts printed out by computer, to indicate jobs that are critical (jobs that must be done as early as possible if the project is to finish on time).

A word of caution is necessary here, however. As with many other management tools, there is a danger of destroying the effectiveness of the method by being too ambitious. A bar chart is above all a visual representation of a plan, and it must be easy to understand. When more than about six different colours or shading patterns are used, much of the visual impact is lost and the coded chart becomes difficult to interpret.

Bar charts for resource scheduling

Coded bar charts are a simple method for scheduling resources on very small projects.

Suppose that a blue bar is used for every job requiring one electrician. If anyone needs to know how many electricians are needed at any time, it is only necessary to count the number of blue bars falling within the relevant time column to find the total number of electricians required.

If the bars are set up on an adjustable board or in a suitable computer system, they can be moved sideways (rescheduled) so that unwanted peaks and troughs in the planned workload are smoothed out, allowing the project to be planned without exceeding the resources available.

This method generally becomes very complicated if there are jobs needing more than one person. However, provided that no job needs more than two or three people, several bars can be used in parallel. For example, if yellow is used as the code for an electrician's assistant and a job is expected to need two electricians plus one assistant, then two blue bars and one yellow would be used, placed side by side. Above these tiny quantities, however, bar charts become quite impracticable.

Limitations of bar charts

There are various physical methods by which bar charts can be constructed on wallboards, allowing users to add, subtract or reposition bars at will. It is possible to schedule more than a hundred jobs on such a chart. *Rescheduling,* however, is a different story. Setting up a complex plan in the first place might take a few days or a week. Adjusting a wallboard chart to keep in step with changes could prove impossible. *Inflexibility* therefore becomes a serious drawback with charts constructed on wallboards. The solution to this problem is to plot the chart using suitable project management software.

Planners using over-complex bar charts find difficulty in casting their eyes along the long rows without going off track. People subjected to prolonged exposure to such work are easily recognizable by their sore eyes or 'planner's squint'. Projects of very long duration may mean that the bar chart periods have to be relatively coarse, not capable of showing individual calendar day dates. These are problems of *interpretation* and *scaling.* A computer-based planning system will, however, allow the data on the bar chart to be supplemented or replaced in a tabular format, in spreadsheet fashion. Data presented in detailed tables, although having less immediate visual impact, can be read more easily and accurately, without the possibility of errors caused by having to read times from a coarsely scaled bar chart.

Linked bar charts

One problem with bar charts is that they cannot easily be used to indicate interdependent relationships between tasks. A simple case study will illustrate this point.

The furniture project

Eaton Sitright Limited is a company that manufactures good-quality furniture for sale to homes and offices. The company wishes to introduce a new design of table and chair to its standard range, and has started a project to design and make a small prototype batch for consumer appraisal and testing. The furniture will be steel-framed, and the table is to be provided with one drawer.

Task number	Task description	Duration (estimated in days)
	Chair	
01	Anatomical study for chair	15
02	Design chair	5
03	Buy materials for chair seat	6
04	Make chair seat	3
05	Buy chair castors	5
06	Buy steel for chair frame	10
07	Make chair frame	3
08	Paint chair frame	2
09	Assemble chair	1
10	Apply final finishes to chair	2
	Desk	
11	Design desk	10
12	Buy steel for desk frame	10
13	Make desk frame	5
14	Paint desk frame	2
15	Buy wood and fittings for desk	5
16	Make desk drawer	6
17	Make desk top	1
18	Assemble desk	1
19	Apply final finishes to desk	2
	General activities	
20	Decide paint colours	10
21	Buy paint and varnish	8
22	Final project evaluation	5

Figure 7.5   **Furniture project task list**

Figure 7.5 lists the main tasks for this project. The jobs are listed in separate chronological order for the chair, and for the desk. The general tasks at the foot of the list apply to the whole project. No attempt has been made in this tabulation to state any relationship between the tasks, but the company's planner can bear these in mind and avoid logical errors when the plans are made.

Figure 7.6 is the resulting bar chart. The planner has been careful not to schedule any job before it can actually take place. For example, the paint colours must be decided before the paint can be purchased. No painting task can start before the relevant article has been manufactured and the paint has been purchased. Although the chart cannot show these relationships, they can be dealt with mentally on this simple project. With a larger project, however, there would be considerable risk of producing a chart containing some logical impossibilities. The danger of such mistakes is increased when jobs are 'shuffled' on large adjustable wallboard charts to smooth out workloads.

Vertical link lines can be added to bar charts to show constraints between jobs. Figure 7.7 is a linked version of the bar chart of Figure 7.6. This clearly shows, for example, that the chair design cannot start before the anatomical study has been completed. Even for this simple project, however, the linked bar chart cannot show every task dependency. It would be difficult to draw the links from 'Buy paint and varnish' to the starts of the two painting jobs without producing crossovers and some confusion (although, in this simple case, these particular crossovers could be eliminated by rearranging the sequence of tasks). Most project management computer programs are capable of plotting linked bar charts, but the results are usually difficult to interpret.

Line of balance charts

Line of balance charts are more complex than bar charts, need more effort to design, and are more difficult to interpret. They are rarely used, but are included here for completeness. There are at least two quite distinct versions.

One line of balance method is a forerunner of MRPII (material requirements planning),and can be used for parts and materials scheduling in manufacturing projects. That method can cope with projects involving repeating batches of a product where the batch quantities differ. A detailed account is given in Chapter 15.

Another line of balance method (described here) is suitable for projects in which a number of identical items have to be produced singly in a planned sequence. The example most often used is the construction project where a number of similar buildings have to be erected on a site. Other uses for this method include the repetitive introduction of identical procedures into a number of different offices, or any other projects that require an identical pattern of tasks to be repeated several times within a planned timescale.

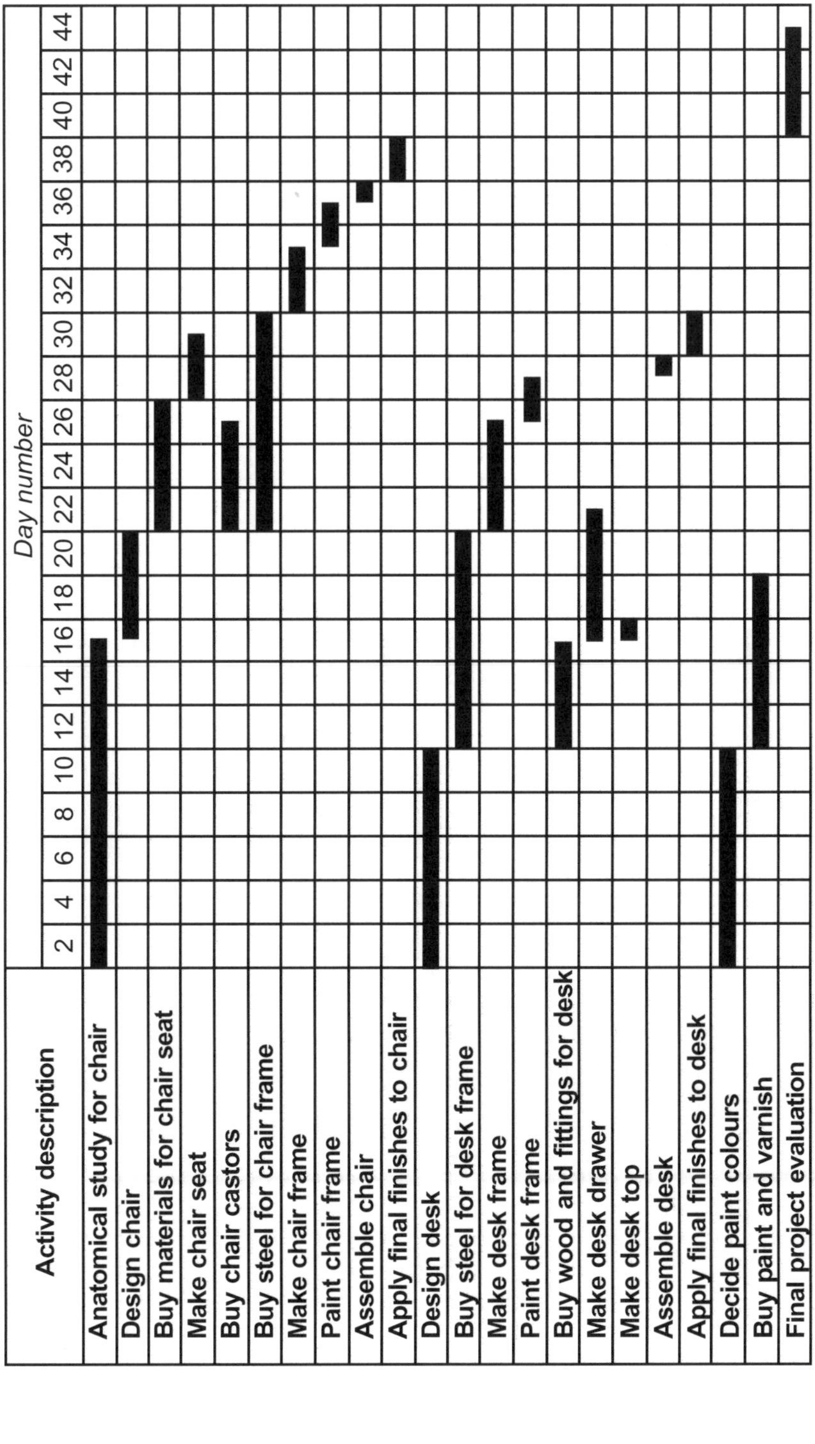

Day number

Activity description	Day number (2–44)
Anatomical study for chair	
Design chair	
Buy materials for chair seat	
Make chair seat	
Buy chair castors	
Buy steel for chair frame	
Make chair frame	
Paint chair frame	
Assemble chair	
Apply final finishes to chair	
Design desk	
Buy steel for desk frame	
Make desk frame	
Paint desk frame	
Buy wood and fittings for desk	
Make desk drawer	
Make desk top	
Assemble desk	
Apply final finishes to desk	
Decide paint colours	
Buy paint and varnish	
Final project evaluation	

Day number scale: 2 4 6 8 10 12 14 16 18 20 22 24 26 28 30 32 34 36 38 40 42 44

Figure 7.6   Furniture project: Bar chart

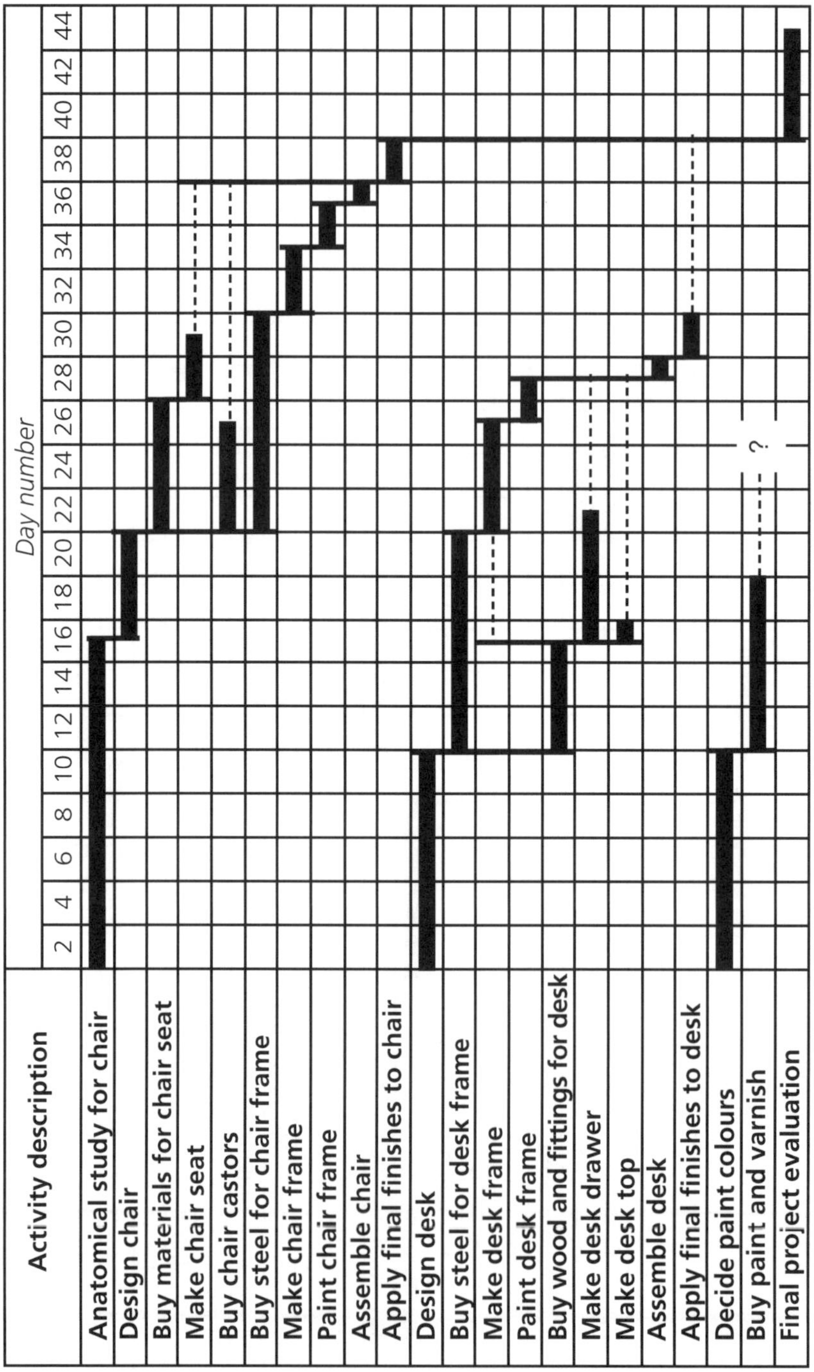

Figure 7.7   Furniture project: Linked bar chart
This chart attempts, but is not able, to show all the links between tasks.

As with simple bar charts, daily progress can be checked against the chart using a vertical date cursor.

Five house construction project

Figure 7.8 is a simple bar chart for the construction of five similar houses on a new estate. The same pattern of tasks is repeated for each house, but the starts of houses 2, 3, 4 and 5 have been progressively delayed to allow the various trade groups to progress from one house to the next.

A line of balance chart can be drawn for this project by rearranging the bar chart from Figure 7.8 to the pattern shown in Figure 7.9. Notice that there are vertical arrows showing the logical links between consecutive tasks. These are constraints arising from the use of shared resources. They mean that each task requiring a particular trade must be finished before the corresponding task can be started on the next house. Brickwork is the longest task, for which two separate teams (Teams A and B) have been planned to speed up the whole project.

Anyone attempting to draw such a chart will soon notice a slight scheduling problem, caused because not all tasks have the same duration. The trades engaged on the shortest tasks might have to stand by and suffer idle periods while their busier colleagues catch up. However, as shown in Figure 7.9, buffers can be introduced as a solution.

Project to build 80 houses

Figure 7.10 is another line of balance chart, again displaying a plan for building houses, but this project is for 80 houses. There are 15 separate tasks in the plan for each house (only five tasks per house were planned for the five-house project in Figures 7.8 and 7.9). Although this chart looks very different from the charts used in the five-house project, it uses a similar method. The principal difference is that, rather than endure the tedium of drawing a bar chart showing in stepped sequence the 1200 separate tasks needed to construct all 80 houses, the drawing has been coarsened. Every set of 80 identical stepped and linked tasks is represented in Figure 7.10 by a single sloping line. The thickness of each line is proportional to the duration of the task at each house. The slope of each line depends on the time allowed by the planner for completion of all 80 identical tasks. The bent line for glazing tasks introduces a time buffer.

When a vertical 'today's date' cursor is placed on the chart, it will intersect each bar to show the number of houses for which the various tasks should have been completed on that day. The scale should be chosen so that the bars slope at the least possible angle from the horizontal. Then the angle between the cursor and the bars will be greater, allowing greater accuracy when reading off the figures.

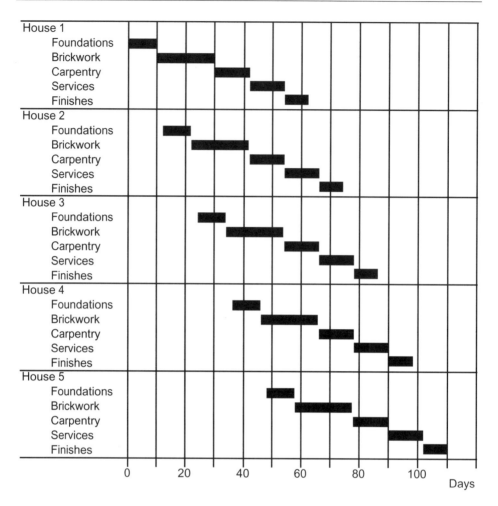

Figure 7.8   Five-house project: Bar chart
This provides the data for the line of balance chart in Figure 7.9.

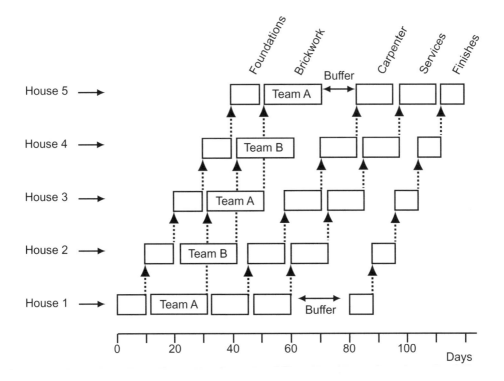

Figure 7.9   Five-house project: Line of balance chart

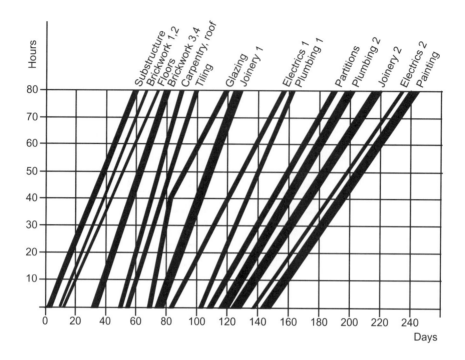

Figure 7.10   Eighty-house project: Line of balance chart

Chapter 8

Network analysis: Logic diagrams and the critical path

This chapter introduces critical path network analysis. Most explanations and examples in the remainder of this book assume that the underlying planning for projects – even where bar charts are used for display, communication and control – will be based on some form of network analysis.

Background

Network analysis is a generic term for several project planning methods which can be traced back to developments in Europe and elsewhere, but their full exploitation was seen in the late 1950s, when they were used with great success and much publicity for the planning and control of US defence projects. The striking improvements demonstrated over earlier methods have since led to their widespread adoption in many industries far removed from either America or defence.

Whereas time-scaled charts are usually very good visual aids that can be understood at a glance, networks can appear strange and unfamiliar at first sight. Proficiency in both the use and understanding of networks requires some initial learning and practice and, perhaps, a degree of aptitude in the application of logical argument.

Network diagrams, unlike bar charts, are not usually drawn to scale. They simply show all the project tasks in their logical sequence and juxtaposition. Networks *can* be set out on a timescale, but their notation is neither intended for, nor ideally suited to, that purpose. Time-scaled network diagrams are not in common use, and will be ignored in this book.

Although network diagrams are weak in their ability to display tasks on a time scale, they have other very significant strengths. When compared with bar charts (including linked bar charts), critical path networks provide the more powerful notation needed to show all the logical interdependencies between different jobs. The planner can ensure, for example, that bricklaying will not be scheduled to start before its supporting foundations are ready or that a company department is not expected to move to its new offices before all the essential facilities are in place and tested. Such logical mistakes are relatively easy to make with bar charts, especially where their size and complexity prevents all the logical links from being shown. Even when a bar chart can be drawn to conform with all logical inter-task constraints, errors will very probably be introduced during updating unless the chart is plotted by a computer running critical path based project management software.

Another great strength of networks is that they allow priorities to be quantified, based on an analysis of all the task duration estimates. Those tasks that cannot be delayed without endangering project completion on time are identified as critical, and all other tasks can be ranked according their degree of criticality.

Networks cannot, by themselves, be used for resource scheduling. In this respect bar charts are superior and easier to understand, provided that the number of activities is very small. However, networks (because they quantify priorities and highlight critical jobs) make a vital contribution to the resource-scheduling process. When a suitable computer program is used, very powerful resource-scheduling capabilities result.

The different network notation systems

Several network systems emerged during the second half of the twentieth century, but these all fit within one or other of two principal groups, determined by the method of notation:

1   **The activity-on-arrow system** (often simply called arrow networks) – the names used within this group include:
    ● ADM (arrow diagrams), CPM (critical path method) or CPA (critical path analysis) – these three names are practically synonymous
    ● PERT (Programme Evaluation and Review Technique), which uses ADM notation but with probabilistic time forecasts
2   **Activity-on-node networks** – these include:
    ● precedence diagrams (PDM), which are by far the most commonly used today
    ● the Roy method (named after its inventor), otherwise known as the method of potentials (MOM or MPM); this is an early activity-on-node system, very similar to precedence notation, now rarely (if ever) used
    ● some very early, no longer used, arrow networks, which placed the activities on the circular nodes instead of on the linking arrows.

There are also systems used in production and materials control that are really networking methods. These are generally outside the scope of this book, but one (line of balance) is described in Chapter 15.

Inevitably, with the passage of time, the distinction between terms such as

PERT, CPA and CPM has become clouded and the terms are often wrongly interchanged (which is no great cause for concern).

Which system should be used?

Network analysis, and particularly the use of arrow diagrams, gave planners a valuable new tool with which they could express the logic of a proposed work plan for their projects. Coupled with the concept of the critical path and the use of float to determine priorities, these were big steps forward. But arrow diagrams still had their drawbacks. Not least of these was the difficulty experienced by early network analysts in trying to persuade their managers and others to accept the new and unfamiliar notation. Gantt charts were still preferred (they still are in many places).

Now the precedence system has become far more popular, and is in widespread use. One reason for this is that precedence diagrams appear more 'user-friendly' to people with no planning experience because they bear a close resemblance to engineering flowcharts. Moreover, although arrow diagrams could show many complex relationships between different activities and events, there were limitations – particularly where it was desired to show activities whose starts and finishes could be allowed to overlap. Precedence networks allow a range of more complex constraints to be shown and planned.

A very strong reason for the use of precedence networks is that modern computer software will only accept precedence notation.

Why, then, does arrow notation survive, and why describe it in this book? Proficiency in arrow notation remains a very useful skill for the planning professional, and I use both arrow and precedence networks, each for a particular purpose. Arrow networks are often better for initial planning because they are faster and easier to sketch freehand. This speed saves valuable time at project planning meetings (which are invariably attended by managers and other senior people). The speed and flexibility of arrow diagrams makes them particularly useful in brainstorming sessions when logic is being discussed and hammered into shape. Later, when the networks are being tidied up, checked and redrawn before input to the computer, it is a fairly simple matter to convert to precedence notation.

Precedence logic is particularly easy to draw and edit on the computer screen, but the small screen size compared with large sheets or rolls of drawing paper limits the size of network that can be seen as a complete 'map'. Each computer screen image is more like a page in an atlas, so that the complete journey from project start to finish through all possible paths cannot be seen without much tedious scrolling up, down and sideways.

I have been told that precedence networks can be produced quickly in team brainstorming sessions if each activity is represented by a Post-it note. These can be stuck on a flipchart or roll of paper as the ideas emerge from the collective brain power. There must, however, be a practical limit to the size of networks that can be compiled by this method.

Which system would you like to read about?

The serious student or professional planner should be aware of both arrow and precedence diagrams, and both are described in this book. The networks for some case studies are given in two versions, allowing the reader to choose one or compare both.

Some people might wish to use networks only on their computers, always drawing them directly on the screen. For those people, arrow networks can have little interest, and they will probably want to skip the next main section of this chapter. For that reason, I have set out the text describing arrow networks and precedence networks as two separate self-contained sections. This has inevitably meant duplicating some of the explanations in the following pages.

Critical path analysis using arrow diagrams

The arrow logic diagram

The heart of any activity-on arrow system is the arrow diagram, logic diagram, or 'network', itself. This differs from the more familiar bar chart in several important respects. Arrow diagrams, in common with all other network methods, are not drawn to scale. Every network is, however, constructed with careful thought to show as accurately as possible the logical relationships and interdependence of each activity or task with all the other activities in the project. Indeed, it is for this reason that networks are sometimes called 'logic diagrams'.

Activities and events in arrow diagrams

Figure 8.1 shows a very simple arrow diagram. Each circle represents an event in the project. An event might be the start of a project, the start of an activity (or task), the completion of a task, or the end of a project. The arrow joining any two events represents the activity, task or time delay that must take place before the second event can be declared achieved. Events are usually shared between tasks, so that a single event might signal the completion of one or more tasks and the start of one or several more tasks. In Figure 8.1 it can be seen that that 10 events are linked by 11 activities.

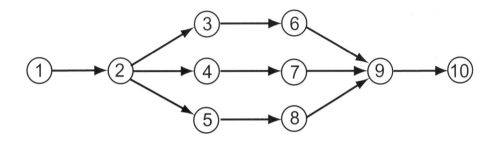

Figure 8.1   The main elements of arrow logic
Each circle represents an event, such as the start or finish of one or more project activities. The arrow joining any two events denotes the activity or time needed for the project to proceed from one event to the next. The number written within each circle is the identifier for the event. In addition to the activity description (not shown here), each activity is identified by its preceding and succeeding event numbers. The first activity here, therefore, would be called activity 1,2 or 1–2. No activity can start until all activities leading into its preceding event have been finished. Activity 2–4, for instance, cannot start until event 2 has been achieved or, in other words, until activity 1–2 has been finished. Similarly, activity 9–10 cannot start before event 9 has been achieved, which means that activities 6–9, 7–9 and 8–9 must all be finished. Networks do not need to be drawn to any timescale, and the length of an arrow has no significance. It is always best, as here, to start and finish a project network at single events.

Jargon

I prefer to avoid technical jargon as much as possible, but readers may occasionally encounter other terms that describe the event circles and activity arrows that make up networks. These strange terms have their origins in the mathematical theory of networks. In this alternative language, the circles are termed 'nodes' and the arrows become 'arcs'. The event at the tail of the arrow (the activity's preceding event) is called the *I* node for that activity, and the event at the arrowhead (the succeeding event) is called its *J* node. Arrow networks are occasionally referred to, therefore, as '*IJ* networks'. This jargon is not necessary for practical project network analysis, but the terms might be found in the literature.

Direction

By convention, activity arrows are always drawn from left to right. This means that the arrowheads are not strictly necessary and could be omitted. Occasionally, when a network is altered or through lack of space on a page, it might be impossible to avoid drawing an arrow vertically or even from right to left. In those exceptional cases the arrowheads *must* be shown so that there can be no ambiguity about the direction of any arrow.

Scale

Unlike bar charts, network diagrams are not usually drawn to any scale. The length of the arrows and size of the event circles have no significance whatsoever.

Identification numbers in arrow diagrams

The numbers written in the event circles are identifier codes that label the events: they allow the events and their associated activities to be referred to without ambiguity. In Figure 8.1 the arrow from event 1 to event 2, for example, can be described as activity 1,2 or 1–2. This labelling is convenient for all arrow networks, and is essential for anyone who still has software capable of processing arrow networks.

Logical dependencies and constraints in arrow diagrams

In any arrow diagram, no event can be considered complete until all the activities leading into it have been finished. Activities leading out of an event must wait for that event to be achieved before they can start. This can be demonstrated by reference to Figure 8.1. Event 9 cannot be considered as being reached or achieved until all three activities leading into it from the left have been achieved. When event 9 has been achieved, but not before, activity 9–10 can start. Activities 2–3, 2–4 and 2–5 must all wait until activity 1–2 has been finished before they can start.

Now, applying the arrow diagram method to an everyday 'project', suppose it is decided to plant a tree in a garden. If an arrow diagram were to be drawn, the result would look something like the sequence shown in Figure 8.2. The interdependence of activities is clear in this case, and only one sequence is possible. The tree cannot be placed in the hole before the hole has been dug, and

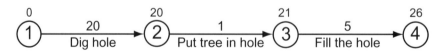

Figure 8.2   Tree project using arrow notation
The numbers written above the activity arrows in this extremely simple example are the estimated task durations. Minutes have been used here, but any time units can be used provided the same units are used throughout the network. Days or weeks are more usual in industrial and commercial projects. The number above each event circle shows the earliest possible time by which the event could be achieved.

there would be little point in filling in the hole before putting the tree into it.

Activity duration estimates and descriptions

One of the most important tasks in any planning operation is to estimate how long each task will take. This is an estimate in units of elapsed time, not necessarily connected with man-hours or other units of work. Estimates for the duration of each activity have been made for the simple tree project, as follows:

Activity	Description	Estimated duration
1–2	Dig the hole	20 minutes
2–3	Position the tree	1 minute
3–4	Fill in the hole	5 minutes

No one needs network analysis to realize that this project is going to take a minimum of 26 minutes to complete. Notice, however, that the estimated duration is written above each activity arrow in Figure 8.2, with a concise activity description written below. Space is usually limited on all networks, so planners must become adept at describing tasks in the least possible number of words.

The estimated achievement time for each event (written above the event circle) is calculated by adding up the estimated durations of all the preceding activities from left to right along the arrow path. These event times are the earliest possible times by which the events can be achieved.

Dummy activities

The network in Figure 8.3 represents a slightly more complex project (without its activity descriptions). Now the configuration is actually seen to be a network of activities, and not just a simple straight-line sequence. As in all project networks, there is more than one path through the arrows from project start to finish. In this example there are three possible routes to the final event 6, one of which flows through the dummy activity arrow linking event 4 to event 3.

Dummy activities (called 'dummies' for short) do not represent actual work, and practically always have zero duration. Rather, they denote a constraint or line of dependence between different activities. In Figure 8.3, therefore, the start of activity 3–6 is dependent not only upon completion of activity 2–3, but it must also await completion of activity 1–4. Alternatively expressed, activity 3–6 cannot start until events 3 and 4 have both been achieved.

Dummy activities are always drawn as dotted arrows.

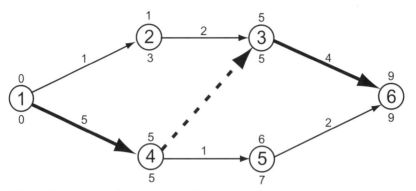

Figure 8.3   An example of arrow network time analysis
The dotted arrow in this network is a dummy activity. A dummy does not represent a real task, and usually has zero duration but it acts as a logical link between events. In this simple network, the start of activity 3–6 depends not only on completion of activity 2–3 but (through the dummy) also on completion of activity 1–4. In other words, activities 2–3 and 1–4 must both be finished before event 3 is achieved. The number above each event circle is its earliest possible completion time, and the number below is the latest pemissible completion time (see text for more details). The longest path through the network is the critical path, shown here in bold arrows. Some networks have more than one equal critical path.

Time analysis with arrow networks

Time units for activity durations

In Figure 8.3 (as in the simple tree project), numbers have been written above the activity arrows to show their estimated durations. Planners should always choose these time units according to their suitability for the project. In the tree project, minutes were the most appropriate unit of time. Days or weeks are most often used in practice for project plans, and weeks have been chosen for this example.

The best computer programs will accept any unit of time from minutes to years. Some computer programs allow different units of time to be mixed in the same project network, but I do not recommend this practice. Mixing time units in the same network can lead to some very peculiar results and messy tabulations when the computer prints out the results. Best practice has always been that the planner chooses a suitable unit and uses it consistently throughout the network.

The forward pass through the network

In the project network of Figure 8.3, the earliest possible time for each event and the earliest possible time for project completion at event 6 have been calculated by adding activity duration estimates along the arrows from left to right. This is always the first step in the full time analysis of any network, and is known as the *forward pass*.

The forward pass process is more complicated in this case than it was in the simple tree project because there is more than one possible path through the network. The earliest time indicated for each event might appear to depend on which path is followed, although only the longest preceding path will give the correct result. The earliest possible completion time for event 3, for instance, might seem to be 1 + 2 = 3, if the path through events 1, 2 and 3 is taken. Event 3 cannot really be achieved, however, until the end of week 5 because of the longer path through the dummy. This also means that the earliest possible start time for activity 3–6 is the end of week 5 (or, for more practical purposes, the beginning of week 6).

Thus the earliest possible time for any event is found by adding the estimated durations of all preceding activities along the path that produces the greatest time. By following this procedure through the network to the end of the project at event 6, it emerges that the earliest possible project completion time is estimated as nine weeks.

The backward pass

Now consider event 5 in Figure 8.3. Its earliest possible achievement time is the end of week 6, three weeks before the earliest possible time for finishing the project at event 6. It is clear that activity 5–6, which is only expected to last for two weeks, could be delayed for up to one week without upsetting the overall timescale. In other words, although the earliest possible achievement time for event 5 is week 6, its latest permissible achievement time is the end of week 7. This result can be indicated on the arrow diagram by writing the latest permissible time underneath the event circle. The result is found this time, not by addition from left to right along the arrows, but in exactly the opposite way by subtracting the estimated durations of activities from right to left (9 – 2 = 7 for event 5).

This subtraction exercise can be repeated throughout the network, writing the latest permissible times below all the event circles. Where more than one path exists, the longest must always be chosen so that the result after subtraction gives the smallest remainder. This is illustrated at event 4 in Figure 8.3, where the correct subtraction route lies through the dummy.

Float or slack

The term 'slack' indicates the amount of leeway available for achieving an event (the difference between its earliest possible and latest permissible times) without jeopardizing the earliest possible completion time for the whole project. The amount of slack at an event also determines the leeway available for starting and finishing activities that pass through the event. Strictly speaking, 'float' is the correct word for the leeway of activities (as opposed to slack for events).

However, 'slack' and 'float' are now used synonymously, and 'float' is the term used throughout this book. There are various categories of float. These are explained in Chapter 10, but can be ignored for the examples in this chapter.

The critical path

When all the earliest possible and latest permissible times have been added to the diagram, there will be at least one chain of events from the start of the network to the end where the earliest and latest event times are the same, indicating zero float. These events are critical to the successful achievement of the whole project within its earliest possible time. The route joining these events is not surprisingly termed the *critical path*. Although all activities may be important, it is those that lie on the critical path that must claim priority for management attention and the supply of scarce resources.

It is always possible that two or more paths through a network will have the same total duration, so that there might be more than one critical path..

Three ways of showing times on arrow networks

The times written on arrow networks usually refer to the events rather than directly to the activities. Project managers, however, need to know the times when each activity should start and finish. Although these times are easily derived from an arrow network, they cannot easily be shown owing to lack of space. This is demonstrated in Figure 8.4, using a fragment from a larger network. All estimates are in days.

Refer to version A in Figure 8.4. This shows arrow network notation according to British Standard BS 4335:1987. This notation is not well suited to freehand sketching (the principal remaining role for arrow networks) because:

1   Relatively large-diameter event circles are required, which reduce the amount of network detail that can be drawn on a sheet of paper.
2   Each event must be drawn carefully, taking time that is not usually available in a brainstorming session.

Version B in Figure 8.4 is a form of notation used in many countries, and generally throughout this book. It allows rapid freehand sketching, and is economical of space on a sheet or roll of paper.

Now consider activity 25–30 in Figure 8.4 (using either version A or B). The time analysis data for this activity are not all immediately apparent from the network. Certainly, its earliest possible start is day 40, the earliest completion time for event 25. The latest permissible start for this activity is the latest permissible time for event 30 minus the activity duration, which is 100 minus 10, giving day 90 (not the day 85 shown as the latest permissible completion for event 25). This

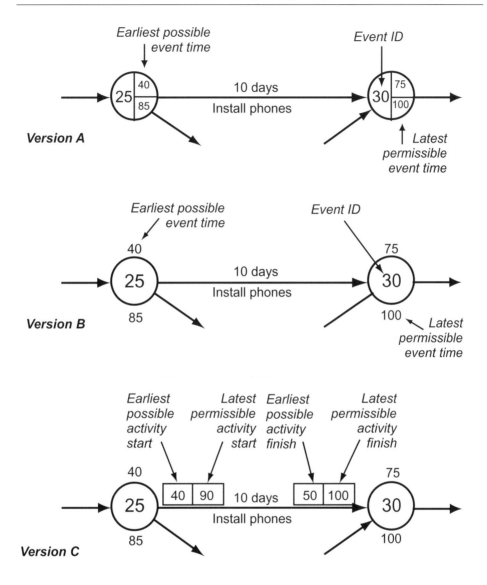

Figure 8.4   Three methods for showing times on arrow networks

arises because other activities entering and leaving events 25 and 30 affect the times for those events independently of activity 25–30.

The 'missing' time analysis data for any activity can be added if desired (and if space and drafting time allows) using version C.

These difficulties do not arise with precedence notation.

Critical path analysis using precedence notation

The precedence system of notation is preferred by many, and has emerged as the dominant method for the following reasons:

- Precedence logic diagrams more closely resemble engineering flow diagrams or block schematic diagrams than arrow diagrams, and are therefore more easily understood by people with no network training.

- Precedence notation allows clear illustration of activities whose starts and finishes do not coincide directly with the starts and finishes of their immediate predecessors and successors. In other words, precedence networks can show activities that can be allowed to overlap each other or which, conversely, must be separated by a time delay.

- Precedence networks are widely supported by available computer software. Arrow diagrams are not.

As with arrow diagrams, precedence networks cannot be used to schedule resources without either conversion into bar chart form (for tiny projects) or the use of a computer.

Activities in precedence diagrams

Figure 8.5 shows the convention for an activity in precedence notation. Although this must be the preferred pattern when networks are drawn by hand, it is an ideal not achieved when networks are plotted by computer because the software will limit the amount of data that can be included in each activity box. Without such limitation, networks would take up far too much screen space and be difficult to plot at a convenient size.

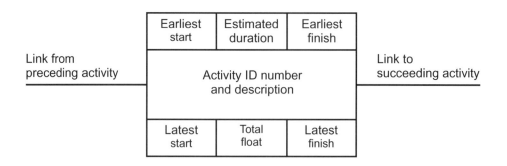

Figure 8.5   An activity in precedence notation

Direction

The flow of work in a precedence diagram is (as for arrow diagrams) always from left to right.

Scale

Precedence diagrams are not drawn to scale. The link lengths or activity box sizes have no significance whatsoever.

Activity identifiers

Every activity is given a unique identification number, usually referred to as its *ID code*. These codes are necessary for computer processing. Activity identification is a little simpler in precedence networks because, unlike their arrow network counterparts, it is not necessary to specify a preceding event code and a succeeding event code. A single code for each activity is all that is required. These ID codes can range from small serial numbers to complex alphanumeric codes, depending on the size and complexity of the networks and the capacity of the computer software for accommodating long ID numbers.

Logical dependencies and constraints

All the activities comprising a project are linked by lines which, unlike the arrows in arrow diagrams, almost always have zero duration.

Precedence notation allows more freedom to express complex interactivity relationships than the arrow diagram method. Activities can, for example, be shown to overlap rather than follow each other in strict sequence. Complex links are described later in this chapter (see Figure 8.17). Their use can be valuable, but is far less common than simple finish–start links. Although most project management computer programs allow complex links, they usually assume finish–start relationships by default. All the precedence examples in this book use finish–start links.

Activity duration estimates and descriptions

The tree project, which was shown as three sequential arrow activities in Figure 8.2, translates easily into the precedence diagram shown in Figure 8.6. The activity duration estimates for this very simple project are repeated below:

Activity	Description	Estimated duration
1	Dig the hole	20 minutes
2	Position tree	1 minute
3	Fill in the hole	5 minutes

The earliest estimated start and finish times for these activities, found by adding up the estimated durations from left to right, have been written in the activity boxes.

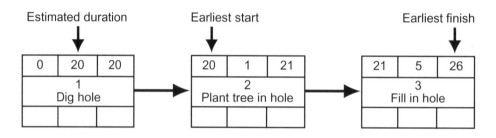

Figure 8.6   Tree project using precedence notation

Dummy activities

A dummy activity is an activity requiring no work and signifying no actual activity or duration. Dummy activities are usually unnecessary in precedence networks, but they can be useful as start and finish activities (see Figure 8.7, for instance) or as interface activities common to two or more different project networks (explained later in Chapter 9). Dummies can occasionally be useful in precedence networks to make the logic easier to follow by eye (see Figure 8.18).

Time analysis with precedence networks

Figure 8.7 is a very simple precedence network (the equivalent of the arrow network in Figure 8.3). The identifier codes in brackets show how these precedence activities correspond with those in the arrow version. All duration estimates are in weeks for this example.

The start and finish activities are not strictly necessary, and have no corresponding activities in the arrow equivalent. They have been introduced here because it is always desirable to start and finish a network at single nodes. Also, when networks are processed by computer it is always best to expect only one start and one finish activity in error log reports. A report of more than one start or finish will then clearly indicate an error in the input data (this point is explained more fully in the error-detection section of Chapter 13, page 309).

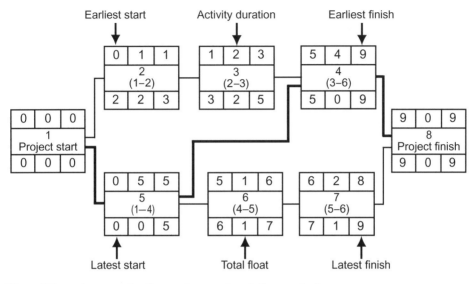

Figure 8.7   An example of precedence network time analysis
The critical path is shown by the bold links. Activity ID numbers in brackets denote the corresponding activities in the arrow version of this network, shown in Figure 8.3.

The forward pass

In the project network of Figure 8.7, the earliest overall project duration possible has been calculated by adding activity duration estimates through the links, passing from left to right. There is more than one possible path through the network, and the path with the longest duration will determine the earliest possible finish time for this project.

The earliest possible start time for activity 4 might seem to be 0 + 1 + 2 = 3 (the end of week 3) if the path through activities 1, 2 and 3 is taken. However, activity 4 cannot start until the end of week 5 (in practice, the beginning of week 6) because it is constrained by the longer path through activities 1 and 5.

By following this procedure through the network to the end of the project at activity 8, it emerges that the shortest possible estimated project duration is nine weeks (with completion at the end of the week 9).

The backward pass

Now consider activity 7 in Figure 8.7. Its earliest possible finish time is the end of week 8, one week before the earliest possible time for finishing the project at the end of week 9 (activity 8). It is clear that activity 7 could be delayed for up to one week without upsetting the overall timescale. This can be expressed as a total float of one week, entered in the centre bottom box of the activity. This result is indicated on the activity box by writing the latest permissible finish time in its bottom right-hand corner. The result is found this time, not by addition from left to right through the network, but in exactly the opposite way, through subtraction from right to left. So the latest permissible start for activity 7 is seen to be $(9 - 2)$ = 7 (meaning the end of week 7 or the start of week 8).

This subtraction exercise must be repeated throughout the network, writing the latest permissible times and floats along the bottom rows of all the activity boxes. Where more than one path exists, the longest must be chosen so that the result after subtraction gives the smallest remainder (earliest time). This is illustrated in Figure 8.7 at activity 5, for instance, where the correct subtraction route lies through the activities 8 and 4.

Float or slack

The term 'float' indicates the amount of leeway available for starting and finishing an activity. 'Slack' is another term for float. There are various categories of float. These are explained in Chapter 10, but can be ignored for the purposes of this simple example.

The critical path

When all the earliest possible and latest permissible times have been added to the diagram, there will always be at least one chain of activities where the earliest and latest times coincide, indicating zero float. These activities are critical to the successful achievement of the whole project within its earliest possible time, and the route following these activities through the network is called the *'critical path'*.

Although all activities may be important, it is the critical activities that must claim priority for resources and management attention.

Case study: Furniture project

The furniture project of the Eaton Sitright company was introduced in Chapter 7, where it was shown that bar charts (Figures 7.6 and 7.7) cannot clearly show the relationships or constraints between all the different activities. Now the project will be planned again using network analysis. Remember that time units are expressed in days for this project.

The task list for the furniture project was given in Figure 7.5, but it is repeated here in Figure 8.8, with one important difference: a column of data has now been added which defines the activity relationships. It does this by stating, for each

Activity number	Activity description	Duration (days)	Preceding activities
	Chair		
01	Anatomical study for chair	15	None
02	Design chair	5	01
03	Buy materials for chair seat	6	02
04	Make chair seat	3	03
05	Buy chair castors	5	02
06	Buy steel for chair frame	10	02
07	Make chair frame	3	06
08	Paint chair frame	2	07, 21
09	Assemble chair	1	04, 05, 08
10	Apply final finishes to chair	2	09
	Desk		
11	Design desk	10	None
12	Buy steel for desk frame	10	11
13	Make desk frame	5	12, 15
14	Paint desk frame	2	13, 21
15	Buy wood and fittings for desk	5	15
16	Make desk drawer	6	15
17	Make desk top	1	15
18	Assemble desk	1	14, 16, 17
19	Apply final finishes to desk	2	18
	General activities		
20	Decide paint colours	10	None
21	Buy paint and varnish	8	20
22	Final project evaluation	5	10, 19

Figure 8.8   Furniture project: Task list

activity, the ID numbers of all activities that must be finished before the new activity can start. It is only necessary to list the immediately preceding activities.

The resulting network for the furniture project is given in Figure 8.9 as an arrow diagram and in Figure 8.10 as a precedence diagram.

Of little consequence now, when computer programs for arrow networks are practically extinct, there are two activities labelled 6 to 14 in the arrow version, Figure 8.9. Had this network been intended for input into a computer, it would have been necessary to add a dummy activity in the path of one of these two parallel activities to create different identifying events.

Time analysis has been completed on both diagrams and, as expected, the data are identical. Figure 8.11 tabulates these data in a widely used format. The tasks have been sorted in this table in ascending order of their precedence ID numbers.

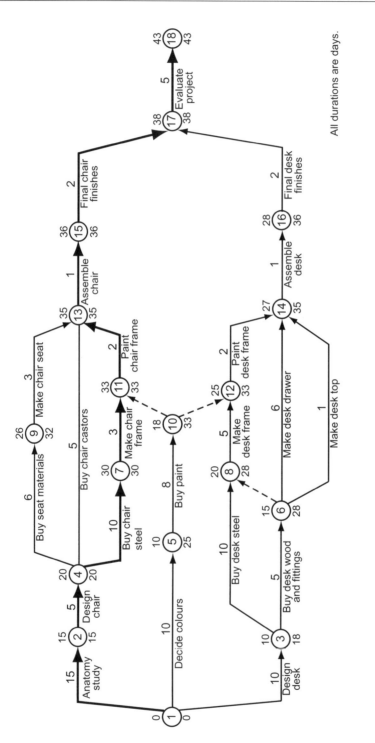

All durations are days.

Figure 8.9   Furniture project: Activity-on-arrow network diagram

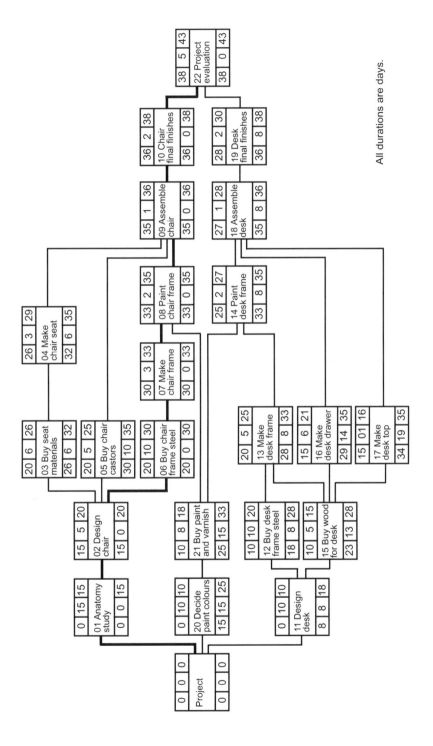

All durations are days.

Figure 8.10 **Furniture project: Precedence network diagram**

ADM only Prec. event	Succ. event	PDM only Activity identifier	Activity description	Duration (days)	Earliest start	Latest start	Earliest finish	Latest finish	Total float
1	2	01	Anatomical study for chair	15	0	0	15	15	0
2	4	02	Design chair	5	15	15	20	20	0
4	9	03	Buy materials for chair seat	6	20	26	26	32	6
9	13	04	Make chair seat	3	26	32	29	35	6
4	13	05	Buy chair castors	5	20	30	25	35	10
4	7	06	Buy steel for chair frame	10	20	20	30	30	0
7	11	07	Make chair frame	3	30	30	33	33	0
11	13	08	Paint chair frame	2	33	33	35	35	0
13	15	09	Assemble chair	1	35	35	36	36	0
15	17	10	Apply final finishes to chair	2	36	36	38	38	0
1	3	11	Design desk	10	0	8	10	18	8
3	8	12	Buy steel for desk frame	10	10	18	20	28	8
8	12	13	Make desk frame	5	20	28	25	33	8
12	14	14	Paint desk frame	2	25	33	27	35	8
3	6	15	Buy wood and fittings for desk	5	10	23	15	28	13
6	14	16	Make desk drawer	6	15	29	21	35	14
6	14	17	Make desk top	1	15	34	16	35	19
14	16	18	Assemble desk	1	27	35	28	36	8
16	17	19	Apply final finishes to desk	2	28	36	30	38	8
1	5	20	Decide paint colours	10	0	15	10	25	15
5	10	21	Buy paint and varnish	8	10	25	18	33	15
17	18	22	Final project evaluation	5	38	38	43	43	0

Figure 8.11   Furniture project: Time analysis

Another, more practical, sort sequence would be in ascending order of earliest start times.

All times are given here are as day numbers. This is typical of a plan where the project start date is not known. As soon as authority is given for a project to start, the start time of the first activity can be converted to the appropriate calendar date, and then all subsequent start and finish times can be given as calendar dates instead of day numbers. A practical working plan would ensure that only working days would be valid for inclusion, so that no task would be scheduled to start, continue or be finished over a weekend or public holiday shutdown. This conversion from numbers to dates is awkward as a mental exercise, but becomes painless when a computer is used.

The network diagrams in Figures 8.9 and 8.10 clearly show all the activity links which the bar charts could not. Time analysis has indicated all the tasks that have zero total float and are therefore critical. Other tasks can be ranked in their degree of priority because those with least total float must take priority over those with more float.

Case study: Gantry project

Another project example will show how network logic and critical path calculation can be used as an aid in planning to reduce project time through effective crash actions. It is assumed here that every crash action carries the penalty of increased cost.

Gantry project explanation

Figure 8.12 shows a steel gantry that has to be set up on the side of a steep hill. The requirements of this small project are quite simple, but one or two points have to be borne in mind about the order in which the work is to be carried out.

The first step in erecting the gantry must be to mark out the site and prepare the foundations. Assume that all other preparations, including the delivery of construction machinery and materials to site, have already been carried out.

The two tower foundations will differ in size, because foundation B will have to support greater weight than the foundation at A. Tower B has to be placed on a prefabricated plinth in order to raise it to the same height as tower A. A final levelling adjustment must be made at base A after the plinth has been erected for B, and this is to be done by taking a theodolite sighting from the plinth top.

All these special requirements are reflected in the project network diagram. All times are in days for this project.

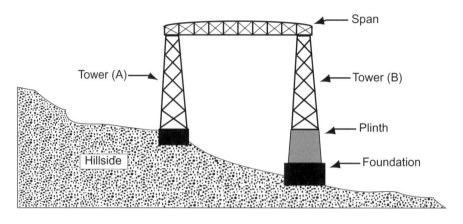

Figure 8.12   Gantry project
This sectional view of a hillside shows the outline requirements of a project to erect a steel gantry.

Gantry project: Network diagram

Figure 8.13 includes two versions of the network diagram for the gantry project. These are the arrow diagram and its precedence equivalent.

Arrow (ADM) version of the gantry project network

Please refer to the upper network in Figure 8.13, the arrow diagram for the gantry project. Note that the dummy 8–9 denotes the constraint imposed on the start of levelling at base A. This ensures that the plinth is erected first, without which no theodolite sighting could be taken.

Time analysis has been carried out according to the procedures explained earlier in this chapter, and the activities lying on the critical path are drawn with bold arrows.

Precedence (PDM) version of the gantry project

The lower network in Figure 8.13 is the precedence diagram for the gantry project. The logic is the same as that shown in the arrow diagram, but it is no longer necessary to use a dummy to control the levelling at base A, since the link from activity 10 to activity 5 does that job.

Activities 4 and 9 are both waiting times while concrete cures. This is hardly work or real activity, and the precedence notation would, in fact, allow these activities to be shown simply by placing links from 3 to 5 and 8 to 10 and giving these links duration values. However, it is always safer to insert activities in the

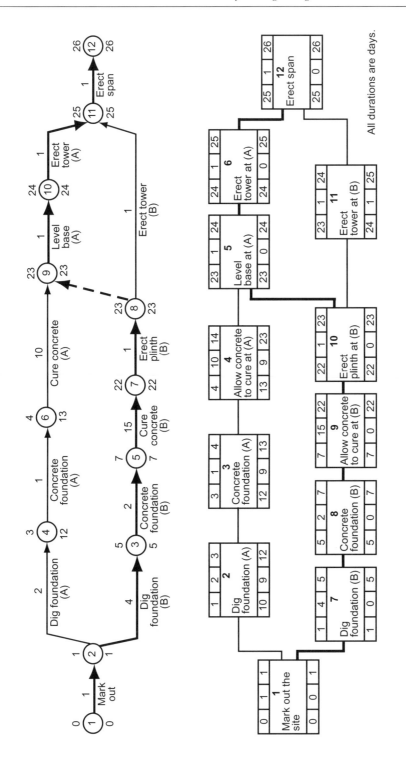

Figure 8.13 Gantry project: Network diagram

The arrow diagram and its exact precedence equivalent are shown here.

All durations are days.

ADM only Prec. event	Succ. event	PDM only Activity identifier	Activity description	Duration (days)	Earliest start	Earliest finish	Latest start	Latest finish	Total float
1	2	1	Mark out the site	1	0	1	0	1	0
2	4	2	Dig foundation for tower A	2	1	3	10	12	9
4	6	3	Concrete foundation A	1	3	4	12	13	9
6	9	4	Allow concrete to cure at A	10	4	14	13	23	9
2	3	7	Dig foundation for tower B	4	1	5	1	5	0
3	5	8	Concrete foundation B	2	5	7	5	7	0
5	7	9	Allow concrete to cure at B	15	7	22	7	22	0
7	8	10	Erect plinth at B	1	22	23	22	23	0
8	9	—	Dummy (arrow diagram only)	0	—	—	—	—	—
8	11	11	Erect tower B	1	23	24	24	25	1
9	10	5	Adjust base level at A	1	23	24	23	24	0
10	11	6	Erect tower A	1	24	25	24	25	0
11	12	12	Erect the span	1	25	26	25	26	0

Figure 8.14   Gantry project: Time analysis

network if paper and computer space allows, because the logic and planner's intentions are then more clearly recorded and made visible. Such 'visibility' will be found very beneficial during subsequent network checking and in the interpretation of reports from the computer.

Time analysis of the gantry project network

The gantry project time analysis results are tabulated in Figure 8.14. The earliest possible completion date is seen to be at the end of day 26.

 If the times in this table are desired as calendar dates (they usually will be), a calendar must be consulted for the conversion, and non-working days (such as weekends and public holidays) must be taken out. As explained for the furniture project earlier in this chapter, this chore is one of many avoided when a computer is used.

Optimized crash action

Critical path analysis, by identifying critical tasks, helps to ensure that scarce resources can be allocated to best effect. Detailed scheduling of project resources is dealt with in later chapters, but there is one specific application of critical path analysis with respect to resources which can be explained here. The resources in question are time and money.

 Suppose that the predicted duration of 26 days for the gantry project is unacceptable to the project customer, and that the shortest programme possible must be devised (even if this increases the project costs). The project manager can consider several options, starting by re-examining the network logic to see if any short cuts are possible and questioning the original estimates. In the gantry project case, no network improvement is thought to be possible, and the project manager is left with the need to consider taking 'crash action' on some or all activities. The following actions might be considered:

- hiring extra labour (which could lead to some inefficiency: doubling a workforce does not always halve the job duration)
- hiring heavier or additional plant
- working overtime on weekdays or at weekends (which will attract overtime payments)
- working all night (again attracting overtime payments, plus additional expense in supervision costs and in floodlighting the hillside and access routes)
- the use of additives to shorten concrete curing time (again adding cost).

 Suppose that, after considering all these possible measures, the project manager has compiled a possible action list. Figure 8.15 shows that list, which includes only those activities for which crash action is thought to be possible.

If all the crash actions defined in Figure 8.15 were to be taken successfully, the total estimated project duration should be reduced from 26 to 15 working days at a total additional cost of £2600. This plan assumes that some people will agree to work through nights and weekends.

However, when the network is examined it is found that there is no point in crashing *all* the activities, regardless of cost. Some have nine days' float, so that shortening their original times by one or two days can have no effect on the project completion date. Money spent on crashing activities that have considerable float will simply be wasted.

There is a theoretical optimum cost/time solution in which the amount of planned crash action and extra cost is planned to best effect, with no additional effort and expense wasted on actions that will produce no result. To approach this optimum state of affairs, the first thing to do is to crash only the critical activities. When this is done for the gantry project, it is found that the original critical path has been reduced so much that its duration is now shorter than that of other paths through the network. Activities that were once critical have been speeded up to the point where they have gained substantial float. This gives two results:

1   The project duration has, as desired, been shortened.
2   The critical path now flows through different parts of the network.

Attention must now be redirected to those activities which lie on the new critical path. They must also be considered for crashing. Taken to its ideal limit, this process can be repeated so that many, if not all, activities become critical. This result will generate multiple critical paths through the network, but should ensure that money and effort are not wasted on crash actions that can produce no further shortening of the project duration. The procedure is not often followed to this extreme, but applying the principle in moderation can bring forward a planned completion date without wasting money on crashing non-critical activities.

Exercise

Using either the arrow network or the precedence diagram of Figure 8.13 and the data from Figure 8.15, try to find a sensible crash option for the gantry project that allows completion in 15 days at minimum extra cost. Do not plan to crash any activity unless that action can shorten the overall achievable project time.

The exercise should reveal that it is not necessary to crash activities 3, 4 and 11. This reduces the total additional costs of crashing from £2600 to £2250, saving £350.

In a typical project network, with many more activities and greater complexity, the outcome could be far less obvious, and a great deal more unnecessary expenditure might be saved. But, for whatever reason a network is drawn, attention and subsequent control usually concentrates along the critical activities.

ADM only Prec. event	Succ. event	PDM only Activity identifier	Activity description and proposed crash action	Normal duration (days)	Crashed duration (days)	Extra cost £
—	—	—	Hire of floodlights to allow all night working	—	—	500
—	—	—	Employment of night supervisor	—	—	750
2	4	2	Dig foundation A using heavier hire plant	2	1	200
4	6	3	Concrete foundation A with extra labour	1	0.5	50
6	9	4	Use fast curing concrete at foundation A	10	5	100
2	3	7	Dig foundation B using heavier hire plant	4	2	300
3	5	8	Concrete foundation B with extra labour	2	1	100
5	7	9	Use fast curing concrete at foundation B	15	8	200
10	11	6	Use extra labour to erect tower A	1	0.5	150
8	11	11	Use extra labour to erect tower B	1	0.5	200
11	12	12	Hire larger crane to erect the span	1	0.5	50

Figure 8.15   **Gantry project: Possible crash actions to shorten the project duration**

No time is lost worrying about incidents or situations which the network demonstrates to be inconsequential.

Any contingency that arises during the execution of a project can be checked against the network to establish its relevance to time and costs. Only those factors which deserve management attention need be reported to executives higher up the line organization. This is, of course, a practical case of management by exception.

PERT

PERT (Programme Evaluation and Review Technique) is very similar to critical path analysis, and the two methods are often confused with each other. It matters little if they are. Construction of the network diagram is carried out in the same way for both methods, the main difference only becoming apparent when the time comes to estimate activity durations.

For PERT, three time estimates are required for every activity:

t_o = the most *optimistic* duration that could be foreseen
t_m = the most *likely* duration
t_p = the most *pessimistic* duration

From these quantities a probable duration is calculated for each activity, on a statistical basis, assuming that the errors will fall within a normal distribution curve when all the project activities are taken as the sample.

$$t_e = \frac{t_o + 4t_m + t_p}{6} \text{ (where } t_e \text{ is the expected time)}$$

This calculation is repeated on all activities in the network, and used to predict the probability of completing the project within the scheduled time. A computer removes the drudgery from these calculations and enables the results to be made available in time for appropriate action to be taken.

Some authorities do not accept that a normal distribution curve is suitable for predicting the spread of estimating errors. Estimates are frequently too optimistic rather than too pessimistic. Allowance for this tendency can be made by skewing the distribution curve deliberately. As an example, the following variation of the formula has been used:

$$t_e = \frac{t_o + 3t_m + 2_p}{6}$$

Whichever statistical basis is chosen, PERT will produce a critical path in the same way as any other network analysis method. The emphasis has changed slightly however, from cost-time analysis and concentration on the critical path, to a more statistical approach, predicting the probability of completing the project by a given date.

Although many users refer to their networks as 'PERT', the term is often misapplied because it is the more straightforward critical path analysis method, with its single duration estimates, that is most widely used.

More complex network notation

Overlapping activities in arrow networks

In Figure 8.16, several versions of a small extract from a larger network are shown. Suppose that this project is for a new bicycle. Three activities are shown: design engineering, drawing, and the procurement of components and materials.

Figure 8.16(a) shows the network fragment as it was originally drawn, with the three activities following each other and bound by rigid start-to-finish constraints. The activities lie on the critical path and contribute 28 weeks to the total bicycle project duration, which is unacceptable.

Re-examination of the network uncovers a fundamental flaw in the logic. Does all the engineering design have to be finished before detailed drawing can start? Of course not. These activities can be allowed to overlap to some extent. Similarly, some of the long-lead purchase items can be ordered in advance, as soon as the designers can specify them; it is not necessary to wait for the final parts lists.

In Figure 8.16(b) an attempt has been made to indicate the permissible overlap of activities by redrawing the network fragment. The start and finish constraints have now been relaxed by inserting dummies, each of which has been given a duration value. Drawing can start two weeks after the start of engineering, but cannot be finished until three weeks after the completion of engineering. Purchasing can begin three weeks after the start of drawing, at which time it is estimated that the long-lead items can be specified. Some purchased items cannot be ordered, however, until the parts list is issued along with the general assembly drawing, and delivery of these late-purchased items is not expected until four weeks after the completion of drawing.

Although no crash action has been planned, the timescale for this small part of the main network has been reduced from 28 to 17 weeks – almost halved. Bicycles can start to come off the production line 11 weeks earlier than if the activity boundaries had been adhered to rigidly.

In arrow notation, overlapped activities, where one task is dependent upon a flow of work or information from another, are called 'ladder networks' or 'ladder activities'.

Although drawn to the correct convention, the logic of Figure 8.16(b) does not

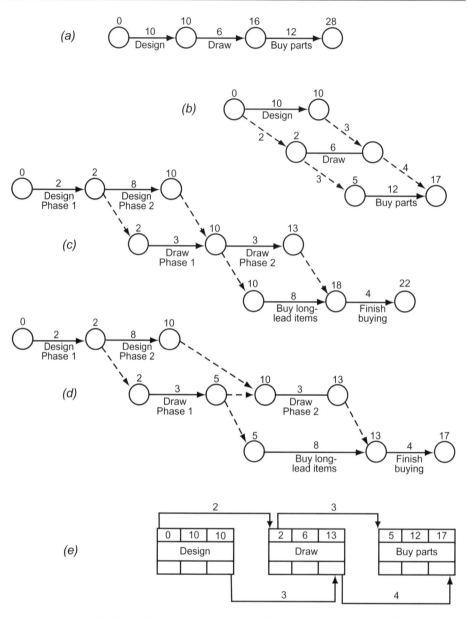

Figure 8.16   **Methods for showing overlapping activities in arrow and precedence networks**

stand up to close scrutiny. It might be assumed that drawing could start two weeks after week 0 even if no engineering had been carried out, and that procurement could start at week 5, whatever the state of engineering or drawing. Clearly this was not the planner's intention when the network was drawn, and alternative networks might be suggested.

In Figure 8.16(c) the same sequence of activities has been depicted but, by splitting engineering into two phases and doing the same with drawing, the true relationships and constraints are more clearly defined. But a different, and wrong, answer has been obtained this time. The mistake lies in the start restriction imposed on buying, which is in fact dependent not on the completion of engineering, but only upon phase 1 of the drawing.

The true picture is obtained by drawing the network in Figure 8.16(d), where all the dummies are correctly placed.

Ladder networks are not a very elegant solution, and other methods for dealing with complex conditions at the boundaries between two activities used to exercise the minds of the planning professionals. Some project management software allowed lags and overlaps to be specified between activities when the data were input. Another useful instruction was to specify two activities as 'tied', meaning that the succeeding activity must start as soon as its predecessor had been finished.

However, most of these problems can now be overcome using the more versatile precedence system. The precedence solution for the bicycle project is shown at (e) in Figure 8.16.

Complex constraints using precedence notation

Overlapping activities and other more complex constraints are best served by precedence notation. Complex, in this sense, means any link between two activities that differs from the usual start–finish constraint (which says that an activity can be started as soon as its predecessor has finished, but not before).

Figure 8.17 shows the four types of precedence links that can be used. Even a normal start–finish relationship, shown in Figure 8.17(a), can be made more complex if required by placing a time value on the link. This would force a delay between the finish of one activity and the start of the next. This type of lag relationship is useful for activities such as waiting for concrete to cure or watching paint dry.

Devaux (1999) gives some useful examples of complex constraint applications.

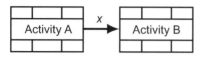

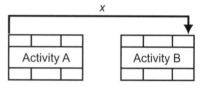

(a) Finish-to-start: Activity *B* cannot start until *x* network time units after the finish of Activity *A*. Most constraints are of this type, but x is usually zero.

(b) Start-to-start: Activity *B* cannot start until *x* network time units after the start of Activity *A*.

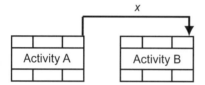

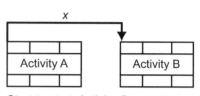

(c) Finish-to-finish: Activity *B* cannot be finished until *x* network time units after the finish of Activity *A*.

(d) Start-to-finish: Activity *B* cannot be finished until *x* network time units after the start of Activity *A*.

Figure 8.17   Constraint options in precedence networks

This diagram shows the different kinds of constraints that can be specified between any two activities in a precedence network.

An interesting comparison between arrow and precedence logic

One apparent disadvantage of the precedence system is illustrated in Figure 8.18. Whenever a significant number of activities have to be linked independently to several following activities, the use of dummies in arrow diagrams can seem to produce a clearer diagram than the precedence counterpart. This can be seen by comparing the arrow network shown at (a) in Figure 8.18 with its precedence equivalent at (b). All parts of Figure 8.18 show the same actual logic.

Although precedence networks do not normally have dummies, these can be introduced artificially as a convenient method for clarifying the logic. The two dummies introduced at Figure 18(c) have produced a dramatic improvement in network clarity without changing the actual logic meaning.

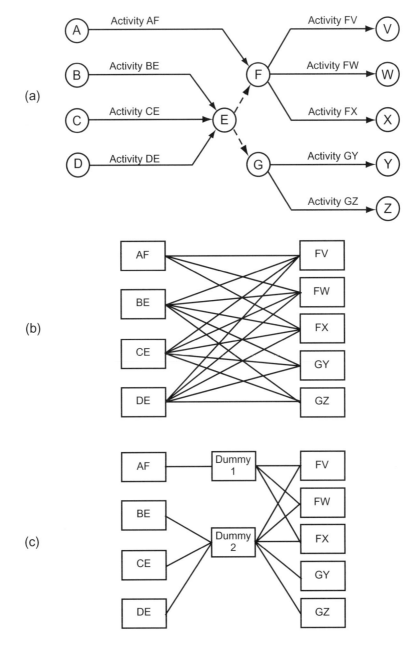

Figure 8.18   Using dummies to clarify cluttered logic

These three networks have identical logic. The network at (b) is the conventional precedence equivalent of (a). Although dummies are not customary in precedence networks, the complex 'road pattern' at (b) can be improved by placing two zero-duration activities (dummy 1 and dummy 2) at the busy intersections.

Chapter 9

Network analysis in practice

The previous chapter introduced project network analysis by explaining the diagramming methods and demonstrating the principles of time analysis. This chapter describes procedures and methods needed to implement project network analysis successfully in practice. Several of the steps described anticipate the use of a computer for time analysis, resource scheduling and reporting.

Developing network logic

Network diagrams provide the notation that enables planners to document the processes for executing a project, and do so clearly, in great detail and in the preferred sequence. This is a valuable tool that should always be fully exploited. Brainstorming is probably the best approach for any new project because it can extract and combine the thoughts of the best available minds.

Arranging a brainstorming meeting

The number of people involved in drawing a network depends to some extent on the size of the project organization. At the smallest end of the scale, individuals will draw networks simply to plan and control their own activities. For larger projects it is customary, and desirable, to have at least one responsible person on hand who can speak for each department or sub-organization involved.

The individuals chosen should be of sufficient seniority to enable them to commit their departments to the resulting plan, and to any specific methods of working or estimates upon which the agreed plan depends.

The network should be drawn rapidly, as large as possible, and in full view of all those who are contributing information. Nowadays, it is easy to draw a network directly using a computer with suitable software. Use of projection equipment means that everyone at the meeting can follow the process. Unfortunately, the computer is not capable of displaying an entire network of any significant size on a single screen, which means that it is necessary to scroll up, down and across the screen to see the whole picture. Ideally, everyone at the meeting should be able to see the whole logic pattern as it develops, and be able to follow every path through from start to finish. A large sheet or roll of paper laid out on a long table or fixed to a wall is still the method that I prefer.

Arrow notation is best suited to the brainstorming purpose, because it can be sketched far more quickly than a precedence diagram. It is always easy to convert an arrow diagram to precedence later, after the meeting, thus saving the precious and costly time of all those attending the meeting.

A useful kit of materials, all designed to save time, comprises:

- a large sheet or roll of paper, arranged so that it can be seen by all those taking part in the meeting
- a supply of sharpened soft pencils
- a soft eraser
- a long ruler
- a template for drawing event circles (which can be a hole carefully drilled in the aforementioned ruler).

Initial networks can be drawn freehand, but a ruler and circle template will help to keep the initial sketch neat and relatively small without adding significantly to the time needed. A sprawling sketch can prove awkward if it causes the network to overflow the sheet when the later stages are reached. Whilst an initial network sketch can be redrawn more tidily after the meeting, if it is not produced with a little care in the first place, it will soon become unreadable and vague because of the inevitable erasures, corrections and additions made during the meeting. It is as well to start the diagram using straight lines, small event circles and with sensible spacing.

Contribution of the planning expert

It has to be assumed that the person who wields the pencil and commits all the working proposals to paper is sufficiently competent to do so. The person entrusted with this task should be as skilled and experienced a network analyst as possible.

The task of the expert will be made easier if everyone present has received some prior training and is able easily to follow the meaning of the network as it grows. Although complete mastery of the art of network logic takes time and practice, the essential elements arc not difficult and can be taught in a few hours.

There are several pitfalls that can rob a potential expert of accuracy and success. Although all network logic is built from only a few simple basic symbols, it is not always easy to assemble those symbols in a way that avoids mistakes. To a great extent, the degree of success depends on the aptitude of the individual. Getting the logic right can be compared to solving a recreational puzzle. Some people see the challenge of drawing networks in that light. Networking can, indeed, be fun.

Give three different project planners the same data for a project, and they would probably produce three different networks, each signifying a different personal vision of how the work should logically proceed. This does not necessarily mean that any of the networks is wrong. Each proposed method of working could be valid, and lead to a satisfactory result.

A skilled analyst should be allowed to control the brainstorming meeting effectively (regardless of seniority). She or he will ensure that the logic develops along the right lines, asking check questions from time to time in order to prove the logic and avoid errors. Check questions can take the following forms:

- 'We've shown work starting on site immediately, but should we deliver some machinery first, or set up a site hut, or deliver some materials?'
- 'Won't it be necessary to check these drawings before they can be issued?'
- 'Is customer approval needed before work can start on this activity?'
- 'Does this steelwork need priming or any other protective treatment before erection?'
- 'Can this tower really be erected as soon as the concrete base has been poured, or will it ooze slowly downwards into wet cement?
- 'This method failed us badly on the last project. Isn't there a better way?'
- 'Does the start of this activity really depend on all these incoming activities?'
- 'OK, you've told me to add this activity marked "transfer all data from old system", but can this be done safely after "install computer", or should we insert an activity for debugging and testing the system?'

A diagram that emerges from the initial meeting bearing the scars of many erasures and changes shows that a great deal of active and careful thought has gone into the logic. The network analyst must never be too lazy or reluctant to erase and redraw parts of the network as the combined brainpower of the meeting develops and agrees the preferred logic.

An error trap in arrow logic

It is possible to introduce logical errors unwittingly as the plan builds up. An example is shown in Figure 9.1, which is a classic trap well known to all experts who use arrow logic during planning sessions.

Imagine that a construction firm is drawing up a network for the planning and control of a new building project. Figure 9.1(a) shows a fragment of this network at an early stage during the planning meeting. Notice that the roof frame cannot be started until the brick walls have been erected because, obviously, it has to be built on top of the walls. The roof frame will be built by a carpenter from wood, so the roof frame also depends on the timber being purchased. All of this is recognized in the network logic at event 30. So far, so good.

Now suppose that the next activity to be added is 'Point the brickwork'.

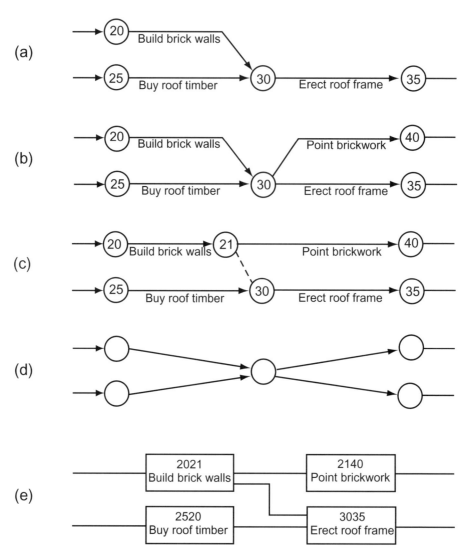

Figure 9.1   A common logic error in arrow networks

The network fragment shown at (a), (b) and (c) is a small section from a construction project network. The incomplete diagram at (a) has been finished with the addition of a fourth activity for pointing the brickwork (b). This addition has introduced an error into the logic. Although the walls must be built and roof timbers purchased before the roof frame can be erected, it is not necessary to have the roof timbers delivered before the brick walls can be pointed. The version at (c) shows how the insertion of a dummy has corrected this mistake. Planners must always question the logic when several activities enter and leave an event, as at (d). 'Does every activity leaving this event depend on *all* the activities entering it?' This kind of mistake is more easily avoided in precedence diagrams, as at (e).

Pointing of the walls can start as soon as the walls have been built, after event 30. The trap is to draw the logic as shown in Figure 9.1(b), simply by drawing the new activity as emerging from event 30. The logic at (b) is wrong because it is not necessary to buy the roof timbers before the brick walls can be pointed. The planner has corrected this mistake by introducing the dummy 21–30, shown in Figure 9.1(c).

The planner using arrow notation must always question the logic when there are multiple input activities and output activities at an event, as in the general pattern of Figure 9.1(d).

The precedence equivalent of this logic, in its correct version, is shown at Figure 9.1(e). It is more difficult to make the logic mistake using precedence. However, it is still good practice, whatever the notation used, to check the logic wherever multiple links enter and leave a node.

Level of detail in network planning

A question often facing planners new to the art is: 'How much detail should we show in the network?' In other words which activities should be included in the network and which should be left out or combined with others?

To some extent this depends on the size and duration of the project, the duration units chosen, the amount of detailed knowledge available and the purpose of the network. A very detailed project network containing 10 000 activities might sound very impressive, but smaller networks are far more practicable and manageable. Also, very big single project networks can prove tiresome (to say the least) when they have to be considered along with plans for other projects in multi-project scheduling systems.

Guidelines

There are several guidelines for deciding the level of detail which should be shown in project network diagrams.

Activities with relatively very short durations

It is probably well to avoid showing jobs as separate activities if their durations amount only to a very small fraction of the expected overall timescale, especially if they do not require resources. Of course, these activities cannot be ignored, but they can be included in the network as parts of other activities.

An example is the preparation of a group of drawings, where a single activity, 'Detail and check sub-assembly X', might be shown, rather than attempting to include a set of separate activities for detailing every drawing, and another set of activities for checking them.

In a project lasting only a few weeks (for example, the overhaul and maintenance of an electricity generating station during a planned shutdown period), it would be reasonable to use network planning units of days or fractions of days, and to include activities lasting only half a day or less. For projects lasting several years, the planning units might be weeks, with very few activities included that have less than one week's duration.

As with all rules, however, there are exceptions. Some activities with very short durations might be so important that they must be included. One example is an activity for obtaining authorization or approval before subsequent work can proceed.

Level of detail in relation to task responsibility

It can be argued sensibly that a network path should be interrupted whenever the action moves from one department or organization to another – in other words, where the immediate management responsibility for executing the work changes. In the days when practically everyone used arrow networks, this concept was easy to define: a new event should be created whenever responsibility progressed from one manager to another (or from one department to another).

A useful guide is to remember that the ultimate purpose of the network is going to be to allow the project work to be scheduled and controlled. In due course, work-to-do lists for different managers will be generated from the network. The network must therefore contain all the jobs needed for these lists. This means that:

- No network activity should be so large that it cannot be assigned for the principal control of one – and *only* one – department or manager.
- An activity that is long compared to the project timescale should probably be broken into two or more activities. This will ensure that the finished plan provides frequent progress monitoring checkpoints.

A network that is sufficiently detailed will enable the following project stages to be identified, planned and monitored or measured:

1   work authorization, either as an internal works order or as the receipt of a customer order or contract

2   drawing and design approvals from the customer (especially where the absence of these might hold up work during the course of the project)

3   financial authorizations from the customer where the contract requires that these be obtained before expenditure can be committed to significant purchases or new phases of the project

4   local authority planning application and consent

5   the start and finish of design for any manufactured sub-assembly, construction work area or significant part of a management change project; if the planned duration of a design task is longer than two or three weeks, it might be

advisable to break the design task down into shorter activities, corresponding to identifiable design phases

6 release of completed drawings for production or construction (probably for specific sets of drawings rather than for individual sheets)

7 the start of purchasing activity for each sub-assembly or work package, signified by the engineering issue of a bill of material, purchase specification or advance release of information for items which are known to have long delivery times

8 issue of invitations to tender or purchase enquiries

9 receipt and analysis of suppliers' or subcontractors' bids

10 following on from (7), (8) and (9), the issue of a purchase order to a supplier or subcontractor (again at the level of work packages and sub-assemblies rather than small individual purchases)

11 delivery of materials to the point of usage – this might be the most significant or last expected item needed for a subsequent project activity; for international projects, this delivery point may be to a ship or to an aircraft, with subsequent transit time shown as a separate, consecutive activity (when responsibility transfers from the supplier to the carrier or freight forwarding agent)

12 the starts and completions of manufacturing stages (in large projects, usually only looking at the entries into and exits from production control responsibility, and again considering work packages or sub-assemblies rather than individual small parts)

13 the starts and finishes of construction subcontracts, and important intermediate events in such subcontracts (see the section on milestones later in this chapter, see page 224)

14 handover events for completed work packages – this would include handing over the finished project (or substantial parts of it) to the customer, but would also ensure that associated items such as the compilation of maintenance and operating manuals were itemized in the network plan.

These are, of course, only guidelines. The list is neither mandatory nor complete.

Level of detail in relation to activity costs

Cost-control methods are described later in this book, but certain aspects of cost reporting and control will be impossible if sufficient attention is not paid to certain activities when the network diagram is prepared.

It is possible to assign a cost to an activity, such as the purchase of materials. If an activity is included on the network for the planned issue of every significant purchase order, then the purchase order value can be assigned to these activities.

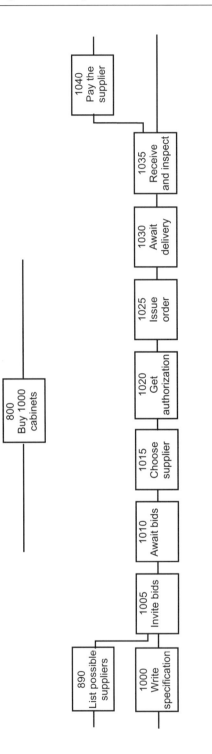

Figure 9.2   Level of detail in a purchasing sequence

Here are two possible extracts from a larger network. Both show a purchasing activity, but in very different levels of detail.

This makes it possible to prepare reports from the computer which will set the times for these costs when the orders are placed, and thus give a schedule of purchase cost commitments.

If another activity is added for the receipt of goods against each of these purchase orders, the same order value can be assigned to these later activities. Using suitable computer techniques (described later), cost schedules can be derived that relate to the time when invoices will become due. The timing of these schedules indicates cash flow requirements.

None of this would be possible with insufficient detail on the network. Figure 9.2 illustrates this case.

The upper network shows the entire purchasing process for a large piece of equipment as one activity. That might be adequate in an enormous project, where it is necessary to restrict the total number of activities and where the project manager can delegate the purchasing activity to the purchasing department with complete confidence. The expanded version of the network, in the lower part of Figure 9.2, lies towards the other extreme. It gives the project manager far more assistance in the preparation of working schedules, and allows more detailed supervision of the purchase process.

Is size important? Should a large network be broken down into smaller networks?

Some companies like to draw outline networks of their projects, perhaps containing only 100 or 150 activities in fairly coarse detail. These are then used as higher-level management controls, but they must be backed up later by more detailed networks produced for the various project departments or participants, and all these networks must be tied together in some way so that their corresponding events or activities are scheduled on the same dates and have the same float.

This correlation can be achieved by designating all the detailed networks as subnetworks of the main control network and by identifying shared events or activities as interface events or activities (see the following section).

Interface events and activities

There are several circumstances in which an activity or event in one network can have a logical link with, or impose a constraint on, an activity or event in another network. The need to identify interface activities or events arises most frequently in projects where the total project network has been broken down into a number of smaller, more manageable subnetworks. This might be the result of a work breakdown or organizational breakdown decision. It could also be that several small network modules or templates have to be merged to constitute the whole

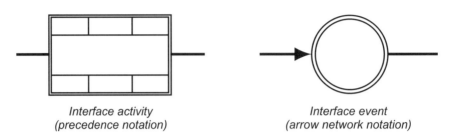

Interface activity   *Interface event*
(precedence notation)   *(arrow network notation)*

Figure 9.3   Network interfaces
Interfaces are nodes common to two or more networks. They are usually depicted with a
double-ruled border.

network (a technique described in Chapter 14). There are occasions when a
common interface appears in more than two subnetworks, for example when
several subnetworks share the same start or finish.

Interfaces should only be allowed for true logical links. They should not be
used in an attempt to depict operational problems such as attempting to delay the
start of an activity until resources come free from an activity in another project.
Such competition for scarce resources requires a different approach, for which
more appropriate methods will be described in the following chapters.

Interfaces are often highlighted on logic diagrams by outlining the event or
activity with double-ruled lines, as shown in Figure 9.3.

Milestones

An important purpose of any plan is to produce a schedule from which project
progress can be managed. Progress checkpoints must be provided at suitable
intervals throughout every network and any schedules derived from it. Events or
activities that have particular significance can each be designated as *milestones*. A
milestone is achieved when the relevant milestone activity is finished in a
precedence network or when a milestone event is achieved in an arrow network.

Computer programs for project scheduling allow reports to be filtered and
printed so that they contain only milestones. These greatly help the assessment of
progress against time and costs, and are of value in reporting to higher
management and (when the contract demands) to the customer.

Estimating activity durations

It is necessary for all activity durations to be estimated either as the network is
drawn, or as soon after as possible. These estimates are for elapsed time, and
might not relate directly to cost estimates.

Units of duration

What units of duration should be used? This can depend on the duration of the project. It may be convenient to use weeks. Days are very often used, and are suggested as the default units in most computer software.

A very useful unit for general purposes is the half-day (0.5), since many projects are conducted on a five-day week basis, and a week then becomes 10 units. Even when the duration extends to several years, the use of half- or one-day units is no problem when a computer is used for subsequent calculations. Resolution of estimates to better than half-day duration is not usually required, but some computer programs can even accept minutes.

Once a unit of duration has been decided, the same unit should be used consistently throughout the network.

Procedure for estimating activity durations

The usual procedure is for the estimates to be added as the network is drawn. Another approach is for the network sketch to be carried from one department to another, each responsible manager adding estimates to the activities for which he or she is responsible.

Some people recommend that activities should be estimated at random rather than in a continuous left-to-right sequence. They argue that estimating sequentially along network paths could lead to early awareness of possible critical activities or programme overruns. In other words, the impartiality of the estimators might become impaired, the estimates being influenced by project demands rather than by the true nature of each job and the time properly required to complete it.

Overtime

Any temptation to assume that overtime will be worked should be avoided, and estimated durations should not be made with overtime working in view. Whilst overtime can often be used to shorten the elapsed time of an activity, it should always be regarded as a reserve resource, to be held back for use as a corrective action against unforeseen (but inevitable) contingencies.

Early consideration of resource constraints and their effect on activity duration

Nothing much has been said so far about possible scarcity of resources and the additional constraints that such problems might impose on the network logic or estimated activity durations.

Consider, for example, the simplest case of a resource constraint, where one particular individual is going to have to perform several network activities single-handed. Assume that this person cannot perform two activities at the same time. The planner, knowing this, might be tempted to add dummies or links to the network to indicate this constraint and prevent any two of these activities from being planned as simultaneous tasks. But if all these activities lie on different paths in a complex network, where should the constraints be placed? Before time analysis has been completed, the planner cannot know in which order all these jobs should be performed.

Similar worries about resources might attach to other activities where the resource requirements are more complex, when several tasks can be allowed to run in parallel or overlap provided that the total resources needed do not exceed the total available.

Fortunately, there is a simple solution to the problem of all such resource constraints. At this stage in the planning, simply ignore them! The purpose of drawing the initial network is to establish the logic of the most desirable work pattern (assuming no resource constraints). Time analysis follows, to establish the amount of float available, which effectively allots priority values to all activities. All of this information provides a sound basis for subsequent resource scheduling, which is a quite separate procedure (described in the following chapters).

Planning and scheduling have to be carried forward one step at a time, and consideration of resource constraints is a step that is not taken when the first network is drawn. However, the planner must use common sense in this respect.

Suppose that an activity requiring skilled fitters has been estimated to require 150 man-hours, and that several people could work on the task if required (without getting in each other's way). The duration for this activity would therefore depend on the number of people assigned. Suppose that the resource/time relationship for this activity is as follows:

●   1 fitter for twenty days
    or
●   2 fitters for ten days
    or
●   3 fitters for seven days
    or
●   4 fitters for five days
    and so on.

The correct approach in these circumstances is for the planner is to ask the manager (or delegate) of the department responsible to say how many fitters would be best for this task, and write the corresponding duration on the network. The possible demands of other activities on these fitters are disregarded at this stage. However, if the company only employs two suitable fitters in total, the planner would be stupid to schedule more than two for this or any other activity. This is where the common sense comes in.

Is the timescale shown too long?

A new network diagram should always be checked to ensure that it reflects the most practicable and efficient way of working. However, it is often found that the first forward pass through an expertly drawn network will predict a completion date that is far too late. The planner will then be under pressure to come up with an alternative shorter plan (which might have to satisfy a delivery promise already made to a customer).

One option is to consider crash actions. This approach was described for the gantry project in Chapter 8. It usually adds costs without adding value to the project, and is to be avoided if possible.

The planner might be tempted to cut estimates arbitrarily, perhaps on the ill-considered advice of other managers, until the work fits neatly into the timescale. That must, of course, never be considered as a valid option unless good reasons can be given showing how the shorter times can be achieved.

A more sensible first course of action is to re-examine the network logic. Are all the constraints shown really constraints? Are all the activities strictly necessary? Could some work be delayed until after initial delivery to the customer? Can any activities be overlapped, so that the start dates of some critical activities are brought forward? Most networks only use simple start–finish relationships, but the experienced planner will always bear in mind the availability of complex precedence constraints and use them in those cases where the project might benefit. When these ideas are used collectively to shorten the project timescale the process is called *fast-tracking*.

If the project duration cannot be shortened sufficiently either by fast-tracking or by crashing alone, the two methods can be combined. What this process might be called is not clear, but the resulting plan will be devoid of float, super-critical, fraught with risk of failure, and will demand meticulous progress control.

A case for drawing networks from right to left

The following case illustrates how a skilled and experienced network planner can control and lead a brainstorming meeting to extract a workable plan from a seemingly hopeless situation. The example also points to a circumstance where it can be better to draw the network from right to left – from finish to start. This is based on a true story which had a happy ending.

Case study

A project had been in progress for several months. Its purpose was to provide prototypes or production models from four related development streams, and assemble them on a stand at a national trade exhibition. The product designs came from different geographical locations in the company, but all were the responsibility of one production management organization, and included the following items:

- prefabricated modular hospital operating theatres
- a range of electronic patient monitoring devices for intensive care purposes
- heart-lung machines and associated equipment
- large steam and gas sterilizers.

The target end date for this project was fixed by the opening date of the exhibition, and was fast approaching. But planning had been a problem because of the coordination needed between different parts of the organization. Indeed, there was no plan at all (let alone a network diagram). The situation had been allowed to drift out of control. The divisional manager therefore called in an experienced network planner, arranged a meeting of all the managers responsible for the various products, and put the network planner in charge.

The planner (let's call her Dorothy) found that no one could say what the current state of progress was. There were so many loose ends that no one knew where to start making a plan. Dorothy asked everyone to concentrate on the end event, with the stand ready for the opening day of the exhibition. This final event was duly drawn at the right-hand end of the network sheet (as a circle in arrow notation). 'I want you to picture the stand just before the exhibition is opened and the visitors pour in', said Dorothy. 'What is the last thing to be done to make the stand ready and presentable?' Slowly, the answer came: 'Vacuum the carpets and generally clean up.' This activity arrow was drawn in front of the final event.

And so the questioning continued, going into more and more detail. The confidence of the members at the meeting grew, and so did the network – from right to left. Duration estimates were added as it went along.

The network continued to expand in a series of logical steps, working through each product to be exhibited in turn, until the diagram finally terminated at the left-hand side in a number of straggling start events. Each start event related to either:

- a particular aspect of the current state of progress
  or
- an activity that had not previously been thought of (indeed, if this network had not been drawn backwards, these forgotten activities would have been remembered too late or not at all).

Now everyone knew exactly:

- the current state of progress
- the tasks remaining, and their sequence
- the time needed, and which jobs were most critical.

There was now a detailed plan from which to issue and progress the remaining work. By adapting the planning tactics to suit the particular project case, order was retrieved from chaos. The exhibition did open on time, with all the products displayed on the stand.

Network analysis as a management tool

Network analysis demands the application of sound common sense, and very little else. When the techniques were first introduced they were regarded with suspicion by many, and tended to be protected by an elitist mystique. That was unfortunate and unnecessary. The elements of network notation are simple. Although a project network can contain thousands of activities, all the basic notation is demonstrated by the simple examples that were shown in Chapter 8.

No special degree of intelligence is required. Anyone with a fair share of mental aptitude could be expected to acquire at least a working knowledge of logic diagram preparation in just one day. However, the method of teaching is all-important; the premature introduction of all but the basic bones of the system must be avoided. It is also sensible to start by practising, to gain competence in using the notation, getting the logic right, and time analysing small networks mentally. All of this should take place before going on to use a computer and more advanced procedures such as cost and resource scheduling.

Those who choose to go through project life in ignorance of the finer points of networking language may find themselves at some disadvantage if called upon to discuss network problems with their more erudite colleagues. Every profession has its own technical language, and without it communication must suffer. Nevertheless, critical path techniques can be applied very effectively by anybody with a grasp of the logical concepts involved. Basic network analysis is a simple but valuable management tool which should never be regarded as a complicated and advanced technique reserved for the specialist.

There is always a danger of trying to be too clever by dotting every 'i' and crossing every 't'. Planning is not a precise technique, and networks will be more effective if they can be kept as simple as possible, although incorporating all the essential activities and constraints. It is very probable that attempts to improve existing techniques arise not because the techniques themselves are inadequate, but because the planners are not able to exploit them properly.

The benefits to be derived from drawing a network are in themselves often worthwhile, even if no duration estimates are made, no time analysis takes place, and the network is not used to control subsequent progress. Networking encourages logical thinking and planning. A network meeting can be regarded as a very productive form of brainstorming. Not only does the notation allow expression of all inter-activity dependencies and relationships, but there is also the important possibility that activities may be brought to light that might otherwise have been excluded from schedules, estimates and (most important) pricing.

It would be unreasonable and unrealistic to expect the project manager to carry out network planning (or any other kind of planning) in isolation. The project manager must be able to count on the support and cooperation of members from every department in the organization. This applies not only to the initial planning session, but also to all subsequent discussions and progress monitoring and network updating. This support will only be possible if suitable training has been provided. Most important of all, encouragement and support must come from the top, from the company's senior management. Once the idea of project planning and control by networks has been accepted throughout the organization, the battle will largely have been won.

Chapter 10

Scheduling resources, Part 1: Principles

Resource scheduling is a complex subject that can be viewed from a number of different standpoints. At the strategic level it can be seen as an important element in formulating the long-range plans of companies. In this book, the subject is treated from the point of view of the project manager, who is more likely to be concerned with the shorter-term operations of the business. However, the techniques described here for project resource management cannot be regarded in isolation from the longer-term strategy, since project and other working schedules contribute vital information to the higher-level strategic planning process.

There are arguments (not discussed here in detail) concerning the attitude of company management to the stability of its workforce. In an organization that cherishes a stable labour force, with job security and long-term career development high on the list of its perceived staff motivators, resource scheduling can be seen as the process of identifying the resources available to the project organization, and then attempting to deploy those resources as efficiently as possible to achieve the business objectives. The number of organizations which take that approach appears to have decreased in recent years. More companies now start by examining or re-examining the needs of the organization, and then match their staff numbers accordingly (which can mean ruthless 'downsizing').

Resource management can also be looked at in other ways, depending on the nature of the business and on management attitudes. In those industries with a high proportion of casual labour, or which subcontract large elements of their work, detailed in-house resource scheduling can usually be confined to the relatively few permanent headquarters staff. Even in those industries, however, some knowledge of future resource requirements is desirable, so that subcontractors can be forewarned for instance.

An organization that handles projects using its own permanent engineering and manufacturing or construction workforce will need to take resource scheduling very seriously. It will have to calculate detailed working schedules that satisfy not only the needs of each individual project, but also the combined effect of all work on the organization's total resource pool. The possible effects of predicted new work must be tested, preferably using 'what-if?' modelling. Information must be gathered on the longer-term work requirements of the organization, so that facilities can be planned and provided for the future expected workload.

What are resources, and which of them can be scheduled?

A project resource is any person, object, tool, machine or sum of money needed for work on a project. Resources can be categorized in several ways, and it is interesting to start by identifying three main classes (the definitions are my own).

Exhaustible resources

Once an exhaustible resource has been used, it is no longer available for use on a project. Replenishment is physically impossible.

Time is the most important exhaustible resource. Time is truly exhaustible. Once spent, it has gone for ever, and can never be renewed. Time is a very special resource needing its own techniques for planning and scheduling. These range from the simple day-to-day diary to the charting and critical path methods described in the preceding chapters.

Fossil fuels (such as coal, oil and natural gas) and mineral deposits (like the ores used in mining) are exhaustible resources. Once the deposits in a particular region have been used up, they cannot be replaced, and the life cycle of the project that exploited them must end.

Exhaustible resources feature in project feasibility and strategic studies and in total life cycle analysis, but (with the exception of time) they do not generally feature in project resource scheduling, and are not considered further in this book.

Replenishable resources

Materials and components obtained through purchasing are replenishable resources. Although stocks of these resources might become exhausted when they are built into a project, they can usually be replenished by buying fresh supplies. The principal methods for scheduling materials come within the realm of stock control and purchasing, but information from project planning provides the control framework for purchasers and stock controllers by stating how much will be needed and when.

Although not considered specifically in this chapter, agricultural crops and their products are replenishable resources. However, they may not all be replenishable in the short term (timber, for example).

Some project management programs can schedule replenishable resources directly, if required. This scheduling might include, for instance, the phasing of materials deliveries to a construction site so that the quantities on site match the rate of progress expected from the project critical path network.

Money, especially when it is scarce, might be regarded by some as an exhaustible resource. Strictly, however, it *is* replenishable. There are many examples of projects where the sponsors have been persuaded to provide more money for an ailing project rather than see it and their initial investment sink into oblivion. As with materials, project management data can determine how much cash will be needed, and when. Cash flow predictions are a form of project resource scheduling, and all competent project management software can be used to generate cash flow schedules.

Re-usable resources

Re-usable resources are assets that are required for use on project work but which remain available for re-use after each task has been performed. They can be compared to catalysts in a chemical reaction: they are necessary to promote the reaction, but at the end they emerge unchanged. Levels of re-usable resources tend to remain fairly stable over the longer term. They might, however, be scarce, in which case their use requires careful planning and scheduling.

People, with their particular skills and aptitudes, are the most common type of re-usable resource. Some might claim that they do not emerge from a project unchanged, but (age apart) they should be available for work on consecutive projects. In a typical organization it is the direct workers rather than the indirect staff (management infrastructure) who have to be scheduled. If, for example, there are only ten people capable of engineering design in a company, it is desirable to schedule the issue of tasks to those people at a rate that never requires more than ten of them at the same time. The process of arriving at such schedules is variously called *resource scheduling, resource levelling* or *resource allocation*. Most of the techniques described in this book are concerned with that particular aspect of resource scheduling. Computer programs can calculate these schedules using data derived from critical path networks.

Industrial plant and machinery, other manufacturing facilities, test centres and so on can also be considered and treated as re-usable resources. Although people and machines are very different resources, the same techniques and computer programs can be used to schedule them, provided that their use can be categorized by a simple code and their quantity can be specified in straightforward units.

Factory or office space is, of course, a re-usable resource. However, its use is difficult to schedule with project management software because one usually has to consider not only the number of space units (square metres or square feet), but also the shape of the space and, sometimes, also its volume. In heavy machine tool engineering projects, for example, machines set up for pre-shipment testing might have to be positioned in the assembly and test bay according to their height and foundation requirements, and it might be necessary to save space by allowing for some machines from different projects to overhang each other. Project management software is not usually capable of dealing with these aspects of scheduling. In practice, the solutions are best left to production engineers (for factory space) or facilities managers (for office space). They would use floor plans or three-dimensional models, either with or without the aid of a computer.

The role of network analysis in resource scheduling

A network cannot be used by itself to demonstrate the volume of resources needed at any given point in project time. In fact, when the network is drawn no considered account can be taken of the resources which will be available. The start of each activity is usually assumed to be dependent only upon the completion of its preceding activities, and not on the availability of resources at the right time.

Naturally, if a planning team knows that, for the sake of argument, a total of four pipefitters are employed in the project organization, they would not estimate the duration of any pipefitting activity at a level which demands the employment of more than four pipefitters on that activity. However, the chance of other pipefitting activities occurring elsewhere in the network at the same time is impossible to deal with when the network is being drawn, because the timing of those other activities cannot be known before the network has been completely drawn and time analysis has been carried out.

In general, therefore, network logic shows only those constraints between activities that are related to the logical, preferred sequence of working. Thus, although a network should be fine in logical theory, it is not always possible in practice to start all activities at their earliest possible times. In fact, if too many tasks clamour for too few resources it might be impossible to carry out the project in the time indicated by the critical path.

This is far from saying that work spent in preparing a critical path network has been wasted, even if resource limitations do cause the earliest possible start times of some activities to appear impracticable. Network construction and time analysis must be seen as the first essential step in the wider process of scheduling resources. Resource constraints are treated as a separate issue, requiring at least one more stage of scheduling after the determination of float and location of the critical path.

Allocating priorities according to float

The results of network time analysis determine activity priorities. When different activities compete simultaneously for the same limited resources, priority rules can be applied so that the resources are allocated where they are most needed. Usually, the activity with least float is given the highest priority.

Case study: Garage project

The principles and some of the problems of resource scheduling can be introduced by considering a simple construction project. Manual methods (as opposed to the use of a computer) are described first, because these demonstrate the underlying processes and provide a useful introduction to the more advanced methods covered in Chapters 12, 13 and 14.

Garage project definition

A small firm of builders has been commissioned to erect a detached garage. The building is to be constructed of brick, with a corrugated sheet roof. This roof will incorporate some transparent sheets as roof lights instead of windows. The doors are to be timber-framed and hung on strap hinges. No heavy lifting is involved in this project, and no activity needs more than two people.

Resources available

The building firm engaged on the garage project is a very tiny outfit, comprising the not unusual father-and-son team. The father, no longer capable of sustained heavy work, is nevertheless a good all-round craftsman with long experience. The son, on the other hand, can best be described as a strong, willing lad, sound in wind and limb but lacking any special experience or skill. This firm's resource availability can therefore be listed as follows:

- Skilled persons – 1
- Labourers – 1

Network diagram for the garage project

Figure 10.1 shows the network diagram for this project. For comparison, this is given in both its arrow and precedence versions. For simplicity, the plan assumes that all materials and construction plant will be on site when needed. The number of activities that can be shown clearly on a book page is limited so, for clarity of illustration, activities allowing time for paint to dry or for concrete to cure have not been included.

All the activity durations have been estimated in days, and assume the small labour force already described (one skilled all-round craftsman and one labourer).

When the network was drawn, no consideration was given to any competition for these very limited resources that might be caused by the possibility of two or more activities requiring them at the same time. The planner knew that any such problems would be resolved in a subsequent separate resource scheduling exercise.

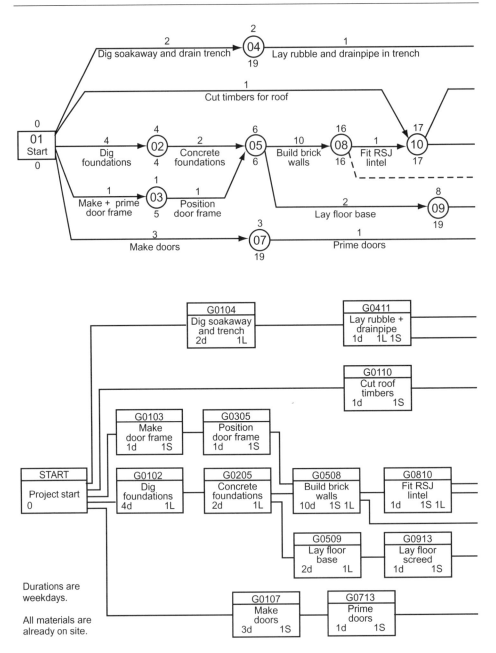

Figure 10.1   Garage project: Network diagram

Follow the garage project case study using either the arrow diagram or its identical precedence counterpart.

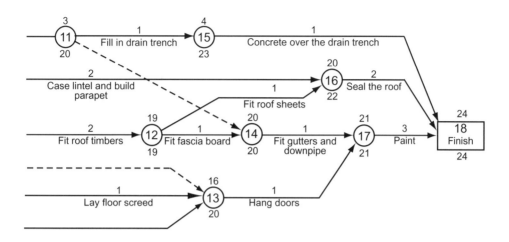

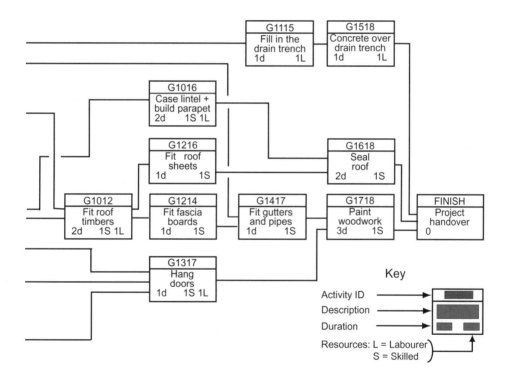

Figure 10.1   *continued*

Time analysis and the calendar

The results of time analysis for the garage project network are given in Figure 10.2, which also provides the task list. If unlimited resources could be used, so that all the earliest possible dates could be achieved, the whole project should take 24 working days. But there is no direct indication from the network or its time analysis of how many craftsmen and labourers would be needed to achieve this result.

All times refer to *close of work* on the given days. Thus an activity scheduled to finish on (for example) day 8, means that it should be finished at close of work on day 8. A job scheduled to start on day 8 means that it could start at the *end* of day 8, which, in practice, really means the *beginning* of day 9.

This rule can be explained best by reference to the arrow diagram in Figure 10.1. A network event (as opposed to an activity) occupies no time itself and its achievement takes place at the instant when all its preceding activities have been completed. Subsequent activities can start at the same instant. Activity 01–02 (dig foundations) starts at time 0, which is the end of an imaginary day 0 or, in reality, the *beginning* of day 1 (the intervening night hours are not recognized as existing by the computer). The estimated duration of activity 01–02 is four working days, which means that its earliest possible completion is at the *end* of day 4. Event 02 therefore takes place at the close of work on day 4. The next activity, 02–05 (concrete foundations) can therefore start on day 4, but that means the *end* of day 4. In practice, therefore, activity 02–05 would not start until the *beginning* of day 5.

Bar chart

Because we are not using a computer in this introductory case, the first step in determining the labour requirements is to convert the network diagram into a bar chart. Figure 10.3 shows the initial result for this project, with every task placed at its earliest possible time.

Please picture the bar chart in Figure 10.3 as having been set up on a wallboard, using strips that plug into holes on a grid pattern, or are otherwise attached so that they can be moved sideways to adjust the schedule as required. Each bar represents an activity on the network, with its length scaled according to the activity's estimated duration.

The bars are coded according to the type of resource needed, black indicating a skilled person and grey for a labourer. Where an activity needs both a skilled person and a labourer, black and grey bars have been drawn side by side.

No activity needs more than one skilled person or more than one labourer.

Prec. event	Succ. event	Activity identifier	Activity description	Duration (days)	Earliest start	Latest start	Earliest finish	Latest finish	Total float	Resources
		START	Project start	0	0	0	0	0	0	
01	02	G0102	Dig foundations	4	0	0	4	4	0	1L
02	05	G0205	Concrete foundations	2	4	4	6	6	0	1L
01	03	G0103	Make and prime door frame	1	0	4	1	5	4	1S
03	05	G0305	Position door frame	1	1	5	2	6	4	1S
05	08	G0508	Build brick walls	10	6	6	16	16	0	1S 1L
08	10	G0810	Fit RSJ lintel over doors	1	16	16	17	17	0	1S 1L
01	10	G0110	Cut roof support timbers	1	0	16	1	17	16	1S
10	16	G1016	Case the lintel and build parapet	2	17	20	19	22	3	1S 1L
10	12	G1012	Fit the roof support timbers	2	17	17	19	19	0	1S 1L
12	14	G1214	Fit fascia boards for gutters	1	19	19	20	20	0	1S
12	16	G1216	Fit roof sheets	1	19	21	20	22	2	1S
01	04	G0104	Dig soakaway and trench for pipe	2	0	17	2	19	17	1L
04	11	G0411	Lay rubble and drainpipe to soakaway	1	2	19	3	20	17	1S 1L
11	15	G1115	Fill in the drain trench	1	3	22	4	23	19	1L
15	18	G1518	Concrete over the drain trench	1	4	23	5	24	19	1L
05	09	G0509	Lay concrete floor base	2	6	17	8	19	11	1L
09	13	G0913	Lay floor screed	1	8	19	9	20	11	1S
01	07	G0107	Make the doors	3	0	16	3	19	16	1S
07	13	G0713	Prime the doors	1	3	19	4	20	16	1S
13	17	G1317	Hang the doors and fit locks	1	16	20	17	21	4	1S 1L
17	18	G1718	Paint all woodwork	3	21	21	24	24	0	1S
14	17	G1417	Fit gutters and downpipe	1	20	20	21	21	0	1S
16	18	G1618	Seal the roof	2	20	22	22	24	2	1S
		FINISH	Hand project over to customer	0	24	24	24	24	0	

ADM only: Prec. event, Succ. event
PDM only: Activity identifier

Figure 10.2   Garage project: Task list and time analysis

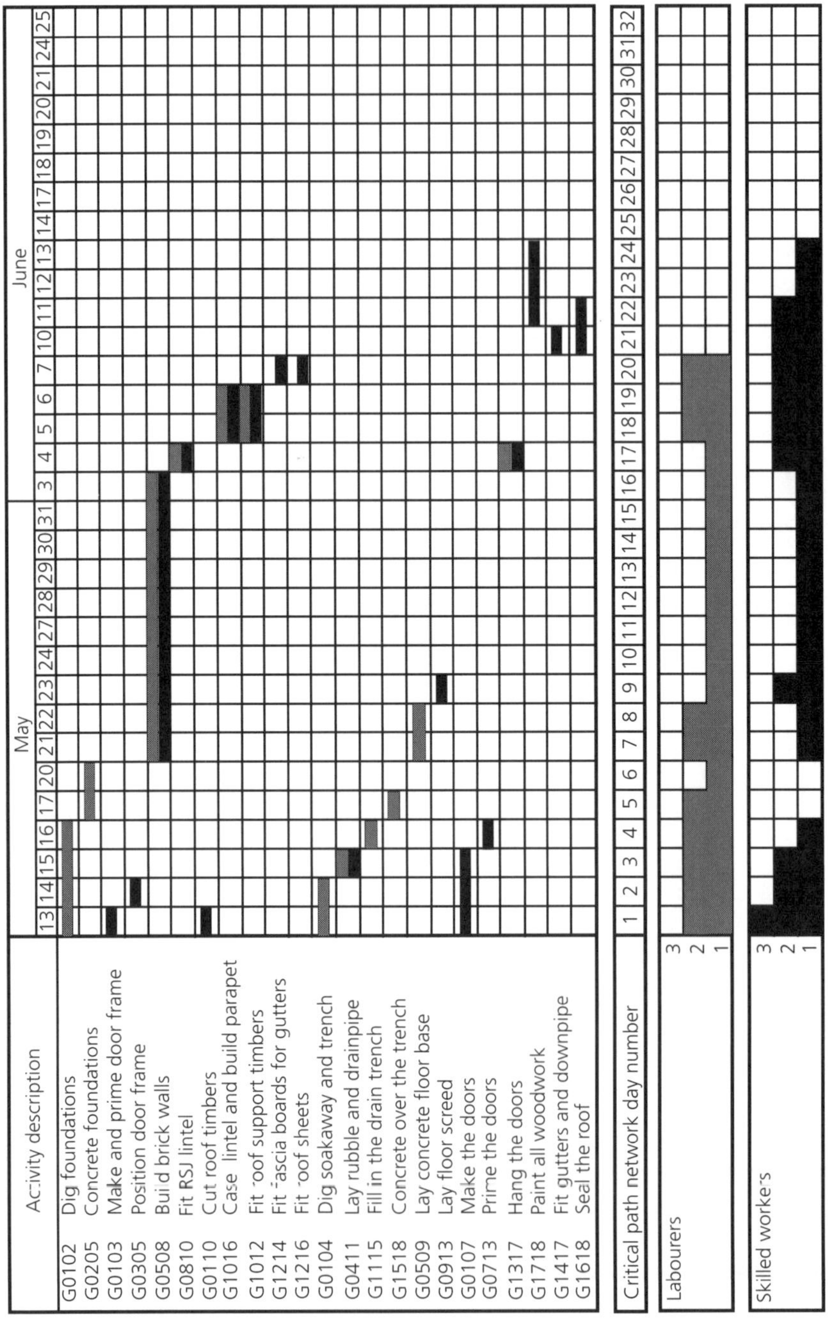

Figure 10.3   Garage project: Bar chart and resource histogram – aggregation
All activities are placed at their earliest starts, giving an unacceptable resource usage pattern.

Calendar and timescale details

The garage project timescale starts at the beginning of 13 May, and network day numbers have been converted into calendar dates for the working schedule. These conversions are valid for the year 2002, and would also apply to 2013. The project calendar has been arranged with no weekend working so that only weekday dates are valid for scheduling. Saturdays and Sundays simply do not exist for the purposes of this schedule. Public holidays have been ignored for simplicity.

The schedule in Figure 10.3 shows that the earliest possible completion date for this project is 13 June. Saturday mornings (not shown on the chart) could be considered as time to be held in reserve against unforeseen contingencies. Evening overtime is another possible reserve resource. However, these possible additional working hours are hidden reserves and must not be built into the initial plan.

Resource scheduling for the garage project

Simple resource aggregation

Each activity on the bar chart in Figure 10.3 is shown starting at its earliest possible time. No thought has yet been given to the resources needed, and it is now time to start putting that right. The resources needed each day to carry out this simple plan are easy to calculate. It is only necessary to add up the number of times a strip of each code occurs in each day's column.

The planned total daily resource requirements are entered at the foot of the chart, as a histogram in our example. The result is, to say the least, unsatisfactory. On some days the workers are expected to be idle; on other days three people will be needed where only one is available. The workload is unbalanced, showing too many peaks and troughs for profitable comfort.

The reason for this uneven schedule is that the planner has shown every job starting at its earliest possible date, regardless of need or priority. Such a plan is known as *resource-aggregated* and it has little practical use except as a step towards obtaining a more practicable *resource-allocated* schedule.

The important principle missed in Figure 10.3 is that many of the jobs are known from time analysis to have float, and the starts of these activities could therefore be delayed to smooth the workload without extending the end date. Using the adjustable wallchart, therefore, it should be possible to reschedule non-critical activities to remove some or all of the unwanted workload peaks.

Resource-limited schedule

If the garage project is to be carried out solely by the father-and-son team, it is obvious that the schedule displayed in Figure 10.3 cannot be implemented. The schedule must be rearranged so that the modest resources available are not double-booked. Using the adjustable chart, the activities can be shuffled around until no column total exceeds the number of people available. When this shuffling is carried out, however, the logic of the network from which the bar chart was constructed must be remembered, and all the constraints between different activities must still be observed.

Figure 10.4 shows the bar chart for the garage project after levelling to produce a resource-limited schedule (see Figure 10.8). The resulting workload histogram is given at the foot of the chart. Project completion has been delayed from 13 June to 26 June. Imposing the resource-limited constraint has therefore extended the timescale by nine working days plus the additional intervening weekend days. However, there is now a smooth resource schedule, perfect for the company because there are almost no idle days and no unwelcome peaks.

Time-limited resource levelling for the garage project

The new resource-limited schedule, although ideal for the contractor, may not be so acceptable to the customer. She is expecting delivery of an expensive new car, and wants to be able to garage it safely. If the new garage cannot be promised in time, the customer may decide, not unreasonably, to look for another contractor.

In these circumstances, several courses of action are open to the small builder. These include the following:

1   Work to the resource-limited timescale of 33 days (Figure 10.4), but make a false promise to the customer that the garage will still be ready and handed over on 13 June. Making such false promises can never be recommended, for commercial as well as for moral reasons.
2   Tell the customer that the project cannot be finished by 13 June – and lose the order as a penalty for telling the unvarnished truth.
3   Revert to the original resource-aggregated schedule shown in Figure 10.3, and take on additional workers, regardless of cost, in order to finish the project in 24 working days.
4   Plan to complete the project within the required 24 working days, accept that additional workers will be needed, but review and adjust the resource-aggregated schedule in an attempt to smooth the workload into a more cost-effective pattern.

Option 4 is one that is commonly taken in project scheduling, and it will work well for the garage project. Remember that this rescheduling of activities can only take place within the constraints imposed by the network logic, so that no activity may be started before all its predecessors have been achieved. Further, if the overall project timescale is not to be extended, no activity may be rescheduled to start later than its latest permissible start time, as determined by network time analysis (shown in Figure 10.2). This means that non-critical activities can be delayed within the float which they possess. Critical activities have zero float, and must therefore always be scheduled to start at their earliest possible times.

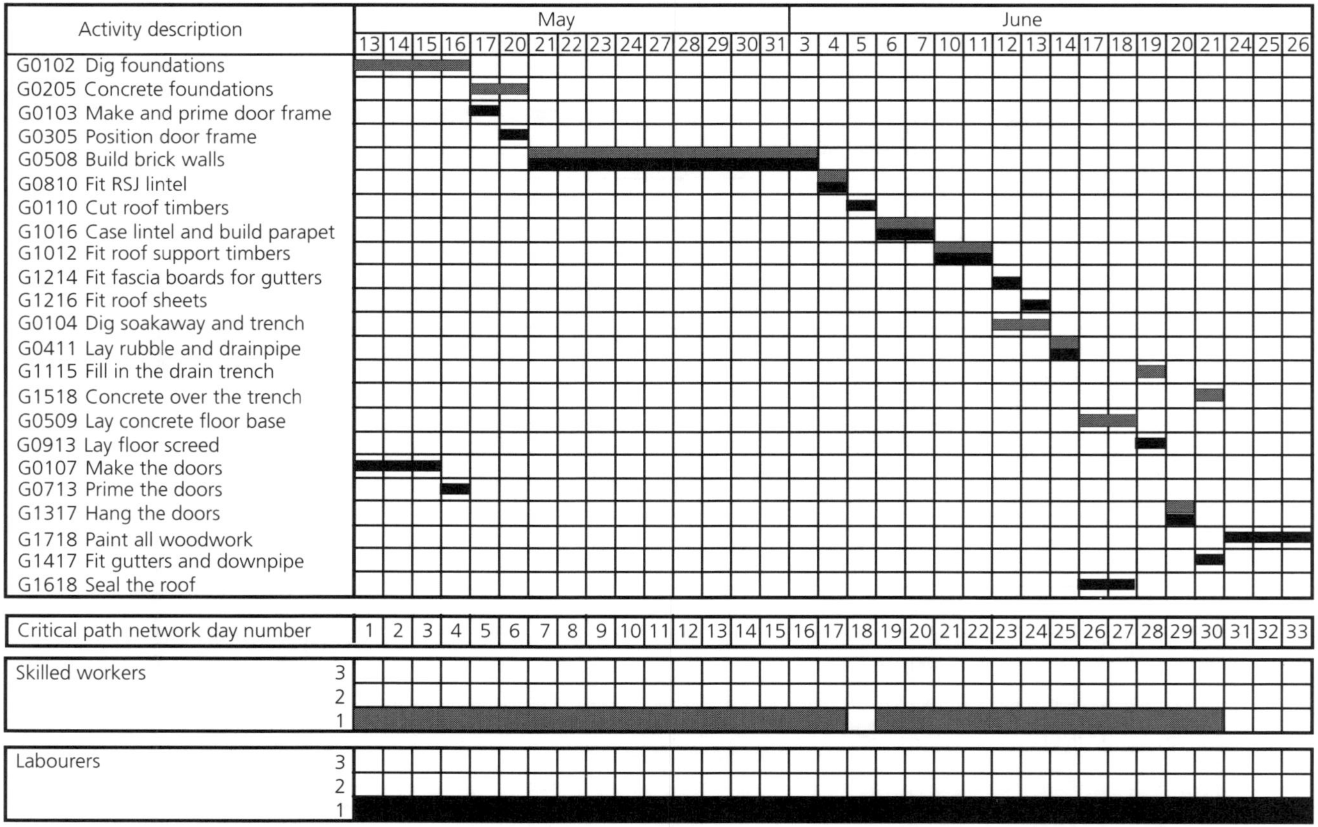

Figure 10.4   Garage project: Bar chart and resource histogram – resource-limited

Tasks have been rescheduled to avoid resource overloads, but this has extended the time needed for the project.

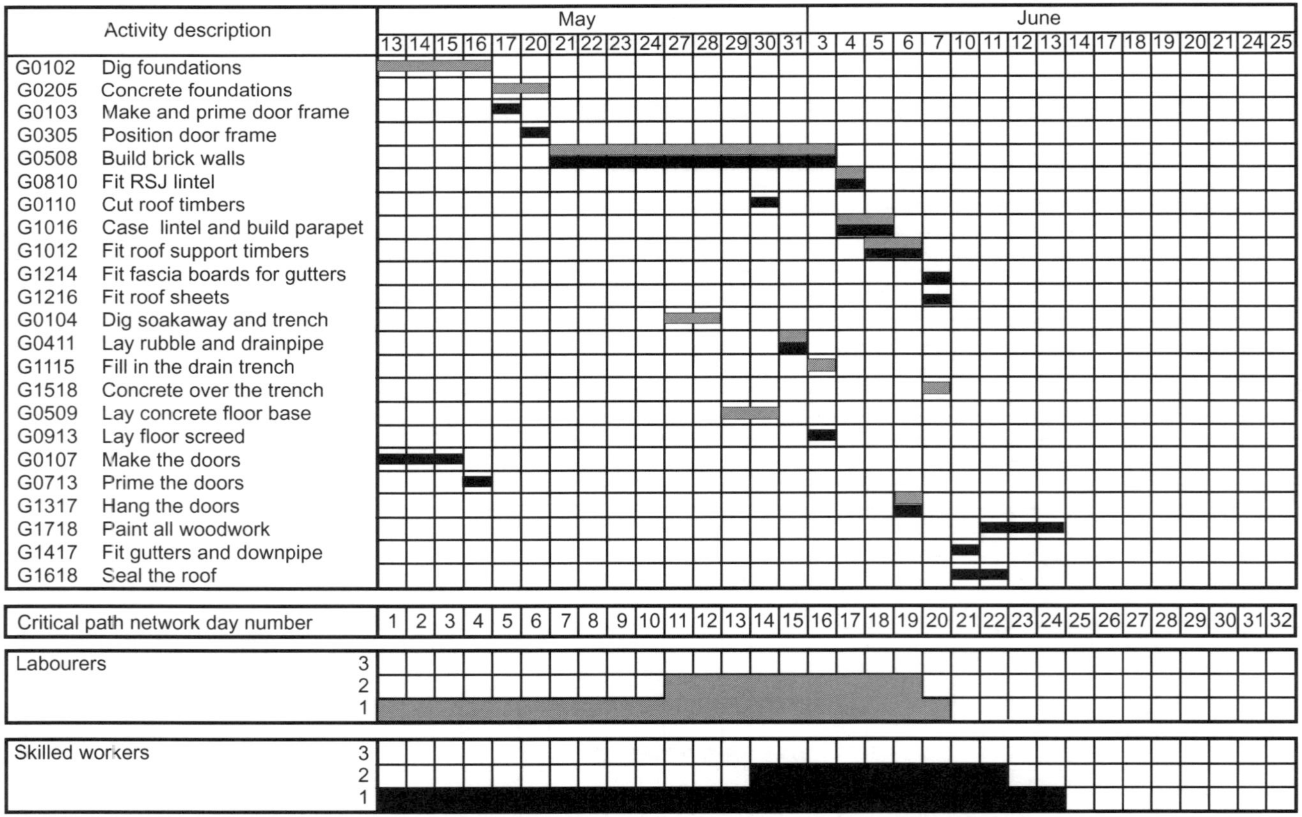

Figure 10.5   Garage project: Bar chart and resource histogram – time-limited

Tasks have been scheduled with time as the priority. Although additional resources are needed, the load pattern has been smoothed to remove uneconomic peaks and troughs. Compare this result with Figure 10.3.

Figure 10.5 is the rescheduled bar chart. The resource histogram at the foot of the chart shows that it is possible to reschedule the project over 24 working days with a resource usage pattern that is far smoother than aggregation, needing only one additional person of each skill category.

Float

The concept of 'float' and the specific definitions for its possible variations are sometimes difficult to comprehend. Since one of the more practical applications of float is found during the resource-scheduling process, it is convenient to illustrate and define float in some detail at this point. The network for the garage project (Figure 10.1) will provide a suitable case for study.

The illustrations in this section are supported by both precedence and arrow network references.

Activity identifiers in the following text are given first for the precedence diagram, followed by their arrow equivalents in brackets.

First consider activity G0913 (09–13), 'Lay floor screed'. For clarity, this activity has been extracted from the main network and is shown as a separate detail in Figure 10.6. Although this diagram has isolated the activity from the network, all the data relative to float are shown. These include the earliest and latest times for both the preceding and succeeding events, and the estimated duration of the activity. A glance at the network fragment shows that the earliest possible start for this activity is (the end of) day 8. The latest permissible finish is day 20.

Allowing for the one day's duration of this activity, it is easy to see that its start (and finish) could be delayed by up to 11 days without causing delay to the activities that follow. This 11 days is the total float possessed by the activity.

If, because of delays in the project or through intentional resource scheduling, the floor screed operation takes place later than its earliest possible time, some (if not all) of its float will be eroded. This will usually have a knock-on effect through the network, robbing some of the float from activities which follow, because they can no longer be started at their earliest possible times.

In fact, the float for any activity must always be seen in relation to how it is likely to affect, or be affected by, the float possessed by other activities in the network. Consideration of these effects gives rise to definitions for various types of float. These definitions will now be given, but it is not necessary to be conversant with all of them.

Before the start of a project, planners and project managers are generally most concerned with *total float*. From the time when resource scheduling starts, and throughout the active life of the project, the focus is on *remaining float*.

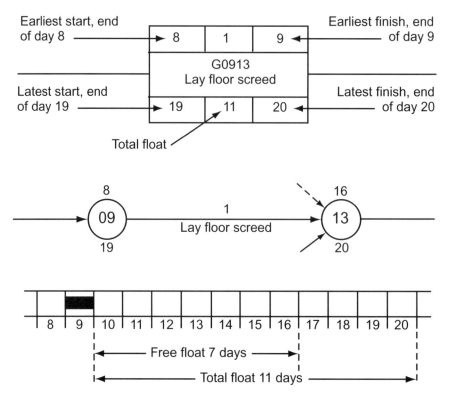

Figure 10.6　　**Garage project: Float analysis of activity G0913 (09–13)**

Total float

Total float is defined as the amount by which an activity can be delayed if all its preceding activities take place at their earliest possible times and following activities can be allowed to wait until their latest permissible times.

Although the total float for activity G0913 (09–13) in Figure 10.6 happened to be equal to the difference between this activity's earliest and latest preceding event times, this cannot always be taken as a reliable guide to the amount of total float available for any activity. This will become apparent by studying another activity from the garage project.

In Figure 10.7, another activity from the garage project, activity G1016 (10–16), 'Case lintel and build parapets', has been isolated and subjected to special analysis. Please refer first to the arrow diagram fragment.

It is seen that event 10 has equal early and late times (17), which should indicate zero float and a critical activity. However, those times apply only to the event, and not to all activities passing through it. Although event 10 lies on the critical path, the path branches at this event and a glance at the whole network in Figure 10.1 shows that the critical path actually misses activity G1016 (10-16).

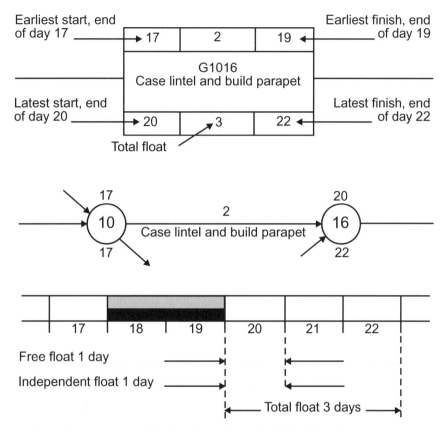

Figure 10.7 **Garage project: Float analysis of activity G1016 (10–16)**

Activity G1016 (10–16) does indeed possess float. The example in Figure 10.7 shows how the precedence notation allows space for the true detail to be shown.

The actual float conditions are illustrated best in the segment of bar chart included in Figure 10.7. It is apparent from this diagram that, using the formal definition, the total float for activity G1016 (10–16) is three days. It is not difficult to calculate this float when the bar chart segment and activity in Figure 10.7 are compared.

> Total float = latest permissible end event time
> *minus*   the earliest possible start-event time
> *minus*   the activity duration

Applying the data from Figure 10.7 to this formula:

$$\text{Total float of activity G1016 (10–16)} = (22–17 – 2) = 3 \text{ days}$$

Free float

Returning to the network diagram in Figure 10.1, suppose that the floor screed activity G0913 (09–13) must be delayed by one or two days owing to the absence of available workmen at the right time. The network shows that the following activity G1317 (13–17), 'Hang doors', cannot in any case start before day 16 because of the restriction imposed by the link from G0508 (dummy from event 08 in the arrow version). This means that completion of the floor screed activity could be delayed from the end of day 9 to as late as the end of day 16 before any ill effect would be caused to its following activities. This float (7 days) is termed the free float of activity G0913 (09–13). However, although any change to the activity within this free float cannot affect following activities, the free float will be eroded if any preceding events are allowed to run later than their earliest possible dates.

Free float is therefore defined as the amount of float available when all preceding activities take place at their earliest possible times and following activities can still take place at their earliest possible times:

> Free float = the earliest possible end-event time
> *minus*   the earliest possible start-event time
> *minus*   the activity duration

Applying the data from Figure 10.6 to this formula:

> Free float of activity G0913 (09–13) = (16 – 8 – 1) = 7 days

Independent float

Now consider activity G1016 (10–16) once again (as shown in Figure 10.7). Notice that it is possible to shuffle this activity around over a one-day period, whatever happens to the schedule for all other network activities. It matters not whether the preceding events are allowed to run up to their latest permissible times, or whether the following events must start at their earliest possible times. This activity can be moved backwards and forwards within one day before any other activity is affected. Because it is entirely independent of all surrounding activities, this small amount of float is called *independent float*.

Defined formally, independent float is the amount of float available when all preceding activities take place at their latest permissible times, and all following activities can still take place at their earliest possible times. The mathematical expression for independent float is as follows:

> Independent float = the earliest possible end-event time
> *minus*   the latest permissible start-event time
> *minus*   the activity duration

Using the data from Figure 10.7 once more:

Independent float of activity G1016 (10–16) = (20 – 17 – 2) = 1 day

The incidence of independent float is rare. Usually, when the above formula is applied to any activity in a network, the result is zero.

Remaining float

The total float possessed by any activity is at risk of erosion from the moment project resource scheduling starts right up to the time when the activity is actually completed. Total float can be reduced, for example, as a result of a conscious decision to delay the planned start of an activity as part of the resource scheduling process (in order to achieve a smoother workload plan). There is also the risk that preceding activities will run late, absorbing some or all of the total float previously possessed by the current activity.

For practical purposes, once a project is started the project manager is not interested in the total float that an activity had in the beginning, when the network was first drawn. It is the residue of the total float still possessed by each uncompleted activity that should concern the project manager. This is the *remaining float*.

Activities with zero remaining float

Activities which have zero remaining float have become critical activities. They should claim priority for resources and for management attention to ensure they are finished without delay, otherwise the project completion must itself be delayed.

Activities with negative float

Suppose that the critical path through a network has a total estimated duration of 100 weeks. The end activity will therefore have an earliest possible completion time of 100 weeks. Barring other considerations, the latest permissible completion time for the project will also be at the end of the 100th week. Time analysis will, in the usual way, produce one or more critical paths back through to the start of the network in which all the critical activities have zero total float. Suppose, however, that those 'other considerations' include a promise to the customer that the project will be completed in 90 weeks. The latest permissible project end date is therefore 10 weeks before its earliest possible date. All activities that were previously on the critical path with zero total float will now have a total float of minus 10 weeks.

Negative float can be caused whenever scheduled target dates are imposed on the end activity, or indeed on any other activity in a project network.

Negative float will appear in any schedule (especially in computer reports) where it is impossible to achieve scheduled target dates for the following reasons:

1   The shortest possible duration of the relevant path through the network to an activity bearing an imposed target date is longer than the time allowed by the target date (that is, an impossible target has been set).
2   Delayed progress prevents one or more activities being finished by their latest permissible finish dates.
3   Activities have to be delayed beyond their latest permissible dates because resources are inadequate.

Needless to say, activities with negative float have become hypercritical. Prompt management action is essential to attempt to expedite them and rescue the project.

Two fundamental priority rules for resource scheduling

The approach to resource scheduling must usually be governed by the choice between two planning options or priority rules: namely, whether the schedule should be resource-limited or time-limited. These options occurred in the garage project earlier in this chapter, but they require further explanation. The choice between these two rules must be made whenever there is a clash between meeting a project-completion date and finding the necessary resources.

Figure 10.8 is a graphical illustration of the resource- and time-limited concepts. The balloon represents a project, which should be imagined as an incompressible fluid of constant volume being squeezed between the two main constraints of time and resources.

Resource-limited scheduling

Resource-limited scheduling results in a plan that never exceeds the declared levels of available resources. This often means accepting a project end date that is later than the earliest possible date predicted from network time analysis. In other words, working within available resource levels is seen as the first scheduling objective, with secondary priority for completing the project in the shortest possible time. This condition is shown in the upper diagram in Figure 10.8.

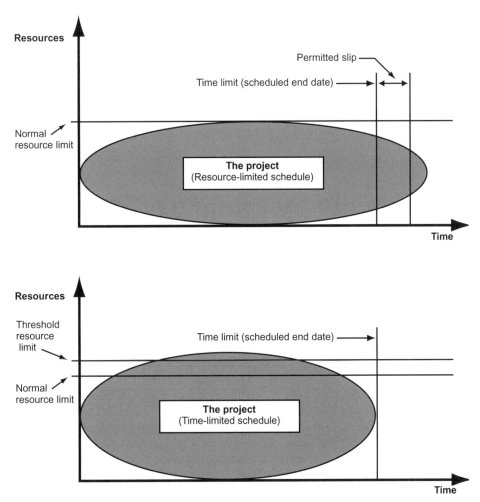

Figure 10.8   Time-limited versus resource-limited priority rules for resource scheduling

Time-limited scheduling

If the completion time is the paramount objective, the planning procedure must be time-limited. The overriding objective in this case is to ensure that the project can be scheduled for completion by a specified date. This date is often the earliest possible completion date indicated by network time analysis (the duration of the critical path), but it might be some slightly later target date.

Time-limited scheduling means that any predicted resource overloads must be accepted, probably on the assumption that these can be made good by hiring subcontract labour or by making other suitable short-term resource arrangements. Even though resource constraints are seen as having secondary priority in a time-limited schedule, the planner should still aim at a smooth resource-usage pattern, avoiding unnecessary interruptions, peaks and troughs in the workload patterns of all the project resources. The time-limited condition is depicted in the lower half of Figure 10.8.

Methods for easing the resource and time restrictions

If either strict resource-limitation or time-limitation fail to produce an acceptable schedule, it might be necessary either to breach the limits or, alternatively, attempt to ease them to allow a compromise solution.

Using threshold resources to extend the resource availability limit

Sometimes it is possible to consider a second tier, or 'threshold' level of a particular resource, to be used in schedules only when all the normally available resources have been allocated to activities, and when the project timescale would otherwise be at risk. An example would be an engineering department with a declared resource strength of 75 permanent staff employees, where the engineering manager knows that an additional 30 engineers could be made available from various subcontract agencies.

When a computer is used for scheduling with threshold resources available, it first attempts to generate a schedule that only uses the normally available resources. The additional resources are only brought into play when the computer is unable to schedule an activity without exceeding the stated amount, or 'threshold', of normally available resources. The schedule might still exceed the target completion date, but at least the use of threshold resources can take some of the strain, as shown in the lower part of Figure 10.8.

In the case of the engineering department, the engineering manager would receive a computer report showing how many of the 30 subcontract people are expected to be needed, with the dates. This should enable the manager to negotiate with the subcontract agencies well in advance for the supply of the additional engineering staff. It would also give the company time in which to arrange for the hire of any necessary accommodation and equipment for them. This is another example taken from real life, where the system worked efficiently, prevented last-minute panics, and allowed plenty of time for seeking subcontracted staff and facilities from the most cost-effective sources.

Specifying alternative resources

It sometimes happens that the start of an activity has to be delayed because the specified resource is not free, although another type of resource exists in the project organization that could be substituted. This state of affairs could occur, for example, in an engineering office. It might be that a specialist in electronic engineering also has skills in control and lubrication design. Some computer programs allow the planner to specify such alternative resources in the initial plan, so that the computer can take advantage of their availability in time of need.

Allowing project end-slip

Some computer software allows the planner to declare an element of acceptable project slip, beyond the preferred target completion date. The computer is then able to make use of this extra time if – but *only* if – resource limits would otherwise be exceeded in a time-limited scheduling calculation. Such end-slip is not counted during time analysis, and float is still calculated from the normal end of the project. Thus if, for instance, a slip period of eight weeks is allowed after the last project activity, the calculated critical path length will exclude this eight weeks: otherwise eight weeks of artificial float would be created to give everyone involved on the project a false sense of security. In the top part of Figure 10.8 the computer has not been able to contain the project within the permitted slip, and the project is scheduled to end late because of the resource limitations.

Summary: The elements of a practicable schedule

An example of how not to schedule

An engineering director I once knew called for a departmental plan, drawn on a sheet of paper covering a long reference table, which was supposed to allocate 30 engineers (identified by their names) to jobs from several projects (actual project orders and possible orders) at weekly intervals covering a period of no less than two years ahead. This elaborate chart therefore needed about 3000 pencilled entries. It cost about ten days of a highly paid chief engineer's time, and involved detailed discussions with the engineering director and other senior people.

The schedule did look quite impressive when it was finished, but it was completely inflexible and difficult to update. Not surprisingly, it therefore became totally useless after only a few weeks. Even if the work plans had been soundly based (which they were not) it is always ludicrous to expect to be able to allocate named individuals to specific jobs on precise dates so far into the future. Even if all expected orders for new projects had been received (they were not), and all the jobs did by some chance happen to materialize in the particular weeks shown on the plan, there would still be a large question mark regarding how many of the 30 named engineers would continue to be employed by the company. In fact, that particular firm was wound up with big debts before the two years covered by the plan had expired.

How it should be done

The following is a useful checklist for determining whether or not a proposed schedule will be of practical use:

1   Is the timescale predicted by the plan achievable?
2   Are all significant tasks included?
3   Are the tasks placed in logical sequence with dependencies between them clearly shown?
4   Will the chosen level of detail allow progress checks against events or activities at reasonably frequent intervals?
5   Does the plan communicate? Is it visually effective?
6   Are critical tasks identified and highlighted?
7   Are all other task priorities quantified?
8   If people or other resources are to be employed directly by the project organization, have those resources been scheduled so that their availability matches the plan?

Manual scheduling methods only provide adequate flexibility in the very simplest cases. The following chapter, which continues the subject of resource scheduling, is based on the assumption that a computer will be used.

Chapter 11

Scheduling resources, Part 2: In practice

The previous chapter introduced some of the principles on which project resource scheduling should be based, particularly with regard to the relationship between critical path network logic, float-determined priorities and the availability of resources. The examples used were purposely kept very simple. Before resource scheduling can be carried out on a more realistic scale, the project manager or planner will be faced with a number of questions that either raise problems or force decisions (especially when data are being assembled for the computer). This chapter continues the subject of resource scheduling by considering some of these questions.

Choice of labour resources to be scheduled

The best modern project management software will allow hundreds of different resource categories to be specified and processed, but the planner who makes too much use of this facility will regret it. Network diagrams, schedules and reports will become very complicated and difficult to manage if every possible type of resource in the organization is entered in the scheduling process. The computer will struggle but fail to produce workload levels that are really smooth and satisfy everyone. Processing time and the risk of errors are likely to increase beyond acceptable levels.

My approach has always been to analyse the organization and working patterns first, pick out the mainstream resources on which project work is heavily dependent (no more than ten categories), and then schedule those as well as possible. Provided capacities for all resources throughout the organization are in the correct proportions, other tasks will probably be scheduled at a rate of usage that unscheduled resources can handle. This is, of course, empirical and my personal view. It depends on a sufficient number of activities in the database for the distribution of times to be approximately normal, so that undue peaks and troughs are not created for the unscheduled resources. Some readers might not agree with this approach, but it always pays to start implementing any new scheduling system as simply as possible. Think big, start small. Other resource types can be added to the database later, if necessary.

Engineering design and drawing

Petrochemical and construction projects

In the engineering design for large petrochemical or construction projects it would usually be necessary to schedule work and headquarters staff resources for each of the main engineering disciplines (civil, structural, mechanical, electrical, piping and so on). This scheduling might be further broken down into engineering, drawing and checking (although computer-aided design can blur these boundaries and reduce the need for such breakdown). The size of tasks for this purpose would not usually go down to the level of individual detail drawings, but would probably encompass groups of drawings for plant or building areas, or for other suitable small work packages.

Manufacturing projects

In the engineering design for manufacturing projects, again confining the scheduling detail to subassemblies and groups of drawings rather than to individual drawings, I have found it sufficient to consider only three resource types during scheduling, designated as follows:

- layout (senior engineers)
- detailers
- checkers or group leaders.

It is recognized that this will not cover every grade of engineering and drawing office staff. For example, many mechanical engineering design activities might also attract a proportion of lubrication and process control design. The common sense approach here (remembering the warnings in the introduction to this section) is to avoid getting into too much detail. If the company knows, from experience, that process control engineering always takes place alongside mechanical design, but typically requires only 10 per cent of the level for mechanical design, then there might well be no need to include process control design specifically in the resource scheduling process. It is then only necessary to schedule the mechanical design engineers.

In such circumstances, process control design activities would not even have to be shown on the network diagram, unless they had particular individual significance. The process control manager can be left to schedule his or her department's work in line with the mainstream mechanical design schedule, and the process control engineering manpower requirements can be assumed as being

10 per cent of those calculated for the mechanical engineers. This approach may not appeal to the fastidious expert or the timid planner, but it saves considerable planning and scheduling effort, and has been proven to be perfectly effective in practice.

Manufacturing

For scheduling projects through a factory, it might again be necessary to choose only two or three key resource types. This selection can be as crude as the following:

- light machining
- heavy machining
- assembly

Or it might involve a few different selections, depending on the organization and its processes.

If this seems surprising, remember that the project planner and project manager are not usually concerned with the day-to-day detail of job scheduling in the manufacturing plant, which is the separate function of production control. The project schedules simply ensure that project work packages are loaded to the factory at a rate consistent with its expected available capacity.

For similar reasons, it is not necessary to be concerned about the fluctuations in resource usage that would normally occur during the course of a group of manufacturing tasks that might be represented on the network and its resulting schedules by a single activity. An example is an activity covering the production of all components needed for a project subassembly. In large manufacturing projects, or when several projects are being scheduled in a total multi-project calculation, it is only necessary to specify an average rate of usage for each production resource, spread evenly over the duration of each production activity on the project network diagram.

The justification for this approach is that each network activity, although perhaps representing several manufacturing operations, is likely to be very small in relation to the total workload of hundreds or even thousands of other manufacturing activities. Workload peaks and troughs of individual activities are so small in relation to the whole that they tend to even out, especially since the activities have been scheduled so as not to exceed the total stated production capacities.

Project resource allocation can therefore ensure that work is fed to the factory at a pace that does not overload the separate production control system, which can then break the manufacturing activities from the project schedule down into detailed factory work schedules.

These arguments concerning manufacturing activities, because they rely on statistical chance, need a fairly large sample. They are best justified when the total manufacturing workload for all projects is represented by at least a few hundred activities. All of this depends on the use of multi-project scheduling (described in Chapter 14).

Choice of resource units

Whenever resource scheduling is intended, it is necessary to decide what units should be used. Simple numerical quantities can usually be used to quantify people of a special skill or from a particular group or department. If 50 labourers are available for allocation to the project, then 50 resource units are entered in the system as the available strength. If eight of those labourers are required to work on a single activity, this might be indicated on the network, computer input, and subsequent schedules as 8LAB (where 'LAB' or some other suitable code identifies the resource as labourers).

Note that an activity can have two, three, or many more different types of resource assigned to it. This was seen in the garage project in Chapter 10, where some activities required both a skilled person and a labourer.

Decimal resource quantities

There are occasions when one or more people working on a project might have to spread their time over several activities simultaneously. Buyers in a purchasing department represent a good example. An average purchasing activity might only involve a buyer intermittently, because most buyers handle several enquiries and orders at the same time. Large projects can impose a heavy and uneven workload on purchasing departments, and the planner might decide that some way must be found to allocate buyers part-time to activities so that project purchasing can take place in the correct sequence of priorities without causing health-threatening overloads.

A group of five buyers might easily have 50 enquiries and purchase orders in various stages of preparation. The planner could overcome this problem by reasoning that the average buyer only spends 10 per cent of his or her time on one task, so that a usage rate of 0.1BUY might be used to show the resource requirement for a typical purchasing activity. A purchase ordering activity with an estimated duration of two weeks and a resource requirement of 0.1BUY would then mean that 10 per cent of a buyer's time must be spread over two weeks for the purchase order to be raised and issued.

Factored units

Some computer programs are unable to accept resource quantities that are not integers. If the software cannot accept decimal quantities, it is necessary to resort to tricks. Factoring is one solution that I have found effective. This approach can be explained by referring once again to a buying department.

In the case of the buyers quoted in the previous section, the units could be factored by ten. Then 10 resource units (10BUY) would represent not ten, but just one buyer. The declared number of available buyers must then also be multiplied by 10. Thus a group of five buyers would be declared as a resource availability of 50BUY. Now when 1BUY is written against a two-week purchase order activity on the network, this actually signifies one buyer spending 10 per cent of his or her time over the two-week activity duration.

If factored units are used, any cost rate specified for the resource must be divided by the factor so that cost reports will be corrected to counteract the large quantities created artificially by the factoring trick. Once again quoting the buyers, suppose that the standard cost rate for one buyer is £150 per day and that days have been used as the standard duration units on the network. Because the units have been factored by ten, the standard daily cost rate for 1BUY unit must be specified as £15.

Competent software will accept decimal quantities, and will not demand the use of factoring or similar tricks.

Use of man-hours

Some programs will allow resources to be specified in terms of man-hours, both as the daily requirement and as the availability. This is allowed even when the activity durations are estimated in days. Thus, when an activity duration of one day is specified on the network, this will be regarded as a resource-usage of seven hours, and seven units of any resource on that activity (when rate constant) means seven hours per day (one person per day). A resource usage of one in this case means only one hour per day, or one-seventh of a person's time throughout the activity. Days might, alternatively, be regarded as eight hours.

Use of man-hour units in this way means that decimal resources and factored resources should not be necessary, provided that the division into sevenths or eighths (rather than tenths) is sufficiently fine.

Rate-constant and non-rate-constant usage of resources

The easiest, and usually acceptable method is to assume that a resource will be used at a constant rate over the life of an activity. Thus if an activity is shown with an estimated duration of one week, needing 1BKL and 1LAB (where 'BKL' is a code for bricklayers and 'LAB' signifies labourers) this means that the job requires one bricklayer and one labourer working full-time for one week. This is known in scheduling terms as a rate-constant use of resources.

Planning for uneven resource usage within one activity is possible with some computer systems. For example, the activity just described might have needed no bricklayer or labourer for two days in the middle of its period, but two bricklayers and two labourers for the last two days. The total resource cost and requirement is the same, but the usage pattern is no longer rate-constant.

In practice, it is seldom necessary to be concerned with such fine detail in project scheduling, especially in large networks where the numbers of activities being scheduled should tend to smooth out any small ripples. The use of most, if not all, resources in a project schedule can usually be considered as rate-constant.

Specifying resource availability levels

Efficiency and the sludge factor

If there are 100 people of one resource type in a department, it might seem reasonable to declare that 100 units of that resource are available to the project. There are, of course, complications. Some of these people will probably be needed for other projects. This problem can be overcome by scheduling all projects together in a multi-project system (Chapter 14).

No department or group of workers ever achieves 100 per cent efficiency. People take time off or work at reduced efficiency for a variety of reasons (illness, annual holidays, dentist, brief visits to the cloakroom, longer visits to the cloakroom, time waiting for work to be allocated, machine or computer failures, training, and so on). Some of these people will also be working on unscheduled jobs, including rectification work and the like.

The answer here is to estimate the level of efficiency for each department or resource type, and to declare a correspondingly reduced level of that resource as being available to the project. If in doubt, start by assuming a relatively low efficiency of 80 per cent, and amend this as experience builds up. So, although there might be 100 people of a particular resource category on the permanent strength of a department, 80 would be the total strength of this resource declared as available for scheduling across all projects. That leaves a 20 per cent sludge factor to cover unplanned absences and downtime, and also to allow for work that is impossible or impracticable to schedule.

Overtime as a resource availability

Projects should not generally be scheduled with the intention of using resources during overtime. This point was made in Chapter 9 in the context of estimating activity durations. It applies with equal force and for the same reasons when the time comes to set up the resource file in the computer. Declared availability levels should be limited to the capacities present during normal working hours.

Planning for changes in availability levels

The availability level for any manpower resource can change during the life of a project, possibly increasing as a result of recruitment or decreasing if redundancy measures have to be taken. The extent and timing of such planned changes should be available from the organization's long-term budgets and manpower plans. These plans will themselves be influenced by the results of project scheduling, so the process is one of cross-fertilization.

Clearly, the resources declared as available for project scheduling need to be kept in step with the forward manpower planning levels. Computer scheduling programs usually allow such changes to be specified. The following is an input format that might be provided by the software for each resource, in this case showing the entry by an expanding company for its expected availability of design engineers (DE):

Resource	Availability start	Availability finish	Quantity
DE	01 Jan 2005	30 Jun 2005	48
DE	01 Jul 2005	30 Sep 2005	50
DE	01 Oct 2005	28 Feb 2006	51
DE	01 Mar 2006	30 Jun 2006	53

The pattern for the declared availability of a manpower resource is therefore likely to be either a continuous, constant level, or a level which varies in one or more steps (up or down) during the life of the schedule according to the relevant departmental manpower plan.

Using different calendars for resource scheduling

The subject of calendars and their application in project management computer software is dealt with at greater length in the following chapter, but (at the risk of some later repetition) it is relevant to mention calendars here briefly in the context of resource scheduling.

Readers will know that computers have an inbuilt calendar in their operating system that recognizes calendar dates over a wide time span. All good project management software can produce schedules using calendars that extend well into the 21st century, which should be more than sufficient to accommodate any project.

The project planner will be offered a default calendar. Unless the planner specifies otherwise, all activities in a network will be scheduled according to that default calendar. This is the calendar that matches day numbers from time analysis to actual dates, depending on how many days are to be worked in each week. The most usual default calendar is a working week of five days. That means that no activities will be scheduled to take place during weekends, and any dates which fall during weekends will not be valid and will not appear in any calculated schedules. So no resources will be scheduled at weekends when that calendar is used.

Weekend and shift working

It sometimes happens that a schedule must allow for a mix of single-shift (normal) working with two- or three-shift working. Perhaps all the office staff, including design engineers, work five days in a week and the factory staff work two or three shifts within each 24-hour period. This will complicate scheduling somewhat. Matters will be even more complicated if some, but not all, people normally work over weekends.

The correct way to overcome these problems is to assign any activity that requires resources over times not allowed in the five-day week default calendar to a new calendar specially created for the purpose. All competent project management software allows the planner to set as many special calendars as the project requires.

One calendar might, for example, allow two shifts per day from Monday to Saturday (inclusive). Another might allow three-shift working for seven days each week. The choice of which calendar to use can be made in some software by assigning special calendars to the different resource categories, but it is more usual to assign special calendars to the relevant activities.

If weekend working is not involved in the mix, the problem of shift working can be overcome simply by multiplying the number of resource units declared as available for an average shift by the number of shifts to be worked. If three fitters are to work on each of two shifts, then six fitters are the total available resource within each working day. That method avoids the use of special calendars.

Holidays

Individuals' annual holidays, provided these are not all taken simultaneously during a plant shut-down, can be treated as a general reduction in the resources stated to be available. This contributes to the suggested 20 per cent reduction mentioned above on page 260.

At least one computer program (*4c*) allows a staff file to be associated with the resource pool. Various employment details of each staff member can be held on file, including planned vacation dates, so that individual holidays and other planned absences can be specified and taken out of the resource availability pool.

Public holidays and other general holidays where no work can take place at all on a project should be determined in advance using diaries or long-range almanacs. These dates must then be removed from the days available for scheduling. Computer programs will allow for this, either by letting the planner remove the relevant days from the default calendar or by providing one or more special holiday files.

International projects might have groups in several countries that have different work patterns, perhaps in respect of religious and national holidays. When activities from all these countries are mixed in the same network and schedule, a separate special calendar can be set up and used to suit each location.

Scheduling labour costs

It will certainly be necessary to schedule estimated expenditure, and computer resource scheduling programs can be used for this purpose. Project management computer programs usually allow a unit cost rate to be specified for each resource, and also allow the planner the alternative option of stating an estimated cost for a whole activity (particularly useful for materials costs and other expenses).

The resulting schedules are very valuable because they set out the predicted project costs against the scheduled project timescale, providing one of the essential ingredients for cost control and cash flow management.

Using resource rates for labour costs

It is possible to declare a cost rate per unit network time for each resource category. In the best programs it is further possible to put in cost rates for threshold resources, recognizing the different costs that must be incurred, for example, in bringing in temporary staff to cover overload conditions. One way in which the computer will calculate the costs for an activity is as follows.

Suppose that an activity has an estimated duration of 10 days (equivalent to 2 calendar weeks on the default calendar) and that its resource requirement is 1 engineer. The cost rate for this resource (engineers) has been specified as £200 per day using normally available staff, and £250 per day for the threshold level. The computer will multiply the normal rate by the duration, giving £(10 × 200) = £2000 as the estimated or budget cost of the activity.

Should the total workload cause the computer to call in resources from the threshold reserve to perform this activity, it would use the threshold rate in the cost calculation and schedule the cost as £2500.

Scheduling costs for materials and other purchases

The estimated costs of materials and equipment can be scheduled by placing budget costs on the relevant purchasing activities on the network, and then allowing the computer to produce timed expenditure schedules. This subject was introduced briefly in Chapter 9, and Figure 9.2 will serve to illustrate the further explanations given here.

Scheduling committed purchasing costs

There are various times during the purchasing process when it might be argued that costs are irrevocably committed, but for all practical purposes the project contractor is committed to the cost of a purchase when the purchase order is issued (although pedants could argue that a firm contract might not exist until the supplier has received and accepted the terms of the order).

So that the total committed purchased materials costs of a project can be scheduled, therefore, it makes sense to place the cost of each purchase order on the relevant 'issue purchase order' activity in the project network. Activity 1025 in Figure 9.2 is an example. By specifying all similar 'issue purchase order' activities with a duration of 1 day, a suitable reporting code and the purchase cost, it is possible to produce schedules of committed materials costs for the project. These reports can be printed as lists or graphs.

If this facility is required, the network diagram must indeed include a suitable activity (such as 'issue purchase order') on which to assign the materials costs for each purchase. If the purchasing department should argue that it takes two weeks to prepare and issue a purchase order, one answer is to precede all the one-day order issue activities with a new set of activities labelled 'prepare purchase order', all with a duration of 9 or 10 working days.

Scheduling cash outflows for materials costs

The project organization's accountants might ask the planners for a schedule indicating when funds have to be made available to pay for purchases. This is really another application of resource scheduling, requiring the planner to work out when all suppliers' invoices are due to be paid.

Once again this can be achieved by allocating the cost of each purchase to an activity within the appropriate purchasing string, but this time an activity must be chosen that occurs after the materials have been delivered and when the invoice is due for payment. One option is to provide a 'goods received' activity, and another is to place the costs on a goods inwards inspection activity. Alternatively, special 'pay' activities can be created (such as activity 1040 in Figure 9.2).

However, most contractors do not pay their suppliers immediately upon receipt of goods. Suppose that the usual delay between accepting goods and paying for them is four weeks (20 working days). This can be scheduled by injecting yet another activity into each purchasing string, with a duration of 20 days, labelled with a description such as 'payment delay' (virtually a dummy activity). In Figure 9.2 this would be placed between activities 1035 and 1040.

Some software would allow the 'pay' activity itself to be given a duration of 20 days, and let the planner treat the money as a non-rate-constant resource with all the usage taken up on the last of the 20 days.

In precedence notation, the same result can be achieved (provided the software allows) simply by allocating a duration of 20 days to the finish–start link between activities 1035 and 1040 (Figure 9.2). However, I prefer to use two separate, consecutive activities ('delay' and 'pay') because that method is more clearly obvious on the network and satisfies an approach that I call 'visible logic'. Although lagging links, distorted resource usage patterns and the end-loading of resources are all possible, these features tend to remain hidden inside the computer, and can cloud the visible logic and make checking difficult.

Logic checking and subsequent comprehension of reports will also be helped if the 'pay' activity can be given a reference that relates directly to its associated purchase order activity. When the network is drawn, the purchase order numbers are unlikely to be known, but an easy solution is simply to use the activity ID codes. Thus, in Figure 9.2, the description of activity 1040 need only read 'Pay 1025'.

Once again, as in the case of the committed costs schedule, the use of a computer will allow a time-related cost schedule to be produced. By allocating a unique reporting code to all these pay activities, the computer is enabled to report only these costs. If this is done after the resource scheduling calculation, all the costs will fall into the correct cash outflow time frame.

Benefits of the computer for scheduling costs

When familiarity is gained with the use of computer systems and the use of filtering, sorting and reporting codes, both of the above methods can be combined, allowing the preparation of schedules and graphs for both committed costs and cash outflows.

Planners who become familiar with a particular scheduling program will learn how to exploit its features to produce the schedules they need. They will, for instance, be able to solve the more complex problem of scheduling the expected timing of stage payments for capital equipment purchases and subcontracts so that these will be included properly in the total project cash outflow schedule. There must be at least one suitable activity in the network that can be identified with every case when a stage payment is expected to fall due. Then the anticipated stage payment amounts can be placed as costs on those activities.

The capabilities and methods of use vary greatly between different computer systems, and there is usually more than one way to achieve a desired result even within one project management program. Even when a program appears not to possess the required capability, there are often 'tricks' that can be employed to produce the output needed. Unit factoring, described earlier in this chapter, was one of such tricks.

Scheduling cash flow

Cash flow schedules can be required to show either expenditure (outflows), corresponding income or savings (inflows), or a combination of expenditure and its consequent income (net cash flows). The concept of scheduling cash flows, especially *net* cash flows presents difficulty to some project staff, whose training and interests usually tend to be technical rather than commercial. Students often provide cash outflow schedules or projected profit and loss accounts in the mistaken belief that these satisfy requests in examination questions for net cash flow schedules.

Cash flow scheduling was described in Chapter 6 in connection with project financial appraisal, which is an important application of net cash flow predictions. This subject deserves further explanation here in the context of resource scheduling. Money is undeniably a basic project resource. Plans which show the expected cash 'outputs and inputs' throughout the life of a project are an important aspect of project resource scheduling.

Reasons for scheduling cash flow in project management

Any organization investing funds in a large project will want to know not only the amount of money required, but also when the money is likely to be required, so that provision can be made with bankers or other financial sources for the monies to be available when they are needed. The cash outflow aspects of purchasing were mentioned in the preceding section of this chapter with this requirement in mind.

Contractors and project managers may also be asked to predict cash flows as a service to the customer. Customers need to know when to expect claims for payment from the contractor. In some projects, customers buy equipment for the project themselves, or at least pay the suppliers' invoices directly and, again, they need to be advised in advance of the likely amounts and timings of these commitments. So project cash flow schedules can serve a dual purpose, helping both the contractor and the customer to make the necessary funds available to keep the project afloat and financially viable.

Method

The essential feature of any cash flow schedule is that it must be compiled by placing each sum of money in the period when it falls due for payment or receipt. The total project payments or income due in each of those periods can then be calculated.

PROJECTS UNLIMITED LTD — Loxylene Chemical Plant for Lox Chemical Company

Project number P21900
Issue date March 2003

Quarterly periods – all figures £1000s

Cost item	Cost code	2004				2005				2006				2007				Total budget
		1	2	3	4	1	2	3	4	1	2	3	4	1	2	3	4	
ENGINEERING	A																	
Design	A105	10	20	50	70	75	50	30	10									315
Support	A110			2	2	2	5	5	5	5	5	3	2	2	2	2	2	44
Commission	A200													2	6	10	10	28
Project management	A500	4	5	7	8	8	8	8	8	7	6	6	4	3	2	2	2	88
PURCHASES	B																	
Main plant	B110					400				500	480			2200			400	4000
Furnaces	B150						60	500			40							600
Ventilation	B175						20	5	5		160	10						200
Electrical	B200					10	5	20	25	25	140							225
Piping	B300						5	5	20	20	40	40	60	20	20			230
Steel	B400			20		80	200	200	200	200								900
Cranes	B500					50							400		50			500
Other	B999		5	25	5	10	20	20	50	5	5	10	5	10	5	2		177
CONSTRUCTION	C																	
Plant hire	C100				2	3	10	10	8	6	4	2	1	1				47
Roads	C200				10	20	40	80	60	5	5							220
External lighting	C250				5				40		5							50
Main building	C300																	
Labour	C310					10	30	100	150	200	400	100	50	40	20	20		1120
Materials	C320					2	10	30	100	200	220	200	100	100	10	5		977
Stores building	C400																	
Labour	C410							20	20	20	20	60	60	30	5	5		240
Materials	C420					10	20	25	15	5	5	5	2	5	10	5		107
CONTINGENCY SUM	Y999					10	20	20	25	30	20	60	35	45	45	50	50	400
ESCALATION	Z999					35	29	74	59	110	136	70	88	322	30	32	85	1070
TOTALS		14	30	104	102	715	519	1132	795	1338	1496	711	827	2802	206	128	619	11538

Figure 11.1   Cash outflow schedule

This is a simple example of a schedule that might be prepared for a customer by the management team of a large project. In some cases the general arrangement, degree of breakdown and even the cost-coding system might have to be agreed with the customer.

Timing

Whether for use in project appraisal or for managing project funds, cash flow schedules are necessarily bound up with project timescale planning. A cash flow schedule for early project appraisal can only be prepared after the timings of key project events have been forecast (perhaps using a very simple bar chart). The more detailed cash flow schedules required for an active project must wait until after the project has been properly scheduled.

The planner must decide how to relate each item of cash flow to its causal activity on the project plan. Stage payments to a subcontractor, for example, might be linked to network milestones (each payment following the planned milestone date by perhaps 30 days). Labour wages and salaries are usually paid in arrears, thus delaying these cash outflows by as much as one month. Suppliers' invoices might be received at the same time as the goods, but they often allow a 30-day period of delay for payment. Similar considerations apply to cash inflows, which can sometimes be delayed by several months when the customer is particularly slow at responding to claims for payment.

The method described here is illustrated by a manual example but the data for cash flow scheduling will normally come from a computer. A method for allocating materials costs to a computer-generated cash flow schedule was described on page 263, but other project costs are more difficult to place in their correct time frames and will require more careful attention to network design and the placement of estimated costs on network activities.

Example of a project cash outflow schedule prepared for a customer

The project represented In Figure 11.1 is for the engineering, purchasing and construction of a chemical process plant to produce the plastic Loxylene. The customer has contracted to pay quarterly on a cost-plus basis, and has asked the contractor for a cash outflow schedule. The timescale is therefore set out as annual quarters in this case.

Each cost item is placed in the period during which payment is expected from the customer. The customer can use the information as a phased budget, to indicate if and when it might be necessary to obtain more funds. Sometimes all the entries on cash schedules and other cost reports will have to be classified according to the customer's own code of accounts or capital appropriation codes.

Example of a net cash flow schedule for a contractor's own use

In Figure 11.2, the Loxylene Chemical Plant project appears again. This time the cash outflows are summarized and augmented by the associated inflows.

Comparison of inflows and outflows, in each quarterly period and cumulatively, will show how the net cash balance is expected to change throughout the project. This should enable the contractor's financial director to

| PROJECTS UNLIMITED LTD | | | | | | | | | | | | | | | | | Loxylene Chemical Plant for Lox Chemical Company | Project number P21900 |
| Issue date March 2003 |

Cost item	2004				2005				2006				2007				2008	Total budget
	1	2	3	4	1	2	3	4	1	2	3	4	1	2	3	4	1	
INFLOWS																		
Agreed loans	50				150													200
Client's payments	10		50	100	200	500	1500	1000	1000	1750	1000	1000	1000	3000	1000	1000	1000	15110
Total inflows	60		50	100	350	500	1500	1000	1000	1750	1000	1000	1000	3000	1000	1000	1000	15310
OUTFLOWS																		
Engineering	14	25	59	80	85	63	43	23	12	11	9	6	7	10	14	14		475
Purchasing		5	45	5	550	310	745	295	750	665	215	457	2242	76	2	470		6832
Construction				17	35	97	245	393	436	654	382	241	186	45	30			2761
Contingency					10	20	25	25	30	30	35	35	45	45	50	50		400
Escalation	35					29	74	59	110	136	70	88	322	30	32	85		1070
Total outflows	14	30	104	102	715	519	1132	795	1338	1496	711	827	2802	206	128	619		11538
NET FLOWS																		
Periodic	46	(30)	(54)	(2)	(365)	(19)	368	205	(338)	254	289	173	(1802)	2794	872	381	1000	3772
Cumulative	46	16	(38)	(40)	(405)	(424)	(56)	149	(189)	65	354	527	(1275)	1519	2391	2772	3772	3772

Figure 11.2   Net cash flow schedule
The cash outflow schedule for this project was shown (in slightly more detail) in Figure 11.1. Now the predicted cash inflows have been added, enabling the project manager to schedule the periodic and cumulative net cash flows.

ensure that sufficient funds are always available to support expenditure on the project, including funding work in progress.

Data sources for net cash flow schedules

Figure 11.3 indicates the logical sequence in which data must be assembled for a net cash flow schedule, such as that seen in Figure 11.2

Everything must start with project definition and the work breakdown, so that the project scope and its principal tasks are all listed. Figure 11.3 demonstrates the importance of the work breakdown, subsequent cost estimates and the project plan. All are key constituents. The net cash flow schedule cannot be prepared without them.

The seven steps of project resource scheduling

Many factors may have to be taken into account before a workable resource schedule can be produced for a project. Some of these factors are depicted in Figure 11.4.

A mathematician faced with a problem containing a number of unknown quantities would adopt a logical approach, and attempt to evaluate the unknowns by solving them one at a time. Project scheduling benefits from this approach, and there are seven recognizable stages leading from potential chaos to a practicable solution. The seven steps are listed and explained in Figure 11.5.

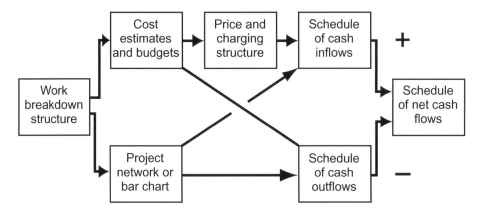

Figure 11.3   Essential elements of a project net cash flow schedule

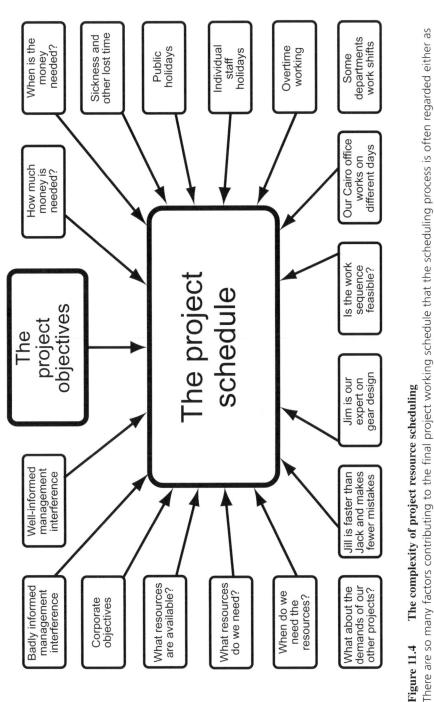

Figure 11.4   The complexity of project resource scheduling

There are so many factors contributing to the final project working schedule that the scheduling process is often regarded either as impossible or requiring an intuitive gift. But no magic is needed. The mystery is removed when the process is carried out in seven sensible, separate steps.

Project scheduling in the corporate context

The approach taken to scheduling must depend on what the schedule is to be used for. In any organization, planning has to be carried out at several levels. These range from overall, strategic corporate long-range plans to the day-to-day allocation of tasks to individual people and machines. Project schedules generally lie between these extremes, and they serve several purposes in the general planning context.

Project schedules (combined with sales forecasts of possible work to come) provide the data from which manpower, financial and other long-range corporate plans can be formulated. These data are not needed in great depth of detail, but they should instead be summarized in quantities that will suit the broad corporate plans that they feed. This is the 'upward-looking' purpose of project schedules, for which they should predict departmental manpower and facilities needed, the types of skills required, cash flows, and the like. If the organization is a joint venture or other company set up to handle a single large project, there is one level of planning less for the company, because the overall project schedule doubles as the corporate plan.

The principal 'downward-looking' purpose of project schedules is to list the jobs that all departments will have to carry out. These are sometimes known as *work-to lists*. The purpose of these lists is to feed work to all the departments in correct sequence, timed to fit in with the needs of the project. Proper resource scheduling leading to the issue of work-to lists should ensure that work is fed to departments at rates that will not cause overloads. It should then be the job of the departmental managers to arrange the lowest layer of scheduling (the last of the 'seven steps'), which is the day-to-day allocation of jobs to individual people according to their availability or particular aptitudes.

The case studies and examples in this book have been kept simple for clarity. In real life, projects are likely to involve many more than the 25 or so activities used in our examples. Project networks with over one thousand activities are not unusual. Worse still, a contractor might have to manage several such projects simultaneously, all in different stages of progress, and all making demands on common resources. It should be apparent that no project schedule can be considered in isolation from other projects being conducted within the same organization, especially when it comes to considering resources. At one time companies had to cope with all planning, even on this scale, using only bar charts on adjustable planning boards. Modern computer systems can do the job more accurately, and with far greater flexibility. The process, called multi-project scheduling, is described in Chapter 14.

Step	Preferred method
1 Define the objectives	
– Technical	Solution, conceptual or feasibility engineering, with the results documented in a project specification.
– Financial	Initial evaluation of the proposed solution. To be revised, refined and developed into budgets after step 2.
– Time	Summary bar chart or simple network diagram, based on experience from similar past projects if possible.
2 Divide the project into its constituent tasks	Prepare a coded work breakdown structure (WBS).
3 Put all the identified tasks into their logical working sequence	Draw a detailed network logic diagram. This might require a brainstorming meeting. Ensure that every task in the WBS is considered.
4 Estimate the duration of every task	Forecast the calendar time needed from start to finish of each task on the network. Task resource requirements should also be estimated but at this stage ignore the possible effect of these on the schedule.
5 Calculate the timing and priority of each task	Enter the network data into a computer and carry out time analysis using suitable project management software. Re-examine the network and task times if the forecast completion date is unacceptable.
6 Reconcile task needs with the resources that can be provided	Use the computer to allocate resources to tasks, using the float from network time analysis to determine priorities when resources are insufficient. Filter reports to produce work-to lists that are specific to every line manager.
7 Assign each task for action	This important step is best left to line managers and supervisors, especially for human resources. Matching people to tasks usually demands personal knowledge of individual characteristics, capabilities and skills.

Figure 11.5   Seven logical steps towards a project resource schedule

References and further reading for Part III

Burke, Rory (1999), *Project Management: Planning and Control,* 3rd edn, Chichester, Wiley

Devaux, S.A. (1999), *Total Project Control: A Manager's Guide to Integrated Project Planning, Measuring and Tracking,* New York, Wiley

Harrison, F.L. (1992), *Advanced Project Management: a Structured Approach,* 3rd edn, Aldershot, Gower

Kerzner, H. (1997), *Project Management: A Systems Approach to Planning, Scheduling and Controlling,* 6th edn, New York, Van Nostrand Reinhold

Lockyer, K.G. and Gordon, J. (1995), *Critical Path Analysis and Other Project Management Techniques,* 6th edn, London, Pitman

Reiss, G. (1995), *Project Management Demystified: Today's Tools and Techniques,* 2nd edn, London, Spon

Weaver, M., (1997), *Managing Resources: Project Planning and Financial Control,* Oxford, Butterworth-Heinemann (an activity pack in a ring-binder with overhead transparency masters and worksheets)

Part IV

Computer applications

Chapter 12

Project management computer systems, Part 1: Preparation

This chapter is an introductory guide to this complex subject, and deals with some of the preparations that are necessary before a computer system can be implemented. Chapter 13 describes the more common aspects of processing project data. Chapter 14 rounds off this part of the book by illustrating some of the more advanced or time-saving techniques available to the experienced planner or project manager.

Scheduling with or without a computer

Time analysis

An expert planner faced with the task of producing and analysing a network for a project containing only a few activities will undoubtedly produce the fastest results by drawing a freehand arrow diagram and analysing it mentally. It is likely to take longer using a computer because of the formalities needed to set up the new project files in the system and enter the data. Time analysis of the small garage project network in Chapter 10 (Figure 10.1), for example, can easily be carried out rapidly using pencil, paper and an average human brain.

University students whose management course includes a project management module might find it easier to draw simple networks for assignments manually, rather than take precious time to learn a software program to do the job. This is a special case. Provided that the network is drawn with reasonable care, and that the use of a computer was not mandatory, some examiners might even prefer to see hand-drawn networks with all the time analysis calculations exposed. When a network is processed by computer, using software such as *Microsoft Project,* time analysis is automatic, the calculations are hidden in the computer, and there is no proof in the resulting plans that the student knows how to make the calculations or understands their implications.

Those planners who use critical path networks but choose not to follow the planning process through to proper resource scheduling may be able to carry out the time analysis of quite large networks without the help of a computer. It is not difficult to trace all the paths through a big network, write the earliest and latest times in by hand, and then highlight all the critical activities. Admittedly, precedence diagrams containing several complex constraints are not quite so easy.

Even if initial time analysis is relatively easy, however, updating a network to accommodate logic changes or new progress information is a very different story. Unless the network is very small indeed, the planner without a computer is faced with the daunting task of having to erase large amounts of time analysis data from the network diagram and start the calculations afresh. Even changing the estimated duration of one activity or a very small alteration to the network logic can mean that calculated times will have to be erased and rewritten throughout the entire network.

Resource scheduling

The arguments for resource scheduling are similar to those for time analysis. A very small project should present no great difficulty to a planner armed with an adjustable bar chart and all the relevant facts. Projects with up to a hundred different tasks can be planned with the aid of such adjustable systems. An initial schedule might take a day or two to set up and inflict some eyestrain on the scheduler, but an effective plan could be made, with well-smoothed resource loads.

The biggest problem with any manual charting method, however, is that it is too inflexible. A change of plan to any except the very tiniest project can result in hours of tedious work in repositioning all the tasks on the chart. This is always coupled with the risk of introducing logical or other errors. Of course, most projects have more than a hundred activities, and manual resource scheduling becomes even more difficult (impossible altogether for really large projects). The job *must* then be given to a computer.

Speed and flexibility

The well-known advantages of using computers for many business applications apply equally to project management. These include the ability of the machine to process large volumes of data quickly and accurately, and to repeat the process just as quickly and accurately to reflect progress made or any change in the project scope or plan. Although it can take a significant amount of time to install all the project parameters and activity data in the computer, the subsequent flexibility to changes and the speed of reprocessing are important assets in project scheduling and control.

Information management

Another important feature of computer systems is that they allow management information to be produced and disseminated quickly and effectively.

With a manual wall chart, the only practical fast way of spreading its information is to photograph the chart and distribute colour prints. A bar chart or network diagram drawn on a sheet of paper or film can, of course, be copied and distributed. But these charts and diagrams are limited in the detail that can be shown clearly. They will usually cover the whole project, so that prints taken from them are not specific to particular departments or managers. The ability of computers to filter, sort, list and print data will be found invaluable in overcoming this problem.

Computer systems allow reports to be generated that are up-to-date, very detailed, but edited so that they are specific to the people or departments to which they are addressed for action. Activities can be listed in any desired sequence, with critical activities highlighted.

If users are provided with suitable personal computers linked to a network, they can interrogate the system at will or work interactively with it. Timesheet and progress information can be entered, for example. The most effective project management programs work across a database, which can often be arranged to import or export data to one or more other company databases to produce a well-integrated management information system.

From the late 1960s onwards computers have been able to do most of the things that we can do today with modern technology. While it is true that the process took longer, involving batch processing on mainframe machines of enormous physical size, resource scheduling was possible with networks containing many thousands of activities, and all the reports needed to manage progress and costs over a large multi-project model could be produced (see the next subsection). The difference now, and probably the most important advance in recent years, has been the ability of computers to communicate information to other computer users, both within a local network and over the Internet. That has brought great benefits in the handling of information, especially in international projects.

Multi-project scheduling

A computer makes it possible to schedule a programme of many projects together, in one combined multi-project calculation. This will take account of the total demands made on the organization's resources, and balance these against the resources that can be made available. Using a computer in this way allocates all work according to critical path network priorities, should result in an acceptably smooth work pattern, and produces important input for the organization's forward budgets, manpower and other corporate plans. Such systems can also be used for modelling, with possible new projects or strategic decisions injected and tested in 'what-if?' calculations. This subject is treated at greater length in Chapter 14.

Project cost management

When estimated cost data are added to activities and resources, the computer can be used to produce project cost estimates and to schedule cash flows. During the course of a project, computers can make comparisons between planned and actual costs and carry out earned-value calculations.

Investment

The use of any computing system obviously requires some investment. For project management, that means investing money in a suitable computer or allocating space in an existing system, and the purchase of software (the cost of which can be significant). At least as important is the time that has to be invested in choosing the system, in implementation and training, and in the initial data preparation for every project. Provided sensible choices are made, all this investment should be well repaid.

Facilities required

Organizational factors

Management support

Before any project can be scheduled by computer, the project manager has to ensure that appropriate facilities are available, most notably the hardware and specialized software. Most of this chapter deals with aspects of the computer software, but even the best possible choice of system cannot guarantee success by itself.

Undoubtedly, a vital factor, as in so many other cases, is the commitment and support provided by the organization's higher management. This includes not only the willingness to commit funds for facilities, equipment and staff, but also active support and encouragement. This encouragement is especially important during the preparation and implementation stages, when initial operating difficulties or the scepticism of project staff at large have the potential to deliver a fatal blow.

Staffing

Although anything but the very simplest project management computer software needs expert operators, there is generally no reason why a large, expensively staffed group needs to be established. There should be at least one person who is expert in the use of the system, and at least one other who can take over in the case of absence or other emergency. Otherwise, the number of people required will depend on the size of the organization and the number of projects being planned centrally.

Techniques exist for greatly reducing the amount of effort needed for network creation and data input. These methods include the use of modular networks or templates, described in Chapter 14. The increase in planning efficiency can be enormous, enabling a large planning operation to be coordinated by only two or three people. However, the central administrator or coordinator has to be in place first, so that the necessary inbuilt learning can be accumulated from which to develop the templates and standardized estimates.

Training

Training must be encouraged and supported by higher management. This is usually understood to mean specialist training for the planners, but a more general programme of education throughout the organization is also essential. This general education should be conducted through internally managed meetings with other managers, supervisors and senior staff to convey the objectives and potential benefits of the proposed system. Although external expert help will almost certainly be needed to train the planners in operating the system, it is best if the general educational training can be conducted by the organization's own staff (most likely by a senior planner).

The general education programme also needs to convey to all key project staff the role that they must play in helping to make the computer system work effectively. If the system is to be networked, this training should include the various functions available at the individual user's screen. Most important, all key project staff must be made aware that the ultimate success of the system will depend on their input, whether this is data for initial project planning, feedback of progress information or adherence to the resulting schedules.

Accommodation

Those responsible for planning deserve space where they can work without interruption during the error-prone data input operations. They also need space for laying out and keeping project network drawings. Although networks can be displayed on the screen, the best way for tracing and checking logic remains the single sheet or roll of paper.

System requirements

The basic system requirements are fairly obvious:

1   computer hardware of sufficient speed and capacity
2   suitable software
3   adequate maintenance and systems support for both hardware and software.

Some of the individual choices might not be so obvious.

Hardware

Computers

Previous editions of this book attempted to give the minimum specification likely to be needed by a computer running modern project management software. However, advances in computer performance are so rapid that it is now unwise to suggest a specification. To some extent the software development keeps pace with computer technology, so that new versions of programs can take advantage of the increased computer memory and power. The minimum specification needed for any particular program should therefore be ascertained from the program supplier.

Printers and plotters

Users will probably find that the printer is the limiting factor when reports are required quickly. Tabular reports are not usually a problem, but some graphics reports (such as bar charts and network plots) can take a long time to print if the wrong combination of program, printer driver and printer is chosen. All programs are able to produce graphics reports in different colours. However, reports in colour are less important if the facilities for photocopying and distributing them in colour are lacking.

When the amount of detail to be reported is greater than that which can be accommodated on a single A4 sheet, the program will usually overflow the data onto continuation sheets. Printing for some reports (especially bar charts and network logic plots) will be made on sheets that must subsequently be cut and pasted together on a grid or matrix pattern. For a single project, with infrequent updates, this is merely a small inconvenience. For busier systems, however, the facilities should include a plotter to allow larger sheet sizes or even rolls to be used.

Software

A brief survey

Early users of project management software were reluctant to grasp all the opportunities provided by the few good systems that existed. Most people were content to run time analysis, print out the results, and attempt to run their projects using the earliest possible dates with little regard for resource constraints. In industries with great flexibility of resources, or where work is typically subcontracted to others who must provide and manage the resources, this disregard of detailed resource scheduling was (and remains) a sensible approach. In many companies, however, real problems existed in trying to finish work on time when no easy way could be seen to allocate scarce resources among all the jobs clamouring for them.

Several programs became available in the 1960s that were advertised as being able to report costs and schedule resources. Only a very few actually worked, notably various K & H Projects Systems products and ICL *PERT 1900*. The K & H technology survives in this market with 4c Systems Ltd, whose product *4c* is among the least-known but probably the most versatile and powerful project management package available anywhere.

Other programs that have earned a high reputation are *Open Plan Professional* (Welcom Software Technology International) and *Primavera. Artemis* is another name of repute.

All of the software so far mentioned is at the 'high end' of the market, among the programs able to run very large networks, with many management features, and well deserving the adjective 'powerful'. Although help screens are provided, the benefits of these systems are likely to be realized only after some initial training.

New products appear fairly frequently, and existing programs undergo change and enhancement. These include not only the 'high-end' systems already mentioned, but a myriad of other packages ranging from very large to extremely simple, and with a corresponding range in price. *Microsoft Project* is by far the most widely known and used package, and versions from *Microsoft Project 98* onwards are very capable and represent good value for money. A selective list of available software is given at the end of Chapter 14.

Maintenance and support

The first year, at least, of hardware and software operation should be covered by guarantees. Thereafter, it is usual for suppliers to offer maintenance and support contracts that cost, typically, between 10 and 15 per cent of the original purchase price per annum.

The user must be assured that the software provider will include free upgrades of the software and its documentation. A very important consideration is the availability of a 'hotline', which the user can telephone whenever difficulties arise. Some companies offer hotline services that fall short of perfection because they are not accessible during all the hours when the user operates or because immediate answers to problems are not forthcoming. Some suppliers are merely agents for programs developed overseas, and they will need to refer some queries back to source for answers. Others are not able to staff the hotline continuously, so that the user who calls with an urgent problem is faced with a message answering service.

Choosing a suitable program

Need for caution

Some programs fail to live up to the claims of their suppliers' publicity. Even some programs which receive good reviews in the independent computing journals are found to be flawed when they are put to the test by planning professionals. The range in prices and performance is enormous, and price is not always an indicator of quality.

Much of the advertising needs to be read with critical awareness and circumspection. Wildly extravagant claims are sometimes made. The word 'powerful' is often misused to describe systems that, although valuable for small projects, do not bear comparison with the programs that can handle large volumes of data across big multi-project databases. This can all be very confusing to the new project manager, and it is easy to waste time and money on systems that fail to live up to their claims or the manager's expectations.

If a program is purchased that fails to perform as expected, the results can be costly, not only in terms of the software itself, but also the investment in training and experimental use and in the effort wasted in pouring data into the useless system. There are two other serious disadvantages when a system fails: namely, the loss of essential confidence and support from others in the project organization, and the reduction in efficiency caused by the absence of the expected project work schedules.

Figure 12.1 outlines the procedure that I have found useful when advising a client on the purchase of 'high end' software.

User's specification and suppliers' questionnaire

The starting point in choosing any but the most cheap and simple new software has to be a carefully reasoned specification of what the project manager's organization needs. The purchaser should approach the software houses with a firm set of objectives which, in effect, state: 'This is what we need, what is your

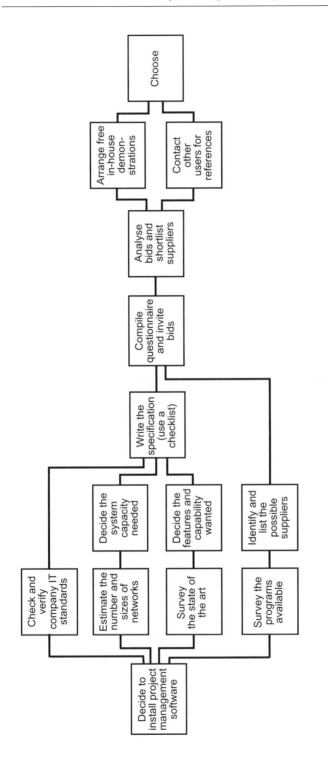

Figure 12.1   Suggested procedure for buying project management software

The steps shown here should reduce the risk of making an inappropriate choice when investing time and money in project management software at the high end of the capability and price range.

Item	Program characteristics
Environment	• Standalone only?
	• Network? (details required)
Ease of use	• Are the drop-down menus helpful?
	• How good are the help screens?
	• How good is the documentation provided?
	• How fast is the expected processing time using:
	(a) our available hardware?
	(b) new hardware as recommended?
Activities	• Maximum number of activities possible in one project?
	• Maximum number of precedence links in one project?
	• Maximum number of activities possible altogether?
	• Maximum number of precedence links possible in system?
	• Maximum number of characters possible in activity ID code?
	• Can activity ID codes be alphanumeric?
	• Maximum number of characters in activity description?
	• Can activities be designated as splittable or non-splittable?
Calendars	• Total calendar time span?
	• How many different calendars can be specified?
	• What duration units are possible with these calendars?
Updating	• What progress reporting methods can be used?
	• Will activities reported as started be at risk of rescheduling?
Reports	• What standard report formats are provided?
	• What are the standard filtering and sorting facilities?
	• How good are the graphics?
	• How fast are the graphics printing speeds?
	• How easy is it to customize reports?
	• Will the system meet our needs for (say) the next five years?
Error detection	• How effective are the error search routines?
	• Are error messages clear and in plain language?
	• Are loops effectively diagnosed, analysed and reported?

Figure 12.2   Checklist for use when buying project management software

response?' This is far better than adopting the weak and more negative stance of pleading: 'What do you offer and how do you think we might use it?'

Figure 12.2 is a checklist of some of the more significant factors to be considered when compiling the user's specification. This checklist will not suit every organization in every detail – some of very advanced possibilities open to the expert have been excluded, and each organization is unique and will have its own special requirements – but it is a convenient starting point. Its most effective

Item	Program characteristics
Resources	• Can resource scheduling be performed?
	• How many different resource types can be specified?
	• How many characters may we use in each resource identifier code?
	• Can resources be assigned to groups or departments?
	• Can threshold resources be specified?
	• Can alternative resources be specified?
	• Any special resource scheduling features?
Cost data	• Can the program assign an hourly or daily cost rate to each resource?
	• Can the program use both cost rates and charge-out rates?
	• Can different rates be specified for overtime or threshold resources?
	• Can an estimated cost be assigned to an activity?
	• What tabular cost reports are available?
	• Can cost/time graphs be produced?
	• Is there a staff timesheet facility?
Templating	• Does the program allow templating?
	• How easy is it to edit templates?
	• Can templates be merged automatically with interface links?
Projects	• How many projects can the system hold?
	• Maximum number of characters in a project identifier code?
	• Can project identifiers be alphanumeric?
	• Can the same activity ID numbers be used again in different projects?
	• Is multi-project scheduling possible?
	• Can projects be allocated to groups for multi-project scheduling?
	• Is what-if? scheduling available to test new project strategies etc?
Operational aspects	• What hardware is recommended?
	• Will the software run on our server?
	• Can the new software communicate with our main database?
	• Are there security safeguards against unauthorized access?
	• If so, how many levels of security are provided?
	• Can we customize these security levels?

Figure 12.2   *continued*

application is as the basis for compiling a questionnaire to be sent to all potential software suppliers.

Without a certain amount of previous experience, the intending user will probably not be competent to write a specification that accurately reflects the future needs of the organization. The specification writer must be a person who is thoroughly familiar with the use of networks, principles of planning and scheduling, and the possibilities offered in general by modern project management

Item	Program characteristics
System Costs	● What is the basic price for a single PC user?
	● What is the basic price for 5 network users?
	● What is the basic price for 10 network users?
	or, how much for our anticipated number of users?
	● Are any optional extras needed and, if so, at what cost?
	● How much training will be needed and at what cost?
	● If training is on our premises, do the training costs include travel, subsistence and accommodation expenses for the trainers?
	● If timesheet capability is to be used, what is the additional cost likely to be for all our timesheet users?
	● If we should need any customization, what is the likely scale of charges?
System support	● Is first-year support and maintenance free of charge?
	● What are the future support and maintenance charges expected?
	● Does system support include free software upgrades?
	● Is there a hotline service for advice and troubleshooting?
	● At what times is the hotline accessible:
	— Normal working hours?
	— Nights?
	— Weekends
	● Are we guaranteed immediate response, and not an answering machine?
	● Was this software developed by the suppliers, or are they simply agents with less in-depth knowledge of the system?
	● How many systems have been sold?
	● How many of those users are in our country?
	● Is there a users' group?
	● Is the users' group supported by the software supplier?

Figure 12.2   *concluded*

software. A considerable amount of internal investigation will be needed to assess the size and nature of projects to be planned, so that parameters can be set for the various minimum capacities of the new software.

Once the user's specification has been written, a corresponding suppliers' questionnaire can be prepared. This simply lists all the requirements of the specification, but converts each statement into a question and leaves the quantities and required characteristics blank for the supplier to fill in and return.

Some skill is needed in setting the questions if the software capabilities are to be probed successfully. For instance, the question 'How many activities can be held in the system?' will often produce the answer: 'The maximum number of activities depends only on the size of the available memory.' But answers to the supplementary questions 'How many characters can be assigned to an activity ID code?' and 'Can ID codes be alphanumeric?' can be more revealing. If the software can accept only three-digit numerical ID codes, there cannot be more than 999 activities in one network.

Investigating the suppliers

Identifying possible suppliers

There are many potential suppliers, and listing all of them might prove difficult. The more important software houses will usually exhibit at project management exhibitions. Other suppliers advertise in journals such as *Project Management Today*. A useful start is to obtain brochures so that those programs which are patently incapable of fulfilling the organization's needs can be eliminated painlessly at the start.

Initial correspondence

Once the questionnaire has been prepared, it is safe to approach the would-be suppliers and invite them to quote. The imposition of a cut-off date for replies is highly advisable.

Some companies will probably fail to reply, even after reminders. Others might reply only to admit, with commendable honesty, that their product will not fulfil all the conditions suggested by the nature of the questions. However, it can be expected that a fair proportion of the questionnaires will be completed and returned.

Shortlisting

The returned questionnaires should be subjected to a formal and fair comparison, so that those products which fail to satisfy one or more vital conditions of the user's specification can be eliminated on a simple 'go' or 'no-go' basis. It is helpful to display all the answers on a matrix chart for this purpose, with each column of the chart allocated to one supplier's product, and with the questions and answers spaced along the rows. This should produce a shortlist of possible suppliers.

Demonstrations

A valuable approach is to invite the shortlisted finalists to visit (separately) and demonstrate their systems. These should be live demonstrations on a computer (not simply audio-visual sales presentations). Such demonstrations can be very revealing, especially when the appropriate questions are asked and when particular tests are requested. The data for these demonstrations and witnessed tests should be provided by the user, so that it is as representative as possible of the projects that will eventually be scheduled. Excepting very cheap packages, most companies should be willing to carry out the demonstration free of charge.

The software purchaser has an obligation to complement the expense and effort asked of the suppliers by providing reasonable facilities for the demonstrator, and by ensuring that all those likely to be associated with the purchase decision process attend all the demonstrations.

Independent referees and other users

Contact with organizations which already successfully use computer systems for project planning and management can be useful: their people should be able to discuss and demonstrate their procedures and so make the intending user more aware of what can be done. The unbiased views of these independent users can also be important for outlining possible problems or limitations. However, many users do not make full use of their systems and fail to derive all the potential benefits, so that a false picture can be gained by consulting them. It might be necessary to employ a specialist independent consultant, at least in the early investigative days.

Making the final choice

It is probable that more than one supplier will be able to satisfy all the more important aspects of the user's specification. Under these circumstances, it is helpful to use a formal bid summary procedure, similar to that described in Chapter 18. Two bid summary tables might be needed: one to compare the technical capabilities, and the other to compare prices and other commercial considerations.

When making the final choice, it is best to start by considering only the most important requirements, so that the user is not overwhelmed by the all the features possible from a powerful project management package. However, the future must be borne in mind, so that the full potential of the user's specification can be realized as confidence and expertise are built up. It could well be advisable, therefore, to purchase a program which is sufficiently powerful and flexible to allow a small-scale start, whilst having the capabilities in reserve for more ambitious use later on.

Special network logic requirements for computer applications

Project management software uses either precedence notation or a form of linked bar charting. With these systems there is no real difference in the methods needed to draw the initial networks or charts.

Collecting start and finish nodes

In some of the earlier programs it was mandatory to have only one start node and one finish node for the whole network. Even with modern programs, this is a convenient arrangement for the following reasons:

- A single start node provides a convenient place on which to hang a scheduled start date for the whole project.
- Similarly, a single finish node provides a place on which to hang a target end date for the project.
- Single start and finish nodes simplify the critical path calculations.
- Having one declared start node and one finish node is useful in analysing error reports. Any other reported starts and finishes can then be recognized as error dangles (see Figure 13.1).

Drawing the network on the screen

It is possible to 'draw' the logic directly on the computer screen (either as a linked bar chart or as a precedence network). Precedence notation is ideal for this purpose, but only very tiny networks can be displayed whole on a single screen at a zoom size large enough to see all the detail.

Although a large network can be viewed by scrolling the screen or by producing interim trial prints, this is not as practicable as starting from a network drawn on a single sheet or roll of paper or film, where the network can be viewed as a whole, and all the logic constraints can be checked by running an inquisitive finger along the various paths. Nevertheless, the facility to be able to edit an existing network from the screen display will be found extremely useful, although it is always advisable to trace the logic through on a printout afterwards.

Preparing for the first computer schedule

Figure 12.3 outlines the principal steps that are typically necessary when attempting to use new software for the first time for project planning and resource scheduling.

Assuming that the program has been properly installed and tested, the first step in setting up the computer schedule for a new project is to prepare and enter all the data. The way in which this is done will depend on the requirements of the particular program, but modern systems are very easy to use in this respect, with screen prompts and help menus available at almost every step.

As users become more familiar with their systems, they should find that data can be entered in a number of different ways: a straight listing of activity data, for example, is quicker than entering the data as a series of responses to prompts. Some programs allow data entry straight into a screen plot of the network, so that links can be dragged into place using the mouse.

Whatever the method chosen for entering data, the information can usually be divided loosely into four main groups. These are:

1 **Project data** – which means the bundle of data that sets up the project file and contains the main details about the project
2 **Calendar information** – from which one or more calendar files will be set up
3 **Resource data** – which is obviously only required if resource scheduling is to be performed, this specifies the codes and descriptions of all the resources to be used, together with their cost rates, availability levels and position in the organizational breakdown structure
4 **Activity records** – with one record for each activity in the network, including its description, duration, and other directly relevant data.

Project data

Basic project data mainly consists of information that has to be entered only once, when each new project file is opened. It includes facts such as the project number and title, name of the project manager, perhaps the customer's name, and so on. The planner might also want to set up codes for different departments or managers in the organization, to facilitate the preparation of edited reports later.

Questions such as system security might also have to be answered at this stage, determining who shall have access to the system and at what level. For example, at the least senior access level (level 9, say), the system user might be permitted to view project schedules on a screen but would not be allowed to change the data on file in any way. On the other hand, the computer technologist might be given complete access to the system (at level 1) with authority to change fundamental parameters or to customize report formats.

Calendars and dates

Most, if not all, project management software allows more than one calendar to be set up and held as a calendar file. By far most important of these is the main or default calendar, which will include all dates except those days on which work may not be scheduled (such as weekends). In many cases this main calendar will be the only one necessary. Most default calendars assume working of five weekdays, with Saturdays and Sundays removed. A task estimated to take ten days will therefore occupy two weeks of the Gregorian calendar.

Holidays will usually have to be taken out of the default calendar. Some systems adopt the alternative approach of allowing a separate holiday calendar file to be set up, in which only the holiday dates are specified. 'Holidays' in this sense usually means public holidays or company holiday shut-downs when no project work can take place.

Care must always be taken when writing or entering dates in numerical form, to ensure that confusion between the American and other conventions does not cause errors. For instance, 01-03-04 means 3 January 2004 to an American and 1 March 2004 to a British person. Most software allows the user to specify the date format.

It is necessary to decide and enter the units of duration that will be used throughout the networks, and to specify how these will relate to each calendar. For example, a standard unit of 1 might be chosen to represent one day, to work with a calendar of five working weekdays within each calendar week. If this were to be the main (default) calendar used throughout the system, then an estimated activity duration of one calendar week would be written as 5 on the network diagram and entered as 5 units in the computer. Most systems allow the user a wide choice of units, ranging from minutes to durations of one month or more.

Some project management programs allow hundreds of different calendars to be specified. Each separate calendar must be given its own identifying file number or name. When the computer calculates schedules, it will work with the main or default calendar unless one of the special calendars is allocated to an activity or a resource. Some examples follow to show why such special calendars might be needed, and how they might be defined. Methods vary from one program to another, and these examples are only a general guide.

Special calendar: Case 1

An organization works only on weekdays. All project work takes place within normal office hours. The project manager has decided that Saturday and Sunday working will never be required. The project manager would like to be able to schedule small jobs with estimated durations as short as one half-day.

Only one calendar (the main calendar) is necessary in this case. The solution for dealing with short duration units could be to specify the standard unit of duration as 0.5 day. This means that each working day will consist of 2 units (which, for practical purposes can be taken as meaning one unit each for the morning and afternoon work periods). The computer will be told that the calendar comprises 10 units in 1 week, with only Monday through Friday as valid dates for scheduling. It is obvious that the same units must be written on the network diagram (so that

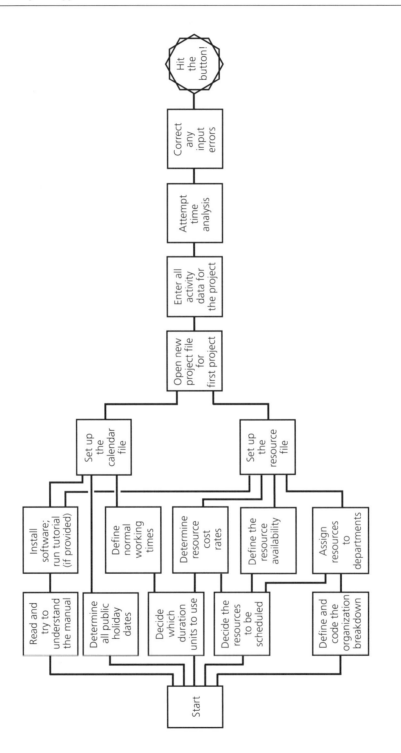

Figure 12.3   Suggested procedure for implementing new project management software
On-site training by the software houses may be needed to achieve full capability.

an activity duration estimated at two Gregorian calendar weeks would have to be written as 20, for example).

The computer will count 2 units as a total calendar day for network time analysis. Work-to lists and all other reports from the system will then show only weekday dates, and Saturdays and Sundays will not be seen as permissible dates for scheduling. Note, however, that network time analysis using this calendar would remain valid for such activities as shipping delays (which do, of course, span weekends), although pick-up and delivery dates could only be reported as taking place on weekdays.

Special calendar: Case 2

Most people in a company work only from Monday to Friday, and they cannot be scheduled as working on Saturdays or Sundays. However, one department does work on Saturdays.

The main (default) calendar in this case might be for duration units of whole days, with only Monday to Friday as valid working days. A second calendar can then be defined, perhaps coded as 'Calendar 2', with 6 days available in the working week, and with only Sundays excluded. Calendar 2 would be called into play whenever appropriate, usually by overriding the default calendar and specifying Calendar 2 instead when data are entered for each relevant activity or (if the software allows) by associating Calendar 2 with the type of labour resource affected.

Special calendar: Case 3

Activities for a project are to be carried out in two or more countries, some of which have different workday and public holiday arrangements. All the activities for the project are contained within one network diagram, and it is not considered desirable or possible to draw a separate network for each country. The whole project is to be planned and progressed from project organization headquarters in London, England.

One solution is to start by deciding where most of the activities will be carried out, and create a main (default) calendar to suit the holiday pattern of the relevant country. Then a special calendar must be created for each country which has a different set of workday and holiday conditions. Activities would then be scheduled against the calendar relevant to the country in which they are planned to occur.

Special calendar: Case 4

A company has at least one department which operates more than one shift within each period of 24 hours. Some shifts operate continuously throughout weekdays and weekends.

A separate calendar can be assigned for each different pattern of shiftworking. For example, 21 work periods would be specified as being equivalent to one calendar week if three shifts are to be worked for all days including weekends. The planner must determine how this will affect the duration estimates written on the network diagram (according to the requirements of the particular computer program).

Other methods for dealing with shiftwork require the use of tricks to obtain the desired results, such as retaining the default calendar but multiplying the number of resources needed for each shift on an activity by the number of shifts to be worked in each 24-hour period. Resource availability levels would have to be factored accordingly. Such tricks are always complicated to apply, and are not generally recommended.

Project start date

It is important to give the computer a datum point from which it will begin the project. This is usually done by imposing a scheduled start date on the first project activity or event. For subsequent updates, a 'time-now' date has to be specified (explained in the section on 'Updating' on page 327).

Scheduled dates (target dates)

The planner might wish to impose fixed target dates on activities anywhere in the network. In some systems it is possible to specify:

- **an early ('not before') date** – the computer must not schedule the start of the activity before the imposed date, this facility might be used, for example, on the first site activity of a construction project, where the date when the previous occupier is expected to vacate the site is known
- **a late date** – an imposed latest permissible date for the start or completion of an activity
- **a fixed date** – some systems allow this by the imposition on the appropriate activity of the same date as both early and late dates.

Other options are usually possible, depending on the software used. Imposed scheduled dates will almost certainly conflict with the dates computed from time analysis, and so will affect float calculations. If an imposed date is logically impossible, negative float will be generated and reported, although programs differ considerably in their ability to indicate negative float clearly.

Resource data

Resource data must be entered if the computer is going to carry out resource scheduling or produce cost reports based on the cost rates of resources.

The planner has to start by deciding how many different resource types are to be considered and scheduled. It is not necessary, and is indeed a mistake, to attempt scheduling every possible department or type of labour employed by the project organization. For example, it is not necessary to schedule canteen staff, cleaners, administrative office workers, and so on. There are usually some direct workers who do not need to be included in the resource scheduling, because their work is provided as a service, or follows automatically on from the work of others who must be scheduled. These aspects were described more fully in Chapter 11.

Mandatory resource data

The following data must be entered for each type of resource deemed necessary for scheduling:

- **Resource code** – a simple identifier code, which often comprises one, two or three characters; examples might include ENG for engineers, BKL for bricklayers, FTR for fitters, TST for a test bay facility

- **Resource name** – the name of the resource type as it will appear in reports

- **Normal availability** – the number of resource units normally available to the program for allocation to simultaneous project activities and the start and finish dates of the period for which they are expected to be available; all competent software will allow for changes in resource levels during the project life cycle; this is achieved by specifying the relevant periods and their associated resource levels, as described in Chapter 11.

Note that it is generally not advisable to declare a total department strength as being available for scheduling. If in doubt, start with either 80 or 85 per cent of the total level. Reasons for this were explained in Chapter 11, under the section 'Specifying departmental resource availability levels'. If a resource is being used with a special calendar for two- or three-shift working, the declared availability level must be reduced even further, to allow for the people to be distributed over the various shifts, and also to take account of their rest days.

Optional resource data

The following optional data can also be entered with most systems for each type or resource specified:

- **Calendar** – the file name of any special calendar against which a particular resource is to be associated and scheduled; this might not be possible with some software; it is more usual to assign the special calendar to the relevant activities, rather than to the resources

- **Cost rate**- the cost expected to be incurred by using one unit of the resource in normal circumstances for one network unit of duration, for example: 1 BKL = £180 per day

● **Threshold resources** – resources above the normal availability level, which the computer may call upon to be used if the project cannot be scheduled using only normal availability levels (see Figure 10.8), examples might include extra hours available by working overtime, or additional staff that could be taken on as temporary or subcontract workers

● **Threshold cost rate** – the cost rate expected when one unit of a threshold resource is used during one network duration period: for example, an overtime rate payable

● **Rate constancy** – the program may allow the user to declare each resource category as rate-constant or non-rate-constant; in the normal case of rate-constant resources, scheduling takes place on the assumption that if two people are needed for an activity, they will be scheduled at the constant rate of two people throughout the activity duration.

For non-rate-constant resources a cyclical pattern of availability can be specified (for example, available for the first five days of every seven-day period). This is not used very often, but it can offer an alternative to the practice of having special calendars, giving the planner another method with which to solve scheduling problems associated with departments that work different numbers of days or shifts.

Other resource data

There are other classes of data associated with resources that depend very much on the software being used. With some systems, one resource type can be given more than one different skill type. It is also possible to assign resources to groups within departments, as part of an organizational breakdown structure. At least one system allows a staff file to be set up, with the names of all project personnel and some of their career details to be entered in the common database.

Priority rules

If resource scheduling is wanted, certain priority rules will have to be defined, although the user might not be asked to make a decision until just before processing takes place. The main rules are:

● whether the schedule is to be time-limited or resource-limited (see Figure 10.8)
● the priority rule for allocating resources to competing activities (a useful choice is to give priority to activities with least remaining float).

Activity records

Activity records comprise the bulk of the data to be entered before the initial run, and it is among these data that most input errors are likely to crop up. A sensible way of going about the task is to have a print of the network diagram to hand, and tick off each activity and each logical link as it is entered into the computer. This will help to prevent errors of omission. It can also prevent duplication, although modern software will not allow duplicate activities to be entered (that is, two or more activities bearing the same ID code).

Mandatory activity data

The following data must always be entered for every activity record, otherwise the computer will not even be able to carry out basic time analysis.

- the activity ID number
- the ID numbers *either* immediately preceding activities *or* immediately succeeding activities
- the type of precedence constraints, if default finish–start links do not to apply; when complex constraints are used, the time duration of the links must also be specified
- the estimated activity duration, given in the units applicable to the specified project calendar.

Optional activity data

Activity descriptions Although it is not mandatory to provide activity descriptions, resulting schedules would not be much use without them. Modern systems allow activity descriptions to contain many characters, but it will generally be found convenient to use sensibly abbreviated descriptions (consisting of perhaps about 30 characters) in order to leave more space for other data in the columns of tabular reports.

Alternative duration estimates Optimistic and pessimistic duration estimates can be added, for use in PERT or risk analysis calculations. This application is relatively uncommon.

Editing and sorting codes A departmental sort code can usually be specified so that reports only contain those activities which are of interest to each manager or department. Codes can also indicate the level of management, so that senior managers might receive summary reports.

A few systems allow various sorting and editing sequences on different parts of the activity data. It might be possible, for example, to use part of the description field as a sort code (perhaps by including a job number or cost code at the start of the description for each activity).

Resource data These codes consist of the resource and the average number of resource units estimated to be required for each resource type. Note that this input can be used not only for resource scheduling, but also for scheduling and reporting costs (provided that cost rates have been specified for all the resources).

Cost The estimated or budget cost of an activity can be included. This method of entering cost data is used for activities that use no declared resources, but which nevertheless incur costs. The most common use is for equipment and materials costs.

Special constraint rules Some advanced programs allow special logic constraints to be defined for an activity. These include tied activities, in which two designated activities must follow each other without delay (for example, concrete pouring followed by curing time).

Splittable activities (applicable only to resource scheduling) Activities may be declared as splittable if interruptions in their progress can be permitted. When this facility is chosen, the program is allowed to split an activity into two or more parts, interrupting the activity so that resources can be diverted for use elsewhere by another activity that has higher priority.

Chapter 13

Project management computer systems, Part 2: Typical applications

The previous chapter listed many of the factors to be taken into account when choosing project management software, and explained some of the preparations and decisions necessary before planning and scheduling can begin. This chapter illustrates the steps needed to create a project schedule, with resources and estimated costs taken into account. The examples were produced using a few different project management software packages from the many that are now available. A few addresses are given at the end of Chapter 14 for those who would like to find out more about the features and availability of these programs.

The welcoming screen

Software varies considerably in its 'user-friendliness'. Some programs (such as *Microsoft Project 2000*) present a blank Gantt chart on the screen as soon as they are booted up, and it is apparent to the user that task data can be typed in immediately.

Other products, such as *Open Plan Professional*, whilst being very powerful and capable systems, have an opening screen that needs some explanation and training before the planner can get started. This is often a price worth paying. The more capable the software, and the more functions that it can perform, the more complicated the various toolbars and drop-down menus are likely to be. Navigation of these menus in many project management software products requires good training and 'hands-on' experience.

Two different approaches to the welcoming screen can be expected, depending on which software is chosen.

1   On booting up the application, the user is presented with a blank Gantt chart onto which all the activity data can be entered. This can usually be changed to a network view, according to the user's preference. When the data are complete, one uses the 'Save' or 'Save as' options from the File menu to store the new project in the system.

2   A screen appears with no prompts. It is necessary to go to the 'File' menu and click on 'New'. In some cases the user must then choose from a range of options in a browser – for instance, 'Project' would be the appropriate selection when entering a new project.

Most programs will allow the project to be saved as a 'baseline', which means that the initial version will be retained unchanged to provide a base against which future updates can be compared to monitor actual performance and other properties against the original plan. Some users, no doubt, find this feature valuable.

Case study project

The project used for the case study throughout this chapter is the same garage project that was introduced in Chapter 10. Its network diagram was originally given in Figure 10.1 in both arrow and precedence versions. The diagram is repeated here in Figure 13.1 for convenience but, as modern software does not cater for arrow diagrams, only the precedence version is relevant to this chapter. The network logic and task duration estimates are unchanged from Figure 10.1, except for giving new ID codes to the start and finish activities (explained below).

Remember that this is a project to build a detached garage for the owner of a private house. The project labour resources comprise a father-and-son team, who run their own construction business. The father is classified as skilled, and the son is a relatively unskilled labourer.

Data for the garage project

Project dates and calendar

The project start date is (or was, depending on when you read this) 10 May 2004. In all cases the standard software default calendars have been used. All the software chosen for these examples use a calendar based on five weekdays. Saturdays and Sundays are therefore removed from the schedule, no resources can be used on these days, and no weekend dates will appear in any schedules. The network diagram in Figure 13.1 includes the estimated duration for each task in days.

Labour resources

The resources needed for each task are shown in Figure 13.1, with 1S representing one skilled person, and 1L denoting one labourer. For this case study the specified resources will be scheduled evenly throughout the duration of the task. The number of man-hours required for a task would therefore change in direct

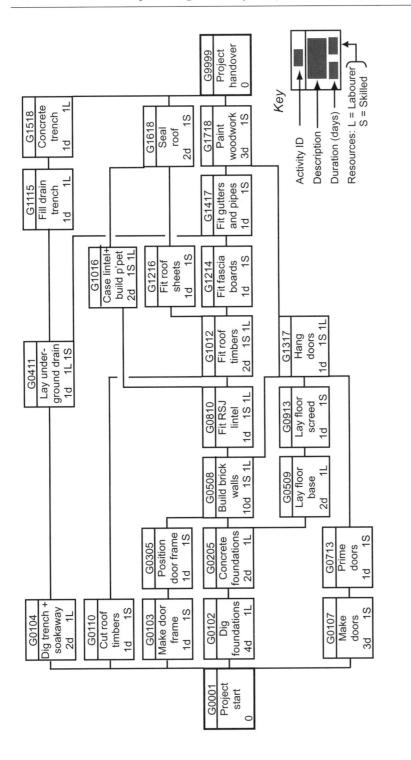

Figure 13.1   Garage project: Precedence network diagram

This is the same project represented in Figure 10.1 but, as this is now to be processed by computer, the arrow diagram is no longer relevant.

proportion to any change (estimated or actual) in the task duration. The quantities 2d 1L 1S on a network task would mean, for instance, a task estimated to last two weekdays, with one labourer and one skilled person working continuously on the task throughout those two days.

Splittable and non-splittable activities

Some resource scheduling software will allow tasks to be split (interrupted and then restarted at a later date) to achieve a smoother usage of resources and avoid overloads. For the garage project, however, the default non-splittable option has been chosen throughout. In most real project cases it is undesirable to interrupt work on a task to divert resources to other work. Continuous, smooth working is always best, if that can be achieved.

Labour costs

There are usually several methods available to the planner for specifying human resource costs. These include a fixed work content for the task, or (my choice here) a cost that is a product of the number of resource units (people) and the task duration. The proportional choice means, of course, that if an activity takes longer than expected the computer will calculate higher actual costs than those originally budgeted in the resource schedule.

For this project, the labour rates chosen are as follows:

- **Skilled worker** – £160 per day. Some software (including *Microsoft Project 2000*) has a default calendar based on an eight-hour day, so the cost for this resource becomes £20 per hour.

- **Labourer** – £120 per day, or £15 per hour.

No overtime working has been assumed, thus there are no overtime premiums to consider.

Labour resources available

All software requires the dates and amounts of resources that are available for the project to be stated before resource scheduling can even be considered. For the garage project, one unit (one person) of each resource type was specified as being available from 1 Jan 2004 to 31 Dec 2004. These dates were chosen to ensure that they would encompass the project period adequately.

A range of dates and numbers could have been entered to allow for any planned expansion or reduction of the workforce in future, and for changes in the resource cost rates.

Activity ID	Activity description	Materials required	Estimated cost £
G0001	Project start	No materials	
G0102	Dig foundations	No materials	
G0103	Make and prime door frame	Wood and primer	50
G0104	Dig soakaway and trench	No materials	
G0107	Make doors	Wood and sundries	300
G0110	Cut roof timbers	Wood	450
G0205	Concrete foundations	Concrete ingredients	150
G0305	Position door frame	No materials	
G0411	Lay underground drainpipe	Pipe	40
G0508	Build main brick walls	Bricks and mortar ingredients	650
G0509	Lay concrete floor base	Concrete ingredients	70
G0713	Prime the doors	Primer and sundries	20
G0810	Fit RSJ lintel over door frame	Rolled steel joist (RSJ)	40
G0913	Lay floor screed	Flooring compound	200
G1012	Fit roof timbers	No extra materials	
G1016	Case lintel and build parapets	Wood and concrete	60
G1115	Fill drain trench	No materials	
G1214	Fit fascia boards	Wood	30
G1216	Fit roof sheets	Sheets and fixings	360
G1317	Hang doors	Locks and hinges	80
G1417	Fit gutters and downpipes	Gutters, pipes, fixings	80
G1518	Concrete over drain trench	Concrete ingredients	20
G1618	Seal the roof	Sealant	30
G1718	Paint all woodwork	Paint and sundries	30
G9999	Project finish and handover	No materials	

Resource code	Resource name		Resource cost per day £
S	Skilled worker		160
L	Labourer		120

Figure 13.2   Garage project: Cost estimates

Cost of construction materials

Figure 13.2 shows the estimated costs of the more important materials for each task in the garage project. These are costs *per task*. Unlike labour costs, these costs are not dependent upon the duration of the task.

Consider, for example, the task to build the garage walls. The quantities of bricks and mortar needed can be estimated accurately, so that when the project starts these materials can be purchased and delivered to the site at a known, fixed cost. This contrasts with the time needed to build the walls, which might (depending on many uncontrollable factors) vary considerably from the original duration estimate. So, labour costs are more likely to vary with task time than the materials used.

However, some software will allow materials usage and costs to be specified at a rate that *is* proportional to task duration for the comparatively uncommon cases when this is more appropriate than the fixed-cost option. Examples include plant hire and (not relevant to this small garage project) some bulk supplies, site fuel costs and site office costs.

Task identifier codes

Task identifier codes are shown on the network diagram. These were originally designed to allow comparison between arrow and precedence networks in Chapter 10. So, G0103 in the precedence diagram, for example, is equivalent to activity 01–03 in the arrow diagram in Figure 10.1.

Now that this project is about to be processed by computer, the ID codes for the project start and finish activities must be chosen sensibly. We could use simply 'start' and 'finish' (as in previous editions of this book). However, I have used instead G0001 and G9999 for the start and finish respectively, so that these start and finish tasks will print out first and last in reports during most sorting sequences.

Task ID numbers in reports processed with *Microsoft Project 2000* are different from the network diagram in Figure 13.1 because this software assigns its own task ID numbers in a simple numerical sequence corresponding to the sequence in which task are entered.

Task descriptions (task names)

The number of characters allowed by the software in the task name field is usually more than adequate. However, abbreviations are usually necessary for task names shown in some graphics reports, such as network diagrams. Some software will simply truncate task names to show only the first few characters. Other packages will allow the user to specify an abbreviated name for every task.

Logic relationships

All relationships in this project are of the finish–start type. No new task can start until all its predecessors have been finished. This is the default assumed by all the software used here. Figure 8.17 showed the other options that can be used, should it be necessary to plan for more complex logical relationships.

Data entry errors

Because there are so many ways in which undetectable mistakes can be made, it pays to be very careful during initial data entry. If a second person can be spared, good practice is to have one person keying in the data, and the other assisting by ticking each item off on a copy of the network as it is entered.

After data entry, it can be very helpful to print a complete activity listing, so that all the data can be checked manually for errors and omissions. The most useful report for this purpose is a list of all activity records printed in ascending order of their ID codes, and with the links to preceding and succeeding activities and the activity durations included. Such a list is invaluable for checking that the logic input to the machine is free from mistakes that might otherwise go undetected.

If the software is incapable of printing such a list, a network plot is an acceptable alternative (see the section on network plotting, on page 312).

Error diagnostics

Whether the computer is to be used for time analysis only or for full resource and cost scheduling, once it has digested all the data its first processing job will be to attempt time analysis. For this it will make forward and backward passes through the network. It will recognize the network logic by means of the identification numbers of all the activities and their specified links. During these backward and forward passes, the program will identify all obvious errors.

All good project management software contains comprehensive error detection routines, designed to recognize particular types of mistakes and report them to the planner for correction (or for confirmation that the relevant data are correct as entered, and that any apparent anomalies were intended). Errors might result from transpositions or other reading errors, keyboard mistakes, entering non-valid control data (for example a date which lies outside the main calendar), or some basic flaw in the network diagram logic itself.

If all the data have been entered correctly there is a possibility that the first attempt at time analysis will work when the appropriate command is given. In the absence of mistakes, the computer will complete the time analysis and write the results to its database. However, unless the network is really small, it can safely be assumed that something will go wrong, and that the computer will produce an unwelcome warning message.

Typical errors

Input errors can be divided into two categories:

1   Mistakes or apparent mistakes which the computer is able to recognize and report back as helpful error messages – examples of these include the following:

- invalid dates (such as 30 February or a target date that falls on a day specified in the calendar file as non-working)
- duplicated activity records (most modern software will not allow duplicate ID codes to be entered)
- dangles (explained below)
- loops (explained below)
- any other anomalies where the computer can recognize conflicting input data – for example, zero duration specified for an activity that also claims to need resources

2   Mistakes which the computer cannot recognize, and which will remain undetected and lead to possible scheduling errors – examples of these are as follows:
- an incorrect activity duration
- an incorrect task name (for example, where two names and ID codes are transposed)
- the wrong type of constraint for an activity in a precedence network
- forgetting to specify the cost of materials for an activity
- entering the wrong resource or sort code for an activity.

Activity data errors which affect network logic

It is not surprising that the most frequent source of input errors occurs in the activity records, since these represent by far the greatest amount of data to be entered. Putting such errors right for large networks can sometimes prove to be an interesting exercise in detective work, with the computer reports merely providing clues. The three main error types are as follows:

1   *Duplicate activities* – If two different activity records have been input with the same identifier code number, the computer will fail to distinguish between them, and will regard them as an error of duplication. It is almost certain that a modern system would report this type of mistake as soon as any attempt is made to enter the second activity record. Earlier systems made the unsuspecting planner wait until after the initial error run. The cause is likely to be one of the following:
- a real attempt to input the same activity twice, which might happen (for instance) if the person entering the data happened to be interrupted, and forgot that the activity had already been entered
- a keyboard error in entering an identification number
- a numbering error on the original network diagram. I am reminded here of an occasion when a colleague of mine was busily engaged in allocating activity ID numbers on a new network drawing that occupied a roll of paper over 5 metres long. There were well over 1000 activities in that project. The drawing was spread over and beyond a double A0-sized drawing board. Halfway through the activity numbering procedure, the

planner was interrupted by a long telephone call. When he returned to his drawing board and picked up his pencil again he had lost his place, forgot the last number added and, as a result, duplicated over 50 activity numbers. The intimidating pile of error warning pages from the computer listed many duplicated activities and several large loops. The disaster took a day and much of a night to put right.

2   *Dangles* – Dangling activities occur whenever records have been created for activities that have no preceding activities (start dangles) or no succeeding activities (end or finish dangles). Clearly, the first and last activities in a network will be seen as dangles. Unwanted dangles occur either because an activity has been omitted by mistake (leaving a gap in a network path), or because a link has been omitted or wrongly specified. In Figure 13.3(a) two dangles have been created because the planner forgot to specify the finish–start link from activity G0509 to G0913. The computer will thus recognize activity G0509 as a finish activity, and G0913 as a start activity. That will, of course, produce large errors in time analysis and the resulting schedules.

3   *Loops* – A loop is a sequence of activities whose logical path forms a

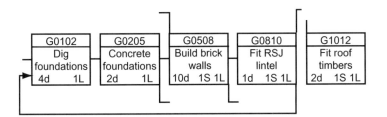

(a)   *Creation of two dangles*

(b)   *Creation of a loop*

Figure 13.3   Garage project: Data errors
Two details from the garage project network diagram, to show how simple data input mistakes can create serious logic errors. Dangles and loops are explained in the text.

continuous loop. This kind of mistake can be caused by entering an incorrect activity number or precedence link, especially by placing a link in the wrong direction. A loop is impossible to time-analyse, and the computer becomes trapped in an endless cycle of activities from which there is no escape.

In Figure 13.3(b) the planner has entered the successor of activity G0810 as G0102 instead of G1012. This has created a loop containing activities G0102, G0205, G0508 and G0810.

The computer program should be capable of listing all the activities contained in a loop. Early (DOS) versions of *Open Plan* produced an error log which contained the words 'Loop detected', then listed the activities within the loop and ended with the chilling message 'Aborted: fatal error'. Now *Open Plan Professional,* in common with some other packages, checks the logic during data entry, and will not allow the creation of a loop.

Other errors

All computer programs contain many more error-checking routines than the three just described. Error reports will be generated, for example, if the planner has tried to enter a target project completion date which precedes the specified project start date (not a very clever thing to do, but easily done at the end of a tiring day by entering an incorrect year).

Other messages will arise if any of the program capacities are exceeded. This would happen, for example, if the network proved to be too large for the computer to handle. Another possibility is that the total project duration might be too long for the specified project calendar.

Network plotting

Network plots are useful both as management control tools and for checking that the correct logic has been input to the computer. The ability to produce legible and useful plots varies considerably from one program to another. The best plots will position all the activities in the best possible pattern, always observing the rule that networks flow from left to right, setting out all the links clearly (especially at crossover points) and placing the activities to use the smallest area of screen or printout possible.

Microsoft Project, especially in versions from *Microsoft Project 2000* onwards, plots very clear networks with all the links shown without ambiguity. The disadvantage is that the standard network plot spreads over many A4 pages, like an atlas. These have to be cut and pasted to form a logic diagram on one sheet. A printer with AO sheet or paper roll capability is needed for best results. A very compact plot can, however, be obtained by choosing to show only the IDs within activity boxes.

Software such as *Open Plan Professional* requires the user to carry out 'placements' from the 'Tools' menu before the program will 'draw' the network on the screen in a sensible layout. These can either be automatic or manual. Manual placements enable the user to drag and drop activities and links on the screen to remove ambiguities where two or more links run along the same path and to make the plot more compact. However, manual placements are time-consuming and inappropriate for larger networks. Other programs use different terms for placements, such as 'Refresh layout'.

4c produces near-perfect network plots that are clear, comprehensive and compact. The garage project, for example, plotted well: even when rescaled to fit a single A4 sheet, links were shown clearly with no ambiguities. The garage network, although legible on a single A4 sheet, is less clear when reduced to the page size of this book. Figure 13.4 therefore shows just a summary plot. The small template examples in Chapter 14 do, however, allow a full-size plot to be shown (Figure 14.9).

Time analysis of the garage project network

With no known remaining data errors, the computer can be commanded to carry out time analysis of the garage project. This involves forward and backward passes through the network to determine the amount of float, and the earliest possible and latest permissible times for the start and finish of every activity. Some software (such as *Microsoft Project 2000*) will carry out calculations and recalculations automatically, without the need for separate commands, as network data are entered.

A project management system will observe any constraints imposed by scheduled dates attached to activities anywhere in the network during time analysis and these will affect float and the route of the critical path.

Microsoft Project 2000 and *Primavera* both present a time analysis tabulation on the same display as a Gantt chart. Whenever a full tabular report is required after time analysis, the column headings can usually be customized to include the following data:

- activity ID
- activity description
- estimated duration
- earliest possible start date
- latest permissible start date
- earliest possible finish date
- latest permissible finish date
- free float (free slack)
- total float (total slack)

The planner can choose many other data fields from competent software for the time analysis table. In particular, these cover cost data, resource requirements,

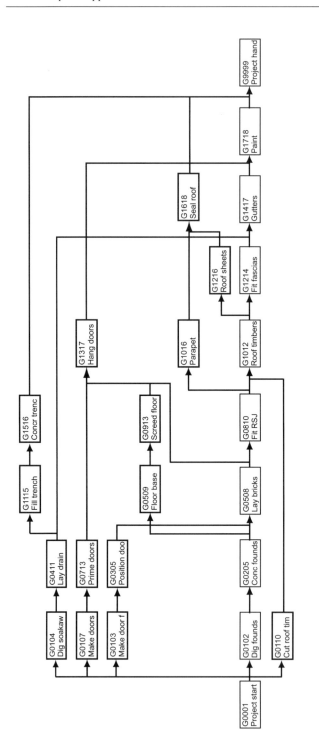

Figure 13.4   Garage project: Summary network plotted by *4c*

Task names had to be severely abbreviated to achieve this compact plot, but this summary is ideal for checking that the network logic has been correctly entered into the computer.

ID	Task name	Duration	Early start	Early finish	Late start	Late finish	Free slack	Total slack
1	Project start	0 days	10 May 04	10 May 04	10 May 04	10 May 04	0 days	0 days
2	Dig trench and soakaway	2 days	10 May 04	11 May 04	02 Jun 04	03 Jun 04	0 days	17 days
3	Cut roof timbers	1 day	10 May 04	10 May 04	01 Jun 04	01 Jun 04	16 days	16 days
4	Make door frame	1 day	10 May 04	10 May 04	14 May 04	14 May 04	0 days	4 days
5	Dig foundations	4 days	10 May 04	13 May 04	10 May 04	13 May 04	0 days	0 days
6	Make doors	3 days	10 May 04	12 May 04	01 Jun 04	03 Jun 04	0 days	16 days
7	Position door frame	1 day	11 May 04	11 May 04	17 May 04	17 May 04	4 days	4 days
8	Concrete foundations	2 days	14 May 04	17 May 04	14 May 04	17 May 04	0 days	0 days
9	Prime doors	1 day	13 May 04	13 May 04	04 Jun 04	04 Jun 04	12 days	16 days
10	Build brick walls	10 days	18 May 04	31 May 04	18 May 04	31 May 04	0 days	0 days
11	Lay floor base	2 days	18 May 04	19 May 04	02 Jun 04	03 Jun 04	0 days	11 days
12	Fit RSJ lintel	1 day	01 Jun 04	01 Jun 04	01 Jun 04	01 Jun 04	0 days	0 days
13	Lay floor screed	1 day	20 May 04	20 May 04	04 Jun 04	04 Jun 04	7 days	11 days
14	Lay underground drain	1 day	12 May 04	12 May 04	04 Jun 04	04 Jun 04	0 days	17 days
15	Fit roof timbers	2 days	02 Jun 04	03 Jun 04	02 Jun 04	03 Jun 04	0 days	0 days
16	Hang doors	1 day	01 Jun 04	01 Jun 04	07 Jun 04	07 Jun 04	4 days	4 days
17	Case lintel + build parapet	2 days	02 Jun 04	03 Jun 04	07 Jun 04	08 Jun 04	1 days	3 days
18	Fit roof sheets	1 day	04 Jun 04	04 Jun 04	08 Jun 04	08 Jun 04	0 days	2 days
19	Fit fascia boards	1 day	04 Jun 04	04 Jun 04	04 Jun 04	04 Jun 04	0 days	0 days
20	Fill drain trench	1 day	13 May 04	13 May 04	09 Jun 04	09 Jun 04	0 days	19 days
21	Fit gutters and pipes	1 day	07 Jun 04	07 Jun 04	07 Jun 04	07 Jun 04	0 days	0 days
22	Concrete trench	1 day	14 May 04	14 May 04	10 Jun 04	10 Jun 04	19 days	19 days
23	Seal roof	2 days	07 Jun 04	08 Jun 04	09 Jun 04	10 Jun 04	2 days	2 days
24	Paint woodwork	3 days	08 Jun 04	10 Jun 04	08 Jun 04	10 Jun 04	0 days	0 days
25	Project handover	0 days	10 Jun 04	10 Jun 04	10 Jun 04	10 Jun 04	0 days	0 days

Figure 13.5   Garage project: Time analysis from *Microsoft Project 2000*

critical status and (once the project has started) progress information. *Microsoft Project 2000* produced the time analysis data shown in Figure 13.5.

Usefulness of time analysis reports

If the project organization has access to unlimited and very flexible resources, or if human and other resource management is to be delegated to subcontractors, a time analysis report can be sufficient for planning and managing the project. Many projects are managed successfully on this basis, using the earliest possible dates as the schedule targets.

In any project where the project activities need people or other resources that are within the project manager's own organization, resource scheduling should always be considered.

A paradox in report dates for activities with zero duration

Some, but by no means all, software will report an activity that has zero duration as being scheduled to finish on the day before it is scheduled to start. This happens, for example, in some *Open Plan Professional* reports.

This is best explained by first considering an activity with a specified duration of one day. Suppose that time analysis gives the earliest start for this activity as 1 June. The computer will recognize the activity as starting at the beginning of 1 June and finishing at the end of the same day. So, in any tabulation, the earliest start will be given as 1 June, and the earliest finish will also be 1 June.

If the same activity had been specified with zero duration, the computer would report a completion date one day earlier than any other activity starting on the same day but having a duration of one day. So it would still declare the earliest start date as being 1 June (which means early morning on 1 June), but the earliest completion date would be given as 31 May (which means the end of work on 31 May). If 1 June happened to be a Monday, with no weekend working allowed, the previous Friday evening would be scheduled as the completion time, so that the tabulation would report the earliest start time as 1 June and the earliest finish time as 28 May.

In fact, close of work time on one day and the beginning of work time on the next working day can, in some circumstances, be regarded as the same point in project time. The intervening hours simply do not exist in the project calendar, and are therefore ignored.

Resource scheduling: The general process

Remembering that the garage project company comprises only two workers, one skilled and one not, it is necessary to perform resource scheduling so that the available resources can be used as efficiently as possible. First, I shall outline the computer process and describe some basic rules under which schedules can be calculated.

Simple resource aggregation

Many early programs could not carry out resource scheduling, even if they claimed to be able to do so. They simply scheduled each activity at its earliest possible date, assigned the estimated number of resources for the period of the activity, and then repeated this for all other activities. No attempt was made to schedule any activity other than at its earliest possible time, and the resulting usage pattern for each type of resource was calculated by simple addition. Resource aggregation by early dates is clearly of very limited use because it produces unworkable schedules, mixing overloads with periods of comparative idleness.

Resource levelling or scheduling

Practically all modern programs, and certainly those used for this garage project case study, are capable of true resource scheduling.

A typical program will attempt to schedule each activity at its earliest possible time, and will 'draw down' the number of resource units for each relevant resource from the total amount specified as available in the project's resource definition file. When each activity ends, its resources are released and returned to the availability pool for reallocation to other activities as necessary.

If insufficient resources remain in the pool for an activity to be started on its earliest date, the computer will make a decision based on priority rules set by the planner.

Priority rules

Influence of float

If the computer has to delay several activities as a result of scarce resources, float is often used to decide which of the competing activities claims first priority. When the computer schedules an activity to take place later than its earliest possible date, it has obviously used up some of the total float originally possessed by the activity and by its following activities. The amount of float left in each case is sometimes called the 'remaining float'. A useful priority rule is to give priority to those activities that have least remaining float.

Time-limited scheduling

Perhaps the most important decision the planner must make regarding resource allocation priorities is to decide whether the schedule is to be resource-limited or time-limited. These rules were explained in Chapter 10 and illustrated in Figure 10.8.

If the time-limited rule is chosen, the computer will schedule all activities at dates necessary to ensure that the project is completed within the timescale specified. Any target dates imposed on the starts or finishes of individual activities within the network would also be given priority. If necessary, the computer will plan for resource usage levels higher than those which have been declared as available.

Resource-limited scheduling

If the computer is operating under the resource-limited rule, it is instructed never to schedule any activity at a date that would cause more resources of any particular type to be needed than the total quantity specified as being available for the project. This means that some activities might have to be delayed beyond their latest (critical) start dates, keeping them waiting until resources are released from other even more critical activities.

Thus, with resource-limited scheduling, the project might have to be extended beyond the earliest possible completion date shown to be possible by the length of the critical path. It might also mean that any target completion dates specified for key activities within the network would have to be ignored.

Effectiveness of resource levelling

It is recognized that resource scheduling by computer may not necessarily produce the smoothest possible pattern of resource usage. Even when a resource schedule is calculated which never exceeds the stated capacity, there can be peaks and troughs remaining that could be ironed out by further calculation.

Imagine that the computer is asked to schedule the usage of electricians on a project, and that a total of five electricians is available within the organization. If the computer is instructed never to schedule beyond the limit of five electricians, it will not do so, and a schedule will be produced that never calls for more than five electricians. That much can be guaranteed. But usage throughout the project life cycle might vary from zero to all five electricians in an unacceptable series of peaks and troughs.

Provided that there was other work for the electricians in the organization, uneven scheduling for one project need not matter. But, suppose that the work on this project means establishing the electricians in overnight accommodation to work on a site away from the headquarters. Then the schedule needs to be optimized, so that the work of electricians is conveniently grouped to allow a level rate of usage and prevent unnecessary travel and wasteful use of accommodation.

Some programs attempt optimization by making more than one scheduling pass through the network. Generally speaking, the computer will produce smoother schedules when it is given the chance to handle a large number of activities and the resource requirements approach the numbers actually available.

Resource scheduling for the garage project

Because the garage project workforce comprises a father-and-son business, the schedule should obviously be resource-limited if possible, because it is going to be very difficult, if not impossible, to augment this tiny labour force. However, I have run both time- and resource-limited schedules for comparison, and to demonstrate the method.

Good software will produce error logs or warning message explaining any adjustments caused by resource limitations or other constraints.

The resource schedules for the garage project were calculated using *Microsoft Project 2000* and *Primavera*. With the project starting on 10 May 2004, project finish using the time-limited rule was predicted as 10 June 2004. It was shown that two skilled and two unskilled people would be needed on certain dates to achieve this result. The histograms produced by *Primavera* are shown in Figure 13.6. The troughs are, of course, Saturdays and Sundays.

When the resource-limited rule was chosen, resources were contained within the one skilled and one unskilled limits, but the project completion date was extended to 23 June 2004. *Primavera* produced a perfect schedule, the histograms from which are shown in Figure 13.7.

Compare these histogram patterns with those produced manually in Figures 10.3, 10.4 and 10.5. The dates cannot be compared directly because the manual versions were calculated for a different project start date (10 May 2002).

Work-to list

One of the most useful types of report available from project management software is similar to the time analysis tabulation shown in Figure 13.5, but with additional columns giving the *scheduled* start and finish dates for each activity. These are the dates recommended for each activity after the resource scheduling process. The resulting schedule is often called a *work-to list*. The report is not simply a list of work that has to be done, it is a recommendation to the relevant managers of the sequence and timing of work to be done – a list to be worked to.

Output reports

A taste of the output report possibilities has already been given, using the garage

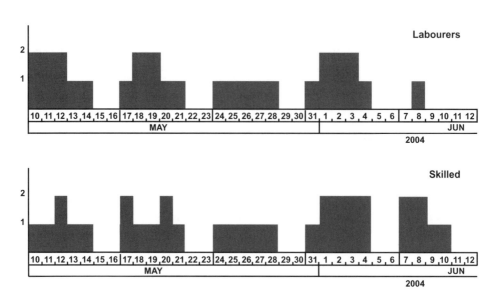

Figure 13.6   Garage project: Time-limited resource histograms by *Primavera*

project data. It is likely that the system will give the user the option of choosing between either a range of standard output reports, or of reports that are adaptable or specially designed to suit the particular needs of the project organization. The commands to be entered for generating reports will depend on the program used.

Proprietary project management software usually contains a range of inbuilt report formats that can be used 'off the shelf', and many of those can be customized from simple drop-down menus. Some programs also give the project manager the option of creating new report formats to suit his or her own project needs, but those need some programming experience. One general word of advice can be given here, however: the beginner would be well advised to start by using the standard formats provided by the system, and think about special report formats later, as confidence in using the system is gained.

Printers or larger plotters can produce network diagrams, Gantt charts and all manner of other graphical displays, enhanced by the use of colour. Work-to lists and scheduled resource requirements can be printed out showing great day-by-day detail. Cost control data can be linked to the schedules, allowing budget cost curves, cost tables and other presentations of planned and recorded expenditure to be printed. Figure 13.8, for example, is a graph from *Primavera* showing daily and cumulative expenditure for the garage project after resource-limited scheduling.

All of these reports can be made available to people inside or outside the project organization via an internal network or through the Internet or other electronic transmission methods.

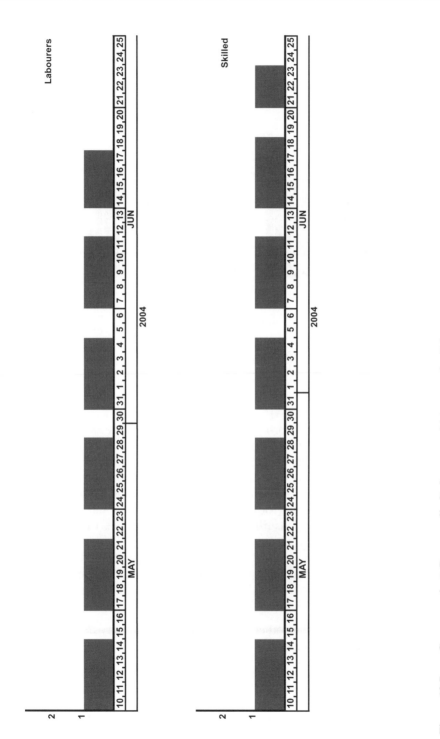

Figure 13.7   Garage project: Resource-limited resource histograms by *Primavera*

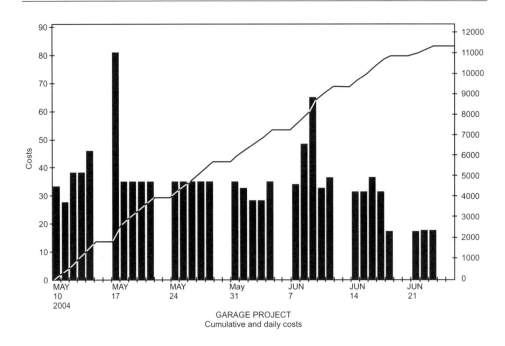

GARAGE PROJECT
Cumulative and daily costs

Figure 13.8   Garage project: Cost report by *Primavera*

Filtering

After a big network has been processed, a very large volume of data is stored in the computer. The quantity of information usually far exceeds that needed for project management. Not only are there a lot of data, but computers are capable of producing output in many different forms, even from a small selection of data. If all possible reports were to be produced, the result might be unmanageable – impressive for its bulk, but not for much else. It follows that the project manager must manage data carefully, ensuring that reports are concise, well presented and as effective as possible for their intended purpose.

The data content of every report must be carefully considered, to ensure that each recipient gets information that is particularly useful or relevant to him or her (preferably on a 'need-to-know' basis). This is achieved by filtering (editing) the project data using one of the following options:

- assigning departmental or other report codes to all activity records
- specifying milestones or key activities
- reporting on selected resources
- choosing some other activity parameters.

Most programs provide a menu from which filtering options can be selected.

If filtering is carefully and properly designed and managed, each departmental manager can be given a work-to list containing only those tasks which he or she is expected to perform or manage. Thus, for example, the purchasing manager would receive information on all purchasing and materials expediting and handling activities.

All unwanted data should be excluded from reports. For example, the planner would probably filter out all activities that are already completed from work-to lists.

Filtering can also be used to exclude information that is secret, confidential or otherwise restricted.

Sorting

Another important aspect of reports is the sequence in which data are presented. This is achieved by the process of sorting.

For example, the person with prime responsibility for planning would need an activity listing sorted according to the activity ID numbers as an aid to checking the input data for errors. A manager responsible for issuing work to a department needs a report that lists jobs in order of their earliest or scheduled start dates. A progress clerk or purchasing expeditor is best served by a report that lists jobs or materials deliveries in order of their planned completion dates.

Design and presentation

At one time, the capability of the computer and its peripheral equipment limited reports to black and white, with text-only output. The very earliest computers used line printers that could only print text, and all of that had to be in upper case. This limited the report possibilities to either pure text tabulations, or to simulated graphics built up from text characters. A resource histogram could, for example, be generated by repeat printing of a single character as the column fill ('X' was always a popular choice). Apart from a few ingenious tricks, the graphics possibilities were few, and the results poor. One line printer from an otherwise reputable manufacturer would burn out some components (the sprag magnets, for those who are endowed with technical knowledge) whenever an attempt was made to print out a succession of lines with no character spaces.

Later, true graphics facilities became available, and some rudimentary colour printing was possible. The results were not particularly successful, processing tended to be slow, special printers or plotters were needed, and some system configurations resulted in printing times that literally took hours rather than minutes. A characteristic of all computer reports during this period, which covered the 1970s and early 1980s, was that reports tended to be classified as either tabular (text-based) or as graphics (often needing a special plotter).

Now, the distinction between text and graphics reports is virtually non-existent.

All systems produce reports that can combine graphics and text as a matter of routine. A common example is in the design of activity data tabulations and Gantt charts: in many programs these are combined reports with the table at the left-hand side and the Gantt chart flowing out to the right. These reports typically allow a considerable degree of choice in 'customizing' their content, scaling, colour scheme and layout style.

The intelligent use of colour to highlight critical activities, or to distinguish other important features of a report, is a valuable asset. This is particularly convenient for users who view the reports on their screens. Reports distributed on paper might require a colour photocopier of suitable size.

A useful combined cost and resource table

Some expert customization might be needed before a report such as that shown in Figure 13.9 can be produced, although one standard *Microsoft Project 2000* report comes fairly close. Figure 13.9, like all the other examples in this chapter, is actually a simulation, closely resembling the computer-produced originals, but redrawn for clarity. The dates agree with the resource-limited schedule for the garage project.

This report shows, correctly, that the estimated total cost of the garage is £11 420. A glance down the table columns shows that the labourer should become free for other work on 18 June 2004, and the skilled person will be able to take up new work from 24 June 2004. This is, of course, only a very simple example.

In past years I have found reports of this type to be immensely useful for manpower planning and other purposes, especially when they showed all the company resources and were calculated for all current projects together (a process known as 'multi-project scheduling', which is described in Chapter 14).

Project summary reports

Most programs make provision for one-page project summary reports, intended as a management overview. If more than one project is contained in the system, some programs will allow summary reports to be printed out concisely for all projects in a type of report sometimes known as a *project directory*.

Updating

Updating is the process of producing a fresh set of schedules and other reports to take account of one or more of the following:

1   a change to the project parameters, an unexpected increase or decrease in the numbers of resources available, changed cost rates, or a newly imposed target date

GARAGE PROJECT SCHEDULED RESOURCE USAGE AND COST

Date	Resource LA: Labourer				Resource SK: Skilled				Task materials £	Cumulative project cost £
	Available	Used	Unused	Cost £	Available	Used	Unused	Cost £		
10 May 04	1	1		120	1	1		160	50	330
11 May 04	1	1		120	1	1		160		610
12 May 04	1	1		120	1	1		160	100	990
13 May 04	1	1		120	1	1		160	100	1370
14 May 04	1	1		120	1	1		160	175	1825
17 May 04	1	1		120	1	1		160	525	2630
18 May 04	1	1		120	1	1		160	65	2975
19 May 04	1	1		120	1	1		160	65	3320
20 May 04	1	1		120	1	1		160	65	3665
21 May 04	1	1		120	1	1		160	65	4010
24 May 04	1	1		120	1	1		160	65	4355
25 May 04	1	1		120	1	1		160	65	4700
26 May 04	1	1		120	1	1		160	65	5045
27 May 04	1	1		120	1	1		160	65	5390
28 May 04	1	1		120	1	1		160	65	5735
31 May 04	1	1		120	1	1		160	65	6080
01 Jun 04	1	1		120	1	1		160	40	6400
02 Jun 04	1	1		120	1	1		160		6680
03 Jun 04	1	1		120	1	1		160		6960
04 Jun 04	1	1		120	1	1		160	65	7305
07 Jun 04	1	1		120	1	1		160	55	7640
08 Jun 04	1	1		120	1	1		160	200	8120
09 Jun 04	1	1		120	1	1		160	360	8760
10 Jun 04	1	1		120	1	1		160	40	9080
11 Jun 04	1	1		120	1	1		160	80	9440
14 Jun 04	1	1		120	1	1		160	30	9750
15 Jun 04	1	1		120	1	1		160	30	10060
16 Jun 04	1	1		120	1	1		160	80	10420
17 Jun 04	1	1		120	1	1		160	30	10730
18 Jun 04	1		1		1	1		160	10	10900
21 Jun 04	1		1		1	1		160	10	11070
22 Jun 04	1		1		1	1		160	15	11245
23 Jun 04	1		1		1	1		160	15	11420
24 Jun 04	1		1		1		1			11420
25 Jun 04	1		1		1		1			11420
28 Jun 04	1		1		1		1			11420
29 Jun 04	1		1		1		1			11420
30 Jun 04	1		1		1		1			11420
01 Jul 04	1		1		1		1			11420
02 Jul 04	1		1		1		1			11420

Figure 13.9   Garage project: A useful resource and cost summary

2   a change in the network logic – this could arise, for example, as a result of a serious technical problem and consequent change of design strategy, or a change in the project scope as a result of a customer modification

3   a desire to produce new schedules that take into account progress made to date.

Some people like to save a baseline model of the project before making any changes, so that they have a permanent record on file of the project as it was originally planned.

Updating frequency

If a schedule has been produced which proves to be practicable in all respects, and if everything goes according to plan, there is no need at all to return to the computer to produce a new schedule during the life of the project. This could very well be the case for a simple project, or for a schedule covering only a very short total timespan. Even more complex projects have been known to run entirely according to their original plans, where those plans were well made and the projects were particularly well managed.

In most projects, however, too many unknown factors lurk. Just when things appear to be on plan, a key supplier fails to deliver vital materials, a design error is discovered that will take weeks to put right, the customer puts in a late modification, or a site supervisor is horrified to see the scaffolding and formwork for a bridge gradually settle into the shape of a graceful bow under the weight of much freshly-poured and liberally reinforced concrete setting rapidly under a tropical sun (yes, it really did happen).

The integrity of a project schedule must be protected at all times. If anything happens that renders a schedule obsolete, it must be updated as soon as possible – otherwise people will lose faith in the plans and disregard them. Updating frequency can be contemplated:

- on an occasional basis, which usually means that, owing to a specific event or change the existing schedules have either become inconvenient to use or are, in fact, wrong
- on a regular basis, which often means monthly.

Regular updating may be needed if the project is very complex, with large volumes of progress data to be digested. For some projects, regularly updated schedules and their resulting reports provide an essential part of reporting to the project client.

For the day-to-day management of project work, it is the current schedule that counts. Updated schedules simply follow to make certain that work yet to be done remains sensibly scheduled. If, for instance, only scrap is produced after six weeks of a manufacturing job, or if it is found that 100 metres of trench have been excavated along the wrong side of a road (another example from real life), the manager does not wait for an updated schedule, but reacts verbally and takes immediate practical action. If the activity was critical, or nearly so, it is obvious that all the stops need to be pulled out at once to put things right. Of course, the schedule must be updated, but that is a consequential process which follows once steps have been taken to sort out the immediate problem.

Method

Changes to network logic or to project parameters are simply a case of replacing data that were entered for the initial run. However, some new steps must be explained in connection with entering progress information.

Time-now date

The first thing to decide before producing a fresh schedule is the date from which the computer is to start new calculations. So a datum point in the calendar has to be chosen, and this is always referred to as *time-now*.

All progress information must be collected and assessed with reference to time-now. The time-now date can be anywhere on the main network calendar, but is likely to be the date on which the updating is carried out.

A future time-now date might be chosen to allow for delays in gathering progress information from the farthest outposts of a project. Supervisors and managers must be asked to report their progress as they forecast it to be at the future time-now (a 'future-time-now' really does sound like a contradiction in terms, and is a difficult concept for some people to grasp initially). Progress reporting for a future time-now does, therefore, introduce a small element of uncertainty, but the degree of such risk is likely to be very small if all the managers are sufficiently competent – and, more important, truthful.

At one time, long delays could be expected between data preparation and the receipt of valid reports. Those were the days of punched cards and batch processing, when a time-now date might have to be chosen one or even two weeks into the future. With modern computing systems, unless there are serious communication difficulties across the organization, time-now can be the present.

Data needed for a schedule update

For every schedule update, the following data must be entered:

● time-now date

● the identifying numbers for all activities which will have been completed since the previous update (as at time-now)

● the identifying number for every activity that is in progress or will be started by time-now; methods for reporting the degree of progress achieved for an activity that has been started vary from one system to another, and most systems allow a choice; typical arrangements allow an estimate of the activity's duration remaining after time-now, or an estimate of the percentage completion at time-now.

Maintaining the schedule status for activities reported as being in progress at time-now

The better computer programs will not reschedule activities reported as being started or in progress. No one wants to receive an updated schedule that calls for a complete work upheaval, with new jobs to be started in place of those currently in progress.

Collecting the data

Producing the first updated schedule will involve the planner in learning a few new commands or ways in which to operate the particular system. But the most difficult (and the most important) aspect of updating schedules for any complex project is the gathering of accurate and reliable progress information. However, this is a problem common to many management systems, and is by no means peculiar to computer project management procedures.

If the schedules are available to project managers over a network, it is usually possible to arrange that they can report progress directly to the system from their own desktop computers.

Chapter 14

Project management computer systems, Part 3: Specialized applications

This chapter concludes the three chapters dealing with project management computer systems by describing a few special applications that can either save considerable planning and scheduling time or provide specialist management information.

Dealing with large networks

In the early days of project planning using network analysis, there were those of us who used to be proud of networks containing thousands of activities. It was common in my experience to work with arrow diagrams drawn on long rolls of paper, so that working prints had to be pinned around two or more walls of an office. Although such plans were cumbersome, they were relatively easy to process on early mainframe computers and the resulting schedules proved practicable and effective.

No doubt people still need and use large networks today, but network diagrams for large projects present special difficulties, illustrated by the following two examples:

1 When a project is of long duration, so that some of its activities extend into the distant future, it is not always possible to predict the course of events with sufficient accuracy to allow detailed planning right through to the final activity. Yet a network plan must be made with a continuous path to the end of the project if time analysis is to be driven correctly by the target project completion date.

2 The size of networks that can be viewed sensibly on a computer screen is very limited. Although there might be no problem at all in entering many thousands of activities into the project file, viewing them is quite another matter. It is not possible to follow the logic of a large network sensibly if it has to be scrolled up, down and sideways across many pages on the small screen.

Rolling wave planning

One method for dealing sensibly with the problem of planning projects that stretch into the distant future has been called *rolling wave planning*. The idea is illustrated in Figure 14.1. The planner compiles the project network with as much detail as is sensible and possible, given the information available at the start of the project. It should be possible to plan at least the first few months of work in adequate detail and with some confidence. Beyond a certain time, however, the information presented to the planner might be vague or non-existent. Activities towards the end of the project may have to be shown on the network as representing relatively large items of work, perhaps even with single activities representing whole work packages.

So the network for a project lasting many years could contain many small activities and detailed logic near the project start, but with the level of detail having to decrease as the plan moves into the future. The later stages would show relatively few, but correspondingly larger, activities as the final completion activity is approached.

When the time arrives for each network update, the planner must review the information available on later activities and, if possible, introduce more detail into

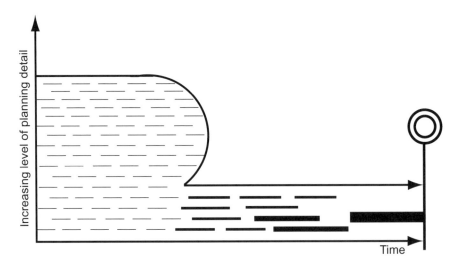

Figure 14.1   Rolling wave planning
It is not always possible to plan ahead in detail for projects that stretch far into the future, yet a continuous path from start to finish is required for critical path analysis. The answer is to show work towards the end of the project in coarse detail, as summary tasks or complete work packages. Each of these summary tasks can be expanded into many more detailed tasks later, stage by stage, when more information becomes available.

those stages of the network. Thus a picture emerges of the planner gradually pushing the level of detail in the network forward, like a rolling wave, as work on the project proceeds.

Hierarchical network breakdown

It is possible to avoid networks having thousands of activities, while still planning in sufficient depth of detail, by breaking the main network down into a series of sub-networks. A logical way of attempting this is to start from the work breakdown structure of the project. Each work package can be planned separately, with its own relatively small network diagram. A summary network is necessary that interfaces with all the sub-networks and makes coherent time analysis possible. Figure 14.2 illustrates this approach, with just a few sub-networks depicted for clarity. Special skills must be learned to make this process work properly, particularly in the coordination of input from work package managers and in the use of interface activities.

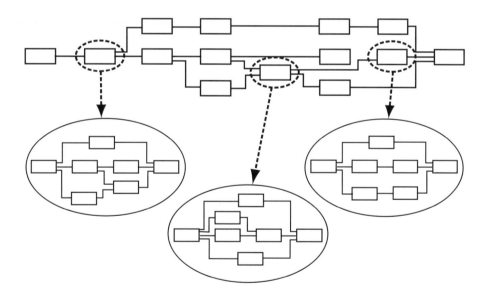

Figure 14.2   Breaking down a large project plan into sub-networks
Big networks are difficult to show on a small computer screen. Prints are better, but often unwieldy. One solution is to produce a project summary network containing only a few large tasks or work packages, and break that down into a series of more detailed sub-networks, all linked logically by interface activities.

Multi-project resource scheduling

Any organization which handles several projects using common resources should not attempt to schedule resources for one project without considering the resources needed by all the others. The organization's managers must therefore look for a way in which to allocate resources over the total company workload, whilst respecting the priority of each project and, indeed, the priority of every activity within each of those projects.

Project management – or at least project planning and scheduling – has now shifted in scale from looking simply at one project in isolation to considering the whole programme of projects. Multi-project resource scheduling is an important part of 'programme management', the name now given to the collective management of projects across a large company or group of companies.

All of this can present an apparently difficult problem. The system has to digest a vast amount of data, priority conflicts must be resolved, and all logical task interdependencies need to be observed. In addition, the result has to be dynamic and responsive to changes, such as design modifications, technical problems, work cancellations, the introduction of new projects, or fluctuations in total resource capacities.

In the past, such planning had to be carried out mentally, using adjustable bar charts, which severely restricted the capability and flexibility of the system. However, as in the case of single-project scheduling, computer systems are available to everyone for this job. The process of scheduling resources across several or all projects is called *multi-project resource scheduling*.

The case for multi-project scheduling

Many companies choose to do without network-based multi-project scheduling or even without resource scheduling at all. In some instances this may not be serious. For example, construction companies which rely mainly on subcontractors for their site work will be able to leave most manpower resource scheduling to the individual firms. Only their head office design and supervision staff will have to be scheduled, and relatively primitive scheduling methods are often used satisfactorily for that limited purpose.

It is in those organizations which employ their own permanent direct labour force for a number of simultaneous projects where multi-project scheduling is more likely to be essential (although it should be remembered that manpower is not the only resource that can be scheduled using project management computer software).

Every company which uses scarce resources for more than one project at a time can derive some advantage from multi-project scheduling. A multi-project schedule has benefits for an organization beyond the planning and control of existing work. The schedule, if properly prepared, is a model of a company's total operational workload. As such, it becomes a powerful aid to manpower and corporate planning. It is even possible to run 'what if?' trial schedules, testing possible new projects in the multi-project model to see what effect these might have on the company's future workload and capacity requirements.

Projects and sub-projects

In multi-project scheduling there is an important difference of scale compared to single-project scheduling. The organization's total workload can be regarded as 'the project'. Each of the former individual projects becomes, effectively, a 'sub-project' within the new total project.

Terminology varies from one software system to another. *Open Plan* and *4c*, for instance, both refer to the total workload as the 'group of projects', with each separate network called a 'project' in the normal way. In other multi-project systems (and often in this chapter), the term 'sub-project' is used to mean each separate project within the total multi-project model.

Activity identifiers

There is a probability that the same activity identifying code numbers will crop up on different sub-project networks. This will be true particularly if the activities for each sub-project are numbered in a simple numeric series.

With some software this can be disastrous. When presented with two or more sub-projects containing duplicated numbers, the computer sees the whole conglomeration of data as one huge error-laden network. The confusion and number of errors generated can be imagined, with all sorts of complex constraints and paths being created across all the sub-projects by mistake. There are several possible solutions to this problem, which depend largely on the capabilities of the software chosen.

One solution is to ensure that duplicate numbers can never arise between different sub-networks. A good way to prevent duplication is to prefix all the activity ID codes within each sub-project with a unique string of characters. The length of this string will obviously depend on the number of sub-projects to be managed, but it is unlikely to be more than two or three characters. Some software can add such prefixes automatically across all the activities in a sub-project network. Project numbers, or parts of them, can provide useful and logical prefixes. It is, however, easy to build up very long activity ID codes. These are best avoided if possible, because long numbers increase work and the risk of human errors. Some of the cheaper systems can only accept ID codes containing perhaps four or six characters in total, which does not allow much space for a prefix.

Fortunately, most software packages do not demand that every number in the overall multi-project model is unique. It is only necessary to make certain that, in the usual way, every identifier is unique within its own sub-project network diagram. The vital point then becomes that each sub-project *must* be given its own identifying sub-project code.

Sub-project identifiers

The computer system will require some means of identifying sub-projects, and that will mean allocating a unique sub-project identifier in each case. Although a simple, short code might suffice, a more elegant solution is to use each sub-project's number as allocated from the organization's standard project register. However, many software packages impose limits on the number of characters that can be used.

System capacity

Software houses are usually very good at producing attractive publicity material which extols the virtues of their products. Many are not so forthcoming when it comes to quantifying the capacities of their systems. A package that can handle tens of thousands of activities in theory is no good in practice if the maximum field width for the activity ID code is too small to accommodate the large numbers needed.

Demands on system capacity are likely to be more severe with multi-project scheduling. The planner will probably need to use more codes, and more characters within each code. There will probably be a more diverse range of departments, groups, resources and skills. Particularly important is the ability of the system to accommodate sufficient characters in sub-project identifier codes. These can easily prove to be the system's limiting capabilities for a particular organization's needs. If the system can only accept numerical codes in a field of two characters, then it can handle no more than 99 sub-projects.

All of these points must be borne in mind when choosing new software. If multi-project scheduling is contemplated, they should be used as the basis for some of the items in the software buyer's questionnaire (described in Chapter 12, and illustrated by the checklist in Figure 12.2).

Managing the multi-project model

The multi-project model can be expected to have a continuous but constantly changing existence. It will comprise a variable number of sub-projects, each with its own different finite life. At regular or irregular intervals, new projects must be added, completed projects removed, and progress information or other changes

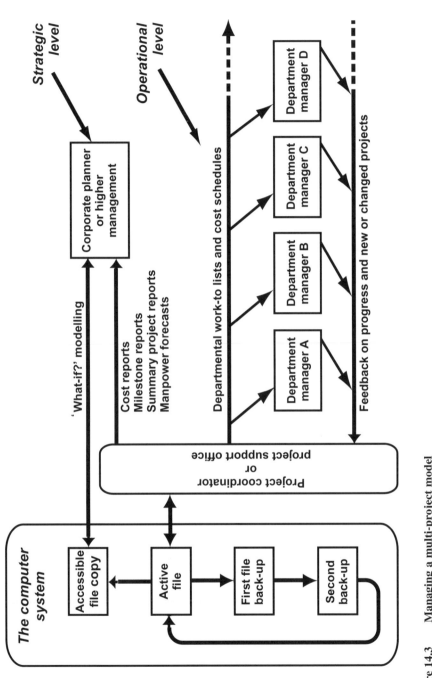

Figure 14.3   Managing a multi-project model

The integrity of the model must be preserved. This can be achieved by allowing access for system changes only through an expert person or group, such as a project support office.

injected for current projects. Managing such a model can be a formidable (but worthwhile) task. Even though individual project networks might be of manageable size, perhaps containing only one or two hundred activities, the total multi-project model for a medium-sized company can easily contain many thousands of activities.

Strict attention to data preparation, system security and updating disciplines must be observed if the whole model is to be maintained in a useful state. This usually means that access levels to the system must be carefully controlled, through entry passwords. Certainly, the data should be accessible for all authorized people to view, but only those with the necessary training and skills should be allowed to enter data or commands that could materially affect the project files and the resulting schedules. Access that can change the system parameters must be even more jealously guarded. Figure 14.3 shows the arrangement that I favour for maintaining the integrity of the multi-project model, while still allowing adequate access for the system users.

The coordination function need not be expensive. It can often be performed by one skilled, appropriately trained person. Training and hands-on experience must, however, be given to at least one deputy. In larger organizations, the project support office can manage the multi-project model.

A less centralized multi-project option

Most of the discussion in this chapter assumes that the organization's project management scheduling will be carried out centrally by people with special skills and training. In many companies, however, the preferred method is to rely on individual managers using their own computers, each running relatively simple and user-friendly software. At one time this approach denied the organization any possibility of multi-project resource scheduling and reporting.

A more recent approach allows a multi-project database to be set up on a server, but with individual project managers encouraged to carry out their own scheduling using their accustomed software (usually a version of *Microsoft Project*) on network-linked desktop computers. Innate Management Systems has developed software dedicated to this approach, claiming interface capability with a database at the server and with other company systems such as accounting, payroll and procurement. *Artemis Views* is another of the project management software systems available that can coordinate data from individual managers who use *Microsoft Project*.

This is an interesting development but, with several users of different planning skill levels entering project files and progress data, it still needs (perhaps more than ever) one or more experts to oversee the core functions to prevent corruption of the model.

Data preparation for the multi-project model

Preparation for multi-project scheduling is very similar to that required for single-project scheduling. A separate network must be drawn for every significant, definable project in the organization. Estimates for durations, costs and resources are made in the normal way, and prepared for input to the computer. All of this follows the methods explained in previous chapters.

Calendars and holiday files will normally be the same as those used for carrying out single-project scheduling in the organization.

Resource definition file

When the resource definition file is established, it will have to be structured for the whole model, rather than for any individual sub-project. This means that the total availability level of each resource will be the total amount of that resource which is available for allocation to all sub-projects.

The use of resources on non-project work must be taken into account when the total multi-project schedule is calculated. Such requirements might include the manufacture of customer spares items for stock, or the setting aside of staff to provide a general inquiry, consultancy or other facility under a service contract with a major customer. The general level of such miscellaneous non-project work must first be forecast for each resource, after which there are two ways in which it can be allowed for in the multi-project model:

1   The total level for each resource in the organization that is declared as being available for projects can be reduced by an amount equivalent to the miscellaneous work (see the section 'Specifying resource availability levels' in Chapter 11, page 260).

2   The non-project work can be introduced into the scheduling calculations as if it were one continuous 'project'. This would require a 'network' (which might need only one activity) having a duration spanning not less than the life of the whole multi-project schedule, and carrying the forecast non-project usage level for each category of resource in the model.

The second of these approaches is less satisfactory, but must be used if the organization wishes to use the results of multi-project scheduling in any corporate manpower planning studies.

Allocation of priorities

Planners are always able to choose from a number of priority rules for allocating resources to activities within each sub-project, just as in single-project scheduling. In the multi-project case, however, there is a further level of priorities to be decided: the allocation of resources between sub-projects.

The ideal solution is to specify target start and completion dates for all sub-projects. These should be (or should be closely related to) the contractual dates committed to and agreed with the various customers. The computer will then carry out time analysis for all sub-projects independently, and calculate float from these imposed target dates. After that, priority claims for scarce resources during multi-project processing should be decided on the amount of float at the detailed activity level. That is the ideal solution.

Senior management, sales managers and individual project managers will undoubtedly have views on priority differences between all the sub-projects in the model. There are occasions, for example, when one customer might be regarded as being more important than another. There is then a risk of interference with the scheduling process, with a desire to force the progress of one or two projects at the expense of others. If the project planner cannot overcome this undesirable external influence, the favoured sub-project will have to be given some form of higher priority by artificial means. This might be achieved by placing an artificially early target completion date on the favoured sub-project.

Some software will allow specific priority levels to be imposed for different sub-projects. The planner will need to ask the relevant software company how the particular system deals with this aspect. However, all such artificial allocation of priorities must be resisted wherever possible. When a successful multi-project scheduling operation has been established, it should earn the benefit of management trust and be left to deal with priorities in its own logical and equitable fashion.

Interface activities

There may be a few instances where it is necessary for one or more sub-project networks to share the same activity or have a linking constraint. In such cases the common activities must bear the same identifier, and be designated as interface activities. Interfaces are highlighted on network diagrams by enclosing the activity box with a double-ruled border.

The incidence of interfaces in multi-project scheduling should be rare. It is not good practice, for example, to use them in an attempt to force priorities between different sub-projects (where reliance on remaining float relative to scheduled target dates is the more sensible option). There are, however, exceptions. One example is in the allocation of final factory assembly space for large items of plant or machinery, where one sub-project cannot be assembled until another has cleared the area. Assembly space for large engineering projects is very difficult, if not impossible, to specify and allocate as a resource using project management programs, because it involves area shapes and can even mean considering headspace and overhangs. In such cases the sequence in which projects arrive in the assembly bay will have to be decided by the planners in conjunction with factory management. Then these decisions will have to be forced into the computer schedules by the use of interface activities or by the insertion of constraints between sub-projects.

It is safer to create special interface activities (with zero duration) rather than designate activities representing real work as interfaces. Two or more common interfaces must be given the same ID number. Some software will accept interface links, but will ignore or corrupt such data as the activity description, duration and resource requirements (because these data are effectively being entered more than once when two or more sub-networks bearing the interfaces are entered and processed together).

Updating intervals

The increased amount of stored data, and the far higher probability of frequent changes, mean that regular updating of the multi-project model will probably be mandatory. 'Updating' in this sense means the declaration of a new time-now and complete reprocessing of all time analysis, resource schedules and cost calculations throughout the model. The frequency of updating will depend on the amount of data and rate of change in the system, but will probably have to be every two or four weeks or calendar month.

Organization breakdown structure and information filtering

With the increased amount of data stored in the multi-project model, even more careful thought has to be given to the organization breakdown structure as it is arranged within the computer. This is essential to ensure that data can be properly filtered to give each departmental manager reports that contain only information that is personally relevant, interesting and useful to him or her.

Output reports can be sorted for each sub-project, so that (sub-)project managers will not be inconvenienced by receiving data for sub-projects being handled by other managers in the organization. All project managers' reports should be similar to those that they might expect to receive from a computer system handling only their own project. Now, however, each manager can have added confidence that the resources needed to meet the schedule are more likely to be available on time, because the organization's total needs have been taken into account.

Activities which are the joint responsibility of two of more managers

Allocation of departmental codes, working group codes, resource codes and activity level codes can all be used to facilitate editing and filtering. A difficulty that sometimes arises concerns activities which cross boundaries and require resources simultaneously from more than one department. One example is from an engineering company where prototype manufactured assemblies are subjected to testing that has to be performed by one department and witnessed by another. How can the system be made to produce a report containing the same prototype test activities for each of the two managers concerned without including non-relevant tasks?

One answer in this particular case is to filter the reports according to the resource codes. Activities using two or more resource types would simply appear in the corresponding number of reports. Where activities involve two separate departments but use no significant resources, there is a simple trick. Artificial resources can be created, to allow sorting on their codes. These artificial resources can be given a cost rate of zero and be stated as being available in numbers that cannot possible constrain resource scheduling. *4c* software makes this subterfuge easier, because it allows specified resources to be deselected for the scheduling process.

Processing time

Whereas the schedule for a small project can usually be calculated in a matter of microseconds, multi-project schedules can take considerably longer. More significant is the time taken to print out reports. If this process is likely to take more than one or two hours, consideration should be given to leaving the equipment to perform the operation overnight or at weekends.

'What-if?' testing

Once a multi-project model has been established, it is likely to be viewed as fertile ground in which to plant trial projects for 'what-if?' testing.

When a new sales opportunity arises, the planner can create a simple summary network to represent the new work and inject it into the multi-project model, carry out complete processing, and report back to senior management on the results. There is no need to draw a detailed network for each trial sub-project, but there should be sufficient summary activities on which to load the estimated resources and to produce an approximate timescale if the organization's total capacity is to be tested realistically. Such testing can be invaluable for influencing strategic management decisions.

System security safeguards must be designed when 'what-if?' calculations are anticipated. All 'what-if?' trials must be carried out on a *copy* of the main model, so that working schedules and the database cannot be corrupted. Some software will allow 'what-if?' testing to be performed with adequate safety. Others will use the main model so that, when the 'what-if?' test ends, the planner has to delete the trial sub-project, reprocess the multi-project model, and hope that the database and schedules will be restored to their pre-test state.

Standard networks

The concept of standard library networks

When a company looks over the plans of its past and current projects, a broad common pattern of working can often be found. It is likely that those project plans will contain common elements – identical work patterns or sub-plans that occur at various stages in most of the company's projects. By analysing past project plans and by carefully considering current working methods it is often possible to identify and use these common patterns as templates, either to produce complete standard network diagrams, or to isolate standard network elements for use as 'building bricks' in larger networks.

It might be argued that the concept of 'standard' networks is a contradiction in terms. Networking is, after all, supposed to inspire logical thought. It was never intended to regiment planning into a stereotyped routine, devoid of creative thought or constructive imagination. Nevertheless, standard networks have proved their worth. When the time allowed for planning is short, standard networks can sometimes prove to be such timesavers that they will be used when the networking process might otherwise have been ignored altogether.

Standard networks developed during brainstorming sessions by a company's most competent staff should represent the ideal sequence for performing project work. As experience is gained, the standards can be gradually improved so that they capture knowledge and ensure that lessons learned in the past are not forgotten.

Some companies fight shy of standard networks and network modules, and either continue to draw a completely new bar chart or network for each fresh project, or skimp the planning process. The excuse most often heard is: 'We are a special case. It can't be done here because we are different from other companies, and all our projects are different too.' Of course, these standardization techniques cannot be applied to *all* projects, but failing even to consider them might deny the firm substantial cost and time benefits.

Standard networks in practice

The easiest type of standard network (whole-project template) to envisage is a complete network that can be applied directly to two or more identical projects, with no need to change any part of the logic or data. Not surprisingly, this condition seldom arises in real life. There are, however, many cases where a standard master network can be devised that will at least act as a general pattern for planning similar projects.

The technique is carried out by first drawing a master network covering all activities required for a project which is judged to be typical of a range of projects carried out by the organization. It is valuable if as many suitably experienced people as possible are consulted or, better, are actually on hand in a brainstorming session when the master network is sketched. The aim must be to produce (within reason) the most comprehensive collection of tasks likely to be encountered, and to plan them in the most efficient and practicable work sequence that can be devised. It is quite likely that this process will reveal some inefficiencies or deficiencies in current working methods and lead to immediate cost-effective changes.

Many companies sell projects that can be designed and built with a range of options. In these cases the standard network should be drawn to include all the options, or at least all the more common options. If, for example, the network is produced for a range of houses to be built with or without a garage, the standard version should include the garage. It is a simple matter for the project manager to strike out the activities not needed for houses ordered without garages.

The master standard network can be kept as 'hard copy' on paper or polyester film, or it can be stored in the computer files. When each new project materializes, the master network is discussed with the project manager or other responsible person, who then takes the following steps:

- Deletes activities relating to options that the customer has not ordered or are otherwise not required.
- Deletes or modifies design activities in the light of any available retained engineering (designs from earlier projects that can be used directly or adapted for the new project).
- Adds any special constraints or new activities needed for the particular project (for example, *A* must be designed before *B*).
- Reviews the standard estimated duration, resource and cost data for all activities according to project complexity.

The modified or edited standard network is then adopted as the network plan for the new project. The original standard network remains on file, unchanged, for re-use. (The standard might be changed if, in the light of much experience, some of its standard estimates or logic should be changed permanently.)

A house construction example

A number of identical or very similar detached houses are to be built by a construction company on different sites and at different times. Here is an obvious case where a network diagram drawn for the erection of the first house must have relevance to all subsequent houses of the same design. The network for the first house could therefore be drawn and filed as a library standard, to be used whenever a house of the same or similar design is to be built. However, although the network configuration (logic) may be identical throughout, it might be necessary to review all the duration estimates for each house according to its particular environment and ground conditions.

An engineering company example

A company making special-purpose heavy machine tools to individual customer orders used the same standard project network templates very successfully in its engineering plants on both sides of the Atlantic. The simplest of these was used solely as a logic diagram, without time estimates. It served as a sequenced checklist for the start-up activities needed every time a new order for a transfer line machining system was received. A slightly simplified view of this network is shown in Chapter 19 (see Figure 19.7).

The same company made full use of standard project networks for its range of adjustable rail milling machines (also known as plano-mills) and scalpers. Machines varied greatly in size, but a typical machine weighed hundreds of tonnes and was built on a bed about 20 metres in length. In spite of big differences in the size and power of these machines, all had similar configurations. Although each of these projects could last up to 18 months and might be valued at several million pounds, the use of a universal standard network kept the network planning cost down to only a few hundred pounds.

When a new order was received, it was only necessary for the chief engineer or project manager to spend an hour or so marking up a copy of the master network template with appropriate estimates and logic changes. The result in each case was a network whose logic embodied all the lessons learned on similar previous projects, yet was fully 'customized' for the particular project in hand.

Templates (standard network modules)

A search through networks from past projects should reveal several small, repeating network elements, perhaps occurring more than once within each network and common throughout all the projects. Two examples follow that show how these can be used as templates to create networks for new projects.

A templating example using paper-based modules

The machine tool company mentioned above reviewed its network diagrams for several special transfer line machine projects. As a result, it was able to break down those networks into areas that could be represented by small, standardized modules or templates. Summarized briefly, this company's breakdown approach was first to divide the main project network into three consecutive sub-networks:

1   engineering design and drawing
2   procurement and machining
3   assembly.

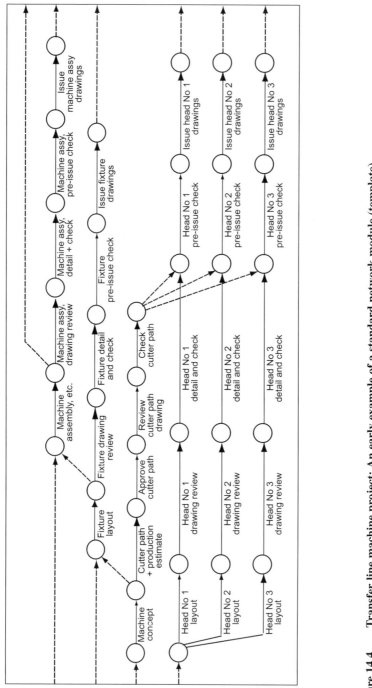

Figure 14.4   Transfer line machine project: An early example of a standard network module (template)

This example includes all the activities needed to design and draw one machine in a transfer line project. This module is for any machine with specially manufactured machining heads. When fewer than three heads are required, the unwanted activities are simply crossed out and ignored. A different module caters for machines with bought-out heads. One standard project start-up module precedes all these design modules. Each design module feeds into sub-assembly modules for purchasing and manufacturing (see Figure 14.5).

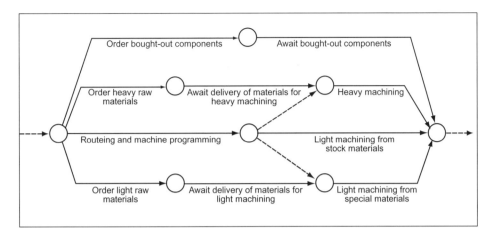

Figure 14.5   Transfer line machine project: Procurement and machining template
This standard network module contains the activities needed to provide the components for one sub-assembly from the design module illustrated in Figure 14.4. These sub-assembly modules feed a final assembly and test module to complete the project network.

Within each of these three main areas, small network modules were identified which could be used for every sub-assembly and main assembly. Examples of these modules are illustrated in Figures 14.4 and 14.5 (arrow notation was in use at the time).

Taken from the design sub-network template library, Figure 14.4 shows the module used for the design of any machine along the transfer line that required manufactured (as opposed to purchased) machining heads.

The module used for machining all the components needed for any mechanical sub-assembly is shown in Figure 14.5. This would be linked into the network by interface events or dummies so that it fitted in between its relevant design engineering and assembly activities (from the preceding and succeeding sub-network modules).

The whole system only needed about 12 different module designs. All of these were printed in suitable quantities on transparent, self-adhesive film and kept as a 'library' for use in the small planning department. Whenever a new project had to be planned, the network was 'drawn' by sticking the appropriate modules on a large piece of polyester film or translucent paper.

This process could be carried out by junior staff, using the sales engineer's block schematic drawing of the transfer line machine as the guide. Standard start and finish modules were available for sticking at the front and back ends of the network, respectively. The project manager was called in to spend an hour or so in modifying, editing and approving the network before computer scheduling.

Event numbers were partly pre-printed on the modules, the planner simply having to complete each number by prefixing two digits from each module's relevant work breakdown (cost) code. This procedure made it impossible to duplicate event numbers by mistake.

Using the company's well-documented past cost records, standard tables were later developed for the duration, resource and materials cost estimates, based on a few simple rules about machine size and complexity.

The network data produced by these methods was fed into the computer to produce work-to lists, resource and cost schedules. The system was fully multi-project across the whole company. The resulting resource schedules and work-to lists were very effective, and resulted in a considerable improvement in cost and time performance. Cost estimates generated from the system were within ± 5 per cent overall of those calculated separately by the company's cost estimating department.

A templating case study using computer-generated networks

The templating example demonstrated in this section was processed using *4c*. The project was given the file name 'Templa' and the title 'Templating Case Study Project'. The project start date was specified as 13 May 2002.

The project

The project for this case study is based on a templating application actually used by a manufacturing company within my own consulting experience. However, I have changed the nature of the product to protect the company's proprietary information. The network templates and full diagrams used here are slightly simpler than their real counterparts, so that the pictures can be kept clear and legible within the confines of a book page.

For every new customer order, the company has to adapt or redesign a number of electronic or electrical sub-assemblies for each generic type of which there is a sub-network template to cover its design and manufacture. The number and choice of these sub-assemblies varies from one project to the next, and all are finally assembled in a cabinet or frame to produce one complete project unit. The cabinet design will depend on the nature and number of sub-assemblies needed for the project. The assembled project unit has to be subjected to final inspection and testing before it can be packed and shipped to the customer. Figure 14.6 illustrates the range of templates held in the 'template library' in the computer, and indicates how the appropriate templates are selected to suit a particular project.

All projects in this company start with a range of similar start-up tasks that can easily be fitted into one standard master project start template network diagram, shown as the upper template in Figure 14.7. This start template is joined to all the following selected sub-assembly network templates by means of interface activity AA9.

The lower half of Figure 14.7 depicts template B, one of the standard sub-assembly templates chosen for this project. Another, template D, is shown as the upper half of Figure 14.8. This project therefore has only two sub-assemblies, designated by the code letters *B* and *D*.

Whichever sub-assembly templates are chosen for any project, they all feed (via interface FF1) to the standard finish template shown in the lower half of Figure 14.8.

To summarize, Project Templa uses four standard templates from the total number contained in the template library. The chosen templates are as follows:

- template case study start, coded TCSAA (mandatory for all similar projects)
- one sub-assembly template type B
- one sub-assembly template type D
- template case study finish, coded TCSFF (mandatory for all similar projects).

Creating the project network

Once the new project had been opened as a project file using the *4c* software, the project templating mode was selected. The screen then displayed the contents of the template library (Figure 14.9 shows a screen detail).

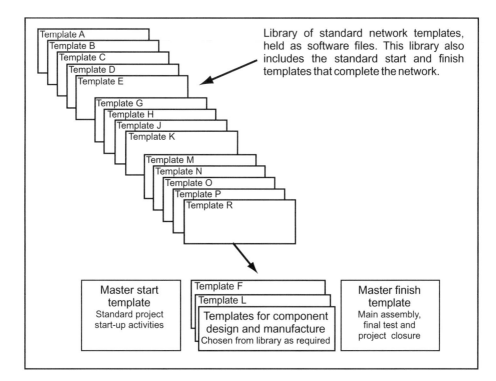

Figure 14.6   Templating case study: The template library principle

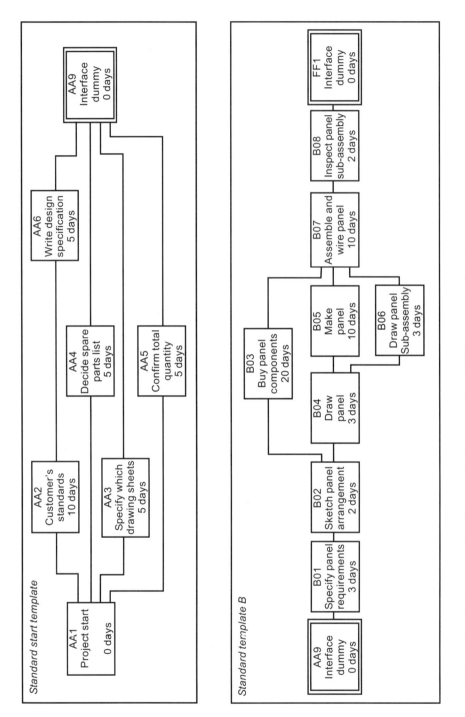

Figure 14.7   Templating case study: The standard start template TCSAA and template A

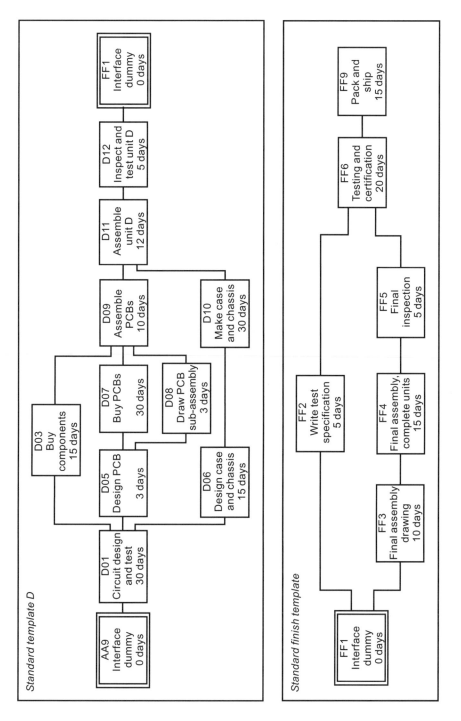

Figure 14.8 **Templating case study: Template D and the standard finish template TCSFF**

The new project network was created quickly and simply by selecting templates TCSAA, B, D and TCSFF (shown highlighted in Figure 14.9). The software then merged all four templates in one quick operation. Figure 14.10 depicts another screen capture from *4c*, showing the complete network in outline. Figure 14.11 is a zoomed-in view showing how the links surrounding one of the interfaces (AA9) have been observed correctly by the software.

A note about template interfaces

One problem with templating is the treatment of inter-template links or interfaces.

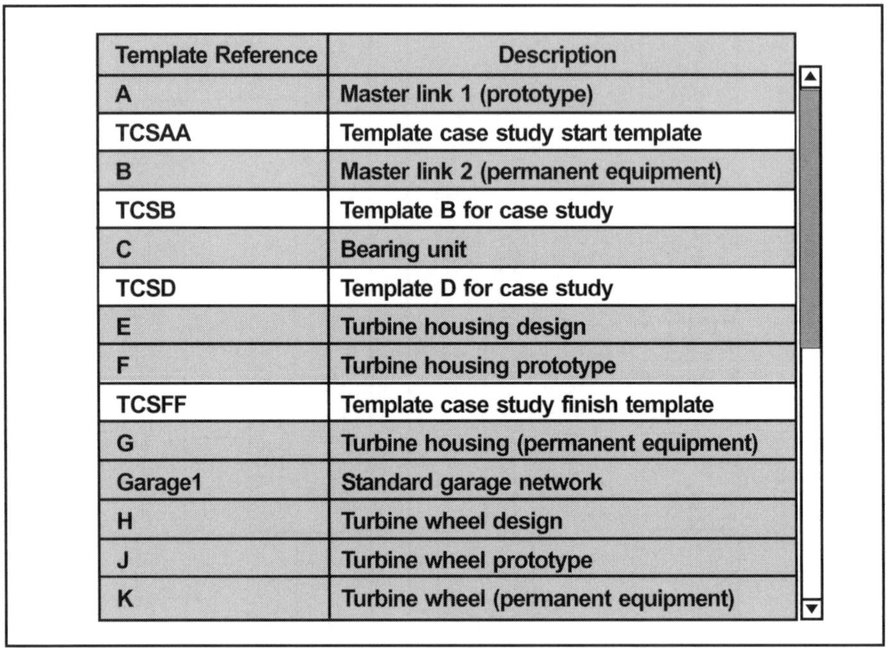

Template Reference	Description
A	Master link 1 (prototype)
TCSAA	Template case study start template
B	Master link 2 (permanent equipment)
TCSB	Template B for case study
C	Bearing unit
TCSD	Template D for case study
E	Turbine housing design
F	Turbine housing prototype
TCSFF	Template case study finish template
G	Turbine housing (permanent equipment)
Garage1	Standard garage network
H	Turbine wheel design
J	Turbine wheel prototype
K	Turbine wheel (permanent equipment)

Figure 14.9   Templating case study: The template library browser
A project network can be produced automatically by selecting the appropriate templates from this browser in the *4c* project management package.

Most programs capable of merging templates into whole project networks do not possess the capability of *4c* and will not observe the links between interface activities on the different templates. The planner will then have to enter these links separately after the merging process. This might be a small inconvenience in some cases, but a checklist of such links will be always be necessary to prevent errors and omissions.

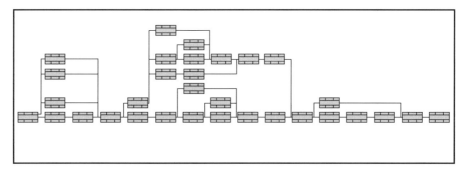

Figure 14.10   Templating case study: Network diagram
The templates were selected from the *4c* browser and merged into this complete project network by a few mouse clicks. The summary view is shown here to save space.

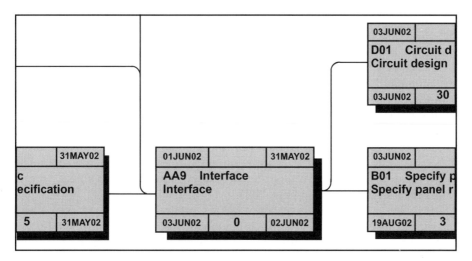

Figure 14.11   Templating case study: A network fragment
Here the detailed network view option from *4c* has been selected. The complete network cannot be reproduced on this small page with clarity, but this zoomed detail shows how the interface connections have been made automatically. This is a function that most other software cannot perform.

Processing

Once the templates have been merged, the project network exists in the computer files as a normal project, available for all processing in the usual way. Figure 14.12 shows the bar chart produced by *4c* for this templating case study project, based on early dates from time analysis.

In the real-life case on which this case study is based, the number of activities in an actual template vary between 15 and 100. A typical project could comprise some 10 templates altogether, perhaps containing about 350 activities. Full resource and cost information is included. With well over 100 projects in the multi-project model at any time, templating saves this company a great deal of time and effort.

Programs for probability and risk analysis

This subject strays into Chapter 24's territory, but is included here because it is also a special application of project management computer software. Whenever investment in a new project is contemplated, the sponsors or managers will want to quantify the predicted results as far as possible before making any commitment. Financial aspects of project appraisal were covered in Chapter 6. In some cases, however, there may be particular concern about timescale uncertainty.

Several project management programs now include a capability for carrying out probabilistic risk analysis. These use statistical methods which can help planners to evaluate the likelihood of an event, such as the most likely (or least likely) project completion date. One of the longest-established such programs is *OPERA*, part of the *Open Plan Professional* project management system.

To use the system, the planner has first to consider every network activity and decide how much confidence can be placed in the estimate made for its duration. Then, in addition to the original estimate, the planner is given an opportunity to express two more estimates for the duration of every activity: the most optimistic, and the most pessimistic. This is the same procedure used for PERT (see the section on PERT in Chapter 8 page 208).

During network time analysis, the *OPERA* program causes the computer to select the optimistic, the most likely, or the pessimistic duration estimate for each activity. The selection will be different for every activity and for each of a number of repeat time analysis runs. The choices are random. It is clear, therefore, that the predicted completion date for a project will depend on chance, with a wide variety of results possible. When the time analysis calculation is repeated many times, a statistical pattern will emerge. Processing speed is so rapid that time analysis of the network can be repeated many hundreds of times in seconds.

This technique is known as a *Monte Carlo simulation*. If the number of iterations (the sample) is sufficiently large, a distribution curve can be obtained to yield a number of useful statistical quantities. Although *OPERA* is demonstrated in this chapter, the results from other software (*Pertmaster*, for example) have a strikingly similar appearance.

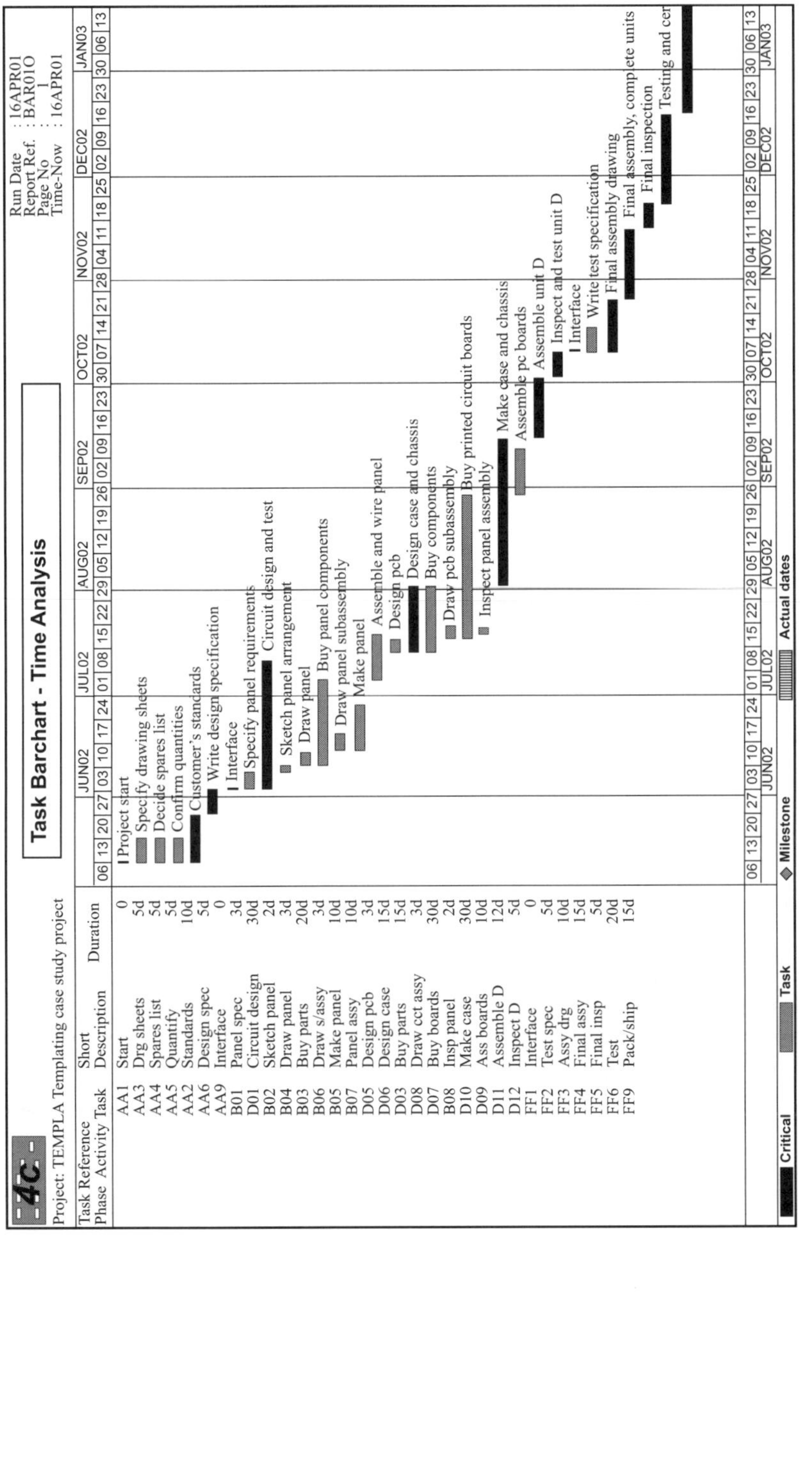

Figure 14.12 Templating case study: Bar chart produced by *4c*

This plan was compiled in a few seconds simply by merging four standard templates.

Risk analysis of the garage project using OPERA

Here is the garage project once more. This time, however, a new task list has been drawn up to show the three duration estimates upon which *OPERA* will base its risk analysis. The data are given in Figure 14.13. The user has a choice of several different distribution patterns. A normal distribution was specified for this case study, and the computer was instructed to run 1000 iterations to find the latest completion date of the project handover activity (G9999). The schedules were resource-limited.

After only a few seconds, the report shown in Figure 14.14 was available (shown here redrawn from a screen view). The chart in this report has two main elements: a frequency histogram, and a graph.

On the scale used in this particular example, each bar in the histogram has a width equivalent to one day. The height of each bar is proportional to the frequency, which means the number of times that activity G9999 has been calculated to finish on that date. The overall pattern, or the envelope of the histogram, conforms to a normal distribution curve, but its steps are coarse because the garage project contains only a few activities and the total range of possible completion dates is limited. With the project starting on 10 May 2004, the most probable completion date after resource-limited scheduling is seen to be 29 June 2004.

There is a slight possibility that this project could be finished as early as 23 June, if all the most optimistic activity times are achieved. The most pessimistic result shows a small risk of the project not being finished until 6 July.

The left-hand vertical scale of the chart gives the proportion of the total results falling in each day, expressed as a percentage. Thus, for example, 15 per cent of the calculations gave the completion date for the garage as 28 June.

The graph shows the cumulative effect: the predicted probability of meeting any given date, as read from the scale on the right-hand vertical axis. At the extremes, there is zero chance of completing before 23 June and maximum, 100 per cent, chance of completing by 6 July. There is a 60 per cent chance that the project will finish by 30 June 2004.

Software sources

The following list is a small but important sample of the wide range of project management software available. *Microsoft Project* is a well-known and popular program which has sold millions of copies in its various versions. Innate Management Systems offer a utility that enables several users of programs such as *Microsoft Project* to pool their project data in a single multi-project model. *Pertmaster* specializes in risk calculations. The other programs listed here are professional, high-level, relatively high-cost systems that require some investment in training but which should repay their users by providing versatility, great

Activity ID	Activity description	Optimistic duration (days)	Most likely duration (days)	Pessimistic duration (days)
START	Project start	0	0	5
G0102	Dig foundations	4	4	7
G0103	Make and prime door frame	1	1	2
G0104	Dig soakaway and trench	2	2	4
G0107	Make doors	3	3	6
G0110	Cut roof timbers	1	1	3
G0205	Concrete foundations	2	2	4
G0305	Position door frame	1	1	1
G0411	Lay underground drainpipe	1	1	2
G0508	Build main brick walls	10	10	15
G0509	Lay concrete floor base	2	2	3
G0713	Prime the doors	1	1	1
G0810	Fit RSJ lintel over door frame	1	1	2
G0913	Lay floor screed	1	1	3
G1012	Fit roof timbers	2	2	4
G1016	Case lintel and build parapets	2	2	5
G1115	Fill drain trench	1	1	2
G1214	Fit fascia boards	1	1	2
G1216	Fit roof sheets	1	1	2
G1317	Hang doors	1	1	2
G1417	Fit gutters and downpipes	1	1	2
G1518	Concrete over drain trench	1	1	1
G1618	Seal the roof	1	2	3
G1718	Paint all woodwork	2	3	4
FINISH	Project finish and handover	0	0	0

Figure 14.13   **Garage project: Duration estimates for PERT or Monte Carlo analysis**

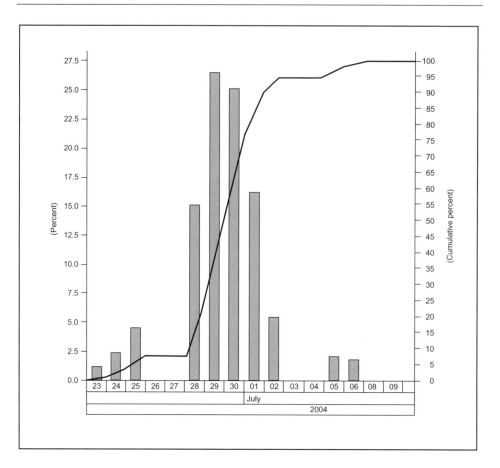

Figure 14.14   Garage project: Monte Carlo analysis
OPERA, part of the *Open Plan* suite of programs, performed 1000 resource-limited schedules for the garage project to produce this probability graph. The activity durations used are those shown in Figure 14.13.

capability and high capacity. UK addresses are given, but some of these companies have headquarters, offices or agents in other countries.

4c	4c Systems Ltd, Knyvett House, 1 Watermans Business Park, Staines, Middlesex TW18 3BA Telephone: 01784 898641 Fax: 01784 898642
Artemis	Artemis Management Systems Ltd, Artemis House, 219 Bath Road, Slough, Berkshire SL1 4AA Telephone: 01753 606 000
Innate	Innate Management Systems Ltd, 1 Christies Warehouse, Wherry Quay, Ipswich, Suffolk IP4 1AS Telephone: 01473 251550
Microsoft Project 2002	Microsoft Ltd, Microsoft Campus, Thames Valley Park, Reading RG6 1WG Telephone: 0870 601 0100
Open Plan Professional	Welcom, 26–28 Church Road, Welwyn Garden City, Hertfordshire AL8 6PW Telephone: 01707 331 231
Pertmaster Professional and Risk	Pertmaster Limited, Epworth House, 25 City Road, London EC1Y 1AA Telephone: 020 7972 0514
Primavera	Primavera, 2nd Floor, Commonwealth House, 2 Chalk Hill Road, London, W6 8DW Telephone: 0208 563 5500

Part V

Purchasing and materials management

Chapter 15

Scheduling parts for manufacturing projects

Materials and parts are just as much resources for projects as money and labour. Although the examples given in Chapters 10 and 11 demonstrated the scheduling of human resources, the same methods can be used for bulk materials. Most project management computer packages can carry out this function, provided that the materials requirements for any network task can be specified in amounts defined by simple units of quantity (tonnes of sand and so on). Project management packages can also be used to schedule the overall loading of manufacturing facilities. But scheduling individual parts and manufacturing operations is a different story.

Manufactured and purchased parts for manufacturing projects lead to different scheduling problems from those associated with the purchase of bulk materials. A great deal more detail is required in manufacturing schedules than can easily or feasibly be included on the main project schedule. Solving the problems of parts scheduling falls more properly within the ambit of operations management than project management (see, for example, Slack et al., 1998). This chapter can, however, provide a glimpse into this subject.

Parts scheduling compared with project scheduling

Parts scheduling requires close analysis of drawings, meticulous attention to detail, and specialized techniques. At one time, the only practicable approach depended on manual methods, often using elaborate compilations of index cards. The amount of work required could be prodigious, especially when attempting to identify and coordinate the usage of parts common to more than one part of the project or, worse still, also common to other projects and routine manufacturing. The methods were cumbersome, prone to error, and could not easily cope with changes. Those methods can be consigned to history and earlier editions of this book. Now the problems of complexity, inflexibility and errors can be solved more easily using computers.

Any system of parts scheduling demands the assembly of data structured on bills of materials or parts lists. Since these documents are products of design engineering, it follows that project parts scheduling cannot take place until design is substantially complete, considerably later in the project life cycle than when the main project schedules are made.

The techniques described in this chapter assume that the project manager already has the main project plans and schedules, and knows when each significant assembly or sub-assembly will be required for the project. That information must be derived from the overall project plan (using critical path networks or bar charts). Then, provided all the human resources and overall manufacturing facilities are scheduled sensibly (at departmental or group levels), production managers are given a time framework into which the manufacture and procurement of parts and smaller sub-assemblies can be fitted.

Activities in overall project schedules cannot usually be chosen to show a depth of detail much smaller than main assemblies, or at least fairly large sub-assemblies. Factory schedules will even have to include all the separate manufacturing operations needed to make each part. Scheduling at the much greater level of detail needed for individual parts must be carried out by the manufacturing organization using their own specialized methods. These manufacturing schedules might contain a mix of specially purchased components, items manufactured within the company's own factory, and other parts which are usually held in store as general stock.

Identifying and quantifying common parts

The parts scheduling task is usually complicated further because some of the parts for one assembly are also used on other assemblies, or even other projects, so that provisioning must take all these different uses into account. Suppose that a project needs 100 cam-operated electrical switching sub-assemblies, all slightly different, but each containing a particular type of microswitch in varying quantities. Someone has to discover how many of these switches are needed in total for the project, and make sure that 100 separate purchase orders for microswitches are not placed. The switching sub-assemblies might easily have other components that must be investigated to discover their total requirements as common items (cams and servo motors, for example).

Batch differences

Another complication arises if a project has to result in more than one similar output batch, produced at different times. Consider, for instance, a defence contractor who is working to produce a 'state-of-the-art' weapons guidance system. The initial contract might be for the design and manufacture of six identical Mark 1 prototype units, to be delivered at two-monthly intervals. An improved version (Mark 2) could be under development before all the prototypes have been delivered, so that Mark 1 and Mark 2 systems are both in different stages of production in the factory at the same time, with some parts common to both batches. While all this is going on, engineering changes can, of course, be expected to affect one or both batches, or even individual units within a batch.

When parts scheduling becomes particularly complex, the project planner or project support office can provide help to the materials manager and production managers by collating all the known parts requirements, listing the assemblies and sub-assemblies on which the parts are to be used, and relating this information to the dates on the project plan. That information can provide the input to a manufacturing requirements package (MRPII).

Filing cabinet project

In this and the remaining sections of this chapter, some aspects of parts scheduling can be demonstrated using a simple manufacturing project. For clarity in these pages this study will not be taken down to the level of individual manufacturing operations, and excludes finishing processes such as plating and painting.

A company has designed a steel two-drawer filing cabinet, an exploded view of which is shown in Figure 15.1. In the first instance, only one cabinet is to be made.

Simple parts listing

All the parts needed for the filing cabinet can be seen in the exploded view (Figure 15.1), and these could easily be listed on a parts list or bill of materials. This might be compiled using a computer-aided design (CAD) system, or manually on a form such as that shown in Figure 15.2. The item numbers on this parts list correspond with those in the circles on the exploded view.

Armed with the simple parts list, the company's purchasing and production control departments would be able to provision all the materials by drawing available items from existing stocks, and either buying or making the remainder. There is no ambiguity about the total required quantity of any item, and no complicated calculations are needed. Everything is detailed on one simple parts list.

Given a target completion date for the single cabinet, it would also be fairly simple to decide when each item must be ordered. Priorities must be given to those parts having the longest purchase or manufacturing lead times.

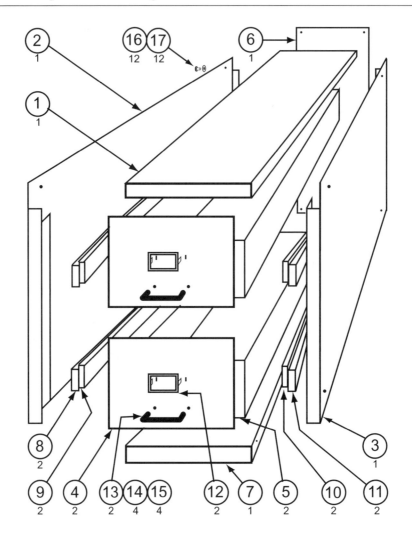

Figure 15.1   Filing cabinet project: Exploded view

Structured parts list

The best sequence of manufacture for the filing cabinet would be as follows:

1   Make individual components and obtain bought-out items.
2   Assemble the parts into sub-assemblies.
3   Carry out the final main assembly.

Item No.	Our part number	Description	Quantity Unit	No	Remarks
01	FC1001	Top panel	Each	1	MF Panel shop
02	FC1002L	Side panel, left	Each	1	MF Panel shop
03	FC1002R	Side panel, right	Each	1	MF Panel shop
04	FC1003	Drawer chassis	Each	2	MF Panel shop
06	FC1005	Rear panel	Each	1	MF Panel shop
07	FC1006	Plinth	Each	1	MF Panel shop
08	A502-A	Runner, outer, left	Each	2	SP Smiths plc
09	A502-B	Runner, inner, left	Each	2	SP Smiths plc
10	A503-A	Runner, outer, right	Each	2	SP Smiths plc
11	A503-B	Runner, inner, right	Each	2	SP Smiths plc
12	A209	Title card holder	Each	2	CS Carter
13	A350	Handle	Each	2	CS Epsom and Salt
14	S217	Screw	Each	4	CS Acme Screws
15	W180	Washer,shakeproof	Each	4	CS Acme Screws
16	S527	Screw, self tapping	Each	12	CS Acme Screws
17	W180	Washer,shakeproof	Each	12	CS Acme Screws

MF = Make
SP = Special purchase
CS = Common stock

Iss	Mod No	Date	Iss	Mod No	Date	Iss	Mod No	Date	Iss	Mod No	Date
A	Prot	4Jun02									
1	-	3Aug02									
2	1	14Nov02									

Drawn by: EFP | Checked by: TQM | Approved *David Woodford*

Heath Robinson Furniture plc   Birmingham   England

Title: Filing cabinet: Elite series Two drawer Without lock | Sheet 1 of 1 sheets | Assembly number: FC1000

Figure 15.2   Filing cabinet project: Simple parts list
This list is derived from the exploded view of Figure 15.1. It shows total quantities without regard for the breakdown into production sub-assemblies.

The simple parts list arrangement shown in Figure 15.2 is not very convenient for the production department because, ideally, they need a separate parts list from which to issue the manufacturing kit for each sub-assembly.

In order to produce these separate parts lists, it is usual for the designer to start by drawing a family tree or 'goes into chart' showing how all the sub-assemblies and individual parts come together for the final assembly. The family tree for the filing cabinet is shown in Figure 15.3. This is a hierarchical structure not unlike the larger-scale work breakdown structure for a project, but the level of detail here goes down to the very lowest level, including every nut, bolt and washer. Further, the tree must show the quantity of each part needed. Coding (part numbering) is essential.

The example in Figure 15.3 reveals that four separate sub-assemblies have to be made before final assembly of one filing cabinet can take place. So the simple parts list of Figure 15.2 has to be structured as five separate lists, one for each sub-assembly, and one for the final main assembly. This arrangement is summarized in Figure 15.4.

While the arrangement of parts lists in the filing cabinet family tree grouping (Figure 15.3) is ideal for manufacturing purposes, it is not so convenient for the purchasing of parts, or for the scheduling of manufacture for parts common to more than one sub-assembly.

For example, the washer, part number W180, is common to two assemblies. It appears twice on the simple parts list of Figure 15.2, where it is an easy matter to add up the quantities to find the total number of washers needed to make one filing cabinet (4 + 12 = 16). On the family tree in Figure 15.3 and on the manufacturing parts lists derived from it in Figure 15.4, this result is not quite so obvious. Anyone glancing at either the family tree or at the five separate parts lists might be forgiven for assuming that only 14 washers type W180 were needed (12 on the final assembly, and two on the drawer assembly). On each of the separate parts lists the washer (and every other item) only appears in the quantities needed to make one particular sub-assembly, regardless of how many sub-assemblies are needed. Of course, the catch is that two drawer assemblies are needed for one filing cabinet, so that the total number of washers needed for one cabinet is 12 + (2 x 2) = 16.

To find out how many of any item must be provisioned in total, therefore, it is necessary to work up through the family tree, multiplying the quantities as necessary. That gives the result for one filing cabinet, which must be multiplied again by the batch size to find the total quantity for each component. So, if the batch comprised 10 filing cabinets, at least 160 washers type W180 must be obtained.

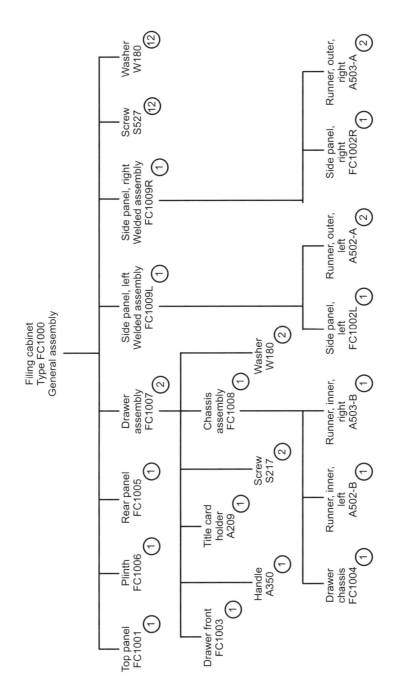

Figure 15.3   Filing cabinet project: Family tree

The family tree or 'goes into chart' shows how the various components and manufactured sub-assemblies come together for the final assembly of one filing cabinet. The encircled numbers are the quantities needed for each sub-assembly or main assembly on the next higher level of the tree.

FC1000 Filing cabinet: Final assembly — Revision 2
Parts list

Part number	Description	Quantity	Remarks
FC1007	Drawer assembly	2	
FC1009L	Side panel, left, welded assembly	1	
FC1009R	Side panel, right, welded assembly	1	
FC1001	Top panel	1	
FC1006	Plinth	1	
FC1005	Rear panel	1	
S257	Screw, self-tapping	12	Acme Screws
W180	Washer	12	Acme Screws

FC1007 Drawer assembly — Used on filing cabinet FC1000
Parts list

FC1008	Drawer chassis sub-assembly	1	
FC1003	Drawer front panel	1	
A209	Title card holder	1	Carter
A350	Handle	1	Epsom and Salt
S217	Screw	2	Acme Screws
W180	Washer	2	Acme Screws

FC1008 Drawer chassis sub-assembly — Used on drawer FC1007
Parts list

FC1004	Drawer chassis	1	
A502B	Runner, inner, left-hand	1	Smiths plc
A503B	Runner, inner, right-hand	1	Smiths plc

FC1009L Side panel, left, welded assembly — Used on filing cabinet FC1000
Parts list

FC1002L	Side panel, left-hand	1	
A502A	Runner, outer, left-hand	2	Smiths plc

FC1009R Side panel, right, welded assembly — Used on filing cabinet FC1000
Parts list

FC1002R	Side panel, right-hand	1	
A5032A	Runner, outer, right-hand	2	Smiths plc

Figure 15.4   **Filing cabinet project: Parts list arranged in sub-assemblies**

Line of balance

An extension of the parts scheduling and collation problem occurs when more than one project is being undertaken at the same time, especially when parts or assemblies used on one project are also required for some or all of the others. The line of balance case study which follows demonstrates some of the principles of complex parts scheduling.

The subject of this case study is the same filing cabinet that was illustrated in Figures 15.1 to 15.4. This time, however, this is a limited-edition filing cabinet to be made in a total quantity of 50, and the orders for the delivery of these have been received according to the first two columns in Figure 5.5. Although this is a small quantity by any manufacturing standards, suppose for the sake of this study that these cabinets must be manufactured in small batches, each batch being initiated by a separate customer order. In all the following calculations calendar dates have been converted into numbers, with the promised delivery time for the first batch taken as the datum (time zero). All other customer delivery dates are related to this datum, shown in the column headed 'Delivery day no.' in Figure 15.5

Customer	Date promised	Delivery day no.	Lead time day no.	Quantity ordered	Cumulative quantity
Jones	7 Oct	0	−32	5	5
Jenkins	11 Oct	4	−28	5	10
Griffiths	29 Oct	16	−16	10	20
Morgan	4 Nov	20	−12	10	30
Edwards	14 Nov	28	− 4	10	40
Williams	26 Nov	36	4	5	45
Evans	2 Dec	40	8	5	50

Figure 15.5   Filing cabinet project: Delivery data

Calculating the quantities and lead times

Simple parts collation takes no account of the different lead times needed to make or buy all the various parts. To create a manufacturing schedule for all batches, it is necessary to reconcile the quantities of all the parts needed with the complex delivery schedule.

The first step in a line of balance calculation is to obtain a family tree for the parts needed to build one complete product. A family tree already exists for the filing cabinet (Figure 15.3), but for line of balance purposes it is more convenient to redraw this tree laterally, so that the sequence flows with time from left to right. The redrawn family tree is shown in Figure 15.6.

Quantities

The number written in the small circle alongside each part number in Figure 15.6 shows, as before in Figure 15.3, the quantity of that part which must be provided to construct one of the sub-assemblies on which it is used.

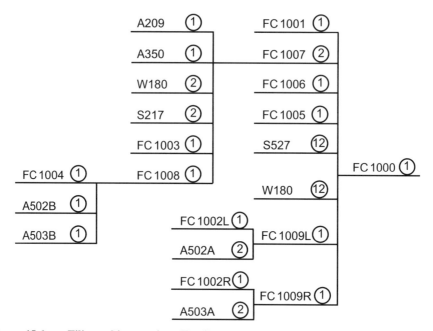

Figure 15.6   Filing cabinet project: Family tree redrawn for line of balance

Lead times

In Figure 15.7, the next step is shown. Squares have been added at every intersection and at the ends of the tree branches, rather in the fashion of event nodes in an arrow network diagram. Indeed, the following steps bear close resemblance to network time analysis.

For each item, the elapsed time between placing an order (purchase order or factory manufacturing order) for each item and the day when that part will be needed must be estimated. These are total duration estimates, which means that all activities such as preparation and issue of orders, machine setting times, suppliers' lead times, shipping times and stores kitting times have to be allowed for in the times. Each estimate has been written below the branch to which it refers. Estimates are in working days, with all figures rounded up to the nearest whole day.

Now the total project lead time for any part can be found, by adding up the individual lead times backwards through the tree, working through every path from right to left. The results are shown inside the 'event' squares.

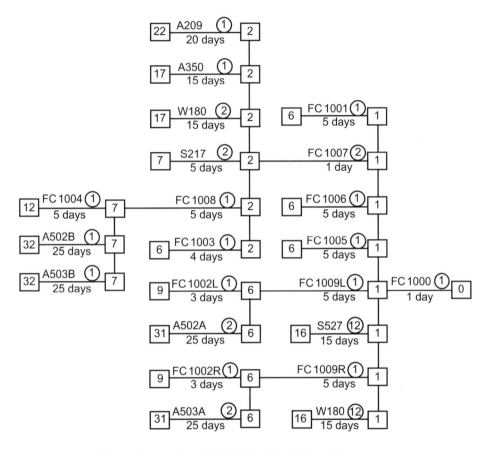

Figure 15.7   Filing cabinet project: Calculation of lead times for parts

The family tree, set up and annotated as in Figure 15.7, now tells us all we need to know about the provision of parts for one filing cabinet. Again taking part A503B as an example, we know that two of these must be provided, and that they have to be *ordered* at least 32 days before the filing cabinet is wanted. If they are not *received* by the seventh day before completion is due, the programme is bound to run late. Notice that, unlike an arrow network diagram, everything on this family tree is critical. All times are latest times. No float exists anywhere. A column has been included in Figure 15.5 to show these lead times as project day numbers, all with respect to the day zero datum.

All of these quantities for a single cabinet must obviously be multiplied by the batch quantity to complete the total quantities needed for each batch.

Time-quantity relationships for multiple batches

Before a series of repetitive batches can be considered, it is necessary to draw a graph showing the cumulative quantities to be delivered against time. Figure 15.8 shows the graph for the filing project (drawn from the cumulative quantities given in Figure 15.5). The time axis is scaled in working days, starting from day zero, which is the first day of the delivery schedule.

Now suppose that day 4 of the programme has been reached and that the current status of production has to be checked against the delivery commitments. Again taking the drawer runner, part number A503B, as an example, the lead time for ordering this part is known to be 32 days (Figure 15.7). Two of these runners are needed for each cabinet. By projecting forward along the delivery graph from day 4 by the lead time of 32 days, day 36 is reached. The graph shows that 45 cabinets should have been delivered by day 36. This means that at day 4 all the runners

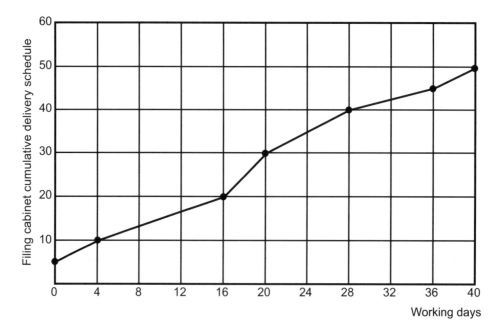

Figure 15.8   Filing cabinet project: Delivery commitment graph

needed to make these 45 cabinets should either be issued, available or on order. In other words a total of 90 parts number A503B must have been ordered.

Not only is it possible to calculate how many parts should have been ordered, it is also possible to work out how many parts from those orders must actually be available in stock or already used. This is done by considering the end 'event' for the relevant part or sub-assembly in each case, instead of its start 'event'. For part A503B at day 4, the result would be based on a lead time of 7 days, which takes the projection on the delivery graph up to day 11. A sufficient quantity of this part must therefore be in stock or issued by day 4 to make 16 cabinets (32 parts).

Data for one complete filing cabinet				Project quantities to be finished or in progress at day 4	
Part number	Used on	Total lead time in days	Quantity	For how many cabinets?	Total number of parts
FC1000		1	1	11	11
FC1001	FC1000	6	1	15	15
FC1002L	FC1009L	9	1	18	18
FC1002R	FC1009R	9	1	18	18
FC1003	FC1007	6	2	12	24
FC1004	FC1008	12	2	20	40
FC1005	FC1000	6	1	15	15
FC1006	FC1000	6	1	15	15
FC1007	FC1000	2	2	12	24
FC1008	FC1007	7	2	16	32
FC1009L	FC1000	6	1	15	15
FC1009R	FC1000	6	1	15	15
A350	FC1007	17	2	31	62
A502A	FC1009L	31	2	45	90
A502B	FC1008	31	2	45	90
A503A	FC1009R	31	2	45	90
A503B	FC1008	31	2	45	90
A 209	FC1007	22	2	38	76
S217	FC1007	7	4	16	64
S527	FC1000	16	12	30	360
W180*	FC1007	17	4	31	124 ⎫ = 484
W180*	FC1000	16	12	30	360 ⎭

*Common part

Figure 15.9   Filing cabinet project: Calculation for line of balance at day 4

In the table of Figure 15.9, similar calculations have been performed for all the filing cabinet parts. The quantities all relate to day 4 of the programme. The start events have been used in this example, so that the total quantities shown include the totals of parts which should be on order, in progress, in stock, or already dispatched in completed cabinets).

Drawing the line of balance chart

Now refer to Figure 15.10, where the data from Figure 15.9 have been converted into chart form. Each separate item has been allocated a column to itself, and the total minimum quantity required is shown as a horizontal line drawn at the appropriate scale height across the relevant column. These quantities are the necessary balance quantities for the programme, and the stepped graph which they form is known as the line of balance. Remember that this whole chart has been calculated with respect to day 4, and is only valid for that single day of the manufacturing programme.

The last step is to find out what the actual progress is and plot these results on the same line of balance chart. The chart should take on an appearance similar to that shown in Figure 15.11, where some imaginary progress results have been assumed and plotted. The fruits of all the calculations and planning labours should now become obvious, since it is clearly seen that any achievement which falls below the line of balance indicates that the delivery schedule has slipped and customers will not receive their cabinets on time.

Using the line of balance chart

In the example, parts W180, S527 and S217 have been purchased in total quantities from the start, because these are inexpensive items and they take up little storage space. Part A350 is seen to be below the line of balance, indicating that more should have been ordered by day 4.

Everything illustrated here relates to day 4 of the delivery programme, and the chart is valid for only for that day. A separate chart would have to be calculated for any other day on this project, which could be from day −32 up to day 40.

The vertical scale can prove troublesome because of the wide range of quantities that might have to be accommodated. This was true to some extent in the filing cabinet example. If the problem is particularly acute, a logarithmic scale can be considered.

Although line of balance charts cannot show the reason for any shortages, they are effective visual displays, and particularly good at highlighting deficiencies. As such, they are useful for showing to higher executives at project meetings, where they save time by satisfying the principle of management by exception.

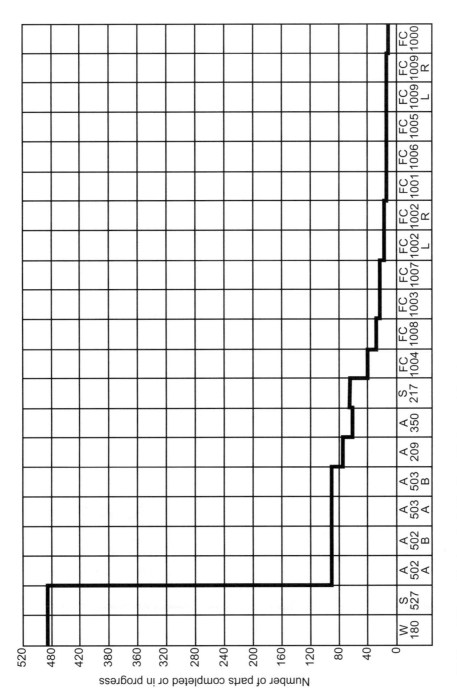

Figure 15.10 Filling cabinet project: The line of balance at day 4

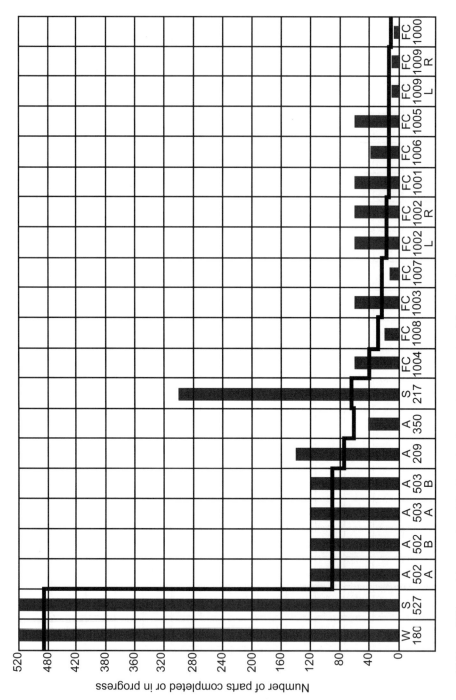

Figure 15.11   Filing cabinet project: The line of balance chart completed for day 4

In practice it is necessary, although even more laborious, to split up the family tree and all the charts into more detail, not just into parts and sub-assemblies, but also into the manufacturing operations needed to make the individual parts. All of these operations would then be allotted columns on the line of balance chart. This might seem a high price to pay for a chart which is only valid for one day, but the line of balance principle becomes far more useful when the results are used not to draw charts, but to plan and initiate work from computer-generated schedules.

Computer solutions

The problems of materials records, collation from parts lists, and timescale planning of manufacturing operations have long been recognized by the computer industry, resulting in techniques such as materials requirement planning (MRP) and its successor, manufacturing requirements planning (MRPII). Any such system still requires the input of considerable amounts of data. Accuracy and proper administration is vital. The underlying methods are not unlike the line of balance technique described above. However, with MRPII, the family tree analysis, parts collation and scheduling is automated. The system is therefore dynamic and responsive to change. Also, with a computer system to list, edit, count, multiply and report on each item, careful watch can be kept on stocks to minimize shortages or excess stocks.

Chapter 16

Purchasing, Part 1: Principles and initial ordering

This chapter deals with some of the general principles of project purchasing and purchase order preparation. The subject is continued in Chapter 17, which concentrates mainly on those aspects of purchasing and materials control that occur after the issue of a purchase order. Chapter 18 describes purchasing procedures in construction and other capital projects, which differ in some respects from those applying to general engineering and manufacturing projects. However, many principles and some procedures are common to all purchasing, so that Chapters 16, 17 and 18 are not mutually exclusive. A further reading list is given at the end of this part of the book.

The importance of purchasing and materials control

Purchasing is a vital function of most projects. Purchasing is also a greedy function, consuming large amounts of time and money. Perhaps a good way to emphasize the importance of purchasing and materials control is to remember that purchased goods and services are likely to account for over half the total project costs. Efficient supply of materials is essential to avoid delays through shortages, the acquisition of goods unfit for their intended purpose, or serious over-expenditure. Competitive buying is important to the financial success of most projects and overspending on material budgets can easily wreck profits. Yet, despite all these factors, purchasing barely receives a mention in most project management textbooks, and is ignored altogether in some (see Figure 16.1). Purchasing deserves the best possible planning and management.

In addition to the issue of purchase orders, the materials management function generally includes inspection or checking of goods upon receipt, and the provision of handling and safe storage facilities. It can extend beyond the boundaries of the purchaser's premises to embrace supervisory expediting and inspection visits to suppliers, making packing and transport arrangements for goods into and out of the firm, port and customs clearance for international movements, and

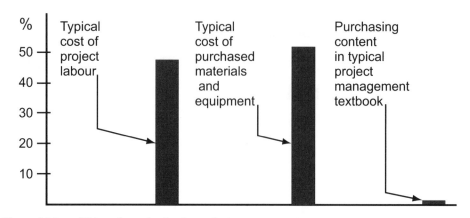

Figure 16.1   Value of purchasing in project management

involvement whenever special provisions have to be made for insurance, credit guarantees and other commercial arrangements.

Another aspect of materials management relates to capital investment. If materials are bought long before they are needed, funds which might have been used more profitably elsewhere are locked up unnecessarily. If the contractor is relying on loan capital, idle materials represent waste in terms of avoidable interest or overdraft charges.

On the other hand, delays caused by materials shortages are likely to be more damaging than premature purchasing. Work might have to stop until the shortages have been made good but the project will continue to attract wages and overhead costs during the idle period. Even if the workers can be given other temporary fill-in jobs, disruption to the scheduled smooth flow of project activity can cause inefficiencies and overspending of labour budgets. If materials shortages delay project completion, final billing will be held up, putting back revenue receipts and damaging cash flow. There could also be contractual penalty payments or other expenses to put profitability at risk.

The purchasing cycle

Some people regard a purchasing department as an office staffed with individuals whose only function in commercial life is to type and send off purchase orders. Unfortunately, this concept may sometimes come too close to the truth for comfort. Where this is the case, any attempt at materials control is condemned to death before birth. Mainstream purchasing activities start long before an order is placed, and do not end until the materials have been delivered and put to use. Where international freight movements are needed, the purchasing department typically makes the arrangements, either directly or (more usually) by cooperation with a freight forwarding agent.

Other purchasing functions can include the establishment of preferred vendors lists, together with assessments of their performance or 'vendor ratings'. Follow-up activities will be required if goods fail to match their specification upon delivery or in service.

The normal sequence of events for a significant project purchase is not unlike that of the project cycle shown in Figure 2.2. In fact, the procurement of any item can be regarded as a mini-project in itself. The project manager is replaced in this analogy by the purchasing department or purchasing agent. Activities in the cycle vary somewhat according to the type of goods or services involved (especially their cost) and the industry, but Figure 16.2 illustrates most of the principal steps in a typical process.

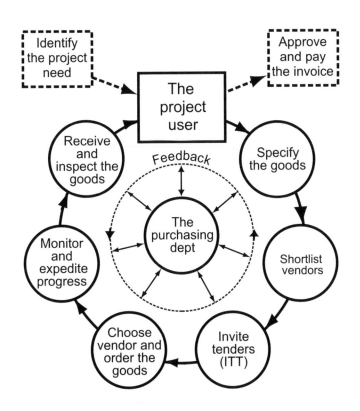

Figure 16.2   The purchasing cycle
Purchase of a significant item can resemble a mini-project. Compare this chart with the project cycle shown in Figure 2.2.

Purchase specification and requisition

The purchasing cycle is initiated by the discovery of a need for raw materials, components or a larger item of equipment. The origin of this discovery may lie in stock control, stores, engineering design, or production control. That will depend on the type of goods, the industry, organization of the firm, and the nature of the project. Once the need has been recognized, action must be started by a request from the project engineers to the organization's purchasing department or agent. This request specifies the goods, and usually starts as an enquiry that asks the purchasing department to obtain details of suppliers, their quoted prices, delivery promises, and their reputation or expected performance. The buyer may recommend or actually choose the preferred supplier.

When the time comes to order goods, a request is made to the buyer which authorizes the purchase and gives all necessary details. This request, duly signed by a responsible person, can be made using one of the following documents:

- a purchase requisition form
- a bill of materials or parts list, with items to be purchased clearly highlighted, and with the total quantities required made clear
- a stock replacement requisition, produced by stores or stock control personnel whenever replenishment of items stocked for general use is required.

Supplier selection

The buyer's first responsibility is to identify a suitable source of supply. Occasionally, only one supplier can be found, or one may be specified on the requisition. Limitation of choice usually arises when goods are highly specialized but, even where there is only one manufacturer, there may be a choice between different stockists. There are, of course, occasions when urgency is the most important factor, when there is simply no time in which to conduct a proper supplier selection procedure. In all other cases (except for low-cost purchases), the supplier should be chosen after the collection and perusal of several competitive quotations.

The buyer would normally be expected to favour the lowest bidder, but this choice must be tempered by knowledge of that bidder's reputation for quality, delivery performance and commercial standing. It is usually undesirable and risky to allow the buyer to choose a supplier without the knowledge and agreement of the relevant project engineer. In some organizations, vested interests or jealously guarded power mean that this essential partnership between the purchasing and engineering departments is lacking. That is always unfortunate, and should be corrected, if necessary by intervention of more senior management.

Purchase order issue

Moving one more step round the cycle, the order has to be prepared and sent to the supplier. This is the most routine and obvious part of the purchasing cycle, usually consisting of typing and printing the order, checking it, signing it, and then either mailing it, or transmitting it to the supplier electronically.

What has this explanation of purchase order preparation got to do with project management? It takes time. Several days or even weeks of valuable project time can be consumed by this mundane, simple activity. Procurement lead time estimates on the critical path network must always allow for such delays. In fact, unless emergency measures are contemplated, two weeks should often be regarded as a minimum estimate for purchase lead times, even for items that can be obtained from the supplier's stock.

An aspect that should particularly concern the project manager is that each purchase order should set out commercial conditions which, once accepted by the supplier as a contract, commit the buyer (and therefore the project) to all implied cost and legal implications.

Order acknowledgement

The supplier will be expected to return an acknowledgement of order receipt, accepting the terms, or at least confirming details of quantity, description, price and delivery. Naturally, these details must be compared with the supplier's original quotation, and the buyer will question any discrepancy. When the order has been accepted by the supplier, a binding legal contract exists (see the 'Contracts' section in Chapter 6, page 142).

Expediting

As far as the purchaser is concerned, the period following the issue of a purchase order will be one of waiting, and a great deal of reliance must be placed on the supplier. That is not to say that the purchaser can do nothing. This is the time when the expediters earn their money by keeping in touch with the supplier to investigate and spur progress. Expediting is not just a process of chasing up late deliveries. It requires communication (including possible visits) with the supplier during the waiting period. This either safeguards progress, or provides an early warning system should the supplier experience any difficulty in meeting the order.

After goods receipt

Receipt of the goods is not the end of the purchasing story. The consignment must be examined at the project site or factory receiving bay to check for possible lost items or damage caused in transit. There might also have been some mistake by the supplier, either in the quantity supplied or in the nature of the goods. Goods inwards inspectors may wish to examine the goods more thoroughly to ensure that they comply with the purchase specification although, in recent years, the tendency has been to place more reliance on the suppliers' own quality procedures.

If the goods are accepted, the goods inwards personnel will record the consignment, usually by preparing and distributing a goods inwards certificate or by copying the supplier's own despatch note (to act as a certificate). At least one copy of the certificate will go to the accounts department, which needs it before it can pay the supplier's invoice. Another copy will go to the buying department, to cut short any further expediting action and close off the file on that particular order. Routeing of other copies might include other departments such as the stores, but this depends on the nature of the firm and the goods.

If the consignment is not received in satisfactory condition for any reason, it will be sent smartly back whence it came, accompanied by a rejection note. Distribution of rejection notes generally follows that of acceptance certificates, but will produce opposite reactions from the various recipients. For example, the accounts department will not pay any associated invoice, and the purchasing department will redouble its expediting efforts.

When the correct goods have been received, they will be passed into stores or placed with project stocks to await use.

If the consignment was ordered for stock used in repetitive production or manufacture, stock records will have to be updated. Then there will follow the customary depletion of stock as usage takes place, until the stock records indicate the need for a fresh purchase order. Then the whole purchasing cycle is set in motion again.

The purchase order

The purchase of an item has already been referred to as a mini-project. It follows that, just as a project needs to be provided with a complete specification, so does a purchase order. There are two main parts to this particular type of specification: a statement of the relevant commercial conditions, and a description of the goods.

A purchase order form is shown in outline in Figure 16.3. This gives some idea of the information needed, but limited space in the illustration has not allowed every item to be shown. A slightly more complete list of the information required on a purchase order is as follows:

1   a purchase order serial number, for identification, filing and possible subsequent information retrieval
2   the name or description of the goods to be supplied
3   the quantity required

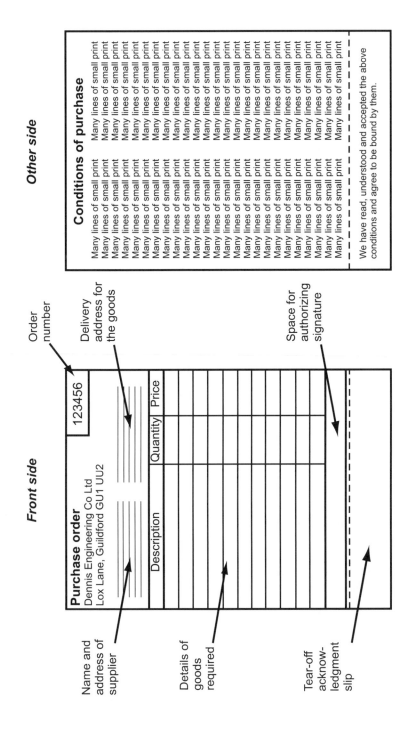
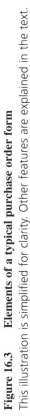

Figure 16.3   Elements of a typical purchase order form
This illustration is simplified for clarity. Other features are explained in the text.

4   the agreed purchase price, as quoted by the supplier and accepted by the purchaser
5   if relevant, the reference number and date of the supplier's quotation document or catalogue item.
6   the delivery date required
7   the address to which the goods are to be delivered
8   the terms on which delivery are to be made (liability for transport, packing, insurance costs, and so on)
9   invoicing instructions
10   an authorizing signature.

Commercial conditions of purchase

It is customary for companies to standardize many of their commercial conditions of purchase and print them on the reverse of their purchase order forms. The set of conditions which follows is based on those used by one company, but each firm must seek its own legal advice and draft its conditions of purchase according to its own experience, needs and current state of the law:

1   **Definitions**
    Company   – means Lox Box Company Limited
    Seller   – means the person, firm or company to whom the company's order is addressed
    Goods   – means the supply and delivery of the goods, materials or equipment in accordance with the company's order together with any subsequent modifications specified by the company
    Contract   – means the agreement between the company and the seller for the supply of goods.

2   **Payment** – Net cash against shipping documents or other proof of delivery unless otherwise agreed (subject to any deductions and retentions authorized in the terms of the order, and subject to the seller carrying out all his obligations).

3   **Prices** – All prices are fixed for the duration of the contract and, unless otherwise agreed, are not subject to escalation charges of any description.

4   **Quality and description** – The goods shall conform to description, be of sound materials and quality, and be equal in all respects to any specification given by the company to the seller.

5   **Indemnity** – The seller shall at his own expense make good by repair or replacement all defects attributable to faulty design and/or workmanship

which appear in the goods within the period of 12 months from date of delivery. The seller shall also indemnify the company in respect of all damage or injury occurring before the above-mentioned period expires to any person or property and against all actions, suits, claims, demands, costs, charges or expenses arising in connection therewith to the extent that the same have been occasioned by the negligence of the seller, his servants or agents during such time as he or they were on, entering on to or departing from the company's premises for any purpose connected with this contract.

6 **Intellectual property** – The seller will indemnify the company against any claim for infringement of letters patent, trademark, registered design or copyright arising out of the use or sale of the goods and against all costs, charges and expenses occasioned thereby except in so far as such infringement is due to the seller having followed the design supplied by the company.

7 **Loss or damage** – All responsibility for any loss or damage, whether total or partial, direct or indirect from whatsoever cause, shall lie with the seller until full and complete delivery in terms of the order shall have been made by the seller. But it is agreed that the company will take all necessary steps to ensure that it does not in any way invalidate any claim which the seller may have against the carrier.

8 **Changes in the work** – No variations of, or extras to the order shall be carried out by the seller unless specifically authorized by the company on its official amendment form.

9 **Subsuppliers** – The seller shall provide a list of all subcontractors or subsuppliers when requested by the company.

10 **Expediting** – The company's expediting staff shall be given access at all reasonable times to the seller's works or offices or those of any subcontractor in order to view or discuss work in progress.

11 **Rejection** – The company may at any time, whether before or after delivery, reject (giving reasons therefor) any goods found to be inferior, damaged or if the seller commits any breach of the order. This condition shall apply notwithstanding that the goods may have been inspected or tested by the company.

12 **Arbitration** – Any dispute or difference arising from the contract shall, on the application of either the seller or the company, be submitted to arbitration of a single arbitrator who shall be agreed between the parties or who failing such agreement shall be appointed at the request of either party by the President for the time being of the Law Society.

13 **Time for completion** – The seller's promised delivery date must be firm, but if delivery is delayed through any cause beyond the control of the seller and immediately such cause arises the seller notifies the company in writing giving full particulars then a reasonable extension of time shall be granted. If delivery is not made within the time stipulated or within any extension of time the company shall be at liberty to cancel the contract without prejudice to any right or remedy which shall have accrued or which shall thereafter accrue to the company.

14 **Title to goods** – Title to the goods passes to the company on delivery to the specified place of delivery as requested by the company.

15 **Law of the contract** – Unless otherwise agreed the contract shall be subject to the laws of England.

Acceptance by the supplier

When the supplier has received the purchase order, complete with its set of conditions, the supplier is expected to acknowledge acceptance of the order. That then establishes a legal contract. The order form shown in Figure 16.3 carries a tear-off acknowledgment slip which is intended to encourage the supplier to accept the standard conditions and other requirements of the order. However, many suppliers ignore such arrangements and acknowledge receipt of the order but supply their own set of standard conditions, which might differ from those of the purchaser.

It is possible for correspondence to develop, with each party to the contract continuing to send to the other the particular set of conditions that it prefers. In the event of a dispute it is then possible that the courts will regard the conditions contained in the last, unanswered letter of such correspondence as those which apply to the particular contract. The inference is that those conditions have not been rejected, and have thus been accepted by default.

Terms of trade used in international business (Incoterms 2000)

When a project proposal involves shipping goods to an overseas customer, or the purchase of goods from abroad, it is important that the boundaries of responsibility for transportation are clearly defined in proposals, contracts and on purchase orders. Incoterms, defined and published by the International Chamber of Commerce, are accepted worldwide as the succinct and definitive method for setting out these boundaries. The terms are listed below, in ascending order of the sender's scope of responsibility. Full definitions of these terms are given in ICC

Publication No. 560 (see International Chamber of Commerce, 2000 in the further reading list at the end this part of the book).

Group E Incoterms (departure)

EXW   Ex works

Group F Incoterms (main carriage unpaid)

FCA   Free carrier
FAS   Free alongside ship
FOB   Free on board

Group C Incoterms (main carriage paid)

CFR   Cost and freight
CIF   Cost, insurance and freight
CIP   Carriage and insurance paid to

Group D Incoterms (arrival)

DAF   Delivered at frontier
DES   Delivered ex ship
DEQ   Delivered ex quay
DDU   Delivered duty unpaid
DDP   Delivered duty paid

Specifying the goods

Bought-out parts, equipment and materials can often be specified by reference to a manufacturer's catalogue or part number. This would appear to be a sufficiently rigid description of the goods. It has to be remembered, however, that most manufacturers reserve the right to modify their designs. If goods are ordered through stockists or factors, then even the company of manufacture might be liable to change. Such a change could be slight and insignificant to most users of the item concerned, but it might render the product utterly useless in a particular case. An example of this would be where a manufacturer changed the material of a component: the catalogue description and illustration might be identical for both versions of the item, but the strength, weight and other physical properties would change.

Sometimes a relevant national standards specification (for example, a British Standards Specification) exists that can be quoted to specify the requirements. There are also many specifications provided by other official bodies, including the armed services. Some companies, however, take no chances, and produce their own drawings and specifications and allocate part numbers themselves. This practice costs a considerable amount of time from professional or technical staff, but has much to commend it. Apart from removing any ambiguity about what is being ordered, provision is thus made for a common part-numbering system, which simplifies stock-handling and purchasing procedures, and eases the burden of the cost office.

This subject of purchase specifications is continued in Chapter 18, with particular reference to procedures used by companies working on complex construction, petrochemical, mining and civil engineering projects.

Case history

An example from my own experience will emphasize the pitfalls of inadequate purchase specifications and point to the type of circumstances where the preparation of special drawings for bought-out components is justified.

A company manufacturing apparatus for hospital operating theatres had a product which had been in very low-volume production over a number of years without significant design change. This unit used three water taps of the elbow-lever action type; these enable surgeons to operate the taps without contaminating their gloved hands. Each tap had a threaded hose outlet. The operating direction of the tap lever and its on and off positions were critical to the correct assembly and operation of the equipment.

No drawing of these taps existed, but for several years the small stock was replenished from the same reliable supplier, which manufactured them specially each time according to a mixture of written instructions on the order form and the manufacturer's memory of past orders.

For various reasons a time came when orders for these taps had to be placed with a succession of different suppliers. A written description of the taps was given with each order, but there was still no drawing. Every conceivable error arose in the subsequent supply of these items. Taps arrived with the wrong hose connecting thread, or with no thread at all. Levers came as wrist-action instead of elbow-lever. Taps were discovered with the levers set at right angles to the required position and, on one occasion, the taps had anticlockwise rotation instead of clockwise. Sometimes consignments were accepted into stores without the errors being discovered until the taps were withdrawn for use.

Eventually, a drawing of an ideal tap was produced. This defined the outline dimensions, general shape, hose connection and the lever operating direction and positions. Thereafter, one copy of this drawing was sent with every purchase order, while a second copy was sent to the goods inwards inspectors to enable them to check each new consignment. Very few mistakes occurred subsequently and, when they did, the goods inwards inspectors were able to spot them immediately and have them rectified by the manufacturer.

The improvement was dramatic, immediate and permanent. All the previous trouble could have been prevented if only the correct procedure to specify the goods had been followed all along.

Timing of orders and deliveries

Early ordering of long-lead items

Engineers and others responsible for initiating project purchases have a duty to identify those items that are likely to have long lead times and ensure that ordering instructions are passed to the purchasing department as soon as possible. This might mean issuing advance information on such things as special bearings, motors, castings and other bought-out components, at times when the relevant assembly drawings and final bills of material remain unfinished or even unstarted.

It is sometimes desirable to issue advance information even when the goods cannot be specified in exact detail, because this gives the purchasing department the chance to get started on obtaining provisional quotations and (in a really urgent case) on reserving capacity in a manufacturer's works by issuing a letter of intent.

Any company with sufficient project experience will attempt to follow such practices as a matter of course. If a project has been planned using a critical path network, any need to issue advance purchasing instructions will almost certainly be highlighted.

Just-in-time

The phrase 'just-in-time' took on a specific meaning with the adoption by some companies of the Japanese approach to purchasing and manufacture which attempts to reduce stockholding to zero and, among other things, relies on suppliers to deliver direct to the workplace 'just-in-time'.

This system relies heavily on establishing a great deal of trust, and the suppliers are expected to be fully responsible for delivering the supplies in the right quantities, at the right time and of the right quality without day-to-day supervision from the purchaser. But these ideals cannot be achieved overnight, and cannot be expected to operate for project purchasing, where regular use of suppliers and repeat orders are not the norm.

As a general rule, it is late or incorrect deliveries (and the shortages which they cause) that will always produce the biggest headaches for project managers, and any decision to delay the issue of a purchase order must be tempered with caution, allowing time for unforeseen contingencies. What would happen, for example, if an important consignment arrived just in time, only to be rejected as being damaged in transit or was otherwise unfit for project use?

Retarded deliveries and call-off orders

There are often reasons why deliveries of project materials should not be called for too early. Materials which are ordered so as to arrive long before they are needed will have to be paid for earlier than is necessary, inflating the amount of money tied up unprofitably in inventory and work in progress. Another problem is that storage difficulties can arise for items delivered prematurely. Some goods have a short shelf life, and will deteriorate if kept too long in store.

Call-off orders

If an order is for a large quantity of parts, deliveries can be arranged to take place in batches, at an agreed rate over a specified period. Of course, the suppliers must be willing to accept such arrangements, but the practice is common. The supplier can either store the balance of the order, or manufacture to suit the schedule. This is known as a 'call-off' procedure, because the items are called off as they are needed for the project. It is older than, but not too far removed from, the just-in-time approach.

Although the deliveries of items in large, repeating quantities brings batch or mass production to mind, some single projects do consume large quantities of materials. For instance, one would hardly consider the building of a large office block as mass production, but enormous quantities of building supplies may be involved. There would be very obvious difficulties if all the supplies were to be delivered before work had begun on site clearance. Chaos would reign, with cement, sand, ballast, bricks and other supplies strewn all over the area. Access for site work would then be impossible, and those supplies which survived without being pilfered or ruined by exposure to the elements would have to be moved before work could start. By indicating the total quantities required for the project, the contractor can gain the benefits of quantity discounts, but the deliveries must be called off only when they are needed.

Now consider a manufacturing project requiring 10 000 small identical electromechanical components, costing £30 each, to be incorporated in sub-assemblies over a period of some two years. These components are small and present no storage problem. But they are not all needed at once, so why commit expenditure of £300 000 too early? Again, a call-off order is indicated, allowing the contractor to delay expenditure, keep inventory down, and improve cash flow, while still reaping the benefits of the discount that can undoubtedly be negotiated because of the large quantity involved.

Commonsense timing

Once it is agreed that materials should be ordered to a project plan, there remain one or two questions regarding the commonsense application of that plan.

Returning to the case of the 10 000 components costing £30 each, there is no question that the order for these items should be arranged on a call-off basis if possible. But what about the inexpensive items such as screws, nuts, washers, solder tags and so on? It would be nonsensical to attempt ordering these items to any plan. Rather, one would see to it that the whole quantity was ordered in advance, and with a generous supply to spare. Rigid control would not be necessary. The application of planning and control would probably cost more than the total value of the materials themselves, and might attract ridicule from the suppliers into the bargain.

Some items will therefore be controlled strictly from the project plan while others will not. Where should the line be drawn? The section on Pareto analysis in Chapter 17 (see page 399) describes one approach but, first, it has to be said that ordering to a plan is not likely to be one of the project manager's chief worries. The more likely problem is one of trying to obtain urgent materials in an impossibly short space of time. When delays occur early in a project, and no let-up of delivery time can be allowed, the remaining part of the work will resemble an incompressible object being squeezed between two irresistible forces. The procurement activity stands a high chance of being trapped in such a squeeze, owing to the tendency of engineers to provide their purchase specifications too late.

Purchase quantities

Problems with orders for small quantities

Purchase orders for small quantities of materials or components are often a specific feature of projects where the work is non-repetitive and confined to the completion of only one end product. In these cases, the purchasing department will be faced with appreciable handicaps when it attempts to achieve short-term deliveries and low costs. A single small component may be vital to the success of a project but, although this component assumes important dimensions in the eyes of the project manager, for the manufacturer it has only nuisance value, yielding small profit and disrupting work on larger orders for more valued customers.

If the contractor is a large company, or part of a big group, there is always a possibility that the supplier may give good service in the fond hope of larger follow-up orders. Although the supplier's optimism might be completely groundless, only a foolish project manager would set out deliberately to discourage it. Similar motives sometimes prompt suppliers to proffer free samples of their wares. Items obtained in this way not only cost nothing, but also can usually be obtained by return of post, or out of a sales representative's brief case. Small stocks are sometimes reserved by suppliers for this purpose, and if the paperwork and formal ordering formalities are circumvented in this way, much valuable project time can be saved. Project managers would obviously be ill-advised to consider planning a project on the basis of materials supplied as free samples, but it should be remembered that some projects have been given the kiss of life by items procured in this way after all other methods have been tried and found wanting.

Items ordered in very small quantities will usually be priced higher than they would be if bought in larger, price-discounted amounts. Other penalties of small quantity orders include higher costs per unit for packing, transport, documentation, and general handling. These are some of the factors which can induce suppliers to charge higher prices for very small purchases.

The lure of quantity discounts

Quantity discounts or other inducements offered by suppliers have led purchasers to buy well beyond their immediate needs. Some reported cases have been spectacular. To take a modest example, suppose that seven special instruments are required for a project, and that the unit price is quoted as £20 000 each for quantities of one to nine, and £17 500 each for quantities of ten or more. The buyer might be tempted to buy ten to take advantage of the discount, although only seven are required immediately. The saving on unit cost, however, will not be worth the cost of three surplus units left on the shelf at the end of the project. Instead of costing £140 000, the units have cost a total of £175 000.

The only possible justification for buying above the net requirement would be to offset expected breakages (in which case a budget must exist) or against a *certain* follow-up order from the customer for spares. Any unjustified inflation of order quantities must be vetoed by the project manager. Surplus stocks can accumulate with embarrassing speed if restraint is not exercised.

Materials purchased for use in continuous or batch production are also liable to become overstocked through the lure of quantity discounts. Overstocking leads to a reduction in the inventory turn ratio (annual sales value divided by the value of stock and work in progress), which increases the amount of investment required in the business compared to the profits generated.

Some suppliers offer personal inducements, perhaps in the form of free gifts or holidays in return for orders. Managers should not allow themselves or their subordinates to be tempted by such offers into purchasing above the needs of the project.

Chapter 17

Purchasing, Part 2: Post-order activities and wider aspects of materials control

This chapter starts by dealing with some purchasing activities that take place after the issue of a purchase order. These activities include the issue of purchase order amendments, expediting, dealing with shortages, and various aspects of stores administration. The chapter concludes with comparisons between the treatment of materials as general stocks and materials purchased and stored specifically for a project. A further reading list is provided at the end of this part of the book.

Purchase order amendments

Should it become necessary to change any aspect of a purchase order after issue, the supplier's earliest agreement should be sought to determine the effect on price and delivery, and to ensure that the proposed change is within the supplier's capability. Once these facts have been successfully established, an amendment to the original purchase order must be issued.

Each purchase order amendment should bear the same reference number as the original purchase order, suffixed by an identifying amendment number (amendment 1, 2, 3 and so on). Purchase order amendments should be prepared on a standard format and authorized in the same way as purchase orders. Amendments must be distributed so that they are received by all recipients of the original purchase order or its copies.

Amendment or new order?

The amendment procedure is often used to add one or more items to an existing order. However, if the introduction of a new item is likely to jeopardize the previously agreed delivery date of any other item on the purchase order, the best policy is to issue a fresh order for the new item, so leaving the supplier to carry on unhindered and with no excuse for failing to meet the existing commitments.

The practice of adding a succession of new items to an existing order can result in a number of partial deliveries, none of which completes the order, so that administration becomes messy. The need to wade through a purchase order plus a pile of amendments in order to discover its total extent and the balance of deliveries and payments outstanding is time-consuming and irritating. Invoice control is likely to be made difficult, and payment disputes can result. Separate orders prevent these difficulties.

Expediting

First reliance on obtaining goods in time to meet the project schedule must be vested in the purchasing department. Once each order has been placed, responsibility shifts (within the purchasing department) from the buyer to the expediter, although in smaller organizations the buyer will fulfil both roles. Expediting, contrary to popular belief, is not just a process for chasing up goods which are overdue for delivery. It is a preventive measure that seeks instead to foresee problems and pre-empt late deliveries.

Routine approach to expediting

Expediting is usually a routine procedure for monitoring the progress of each order, so that suppliers can be encouraged to deliver on time, and to allow adequate warning of any possible delay.

One common expediting method consists of marking each purchase order record with flags (in a card index or computer system) signalling the dates when reminders to the supplier would seem propitious. As each reminder becomes due, a standard message can be sent, tactfully asking the supplier to confirm that work on the order is going according to plan.

More urgent expediting methods

The expeditor should react promptly and firmly whenever the reply to a routine expediting enquiry is unsatisfactory. The special efforts of the purchasing department should not stop until the supplier has either shown the necessary improvement or has actually delivered the goods.

Sometimes a new method of approach to the supplier can produce the desired result. An offer to arrange collection of the goods from the supplier's premises will, for instance, make the supplier aware that the purchaser is willing to participate constructively and that, on this occasion at least, there is genuine urgency.

A carefully composed letter, explaining why a particular item was urgently wanted for a vital export order once reduced a quoted delivery time from 16 weeks to an actual 14 calendar days, even though the order was for just two small flexible drive shafts which had practically no profit value to the supplier and (because the shaft lengths were not standard) caused the supplier to interrupt a high-volume production run of automobile tachometer drives and make a special machine set up. Similar letters were sent to two other suppliers on that particular project, and they achieved almost the same degree of success in getting the parts on time.

Perhaps the written word in general carries more weight than a telephone call (which is easily forgotten). Messages printed on paper are tangible objects that remain under the eye as a constant reminder and, if properly addressed, will reach senior managers in the suppliers' organizations.

Alternative sourcing

When expediting appears to be failing, the design engineers might be able to suggest an alternative item that can be obtained more quickly. The solution might instead mean finding another source of supply. If the original order does have to be cancelled because the supplier has failed to make the agreed delivery, there should be no penalty for the purchaser, because the supplier has broken the contract by failing to fulfil the delivery conditions.

Commitment and motivation

The purchasing department will not usually be directing all its attention to one project, unless it is very big. Quite understandably, each purchasing order which passes through its hands could be regarded by the expediters as just another routine job.

Projects of sufficient size can justify the allocation of a buyer, or even a group of buyers and expediters, to the project. These staff should be seconded to the project from the purchasing department if possible, but they might have to be recruited specially as temporary staff or contract staff.

Special staffing should be particularly effective in a project team organization, because the reporting line is to the project manager rather than to the materials or purchasing manager. The buyer and expediter (they might be the same person), as part of the team, should identify themselves more closely with the success or failure of the project and thus be more highly motivated

The project manager should be motivated by a sense of personal involvement with the success of the project. He or she will perhaps realize that their own career prospects can be closely linked to the success of the project. This realization should spur the project manager on to exercise initiative, perseverance, tact and (in the last resort) guile. For these reasons the project manager can sometimes be successful in preventing or clearing a shortage which has been accepted by others as inevitable. The effective project manager refuses to accept defeat, and explores every avenue until a solution is found.

Intervention by the project manager

If the supplier definitely cannot deliver on time, the project manager must be brought into the picture. He or she can then decide on just how important the delay is likely to be, and authorize emergency measures if these appear to be justified. In the last resort the project manager must feel free to intervene in the expediting process, even if this brings accusations of interference from the purchasing manager. The earlier examples illustrating the success achieved by writing special letters were cases where the purchasing department's routine procedures had failed to improve the suppliers' promises, and the project manager refused to accept defeat and wrote letters to the suppliers himself.

Shortages

Jobs are sometimes delayed because of materials shortages, or have to be started before all the necessary materials have been assembled. This usually happens because, in spite of expediting, a supplier has failed to deliver on time. However, shortages can arise through many causes. These include breakages, theft, failure to notice low stock levels, incorrect specifications, purchasing mistakes, design mistakes, design changes and a variety of other reasons.

No project manager likes to see any job delayed because of shortages, and no one wants to start a task before being assured that all the materials are available to carry it through to the finish. Shortages do occur in projects however. Shortage lists are one way for bringing them to the purchasing manager's attention for action. Shortage lists can be used on any project – for factory materials or for shortages on a construction site.

Shortage lists

A shortage list is a communication from the project manager (or more junior manager) to the purchasing department conveying a request for urgent action to make good a materials shortage. The essential elements of a shortage list are depicted in Figure 17.1, which is a clerical version of the procedure. A shortage list must:

- be quick and easy for the manager or supervisor of the affected task to use
- describe the missing materials by type and quantity
- give precise information to the purchasing department so that the purchase order can be identified quickly and the supplier contacted.

Shortage list	Project:		Date issued::		
	Department:		Issued by:		
To the purchasing manager. The items listed below have not been received and are critical to progress. Please expedite and report as soon as possible.				Is work held up? Yes/No	
Order No (if known)	Description of materials or equipment	Quantity needed	When needed	Reply from purchasing manager	

Figure 17.1   A shortage list format

In addition, a shortage list system should:

● state the degree of urgency
● allow feedback, so that the project manager or supervisor involved can be told when to expect delivery.

The storekeeper, foreman, supervisor or manager who discovers that there are shortages on a job would enter all the relevant information on a shortage list and transmit it to the relevant buyer by the quickest available means. Depending on the type of project, the shortage list information might be made available to shop floor progress chasers, site foreman, storekeeper and, of course, the project manager.

The procedure should provide that the buyer reports back to the originator on what is being done to clear the shortages.

The Pareto principle and stock management

Firms which order many varied items for general production as well as for manufacturing projects have at their disposal a method for deciding which materials can be ordered in bulk without special controls, and which need more rigid degrees of authorization, planning and control. This method is based on the Pareto principle.

Vilfredo Pareto (1848–1923) was an Italian sociologist and economist whose work included studying the distribution of wealth across the general population. From his census results, Pareto found that 80 per cent of the total wealth was typically distributed among only 20 per cent of the people. Pareto's discoveries have led to the general acceptance and use of the 'Pareto principle', otherwise known as 'Pareto's law' or the '80/20 rule'.

In general terms, the assumption made is that, in any 'population' of items, 80 per cent of their total value or effect will be spread over only 20 per cent of the items. These 20 per cent are sometimes referred to as the 'significant few'. The converse is, of course, that 80 per cent of the items (the insignificant many) account for only 20 per cent of the combined value or effect.

Applied to stock control, the Pareto principle means that 80 per cent of items purchased or held in stock can be expected to account for only 20 per cent of the total inventory value. The implication is that management control should not be dissipated on these less expensive, insignificant many items, but should be concentrated instead on those items where it will do most good, namely on the more valuable and significant 20 per cent.

If a company cares to take the time and trouble, it can list its purchased goods (usually confined to general stock items) in descending order of their inventory value, analyse the ranking, and allocate each item into either the 20 per cent or 80 per cent groups.

The ABC extension of the Pareto principle in stock control

A common variant is to divide stock into three, rather than two, categories, with the items labelled as category A, B or C. A typical classification would be as follows:

- **Class A** – the significant few, the 20 per cent of the stock 'population' that accounts for 80 per cent of the total inventory value
- **Class B** – the middle range, a further 30 per cent of the stock that accounts for another 10 per cent of the total inventory value
- **Class C** – the remaining 50 per cent of stock items, the insignificant many accounting for only 10 per cent of total inventory value.

Reordering of these items would then be controlled as follows.

Items in Class A

Stores issues must be properly authorized. Each fresh order must be justified against specific requirements, and the purchase must be authorized by a senior manager.

Items in Class B

Stores issues must be properly authorized. Stock replenishment orders are triggered when stock records show that the stockholding has fallen to a predetermined minimum level, and the re-order quantity is calculated to restore the stock level to a predetermined maximum (this is called the 'max-min' system of stock control).

Items in Class C

This group typically includes items such as small screws, nuts, washers and consumables. Stores issues are less rigorously controlled, and some items may be left out in open bins or racks. The two-bin method is commonly used for re-ordering. Two bins are held in stores. When the stock in one bin has been exhausted, the second is brought into use, and fresh stocks are ordered automatically to fill the empty bin.

Project or stock purchasing?

Projects supplied completely from stocked materials

Imagine a large factory churning out a varied range of products in quantity, and suppose that this company does not operate the just-in-time system of purchasing, but holds comprehensive stocks of all possible materials requirements. If a special manufacturing project were to be handled in this environment, it is just conceivable that it could be completed entirely from stock materials and components, with no need for any special project purchasing whatsoever – an unlikely possibility, certainly, but not absolutely impossible if the project happened to be in the firm's customary line of business.

This kind of stock purchasing attracts high inventory holding costs for the company, but it provides local cost advantages from the point of view of a project manager. There is no need to buy any materials in small quantities, but rather one could order in economic batch sizes, so that the standard costs of materials charged to the project appear low. No special arrangements for materials storage need be contemplated, although the project manager would be well advised to ensure that the storekeepers reserve or 'pre-allocate' any essential materials and components.

Projects supplied entirely from special purchases

Now consider a company which carries no stocks. Every time a new project appears on the scene, each single item must be ordered, right down to the last nut, bolt and washer. This is an example of 'project purchasing', which for manufacturing projects might seem just as improbable as the stock purchasing case (although it is the norm for some other types of project).

There are definite advantages to be gained by adopting a project purchasing policy but, before moving on to discuss these, one or two of the disadvantages should be mentioned.

The most serious drawbacks of project purchasing in manufacturing projects occur when a company is running more than one project at a time in the same factory. With project purchasing in operation, any parts common to two or more of these contracts must be ordered and stored separately. Individual order quantities are therefore smaller, so that quantity discounts are forfeited or reduced. Such purchases increase the company's total inventory (and therefore inventory holding costs) because safety stocks to allow for losses, breakages and scrap have to be held in more than one place (perhaps even as many places as there are projects). Two or more separate stores occupy more floor space than one combined store of the same total capacity. Administration costs (including security) must be higher. Why, then, should project purchasing ever be considered?

Of course, the situation is different for construction and other companies whose projects are built on several sites remote from the company's premises, where materials have to be delivered to site by the suppliers. In these cases all materials handling and storage is specific to each project, and project purchasing is the obvious and usual method.

Several very good reasons exist for advocating project purchasing and storage for manufacturing projects wherever the size of the project and the nature of the operations allow this to be arranged conveniently. One of these is that it facilitates the physical pre-allocation of materials for a project.

Information for cost and budget analysis

Another advantage afforded by project purchasing over stock purchasing, for any type of project, is the improved cost and budget analysis which it allows. This is illustrated in Figure 17.2, which compares the cost data obtained by three different methods for the same project materials.

All the curves have one thing in common: each has been drawn by adding together the materials expenditure on a month-by-month basis as soon as the data are known. The only difference between the curves is the information route through which the cost data have been obtained.

Cost data from stores issues

Curve *C* in Figure 17.2 is the only graph which could be derived in all circumstances, whether stock or project purchasing had been adopted. In this case,

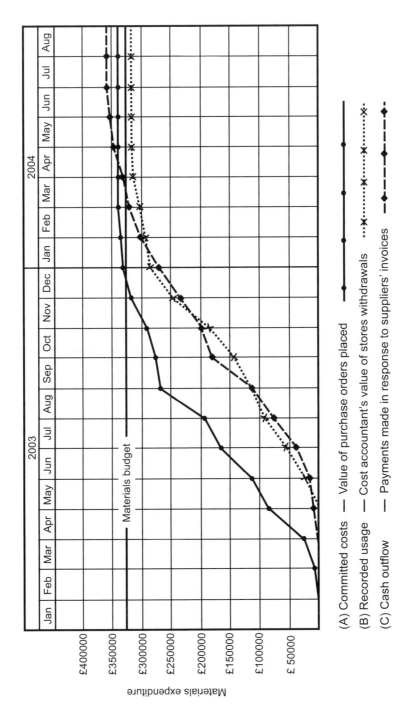

(A) Committed costs — Value of purchase orders placed ————•————

(B) Recorded usage — Cost accountant's value of stores withdrawals ⋯⋯✕⋯⋯✕⋯⋯

(C) Cash outflow — Payments made in response to suppliers' invoices — — ◆ — —

Figure 17.2   Three methods for recording the cost of project materials

the materials costs have been found by valuing all the items listed on stores requisitions or similar paperwork (usually at standard cost) as the items have been withdrawn from stores for use on the project.

Errors can arise owing to discrepancies between the amounts listed and the amounts actually issued or used. Valuations can also be inaccurate if outdated standard costs have been applied. These errors ought not to be significant, however, unless there are serious shortcomings in the stores or costing administration. The real disadvantage of this most usual form of costing – a time penalty – only becomes apparent when the results are compared with those obtained from alternative methods. It is not called 'historic costing' for nothing.

Cost data from committed costs

Project purchasing (or 'contract purchasing') allows the material costs to be picked up as each purchase order is issued, which is when the costs are committed, rather than when they actually occur. Plotting data obtained in this way gives a good indication of the expenditure committed well in advance of the time when the materials will actually be used. Any items already available from general stocks, and which are not to be ordered specially for the project, must, of course, be allowed for and included in the total commitment. This is easily accomplished: all that is necessary is to withdraw these stocks from production stores in advance and pre-allocate them by transfer into the project stores. The requisitions used to withdraw these materials from production stores can be costed at their standard cost, and the costs added to the total project commitment.

Curve *A* of Figure 17.2 shows how data from committed materials expenditure can give the earliest possible warning of the need for action when budgets are in danger of being overspent. Once again, discrepancies from valuation errors can intrude if allowances have to be made for materials used from general stocks but, as before, these errors should be too small to destroy the validity of any trend indicated.

Analysis of committed expenditure is the most effective method for monitoring the amount spent on equipment and materials and for predicting the project total. The method is not the most accurate, however, and is of less use in measuring the amount actually spent in the final event, for reasons which will become apparent on considering Curve *C*.

Cost data from suppliers' invoices

Payments made against suppliers' invoices provide the most accurate account of purchased materials costs for a contract. Project purchasing is an essential condition, otherwise all invoices cannot easily be related to the project being costed. Curve *C* in Figure 17.2 shows how type of cost information can build up as the project progresses.

Note that Curve *C* lags behind both the other two curves by an appreciable period. Most invoices will be paid only after the goods have been received. In fact, the customary office procedures for invoice checking and approving payment must mean the lapse of at least another week or two before the cheques are raised and signed. Suppliers do not always submit their invoices promptly, or they make mistakes, which can introduce further delays before payments are made. These payment time lags provide some useful free credit for the purchaser, but they also put back the date when the true project costs can be assessed.

The significant fact which emerges here is that information derived from suppliers' invoices is far too late to be of any use whatsoever in budgetary control. By the time the facts are known, the money has long since been committed and nothing can be done. This emphasizes the importance of measuring and controlling project purchase costs at the point of commitment, which means when the purchase orders are issued.

Comparative accuracy

Before leaving Figure 17.2, observe that all three curves attain different final levels. In this example the differences have been exaggerated deliberately, and in practice no more than about 5 per cent of the total material costs should separate the highest and lowest asymptotes.

The curve of committed costs (Curve A), did not quite reach the true final cost value (Curve C) owing to slight differences between suppliers' quotations (the amounts shown on the purchase orders and used to compile Curve A) and the final prices actually invoiced. These extra costs arose because one or two purchase orders were placed after the suppliers' quotations were time-expired, and because of incidental expenses, such as freight, packing, insurance, and port and customs duties that were not originally taken into account.

Curve B (materials actually withdrawn from project stores) also fell slightly short of the real total as shown by Curve C. This could imply that some over-ordering took place (leaving some goods in stock at the end of the project). Changes to the scope or specification of the project during its execution might also have led to materials being left unused in stores. When surpluses are accumulated in this way, these should really be written off as a charge against project profits, unless they can be returned to the suppliers for full credit or used elsewhere on other projects. Otherwise, the surplus materials will only have to be written off at a later date.

Project purchasing as a condition of contract

Some projects where reliability and safety are paramount (for example, in the aerospace, defence and nuclear industries) demand that all items are purchased against certification of fitness for use. Even raw materials will be included, and samples may have to be tested in independent laboratories.

Another important quality aspect is 'traceability'. Suppose that a component fails in an aircraft in service. Good traceability will allow the original source and batch of the failed component to be traced. This, in turn, will allow all other components from that batch to be traced so that they can be replaced to avoid problems in all the other aircraft that might be affected.

These conditions mean that the choice between stock purchasing and project purchasing has been taken out of the contractor's hands. Project buying has, in effect, become a condition of contract.

Incidentally, the additional inspection, documentation and storage measures required to satisfy these conditions will inflate the cost of project purchases and materials handling, and should, if possible, be allowed for in the contract price.

Stores administration

Most problems arising out of the physical storage of goods can be resolved into a few well-defined categories:

1 **Accommodation** – requirements for floor space, racking and shelving, stockyards, and so on
2 **Labelling** – marking the goods so that they can be identified later without ambiguity
3 **Location** – recording the place where the goods have been stored so that they can be found when they are needed
4 **Preservation** – paying attention to possible deterioration, limited shelf-life, cross-contamination between different materials and the storage environment generally
5 **Handling methods and equipment**
6 **Health and safety** (particularly associated with handling methods and hazardous materials)
7 **Clerical routines** (whether manual or computerized)
8 **Security** – prevention of theft, wilful damage or misallocation
9 **Records and information systems.**

Some of these items will now be discussed briefly.

Accommodation

With the exception of just-in-time systems or the clearance of shortages, a decision usually has to be made about where incoming materials should be stored. The solution could be a very simple matter of placing a consignment of components in a bin on a vacant rack. On the other hand, the problem could be a large truck, taking up all the space in the goods inwards bay, and crammed to overflowing with bulky goods that cannot be unloaded because there is nowhere to put them. Problems of this type differ from purely mental worries. They possess a sickening and grotesque physical reality that can raise blood pressures and inflame human passions to dangerous levels. A truck driver who has travelled overnight on a long and tiring journey will not be disposed to offer any suggestions about where the goods can be put – at least none which might prove constructive.

Space problems are generally brought about by lack of foresight and inadequate planning. This is an area in which the project manager should be well equipped to contribute. Space is just as much a project resource as labour. It might seem feasible to include these space requirements in the project resource allocation planning, but this is particularly difficult, and is seldom done in practice because the problem is three-dimensional and not suitable for the usual project management computer software. A simpler, and effective, alternative is to provide the manager responsible for materials control with a schedule of project purchasing activities, derived from the critical path network or bar chart (whichever is in use) and sorted according to their expected delivery dates.

Labelling

Correct labelling of stored items is essential, otherwise mistakes in issuing are bound to arise. Stores staff cannot be expected to identify all the varied items needed for a project by their appearance alone. All parts must be given numbers so that ambiguities are not possible. A standard part-numbering discipline, originating from the design office, is a necessary basis for a stock identification system. Each consignment will be marked with the correct part number on receipt into stores and, provided that the number and the goods do not become separated, identification is then made simple. Raw materials can be given the specification number as identification, in some cases backed up by dimensions. Commonly used raw materials, such a metal stocks, can be painted with colour codes.

Location and retrieval

Location and retrieval of materials is a problem proportional to the size and layout of the stores. Valuable project materials have been known to vanish, causing urgent and expensive re-ordering, only to reappear at the back of a dusty shelf long after the project has been finished. The remedy is to give every rack, shelf, and bin an identifying 'address', which is usually a simple alphanumeric code. Stock records will show the stores address code (often called the 'bin number', even where no actual bin exists) against every item held. This is, of course, the common procedure in any well-run store or warehouse.

Physical pre-allocation of materials

One advantage of special project purchasing arises from a weakness inherent in most stock pre-allocation systems. The only safe method for pre-allocating materials for use on forthcoming project work is to withdraw them from general stock and place them in a separate project store. If this is not done, it is certain that – whether pre-allocation is practised or not – some of the stock will be used on other work, and so will be unavailable for the project when needed. Cheery assurances from the storekeeper that the deficient items are 'on order' or 'expected any day now' will not be well received. A project cannot be completed with empty promises.

Preservation

Any materials which are particularly susceptible to deterioration through mechanical shock, heat, cold or damp must be suitably protected. Some articles will deteriorate under any conditions, and must be used within a short time. Heat-developed photographic materials and some dry batteries are examples, and these must be issued in a first-in, first-out sequence. Certain raw materials are not suitable for storing in close proximity to each other because of the risk of damage through cross-contamination. For example, a prudent person would not store strongly scented soap alongside tea.

Security

Safe custody and security of stock demand that the storage area can be locked up outside normal working hours. At other times, stores entry will usually be restricted to authorized stores personnel. Regulations such as these are designed not only to prevent theft, but also to minimize the possibility of irregular or unrecorded withdrawals. Construction site stores are particularly vulnerable and need special protection, which can include a full-time watchman, dogs, patrols, high fencing, alarms, closed circuit television, security lighting, and so on.

Irregular removals are not all due to theft. They might arise from surreptitious attempts at making good losses, scrap or breakages on the site or workfloor. Over-zealous activity to clear shortages on one project could lead to unauthorized taking of stock pre-allocated for other projects.

Stores records and information systems

Information systems must be designed and implemented to provide accurate feedback of all material movements (arrivals and withdrawals) for stock control and cost accounting purposes.

Stores receipts are documented by goods inwards notes or, in the case of items manufactured within the premises, some form of completed job ticket, inspection ticket or stores receipt note. Serviceable items returned to stores for stock because they are no longer required for any reason must be similarly documented.

Issues from stores are usually authorized and documented by stores requisitions, bills of materials, stores issue schedules or parts lists. These withdrawals must be reported against job numbers to the cost office. Those responsible for stock control will rely on this information to maintain stock records as accurately as possible, and re-order where appropriate.

Materials management as a shared or common service

Unless a project store has been set up specially within the project organization, project managers generally have no direct control over the materials management operation. The usual arrangement in a manufacturing company is for the purchasing and stores departments to operate as common services, often combined organizationally with other materials functions such as goods inwards and despatch under the command of a materials manager. The project manager is usually entirely dependent on the materials manager and the stores organization for all materials handling aspects of the project. The project manager may even be denied access to secure stores areas.

Reliance on common services can always cause problems for a project manager, where there might be a clash of priorities, and with any attempt at random independent checking regarded with suspicion – even hostility – by the common services manager, who regards the project manager's interest in the department's performance as unwarranted interference. In fact, the project manager might actually have less direct access and control over a common services department within the company than he or she has over an external supplier of goods and services, where at least the purchase contract will probably give right of access for expediting and on-site inspection purposes.

A true story

Here is an example to illustrate how reliance on common services can let a project manager down. A company in the UK was carrying out a project to manufacture and install two prefabricated operating theatres in a Scandinavian country. The parts for these theatres were derived from common stocks, packed and shipped to the project site by the company's common services division. The highly experienced installation crew, which reported to the project manager, was flown out to the site as soon as all the materials had reached their destination.

The hospital authorities arranged for the initial erection of the main frames to be given full publicity, signifying the proud results of their new investment. Each of these operating theatre frames comprised eight legs, bolted to a welded top frame (so that each theatre skeleton resembled a large spider). Having marked out the floor accurately for the first theatre, members of the site team stood holding eight legs in position while, watched expectantly by the media and local dignitaries, the first top frame was lowered gently into position by a hoist. Of course, it did not fit: the common services division had packed and despatched the wrong top frames.

If there is anything worse than being made to look foolish, it must be suffering that indignity under the bright lights of publicity. The acute embarrassment of the project manager and the company was the result of failure by a common services division over which the project manager had no direct control.

The immediate remedy in that case was for the common services division to airfreight two correct frames to the site – an expensive operation because the large steel frames were heavy and bulky. The longer-term remedy in such cases is usually more difficult, but involves motivating common services to improve its service to the project through a mixture of education, persuasion and (if necessary) mobilizing support and action from the company's senior management.

Chapter 18

Purchasing, Part 3: Procedures for capital projects

Chapters 16 and 17 dealt with general principles of purchasing and materials management. The subject of project purchasing is continued in this chapter, but with more emphasis on obtaining equipment for capital projects (such as civil engineering and large construction projects or projects for the engineering, design and construction of petrochemical and mining plants). Some of the procedures described (such as the specification documents and bid summary procedures) are also applicable to the purchase of high-value equipment for any kind of industrial project. A further reading list is provided at the end of this part of the book.

The purchasing organization

Figure 18.1 shows some of the important elements that might be found in a project purchasing organization. It has to be stressed that there are many ways in which such elements can be organized, and the arrangement in Figure 18.1 is deliberately drawn in very general terms. Some elements have been omitted in order to keep the diagram simple: for example, the suppliers might employ specialist export packing companies and (organized by the shipping agent) there might be shippers, road hauliers, airlines, insurers and many other participants. It is also possible that the project client or the financing organization that is advancing funds for the project might wish to safeguard its own interests through the services of an independent consulting engineer.

In Figure 18.1 the client (often called the owner) is shown as dealing through a managing contractor, with all the other elements shown as separate entities. Among the many possible organizational variations, some of these elements could be part of the managing contractor's own company. In another case, the managing contractor might be a professional project management organization, employing or controlling a main contractor that owns and operates some or most of the elements. Variations could be listed *ad nauseam* and thus it would be unwise here to describe the organization in Figure 18.1 as 'typical'.

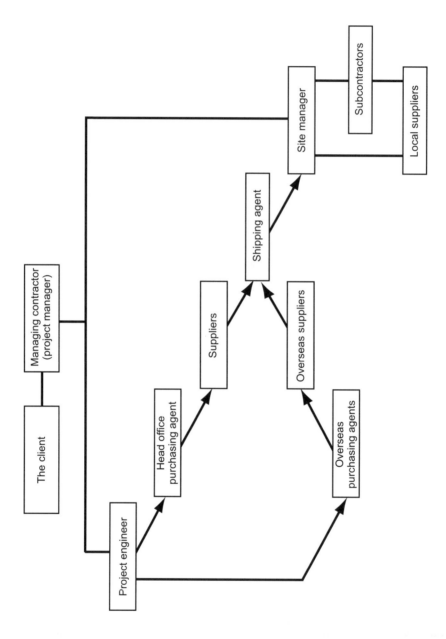

Figure 18.1   Elements of a purchasing organization for a large international project

The purchasing agent

One particular organizational aspect must be mentioned before passing on to a more detailed description of purchasing procedures. This concerns the identity and location of the purchasing agent.

The purchasing agent could be an independent organization, the contractor's purchasing department, or even the client's own purchasing department. There can also be various combinations of these arrangements. In an international project, the client's purchasing department might, for convenience, issue purchase orders to local suppliers, leaving the managing contractor's head office purchasing department to deal with other suppliers worldwide (possibly operating through purchasing agents overseas where their location and local experience provides for greater efficiency). Throughout the remainder of this chapter, the term 'purchasing agent' is used to mean the purchasing authority that happens to be responsible, irrespective of where that authority is located.

Figure 18.2 will serve to introduce the principal procedures needed to obtain project equipment (and other supplies, such as steelwork and piping) and transport it to site. The organizational functions shown in this diagram are based on an actual international project.

Purchase control schedules

Purchase control schedules list all the significant items of equipment required for a project, and are used by the project engineers as registers from which to control the serial numbering and preparation of purchase specifications.

Format

Figure 18.3 shows the layout of main and column headings for a typical purchase control schedule page. This particular example has columns allowing for the entry of both timescale and cost data.

Inclusion of scheduled dates

If purchase control schedules are to be used for controlling progress throughout the purchase cycle for each item listed, a separate column must be provided for every significant event in the purchase cycle so that target dates can be shown. This means using a format considerably more complex than that shown in Figure 18.3, and the amount of schedule data to be entered on purchase control schedule forms becomes considerable. The data must be kept up to date with changes in the project schedule.

→	1: List requirements	2: Prepare project plan	3: Prepare enquiry specifications	4: Enquiry request	5: Issue of enquiries (ITTs)	6: Suppliers' bidding
Project manager		Draw critical path network and process by computer. Write dates to the purchase schedules	Responsible to the client for scheduling, initiating and supervising all project activities, and for successful completion of the project in all respects. Submits regular cost and progress reports to the client.			
Project engineer and design team	List all equipment requirements on PURCHASE SCHEDULES	Assist the project manager with planning the network logic and estimating task durations	Write a provisional purchase specification (ENQUIRY SPECIFI-CATION) for each item of equipment to be purchased	Send a REQUEST FOR ENQUIRY to the purchasing agent and recommend possible suppliers	Provide technical support to the purchase agent throughout the enquiry phase, including discussions with suppliers and assessment of suppliers' requests or proposals for amendments to the purchase specifications	
Purchase agent		Assist the project manager by providing estimated times for purchasing tasks and suppliers' delivery times		Maintain records of suppliers from which to augment the project engineers' suggested list of sources	Issue an invitation to tender (ITT) or PURCHASE ENQUIRY for each item. Send to jointly recommended suppliers	
Equip-ment suppliers						Prepare bids and submit them to the purchase agent on or before the relevant closing dates

Figure 18.2 Stages in the purchase of equipment for a large international project

	7: Evaluation of suppliers' bids	8: Approval and authorization	9: Purchase specification	10: Purchase requisition	11: Purchase order	12: Order fulfilment
The client		Study recommendations and approve and authorize major purchases				
Project manager	Responsible to the client for scheduling, initiating and supervising all project activities, and for successful completion of the project in all respects. Submits regular cost and progress reports to the client.					
Project engineer and design team	Analyse and compare suppliers' bids. Discuss and jointly agree the most suitable supplier.		Review changes to the enquiry specification and rewrite as the PURCHASE SPECIFICATION	Issue a PURCHASE REQUISITION to the purchase agent. Attach the purchase specification	Technical support to the purchase agent throughout the enquiry phase, including assisting, if required, during witnessed inspection and testing at the suppliers' premises	
Purchase agent	For major items, recommend to the client and request authorization to purchase				Issue a PURCHASE ORDER to the successful bidder. Attach the purchase specification. Ask for acknowledgment and acceptance	Arrange expediting and inspection. Monitor progress and verify any claims for stage or progress payments
Equipment suppliers					Acknowledge receipt of the purchase order and acceptance of its terms.	Proceed with supply. Provide facilities for the buyer's inspection and witnessed tests, if required

Figure 18.2   *continued*

	13: Export preparation	14: Suppliers' documentation	15: Transport and shipping	16: Port and customs clearances	17: Site receipt and storage	18: Final payment
The client						Pay the supplier or subcontractor according to the contract terms
Project manager	Responsible to the client for supervising all project activities and for successful completion of the project in all respects					
Project engineer	Technical support and liaison throughout, including asissting, as required, with final commissioning on site					
Purchase agent	Ensure suppliers observe packing, marking and documentation instructions. Liaise with freight forwarding agent. Report to the project manager regularly and on demand. Act to replace lost or damage materials.					Certify final payment
Equipment suppliers	Pack goods and mark crates in accordance with purchase order and specification	Provide drawings, test certificates, and instructions for installation, operating and maintenance	If required by the purchase order, arrange for attendance on site during installation and commissioning and for training the client's personnel in the safe and efficient operation and maintenance of the equipment supplied			
Freight forwarding agent	Arrange export and shipping documents. Book ship or aircraft		Consolidate consignments. Monitor and progress the movement of goods through all stages of shipping, airfreight, road and rail transport, either directly with carriers or through associated overseas agents. Facilitate port and customs clearances. Advise the purchase agent immediately if problems arise			
Site materials controller				Liaise with the freight forwarding agent or local representative to progress transit of goods from port of entry to project site	Arrange handling equipment and secure site storage. Examine goods on arrival. Certify safe receipt. Report shortages or damage	

Figure 18.2   *concluded*

Purchase schedule for Loxylene Plant (Huddersfield)						Page of			
Subschedule for storage tankhouse code LX 5150-450						Issue date:			
Spec. no.	Rev. no.	Description	Qty	Supplier		Order no.	Amdt no.	Date needed	Cost on-site

Figure 18.3   Page heading for sheet 1 of a purchase control schedule

At the time when it was necessary to use entirely manual methods for compiling purchase control schedules, the entry of planned target dates was a tedious and expensive chore. Even with computer-controlled scheduling, difficulties remain. It is not likely that every item of equipment or supplies shown on the purchase control schedule will be represented by a separate chain of activities on the project network diagram. Even where this is the case, the degree of detail allowed on the network might not depict and date all parts of the purchase cycle.

There are several possible remedies to reduce the amount of clerical work needed – or, indeed, to eliminate it altogether. All of these require that the degree of planning detail on the critical path network is adequate and chosen with common sense.

One approach would be to represent every item of equipment by a separate activity chain on the network. Then every date needed for control could come off a computer-generated work-to list that acts as the purchase control schedule. The arrangement would be dynamic and flexible to change. The big snag with this method is that the degree of detail needed would be difficult to achieve and manage. The network would become huge and unmanageable.

A more practicable approach is to plan all items of equipment on the network in groups according to the areas in the finished project where they are going to be needed. For example, all the pumps for a particular plant area might be represented on the network simply as 'pumps for bay 3', even though there might be many of these pumps, occupying one or more sheets of the complete purchase control schedule. The equipment on the purchase control schedule sheets can be listed in a separate block for each plant area group. The schedules can then:

- simply refer to the relevant activity ID code for each group of equipment items or
- show all the dates in detail, derived and printed from the project management database (with identical dates shown for each item of equipment within the same group) or
- a combination of both of these.

Preparation of purchase control schedules

An effective arrangement for the preparation of purchase control schedules is to ask each project engineering discipline group (civil, structural, mechanical, piping and fluids, electrical, process control, and so on) to prepare a separate schedule of the equipment for which it is responsible. Apart from the obvious common sense technical advantages of this approach, it can greatly simplify the allocation of purchase specification serial numbers.

If the project is of any significant size, or if the company procedures so demand, the schedules can be broken further down into sub-sets according to the various project plant sections. Thus the total set of purchase control schedules for a project could be arranged as shown in Figure 18.4 (which also shows how serial numbers might be allocated).

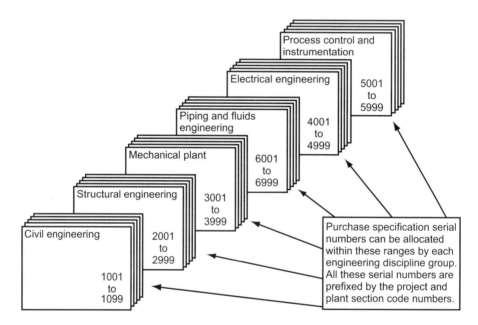

Figure 18.4   A complete purchase control schedule

Distribution

During the project execution, it is usual to merge all parts of the purchase control schedule into the complete schedule for the project. This complete version is then made available to all the engineering discipline groups (along with the drawing schedules), to the purchasing agent, and possibly to the client. Once the site management team has been set up, it too should receive the schedules to allow pre-planning of storage facilities and to assist in the planning of work on site.

Updating

Purchase control schedules contain much information which is liable to considerable change from various sources as the project proceeds, and therefore must be kept up to date.

If everyone using the schedules has access to them over a computer network, the problems of issue and revision status are largely avoided. If, on the other hand, schedules are to be distributed as hard copy, they must be re-issued at regular intervals and subjected to rigid version control (by specifying the relevant revision number).

When the project is finished the purchase control schedules, because they list all the purchase specifications, become part of the essential documentation that records the 'as-built' state of the project. The final version must therefore be archived (along with the drawing control schedules).

Purchase specifications

Preparation

The importance of specifying goods properly was stressed in Chapter 16 and illustrated by an actual case history concerning the purchase of a simple component (a tap for use on operating theatre equipment). In that case, the technical purchase specification consisted of one small drawing. It was only necessary to supply a print of the drawing with each new purchase order and to quote the drawing's serial and revision numbers on the purchase order form.

Clearly, the physical requirements for many project materials, components and equipment cannot be expressed on a single drawing. It is often necessary to prepare a full written specification, which might take many hours of a professional engineer's time to design and compile. In many cases, these specifications start life in provisional form, and are developed as other design work proceeds. When potential suppliers are approached, they might make suggestions that could further influence the final content of some specifications.

It is therefore convenient to identify two stages in the preparation of a purchase specification.

1 **The enquiry stage** – The purchase specification starts life as an enquiry specification. This is issued by the project engineering department to the purchasing agent under cover of a 'request for enquiry' or similar document. The purchasing agent sends the enquiry specification to potential suppliers along with a standard 'invitation to tender (ITT)', request for quotation (RFQ) or 'enquiry letter'.

2 **The purchase order stage** – When a supplier has been chosen, the enquiry specification is reviewed and updated to include all changes resulting from

discussions with the supplier. The enquiry specification has now become the purchase specification, which is re-issued to the purchasing agent by the project engineering department together with a purchase requisition. The purchasing agent then issues a purchase order to the chosen supplier, with the purchase specification attached.

There need be no difference in the method for preparing enquiry and purchase specifications, and the same format can be used for both. An example of a set of specification sheets is shown in Figures 18.5, 18.6 and 18.7.

Specification serial numbering

A possible numbering system for enquiry and purchase specifications was illustrated in Figure 18.4. Since the final purchase specification is derived from (or may be identical to) the initial enquiry specification, the serial number first allocated should be retained throughout all stages, if possible. This seems logical and straightforward, but there are pitfalls for the unwary. These are mentioned later in this chapter.

Issuing specification amendments or revisions

When a specification is first issued (say at revision 0), all the individual sheets should also be labelled as 'Revision 0'. Then the whole specification can be referred to confidently, without ambiguity, as 'serial number so-and-so, at Revision 0'.

When changes occur, it is not likely that every sheet of a multi-page specification will be affected. Some sheets may need changing, whilst others remain unaltered. It may also be necessary to insert additional sheets. Then an amended specification could contain some sheets that are still at Revision 0, whilst other sheets in the same specification bear different revision numbers.

A sensible way to define the correct composition of a revised specification is to attach a contents list at the front which shows the correct revision number for every sheet. The revision number of the contents list itself will be the same as the highest-numbered revision to be found among the sheets. Figure 18.5 shows a design used by one company for such a front sheet.

Each revision should be issued to every person in the project organization who received the original issue, and relevant suppliers must also be included.

Some companies only re-issue sheets that have changed (always including a fresh front sheet, of course). Others re-issue the whole specification each time. Total re-issue may have to be considered where the clerical proficiency of recipients is in any doubt (in other words, for those not directly supervised by the project manager and who cannot be relied upon to incorporate amended sheets or discard obsolete sheets correctly in their specification copies).

SPECIFICATION

This specification comprises the sheets listed in the following table. At each revision only revised or additional sheets will be issued, together with a revision of this front sheet.

Sheet	Rev	Sheet	Rev	Sheet	Rev	Sheet	Rev	Sheet	Rev	Sheet	Rev

ATTACHMENTS

The following attached documents form part of this specification:

SUMMARY OF REVISIONS

Rev No	Date	Brief description of each revision

APPROVALS

Originated by:	Checked by:	Senior engineer:	Project engineer:

Client —
Project —
Plant —
Discipline —
Title —

—	Spec. No:	Rev. No:	Sheet
			1

Figure 18.5   A purchase specification: Front sheet

Example of a form used by one company to head every enquiry and purchase specification. The grid at the top lists all the sheets comprising the complete specification, and was important when several amendments resulted in the specification containing sheets with different individual revision numbers.

SPECIFICATION

DRAWINGS AND OTHER DOCUMENTS

1   SCOPE OF SUPPLY. Complete engineering drawings, installation instructions, operating/maintenance manuals, parts lists and recommended spares lists for all equipment and services covered by this specification.

2   QUANTITIES:
Drawings for approval – 3 prints
Final drawings   – 1 transparency or master in approved electronic format
Test certificates   – Original plus 5 copies, all signed
Other final documents – 6 copies

3   LANGUAGE: English

4   IDENTIFICATION: All documents shall bear the purchase order number under which this specification is issued, appropriate equipment and tag numbers as specified, and the purchaser's drawing numbers (when supplied).

5   REVISIONS: Any drawing revised after initial submission shall be resubmitted immediately, showing details of changes and the new revision number.

6   CERTIFICATION: Final drawings shall be certified as accurate.

7   AS-BUILT DRAWINGS: Where the specification includes installation and erection, as-built drawings reflecting any on-site changes shall be submitted as soon as possible after the work.

8   DATE OF SUBMISSION: All documents shall be submitted on or before the dates specified in the purchase order delivery schedule.

9   APPROVAL: All drawings for equipment specially designed to meet this specification shall be submitted for approval before manufacture unless otherwise agreed.

10 TEST CERTIFICATES: These shall show the British or other agreed national standard or code under which the tests were performed.

11 LUBRICATION REQUIREMENTS. Recommended lubricants and quantities sufficient for one year's operation shall be specified.

12 SPARES LISTS. Lists of recommended spares shall be given, suitable for one year's operation under the specified conditions. Each item shall include:
Identification, part or serial number
– Maker's name and reference
– Quantity recommended
– Current price and delivery

EQUIPMENT MARKING AND IDENTIFICATION

Each item shall be identified by its mark, equipment or tag number by the method indicated thus: ✓

☐ Painting   ☐ Wired-on stamped metal tags   ☐ Stamped nameplates

☐ Other, as specified later in this specification. See sheet number: _____

INSPECTION AND TESTING

Documented inspection and testing is required, as indicated in the following tables thus: ✓

Inspections by the purchaser	Required?	Testing required	Unwitnessed	Witnessed
During manufacture		Standard works		
Final inspection		No load running		
Of packing		Full load performance		
As specified later on sheet number		As specified later on sheet number		

Title		Spec. No:	Rev. No:	Sheet
				2

Figure 18.6   A purchase specification: Second sheet

This lists various standard requirements, and also acts as a checklist for engineers. The main technical description follows on continuation sheets (Figure 18.7).

SPECIFICATION			
Title	Spec. No:	Rev. No:	Sheet

Figure 18.7   A purchase specification: Continuation sheet

As many of these sheets as necessary follow the first and second sheets to describe the equipment or services to be purchased. Standard texts are held in computer files for regularly purchased items such as pumps, valves, electric motors, and so on.

These remarks on issuing revisions apply to any multi-page documents that are subject to change and re-issue, such as drawing and purchase control schedule sets.

Specification library

For equipment which is purchased often, such as pumps, valves, piping, motors and so on, an experienced project engineering organization will avoid the chores and risks associated with preparing a new specification for every occasion by developing a library of standard material and equipment specifications. The texts of these can be held on a computer file, to be extracted, adapted as necessary, and used to prepare the specification for each new requirement.

Purchase enquiries

So that the enquiry process can be put in hand, the project engineers will send copies of the enquiry specification to the purchasing agent, asking the agent to issue a formal invitation to tender or purchase enquiry. The project engineers may have a good idea of which suppliers should be asked to bid and, indeed, they may already have discussed the requirements with some possible suppliers in advance. Provisional quotations might have been obtained from potential suppliers for some of the more expensive items when the project cost estimates were first prepared.

The project engineers can use a form similar to that shown in Figure 18.8 to convey their instructions and suggestions to the purchasing agent. Some of the information may be commercially confidential, not to be disclosed to bidders, and the purchasing agent will substitute his or her own official covering letter or standard form when sending out the enquiries to suppliers. The purchasing agent would usually be given authority to add potential suppliers to any list put forward by the project engineers.

Enquiries should always be conducted in such a way that they encourage suppliers to submit their quotations according to a common format. Then all the bids can be compared on a like-for-like basis.

Distribution of purchase enquiry documents

In the relatively simple organizational arrangement where the purchasing agent is part of the main contractor or project engineering company, and where the purchasing and project engineering departments are located in the same building, there should be no problem with the distribution of enquiry instructions and in communicating quotations and subsequent progress. Circumstances become a little more difficult when the purchasing agent is part of an external organization,

REQUEST FOR PURCHASE ENQUIRY

To: (Purchasing agent)

Date:
Our reference:
Your reference:

Please obtain bids for the goods or services described in the attached specification.
Note the following requirements:

Vendors	*Bids*
☐ Only those listed below	☐ Forward bids as soon as received
☐ Those listed plus those of your choice	☐ Forward all bids after closing date
☐ Suitable vendors of your choice	☐ Supply a commercial bid summary

The closure date for receipt of bids should be:
Our required on-site delivery date is:
The recommended standard packing category is:
Your technical contact for this purchase is: Telephone:
Recommended vendors:

Notes and special requirements:

_____
Project engineer

Client   –
Project   –
Plant   –
Discipline –

Title		Spec. No:	Rev. No:	Sheet

Figure 18.8   A purchase enquiry request

Example of a form used by one company's engineers to instruct their purchasing agent to issue an enquiry letter, request for quotation (RFQ) or invitation to tender (ITT) to potential suppliers. The project engineer would provide the accompanying specification.

and more difficult still if that external organization happens to be located far away from the project engineers or overseas. Matters can become very complicated where a project requires more than one purchasing agent, perhaps with one in the client's country, one in the country of the main contractor, and others operating in other countries to provide local expediting and inspection services.

It is sometimes necessary to keep purchasing agents informed by sending them copies of enquiries and specifications which are intended for initial action by another purchasing agent in the project organization. Although each such enquiry (and any subsequent requisition) bears the name of the purchasing agent responsible for taking action, there could be a risk of another agent taking action as a result of receiving a copy that was only intended only to keep the agent informed. The project engineering company might wish to consider colour-coding each batch of documents (by printing or photocopying them on coloured paper stock), with a different colour chosen to represent each of the purchasing agents. Then everyone on the project would know, for example, that a pink set of enquiry documents was for the action of the agent in Lagos, yellow sets were for the agent in Buenos Aires, while plain white sets were always intended for action by the purchasing department in the contractor's head office. This measure, especially when followed through to the documents used during the actual purchasing stage, can help to prevent unfortunate and expensive mix-ups where two different purchasing agents follow up the same enquiry and, in the worst case, place duplicate orders for the same goods.

The impact of European Directives on Public Sector Purchasing

Readers working in the public sector should be aware of the requirements imposed by the following European public procurement directives.

- 93/36/EEG for the supply of products
- 93/37/EEG for the design and construction of public works
- 92/50/EEG for the provision of services
- 92/38/EEG for suppliers, works and services in the utilities sectors.

These regulations apply to advertisements of contract tender opportunities where the contract value exceeds a specified threshold amount. Thresholds are updated every two years, but at the time of writing (2002) the directives for services and supplies operate for contracts above £100 410, and the works directive threshold is £3 861 932.

The aim of these directives is to achieve fair competition and work opportunities throughout the EU. Opportunities for new contracts may not be advertised in the UK before a contract notice has been sent for publication in the *Official Journal* of the EU. There are exceptions for contracts for secret work.

Guidance is necessary in deciding how to calculate the threshold values, in the relative timings between notifying the *Official Journal* and advertising in the UK, and on methods for transmitting notices to the *Official Journal*. In the UK, the Inland Revenue is a good source of information. A good place to start is their Website at: <http://www.inlandrevenue.gov.uk/manuals/pummanual/specific guidance/pum4070.htm>.

Dealing with suppliers' queries during the bidding period

Some contractors' engineers become involved in discussions with suppliers during the bidding period, answering questions and perhaps listening to alternative proposals. However, there is a procedure that is intended to promote fair dealing when the purchaser answers queries from one or more bidders who require clarification of the enquiry details. This procedure requires that the bidder's question, together with the purchaser's answer, is distributed as soon as possible to all the other bidders. Then all bidders are given access to the same information, and no one has an unfair disadvantage. Anonymity of suppliers who raise questions should be preserved.

Bid evaluation

Bid summary tabulation

Companies which have to make high-cost purchases as a regular part of their project operations develop standard procedures for evaluating competitive tenders. The method typically used requires that information received from bidders is tabulated on a summary form which allows direct comparison of quoted prices, promised delivery times and other critical factors. An example of a bid summary form is shown in Figure 18.9.

Estimated packing, carriage, insurance, port and customs costs arising from foreign bidders have to be included, and all cost estimates and prices must be converted into the same currency. These steps ensure that the total delivered costs are compared in every case on a like-for-like basis.

Promised delivery dates are compared on the bid summary, again not forgetting that the critical factor is the expected arrival date at site, and not simply the suppliers' ex-works dates.

Technical evaluation of quotations must, of course, be a matter for the relevant project engineer. Sometimes this has to be done in collaboration with the client's own engineers. The bid summary form illustrated in Figure 18.9 is not suitable for making a detailed technical analysis (although it might be possible to devise other summary forms that could help). Once a technical preference has been identified, however, this can be noted on the bid summary form, where it must count heavily towards the final choice of supplier.

BID SUMMARY							
SELLERS ⟶		A	B	C	D	E	F
Country of origin							
Bid reference							
Bid date							
Period of validity							
Bid currency							
Project exchange rate							
Item	Qty	Description	Price	Price	Price	Price	Price	Price
Total quoted ex-works							
Discounts (if any)							
Packing and export prep cost							
Shipping cost							
Customs duty and tax							
Local transport cost							
Estimated total cost on site							
Delivery time ex-works							
Estimated total transport time							
Total delivery time to sit							

RECOMMENDED BY THE PURCHASING AGENT:

_____

_____

                                              ....
                                              For purchasing agent

RECOMMENDED BY THE ENGINEER:

_____

_____

                                              ....
                                              Project/ senior engineer

RECOMMENDATION TO THE CLIENT:

_____

_____

                                              ....
                                              Project manager

Specification title:	Specification number:

Figure 18.9   A bid summary example

Bid summaries are used to compare bids on a like-for-like basis. Prices should be compared on the basis of total delivered cost to the project location. All currencies should be converted to the project control currency.

Choice of supplier

Recommendation of the successful bidder is usually the responsibility of a senior member of the project engineering staff, but in many cases the client will wish to have sight of the bid summary analysis and approve the conclusions reached (even in cases where the project engineering staff belong to a main contractor with complete contractual management authority). Whether or not the purchasing agent is involved in the final choice of supplier depends on the organization, but the advice of a properly competent and experienced agent must never be ignored, and it will be assumed here that the engineer and agent will agree jointly on the choice of recommended supplier.

Whenever a difficult final decision has to be referred to higher authority, the client or another third party, the task will be easier if all quotation data have been set out carefully on a bid summary form that also carries the recommendations of both the engineer and the purchasing agent.

Sealed-bids evaluation

Bid summary forms can be used by a purchaser to help evaluate bids for very high-value purchases and for letting valuable contracts and subcontracts, but it is more likely that these would be subjected to a formal sealed bids procedure.

In its strictest form, the sealed-bids procedure requires each bidder to submit two packages on or before a set date. One of these packs contains a specified number of copies of the technical proposal, but no price details. The other pack is the sealed commercial bid, which must include all prices, cost rates and other commercial details.

The purchaser opens the technical bids first and evaluates these carefully, eliminating all bidders whose proposals appear to fall short of the technical and quality requirements, and disqualifying any others who have contravened the rules of the game. The commercial bids are returned unopened to these unsuccessful bidders.

The shortlisted survivors are then invited to attend a presentation meeting at which all their sealed commercial bids are opened and laid bare, after which the successful bidder is chosen.

Relevance of formal bid evaluation to project cost control

Much time and effort are devoted to procedures and computerized systems for collecting and reporting the costs of material and equipment purchases after the purchases have been made. Although *cost reporting* is an essential part of project management, in the case of materials expenditure it is nothing more than *reporting*. It is not *cost control*. It is in the project engineering, enquiry and bid summary stages, before the purchasing contract is made, where the expenditure die is cast. If over-expenditure is detected after the costs have already been committed in the shape of a requisition to the purchasing agent and the issue of a purchase order, the only remedy left to the project manager is to crawl into a quiet corner and have a good cry.

Purchase requisitions and orders

When recommendations from the bid summary have been approved and the expenditure authorized, a purchase requisition can be issued to the purchasing agent by the project engineers (see Figure 18.10). Again, a correct purchase specification must accompany each requisition. As in the case of the purchase enquiries, the requisition contains specific instructions for the purchasing agent and, as before, some of the commercial information on the requisition might be confidential between the project engineers and the agent, not to be passed on to the supplier. The agent will remove the requisition from the specification, and attach in its place a purchase order (which might be similar to that shown in Figure 16.3).

The distribution of requisitions will probably be similar to that for enquiry requests and, if a colour-coding convention has been used to indicate which of several possible purchase agents must take action, the same colour convention can be followed through to this requisition stage. But then comes an important difference: the enquiry documents were only requests, but the purchase requisition actually vests authority in the purchasing agent to issue the official order and sign it on behalf of the contractor, with the intention of binding both supplier and purchaser to a contract.

Purchase requisitions must therefore be authorized at a suitably senior level in the project. There may be a case for grading the level at which various individuals can sign, according to the levels of committed expenditure (a system which can be abused by anyone smart enough to split an order that exceeds his or her limit of authority into a number of smaller orders that individually do not). It is not unusual to require the project manager's signature on all significant requisitions: for some particularly important or sensitive items, the client's authorization may also be needed.

Correlation between specification, enquiry and order numbers

The filing, retrieval and general handling of purchase documents would be a great deal simpler if the initial enquiry, the specification and the resulting purchase order could all have the same reference number.

Although it is often possible to use the specification number as the enquiry

PURCHASE REQUISITION

To: (Purchasing agent)

Date:

Our reference:

Your reference:

☐ Please issue a purchase order
☐ Please also make all arrangements for transportation
☐ Please issue an amendment to the purchase order
for the equipment, materials or services detailed in the attached specification

VENDOR (name and address)

Quotation reference and date

CONSIGNEE (name and address)

SPECIAL INSTRUCTIONS

Inspect in accordance with specification   ☐

Recommended degree of expediting is: intense ☐   normal ☐   none ☐

Recommended standard packing category is   ☐

Other (see continuation sheet attached)

PRICE		DELIVERY	
Basis:		Original delivery promise:	
Original budget			
Original quote		Current delivery promise:	
Previous amendments			
This amendment		Required delivery to consignee:	
TOTAL PRICE NOW			

APPROVALS

Originated by	Senior engineer	Project engineer	Project manager
Client —		Project number:	
Project —			
Plant —		Specification number:	Revision
Discipline —			
Title:		Requisition number:	Amendment

Figure 18.10   A purchase requisition

When properly approved (and usually supported by a purchase specification), the requisition instructs and authorizes the purchase agent to issue a purchase order.

number, various events can intervene to prevent the same number being carried through to the purchase order. Not least of these is that each particular purchasing agent (and there could be more than one for the project) might wish to use his or her own standard order numbering system.

The supply of materials listed in several specifications might be consolidated into one purchase order. It might be advantageous, for example, to collect all the requirements for valves together and order them all from one supplier on a single purchase order. In that case, several specifications would have to be attached to the purchase order, all with different numbers.

An even more difficult complication arises when it is decided to order materials defined in one specification as two separate orders, placed with different suppliers (which means that the original specification must be amended or split to suit the different suppliers, and will generate two requisitions as well as two purchase orders).

The authority responsible for project procedures must ensure that all these factors are considered, and that, if a common numbering system is impossible, the system adopted allows all the related documents to be adequately cross-referenced. The organization which provided the forms that I have adapted to illustrate this chapter used the following procedure:

1   Enquiry specifications were allocated serial numbers from the purchase control schedules, in the manner indicated by Figure 18.4.

2   Purchase enquiries were given the same numbers as the specifications which accompanied them.

3   A completely different series of numbers was used for requisitions, allocated from registers, and with a different series for each purchasing agent. These series were distinguished from one another by the use of a different letter prefix to denote the agent responsible. Every requisition also carried a cross-reference to the specification or specifications which accompanied it.

4   The purchasing agents were persuaded to use the requisition numbers as their own purchase order numbers. This acceptance by the agents was made easier because each had been allocated his or her own continuous series of requisition numbers, which automatically meant that a purchase order system using the same numbers would have no awkward gaps left in the sequence of numbers issued. As with the requisitions, each purchase order also carried the number or numbers of all attached specifications.

Thus several different numbering systems were agreed and had to be accepted, all running together in the same organization and on the same projects. There was, however, full cross-referencing between all the vital documents.

Assuring quality and progress

Suppliers' procedures

The manufacture of each item of special capital equipment is itself an industrial project, demanding (on a smaller scale) project management techniques similar to those used on the main project. A feature of project equipment purchasing is that the buyer should take a detailed interest in the vendor's own project management and quality procedures.

Several large companies and government departments insist that those who supply them with project equipment or carry out sub-contracts at least use critical path analysis, and that they will probably be expected to show that their quality policy and procedures satisfy the requirements of the International Standard ISO 9000 series. It is not unknown for purchasers to offer advice to vendors in establishing their own internal systems.

Some UK Government purchasers might also wish to ensure that their suppliers are aware of, and implement, the PRINCE2 project management structure and principles (<http://www.ogc.uk/prince>).

Inspection and expediting visits

The purchaser might wish to arrange visits to a supplier's premises to check on progress, inspect the quality of workmanship, or witness tests. Such visits are sometimes linked to the certification of suppliers' claims for stage payments.

There are several ways in which responsibility for carrying out inspection and expediting visits can be allocated or delegated. Where suitable engineers are available to the purchase agent concerned, it is often convenient for the agent to arrange visits which combine the inspection and expediting functions. Where specialist engineering attendance is needed for inspection or to witness tests, the project engineering organization might send one or more of its own engineers to assist the purchasing agent. To avoid expensive overseas travel when foreign suppliers are involved, it is sometimes possible to engage a local professional engineering company to undertake the inspection and expediting visits.

Whatever the arrangement for staffing the inspection function, the project engineers must make arrangements (usually through the purchasing agent) for the inspectors to receive all necessary drawings and specifications, the purchase order, and all revisions to these documents. Some companies are also able to provide the inspecting engineers with checklists, to help ensure that no vital point is overlooked when they make their visits.

INSPECTION/EXPEDITING REPORT				
Report number	Sheet 1 of	Date this visit	Date of last visit	Inspector/expediter

MAIN SUPPLIER DETAILS

Name _____

Address _____

_____

Supplier's reference _____

Persons contacted _____

_____

Equipment _____

_____

_____

_____

Contract delivery date

Current delivery estimate

Plans for next visit

Date _____

To expedite ☐
To continue inspection ☐
Final inspection ☐
To inspect packing ☐

SUB-SUPPLIER DETAILS

Main supplier's order number _____

Name _____

Address _____

_____

Sub-supplier's reference _____

Persons contacted _____

_____

Equipment _____

_____

_____

Agreed delivery to supplier

Current delivery estimate

Plans for next visit

Date _____

To expedite ☐
To continue inspection ☐
Final inspection ☐
To inspect packing ☐

ORDER STATUS SUMMARY (see attached sheets for details)

Assessed progress by (weeks)	Tests witnessed?	Complies with spec?	Released for packing?	Released for shipping?
Early ☐	Yes ☐	Yes ☐	Yes ☐	Yes ☐
Late ☐ ____	No ☐	No ☐	No ☐	No ☐

ACTION REQUIRED	ACTION BY
	Specification No	Revision
Title	Purchase order No	Amendment

Figure 18.11   An inspection and expediting report

A convenient format for summarizing the results of visits to equipment manufacturers.

Quality and progress reports

The project manager (and sometimes the client) might want to see a quality and progress report from the relevant purchasing agent following every formal visit to a supplier. The inspecting engineer or expediter will probably be asked to use a convenient standard summary form for this purpose, an example of which is given in Figure 18.11.

Vendors' documents

Provision must usually be made for the project engineers to receive and approve documents from the supplier for items which are manufactured specially for the project. The term 'vendors' documents' is usually applied, although the providers of the goods might also be referred to as manufacturers, sellers, suppliers or subcontractors.

The first step in ensuring the timely receipt of vendors' documents is to make certain that the obligations for providing them are always spelled out clearly on the purchase orders or their attached purchase specifications.

The nature of vendors' documents

Foundation, capacity and installation drawings

In addition to general layout or assembly drawings, there is usually a requirement for the early availability of installation instructions. With heavy plant and machinery, for example, foundation drawings, power supply requirements and overall weights and dimensions are all vital information, the lack of which could hold up design work on the project. Obtaining such information, and progressing any necessary approvals, is all part of the expediting process.

Other vendors' documents

When the equipment is delivered, a final set of drawings, certified test results, operating and maintenance manuals and a recommended spares holding list will probably be needed. In some cases, suppliers may be required to supply documents translated into a foreign language, according to the nationality of the project end-user.

Retention of vendors' documents

The project engineering company will have obligations to provide backup ('post-project service') to the client after project handover. These obligations usually extend beyond the initial guarantee period, and can involve the provision of advice or services in maintaining, repairing, replacing, operating, modifying or extending the plant.

Much of the installed plant in a large industrial project will incorporate equipment purchased from third-party suppliers. The project client will need to find and consult relevant vendor documents for many years after project handover. The contracting company will therefore need to store a complete project set of vendors' documentation safely in its own files or archives if it is to provide an adequate post-project service.

It is not sufficient to rely on being able to obtain additional or replacement copies from all the various suppliers in the future. The commercial world is a volatile place. Some original suppliers might lose or destroy their records, be swallowed up in mergers or take-overs, or simply cease trading.

Serial numbering

A great number of vendors' drawings and other documents can accumulate in a large project, and the project engineering company must make certain that it will be able to find any of these quickly if the client reports operating difficulties, or if the documents are needed again for any of the other reasons already listed. Thus copies of vendors' documents are usually numbered serially and recorded in registers before filing. To ensure that any of these documents can easily be found again in the future ('location' and 'retrieval' are the buzzwords), the files must be arranged in some recognizable and logical sequence. This might be based on specification numbers, requisition numbers, purchase order numbers, or the company's standard project work breakdown coding system.

Indexing

A cross-referenced index might have to be created so that, for example, a file can be found if only the equipment specification number or the supplier and approximate date of supply is known.

If vendors' documents are kept in a secure file (for example, in an off-site vault) an index of those documents must be kept with them.

Shipping, port and customs formalities

Marking and labelling

The purchasing agent must ensure that every consignment is properly marked before it leaves the supplier's premises. It is customary to include instructions for marking in the purchase specification or as a sub-set of conditions to the purchase order. Marking will usually involve suppliers stencilling easily recognizable markings on packing crates so that each item can be clearly identified through all stages of its journey and, not least, by the site personnel when it finally arrives. The purchase order number usually has to be included in all markings.

Freight forwarding agents

It is best to entrust arrangements for long-distance transport, shipping, airfreight, seaport and airport and international frontier formalities to a specialist organization. The purchasing agent will undoubtedly have considerable experience and expertise, but the employment of a reputable freight forwarding agent will be invaluable.

Freight forwarding agents operate through worldwide organizations, They have their staff or representatives stationed at most of the world's ports and airports and, through modern communication networks, are able to monitor the progress of every consignment through all stages from initial loading to final delivery.

Collaboration between the purchasing agent and a freight forwarding agent can achieve benefits from the economy of scale obtained when different consignments are consolidated to make up complete container loads.

The combined expertise of the purchasing and freight forward agents can be a great comfort to project staff confronted for the first time with the need to deal with the formidable array of documents associated with the international movement of goods. Failure to get the documentation right first time can lead to delays, the impounding of goods, and to legally imposed penalties.

Local knowledge provided by the forwarding agent's contacts in the countries along the delivery route can yield important information about the type and capacity of port handling facilities, warning of any unusual congestion or industrial disputes (with suggestions for alternative routes), and details of inland road and rail systems (including size and weight restrictions). For example, the agent in one case was able to prevent an expensive mistake in the shipment of structural steel sections by pointing out that a local railway company operated a particularly tight restriction on the maximum length of loads, because their route included tunnels with unusually sharp curves. At a port, the local agents were able to warn about a peculiar security problem, where the local shanty town inhabitants were always on the lookout for fresh supplies of building timber. If such timber happened to exist in the shape of well-constructed packing crates protecting expensive project equipment standing on the dockside – well, who could blame them?

Purchase order status reports

The purchasing agent is usually required to keep the project manager informed of the progress status of all current purchase orders. This responsibility, in addition to the inspection and expediting reports already described, extends through all stages of the journey to the project site. This reporting can be done by means of regular order status reports, which list all purchase orders in progress, giving outline details of shipping and delivery dates, and highlighting any problems and corrective actions.

Order status reports duplicate, to a large extent, the information contained in the purchase control schedules prepared by the engineers, but the listing sequence will be different. Only active orders are included, and these will probably be listed in sequence of their purchase order numbers rather than their purchase specification numbers.

If a common computer database facility can be made available simultaneously to the project engineers and the purchasing agent, the purchase schedules and order status reports can be integrated to save much clerical work. However, what tends to happen in practice is that no matter how cleverly the computer system or manual method has been devised, much of the progress data (especially from overseas) simply doesn't get into the system in time to be of any use.

Efficient communications and dedicated, regular reporting by all the purchasing agents and freight forwarders involved on the project are essential if purchase order status reports are to be of any value.

It is also important to arrange the reports so that potential or real problems are highlighted, and not lost in the larger amount of detail reporting routine transactions that are proceeding according to plan.

Case history

A UK-based company was engineering and managing several projects for an African client. There was a requirement to coordinate all the order status data from several purchasing agents, one in the British Home Counties, one in South Africa and another in Zambia. Purpose-built computer equipment was purchased on the recommendation of the company's computing manager (who, no doubt, meant well). The intended purpose of the system (its only declared purpose) was to coordinate the progress data contained in weekly reports from the three purchasing agents and various freight forwarding agents, and process this information to update and print one integrated weekly purchase order status report for distribution to each client and throughout the project engineering organization.

The system was a complete failure from the start, simply because it was starved of data. With the communications difficulties for that group of projects, it was not practical to expect agents overseas to deliver comprehensive reports on the movements of materials and the progress of purchase orders, all supposed to arrive at company headquarters reliably, accurately, and on the same day of every week. Further, the company did not have direct authority over all the agents involved, and so was not able to insist on such reports.

The company tried for over a year to sell the redundant computer equipment but, in the manner of all computer hardware, it quickly became obsolete. It had had cost many thousands of pounds. Eventually the company sold it to me for £10 as scrap, and I was able to use its components to make an electronic organ. By then the computing manager had left the company, so he did not have to face the music.

References and further reading for Part V

Cavatino, J. and Kauffman, R. (2000), *The Purchasing Handbook,* 6th edn, Maidenhead, McGgraw-Hill

Cox, A. (1998), *Strategic Procurement in Construction,* London, Thomas Telford

Croner's Reference Book for Exporters, Kingston-upon-Thames, Croner Publications (by subscription, updated monthly)

Croner's Reference Book for Importers, Kingston-upon-Thames, Croner Publications (by subscription, updated monthly)

Erridge, A., Fee, R. and McIlroy, J. (2001), *Best Practice Procurement,* Aldershot, Gower (in association with IPSERA)

Farmer, D. and van Weele, A.J. (Eds) (1995) *Gower Handbook of Purchasing Management,* 2nd edn, Aldershot, Gower

Fearou, H., Flynn, A., Fraser Johnson, P. and Leenders, M. (2002), *Purchasing and Supply Management*, Maidenhead, McGraw-Hill/Irwin

International Chamber of Commerce (2000), *Incoterms 2000,* ICC publication No. 560, Paris, ICC Publishing SA (available from ICC national committees throughout the world in many languages, or order online at <http://www.iccwbo.org/incoterms/order.asp>)

Slack, N., Chambers, S., Harland, S., Harrison, A. and Johnston, R. (1998), *Operations Management,* 2nd edn, London, Financial Times/Prentice-Hall (comprehensive, well-written, reasonably priced and recommended)

Wallace, T.F. (1995), MRPII – *Making it Happen: The Implementers' Guide to Success with Manufacturing Resource Planning,* Chichester, Wiley

Part VI

Managing work and costs

Chapter 19

Managing project start-up

Once authorization has been received, the project ceases to be merely an object for planning and speculation, and becomes instead a live entity to which the contractor is fully committed. For the purposes of achieving all the project objectives, whether technical, budgetary or timescale, the appropriate project organization has to be set up and all participants must be made fully aware of the particular roles they will be expected to play.

A common risk to projects is failure to start work on time. Very long delays can be caused by prevarication, legal or planning difficulties, shortage of information, lack of funds or other resources, and a host of other reasons. All of these factors can place a project manager in a difficult or impossible position. If a project is not allowed to start on time it can hardly be expected to finish on time.

Project authorization

Receipt of authority to proceed

Project authorization usually means that the contractor has been instructed by the customer or client to proceed with the project on terms that have previously been negotiated and agreed. This authorization might be in the form of a special contract, a purchase order or (less desirably) a letter of intent. But some of the procedures in this chapter are equally applicable to 'in-house' projects, where the customer is the corporate body and the contractor is a division or department within the parent organization. In-house projects are often authorized by an internal memorandum issued by the senior management to the department or project manager responsible.

Project registration and numbering

Once a new project has entered an organization, it has to be formally 'entered into the system' so that all the necessary accounting, planning, progressing and other administrative procedures can be put in place.

One of the very first steps is to allocate an identification number to the new project which, depending on the procedures of the particular contractor, will be used henceforth as a basis for drawing numbers, cost codes and other important project documentation. Numbering systems were discussed in the cost-coding section in Chapter 4 (see page 96).

Project numbers are usually derived serially from a register, which might be a loose-leaf book or a computer file. A typical sheet suitable for a loose-leaf system is shown in Figure 19.1.

The purpose of a project register is, of course, not only to allocate numbers. The register of current projects lists all authorized work within the organization against which time may legitimately be booked on timesheets and against which the costs of project materials and expenses may be charged. When projects are closed, it is useful to keep the register information in a secure but accessible archive.

Each project entry in the register should identify (and therefore associate) the following data:

● project title
● start and (eventually) closure dates
● project manager responsible
● project number.

Ideally, the register should also identify:

● the customer
● the customer's order number or letter reference.

Whenever it is necessary to retrieve information about a project, current or long past, the project register or its archived information is usually the best – even the *only* – starting place. In most management information systems or archives, the project number is the essential element leading to the various document files and project data. But the project number might not be known or remembered. Very often, historical searches start with only a vague recollection of the project description, or the name of the customer, or the approximate dates. A well-kept register will enable any project to be identified even when only one or two of the associated data items listed above are known.

Internal project authorization document

The first step towards project implementation in any well-run company is the issue of an authorization document. Entitled 'project authorization' or perhaps 'works

Project register

Project number	Project title	Project manager	Customer	Date opened	Comments Special restrictions	Date closed

Date of last revision

Figure 19.1   A project register page

order', this document carries essential data that define the levels of expenditure authorized (the departmental and purchasing cost budgets), planned start and finish dates, details of the customer's order, pricing information, invoicing and delivery instructions, and so on. One necessary item on a project authorization is the signature of a member of the contractor's senior management. This is the signal that the project is properly authorized, that work can begin, and that costs can be incurred or committed. Project authorizations are often issued for internal management projects because they, like any other project, must be subject to formal planning, budgeting and control.

Format and general content

Project authorizations are usually summarized, often to the extent that all information can be printed on one side of an A4 page. This can be true even for large capital projects. Precise project definition is achieved by listing the relevant technical and commercial documents on the authorization form. If, for example, the project has been won after in-depth negotiation of a detailed contract, coupled with the discussion of technical and commercial sales specifications, the project authorization must identify these documents without ambiguity by giving their serial numbers and all approved amendments or revision numbers.

Figure 19.2 shows a works order form of the type which has been used for many years in manufacturing companies handling special projects. The information on budgets and schedules is necessarily brief, and is provided on the form only to allow outline planning and to place overall limits on the amount of expenditure authorized. Detailed budgets and work-to lists usually take some time to prepare, and may be delayed by a week or two after the works order issue.

Figure 19.3 shows a project authorization form used by a mining engineering company to initiate and authorize projects ranging from small feasibility studies and minor plant extensions to very large capital projects. Again, the form only summarizes the essential points (although this company did tabulate more detailed budgets on the reverse side of the form). A fairly comprehensive management information system was in use, and the form was designed to provide the basic input data to the system (as well as informing departmental managers about the new project).

Charter and contract

Some organizations invoke a lengthy authorization procedure that consists of a project charter, followed by a contract. The charter is a form of specification that sets out the principal objectives and is prepared for consideration and approval by the company's senior management. Once the charter has been approved, a separate and subsequent exercise is undertaken to translate it into a contract, which is a working document that establishes the project in the organization under the nominated project manager. The contract is internal, between the project manager and senior management – and, indeed the project manager is sometimes (misleadingly) called the 'project owner' in this context.

Once a firm order has been received from a customer, all haste should be made to get work authorized and started as soon as resources can be made available. Time is usually scarce in project management. For that reason, my own view is that the charter-and-contract method is somewhat cumbersome, expensive to administer, and can delay the start of work unnecessarily.

Distribution

Project authorizations are generally issued to all company departments for general information, but the supporting technical and commercial documents are handed over only to the project manager. It becomes the project manager's responsibility thereafter to ensure that all other managers in the organization are made aware of project requirements in detail, and sufficiently in advance to enable them to make any necessary preparations.

Authorizing work without a contract or customer's order

The customary rule

One of the first things that all well-taught managers know is that no expense shall be committed on any project unless the customer's written authority to proceed (and promise to pay) has first been obtained. The risks taken by anyone disobeying this golden rule should be obvious. Once the customer knows that the contractor has already become committed to actual costs, the contractor's bargaining position in any contract negotiations has been weakened. Worse still, if the customer's mind changes altogether and the project does not eventually go ahead for any reason, all the contractor's committed costs may be forfeit. For these very sensible reasons, the internal project authorization document will not normally be issued unless the customer's written authority to proceed has been obtained.

Breaking the rule

In spite of convention, there might be occasions when a very limited amount of work can be authorized before receipt of a firm order from the customer.

This poses a risk. Indeed, to many work-hardened managers it will sound like heresy. Nevertheless, provided the risk can be quantified and contained within controlled limits, it is often possible to gain several weeks' progress in the project calendar for the expenditure of only a tiny fraction of the total project costs. Of

Works order		Project number

Customer

Delivery address (if different)

⌐　　　　　　　　　　　⌐ ⌐　　　　　　　　　　　　⌐

L　　　　　　　　　　　　⌐ L　　　　　　　　　　　　⌐

Project title

Drawings, specifications and other documents defining this project	Number	Rev

Budget summary	*Hours*
Engineering design	
Design after issue	
Works	
Assembly	
Final testing	
Installation	
Commissioning	
Materials, services and expenses	£

Schedule summary Project start and finish dates are firm. Others subject to detailed planning.		
	Start	*finish*
Design and drawing		
Purchasing		
Manufacturing		
Assembly		
Final test		
Install and commission		
Overall project dates		

Commercial summary	Contract type and total price
Sales engineer:	
Sales reference:	
Customer's order no.	

Notes/limitations

Authorization (subject to any limitations listed above)

Project manager assigned:　　　　　　　Authorized by:

Distribution

Chief engineer ☐	Project manager ☐	Works director ☐	Materials manager ☐	Quality manager ☐	Accounts manager ☐	Office manager ☐

Figure 19.2　　Works order
Example for a manufacturing project.

PROJECT AUTHORIZATION

Client _____

Scope of work _____

_____

_____

_____

_____

Source documents _____

_____

_____

Project number (to be entered by accounts department) [ ][ ][ ][ ][ ][ ]

Project title (for computer reports) [ ]

Project manager (name) _____ Staff number [ ][ ][ ][ ]

Project engineer (name) _____ Staff number [ ][ ][ ][ ]

Project start date (enter as 01-JAN-03) [ ][ ]-[ ][ ][ ]-[ ][ ]

Target finish date (enter as 01-JAN-03) [ ][ ]-[ ][ ][ ]-[ ][ ]

Contract type:

Reimbursable [ ]   Lump sum [ ]   Other (Specify) _____

Estimate of man-hours

Standard cost grade	1	2	3	4	5	6	7	8
Man-hour totals								

Notes:

....
Authorization (1)   *Authorization (2)*

Project manager	Marketing	Contracts dept	Purchasing		
Project engineer	Central registry	Cost/planning	Accounts dept		

Figure 19.3   Project authorization
A form used by a mining engineering company.

course, no orders for supplies can be placed, but it might be possible to carry out activities from a preliminary checklist, such as those tasks in Figure 19.7, without committing more than one or two people over the limited period concerned.

Naturally, such advance work in the absence of a customer order will only be authorized where this strategy has some advantages for the contractor. These advantages might include the avoidance of possible trouble later on, if the overall project timescale is seen to be particularly tight. If the contractor foresees a trough in the organization's total workload, it may suit the contractor to carry out preliminary work so that full-scale work on the project can start as soon as the order is received, thus pulling work for the new project forward. Conversely, doing absolutely nothing and waiting until the official order is received from the customer could mean that the main project workload will be delayed until it interferes with work for other projects.

Graphs of project expenditure plotted against time display a characteristic *S* shape (see Figure 19.4). The rate of expenditure usually starts very slowly, increases greatly during the middle part of the project life cycle, and then falls off again as the project nears completion. Any talk of authorizing advance expenditure must be limited to the first few weeks, when the rate of expenditure is very low and confined to preliminary internal engineering tasks. Steps must be taken to ensure that the expenditure rate remains low. Any decision to allow advance work is always risky, and this must be reflected in the conditions listed in the authorizing document. A preliminary issue of the project authorization can be used but only with the following provisos:

- Authorization should be limited to allow only one or two named individuals to do the work.
- The project accounting system should be programmed to reject time booked by people who are not on the authorized list.

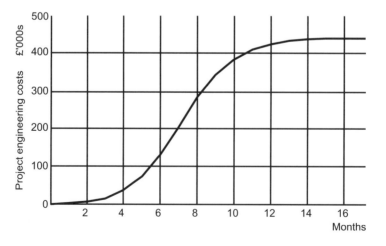

Figure 19.4   Typical cost-time relationship

- No materials or equipment must be ordered.
- There must be a total budget allocation for this work, regarded as the 'write-off' value of the risk.
- The work to be done should be defined and confined by a checklist or schedule.
- Progress and costs must be monitored and reported to senior management so that work can be stopped immediately at any time.

Preliminary organization of the project

Even when a clear technical specification has been prepared, there are often many loose ends to be tied up before actual work can start. The extent and nature of these preliminary activities naturally depend on the type and size of project.

Transfer from the sales organization to the project manager

One of the very first tasks is to appoint the project manager.

A desirable procedure in large projects with a high degree of complexity might be to seek out the senior sales engineer who spearheaded all the conceptual engineering studies during the proposal phase, and allow that person to take the actual project through to completion. In that way, what is eventually built should be what was actually sold. In most cases, however, this is not practicable. Another way must be found to ensure that the project is handed over from the sales organization to the fulfilment end of the business in such a way that there is no ambiguity about what has to be done, when, and at what cost.

For this purpose, the sales engineers must prepare a definition package or specification, detailing all the technical and commercial commitments in the contract. This package can be given to the new project manager. It will help to ensure that he or she is accurately and fully informed from the start.

Charting the organization

When the project manager has been named, an organization chart (sometimes, unfortunately, called an *organigram*) should be drawn up and published to show all the key people or agencies concerned with the project. It must include senior members of all external groups who are to have any responsibility in the project. If the organization is large, the usual arrangement is to produce an overall summary chart, and then draw a series of smaller charts that allow some of the groups to be shown in more detail. Depending on the actual arrangements, an overall project organization chart might have to show:

1   key elements in the contractor's own organization, obviously including the project manager
2   management teams working away from the contractor's head office (especially site teams on construction projects)
3   principal subcontractors
4   external purchasing agent (if employed), together with any outside groups responsible for expediting, equipment inspection and shipping arrangements
5   independent consultants, acting either for the customer or the contractor
6   representatives of government or local government departments (if relevant).

Responsibility matrix: Deciding who does what

People must know what is expected of them. One tool which can assist the project manager to allocate responsibilities is the *responsibility matrix*, an illustration of which is shown in Figure 19.5. The job titles of key members of the organization are listed above the matrix columns, and various important task types are listed along the rows. Symbols are place at the appropriate matrix intersections to show primary and secondary responsibility for each of the task types listed.

The responsibility matrix is best suited to dealing with task categories rather that listing all the detailed tasks themselves. For example, it can show the person responsible for approving new designs in general, but it is not the place in which to list all the drawings that carry those designs.

Correspondence and other documents

The contractor will be well advised to take control of procedures for project correspondence and document handling seriously. The contractor could easily be placed in a difficult position if vital letters or other documents were lost. It is necessary to ensure that positive steps are taken to deal with the routeing and control of documented information, both within the home office and between all external parts of the project organization.

Documents: Deciding who gets what

Most projects generate a great deal of paper. Once all the planning, control and administrative procedures have been decided, all the associated forms, expected reports and other types of documents can be listed. It is then possible to consider each of these document types in turn and decide who needs to receive copies as a matter of routine. This should usually be on a 'need to know' rather than 'nice to have' basis (except that all requests for documents from the customer must

Task type:	The client	Project manager	Project engineer	Purchasing manager	Drawing office	Construction manager	Planning engineer	Cost engineer	Project accountant	and so on
Make designs		+			●					
Approve designs	●	■	+							
Purchase enquiries		■	+	●						
Purchase orders	■	■	+	●						
Planning	■	■	+	+	+	+	●	+		
Cost control		●		+		+		+		
Progress reports		●	+	+	+	+	+			
Cost reports		●		+		+		+	+	
and so on										

● Principal responsibility (only one per task)
+ Secondary responsibility
■ Must be consulted

Figure 19.5   **Linear responsibility matrix**
A matrix tool to help decide who does what.

obviously be looked upon favourably, unless these would give away information that the contractor wishes to remain confidential).

If the documents are to be made available in electronic form, accessible over a network, it might be necessary to impose different levels of access for security purposes, thus preventing unauthorized people from seeing sensitive or confidential data.

Once the regular distribution or availability of documents has been agreed, the decision can be depicted on a chart arranged as a matrix. This is, of course, secondary to the responsibility matrix shown in Figure 19.5. Each authorized recipient can be named and allocated a vertical column, and each category of documents can be allocated a horizontal row. A tick in the square at each grid intersection shows that access is permissible. Alternatively, a number written at the intersection shows how many hard copies of the relevant document each person should receive. Figure 19.6 illustrates the principle.

Document type: **Recipient:**	The customer	General manager	Project manager	Project engineer	Works manager	Production control	Buyer	Quality manager	Accountant		and so on
Bought-out parts lists				1		1	2	1			
Material specifications				1			1	1			
Purchase requisitions				1			1*				
Purchase orders							1		1		
Shortage lists			1			1	1				
Committed cost reports		1	1	1			1		1		
Drawing list			1	1	1						
Drawings for approval	1			1*							
and so on											

1	Number of copies per recipient
*	Retains original signed document

Figure 19.6   Document distribution matrix
A matrix tool to help decide who gets what.

Internal routeing of hard copy documents

There is always a risk that documents will be received safely by a company, only to be lost or misrouted within the organization.

There is a useful discipline which can be imposed to help prevent this problem, and to ensure that every document reaches the person who should take appropriate action. This procedure is based on the concept of two levels of distribution:

primary and *secondary*. The following description explains how this concept can be implemented. The case described here is for incoming project documents, but copies of outgoing correspondence can be distributed in similar fashion.

Primary distribution of incoming documents

Each original letter is date-stamped on receipt and placed in central files. Sufficient copies are sent to the project manager, together with any enclosures from the original letter, to allow him or her to arrange for secondary distribution. The number of copies would be specified in the project manual, or in some other written procedure.

Secondary distribution

The project manager (or delegate) considers who should answer the incoming letter and take any necessary action. An action copy, with enclosures, is passed to the chosen individual. One copy is placed in project office files (the project support office, if such exists), and the project manager may decide to direct copies to other managers or staff for information.

The copy intended for action must be clearly indicated as such, to ensure that action is not duplicated by the recipient of a copy intended only to give information.

Nominated addressees or contacts

It is good practice for each organization to nominate one of its senior members to act as a control point for receiving and sending all formal written communications and technical documents, however these are transmitted. Each nominated addressee then becomes responsible for seeing that the documents or the information contained in them is made known to all relevant people within their own organization.

Document transmission methods

International projects, where the contracting organization is overseas from the customer, construction site or other project groups, demand careful attention to the transmission routes of documents that must be sent as hard copy. If normal mail and airmail services are too slow or otherwise inadequate, a specialist express postal service or the use of an international courier company should be considered.

Airfreight can be used for bulky consignments of drawings or other heavy documents. When valuable documents have to be sent quickly to any overseas location, use of a regular air courier service means that the courier company can monitor or even accompany each consignment through all stages of its journey, with all movements and aircraft transfers under the surveillance of the agent's network. Such specialist services obviously reduce risk of losses and delays.

Good liaison between the company's travel department and the mailroom will ensure that travellers can be identified who might be persuaded to carry documents in their hand baggage, but this arrangement is often abused, and individuals expecting to visit a site for a meeting or a short inspection can find themselves weighed down with an alarming heap of excess baggage.

At some overseas destinations, the customs authorities can delay release of documents, and the contractor should always seek the professional advice of a carrier or courier familiar with the required route. Local industrial disputes can cause complete hold-ups or frustrating delays. In other cases, customs authorities have been known to be awkward for no apparent reason – in one case known to me, a consignment of drawings intended for a project site was held at a US airport while the customs authorities demanded payment of duty based not on the intrinsic value of the drawings, but on the value of the whole project! The solution in that case was to abandon the drawings (they are probably still in the customs shed) and send a duplicate set through another route.

Serial numbering of correspondence documents

If a large amount of regular correspondence is expected, all the parties likely to correspond with each other can agree to use letter-reference serial numbers, prefixed with their own codes. Based on an actual case (but with fictitious names) here is an example of how correspondence was numbered on one project from my experience. The project contractor was Alternative Engineering Limited (AEL) and its overseas client was Quaint Smelters Inc. (QSI) All serial numbers start at 0001.

	From AEL to QSI	*From QSI to AEL*
Letters	AQL 0001	QAL 0001
Faxes	AQF 0001	QAF 0001
Document transmittal forms	AQD 0001	QAD 0001

Apart from making consecutive filing and subsequent document retrieval easier, the use of a continuous series of numbers means that any gap in the sequence of numbers received at either end indicates a possible loss in transit that needs investigation.

The allocation of serial numbers requires some form of central register, to be administered by a suitable secretary or clerk (perhaps located in a project support office). Such formal procedures are really only suited to the despatch of documents that have particular contractual or technical significance, or for bulk consignments of documents such as drawings and specifications. E-mail correspondence, where many individuals on a single project can communicate immediately with others worldwide from their desks, does not lend itself to such formality, and it is up to the senders to ensure that their messages have been properly received and understood.

Document transmittal letters

Consignments of drawings and other documents which are not accompanied by a serially numbered covering letter should be given consignment numbers, and this is best achieved by the use of standard 'document transmittal letter' forms. These are little more than packing lists, but each is given a serial number and copies are retained on file as a record of what was sent. In the case of the US customs problem mentioned above, for example, the file copy of the relevant document transmittal letter listed all the drawing prints in the impounded consignment, enabling a duplicate set of prints to be made and sent.

Correspondence progressing

Companies with a large volume of project correspondence arrange for a coordinator to ensure that every letter or other document that requires an answer is dealt with without undue delay. The same person will also follow up any possible losses in transit, apparent from gaps in the sequence of serial numbers received.

Project engineering standards and procedures

Special design standards

The contractor will have to investigate whether or not the project calls for any special design standards, safety requirements, or compliance with government or other statutory regulations.

Drawing numbers and drawing format

It is often agreed that the drawings made for a project are the property of the customer, who will expect to be provided with a complete set of drawings at the end of the project and file them in their own system (the contractor would, of course, retain one set). In such a case, the contractor will probably have to discuss and agree the drawing numbering system to be used for the project. Common practice is to number each drawing twice, using the customer's system and the contractor's normal standard, and then cross-reference these in the computer or drawing register.

The drawings may have to be laid out to the customer's own standard drawing format or drawing sheets, in which case the contractor must obtain supplies before drawing can start. If the sheets are of a non-standard size, this might also mean purchasing new equipment for filing hard copies.

Choice of project planning and control procedures

Companies accustomed to carrying out large projects may have at their disposal a considerable range of planning and control procedures. At the start of each new project, these can be reviewed to determine which are appropriate for the particular project. Factors affecting this choice are the size and complexity of the project, the degree of difficulty and risk expected in meeting the end objectives, the number and locations of outside organizations and, last but never least, the wishes or directions of the customer.

Project manual or procedures manual

For some projects, contractors will compile a project manual (otherwise known as a 'procedures manual' or 'project handbook'). This will list the particular procedures that will apply to the project. Listed below are just some of the items that a typical project manual might include:

- names and addresses of key organizations taking part in the project, not forgetting the customer
- the names of key personnel in those organizations, particularly highlighting those who are the specific points of contact for various project matters
- organization charts
- drawing numbering system
- method of project planning and scheduling to be used
- type and frequency of project cost and progress reports to be produced
- linear responsibility matrix
- document distribution matrix
- incoming and outgoing correspondence prefix codes, if used.

Physical preparations and organization

Physical preparations must be made for any project that requires accommodation, plant, equipment, services such as gas, electric power, compressed air, water, and so on. There is no typical case, because the requirements of every project depend very much on the nature of the project and the practices of its contractor. At one end of the scale is the project which will simply follow another in a factory, using the same staff, management and facilities. At the opposite extreme is the international project involving several large companies and a construction site in the middle of a desert with no communicating rail or road, and no other infrastructure. In the latter case, making physical preparation for the main project is, in itself, a collection of very large sub-projects.

Any discussion in this chapter must therefore be in general terms. Nevertheless, one or two important, general principles can be mentioned.

Importance of checklists

All project managers will know the feelings of frustration caused during the initial days and weeks when, keen to start, and with deadlines to meet, real work has to wait because there is no information, no staff, and there is a general lack of other facilities. Lack of information is often the worst of these problems – not necessarily about the main objectives and features of the intended project, but more likely about a hundred-and-one annoying details which have to be resolved before work can start.

The value of checklists is mentioned in several places in this book, and no apology is needed or made for giving additional space to this subject here. Standard checklists, applicable to all projects, present and future, can be used as questionnaires to pre-empt information requirements. The best checklists are developed and refined gradually through experience, so that lessons learned on one project are remembered, added to those already learned, and then put to use on projects which follow.

Construction site example

An instance where a checklist is particularly useful is when a construction site organization has to be established, especially when this is to be overseas. Even for an experienced organization, that can be an enormous operation. All sorts of questions have to be asked, and answered. Some questions should already have been answered when the proposal was researched (see Chapter 3, Figure 3.3). When the project becomes real, the questions and answers are of a more definite and detailed nature. Some examples follow:

- How many people are going to be needed on site?
- How many of these will be:
  - our own permanent staff, on overseas assignment?
  - our own fixed term contract staff, hired for the purpose and duration only?
  - local recruits (Will they need training?)
  - client's staff who will be on site?
  - sub-contractors and their staff?
- What accommodation will be required?
  - How much?
  - What standard?

- – Who is responsible for providing it?
- – Rent-free?
- What are the immigration rules?
  - – Passports and visas?
  - – Work permits?
  - – Any racial prejudices?
- Local employment laws and practices?
- What about expatriates' wives and families?
- Standard terms of employment?
- Pay and taxation arrangements?
- Insurances:
  - – Staff-related?
  - – Work-related?
- Staff medical, welfare and leisure facilities?
- Climate?
- Site access:
  - – Road?
  - – Rail?
  - – Air?
  - – Other?
- Vehicle fleet
  - – Personnel carriers?
  - – Freight carriers?
  - – How provided?
  - – How managed and maintained?
- Site plant
  - – What is needed?
  - – When?
  - – How provided?
  - – How maintained?

… and so on for page after page, covering all aspects of the site and its legal, political and physical environment.

These questions need to be answered as completely and as early as possible. The better the checklist, the earlier and more completely the answers will be obtained.

Getting work started

The kick-off meeting

When the newly appointed project manager has collected his or her wits and absorbed the contents of the project specification (which will probably entail some late nights), the most urgent job is to mobilize all the project resources and tell the key participants what is expected of them.

This process takes place in different stages and by a variety of methods. The first executive action of the project manager is usually to call an initial meeting, often called the 'kick-off meeting', which gives the project manager the opportunity to outline the main features of the project to managers whose departments will work on the project, and to the most senior design staff and other key people. If the project is organized as a team, the project manager will have the advantage of talking to people who are directly responsible to him or her. If the organization is a matrix, the task is more difficult – even getting people to attend the meeting becomes more a question of invitation and persuasion rather than issuing a direct summons.

Whatever the circumstances, the skilled project manager will make the best possible use of the initial meeting to get the project off to a good start. Everyone who attends the meeting should leave with a clear picture of the project's objectives, the part they are expected to play in achieving them, and a sense of keenness and motivation to get on with the job.

Issuing initial planning information

It must be assumed that some degree of work planning has been carried out, either in advance or immediately following the receipt of an order or other form of authorization. The resulting plans and schedules will do no good at all if they are merely hung on a wall and regarded thereafter as objects to be gazed at and admired. The project manager must make certain that the contents of these schedules are made known to every key person in the organization, preferably using well-targeted work-to lists.

It is unlikely, at this early stage, that the plans will exist in sufficient detail for issuing and controlling work on mainstream activities, but two aspects of planning at this initial stage must be mentioned:

1   Although the first bar chart or outline network planning might have been drawn up in very coarse detail, and with vital gaps in precise knowledge of how the project is going to be conducted, those early plans will probably have been used in the project proposal. It is highly likely that, when authorization is received, the overall time framework for the project will already have been established, because of delivery or completion promises made to the customer.

2   Although no detailed plans exist, none should be required right at the start, when the main task is to resolve questions of the type depicted in Figure 19.7.

Two sets of initial plans should therefore be available for issue right at the start.

The first of these is the summary plan giving committed dates for the whole project. This should accompany the works order or other project authorization document. It might be a bar chart. For this purpose, it can simply be a tabulation of the key dates.

The other issue is the checklist and plan for preliminary activities, which the

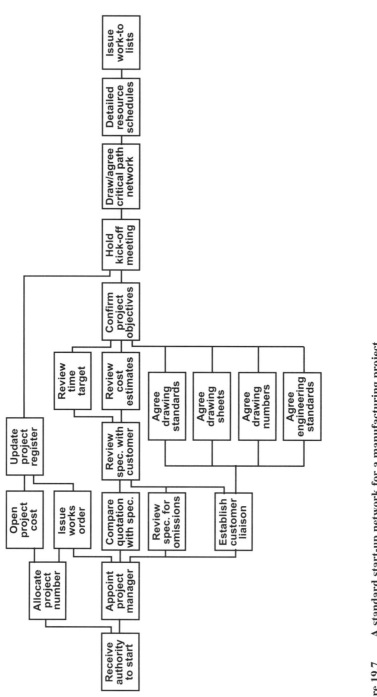

Figure 19.7　A standard start-up network for a manufacturing project

Most companies should be able to develop a standard network to serve as a checklist for the first week or two in the life of new projects. Even without duration estimates and time analysis, these networks can bridge the gap between project authorization and the issue of detailed work-to lists.

project manager will need in order to get the project started in a logical, systematic and efficient way. One urgent job during the early period covered by this checklist must, of course, be to make the detailed plans and working schedules (usually worked and reworked until they satisfy the delivery commitments already made in the project proposal).

Checklist and plan for preliminary activities

Every contractor develops expertise according to the particular industry in which it operates. The contractor learns the sort of preliminary activities that must always be carried out to establish procedures and design standards before a typical project can start. A sensible contractor will write these into a standard checklist. One company designed such a checklist in the form of a network diagram, a copy of which was used at the start of each new project. Time estimates and time analysis were never used on this standard network. It was used only as a checklist, but its value lay in the fact that it listed all likely preliminary activities in their logical sequence. A simplified example is shown in Figure 19.7.

Issuing detailed planning and work instructions

Importance of personal agreement and commitment

Enough has already been written in earlier chapters about the methods available for producing plans and working schedules. If the project is of any significance at all in terms of its size, complexity or perceived importance, it must be taken for granted that detailed planning will be performed, and that this will involve input from at least one senior representative from every key project function. This involvement might mean full attendance at an intensive network brainstorming session, or it could mean, instead, asking these key representatives to view, review and approve a network produced automatically from templates or other standard library data (see Chapter 14).

Each key participant must therefore have some share in formulating and agreeing the detailed plan. This is just as it should be, because no plan can be imposed successfully in isolation. It must carry the acceptance and support of those who are to be bound by it.

As soon as detailed planning has been carried out, the computer can be instructed to analyse the network, carry out resource allocation (if required) and produce a work-to list for every project department.

Issuing work schedules: Targeting action instructions

Dissemination of programme information must be made far more effective than the simple blanket distribution of common schedules to all and sundry. Instead, each department should receive a work-to list showing only those tasks for which it is responsible. Instructions are often ignored when they are issued to too many people, instead of only to the person who is expected to arrange for action. If an instruction is issued in a document that goes to more than one department, each may do nothing, and rely instead on the other to carry the instruction out. There is also a slighter risk that some tasks might be performed twice. Work-to lists were described in Chapter 13.

Such risks exist when project networks or other schedules are distributed to a wide number of departments or people without any explanation or precise instructions for action. Properly filtered work-to lists, on the other hand, possess the advantage of being specific to their addressees, so that management responsibility for each item on each list is the clear responsibility of the recipient.

Work-to-lists usually need be provided in detail to cover only a few weeks ahead, but longer-term summaries may have to be given to help departmental managers to recruit or reserve the necessary people. All of this is readily achievable with the filtering and sorting capabilities of project management software.

Departmental manager's authority

The instructions or reminders contained in work-to lists should in no way detract from the personal authority vested in each departmental manager. Although the source of each instruction is the project manager's office, the information should derive from the detailed project plan that was first made, reviewed and agreed with the departmental managers themselves. The authority of these managers, far from being undermined, should actually be reinforced.

Each manager receives a list of the work required of his or her department, but is free to allocate the work to individuals within the department and to direct and control it. With work-to lists resulting from sensible resource scheduling, there should be no chronic departmental overloads (temporary overloads will always remain a risk). These managers are in fact provided with more effective tools which should help them to control the activities within their particular groups.

Work-to lists for manufacturing

Work-to lists for manufacturing would normally be sent to the production manager or production controller, who would continue to issue works orders, job tickets, route cards or any other form of document demanded by the customary procedures used throughout the manufacturing organization. The levels of detail shown in project networks (and, therefore, in the resulting work-to lists) are bound to be far coarser than those needed for the day-to-day (even minute-to-minute) planning and control of factory operations. Work-to lists will probably provide the expected start and required finish dates for each assembly and sub-assembly. It is highly unlikely that any work-to list derived from the project schedule will specify a greater degree of parts or work breakdown.

The manufacturing organization will therefore use its production engineering, planning and control facilities to interpret drawings, identify the parts and materials required and carry out detailed production scheduling. This must be done to satisfy the dates given on the work-to lists but, provided that project resource scheduling was used, the overall rate of working implied by the work-to list should lie within the capacity of the manufacturing plant.

Engineering design

In engineering design departments, the work-to lists are more likely to be used for controlling day-to-day work without need for the additional documents and procedures always required in manufacturing departments.

However, networks are not always drawn with sufficient breakdown detail for the day-to-day allocation of work, and it might still be necessary for managers and supervisors to arrange for very detailed activities to be listed manually. For example, drawing and purchase control schedules are usually required to show a greater level of detail than is feasible on the project network diagram. A single network activity usually summarizes a group of drawings needed for a small work package or sub-assembly, and it is not usually desirable or possible to have a separate network activity for every individual project drawing. A similar argument applies to purchases and purchase control schedules.

In most engineering design offices and other software groups, highly qualified staff can be found whose creative talents are beyond question. But, while their technical or scientific approach to project tasks might be well motivated and capable of producing excellent results, there is always a danger that these creative souls will not fully appreciate the importance of keeping within time and cost limits. The inclusion of estimated costs and target completion dates on work-to lists can help these specialists to become more aware of their commercial responsibilities.

Drawing and purchase control schedules

Drawing schedules list all the drawings which have to be made for a project. They are similar to a drawings register, and can be used for the allocation of drawing numbers, provided that such numbers are contained within blocks of numbers reserved in the company's central drawing register. Drawing schedules are specific to the project, whereas the central drawing register is a general company record, listing all drawings made for all purposes. A headings format for drawings schedules can be seen in Chapter 24, Figure 24.2.

Purchase schedules list all items of equipment to be purchased for a project, and are used to allocate technical specification serial numbers (and possibly enquiry, requisition and purchase order numbers too). They are to the large project what the parts list is to a small manufacturing project. An example of a headings format is shown in Figure 18.3.

Drawing schedules and purchase schedules were prepared by hand before the age of computers, and they also had to record the progress made on each item listed. But they were really too inflexible for this purpose, and the extensive use of erasers was called for when new revisions were issued or when progress information had to be updated. The schedules should be set up in a computer system: either used as a straightforward word processor, or in a relational database system linked to the network schedule.

When the project is finished, the drawing and purchase control schedules have to be updated to show all the final drawing numbers with their correct revisions, and all the purchase specification numbers and their final revisions. The schedules then define the 'as-built' condition of the project. They are similar to the build schedule documents that will be described in Chapter 25, the principal difference being that drawing and purchase schedules define a single project, whereas build schedules are particularly useful for defining manufactured products that are made in two or more different versions.

Chapter 20

Managing progress

Figure 20.1 depicts a familiar roadside sign. It warns us of forthcoming disruption and inconvenience to our journeys, but promises better things ahead, when the

Figure 20.1   A familiar sign
Will this project start and finish on time?

road has been repaired and our travel has been made smoother and safer. But, when we analyse the message of the sign in more detail, what credence can be given to its purported facts? We can be reasonably certain about the last part of the statement: 'Delays possible'. It is likely, however, that the first day of July will come and go with no sign of activity. Perhaps by the middle of the month things might start to happen, with the arrival of machinery and the erection of temporary traffic signals and other impediments to the free flow of traffic. After that, the promised six weeks might drag out to ten or even twelve weeks.

Road repair operations such as those depicted in Figure 20.1 are usually quite simple projects, yet we often see the kinds of problems I have described. Managing the progress of larger projects obviously poses greater difficulties, with far more complexity in the organization and the number of tasks. This chapter is about helping to prevent such project failures. It starts from the premise that an effective schedule has been produced, and that all key project participants know, and have agreed to, what is expected of them. It then discusses various methods by which work can be monitored and progressed so that the intentions of the scheduler are carried out.

Project progressing as a closed-loop control system

One prerequisite for any control system is a method for measuring the effect of any command given. The information so derived can then be fed back to the command source so that any errors can be corrected by modifying the original command.

An artillery commander watches the placing of his shots, and uses the results of each miss to correct the aim of the gunners. In electrical circuits, error signals can be generated which are proportional to positional errors of moving parts, the incorrect amplitude of output voltages, or waveform distortion. Those error signals can be put to good use by feeding them back into the system's input, in opposite polarity or phase, so that they almost balance out (and therefore correct) the unwanted abnormality.

If no use is made of the error signals, the system is said to be operating as an open loop. When the error signals are connected back to the input, the loop is closed. Project progressing, as a control system, is no exception. For every instruction sent out, errors have to be detected and corrective feedback applied. The competent project manager will ensure that these corrective actions do take place, so that the control loop is effectively closed. Because of the particularly close electronic analogy this process, illustrated in Figure 20.2, is called *cybernetic control*.

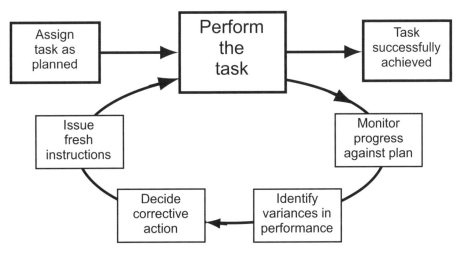

Figure 20.2   A control loop

Management by exception

With any system of control feedback, it is the error signals or messages that are significant, because these are the factors that can generate corrective action. In the management context, the errors or divergences from expectations are called *variances* or, more generally, *exceptions*. The sensible approach of concentrating management reports and attention on exceptions is known as *management by exception*.

Management by surprise

There is an alternative management approach that relies only on outgoing instructions, with no feedback or error signals. This is called *management by surprise*. The manager feeds in work at one end of the system, and is surprised when it fails to come out at the other!

Routine collection of progress data

Whatever the method used for progress feedback, care must be taken to avoid either ambiguity or undue complication. The simpler the method, the more likely the chances of persuading all the managers involved to return data regularly on time. Even so, training all key participants to adopt the regular routine of progress reporting often provides project managers with a real test of their mettle. Many attempts at project control break down because this particular process cannot be established reliably.

Use of task lists or work-to lists as progress returns

Active projects depend on two-way communication between the project manager and every departmental manager. For every work instruction issued, information on the resulting progress must be fed back regularly.

If the instructions are to be conveyed from the project manager to participants by way of work-to lists, there is no reason why the same procedure should not be applied in reverse to feed back progress information. The only missing item is a document complementary to the work-to list. This gap can be filled by:

● the use of specially designed progress return forms
  or
● direct input to the computer via a network
  or
● line managers annotating copies of their work-to lists.

Some project management software packages allow space for comments on their work-to lists. The example in Figure 20.3 is redrawn from a report one version of Open Plan included in its standard range of reports. This example serves as a work-issue notice that can then be annotated with progress information by the departmental manager and returned to the project manager on a later pre-specified date.

For every task on the current work-to list, the project manager will need to be told about progress in one or more of the following ways:

● The task has not been started as planned, for the reasons given.
● The task has just been started.
● The task is in progress, with an assessment of the percentage of the task completed.
● The task is in progress, with an estimate of the remaining duration to completion.
● The task is in progress, with an estimate of the completion date.
● The task is completed.

Time-now date

All progress data should be given with reference to the next *time-now date*, which is the date chosen to act as a reference point from which time analysis and rescheduling will be calculated. The time-now date is important when computer files are updated periodically under the supervision of the project manager or a

ID	Description	Orig dur	Scheduled start	Scheduled finish	Rem dur	% 100	% complete	Progress expected at next time-now Comment
1	Project start	0	13MAY02	13MAY02	0	0		
2	Make and prime door frame	1	13MAY02	13MAY02	1	0		
3	Dig foundations	4	13MAY02	16MAY02	4	0		
7	Position door frame	1	14MAY02	14MAY02	1	0		
4	Make doors	3	15MAY02	17MAY02	3	0		
8	Concrete foundations	2	17MAY02	20MAY02	2	0		
9	Prime doors	1	20MAY02	20MAY02	1	0		
11	Lay bricks for walls	10	21MAY02	03JUN02	10	0		
13	Fit RSJ lintel	1	04JUN02	04JUN02	1	0		
18	Case lintel, build parapets	2	05JUN02	06JUN02	2	0		
12	Lay floor base	2	07JUN02	10JUN02	2	0		
6	Cut roof timbers	1	07JUN02	07JUN02	1	0		
17	Screed floor	1	11JUN02	11JUN02	1	0		
21	Hang doors	1	12JUN02	12JUN02	1	0		

Project: Garage

GARAGE PROJECT

Activity progress update questionnaire

Page: 1

Report date: 16APR02

Figure 20.3   A combined work-to list and progress questionnaire

project support office, particularly when a complex multi-project model is involved.

All people asked to provide progress information, whether direct from terminals or on paper, must be told the next time-now date as far in advance as possible. The planner will usually choose this time-now to be either the date on which rescheduling is to take place, or a day or two later. Progress reporting against a time-now therefore expects managers to forecast slightly ahead when assessing their results.

If the schedules have to be updated frequently, as a result of changes or for any other reason, reprocessing might have to be arranged at regular intervals. If the intervals are regular, the rescheduling dates and time-now dates can be announced and annotated on calendars for many months ahead.

Frequency of progress data collection

Progress feedback should be arranged at fairly frequent intervals, typically more often than the issue of revised work-to lists. Weekly intervals are suggested. If the intervals are too long, some problems might not come to light in sufficient time for corrective action to have any effect.

Continuous, direct progress data input

It is often practicable for departmental managers to be given direct access to the computer files through their own terminals. These managers can then report progress by this direct, 'real-time' method.

The project manager will want to be assured that progress information fed directly to the computer in this way, without first being subjected to checking and critical examination, emanates only from reliable and reasonably senior staff. False statements could lead to subsequent errors in network analysis, future resource allocation and work-to lists. If the computer system is holding a large, complex multi-project model, the group or person responsible for scheduling will always be wary of any input that could corrupt the files and cause many hours of restoration work.

Although project progress information will be updated continuously by the direct input method, the work-to lists and other schedules will probably be revised and reissued only when the planner decides that data reprocessing is necessary. This decision must be made by the planner in advance, and the next time-now date must be announced as soon as it has been decided.

Questions of logic

If the progress information is being gathered on forms, rather than by direct input to the computer, there is another question that the perceptive project manager needs to ask for each task reported as complete. The vital question is:

Can this activity's immediate successor(s) be started?

This question (not usually asked or possible to answer when progress information is being keyed into the computer) is the acid test of whether or not an activity has truly been completed. If the network logic is correct, then an activity cannot strictly be reported as complete if its immediately following dependent tasks cannot be started.

An alert project manager will recognize the danger behind a progress return which says that the percentage progress achieved is 99 or 100 per cent, but that the next activity cannot start. This could mean that the progress claimed has not in fact been made. This anomaly also occurs when a design engineer has completed a batch of drawings, but refuses to release them for issue through lack of confidence in the design, or because he or she feels that (given plenty of time) the drawings could be improved, or for some other non-essential personal reason.

Sometimes an activity can be started even though one or more of its predecessors is still in progress. For example, a design activity, although not complete, could be sufficiently advanced to allow the release of procurement lists for long-lead items. A network diagram cannot indicate all such possibilities and opportunities for speeding progress might easily be missed it the right questions are not asked.

Activities are, in fact, quite often reported as started before one or more predecessors have been reported as finished. This is in contradiction to the logic enshrined in the network, so that, when it happens, it indicates that the network constraints were not absolute. Nevertheless, if that is the situation, it has to be accepted and reported to the computer accordingly. The computer will probably report such activities as being started 'out of sequence'.

Some programs allow the planner to choose an option which allows out-of-sequence scheduling to be performed. This option is likely to be invited during the preliminary screen dialogue when time analysis is requested. A typical form of question asked by the program is: 'Observe network logic: Yes or No?'

The non-routine approach to progressing

Management by walking about

The routine methods described above for collecting progress information can work properly only in an ideal world. They paint a picture of the project manager working entirely from behind a desk, issuing instructions and receiving reports while the project proceeds smoothly on to its successful finish. While the establishment of efficient routine systems is a commendable and necessary aim, more is needed. The project manager must be prepared to depart from the routine and his or her desk from time to time, making visits and spot checks, giving praise or encouragement where due, and viewing physical progress at first hand. This process is sometimes aptly called *management by walking about*.

Visits to sites or production areas are particularly useful when two or more visits are made some little time apart, so that progress (or lack of progress) can be noted. Construction site photographs should be taken on such visits, to check progress and as a permanent record of the project as it develops.

Staff at all levels in a project organization like to feel that their efforts are being noticed and appreciated, and personal interest from the project manager during walkabouts is likely to be a valuable motivator. I knew a large engineering organization once where the engineering director spent all his time luxuriating in a large office filled with expensive period reproduction furniture and protected from the external world by an outer office, equally well furnished, containing his devoted secretary. Most design staff working in the adjacent general offices never saw their director. They were actively demotivated by this arrangement and, indeed, used to declare that the engineering director did not actually exist, but was simply represented by an empty office and a secretary.

Statistical checks

One very useful occasional check is to ask how many people in a department, or staff of a particular grade, are actually working on the project. The answer can then be compared with the manpower planned at that date. Comparison of scheduled and actual cost curves can also be made, but the headcount is quicker, more positive, and likely to produce earlier warning of a potential problem.

Example of a low rate of working measurement

Suppose that 35 design engineers are supposed to be working on scheduled activities on a given date. If only 18 people can be identified as working on the project, something is obviously very wrong somewhere. Although routine progress returns might indicate that everything is more or less on course, the headcount shows that work on the project in the design department is not taking place at the required rate.

Closer investigation might reveal that the project design is held up for lack of information, that work for another project has been given priority, or that the department is seriously understaffed. The project manager must take action to set the right number of people to work.

When the rate of expenditure seems right

Now suppose that the project manager has carried out two checks on a project, as a result of which it is found that both the use of manpower and the rate of expenditure appear to be on target.

There used to be (perhaps there still are) people who would gladly accept such results as indicating that all was well with their projects, mistakenly believing that if the scheduled number of people are actually found to be working on a project (or if the costs *recorded* to date are in line with the costs *planned* to date), then progress must also be on course. Of course, no sensible modern project manager would make such an assumption, because it is necessary also to assess the value earned from the expenditure. This argument will be developed further in Chapter 22.

Managing subcontractors and agency employees

Most companies use subcontractors. They can be used in a variety of ways, the most common of which include the following:

1   to undertake tasks which require expertise or facilities that lie outside the main contractor's own capabilities (for example, heat treatment, plating and anodizing, gear cutting, chemical analysis, certification testing); this form of subcontracting is typically handled and progressed through the contractor's standard purchasing procedures, and will not be discussed further in this chapter

2   to provide additional 'temporary' staff to work in the contractor's own premises to cover work overloads or to substitute for permanent staff who are absent for any reason

3   to undertake specified tasks externally, on the subcontractors' own premises, where the main contractor's accommodation, plant or workforce would otherwise be overloaded

4   to work on a construction site, carrying out the various trades or specialist services – a very brief account of construction site management is given later in this chapter.

Temporary staff working on the contractor's own premises

The supply of temporary staff for all kinds of duties has become accepted practice, and many agencies exist, some specializing in particular trades or professional skills.

Some companies regard the employment of agency staff as a temporary expedient, to be undertaken to cover staff shortages caused by holidays, sickness or sudden work overloads. However, there are companies who plan always to keep a proportion of their total workforce as temporary staff, because this provides flexibility in the event of workload fluctuations and reduces the possibility of having to make permanent staff redundant when the order book is less than full.

Planning for availability

Whenever agency staff have to be used, especially if the numbers are significant, the search for suitable agencies and ensuing negotiations should take place as early as possible so that manpower can be reserved at reasonable rates and with some guarantee of adequate performance. Project disasters excepted, the use of project resource-scheduling techniques (such as those described in earlier chapters) should provide adequate and sufficiently accurate forewarning. The project manager should ensure that the selected agencies are given sufficient notice to mobilize or reserve their own resources. Care should be taken, however, to avoid long-term commitments and the payment of retaining fees – a request sometimes made by subcontractors on the grounds that they cannot otherwise guarantee to have people available when required. In my experience such retainers are unnecessary, and I have never agreed to them.

Supervision

From the project control point of view, although the use of short-term agency staff may be unavoidable, there are risks of errors and inefficiency in all cases where the tasks require a good understanding of the company's procedures and working practices. In those cases some time and money must be dedicated to providing initial or induction training. Longer-term temporary staff can often settle into an organization and acquit themselves well, becoming indistinguishable from the permanent employees until the fateful day arrives when there is no more work for them.

All temporary employees working on the contractor's own premises should normally come under the day-to-day supervision of the company's own departmental managers, and work should be issued, progressed and measured according to the same project management procedures that govern permanent staff. The only additional feature is to ensure that invoices received from the various agencies claim for the hours actually worked, and at the agreed rates. Verification of hours worked is achieved using weekly timesheets. Agencies will generally expect their staff to fill in the agency's own brand of timesheets, and these will be used as the input documents for the resulting agency invoices. However, for detailed and accurate recording of task times worked against appropriate project cost codes, contractors will probably require agency staff also to record their time using the contractor's own internal timesheet procedures.

Temporary staff working in outside offices

An extra dimension of risk is added when tasks are entrusted to staff who cannot be accommodated within the contractor's own premises. In those cases, work allocation and day-to-day supervision is usually delegated to the subcontractor's own management. The main contractor will want to take steps to ensure that design quality does not suffer, and that the hours claimed by the subcontractor equate to the hours actually worked. The outside offices may be situated at a long distance from the main contractor's offices.

Liaison engineer

One way to overcome these problems is to place a supervisor in the external office, which, of course, will require the agreement of the subcontractor. A more usual approach is to appoint one or more of the company's permanent engineering staff as 'subcontract liaison engineer'. The liaison engineer's task is to visit the external offices at very frequent intervals, making certain that the project design standards are known and followed, taking out new work, collecting completed work, monitoring progress and answering routine technical queries on the spot.

Revealing float and budget data to external agencies

Managers differ in their opinions regarding the revelation of float and budget information to subcontractors. There are arguments for and against.

I prefer to tell subcontractors the amount of float available, because this information can be used to decide genuine priorities, and also as the main factor in deciding whether or not overtime working (and therefore overtime premium costs) are justified. The additional costs of overtime should usually be accepted for work on critical tasks that are late or in danger of becoming so.

Other companies will have different views. Some will argue that the only schedule information needed by the subcontractor is the scheduled start and finish date of each task, regardless of float.

If in doubt, a compromise can be suggested. Subcontractors should be told if any job has zero or negative float. For all other jobs, the subcontractor might infer that float exists, but they will not be told how much – only that the work is expected to start and finish on the dates scheduled.

Budget data have to be treated differently. I take the view that if the available budget is revealed on each subcontract order, then the subcontractor will be tempted to spend and claim costs up to that budget. If, on the other hand, the estimates are kept out of sight, progressing work within the scheduled dates should suffice to stop the work from overrunning its budgeted costs.

Effective costs: A paradox

When using about ten different subcontractors for an engineering company in the British Midlands, I reached the following conclusions:

● All the companies chosen performed well in respect of their work quality.
● The terms for recovering expenses and for charging travel time varied considerably.
● The hourly rates quoted varied considerably from one company to another.
● The hours actually booked for equivalent jobs also varied from company to company – in inverse proportion to the hourly cost rates.

Those companies which quoted the higher hourly rates were therefore not necessarily the most expensive to use, because they tended to claim fewer hours and expenses for the equivalent amount of work. In fact, there was little variation in the real costs of using all these subcontractors.

Special arrangements to protect standards and design quality

If significant design packages are subcontracted to external offices, there is a danger that the results might not properly match the project design concept, or that the solutions adopted would differ from those normally preferred by the company.

Most reputable companies would not allow new permanent staff to work unsupervised on their initial work, or before undergoing some basic training and induction into the company's preferred practices and standards. The same argument applies to external staff entrusted with design tasks.

This problem can be overcome to a large extent by nominating one or more members of a subcontractor's senior design staff as a 'key engineer'. Each key engineer can be invited to work in the contractor's main design office for a few weeks, working under competent guidance and absorbing the company's standards and practices.

A package of work is then selected for the external design office. The key engineer carries out the basic design and layout drawings for this work package in the contractor's main office. When this work has been checked and approved, the key engineer returns to the external office, where he or she supervises other subcontract staff in the detailing and checking of all the drawings needed to complete the work package.

As experience is gained, the main contractor will eventually allow some original design work to be carried out in the subcontractor's office, regarding the key engineer as a kind of agent or external supervisor.

Routine priority allocation in manufacturing projects

Occasions will arise when work cannot be carried out by manufacturing departments in a sequence that suits every project schedule. If the production control department were able to pick up all orders and load them sequentially, or according to their own machine and manpower schedules, no serious problem need arise. Sooner or later, however, an order is going to be placed which is wanted urgently, and the production controller will be asked to displace other orders in favour of the newcomer.

ABC system

Some organizations attempt to allocate order priorities, labelling their works orders with the letters A, B or C (for example) to indicate the degree of urgency attaching to each order. A job carrying Priority A would be perceived as being more urgent than jobs at Priority B, leaving Priority C jobs as the poor relations. It is not difficult to imagine why such systems break down. Delayed C orders will eventually become wanted urgently, but will continue to be labelled and treated as C orders. In the end, everyone will label their orders as A priority, so that everything is wanted at once and nothing in fact receives special attention. As W.S. Gilbert points out in *The Gondoliers* (1889):

When everyone is somebodee, then no one's anybody.

Wanted-by dates

A preferable arrangement is to schedule orders by 'wanted by' dates. The production controller can then attempt to schedule to meet these dates, and inform those who are likely to be disappointed. If any project item is expected to be delayed beyond its critical date, the possibility of subcontracting the work can always be considered.

Resolving conflicting priorities

Special project work often has to take its place in the production organization alongside routine manufacturing work or jobs for other projects. Conflicts can arise between jobs with different priorities, and it is indeed a brave person who attempts to intervene between two rival project managers who are fighting for the same production resources.

Critical path analysis and multi-project resource scheduling are the logical ways to decide priorities but, unfortunately, some managers are not over-impressed with logical reasoning when they see their projects being delayed in favour of other work. If such problems cannot be resolved on the spot without bloodshed, a sensible approach is to refer the problem to a third-party arbitrator – preferably a manager at a more senior level in the organization, capable of assessing the relative merits of the conflicting jobs.

When the news is bad

How bad?

When jobs start to run late, the first thing the project manager must do is to consider the effect that this is likely to have on:

1   the current project
2   projects or other work queuing in the pipeline
3   last, but certainly not least, the customer.

On rare occasions, late running might be acceptable and require no action. Usually, however, some degree of corrective action is needed. The project manager must then assess the situation, decide the appropriate action, and implement it.

Late jobs with free float

If the recalcitrant work has enough free float to absorb the total expected delay, then all that needs to be done is to ensure that the work is expedited and finished without further interruption, within the available free float time.

Late jobs with some total float

Total float has to be treated with more circumspection than free float, because any total float used up by late working early in the programme will rob later tasks of their float. So those jobs which possess total float but no free float should, wherever possible, be expedited to bring them back on schedule.

Remember that purchasing and manufacturing departments have always suffered at the hands of project managers by being expected to perform miracles when all the total float has been used up long before work enters the purchasing and manufacturing phases.

Late jobs with zero or negative float

If critical tasks (tasks with zero or negative float) are late, then special measures must certainly be taken. It might be necessary to accept more expensive working methods to expedite these late jobs and bring them back on schedule. If a task budgeted to cost £1000 is in danger of running several weeks late and jeopardizing the handover date of a project worth £1 million, then obviously it would be worth spending £10 000 or even more on the problem task if that could rescue the project programme. The project manager must always view the costs of expediting individual activities against the potential effect on the whole project.

Corrective measures

Orthodox measures

Corrective measures will only be successful if they are taken in time, which means that adequate warning of problems must be given. This will depend on monitoring progress regularly against a well-prepared schedule that is kept up to date.

Working overtime, perhaps over one or two weekends, can sometimes recover time. The project manager will be thankful on such occasions that overtime working was held back as a reserve and not built into the schedules as normal practice. Used occasionally, overtime can be an effective help in overcoming delays. Used regularly or too often, however, the law of diminishing returns will apply, with staff permanently tired and working under pressure, leaving inadequate reserves for coping with emergencies.

If problems are being caused by shortage of resources, perhaps these could be made available from external sources by subcontracting, or there might be additional capacity somewhere else in the contractor's own organization that could be mobilized.

The network logic should always be re-examined critically. Can some tasks can be overlapped, bypassed or even eliminated? Is there any task that could wait until after the main part of the project has been delivered?

If all else fails, try to find out what the customer's reaction would be to late delivery. If, for instance, the project is to install new machinery in a brand-new manufacturing plant, it could be that the customer's own building programme is running late, so that a later delivery date can be negotiated with no one being inconvenienced.

Unorthodox measures

Special motivational measures, incentives, or even unorthodox actions can sometimes give progress a much-needed boost, provided that these measures are legal, not repeated too often, and used sensibly.

Example 1

On one occasion, an export project for the central monitoring of hospital patients electronically, already many months late, was being subjected to further delays by the threat of engineering modifications. The project manager and chief engineer almost came to blows. The project manager booked space on a ship, challenged the assembly crew by placing a small bet with them that they could not meet the deadline, and told the chief engineer that any remaining essential modifications (cutting ventilation holes in panels) would have to be carried out on site. The assembly crew volunteered to work continuously for three days and nights. At triple rates, the overtime payments were enormous, but the consignment went on the ship as planned.

Example 2

An operation for the routine maintenance and servicing of a large fleet of helicopters was causing trouble for an organization because too many aircraft were out of service at any time. Intensive progressing action by management cut the time for each aircraft's annual service from nine weeks to six weeks. The most successful ploy used was to offer the maintenance crews extra leave equivalent to the time saved.

Example 3

A project manager had to rely on the manufacturing department in his company, over which he had no executive authority. Day after day he was distressed to see partly fabricated steel components for his project stacked in the factory with no sign of progress. Representations to management, first at junior and then at senior level, had no effect.

During one lunch break, when the factory was deserted, this project manager took three strong colleagues into the factory, selected a large component weighing about 75 kilograms, carried it into the works manager's office and laid it across his polished desk (which, unfortunately, was scratched in the process). The result was immediate, explosive, extremely unpleasant, but completely effective for that project and its successors.

In all of these examples, success was achieved through the project manager's determination and by motivating (in different ways) the key people.

Immediate action orders

One solution to the handling of really urgent priorities relies upon the use of special *immediate action orders*. These are printed on highly distinctive card or paper, either brightly coloured or covered with vivid red or bright orange stripes. Fluorescent ink is ideal. An example is illustrated in Figure 20.4.

Special procedures

Special measures are necessary to ensure that a proper degree of urgency and respect is always afforded to immediate action orders:

1   Immediate action orders must be designed so that they stand out easily from all other documents, and cannot be ignored.
2   Each order must be authorized at very senior level (for example, the managing director).
3   Only one immediate action order may be in force in the organization at one time.
4   Immediate action orders must be hand-carried from department to department, and from work station to work station, with the date and time of entry and exit stamped against each operation.
5   Every department named for action on an immediate action order must give the specified work absolute priority and interrupt other work if necessary – *immediately.*
6   All possible means must be devoted to achieving the work specified, which might mean incurring high expense. For example, a vehicle or aircraft may have to be sent to collect vital components or materials. Special prices might have to be paid to suppliers to compensate them for any urgent action.

An immediate action order case history

The problem

A project for a complex defence weapons system was under way, part of which was a rocket-borne radar unit. One of the components was a miniature high-voltage transformer and, at the time of this incident, a single prototype was being made. The transformer was highly specialized, and required intricately machined parts, very careful winding, and awkward assembly. Because of the combination of small size and high voltages, the transformer had to be encapsulated in epoxy resin before it could be used or even tested. This meant that, in the event of failure, none of the components could be reclaimed and used again.

During final testing, the transformer flashed over and burned out. This left the project without a key component, and with an apparent design problem regarding this transformer. The prototype had taken six weeks to produce, with rigid inspection routines imposed throughout because of the requirements of HM Government. The idea of having to wait a further six weeks for a replacement, on

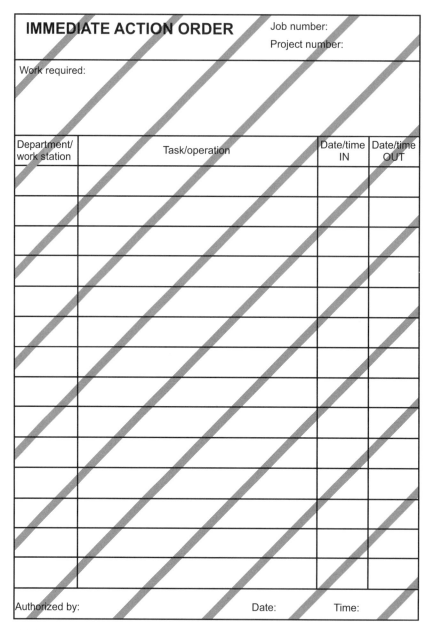

Figure 20.4   Immediate action order
Vivid orange stripes make this document difficult to ignore.

top of the delay while the engineers sorted out the design problem, was simply out of the question.

The solution

The project manager prepared an immediate action order to cover all the actions needed to produce a new fully tested transformer. The order was authorized, but only after the project manager had convinced the company's general manager that the transformer really was critical, and desperately needed.

The first result of issuing the immediate action order was to preclude the possibility of any further immediate action orders being issued. Only one was allowed to be in force at any time.

A progress chaser was assigned full-time to the order, and he started by taking it to the chief engineer, placing it on his desk, and stamping the date and time of arrival against the 'investigate failure and modify design' operation. The investigation was put in hand immediately, and the failure of the first unit was considered to be due to the presence of air bubbles in the encapsulating resin. The engineers modified the design slightly to reduce the risk of air being trapped during the moulding process.

The presence of an impatient progress chaser with a time stamp in his hand, the general manager's signature, the vivid design of the order sheet, and the knowledge that a post mortem examination would be carried out afterwards to look at all the in and out times caused such a flurry of activity that modified drawings were issued within about one hour of the immediate action order being signed.

When the order reached the manufacturing department, one of the first operations required the use of a milling machine, but all machines were in use. Another job was therefore stopped and removed, half finished, from a milling machine. Work was started at once on the manufacture of a new bobbin, and all the other small components were made ready within a very short time.

The quality management department had been warned in advance, and they inspected and passed the work without delay, but they did ensure that the required quality standards were maintained. The progress chaser stayed with the job, and continued time-stamping the order in and out of each department or work station, through winding, assembly, resin encapsulation and final testing.

Success

The modification proved successful, and the new transformer passed all its performance tests.

Without the impetus given by the immediate action order, this job would undoubtedly have taken at least six weeks. It took only three days. Of course, the cost was high, and might have been higher still had any special actions been needed to get materials. But the programme was saved. In total terms, the cost of crashing all the transformer activities was far outweighed by the cost saving made by preventing a six-week slippage of the whole project.

The reasons why such success was achieved should be appreciated. In the first place, the order was sufficiently rare to command attention from all concerned. It was not 'just another high-priority order'. Further, the high level of authorization carried on the document, together with the sense of urgency created by time-stamping the start and finish in every department, left no doubt in any mind regarding the genuine nature of the crash action request.

If special cases for priority are to be allowed, these must be strictly limited in number. But, once any job has been given top priority status, then all the force and weight of management must be used to back up that decision and ensure that the job is carried right through without interruption. There must be no half measures.

Haste versus good management

When a project is at risk of running late, there is always a danger that corners will be cut at the expense of accuracy or quality.

Risk of errors and increased after-issue work

A large quantity of changes and 'after-issue' work arising from design errors could be the result of undue haste or crash actions.

In normal circumstances all drawings, specifications and design calculations would be carefully checked. Design integrity is often proved by means of a prototype or laboratory model. These activities occupy valuable time but, if considered essential, they have to be performed. If ever an engineer has to make a conscious choice between speed and design confidence, the decision must be based on careful consideration of the possible consequences of error. It must be accepted that occasions will arise when risks have to be taken, but these must never be at the cost of ultimate performance and safety.

Examples

Suppose, for example, that a small electronic package had to be produced in a great hurry for an urgent project and that, because design information was still awaited from engineers working on another part of the system, the values of certain components could only be guessed within fairly broad limits. The designers might feel justified in issuing the drawings and allowing production to proceed, knowing that any necessary component or simple wiring changes could be made during final testing and commissioning. The small risk involved would easily be justified if the project were running very late.

If, however, the circuit changes envisaged would mean changing the layout of a printed circuit board which was difficult to design, expensive to manufacture, had a long purchase lead time and was needed in significant quantities, then the engineers would need to be very certain of their design accuracy before releasing the drawings. Similarly, if a huge metal casting or weldment had to be purchased at considerable expense and then subjected to many hours of accurate machining by skilled operatives, a design error could be disastrous.

Increased reliance on subcontractors

A common result of attempting to increase the rate of working is a short-term work overload, leading to increased use of subcontractors.

For work that is accurately specified in manufacturing or construction drawings, the quality control function has clear parameters against which to assess the work. However, if there is undue pressure on the design engineering department, this could lead to a demand for subcontract augmentation of the design function at a level normally considered to be unacceptable. Subcontractors or temporary staff might have to be engaged at higher rates than usual, and with insufficient or no time available in which to investigate their background and proficiency.

Subcontract design staff cannot be expected to identify themselves with the project or with the company's design philosophy and corporate image to the same degree as permanent employees. Their motivation will be different because their career aims lie elsewhere. Their performance may be at higher risk because they are unaccustomed to the regular practices and standards of the firm into whose activities they have suddenly been thrust.

Guidelines were given earlier in this chapter for supervising subcontractors under normal planned conditions: the real dangers come when the organization is seriously overloaded.

Unreasonable management pressure: a case study

Pressures other than project delivery dates can also cause undue haste and put quality or reputation at risk.

The project environment

An electronic engineering company was carrying out a project for the design and manufacture of a prototype system comprising a considerable number of expensive electronic units. The customer was a large aircraft company, and the work was being performed to rigorous defence contract quality requirements.

Divisional managers in the electronics company were always put under pressure to achieve pre-set monthly billing targets and, on civilian projects, invoices were sometimes mailed early, before the goods were quite ready for dispatch, simply to beat the end-of-month billing deadline. Provided dispatch followed within a few days, no great harm was done.

For the defence project in question, invoices could only be mailed when they were accompanied by final test certificates, and these had to be signed by the company's chief inspector.

The big mistake

On one memorable occasion, the chief inspector allowed himself to be coerced or 'pressurized' into signing a test certificate for a piece of equipment before the test had actually been carried out. The project office was therefore able to attach the test certificate to an invoice for several thousands of pounds, and mail both to the customer before the end-of-the-month target.

The inevitable happened. The unit failed its test in spectacular fashion, with clouds of expensive smoke and a panic call for fire extinguishers. The unit had been the only one of its type, with no replacement in the production pipeline. Yet the customer had been led to believe that the unit was finished, tested to rigorous standards, packed and ready for dispatch.

The electronics company had no option but to blush heavily, tell the truth, ask for the invoice and test certificate to be returned, and offer profuse apologies (which were, fortunately, accepted).

Construction site organization and management

The organization and management arrangements at a construction site obviously depend on the size and duration of the project, and on the location of the site.

Coordination and planning

The need for planned coordination is self-evident. Otherwise bricklayers might arrive to start building walls before the footings had been finished, electricians would turn up too early, the roofing contractor might arrive after the scaffolding had been removed, construction plant and building materials would be unavailable when wanted, or in places where they were not wanted, and so on.

Facilities

The main contractor will have to ensure that adequate site office provisions are made, with the usual facilities such as furniture and filing cabinets, telephones and other communications equipment, computers, stationery and a photocopier, all probably housed in a site hut or other temporary accommodation. Space or more detailed provision must also be made for site supervisors and others from the more important subcontractors. All of this is routine, established practice which no competent main contractor or site manager needs to be told.

However, the situation becomes far more complex when the project is very large and the site is remote. There may be no communications, power or water supplies. Setting up the site facilities and making all local arrangements then becomes a big project in itself, requiring very detailed planning well in advance. The main contractor might have to coordinate the provision of roads, temporary accommodation for site management and workers, secure stores, catering facilities, hospital, banking arrangements, and much more.

This is yet another case where the value of a checklist developed from previous experience is likely to be invaluable.

An organization for the site of a large construction project with no special communications or location difficulties is shown in Figure 20.5.

Quality

The need to monitor should be obvious and, where the site is within the jurisdiction of a local authority, the local building inspector might be one of many who would be watching the quality of workmanship, materials and building methods. In addition to the main contractor's engineers, the subcontractors' own managers should be supervising their work. Architects, surveyors, and even the client, could be expected to take more than a passing interest. On some projects the client might appoint its own independent expert representative or consulting engineer to check on quality and progress.

With all these people bearing and sharing responsibility for quality, why should anything ever go wrong? When it does, some months after the building has been occupied, the main contractor might have quite a problem in deciding where to lay the blame and how to pass on the costs of rectification. Adequate records of all site meetings, subcontract documents, inspection reports, site incidents, photographs, and so on, should all be filed safely back at head office for subsequent retrieval.

Progress measurement

The monitoring and measurement of progress has to be carried out not only to maintain the programme, but also to enable the subcontractors to generate claims for payment. These claims will have to be certified by an independent quantity surveyor. The main contractor, in turn, will probably be billing the client for progress payments on the total project, and these claims too must be supported by certificates.

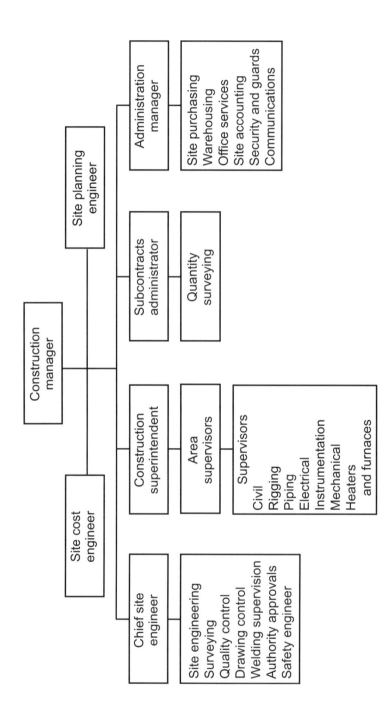

Figure 20.5   **A construction site organization**

Conduct of project meetings

Administration

The chairperson bears responsibility for the conduct and arrangement of meetings. The project manager will often be in the chair, but this is not always the case. On manufacturing projects it is possible that some progress meetings will be chaired by a production manager. Architects often chair progress meetings for construction projects.

As with any meeting, proper administrative arrangements should be made. These should ensure, for example, that:

- A meeting room has been reserved.
- Appropriate visual aids are in place and functioning.
- There is adequate ventilation.
- Visiting members are met and conducted with courtesy to the meeting room.
- Messages and incoming telephone calls are not allowed to interrupt the proceedings.
- Refreshments are provided, if appropriate.

All those invited to the meeting should be given an agenda in advance, so that they have time to prepare their arguments and produce data or exhibits.

Timing

Overnight accommodation might have to be arranged for delegates travelling long distances. Otherwise, meetings should not be timed to start too early in the day if that would cause inconvenience to visiting delegates (especially those from the client).

Some argue that meetings should be scheduled for mid- to late afternoon, so that there is an incentive to get proceedings over and done with as quickly as possible. On the other hand, people tend to be more alert early in the day, and more creative and collective brainpower is likely to be available then to deal with any knotty problems. The chairperson will have to decide which option is best for the particular occasion and the types of people expected to attend.

Resolving arguments or conflict

Arguments sometimes break out during meetings. These may not be altogether undesirable because meetings must be kept alive, with enthusiasm encouraged (always provided that any heat generated can be contained within extinguishable limits). However, arguments must be resolved within the meeting, so that agreement is reached before the members disperse. If this is not done, continuing friction can result, which is an entirely different condition from healthy enthusiasm and team cooperation.

In project work, responsibilities often fall between two or more departments, one of which can usually manage to lay blame at the other's door for any shortcomings or apparent negligence. Manufacturing problems or delays, for instance, might be blamed on poor design or on unwarranted rejections by inspectors. On some occasions these criticisms will have some foundation. At other times they will not. When such conflicts arise, they must be resolved quickly. Unprofitable stalemate conditions must not be allowed to persist and disrupt team harmony.

The chairperson has a clear duty to discover the true facts which underlie any interdepartmental problems, not so much to apportion blame, as to ensure the continued progress of the project for which he or she is responsible. Often an impasse is reached where two departmental managers give separate and conflicting accounts of the reasons for a common problem. There is only one way to overcome such arguments. The opposing individuals must be allowed to confront each other in the presence of a responsible mediator, which in this case must usually be the chairperson. Each individual should now be more reluctant to make excuses which vary from the exact truth, because he or she knows that instant denial of any unjust criticism will be forthcoming from the other department. More constructively, the person-to-person discussion removes the communication delays that can exist between impersonalized departments, often allowing solutions or compromises to common problems to be agreed on the spot.

Was the meeting successful?

When a meeting breaks up, it will have been successful only if all the members feel that they have achieved some real purpose and that actions have been agreed which will benefit the project. Demands made of members during the meeting must be achievable, so that promises extracted can be honoured.

Issuing the minutes

Publication of the minutes must be undertaken without delay, to ensure that they do not become outdated by further events before distribution. Minutes should be clearly and concisely written, combining brevity with clarity, accuracy and careful layout, so that each action demanded can be seen to stand out from the page. Documents that are too bulky may not even be read by everyone. Short, pointed statements of fact are all that is required.

No ambiguity must be allowed after any statement as to who is directly responsible for taking action. Every person listed for taking action must receive a copy of the minutes (an obvious point that is sometimes overlooked). Times must be stated definitively. Expressions such as 'at the end of next week' or 'towards the end of the month' should be avoided in favour of actual dates.

A simple meetings control form

Trevor Bentley (1976) described a simple form and set of rules which I have found effective for the management of meetings. The control form, an adaptation of Bentley's design, is shown in Figure 20.6.

The person calling the meeting (the chairperson) fills in the agenda on a form and lists all those invited to attend, after telephoning some or all of them first to agree the time and place. Copies of the form are then distributed to all the members, preferably about a week in advance.

When the meeting takes place, the chairperson's copy of the form is used to record the proceedings. The first action is to tick or encircle the names of those who actually turn up. Decisions and actions agreed during the meeting are entered on the chairperson's copy during the progress of the meeting.

Just before the meeting breaks up, the chairperson's copy of the form, now complete with all its annotations, is photocopied. Each member of the meeting is given a copy as he or she leaves. Thus instant issue of the minutes is achieved. Further, all the decisions taken and actions are recorded exactly as they were agreed during the meeting.

Bentley recommends that an additional copy of the completed control form should always to be sent to the chairperson's immediate superior. Then, when any meeting fails to result in any positive decisions or actions, the meeting chairperson would be asked to explain why the meeting had been called and what purpose it had served.

Progress meetings

Any project manager worthy of the title will want to make certain that, whenever possible, his or her tactics are preventive rather than curative. If a special meeting can be successful in resolving problems, why not pre-empt trouble by having regular progress meetings, with senior representatives of all departments present?

Regular progress meetings provide a suitable forum where essential two-way communication can take place between planners and participants. The main purposes of progress meetings emerge as a means of keeping a periodic check on the project progress, and the making of any consequential decisions to implement corrective action if programme slippages occur or appear likely.

Meeting action sheet	Meeting/project reference number
Date, time and place	
Those to attend: **Meeting called by (chairperson):**	

Purpose of meeting and agenda:

Decisions agreed:

Actions agreed:	Action by whom?	Action by when?

Figure 20.6   A combined meeting agenda and action sheet

These action sheets are great time-savers. They even allow the minutes to be issued as the meeting closes.

Source: After Trevor Bentley (1976), *Information, Communication and the Paperwork Explosion*, Maidenhead, McGraw-Hill.

Keeping to the subject

There are certain dangers associated with the mismanagement of progress meetings. For instance, it often happens that lengthy discussions arise between two specialists on technical issues that should be resolved outside the meeting. Such discussions can bore the other members of the meeting, waste their scarce and expensive time, and cause rapid loss of interest in the proceedings. Although it is never possible to divorce technical considerations from progress topics, design meetings and progress meetings are basically different functions which should be kept apart. Discussions should be kept to key progress topics, with irrelevancies swept aside.

Frequency of progress meetings

The frequency with which meetings are held must depend to a large extent on the nature of the project, the size and geographical spread of its organization, and its overall timescale.

On projects of short duration, and with much detail to be considered, there may be a good case for holding progress meetings frequently, say once a week, on an informal basis at supervisor level. For other projects, monthly meetings may be adequate. Meetings at relatively junior level can be backed up by less frequent meetings held at more senior level. Project review meetings, which can cover the financial prospects as well as simple progress, can also be arranged: the company's general manager may wish to attend such meetings, and for some capital projects the customer might also want to be represented.

Meetings held more frequently than necessary create apathy or hostility. Departmental supervisors and managers are usually busy people whose time should not be wasted.

Progress meetings abandoned

The above account of progress meetings adheres to the conventional view that progress meetings are an accepted way of project life. Here is some food for less conventional thought.

A heavy engineering company had long been accustomed to holding progress meetings. Depending on the particular project manager, these were held either at regular intervals, or randomly whenever things looked like going badly adrift (most readers will have encountered such 'firefighting' meetings). Several projects were in progress at any one time, and the permanent engineering department of about sixty people was often augmented by as many as eighty subcontracted staff working either in-house or in external offices.

Meetings typically resulted in a set of excuses from participants as to why actions requested of them at previous meetings had been carried out late, ineffectually, or not at all. Each meeting would end with a new set of promises, ready to fuel a fresh collection of excuses at the next meeting. This is not to say that the company's overall record was particularly bad, but there was considerable room for improvement, and too much time was being wasted at too many meetings.

Senior company management, recognizing the problem, supported a study which led to the introduction of critical path network planning for all projects, using a computer to schedule resources on a multi-project basis (at first confined to engineering design and drawing activities). The computer printed out detailed work-to lists. Two progress engineers were engaged: one to follow up in-house work, and the other to supervise outside subcontractors. Both engineers had the benefit of the work-to lists, which told them exactly which jobs should be in progress at any time, the scheduled start and finish dates for these jobs, how many people should be working on each of them, how many people should be working in total on each project at any time, and the amount of remaining float available for every activity.

By following up activities on a day-by-day basis in accordance with the work-to lists, these two progress engineers succeeded in achieving a considerable improvement in progress and the smooth flow of work. If a critical or near-critical activity looked like running late, stops were pulled out to bring it back into line (by working overtime during evenings and weekends if necessary). Fortunately, all the staff were cooperative, grateful (in fact) for the new sense of order created in their working lives.

After several months under this new system it dawned on all the company managers that they were no longer being asked to attend progress meetings. Except for kick-off meetings at the introduction of new projects, progress meetings had become redundant.

Project progress reports

Internal reports to company management

Progress reports addressed to company management will have to set out the technical, fulfilment and financial status of the project, and compare the company's performance in each of these respects with the scheduled requirements. For projects lasting more than a few months, such reports are usually issued at regular intervals, and they may well be presented by the project manager during the course of project review meetings.

Discussion of a report might trigger important management decisions that could lead to changes in contract policy or project organization. For these and many other reasons, it is important that data relevant to the condition and management of the project are presented factually, supported where necessary by carefully reasoned predictions or explanations.

Information in these reports may contain detailed information of a proprietary nature. They might therefore have to be treated as confidential, with their distribution restricted to a limited number of people, all within the company management.

Exception reports

There is another type of internal management report in addition to the detailed management reports just described. These are the reports of *exceptions*, and are confined in scope to those project factors that are giving rise to acute concern, and which must receive immediate attention if the project is to be held on course. If the report is to do with costs, the exceptions will probably be listed as 'variances', but variances are so-called whether they are adverse or advantageous divergences from plan.

Exception reports can be contained in documents such as adverse cost reports, materials shortage lists or computer printouts of jobs running late. At the other extreme, an exception report might be the frenzied beating on a senior manager's door by a distraught project manager who feels that his project and his world have suddenly fallen apart.

Before allowing any exception report to be passed to more senior management, the project manager must first be certain that some remedy within his or her own control cannot be found. Once it has been established that events are likely to move out of control, however, the project manager has a clear duty to apprise senior management of the facts without delay.

All of this is, of course, following the sensible practice of management by exception. This seeks to prevent senior managers being bombarded with large volumes of routine information which should be of concern only to supervisors and junior managers. The intention is to leave executive minds free to concentrate their efforts where they can be employed to the best advantage of the company.

Reports to the client or customer

The submission of formal progress reports to the client or customer could be one of the conditions of contract. If the customer does expect regular reports then, quite obviously, these can be derived from the same source which compiled all the data and explanations for the internal management reports. Some of the more detailed technical information in the internal reports may not be of interest to customers or relevant to their needs. Customer progress reports are therefore, to some extent, edited versions of internal management reports.

Whether or not financial reports of any type are to be bound in or attached to customers' progress reports will depend on the main contractor's role in each case. Under some circumstances, cost and profitability predictions must be regarded as proprietary information, not to be disclosed outside the company. In other cases, the project manager may have to submit cost summaries or more detailed breakdowns and forecasts.

Although customer reports may have to be edited in order to improve clarity and remove proprietary information, they must never be allowed intentionally to mislead. It is always important to keep the customer informed of the true progress position, especially when slippages have occurred that cannot be contained within the available float. Any attempt to put off the evil day by placating a customer with optimistic forecasts or unfounded promises must lead to unwelcome repercussions eventually. Nobody likes to discover that they have been taken for a ride, and customers are no exception to this rule.

Chapter 21

Managing costs

Cost management is not a separate function of project management. While it is true that some people specialize in the cost aspects of project management, possibly holding titles such as 'cost and planning engineer' or even the more specialized 'cost engineer', their roles are part of a far wider framework of project cost control, which must involve many people working throughout the project organization.

Cost management means far more than the control of expenditure. It also includes the control of revenue, making sure that all possible and justifiable income is recovered from the customer or other possible sources. Cost management involves ensuring not only that the amounts of money spent and received are in accordance with budgets, but also that the timing of each transaction is appropriate.

Objectives of project cost management

What are the objectives of project cost management? There are several possible answers to this question, depending upon the datum from which the cost objective is measured.

The cost control aspect

Many things can happen during the life of a project to alter the expected rate and magnitude of expenditure. The direction of change is usually upwards. Some of the reasons may be unavoidable or unforeseen but, in many cases, the fault will lie somewhere within the project organization. The principal purpose of cost control is to ensure that no preventable wastage of money or unauthorized increase in costs is allowed to happen.

A common misconception is to confuse cost *reporting* with cost *control*.

Accurate and timely cost reporting is essential but, by itself, cost reporting is *not* cost control. By the time overspending is reported, the damage has been done. Cost control must be exercised before or when the costs are being committed.

Adherence to the contractor's own cost budgets

Taking the narrowest view, the project contractor should be concerned (for many obvious reasons) that the project is completed successfully without exceeding the contractor's own planned costs (authorized budgets). In many cases, this is the only cost objective set for the project manager. Most of the conventional cost reporting and control procedures, including those described in this and the following chapter, are aimed at achieving that objective.

In some cases (internal projects, for example) budgets are the only cost consideration. There is no profit to be safeguarded, simply the need to keep spending within the amounts previously authorized by the organization's senior management.

Where there is a profit objective, it must be remembered that profits are fragile and easily destroyed by overspending. When a company is operating in a highly competitive market, margins will have to be kept low. The need to stay within budget then becomes even more critical: the company's future prosperity and existence might depend on it.

Responsibility to the project purchaser

The contractor usually has some degree of responsibility for ensuring that the project purchaser's cost objectives are also satisfied. The most obvious manifestation of this is the firm-price contract, in which the contractor's firm *price* is the customer's firm *cost*. Unless the customer rocks the boat by asking for changes, or the contractor goes bankrupt or is otherwise unable to finish the project successfully, the customer can plan capital expenditure with confidence against a fixed budget.

In cost-plus projects, where the contractor is able to mark up costs and pass them on to the client with no fixed price limit, there is less incentive for the contractor to limit costs. In fact, the converse can be true: the greater the amount spent, the greater will be the 'plus' or profit. A long-running cost-plus service contract or an ill-defined reimbursable cost project can be regarded as a gravy train. Then the contractors have an ethical, but difficult, duty to ensure that:

● only legitimate costs are claimed
● work is carried out as efficiently as if the contractors were spending their own money.

Where large capital investments are involved, the managing contractor's project manager can have a specific cost management duty to the client, which broadens the cost objective further. The project cost management function then extends to predicting and reporting costs to the client, working with the client to help schedule and control expenditure and marshal the necessary funds.

A checklist of cost management factors

1   Cost awareness by those responsible for design and engineering, preferably involving a 'total cost' approach
2   Cost awareness by all other project participants throughout the life of the project
3   A project work breakdown which yields work packages of manageable size
4   A code of accounts system which can be aligned with the work breakdown structure
5   Cost budgets, divided so that each work package is given its own share of the total budget
6   A cost accounting system that can collect and analyse costs as they are incurred, and allocate them with minimum delay to their relevant cost codes
7   A practicable work schedule
8   Effective management of well-motivated staff, to ensure that progress meets or beats the work schedule
9   A method for comparing expenditure with that planned for the work actually done
10 Effective supervision and quality control of all activities, with the aim of getting things right first time
11 Proper drafting of specifications and contracts
12 Discreet investigation to ensure that the customer is of sound financial standing, with sufficient funds available to make all contracted payments
13 Similar investigation, not necessarily so discreet, of all significant suppliers and subcontractors new to the contractor's experience
14 Effective use of competitive tendering for all purchases and subcontractors to ensure the lowest costs commensurate with quality and to avoid committing costs that would exceed budgets
15 Appropriate consideration and control of modifications and contract variations, including the passing of justifiable claims for price increases on to the customer
16 Avoidance, where possible, of unbudgeted dayworks on construction contracts
17 Where dayworks are unavoidable, proper authorization and retention of dayworks sheets
18 Strict control of payments to suppliers and subcontractors, to ensure that all invoices and claims for progress payments are neither overpaid nor paid too soon

19   Recovery from the customer of all incidental expenses allowed for in the contract charging structure (for example, telephone calls, printing, travel and accommodation)

20   Proper invoicing to the customer, especially ensuring that claims for progress payments or cost reimbursement are made at the appropriate times and at the correct levels, so that disputes do not justify the customer delaying payments

21   Effective credit control, to expedite overdue payments from the customer

22   Occasional internal security audits, to prevent losses through theft or fraud

23   Effective and regular cost/progress reports to senior management, highlighting potential schedule or budget overruns in time for corrective action to be taken.

Some of these factors were covered in earlier chapters. Others are considered in greater detail in the remainder of this chapter and in Chapter 22.

The total cost approach

The total cost approach is a way of regarding costs holistically, solving logistical problems or otherwise planning to achieve the lowest overall cost. This approach can be used in a wide variety of situations. It has been used, for example, in distribution logistics where decisions have to be made about the location of warehouses and designation of transport methods so as to achieve the lowest possible total distribution costs of retail goods.

Total costs in project management

In the context of project management, total cost considerations mean that managers in the project organization work together, each considering unselfishly how the work contribution of their department is likely to affect the costs incurred by other departments. One example is where a suggested change in design approach, although resulting in greater design difficulties and costs, might save considerable time and money in the resulting production or construction methods. The total cost approach can therefore mean increasing the planned expenditure in one department in order to generate greater cost savings in the rest of the organization.

Example

I was once privileged, in the role of planning consultant, to witness a convincing demonstration of the total cost approach in action. The scene was a project planning meeting in the engineering director's office of a company in the USA. The company was about to start three new projects, each for the design and manufacture of special-purpose heavy machining equipment for external customers. The engineering director was in the chair. Also present at the meeting were the chief engineer and other senior engineers, and (significantly) the manufacturing manager and his senior production engineers.

Various design proposals were passed back and forth between the design engineers and the production people and, one by one, design approaches were agreed that would lead to the lowest total company cost, while maintaining high quality standards. A high level of enthusiasm, motivation and cooperation was generated from the start.

The three projects, planned with multi-project resource allocation and given effective project management, were all subsequently completed on or before time, and well below their originally budgeted costs (that is, below the total cost levels previously experienced by the company for comparable projects).

Involving the customer

The true total cost approach should extend to include the costs to be incurred by the customer after the project has been handed over. These are the costs of operating and maintaining the installed equipment or plant. The customer might have to be convinced of the contractor's good intentions, because a higher initial cost might be needed as a justifiable investment in reducing the total life cost.

Example

This principle is well known to the US company mentioned above, which has widened its total cost approach to involve its customers in continuous design, quality and cost discussions.

The special-purpose machines are sold to customers for machining components in the customers' plants (typically performing all the operations needed to convert rough castings into finished components). Many of these components are complex, such as gear cases, cylinder heads or cylinder blocks for the automotive industry.

In a typical project development, the concept and design of the machines to be supplied, the design and development of the customer's components, and the planned methods for operating and maintaining the machines all form part of continuing discussion and cooperation between the supplier's engineers and the customer's engineers.

This process is variously called *integrated engineering*, *simultaneous engineering* or (most commonly) *concurrent engineering*. It strives to achieve the customer's performance and quality requirements at lowest total cost, resulting in a deal that benefits both companies.

Budgets

Plainly, the initial project budgets should be derived from the cost estimates used when the tender or internal project proposal was prepared. If the target profits are to be achieved, the final version of these cost estimates must become the authorized levels of expenditure. The project work breakdown structure should then allow these estimates to be allocated as budgets for all the departments engaged on the project.

Budget timing

It is not only the top budget limits that are important, but also the rate at which expenditure is scheduled to take place. When plotted as a graph against time, the typical cumulative project expenditure describes an *S* curve (see Figure 19.4, for example).

Budget breakdown

The total budget should spread over the project work breakdown structure so that there is a specified budget for each work package.

The relationship between the work breakdown structure and the project cost coding system is very important. For true measurement and control, each budget element must correspond to an identifiable and measurable work package, and each budget element and its associated work package must share a common, unique cost code. This subject was dealt with in detail in Chapter 4.

Labour budgets

Use of man-hours

It is often said, with good reason, that managers and supervisors should be given their work budgets in terms of man-hours rather than as the resulting costs of wages and overheads. The argument is that a manager should never be held accountable for meeting targets where he or she has no authority to control the causal factors. Project managers are rarely responsible for wage and salary levels, increases in wages and salaries, and company overhead expenses. They are, however, responsible for progress and (through supervision) the time taken to complete each work package.

In these chapters it is therefore assumed that each manager with budget responsibility will be given, and will be expected to observe, the man-hour budget for every work package under his or her control.

Relationship between cost budgets and activities in the project network diagram

If resource scheduling is in use, then each work package from the work breakdown structure should be represented by an activity or group of activities on the project network diagram.

This means that, for every work package, there are two different sources for the estimated costs:

1 the cost estimates used for the work package in the final version of the project proposal document
2 the costs implied by the duration and resource quantities estimated for the relevant activities in the project network diagram.

Provided the customary rate-constant approach is used when specifying activity resources, the man-hour content estimated for each network activity will be the estimated duration of the activity expressed in hours multiplied by the number of resources specified.

For example, suppose that a company works 7 hours per day, and that an activity has an estimated duration of 15 days, with two designers specified as the resources required. This implies an estimated man-hour content for that activity of 7 x 15 x 2, which is 210 hours. If all the activities relative to a particular work package can be identified, it should then be possible to compare the network derived estimates with those in the budget (from the project proposal estimates).

Time does not always allow such comparisons but, when it does, it is unlikely that both estimates will agree exactly. However, there should be no serious discrepancy in the broad totals. If the network estimates appear to exceed the budget estimate, then prompt investigation is necessary to find the reason. At least the warning of excess expenditure will be early.

Budgets for purchases and subcontracts

Budgets for purchases and for subcontracts have to be expressed in the appropriate project currency. Relevant packaging, transport, insurance, duties and tax must be included.

Timing

Figure 17.2 showed that the *S* curve for purchasing and subcontracts can be drawn in different versions, displaced in time depending on which dates the budgeted expenditure is timed. The three options are as follows:

1 the dates when orders are placed (the committed costs) – this is the earliest possible time for monitoring the costs of materials, and the most useful for assessing performance against budget

2   the dates when invoices from the suppliers of goods and services are due to be
     paid (the actual costs)

3   particularly for manufacturing projects, job costing that depends on the
     evaluation of stores requisitions (when the materials are withdrawn from
     stores for use on the project) – that can often be long after the suppliers'
     invoices have been paid.

The costs of purchases are determined during the processes of purchase
specification, purchase enquiry and, especially, during the negotiation and issue of
purchase orders. Once the orders have been issued, the costs are committed. For
that reason, purchasing cost control is dependent upon the procedures described in
Chapters 16, 17 and 18.

Currency units

The currency units used are obviously important. For projects conducted entirely
within the borders of one country, there should be no problem, and the national
currency is the natural choice for all budgeting and reporting purposes. If the
project is to use imported services or materials, the logical method for expressing
both the budget and the expenditure is to convert all sums into the 'home'
currency, being careful to state the exchange rate used in each case.

When a project involves working for a foreign client, the contractor may be
obliged by the terms of the contract or the agreed project procedures to prepare
budgets and report all expenditure in the currency of the client's country, or in
some other international currency (such as US dollars). The currency chosen may
then have to become the control currency for the project. Again, it is essential that
the exchange rates used are shown.

Budget changes

Budgets on most projects are not static. They increase each time a contract
variation order results in an agreed increase in the project price. At any time it
should be possible for the budget to be stated in terms of its initial amount,
additions subsequently approved by the client and, therefore, the total current
budget. If possible, these changes to the budgets should be made at work package
level so that all parts of the budget remain up to date and valid.

Taking authorized budget changes into account, as time proceeds the typical
project budget graph should resemble an *S* curve on to which a stepped rise has
been grafted for every significant addition to the budget.

Adjustments for below-the-line allowances

If the project spreads over more than a few months, cost escalation and (for international projects) foreign exchange rate fluctuations will probably have to be taken into account. Any relevant below-the-line provisions for such changes made in the original project estimate, provided they have been built into the pricing or charging structure, can be regarded as 'reserve budgets'. Appropriate sums can be 'drawn down' from these reserves from time to time as necessary to augment the active control budget.

Cost-collection methods

It can be assumed that every established company will have procedures in place for collecting, analysing and recording project costs. It is vital that this analysis and reporting, of both incurred and committed costs, is carried out promptly. If the figures are a month or more old when they reach the project manager, what chance does he or she have of taking action in time to reverse any bad trend?

Most of the procedures for collecting costs and allocating them to the project cost codes are the responsibility of the company's cost accountant. Provided that the accounts department does its job properly, it is the reported figures rather than the day-to-day operation of the cost accounting procedures that usually concerns the project manager. There are, however, one or two areas where the project manager and others outside the accounts department have specific responsibilities for ensuring that cost collection is as accurate and timely as possible. The remainder of this section describes some of these areas.

Labour costs

General time sheets

A common method for recording and collecting the time spent on projects by professional and other direct office staff on projects is to ask each individual to complete timesheets at regular intervals. Timesheets are usually compiled weekly and require each person to enter the time spent against each relevant cost code or job number, probably expressed to the nearest half-hour. An example of a weekly timesheet is shown in Figure 21.1.

An important part of the procedure is that the person's supervisor should check and verify the entries before adding an approval signature.

Whatever the method used for collecting labour costs, the time records should be as accurate as possible. If the project is organized as a team, so that everyone works on the project all the time, the only errors to be expected would be in allocations to subcodes within the project. If, however, the organization is a

Timesheet

Name: _____

Department: _____

Staff or clock number: _____

For week ending: _____

For accounts department use only

Job number	Saturday	Sunday	Monday		Tuesday		Wednesday		Thursday		Friday	
			Normal	Overtime	Normal	Overtime	Normal	Overtime	Normal	Overtime	Normal	Overtime

Notes: Fill in times to the nearest half hour. For holidays use job number 0099, sickness 0098; authorized special leave 0097; waiting or idle time 0096

Signature: _____

Approved by: _____

Figure 21.1   A weekly timesheet

matrix, people might be working on more that one project during a week, or even on the same day, and the apportionment of time between projects becomes more subjective and open to error or abuse.

Staff often have times when they work less efficiently or actually waste time, and there is always a risk that such time will be booked wrongly to the most convenient number available. People should be encouraged to fill in the entries on their timesheets every day. If this chore is left until collection of timesheets at the end of the week, mistakes will inevitably be made as individuals strive in vain to remember what they were doing earlier in the week.

Timesheet errors on firm-price contracts can throw up false profit and loss assessments and reduce the value of historical cost records for future analysis and comparative cost estimating.

In cost-plus contracts, timesheet mistakes will result in billing errors to the customer, which could be at best unethical and, at worst, fraudulent.

Timesheets should therefore only be signed as approved by those nominated as being authorized to do so. It may be necessary introduce a higher-level check by arranging for a suitable independent person to carry out an occasional timesheet audit. In cost-plus contracts, the customers will probably *insist* on some such safeguard.

Timesheets for agency staff

Staff supplied by external agencies to work in the contractor's offices will be provided with their own agency timesheets, which the project contractor is expected to sign to show that the company agrees with the hours for which the temporary employee will be paid by the agency, and which will eventually appear on the agencies' invoices. These timesheets are rarely suitable as project cost records, and it will probably be necessary to ask the agency staff also to fill in the contractor's own timesheets (which can be colour-coded if required to distinguish them from the timesheets used by permanent staff).

The time spent by agency staff working in agency offices will usually be charged weekly, supported by detailed timesheets from the agency. The contractor may wish to specify and supply the timesheets that are to be used. Checking and correct authorization are obviously important, and the contractor may decide to arrange random, unannounced inspection visits to the external office as a precaution against fraud.

Direct input of timesheet data to the computer

Some of the more powerful project management software systems, when networked, allow staff to key in their timesheet data directly. This procedure can save considerable time, but the following must be borne in mind:

● Checking, auditing and approval are more difficult to arrange, and errors can be expected.

- The system will not work unless everyone is clear about the cost codes to be used, and how these compare with the task information on file.
- There will be additional system costs, which can be considerable, and might be a multiple of the number of staff who will enter data.

Although project management packages with timesheet facilities are valuable for recording costs on projects, their use can give rise to management accounting difficulties, because in management accounting all times have to be collected, including hours spent on non-productive work. An alternative arrangement is not to use the project management package, but to ask staff to key their times into the company's management information system instead.

Casual work from subcontractors

A common method for dealing with miscellaneous work carried out by subcontractors depends on the use of dayworks sheets.

Some such subcontractors submit their bills infrequently, or only after very long delays. It can prove very difficult trying to reconcile invoices received six months or even longer after the work has been done, especially since dayworks sheets tend to be scrappy tear-offs from duplicate pads. Even longer delays between the work dates and receipt of final invoices have been known.

One instance I remember concerned a project for various external and internal improvements to an office building in central London. In addition to the work specified in the original fixed-price contract, there were numerous incidental costs, such as miscellaneous plant rentals, the provision of rubbish skips, rental charges for a site hut, sundry materials, and many other small additional tasks carried out at the request of the office occupier. All of these extra costs were recorded as they were incurred on hundred of dayworks sheets, each signed by the office manager. The total project costs exceeded £100 000, much of which was attributable to the dayworks. The project lasted many months and the construction company, well known in the City of London, submitted its invoice as almost a year late. There was no dishonesty, but the lapse of time made the invoice extremely difficult to check and approve. The services of an independent quantity surveyor were required, at extra cost, before the invoice could be reconciled and passed for payment.

It is important that any company employing contractors or subcontractors checks, approves and retains copies of all dayworks sheets until the relevant invoices have been received and cleared for payment.

Purchases and subcontracts

It can be assumed that the organization's purchasing, accounting and stores procedures will ensure that the costs of materials and bought-out equipment are always collected and recorded. The routine cost accounting systems would normally cover costs associated with the payment of invoices, and the later job costs when materials are issued from stores for manufacturing jobs.

However, whenever the project is of the kind where equipment, materials or subcontracts are ordered specifically for use on the project, the project manager should be concerned particularly to see that a system is in place for recording and tabulating the values of purchase orders as they are placed. This information, at the time of commitment, will give the earliest possible indication of cost trends against the budget (see Figure 17.2). It is unlikely that the purchasing organization or the company's cost accounting procedures will be set up to record committed costs in this way, and the project organization might need to establish its own procedure for this purpose.

Incidental expenses

Some contracts allow the contractor to claim reimbursement of sundry expenses such as telephone calls, printing, photocopying and some clerical tasks. This is often the case with companies in the mining and petrochemical industries, and for some professional organizations such as architects and legal partnerships.

Such costs can prove very difficult to collect. In organizations carrying out several projects simultaneously it can be awkward to isolate the costs associated with one client or one project. However, the effort should be made if possible.

Although it is unlikely that the sums involved will be large compared with mainstream project activities, they are usually significant and worth recovering. In particular, every expense which can be charged directly against a project should be so charged. Otherwise these expenses will simply inflate the general overhead costs, which must always be kept as low as possible if the contractor is to remain competitive in the market. Suggested collection methods include:

- the use of a simple requisition system for all bulk photocopying and other reprographics services, with mandatory use of client or cost codes

- mandatory use of cost codes on petty cash vouchers and all expense claims forms

- the installation and proper day-to-day management of an automatic call logging system covering all telephone, and facsimile lines. In one case in my experience, this measure reduced a company's total annual communications bill from £100 000 to £50 000 by preventing fraudulent use, and £25 000 of the remaining £50 000 was recovered from clients. So, £75 000 was removed from the company's overhead. That was many years ago, and these figures could be multiplied by ten for a comparable case today.

Audits

The need for timesheet entries to be checked and approved by managers and supervisors has already been mentioned. This is, in effect, a form of auditing. It helps to protect the client of a cost-plus project from being overcharged. Incidentally, it also helps to ensure that archived records of fixed-price projects will be relatively free from errors, and therefore of more use when making comparative estimates for future projects.

Any company must always be aware of the possible risks when any manager or other member of staff has authority to commit expenditure or authorize payments on its behalf. Even where complete trust exists between senior managers and their subordinates, the procedures should be audited and, where necessary, amended to reduce the possibility of fraud.

A company should set financial limits above which any manager must seek superior approval before authorizing any particular item of expenditure (for example, a purchase requisition). Payment of the resulting suppliers' invoices should be authorized by a responsible person other than the signatory for the purchase orders, providing an independent check and reducing any temptation for a buyer to order goods or services for their own use.

Rules should be laid down as to the levels of hospitality or gifts that those with purchasing authority may accept from suppliers and subcontractors. These should be drafted carefully so that they do not destroy normal goodwill and accepted moderate practices, but instead deter managers from receiving pecuniary benefits that might tend to corrupt, distort judgement, or generate feelings of obligation to one source of supply.

Petty cash vouchers are open to misuse. I remember a case where a (previously) respected member of the purchasing department regularly made small purchases of sundry stationery items, claiming reimbursement against petty cash vouchers. All would have been well if she had not made a common practice of adding considerable amounts to each voucher after its approval by an authorized signatory. Thousands of pounds could have been saved if a procedures audit had been carried out.

Comparing actual costs with planned costs

This chapter has described some of the measures needed to establish a project budgeting and cost recording system, as a preliminary step towards implementing effective cost management.

The next step is to decide how to make use of cost measurements, and how to analyse and compare these with the work schedules and budgets in order to effect cost control. This will be discussed in the next chapter.

Chapter 22

Earned-value analysis

The previous chapter outlined principles and practices for the establishment of project budgets and the collection of cost data. This chapter continues the subject of cost management by describing techniques that can evaluate performance against budgets, analyse trends and attempt a prediction of the total final project costs. The tools described are important ingredients of an effective system for cost control because they can provide management information in time for corrective action to be taken.

Milestone analysis

Milestone analysis is one of the simpler methods which managers can use throughout the project life cycle to compare the actual costs and progress experienced with the costs and progress planned. The method is less effective and less detailed than others described later in this chapter, but it has the merit of needing a relatively modest amount of management effort to set up and maintain. It also requires less sophisticated cost accounting than other methods, and can be used when project schedules are not particularly detailed.

Perhaps the best way to demonstrate the benefits of milestone analysis would be to consider what happens when actual costs are compared against budgets with no milestones or other corresponding information about progress.

Cost monitoring without milestones

Figure 22.1 shows the kinds of curves that might result if total project costs are recorded regularly and plotted on a graph against time and the budget.

The practice depends on first plotting a graph of expected costs against time. Such graphs are sometimes known as *time-scaled budgets*. The time-scaled budget in Figure 22.1 is represented by the dotted curve. This curve was plotted by

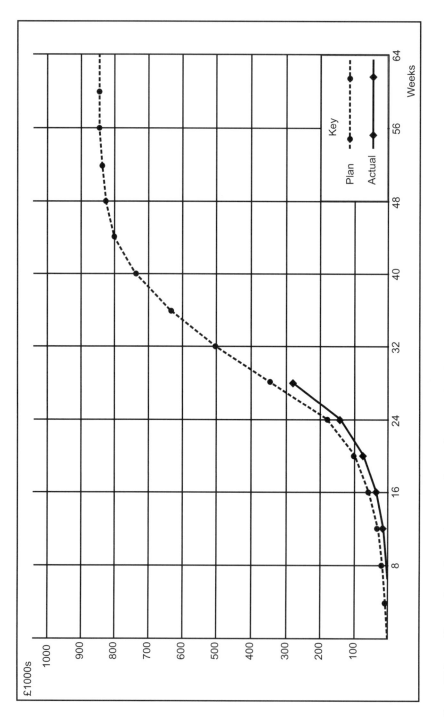

Figure 22.1   Comparison of actual costs against a time-scaled budget
Comparisons such as this mean little unless the corresponding achievement is measured.

combining information from the cost estimates and the project plan, so that the estimated costs for all work packages are included in the curve at their scheduled times. The project manager should, therefore, be able to consult the graph at any time during the execution of the project to find the amount of total project costs that should have been reached if all is going to plan.

In the absence of a suitable work breakdown with budgets it would not, of course, be possible to draw a time-scaled budget curve. In that case, the best that could be done would be to draw the budget as a straight line joining two points, starting from zero cost at the graph's origin and reaching the total estimated cost at the planned completion date. That approach can be dismissed as being of no use whatever.

The actual cumulative project costs can be plotted at suitable intervals on the same axes as the time-scaled budget. If the costing system is at all reasonable, it will be possible to plot these costs fairly accurately. This has been done in Figure 22.1, where it can be seen that actual costs have been recorded up to the end of week 28.

Interpreting the result

Graphs that attempt to compare actual costs with the time-scaled budget, even when they are plotted with great care, are of very limited management use as they stand. The missing piece of information in Figure 22.1 is the corresponding progress or achievement.

At one extreme, if no money is being spent at all, then it is a fair assumption that no progress is being made either. It is also true and easily understood that a significantly low rate of expenditure usually indicates an inadequate rate of progress and achievement. Unfortunately, some managers then proceed to make the less acceptable assumption that if expenditure is being incurred at the planned rate, then progress and achievement must also be either on plan or 'about right'. This is a very rough and ready guide that can lead to dangerously wrong conclusions.

Suppose that the project illustrated in Figure 22.1 has been running for 32 weeks, when the planned expenditure should then be £500 000. There are people who would be well satisfied on being told that the reported expenditure is at or just below £500 000. But those people fail to ask all the vital questions which should be considered by any project manager, namely:

1 How much have we spent to date?
2 What should we have spent to date?
3 What have we achieved so far?
4 What should we have achieved by this time?
5 What are the final cost and delivery prospects for the project if our performance continues at the current level?

Milestone monitoring can help to answer some of these questions.

Explanation of the milestone method

Identifying milestones

The first requirement in milestone analysis is to understand what is meant by a milestone. A milestone denotes a particular, easily identifiable stage in the progress of a project towards completion. It might be acceptance by the customer of a final design concept or layout drawing, the issue of a package of drawings for work to begin, the day when a building is made watertight so that internal trades can start, the date when electrical power is first switched on to a new installation, or any other such occasion.

When arrow networks were in common use, it was usual to designate network event circles as milestones. Remember that an event in an arrow network represents the instant in time when all preceding activities can be declared finished. Now all computer-processed networks must be drawn in precedence notation and there are no events as such in the networks – only activities. The software overcomes this difficulty by allowing the user to designate appropriate activities as milestones. Each milestone is then achieved when the relevant milestone activity is finished. This becomes a little complicated when a true project milestone depends on completion of more than one parallel activity. Precedence notation, however, is very adaptable, and it is easy to solve this problem by creating milestone events artificially. All that is necessary is to insert milestone activities with zero or unit duration at the appropriate network intersections. This is rather similar to the creation of artificial dummies, demonstrated in Figure 8.18.

Milestone analysis therefore starts by choosing and naming the achievements that can most effectively be used as project milestones. Ideally, milestones should coincide with the completion of packages from the work breakdown structure. That approach will be assumed in the remainder of this discussion.

Plotting the budget/milestone plan

For each milestone, two pieces of data are required. These are:

1   the date on which the milestone is scheduled to be achieved
2   the estimated cost or budget for the associated work package (that is, the expected cost of all the work needed to achieve the milestone).

When all milestone data are available, the milestone/budget curve can be plotted. This process starts by sketching the time-scaled budget curve. The position of each point is determined by matching the cumulative cost estimates for the project work packages against the planned achievement dates for those work packages. It might be necessary to use all the constituent tasks, rather than complete work packages, to produce sufficient points on the graph. Care must be taken to ensure that no estimated costs are left out, so that the budget curve will reach the cost estimated for the project. So far this is similar to the process used to produce the time-scaled budget curve in Figure 22.1.

To complete the budget/milestone graph, symbols must be added to the budget curve to represent all the milestones. Each milestone must be positioned on the budget curve at the date scheduled for its completion.

Plotting the graph of actual expenditure and milestone achievement

To be able to plot the graph of actual expenditure for comparison against the plan, two further items of information must be collected:

1   the date on which each milestone was actually achieved
2   the project costs actually incurred (including committed costs of purchased items) at the end of each cost monitoring period.

It must therefore be assumed that a procedure exists for recording the total costs actually incurred and committed for the project at suitable intervals. These intervals might be weekly or monthly, and will depend to some extent on the life cycle time for the project.

The actual costs can be plotted as a graph on the same axes as the time-scaled budget. Points on the graph should be highlighted by symbols that indicate the actual completion date for each milestone. To allow sensible comparison of the planned and actual graphs, it helps enormously if all the milestones can be given simple numbers. If the milestones marked on the budget curve are, for example, numbered 1, 2, 3, 4 and so on, the corresponding points on the actual cost graph can carry the same numbers to make comparison easy.

A milestone analysis example

A construction project lasting just over one year is the basis for this example, and Figure 22.2 displays the relevant graphs.

The dotted curve in Figure 22.2 shows the time-scaled budget for the project, drawn by combining data from the project schedule and the authorized cost estimates. Thirteen milestones have been identified for the project, and the schedule and cost data for these are tabulated in Figure 22.3.

Each milestone has been indicated on the planned curve by placing a circle at the time when it should be achieved. The numbers within the circles identify the particular milestones.

Monitoring method

Actual cost and progress data have been gathered up to the end of week 30 for this project, and these are included in the tabulated data shown in Figure 22.3. The results have been plotted, at two-weekly intervals, as the solid line curve in Figure

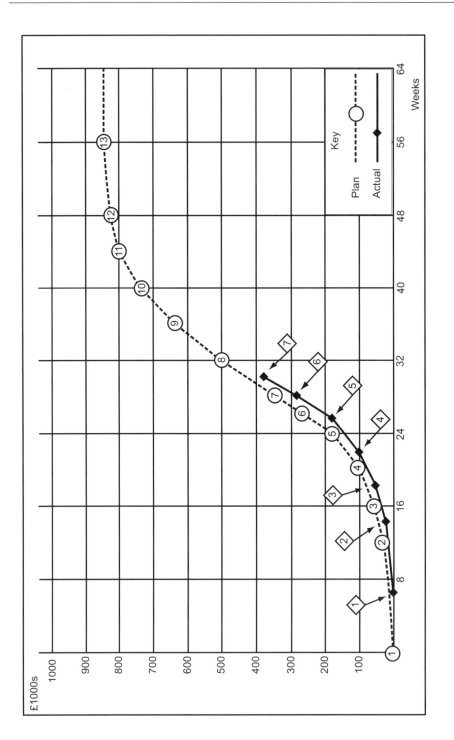

Figure 22.2   Project cost and achievement comparison using milestones

Milestone description	Schedule (week number)		Cumulative cost £1000s	
	Plan	Actual	Budget	Actual
1 Project start authorized	0	6	0	0
2 Design approved	12	14	25	20
3 Drawings issued for building	16	18	60	55
4 Foundations completed	20	22	100	100
5 Drawings issued for services	24	26	180	180
6 All equipment for services ordered	26	28	275	290
7 Walls built to eaves	28	30	345	385
8 Windows and doors finished	32		500	
9 Roof on, building watertight	36		630	
10 Wiring and plumbing finished	40		730	
11 Services installed and tested	44		795	
12 Internal finishes completed	48		825	
13 Site and building handover	56		845	

Figure 22.3   Data for a milestone chart
These data were used to compile the chart shown in Figure 22.2.

22.2. Any milestone passed during each two-weekly period has been indicated on the actual cost curve by means of a diamond containing the milestone's identification number.

Interpreting the results

Of course, if all is going exactly according to plan, the budget and actual graphs should lie together on the same path and the milestone points should coincide. When they do not, investigation should give some indication of the project cost and achievement performance to date.

Imagine that you are the general manager of the construction company responsible for this project and that it has been running for just over eight weeks. If you look at week 8 on Figure 22.2 you will see that milestone 1, project start, has been achieved six weeks late, as indicated by the position of the diamond compared with the circle. The very low costs recorded at week 8 indicate that little or no activity is taking place. So, you can easily see that the project has started late, and that more effort is urgently needed if progress is to catch up with the plan.

When you receive your updated milestone chart at the end of week 14, it tells you that milestone 2 has been reached. It should have happened at week 12, but the project has now been pulled up from being 6 weeks late to only 2 weeks late. Costs recorded up to week 14 are £20 000. These costs compare with a budget of £25 000 for achieving milestone 2. Expenditure at week 14 should have reached about £45 000 (the dotted curve). So you conclude that the project is still running slightly late, but that the rate of expenditure is lower than plan, so extra effort is needed. You are, however, getting value for the money spent because milestone 2 was achieved for £5000 less than its estimated cost.

If you continue to observe the chart at consecutive two-weekly intervals, you can see how it depicts the changing trend. In particular, the cost performance gradually deteriorates. One significant report from the project manager is the milestone chart updated to the end of week 28. The graphs indicate that milestone 6 should have been achieved at week 26 for a project cost of £275 000. However, you can see from the graphs that milestone 6 has only just been reached at week 28 at a cost of £290 000. So the project is not only still running 2 weeks late but is also £15 000 over budget.

By week 30, it is apparent that the project programme, as indicated by milestone 7, continues to run 2 weeks late, and the costs at £385 000 have risen to £40 000 over the corresponding budget for milestone 7.

Without the milestones as measuring points, none of this analysis would have been possible.

Need for replotting

If a change in project scope or any other reason causes rescheduling of work or costs, then the data for future milestones will obviously change too. The curve of predicted expenditure and milestones will have to be amended at each significant authorized change so that it remains up to date and a true basis for comparison of actual costs against plan.

Disadvantages of the milestone method

The milestone method suffers from a few disadvantages. These include the following:

1   The information that can be extracted for management use in controlling the project is often obtained after the damage has been done, and certainly much later than the predictions possible with more detailed earned-value analysis (described below).
2   If programme slippages are going to occur very often, the curves may have to be redrawn frequently, unless a computer can be used or some very flexible charting method is devised.
3   The method takes only an approximate account of work in progress (work packages which have been started, but where the milestones have yet to be achieved).
4   The method only shows coarse trends rather than the more detailed measurements obtainable with earned-value analysis.
5   It is not easy to use the results of milestone analysis to predict the probable final outcome for the project.

However, the method involves comparatively little effort, is a considerable improvement on simple cost versus budget comparison, and may therefore commend itself to the busy project manager.

Earned-value analysis

Earned-value analysis can be regarded as the missing link between cost reporting and cost control. It depends on the existence of a sound framework of planning and control, including the following:

- a detailed work breakdown structure
- a correspondingly detailed cost-coding system
- timely and accurate collection and reporting of cost data
- a method for monitoring and quantifying the amount of work done, including work in progress.

The earned-value process aims to compare the costs incurred for an accurately identified amount of work with the costs budgeted for that same work. It can be applied at the level of individual tasks or complete work packages, and the data are usually rolled up for the whole project. The procedure uses the results to produce a cost performance index. If everything is going exactly according to plan, the cost performance index will be 1.0. An index less than 1.0 indicates that the value earned for the money being spent is less than that expected.

Importance of work breakdown structure

The first stage in establishing an effective procedure for assessing achievement is to decide which work elements are to be subjected to measurement, analysis and reporting. In fact, this choice should be clear; the work packages from the project work breakdown, together with their cost estimates or budgets, must provide the framework. It is important to carry this breakdown through to the level of activities performed by individual departments or work groups, so that each responsible manager or supervisor can be given quantified objectives that can be monitored by the earned-value process.

Earned-value nomenclature and definitions

The following are a few of the names and abbreviations used in earned-value analysis. The list is not complete, but includes the most commonly used terms.

Abbreviation	*What it means*
ACWP	Actual Cost of the Work Performed at the measurement date.
BCWP	Budgeted Cost of Work Performed – This is the amount of money or labour time that the amount of work actually performed at the measurement date should have cost to be in line with the budget or cost estimate. It is usually necessary to take into account work that is in progress in addition to tasks actually completed.
BCWS	Budgeted Cost of Work Scheduled – This is the budget or cost estimate for work scheduled to be complete at the measurement date. It corresponds with the time-scaled budget.
CPI	Cost Performance Index – This factor indicates the measure of success in achieving results against budget. Anything less than unity indicates that the value earned from money spent is less than that intended.
SPI	Schedule Performance Index – This can be used as a measure of progress performance against plan, but is less commonly used than the CPI. Anything less than unity shows progress slower than that planned.

These quantities can be used in the following expressions:

$$CPI = \frac{BCWP}{ACWP}$$

$$SPI = \frac{BCWP}{BCWS}$$

Brick wall project: A simple example of earned-value analysis

For this example of earned-value analysis I have chosen a project comprising one main activity for which progress can be measured quantitatively without difficulty or ambiguity.

Imagine a bricklayer and a labourer engaged in building a new boundary wall enclosing a small country estate. If the amount of progress made had to be assessed at any time, work achieved could be measured in terms of the area of wall built or, more simply here, by the length of wall finished.

The scope, budget and schedule for this project have been defined by the following data:

- Total length of wall to be built = 1000 metres
- Estimated total project cost = £40 000
- Planned duration for the project = 10 weeks (with 5 working days in each week = 50 days)
- The rate of progress is expected to be uniform and linear.

When the above data are considered, the following additional facts emerge:

- Budget cost per day = £800.
- Planned rate of building = 20m of wall per day.
- Budget cost for each metre of wall finished = £40.

At the end of day 20 the project manager has been asked to carry out an earned-value analysis. The actual and planned data for the end of day 20 are as follows:

- Work performed: 360 metres of wall have been completed.
- ACWP (Actual Cost of Work Performed): £18 000. This is the total project cost at the end of day 20.
- BCWS (Budget Cost of Work Scheduled): 20 days at £800 per day = £16 000.
- BCWP (Budget Cost of Work Performed): 360 metres of wall should have cost £40 per metre, or £14 400.

Cost implications

The cost implications of these data can be analysed using earned-value analysis as follows:

$$\text{The Cost Performance Index (CPI)} = \frac{\text{BCWP}}{\text{ACWP}} = \frac{14\ 400}{18\ 000} = 0.8$$

The implication of this for final project cost can be viewed in at least two ways:

1 We could divide the original estimate of £40 000 by the cost performance index and say that the predicted total project cost has risen to £50 000, which gives a forecast cost variance of £10 000 for the project at completion.

2 Alternatively, we can say that £18 000 has been spent to date and then work out the likely remaining cost. The 360 metres of wall built so far have actually cost £18 000, which is a rate of £50 per metre. The amount of work remaining is 640 metres of wall and, if this should also cost £50 per metre, that will mean a further £32 000 predicted cost remaining to completion. So, adding costs measured to date and remaining costs predicted to completion again gives an estimated total cost at project completion of £50 000.

Schedule implications

Earned-value data can be used to predict the likely completion date for an activity or a project, although a straightforward comparison of progress against the plan is probably an easier and more effective method. If the earned-value method is used, the first step is to calculate the Schedule Performance Index. For the wall project at day 20, the SPI is found by:

$$SPI = \frac{BCWP}{BCWS} = \frac{14\ 400}{16\ 000} = 0.9$$

The original estimate for the duration of this project was 50 working days. Dividing by the SPI gives a revised total project duration of about 56 days.

Methods for assessing progress

Most earned-value analysis must be performed not just on one activity, as in the brick wall project just described, but on many project activities. At any given measurement time in a large project, three stages of progress can apply to all the activities:

1   Activity not started – earned value is therefore zero.

2   Activity completed – earned value is therefore equal to the activity's cost budget.

3   Activity in progress or interrupted. For construction projects, as in the case of the brick wall project, earned value for work in progress can often be assessed by measuring actual quantities of work done. For other less tangible tasks, it is necessary to estimate the proportion or percentage of work done, and then take the same proportion of the current authorized cost estimate as the actual value of work performed.

Earned-value assessment for an engineering design department

When reviewing the progress of all engineering design activities in a project, one approach is to determine how many drawings and specifications are to be produced, and then divide this number by the number of drawings actually issued, multiply the answer by 100 and declare this as the percentage of design completed. Although some companies do use this method, it is really too crude because it fails to take into account all the conceptual design work needed, and assumes that the work involved in producing one drawing is equivalent to the amount of work needed to produce any other drawing. However, the method can be used in limited cases, such as for a department which is producing a large number of similar drawings, like electrical wiring or piping diagrams.

In most design jobs the only way to assess progress is to ask the engineer, or the engineer's superior, for an estimate: 'What percentage of this task do you consider has been achieved?', or, perhaps more provocatively, 'How much longer is this job going to take?' This process must be carried through all activities in the project.

In the case of the bricklayers in the wall project, the answers obtained were objective, accurate and proof against fear of contradiction. Many other jobs on a project, especially the software activities, are far less straightforward and much more difficult to assess quantitatively in terms of progress achieved. The engineer may be guilty of unwarranted optimism or poor judgement when giving a progress report. This is the penalty that must be paid when changing from an objective to subjective assessment of progress. Nevertheless, there is no need to abandon the quest. At least an answer of sorts can be extracted and, although by no means perfect, surely this is better than having no answer at all?

Work-in-progress assessments will inevitably be less accurate than the data for completed activities. However, because work in progress should account for only a small proportion of the total work, assessment errors should be diluted by the larger, more reliable, estimates for jobs that are definitely finished. This will, of course, be less true for short-term projects, or at the start of any project, where the proportion of work in progress to completed work may be higher. If the individual activities are large, owing to insufficient work breakdown, then again the work in progress could rank high because it will take correspondingly longer to cross off the completed activities.

Example

An earned-value calculation in an engineering design department is demonstrated in Figure 22.4 using a manual method. In this example, an engineering project is well under way. The total department estimate (the total potential earned value) is seen to be 2975 man-hours.

An analysis of the work completed or in progress reveals that the BCWP (budget cost of work performed) is 1389 man-hours. This is the project earned value at the measurement date.

Against this achievement, the ACWP (actual cost of work performed) is seen to be 1142 man-hours. This figure represents all the hours actually booked to these jobs on timesheets. Although 46.7 per cent of the work has been done, only 38.4 per cent of the budget has been spent. This is a good result, and indicates that work generally is costing less than the budget.

Dividing the BCWP by the ACWP for this project gives a cost performance index or CPI of 1.22. If things are allowed to go on in the same way, the project budget of 2975 hours is likely to be underspent. Dividing by the CPI predicts a

Earned-value analysis

Department: Engineering   Date: May 2002

Project: Sensor and servo control unit   Sheet: 1   of: 1

Activity	Budget man-hours	Per cent achieved	Earned value BCWP	Actual cost ACWP
0001 System design	350	100	350	255
0002 Write system specification	35	100	35	35
0003 Design +25v power supply	105	100	105	140
0004 Breadboard stage	70	100	70	35
0005 Package	70	100	70	40
0006 Prove prototype	35			
0007 Write test specification	35			
0008 Design +10v power supply	105	100	105	65
0009 Breadboard stage	70	100	70	50
0010 Package	70	50	35	25
0011 Prove prototype	35			
0012 Write test specification	35			
0013 Design -15v power supply	105			
0014 Breadboard stage	70			
0015 Package	70			
0016 Prove prototype	35			
0017 Write test specification	35			
0018 Design sensor circuit	350	100	350	288
0019 Breadboard stage	105	100	105	124
0020 Package	105	40	42	50
0021 Prove prototype	70			
0022 Write test specification	35			
0023 Design servo and controls	175	20	35	15
0024 Breadboard stage	140			
0025 Package	70			
0026 Prove prototype	105			
0027 Write test specification	35			
0028 Design main frame	70	25	17	20
0029 System testing	70			
0030 Environmental tests	70			
0031 Write production test spec.	140			
0032 Write operating manual	105			
Departmental totals	2975	46.7	1389	1142

Figure 22.4   Earned-value analysis for an engineering department
Budgets, progress and actual costs can be compared on a sheet such as this as a preliminary step in predicting the final project expenditure.

final engineering design department expenditure of only 2438 man-hours. The accountants would call this a positive variance of 537 man-hours.

Earned-value analysis for manufacturing

Production departments, at first sight, might seem to be a very different proposition from the engineering design department just considered, being concerned with hardware rather than software and far removed from the abstract world of design and development. Fortunately, however, there is no practical reason preventing use of similar methods to cover all production activities. In fact, the process is made easier, since one is dealing not with theories and subjective assessments, but with the tangible fruits of productive labour.

Choice of manufacturing cost centres for analysis

Production activities often employ a wide range of different labour grades drawn from several departments. Which of these should be subjected to achievement analysis must depend to some extent on the degree of control considered necessary.

It is probably unwise to attempt a detailed analysis for every conceivable cost centre. Over-ambition in this direction, leading to a multiplicity of facts, figures and prediction curves, could involve so much effort for so little return that disillusionment with the whole process of earned-value measurement would soon set in.

Probably the best course is to analyse the performance of departments, rather than individual labour grades or machines and other facilities. In this way, each departmental manager can be provided with a feedback of departmental performance against budgets. Each chosen cost centre must be analysed regularly and given its separate place in the achievement measurements, so that effective cost versus budget comparisons can be made.

Cost accounting

Steps must be taken to ensure that the collection of cost data from production aligns with the project work breakdown. This is achieved using a structured cost-coding system, and by paying particular attention to the allocation of job numbers. The time booked to every production operation will then be recorded against a number which incorporates an identifier code, enabling the work and its costs to be related to the correct project task. This system and the cost-coding methods will become clearer by reference back to Chapter 4.

Level of detail for manufacturing earned-value analysis

The basis for allocating work values to each production activity derives from the project work breakdown, together with its associated estimates. For the purposes of earned-value analysis it is not necessary or desirable for the project manager to consider production task breakdowns in any greater detail than the tasks identified in the work breakdown and overall project schedule.

Earned-value analysis for subcontracts

Earned-value measurement may have to include subcontracted activities. However, if the subcontracted work is being obtained on a fixed-price basis, the subcontractor carries the financial risk, and earned-value measurements for internal control are the prime responsibility of the subcontractor.

The project manager will have to pay close attention to the measurement techniques used by subcontractors whenever they submit claims for progress payments. Such payment claims must be made against the achievement of recognizable events or be supported by certificated measurement. It is those results or other reports from the subcontractors that the project manager must include in the earned-value picture for the whole project.

Earned-value analysis prediction reliability and implications

Early predictions of final costs always tend to be unreliable. There are at least four principal reasons for this:

1   Estimates of progress, or of work remaining to completion, are only judgements, and people usually err on the side of optimism.

2. During the first few weeks or even months of a large project, the sample of work analysed in earned-value calculations is too small to produce valid indications of later trends.

3. There is no guarantee that the performance levels early in a project, even when they have been accurately assessed, will remain at those same levels throughout the remainder of the project.

4. Although many activities, especially in design, might be declared as 100 per cent completed, it is inevitable that further work will be needed when questions arise as drawings and specifications are put to use in manufacturing or construction. It is quite likely that some drawings will have to be reissued with corrections or modifications. Unless due allowance has been made

elsewhere for this 'after-issue' work, the project budget might eventually be exceeded.

What if the prediction is bad?

Suppose the actual hours recorded in the example shown in Figure 22.4 had exceeded the earned value, so that the resulting prediction indicated final costs in excess of the budget. The first thing to be noted is that the project manager should be grateful to this method for producing the earliest possible warning. Escape may be possible even from an apparently hopeless situation, provided suitable action can be taken in time.

Stricter control of modifications should help to curb unnecessary expenditure and conserve budgets. While changes requested by the customer will be paid for, and so should augment the budget, all other requests for changes must be thoroughly scrutinized before authorization. Only essential unfunded changes should be allowed. Change control, a very important aspect of project management, is described in Chapter 23.

In the face of vanishing budgets, the demands placed on individuals will have to be more stringent, but this can only be achieved through good communications, by letting all the participants know what the position is, what is expected of them, and why. It is important to gain their full cooperation. The project manager will find this easiest to achieve within a project team organization. If a matrix organization exists, the project manager must work through all the departmental managers involved to achieve good communications and motivation.

The performance of individuals can often be improved considerably by setting short- and medium-term goals or objectives. These must always be quantifiable, so that the results can be measured objectively, removing any question of favouritism or bias in performance assessment, and helping the individual to monitor his or her own performance.

In the project context, these personal objectives must be equated (by means of the work breakdown structure) with the objectives of time, cost and performance for the project as a whole. The three objectives go hand in hand and, if work is done on time, the cost objective should be met. Although all the objectives should have been set at the start of a project, they can be reviewed if things are going wrong and budgets appear to be at risk. However, care must be taken not to set objectives that cannot possibly be met.

If, in spite of all efforts, a serious overspend still threatens, there remains the possibility of replenishing the project coffers from their original source – the customer. This feat can sometimes be accomplished by re-opening the fixed-price negotiation whenever a suitable opportunity presents itself. An excuse to renegotiate may be provided, for example, if the customer should ask for a substantial change, or as a result of economic factors that are beyond the contractor's control. Failing this step, smaller modifications or project spares can be priced generously to offset the areas of loss or low profitability. Care must also be taken to ensure that every item that the contract allows to be charged as an expense to the customer is so charged.

Remember that, without earned value analysis, forewarning of possible overspending may not be received in time to allow any corrective action at all. The project manager must continually examine cost trends, rather than simple historical cost reports. When the predictions are bad, despair is the wrong philosophy. It is far better to carry out a careful reappraisal of the remaining project activities and explore all possible avenues that might lead to a restoration of the original project profit targets.

Evaluating cost performance for materials and bought-out equipment

Measurement of purchasing achievement, in terms of the cost of materials, components and equipment against their estimates, differs considerably from the measurement and consideration of labour costs. If a person is asked to work on a particular job, the hours and associated labour costs are incurred then and there. If ten hours are worked, ten hours should be booked against the appropriate job number, and ten hours will appear in the records as the cost of the job. Purchase orders, on the other hand, are usually originated well in advance of the time when the goods will be received and invoiced, and there may be a further delay before they are actually used. The costs are committed irrevocably some time before the day of reckoning arrives.

It must therefore be stressed that purchasing cost control is exercised when each order is placed. Once an order has been issued which, for any reason, is priced higher than the budget, then it is too late to avoid spending over budget.

The procedures which follow can only contribute to cost control in the sense that they will indicate adverse trends as early as possible. If poor purchasing performance has been experienced early in the project, the best that can be done is to ensure that an improvement takes place when the remaining orders are committed.

Graphs of cumulative expenditure on purchases

A curve can be plotted to show the cumulative value of purchase orders as they are placed. This is a curve of committed expenditure which can be compared with the original budget. An example was given in Figure 17.2.

Any curve showing materials commitments will be far more useful if a budget comparison curve is first plotted on the graph, like a track along which the committed expenditure is expected to run as the points are plotted. The points for plotting the time-scaled budget for materials must be calculated by adding together the materials cost estimates for each task, and timing them according to the dates when the orders are scheduled to be issued, not forgetting to include the value of common stock items. Inclusion of milestones on the graph (as described earlier in this chapter) will enhance its value.

Allowance for materials issued from common stock

If a curve of material commitments is to be drawn, care must be taken to allow for any materials that do not have to be ordered specifically for the project, but which will be issued from normal stocks. The quantities of these stock items must be estimated, and their costs have to be added to the cumulative totals in the curve so that the predicted cost shown reflects the total materials cost for the project.

Tabulations for material purchase costs

Another, more accurate, approach to monitoring purchasing cost performance is to tabulate actual costs against the corresponding estimates whenever a new purchase order is issued. If this is done at regular intervals a pattern will emerge which shows, for all the orders committed to date, whether any trend towards over or underspending is emerging. The experience gained can be used in carrying out regular reviews of the cost estimates for all goods yet to be ordered. This will allow regular predictions to be made of the total materials expenditure, so that these can be compared with the authorized budgets to help in updating the forecast project profitability.

Where it is intended to use this method, four sets of data have to be gathered:

1   the total value of all orders already placed
2   the total estimated value of all purchase orders yet to be placed (using the task list or purchase control schedule as a check)
3   the cost of any materials already issued from general stock
4   the estimated cost of any materials still to be used from general stock.

Surplus materials

When the final reckoning of project material costs is made, the total cannot be restricted only to those materials that have actually been used, scrapped or wasted. Any items which have become surplus to requirements must be included in the total. Such surpluses may have resulted from over-ordering, design modifications and other causes. The only surplus stocks that need not be taken into account are those which can be returned to the supplier for full credit, or which can be used profitably on a known alternative project for which a firm order exists.

There is often an understandable reluctance to write off materials left over at the end of a project. Individuals are sometimes tempted to take these items into general stock in the hope that one day, some time in the future, possibly, they may eventually become useful. It is surprising how quickly a storage area can become completely cluttered with such stock. Not only can large volumes of storage space be taken up, but also the value to be written off can eventually accumulate to embarrassing proportions if it is allowed to mount up unchecked. The day of reckoning has to come, and it is better to recognize stock as redundant at the time when it first deserves that description.

Effect of project changes on earned-value analysis

Every change introduced into a project can be expected to have some effect on the level of achievement attained by the departments involved. Before this effect can be measured, one significant question must always be answered:

> Can the customer be held liable for any additional costs, or must the additional work be paid for out of the existing budget (and, therefore, out of the potential profits)?

Control of project changes is dealt with in the following chapter. It can be assumed that, long before any modification reaches the stage of implementation, the change committee or other designated authority will have ensured that every approved change is clearly defined as 'customer funded' or 'unfunded'.

Unfunded modifications

Each unfunded change will affect the total workload remaining, usually with no corresponding change to the authorized budgets. In most cases changes increase the remaining workload, so that the proportion of earned value achieved is depressed in all the departments affected.

It should be possible to make an appropriate correction to the achievement measurement for each department to allow for unfunded changes. Each modification would have to be added to the task list, along with a cost estimate for the additional work needed. However, change costs are often extremely difficult to estimate and record, because of the way in which the work is intermingled with the original task affected.

There can, of course, be no corresponding increase in the authorized budget. But for practical purposes, such adjustments are unnecessary, and unfunded modifications can be ignored, provided:

● They are not too numerous or horrendous.
● They do not cancel out work already reported as achieved.

Work on unfunded modifications will therefore show up as apparent overspending

– which is, of course, just what it is. Earned-value predictions will be self-correcting as these overspends are picked up, even if they are not immediately identifiable as being expressly due to unfunded modifications.

Completed work rendered void by unfunded changes

Unfunded changes that nullify work already carried out must always be taken into account by erasure of the relevant earned-value elements from the records. This should be done for every department affected, and either whole tasks or parts of them may have to be reinstated into the remaining workload. In this way, the earned-value calculations can be kept on a true course.

Taking an example, suppose that in the case illustrated by Figure 22.4 there arose a modification which demanded a complete restart of activities 0018, 0019 and 0020 (the sensor circuit design). Earned value for this item would have to revert to zero, which would mean subtracting 497 man-hours from the column total of earned value. This would cut the earned value for the project back from 1389 to 892 man-hours. The CPI has been cut from 1.22 to 0.78, and the predicted cost at completion becomes 3809 man-hours.

Customer-funded modifications

Funded changes can be considered as new tasks, for addition both to the task list and its authorized budgets. The customer should be asked to pay for any work which is scrapped as a result of the change, in which case that work can be considered as having been sold and, therefore, achieved. It need not be subtracted from the achievement tally.

The project ledger concept

A picture has now been built up of a collection of methods by which data can be displayed on graphs or in tables to show the predicted and measured performance of each department against plans and budgets. Successful budgetary control and cost prediction obviously require a certain amount of accurate book-keeping, not only within the boundaries of the accounts department, but also under the administration of the project manager.

The dossier of progress assessments and budgets, all collated with respect to the project task list, can be regarded as a project ledger, with two sets of balancing entries:

1 The ledger account is credited with the initial cost budgets plus any authorized additions, such as those arising from customer-requested changes and contract variation orders.
2 The earned values achieved are debited from the ledger as they are reported.

At any time it should be possible to consult the ledger in order to recalculate the cost performance index for the project or parts of it, and to predict the costs remaining to completion.

The ledger will most probably be set up in a computer, either in a central management information system or using one of the more powerful project management packages.

Predicting profitability for the whole project

Once a basis has been established for the collection of earned value statistics from all parts of the project organization, it is a logical and progressive step to put all these results together into a composite prediction of total project costs.

Of course, the first such prediction is that made before the start of the project, when the initial cost estimates and budgets are prepared and when progress can confidently be declared as zero.

Subsequent analysis and cost predictions can be regarded as a continuous process by which the original estimate is steadily refined. As more work is completed, the total estimate to completion contains an increasing proportion of actual cost data, so that the predictions should become more accurate.

For cost-control purposes, it is necessary that these data are presented in a way that shows unwanted trends as early as possible, before it becomes too late for anything to be done.

Graphical prediction method

Cost predictions can be plotted on a graph against project time for direct comparison with the budget, so that any upward or downward trends can be seen clearly and early.

Before the cost data for all the various departments or groups can be brought together and combined with the cost of purchased equipment and materials, they must all be expressed in terms of one common denominator, which must be the control currency for the project. The man-hour units that were appropriate for scheduling and supervisory control must now be converted into costs, using the appropriate rate for each labour grade. The man-hour records must, however, be kept, because these will provide the stable and reliable yardsticks (unaffected by cost inflation) when comparative cost estimates for future projects are made.

Cost monitoring and prediction are aimed primarily at containing costs within budgets but, when a project has been sold commercially for profit, the profit becomes the end objective. Accordingly, the final prediction graphs should relate the cost and budget levels to the effective net selling price. Both the targeted and predicted gross margins will be displayed so that, as time passes, a wary eye can be kept on the likely outcome. The budget and price levels will have to be

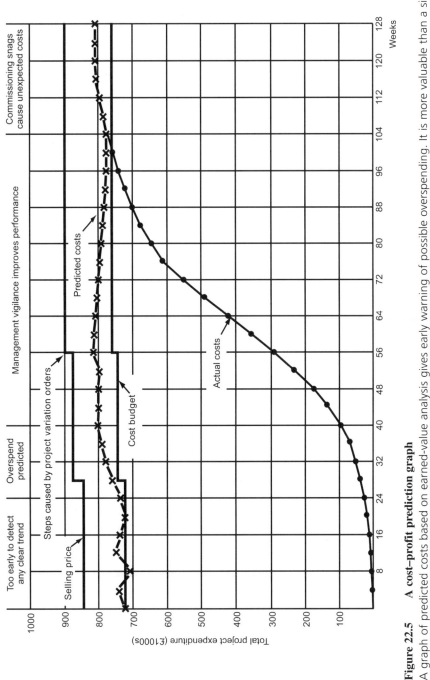

Figure 22.5   A cost–profit prediction graph

A graph of predicted costs based on earned-value analysis gives early warning of possible overspending. It is more valuable than a simple curve of actual costs.

readjusted whenever a variation order or other change is introduced that affects the contract price.

Figure 22.5 shows the type of curves that can result from the regular plotting of cost predictions for the whole project. This contains the following two curves:

1   a curve of cumulative recorded expenditure for the whole project, plotted at four-weekly intervals – the materials and bought-out equipment costs have been included at the time of commitment, and not at the time of invoice payment (which would be too late for control purposes)

2   a curve showing the final cost prediction from earned-value analysis calculations made at four-weekly intervals.

In this example, the project has been finished. It is possible to recapture some of the sense of occasion that would have existed during the active stages of the project by placing a piece of card over the diagram and moving it from left to right to expose the graphs in four-weekly steps.

The first point plotted on the prediction graph, taken at zero project time, is the initial prediction for project expenditure before it has been influenced by actual experience. In other words, this is the original estimate and budget taken straight from the total task list and work breakdown.

The next three or four points on the prediction graph display rather startling variations because they are based, in statistical parlance, on samples that are too small. These early results also contain a high proportion of assessed progress rather than activities that have definitely been completed. As time proceeds and the tally of completed work begins to mount up, it is not very long before a more consistent trend shows, so that, after a few months, the results carry sufficient weight to be taken seriously in determining any need for corrective action.

At about the 24th week, a fairly consistent overspending condition begins to show. Any manager faced with the prospect of overrunning budgets must take some action, and a degree of success in holding down the rate of expenditure was obviously gained in this case. The rate of overspending is seen to decline, to be followed by a long period in which the cost performance steadily improves.

In most projects a danger exists that expenditure will not be cut off immediately when the last scheduled task has been finished. Clean-up operations, on-site activities, drawing corrections and commissioning problems are all possible causes of last-minute additions to costs. Sometimes feverish activity takes place during the final phases of a project in order to get it finished on time, and this too can give rise to unexpected expenditure. Something of this nature has obviously happened over the last weeks of the project in Figure 22.5.

Now compare the graph showing predicted expenditure with that drawn to record actual costs. The curve of actual costs is cumulative, showing the total build-up of costs rather than just the costs incurred during each period of measurement. Notice how much more information can be gleaned from one glance at the prediction curve than can be derived from the cumulative cost curve, especially during the early and middle parts of the project. The overspending

Project cost report summary

Project title:

Project number:

Page   of

Report date:

A Item	B Cost code	C Original budget	D Authorized budget changes	E Authorized current budget C+D	F ACWP	G BCWP (assessed)	H CPI	J Forecast costs remaining (E-G)/H	K Forecast costs at completion F+J	L Forecast variance at completion E-K

Figure 22.6   A tabulated project cost report
A tabular project report that uses earned-value analysis to forecast costs remaining to completion.

danger is simply not shown up at all by the actual cost curve until very late in the project, at which time it is far too late to take any corrective action.

Spreadsheet presentation

Project cost summaries and predictions are commonly presented in tabular or spreadsheet form. Figure 22.6 shows a widely used arrangement, suitable for preparation from purely clerical methods or from computer systems. Tables such as this are typically bound into regular cost and progress reports, often produced at monthly intervals. A description of this format on a column-by-column basis will serve to round off this chapter with a reiteration of the principles embodied in the interpretation of cost and progress data. The spreadsheet columns have been labelled A, B, C and so on, for ease of reference.

The report form is headed with the project title and project number information. The report date is important, being the effective common reference date for all measurements and progress assessments.

The time lag between the effective report date and the actual report issue date depends on the size and complexity of the project to a great extent: it obviously takes more time to collect results from a project spread over a large, geographically scattered organization than it would where the whole project is conducted within one office or factory. Nevertheless, all possible steps must be taken to produce these reports before they become outdated and too late to provoke a constructive management response.

Column A lists the main work packages from the project work breakdown. This list must include all cost items, including software tasks and summarized miscellaneous items. If more detail is required, this can be provided on backup sheets.

Column B gives the cost code for every item. This makes it easier to refer back to the original estimates and budgets and to audit the data presented.

In column C, the original budgets for the work packages are shown, and these add up to the total original project budget at the foot of the column. This is the cost budget originally authorized and approved, which should be equal to the original cost estimates. Consideration must be given to the inclusion or otherwise of escalation and other below-the-line estimates, and it may be necessary to add explanatory notes in the accompanying report text.

As the project proceeds, it can be expected that a number of variations or modifications will arise that are agreed with the client, and for which the client will pay. These must obviously increase both the project revenue and the budget. Budget increments from this cause are listed in column D. These, when added to the original budget for each project section, give the current revised authorized budgets, in column E (the current budget).

In any project of significant size there are usually variations under consideration or awaiting approval that could ultimately affect the budget (and progress assessment). Until such variations have been agreed with the client, it is obviously not possible to take the additional revenue for granted. It may nevertheless be of considerable interest to know the value of any such proposals which happen to be 'in the pipeline' at the report date. Although not shown in the example of Figure 22.6, a column can be included in the report layout, if desired, to give this advance information.

Column F lists the costs actually recorded as at the report date. These comprise the Actual Cost of Work Performed (ACWP), and include the following:

1. all labour hours booked to the project (on timesheets or job tickets), converted at standard cost or other appropriate rates into the project control currency

2 overheads and administrative costs

3 payments for directly relevant insurance premiums, licences, legal fees and consultants' fees

4 payments made to, or legitimately claimed by, subcontractors

5 the cost of all materials committed, which includes the cost of all materials and equipment already used or delivered, plus the value of all other materials and equipment for which orders have been placed at the report date; in all cases freight, packing, insurance, agents' fees and duties paid or committed must be included

6 any other costs incurred or committed up to the report date that can be directly attributed to the project.

Column G is obtained as a result of earned-value analysis using the methods described earlier in this chapter. It shows the assessed earned value of all project work performed at the report date.

In column H, the cost performance index has been calculated from the data in columns F and G. If the CPI is shown on an item-by-item basis, as here, any variation between the different work packages might be useful management information.

Column J forecasts the costs remaining to completion, obtained by factoring estimates for work remaining by the cost performance index.

Column K indicates the best prediction possible of the final total project costs at completion. As time passes, the forecast element of this figure will decrease, the proportion of actual costs will increase, and the final prediction will grow more accurate.

The final column, L, highlights any variances between the authorized budgets and the predicted final costs.

Post-mortem

When the project is finished and the final costs become known, an investigation can be conducted to compare the actual expenditure with the original estimates. Such post mortem examinations are obviously far too late to be of benefit to the completed project, but they can be helpful in pointing out mistakes to be avoided when estimating or conducting future projects.

Chapter 23

Managing project changes

No project of any significant size can be expected to run from start to finish without at least one change. The exception to this rule might exist as a project manager's dream of Utopia, but is unlikely to assume any more tangible form.

My definition of a project change is:

> a departure from the approved project scope or design as indicated by a change to any contract, drawing or specification after its approval and issue for action.

Changes can arise from a customer's request that changes the project scope or specification, a self-inflicted engineering design modification, or through some reason during work on the project that causes the finished result to differ in some respect from the issued drawings, specifications or other formal instructions. Changes (and therefore change management) can sometimes be needed even after the project has been finished and handed over to the customer. Figure 23.1 shows many routes through which changes can develop.

Classification of changes

Changes can usually be placed in one of two principal commercial categories. One way to define these categories is to ask whether the change has originated within the project organization or whether it has come from the customer. There are, however, some borderline cases which cannot be put into either of these classifications but which contain elements of both. A more useful way to classify changes from the commercial point of view is to label them as 'funded' or 'unfunded'. For a funded change, the customer must take responsibility for the change and pay for it. For unfunded changes, the contractor will have to absorb all the costs, with consequent risk to budget limits and expected profits. Whether or not a change is to be funded or unfunded will greatly influence how it is considered for authorization.

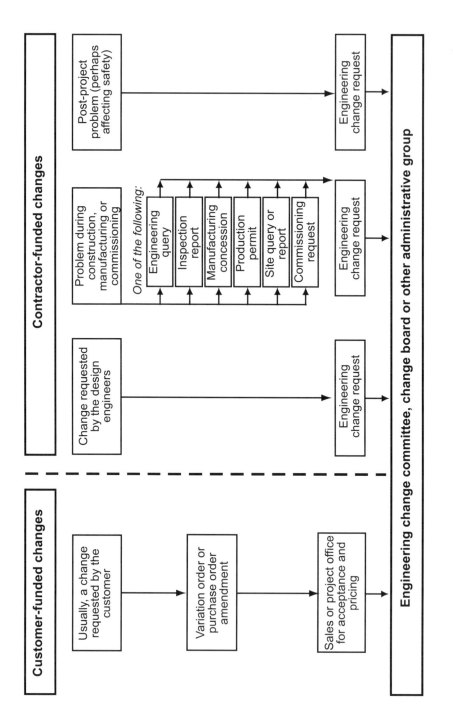

Figure 23.1   Some origins of project changes

Funded changes

Changes to the specified project requested by the customer automatically imply a corresponding change to the contract, since the project specification should form part of the contract documentation. If, as usually happens, the modification results in an increase in the contractor's costs, a suitable change to the contract price must be negotiated. The delivery schedule may also be affected, and any resulting delays must be predicted, discussed and agreed.

Customer-funded modifications may possess nuisance value, and can disrupt the smooth flow of logically planned work, but they do nevertheless offer the prospect of compensation through an increase in price and possibly an increase in profit. When a customer asks for a change, the contractor is in a strong price-bargaining position because there is no competitor and the contractor has a monopoly.

Customer-funded changes are usually documented as purchase order amendments or contract variation orders (otherwise known as project variations).

Unfunded changes

If a contractor finds it necessary to introduce changes for reasons unconnected with the customer, it is hardly likely that the customer could be expected to pay (unless the changes are covered by some contingency for which provision was made in the contract). The contractor must be prepared to carry the additional costs, write off any scrapped work, and answer to the customer for any resulting time delay. For these reasons, contractors must be particularly wary about allowing unfunded (which really means contractor-funded) changes to proceed.

The procedure for introducing an unfunded modification into an active project usually starts by raising a document called an engineering change request, engineering change order, modification request, or some permutation of these terms. Some reasons for unfunded changes are shown in Figure 23.1, and the relevant documentation is described later in this chapter.

Permanent and temporary changes

Changes can be further classified as permanent or temporary.

Permanent changes are carried out with the intention of leaving them permanently embodied in the design and execution of a project, and they will remain recorded in drawings and specifications to show the true as-built condition of the competed project.

Temporary changes may be needed for expediency in getting a project finished, but they are carried out with the intention of either removing them or converting them to some alternative permanent change at a later, more convenient time.

Authorization arrangements

The effects of any change, whether customer-requested or not, may be felt far beyond the confines of the project area that is most obviously and directly affected. This could be true of the technical, timescale or cost aspects. Most projects have to be regarded as a combination of technical and commercial systems, in which a change to one part can react adversely or beneficially with other parts of the system. Such reactions can bring about consequences that the change's originator may not have been able to foresee.

For these reasons alone it is prudent to ensure that every proposed change is considered and approved by selected key members of the project organization before it can be implemented. This precaution means that the overall effects can be predicted as reliably as possible. These selected referees form the 'change committee' or 'change board'. In some organizations, perhaps in larger companies, the change committee might be a properly constituted body that meets regularly in formal meetings. In small project organizations, the arrangement is usually far less formal, but there must nevertheless be some means for change consideration and approval at senior level.

The change committee or change board

In many companies engaged on project work, a regular panel of experts is appointed to consider changes and decide how they are to be handled.

Departmental managers should be included in or represented on the committee. These must include those who are able to answer for the safety, reliability, performance, cost and timescale consequences of changes, the effects on work in progress, on purchases, and on the feasibility or otherwise of introducing the change into manufacture or construction.

In some cases – especially in projects involving the nuclear industry, aviation, defence or other cases where reliability, safety or performance assume great significance – two key members of the committee represent:

- the *design authority* – typically the chief engineer
- the *inspecting authority* – a person such, as a quality manager, who should be independent and able to make assessments on the basis of quality alone, without commercial pressure.

Change committee meetings

Change committees for large projects often meet on a frequent, regular basis, dealing with change requests in batches. Others avoid meetings by circulating requests around the committee members, so that each member considers the effect of the proposed change on his or her own area of responsibility. Each method has its advantages and disadvantages. If formal committee meetings take place at monthly intervals, the wait for change decisions can hold up progress or result in the greater disruption to work that late changes cause. On the other hand, frequent committee meetings take up too much members' time. Informal committees, not meeting collectively but relying instead on the circulation of documents, suffer from a communication problem and can take longer to discuss and resolve misunderstandings or make decisions. Neither approach can be classified as right or wrong, but it will be assumed here that a formal procedure exists, with a change committee meeting at regular intervals (perhaps weekly).

Decision criteria

When each change request is considered for approval, the committee must weigh up all the possible consequences before making its decision. Points which need to be examined are listed below (not necessarily in order of importance):

- Is the change actually possible to make?
- Is it a customer-requested or a self-inflicted change?
- What is the estimated cost of the change?
- Will the customer pay? If so, what should be the price?
- If the change is not customer-requested, is it really necessary? Why?
- What will be the effect on the project timescale?
- How will safety, reliability and performance be affected?
- If several identical sets of equipment are being produced, at what point in the production sequence should the change be introduced?
- Will scrap or redundant materials be created?
- Are any items to be changed retrospectively? Are these:
  – in progress?
  – in stock?
  – already delivered to the customer or otherwise built into the project?
- What drawings, specifications and other documents will have to be modified?

Figure 23.2 illustrates some of the steps in the change handling process.

The change committee's response

When the committee has considered all these questions, it has the following options:

- Authorize the change as requested.
- Give limited approval only, authorizing the change with specified limitations.
- Refer the request back to the originator (or elsewhere), asking for clarification or for an alternative solution.
- Reject the change, giving reasons.

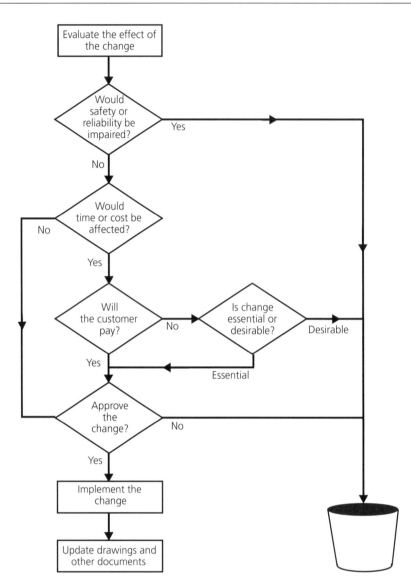

Figure 23.2   Decision tree for change requests

General administration

Use of standard change request forms

Individuals who wish to request a change should always be asked to put their request in writing. This chapter is written on the assumption that all such requests will be addressed to a change committee. Where the organization does not operate a formal change committee, a suitably senior member of the organization, such as the chief engineer, should be designated as the person responsible for considering and authorizing changes.

To save the committee's time and to ensure that all requests are properly controlled and progressed, some kind of standard change request form must be used. This form should be designed in such a way that the originator is induced to answer in advance all the questions that the change committee will want to ask. In some projects, even the customer can be persuaded to submit change requests using the contractor's standard forms.

Because there are several routes along which changes can arise within any organization (see Figure 23.1) there are usually several different forms that can result in change requests. These forms are illustrated later in this chapter (see page 555). However, the administration procedures described here are generally applicable to all of these different forms.

Change coordinator

In any project organization where changes are expected (which really means *all* project organizations), it is advisable to nominate a change coordinator. This is not usually a full-time role, and the person chosen will probably carry out other clerical or administrative duties for the project. The change coordinator may reside in a contracts office, the project manager's administration group, project support office, the engineering department, or in some other department. His or her duties are likely to include:

● registering each change request and allocating serial numbers
● distributing and filing copies of the change documents
● following up to ensure that every request is considered by the change committee without avoidable delay
● distributing and filing copies of the change documents after the committee's instructions have been given
● following up to ensure that authorized changes are carried out and that all drawings and specifications affected by the change are updated and re-issued.

Numbering and registration

Upon receipt of any change request, the coordinator should enter brief details in a register. Apart from their initial use in allocating serial numbers, change registers are important for several other reasons, which include the following:

● to provide a base from which each change request can be progressed through all its stages, either to rejection or to approval and full documentation and implementation

● to record changes in budgets and, if appropriate, prices so that the current valid budgets and prices will always be known

● to provide a search base that allows tracking back ('traceability') so that the origins of all design and commercial changes can be found or verified, both during the life of the project and afterwards.

Change registers can be pages in a loose-leaf folder or, subject to safeguards against accidental erasure and loss, they can be held in a computer. Separate registers should be kept for project variations, engineering change requests, engineering queries, production permits and inspection reports. Usually, a slightly different register format is used for each of these registers, but Figure 23.3 shows a fairly typical layout.

The change coordinator must allocate serial numbers from the appropriate register. The numbering systems should be kept simple, but must be designed so that no number is repeated on another project or in another register. The simple solution is to prefix each change with either the project number or a shorter code that is specific to the project, and to add one or two letters which denote the type of change. For example, if the project number is P123, engineering change request forms might be numbered in the series P123/ECR001, P123/ECR002, P123/ECR003 and so on. Concessions or production permits for the same project could be numbered in the series P123/PP001, P123/PP002, P123/PP003 and so on.

Distribution

The change coordinator's first duty after registering each change request is to arrange for its distribution. This process will be speeded up if the forms are stocked in multi-part sets or distributed via a network.

A typical distribution for any change request might be:

● engineering manager or chief engineer (who may wish to arrange further distribution within his or her department)
● change committee chairperson (the original 'top copy')
● other change committee members.

The originator should retain a copy, and the coordinator will keep another in a 'changes pending file', with a different file for each type of form in use.

Progressing

To prevent undue delays, or even the risk of forgotten requests, change registers should be designed to highlight all those requests that are 'active': this means all requests which have yet to be approved or rejected. For example, a column can be

Register								Project number:			Sheet number:	
Serial number	Originator		Date requested	Brief details or title	Approved? (Yes or No)	Date of final distribution	Budget change (if any)
	Name	Dept					

Figure 23.3   A general-purpose change register
This can be used to serial number, register and progress change requests. Requests might be received as project variation orders, engineering change requests, engineering queries, concessions and production permits. A separate register should be used for each of these document types.

provided on the register sheet headed 'Final issue date' or something similar. The absence of a date in that column tells the coordinator that the change is still active and in need of monitoring and progressing.

Ideally, the coordinator should be able to use the registers to follow up the action after approval, to ensure that the relevant drawings and specifications are updated and re-issued.

Estimating the true cost of a change

Most changes will add to the cost of a project. Changes made late in a project often attract higher costs than those introduced earlier, because sunk costs are then higher and late changes can cause greater disruption to work in progress, causing scrap and rework.

It is not always appreciated that the total costs of an engineering modification can far exceed the straightforward estimate of costs directly attributable to the modification itself. A simple example will help to demonstrate some of the extra incidental costs which can be introduced when a change is made to a project.

Case study: Competition car project

Suppose that a project is in hand to produce two competition cars within the main factory of AB Cars Ltd (the ABC company), whose primary work is the quantity production of cars for sale to the general motoring public. The two special cars are being supplied to another company, Universal Wheeled Vehicles (UVW) Ltd. This is a normal commercial contract specified in UVW's purchase order to ABC. The two competition cars are identical. Although these cars are built from standard components, practically everything about them is special. The engines originally specified are standard production units from the works stores, but they will have to be stripped down, modified, rebuilt and bench-tested before they can be fitted.

During final assembly of the two cars the ABC company is informed that the two engines will not comply with the competition rules, a mistake which has arisen because UVW did not realize that its copy of the rules was out of date. UVW is therefore liable for any additional costs, and has submitted an amendment to the original purchase order.

Suitable replacement engines are not available within ABC, but engines that will satisfy the competition rules can be purchased as modified stock engines from an outside company. These engines require different mountings, and some changes to the inlet and exhaust configuration.

Asked to forecast the cost of this change, ABC's cost estimator might produce a set of figures something like those shown in Figure 23.4.

In reality, however, it might take 12 weeks to get the new engines modified, prepared and delivered, during which time the project might have to be shelved

```
Labour costs:                                          £          £
        Cost of removing old engines
                5 hours at £20 per hour        100
        Cost of preparing two new engines
                60 hours at £20 per hour       1200
        Cost of modifying engine mountings
                10 hours at £20 per hour       200
        Cost of fitting new engines
                20 hours at £20 per hour       400
        Sundry other charges
                10 hours at £20 per hour       200
        Testing and fine tuning
                30 hours at £20 per hour       600
Total direct labour cost                                        2700
Overheads at 80 per cent                                        2160
Materials:
        Two bought-out modified engines       6000
        New exhaust manifolds                  600
        New inlet manifolds                    400
        New fuel injection equipment           300
Total materials                                                 7900

Basic estimate                                                 12760
Contingency allowance (5 per cent)                               638

Estimated total factory cost of modification                   13398
Mark-up (40 per cent)                                           5359

Additional project price for changing two engines              18757
```

Figure 23.4   Car project: Estimated modification cost

temporarily. Even assuming that the fitters could be gainfully employed elsewhere in the works, it is unlikely that the total costs of the change would be limited to the basic £12 760 estimated. The cars, together with work benches, jigs, cradles, measuring equipment and special tools would probably occupy some 100 square metres of prime workspace. Even when no work is taking place, this accommodation still attracts costs in terms of rent, business rates, heating, maintenance, cleaning, insurance, security and so on. These costs might amount to £300 per square metre per annum.

Here is an example of overhead under-recovery (the concepts of absorption costing, standard costing and the recovery of overheads were outlined in Chapter 4). The cost of providing 100 square metres of idle factory floor space for 12 weeks would be nearly £7000, a sum not recovered in the selling price calculated in Figure 23.4.

Other projects for which the space and facilities are needed could suffer from a knock-on effect from the delay. Also, failure to meet the programme in the early part of a project can be reflected in increased activity later on, and this can cause problems and additional costs as a result of crash actions and overtime working.

Modifications often affect stocks of materials by making them redundant. It is not uncommon for items of quite high value to be forgotten completely, simply because they are out of sight in a store.

A direct result of the error in starting with the wrong engine might be that the cars are not ready in time for the competition, leading to damaged prestige and possible loss of prize money and other benefits.

If the error in choosing the wrong engines had been the fault of the ABC company, and not that of UVW Ltd, matters would have been far worse. The change would have to be classified as unfunded but essential, and the contractor would have to bear all the costs, both estimated and hidden. It would then have been quite likely that the UVW would seek compensation from ABC for its losses by way of liquidated damages or by invoking a contract penalty clause for late delivery. The order might even be cancelled (with no possibility of redress, because ABC would have been judged to be at fault).

Checking all the possible cost factors

It is not reasonable to expect that all individuals will inevitably include all possible costs of modifications in their estimates, although this would be the ideal aim.

In fact, the project manager must learn to expect that omissions of important cost factors are likely in many estimates. He or she will become experienced in asking significant and probing questions as a matter of routine, so that the cost estimator's train of thought can be reset:

● Is there to be no inspection on this job?
● Are stocks affected?
● Does the prototype have to be modified too?
● What will the delay cost? Is this going to hold up other work and, if so, what will that cost?

Such questions must always be asked in the quest for the whole truth about the costs of changes.

Recording the actual cost of a change

Some of the difficulties to be expected in assessing the true costs of a design change have now been outlined, and it is apparent that there are many factors which can easily be overlooked. Nevertheless, an estimate can be made in most cases, and this can be used to work out and justify any possible increase in price that the contractor feels able to demand.

Recording the actual costs of a modification can prove to be a far more difficult undertaking: it may even be impossible. Difficulties underlying the measurement and recording of actual modification costs may not always be appreciated by some managers and others who, quite reasonably, would like to know just how much their budgets are being affected by changes.

Example

Suppose that a modification is to be performed on a 'fuzzelbox', which is a complex piece of electronic equipment containing over 1 kilometre of wire, thousands of electrical connections, piping and valves and many other components.

First, take the case where the fuzzelbox has already been assembled, inspected and fully tested. Here there need be no problem in identifying the cost of the change, because a fresh works order or job ticket can be issued for the modification work and materials, complete with a new cost code. All the subsequent work of stripping, changing, inspecting and re-testing can be attributed directly to the change.

Now consider the different (but frequent) case in which drawings and specifications are modified during the course of production work. The fuzzelbox is in a semi-completed state, so that the modification will add new wires, delete others, re-route wires and pipes not yet installed, and result in changed connections and components. How can anyone be expected to record accurately that part of the work which is directly attributable to the modification?

It is quite possible that many changes will occur on a job of this size before it is finished, so that the only apparent and measurable effect on costs will be an increase of expenditure compared with the initially estimated production costs. This situation has to be accepted and, if the modification costs are needed for any purpose, they will have to be estimated.

Forms and procedures

This section describes some of the routes through which changes can reach a project, together with their origins and associated forms (these routes were illustrated in Figure 23.1). The authorization and general administration procedures already described in this chapter will apply generally to all of these forms.

When is a formal change procedure necessary?

When a designer, in a fit of rage or despair, tears up a drawing or clears the computer screen and starts again, there is no need to invoke a formal change engineering procedure. Any new design might have to undergo many such interruptions and changes before it is committed to a fully checked and issued drawing. This is all part of the normal, creative development process. Provided that the design intentions remain within the requirements of the design specification, any internal changes made before drawings are formally issued are not generally considered to be modifications or engineering changes, even though they might prove expensive.

Some companies circulate early, pre-issue drawings for discussion, advance information or approval. These issues are often distinguished from the fully released versions by labelling them as 'revision A', 'revision B', and so on, changing the revision numbers to the series 0, 1, 2 and so on to denote official releases. A rule might therefore be suggested that formal engineering change procedures need only be applied to drawing revisions made after the first issue for manufacturing or construction. But such a rule can prove unworkable if preliminary issues are made for the manufacture of a prototype, in which changes must be properly controlled.

Another reason for invoking formal procedures is found whenever there is an intention to depart from the design specification, especially when the development work is being carried out for an external customer. This, again, is a case for using the formal change procedure before any drawing has been issued for manufacture or construction.

Some rule or criterion is needed that can determine at which point in the design process the formal change procedure should be introduced. The question to be asked is: 'Will the proposed change affect any instruction, specification, plan or budget that has already been agreed with other departments, the customer, or other external organization?' If the answer to this question is 'Yes', the probability is that formal change committee approval will be needed.

Design freeze

Sometimes project organizations recognize that there is a point in the design and fulfilment of a project after which any change would be particularly irksome, inconvenient or potentially damaging. This leads to the announcement of a design freeze, after which the change committee will refuse to consider any change proposal unless there are compelling reasons, such as safety or a customer request. Ideally, the customer should agree to be bound by the design freeze. In some companies the design freeze stage is called 'stable design'.

Project variation orders

Changes requested by the customer which affect price, delivery or any other aspect of the original purchase order or contract require formal documentation. The request document should fulfil the following functions:

- It amends the purchase order or contract, and describes the change.
- It authorizes the contractor to make the change.
- It promises payment.
- It records agreement to any associated timescale revision.

Where the original contract was in the form of a purchase order, the customer will usually request a change by issuing a purchase order amendment (see Chapter 16). In other cases, especially for projects involving construction, changes are recorded on project variation orders (sometimes called simply 'project variations' or 'contract variations'). An example is given in Figure 23.5. Similar changes arranged by a main contractor with site construction subcontractors are often known as 'site variation orders'.

A procedure for simple, repetitive project variations

In projects where a considerable number of small changes are expected, it may be possible to streamline all the change procedures, perhaps with a prearranged scale of charges. Naturally, such a procedure must be restricted to changes of a routine nature, where safety and reliability cannot be affected. Provided that the scope of a change can be defined adequately, and that the work can easily be identified separately from other project work, the costs of small changes can be recovered on some agreed time and materials basis or, for construction projects, against an agreed schedule of rates per units of measured work.

Example

Here is an example which shows how simplified change procedures can be used to avoid the need for hundreds of purchase order amendments or contract variations. For the project in question, a contractor was engaged on a defence contract for designing and building automatic test equipment for the electronic systems installed in military aircraft. Each complete tester was housed in a trailer which could be towed out to an aircraft, connected by cables, and left to carry out a whole range of measurements, 'go' or 'no-go' checks and diagnostic fault-finding routines. The testers were controlled by computers, programmed by special tapes.

Every time the aircraft manufacturer (the customer) wanted to change any of the test parameters, a small amount of software reprogramming was necessary in the test equipment. This happened at least daily during months of prototype

Project variation order	PVO number:
	Project number:
Project title:	Issue date:

Summary of change (use continuation sheets if necessary):

Originator: Date:

Effect on project schedule:

Effect on costs and price: Cost estimate ref:

Customer's authorization details:	Our authorization:

Distribution:

Figure 23.5   Project variation order

commissioning. Some changes also required one, two or three wires to be re-routed. Attempting to estimate the cost of each change and subjecting it to the formal change committee procedure was out of the question. Yet every change had to be recorded for later incorporation into drawings, and every change had to be invoiced and paid for.

These difficulties were resolved by both companies agreeing to the use of simple, serially numbered, all-one-price program change request forms. These documented the details of each change, were authorized by the signature of the customer's senior engineer at the test site, and accepted for on-the-spot action by the contractor's senior commissioning engineer. A copy of each change request form was returned to the head office of the contractor, who kept the relevant drawings and programming records up-to-date. Invoices were sent to the customer periodically, each claiming payment for a batch of changes identified by their serial numbers.

The system was limited by mutual agreement to include only the simple changes needed to alter measurement data or test-point switching. Hundreds of changes were requested, actioned and charged for against these very simple pre-priced request forms, saving valuable time at the commissioning site, with the contractor collecting a satisfying level of revenue, and the customer avoiding the expense of preparing, negotiating and issuing the more formal type of order amendment.

Engineering change requests

The purpose of an engineering change request is to describe, document and seek formal permission for a permanent design change. The change may be unfunded, or it might be the result of a project variation order and therefore funded. Engineering change requests of the type shown in Figure 23.6 are used widely in engineering projects, although they may be known by different titles, invariably abbreviated to sets of initials. The following are among those which may be encountered:

- ECR – Engineering Change Request
- ECO – Engineering Change Order
- MR – Modification Request.

There is no reason why any person, however junior, should not be allowed to originate an engineering change request, because it can have no effect until it has been authorized by the change committee. The method for completing the form should be self-evident from Figure 23.6.

Concessions or production permits

Manufacturing departments, faced with the need to keep to a budget or to accomplish work within a scheduled timescale, sometimes find that they need to depart from the specific instructions contained in the manufacturing drawings to

Engineering change request	ECR number:

Engineering change request   ECR number:

Project title: Project number:

Details of change requested (use continuation sheets if necessary):

Drawings and other documents affected:

Reason for request:

Originator: Date:

Emergency action requested (if any):

Effect on costs: Cost estimate ref:

Will customer pay? Yes ☐   No ☐   If yes, customer authorization ref.:

Effect on project schedule?

COMMITTEE INSTRUCTIONS: CHANGE APPROVED ☐   NOT APPROVED ☐
Point of embodiment, stocks, work in progress, units in service, special restrictions etc.

Authorized by: Date:

Figure 23.6   Engineering change request

achieve their objective. Naturally, the quality control department will keep a wary eye open to ensure that no unauthorized shortcuts or botching are allowed.

Suppose, however, that a drawing specifies the use of chromium-plated screws, but that these are simply not available when required. The purchasing department may be able to obtain alternative screws with a cadmium-plate finish, or possibly some other thread size could be substituted. If the production team decided to make this substitution without reference to the design engineers, there would be a danger (remote in some companies) of an inspector noticing the difference and rejecting the work because it deviated from the drawing.

But would the use of these alternative screws really matter? It all depends, of course, on the actual circumstances, and whether the screws are in a prominent position where they will be easily seen if they do not match adjacent chromium parts. Someone has to decide, and either authorize or reject the change.

Other requests for concessions might not be simply cosmetic. The use of alternative materials, different adhesives, acceptance of wider tolerances, are all reasons for originating requests for concessions. These might represent a risk to performance, reliability, safety or interchangeability. As a general rule, therefore, concessions require the formal approval of the design authority.

Concessions (or production permits) usually fall into the classification 'temporary changes'. It is unlikely that the drawings will be updated to accommodate the change, it being assumed that the manufacturing department will either be able to adhere to the drawings in any future production, or will apply for a further concession.

Procedures for requesting concessions vary greatly from one company to another. They can range from the very informal 'Is it all right if we do it this way instead, George?' to a rigid discipline supervised by the quality control department. Rigid procedures can be expected in the defence, aerospace and nuclear industries, and in any other case where safety and quality rank high as objectives. Figure 23.7 shows a suitable form.

The reasons for instituting a formal concession discipline are fairly obvious, because any departure from the instructions contained in issued drawings or specifications must be either disallowed or treated with a great deal of caution. Concession records may have less significance than other project records once a project has been finished and handed over to the customer. Nevertheless, they can prove useful in the quality and reliability control function. Concession records are part of the project records which a contractor needs to keep in order to trace the possible causes of poor performance, faults or failures in equipment after delivery. If one of a number of identical units should fail in service, it could be vital to trace all other units containing the same concession in order to prevent further failures.

The procedures associated with the granting of concessions can exist in a variety of permutations and combinations of the methods described in this chapter. Whichever method a company decides to adopt, the concession register will be complementary to the manufacturing drawings, modification records, inspection and test records and build schedules in defining the exact composition of the completed project.

Production permit/concession

Production permit/concession

Drawing/spec. number: Application number:

Revision number: Project or job number:

Batch or product serial number(s) affected:	Is work held up?
	Yes: ☐
	No: ☐

Application to allow non-compliance with the above drawing or specification as follows:

Reason for this application:

Requested by: Department: Date:

Engineering assessment

   Performance/reliability?

   Health and safety?

   Interchangeability?

For Engineering Department: Date:

Decision

   Granted: ☐   ------------------------------   ------------------
                   For design authority   Date
   Refused: ☐   ------------------------------   ------------------
                   For quality/inspecting authority   Date

Figure 23.7   Production permit or concession
Used for authorizing and documenting departures from drawings, specifications or other manufacturing instructions.

Engineering query notes

A feature of project manufacturing is that the drawings are usually completely new and untried. It is not surprising, therefore, that a higher incidence of problems in manufacture or construction is a characteristic of project work. These problems can range from design errors to difficulties in interpreting the manufacturing instructions. Design errors must, of course, be corrected by the re-issue of amended drawings, for which the full-scale engineering change procedure will usually be invoked. Simple problems associated with the interpretation of drawings can be resolved by an explanation on the spot from the appropriate engineer. Between these two extremes lies a no man's land of production difficulties which are not a direct result of design errors, but which demand more than a simple explanation to get production on the move again.

In some firms, any problems that cannot be resolved on the spot are channelled into a formalized 'engineering query' procedure, which relies on the use of forms similar to that shown in Figure 23.8. The general idea is that the production individual who comes up against a problem explains the difficulty on one of these forms and submits it to the engineering department for investigation and reply. Naturally, this system can only operate effectively and be accepted if each query is afforded reasonably urgent consideration. The advantages provided by adopting this routine are that all queries can be registered and progressed by the coordinating clerk to ensure that none is forgotten. Regrettably, one engineering director whom I knew preferred the formal system because it kept production personnel, together with their overalls, oil and grease, out of the nice clean engineering design offices.

Example

Suppose that a specified adhesive, when used according to the appropriate process specification, failed to produce the specified bond strength, so that when the unfortunate production employee removed the clamps his or her careful work disintegrated into its constituent parts. The production team would need to ask the engineers what to do, and they could use an engineering query note for the purpose.

If this problem proved too difficult to sort out on the spot, the engineers might be forced to return the query note with a temporary solution suggested. The instruction might read: 'Clean off adhesive, and use six equally-spaced pop rivets instead. This instruction applies only to batch 1. Drawings will be re-issued with a new adhesive specification for batch 2.'

Engineering query note		
Engineering query note		
Drawing/spec. number:	EQN number:	Is work held up?
Revision number:	Project or job number:	Yes: ☐
Other relevant drawings or specifications:		No: ☐
Details of query or problem:		
Query raised by:	Department:	Date:
Answer:		
For Engineering Department:		Date:
Engineering follow-up action required (if any):		

Figure 23.8   Engineering query note

Conversion from engineering query to production permit

If, as in the above example, an engineering query note is returned to a production department with instructions that conflict with those given in the manufacturing drawings, the query note becomes a document that carries authority to deviate from drawings. It has therefore become a concession or production permit.

Because engineering query notes are often converted into concessions in this way, companies that use them should consider combining the concession and engineering query systems into one procedure, with a single common-purpose form designed to cope with both needs.

Inspection reports

Suppose that a block of extremely expensive raw material has been subjected to many hours of machining by highly skilled operators but, on final inspection, one of the measurements is found to be marginally outside the limits of tolerance. Too much material has been cut away; the error has resulted in the work being undersized and no rectification is possible. Any inspector would have to reject the job. In many companies the inspector would fill in an inspection report ticket or form, detailing the 'non-conformance'.

The relevant design engineers, if shown the inspection report, might decide that the error was too trivial to justify scrapping such an expensive workpiece. Perhaps it could still be used for the project or, alternatively, it might be possible to use it for a prototype assembly, on the understanding that it must never be re-fitted into another assembly. A design engineer having the appropriate authority might feel able to annotate the inspection report accordingly, thus countermanding the inspector's rejection.

This is another method by which a job can be passed through an inspection stage, even though it does not conform to the issued drawings. The inspection report has been translated by the design authority into a concession or production permit.

Figure 23.9 shows an inspection report form which has been designed so that it can be converted into a concession in appropriate cases.

Version control for modified drawings and specifications

It is necessary here to consider one or two pitfalls that can trap the unwary project engineering staff into issuing drawings or specifications that are not what their revision numbers would make them seem to be.

Inspection report		Report number:
Project number:	Job number:	Report date:

Details of work inspected or tested:

Drawing number: Revision:

Specification number: Revision:

Batch or serial number(s) affected:

Details of non-conformance:

-------------------------------- Inspector/tester

Application for concession (if required)
    The above non-conformance will not affect reliability, safety or interchangeability
Further comments

Agreed
Refused:

Requested by: -------------------   ------------------- Design authority

Disposal instructions

    Scrap and remake: ☐

    Rectify and re-inspect/retest: ☐

    Concession granted: ☐

                                For inspecting authority/quality manager

Figure 23.9   Inspection report format

Issue of incorrect versions

Diazo prints and translucent 'reproducibles' or 'submasters' are easily recognizable as copies, and are thus unlikely to be confused with original documents. With today's reprographic techniques and digital plotters, however, copies of drawings are indistinguishable from their originals. Drawings produced from CAD software can be plotted at will on plain paper, so that more than one apparently original version of any drawing can easily exist.

Unless rigid safeguards are introduced, any designer can alter the design information in the computer and then cause a new 'original' to be produced without making the necessary change to the drawing or revision number. Unless there is a central drawings registry for the control and issue of drawings, there is no independent check to prevent such mistakes, and measures must be devised to prevent the issue of drawings with incorrect revision numbers.

Example

I once asked a design department to produce a small group of drawings for fitting out a new design office. The designs were first class. The designer started by creating an accurate master outline drawing of the building. This outline drawing was used as the basis for a number of other drawings, covering proposed partition layouts, electrical distribution and lighting, and staff seating arrangements. Unfortunately, the designer issued every one of these drawings with the same serial number – that of the original outline drawing. In this case it was the first project designed on a brand new CAD system, so perhaps there was some excuse, but the drawings reached the local authority planning committee before the mistake was noticed.

The interchangeability rule

The usual practice when a drawing is changed is to re-issue it with a new revision number. If, however, a change results in a manufactured component or assembly being made different from other items with which it was previously interchangeable, it is not sufficient merely to change the drawing revision number. The drawing number itself (and therefore the part number) must also be changed.

This is a golden rule to which no exception should ever be allowed, whether the item is a small component or a big assembly.

Example

Suppose that a project requires the use of 1000 small spacers, and that after 500 had been produced in brass the design was cheapened to use mild steel. These spacers are truly interchangeable, and the part number need not be changed. But the drawing for the steel spacers would be given a new revision number.

Now suppose that the spacer design had been changed from metal to moulded nylon because on some later manufactured assemblies it became necessary for the spacers to be electrically insulating. The old metal spacers can no longer be used on all assemblies. The metal and nylon spacers are not interchangeable. The drawing for the nylon version of these spacers must therefore be given a new drawing number.

Emergency modifications

We live in an impatient age, and project time can usually be regarded as a scarce commodity. If the need for an essential modification is discovered during the active production phase of a programme, there may simply be no time available in which to issue suitably changed drawings. There are right and wrong ways to deal with this situation, and the following case history is an example of the latter.

Case history: – The Kosy-Kwik Company

The project setting

Kosy-Kwik was a company which specialized in the design, supply and installation of heating and air-conditioning systems. In 1990 it was awarded a contract, as subcontractors to a large building group, to plan and install all the heating and ventilation arrangements in a new multi-storey office block commissioned by the Coverite Insurance Company Ltd, which wished to use it for its headquarters. Two engineers, Clarke and Jackson, were assigned to the project. Whilst Clarke was given overall design responsibility, Jackson was detailed off to plan the central control panel and its associated controls and instrumentation.

Early difficulties

We join the project near the end of the preparation period in the Kosy-Kwik factory. By this time most deliveries of plant and equipment had been made to the Coverite premises, except for the control panel, which was still being fabricated, later than scheduled.

Jackson was a conscientious engineer who took a great interest in his jobs as they passed through the factory. He was in the habit of making periodical tours, in order to keep a check on progress and the results of his design. It was during one of these tours that Jackson was approached by the sheet metal shop foreman. It appeared that the Coverite control panel, now nearing completion, was weak and wobbly.

Jackson could only agree with the foreman. The front panel was indeed decidedly flimsy, as a result of a glaring design error in specifying a gauge of steel that was far too thin. Delivery of this panel to site was already late, and threatened to delay the whole project. There was simply no time available in which to start building a new control panel. In any case, the extra cost would have been unwelcome. A simpler solution had to be found – a rescue package in fact.

Marked-up drawings

The engineer asked the foreman to weld some suitably chunky pieces of channel iron to the rear face of the panel in order to stiffen it. The foreman agreed, but was worried about getting the job past the inspection stage with the changes. 'No problem!' said Jackson, who took a pen from his pocket, marked up the foreman's copy of the drawing with the channel iron additions, and signed it to authorize the alteration.

The modification was successful. Everyone concerned was very relieved, not least Jackson, whose reputation had been likely to suffer. Only a few hours were lost, and the panel was duly delivered. The remainder of the project went ahead without further mishap, and the Coverite Insurance Company Ltd joined the long list of Kosy-Kwik's satisfied customers.

The follow-up project

In the summer of 1995, Kosy-Kwik were awarded a follow-up contract by the Coverite Insurance Company. Their offices were to be extended, with a new wing to house computer services and staff. Coverite were working to a well-planned but tight schedule, which demanded that the new wing should be opened on the first working day of 1996. Because of the rigid timescale restrictions, several contract conditions were imposed on Kosy-Kwik. In particular, the only complete shut-down period allowed for the existing heating and ventilating plant (for connecting and testing the additional circuits and controls) was to be during the Christmas break. Otherwise the Coverite Company would suffer loss of work by their office staff. There was also to be a penalty payment of £400 for every week or part of a week by which Kosy-Kwik failed to meet the scheduled end-date.

During the five years which separated these two projects, several changes had occurred in the Kosy-Kwik organization. Clarke received a well-deserved promotion to a remote branch office, where he became area manager. Jackson retired to enjoy his pension. The engineering department expanded, and attracted several new recruits. Among these was Stevens, an experienced contract engineer. He had no means of contact with Clarke or Jackson, and was unlikely ever to meet either of them.

Preparation for the new project

Stevens was appointed as engineer in charge of the new Coverite project. He knew that the best policy would be to prefabricate as many parts of the project as possible in the factory. This would reduce the amount of work to be done on site, and ensure that the final link-up and testing could be accomplished during the Christmas break. Stevens found a roll of drawings labelled 'Coverite Project' in a dead file drawer, dusted them off, and set to work.

Most of the system was found to be straightforward, and the final tying-in with the existing installation was to be achieved by providing the installation engineers with a bolt-on package that could be fitted to the original control panel. This package was duly designed, manufactured and delivered to site along with all the other essential materials. By the time Christmas arrived, all equipment, pipes and ducts were in place in the new part of the building. All that remained was for the final installation team to arrive, shut down the plant, modify the control panel with the kit provided, and then test and set up the whole system.

The installation attempt

Early on Christmas Eve, two Kosy-Kwik fitters were sent to shut down the plant and start work on the control panel. Their first job was to cut a large rectangular hole in an unused part of the original panel in order to fit the new package. A template had been provided for this purpose, which they now placed in position. When they started cutting, the engineers met unexpected resistance in the shape of several large channel iron ribs welded to the rear face of the panel. The engineers had come prepared only to tackle the thin sheet shown on the old drawings. It took them over two hours and many saw blades before the hole was finished. Then they found that the connections to the new control package were fouled by what remained of the channel iron. Worse still, the panel was now weak and wobbly again.

The two engineers were experienced and trained as skilled installation fitters, but were equipped neither materially nor mentally to deal with problems of this magnitude without help. They suffered an acute sense of frustration and isolation, although they found different (shorter) words with which to express their feelings.

A cry for help was indicated. Unfortunately, however, the response to their impassioned telephone call to Kosy-Kwik headquarters was less than satisfactory. Against the background accompaniment of a spirited office party, they learned that all the senior engineering and management staff had already left to start their holiday. The operator wished the fitters a 'Merry Christmas' and suggested that they 'Have a nice day.' The two engineers interpreted these greetings as good advice, gave up and went home to start their unexpected holidays.

The extra cost

There is no real need to dwell at length on the consequences of this case, or to describe the scenes of anguish and recriminations back at headquarters in the New Year. A short summary of the additional cost items follows:

		£
1	Design and manufacture new control panel modification kit	3500
2	Cost of time wasted time during first visit of the two fitters	250
3	Cost of repairing weakened panel, on site	180
4	Contract penalty clause, 4 weeks at £400 per week	1600
	Total additional costs, directly attributable	5530

Post-mortem

A retrospective glance at the circumstances leading to the disastrous consequences of the Coverite project provides a useful basis for describing a more reliable method of dealing with very urgent modifications.

In this example, all troubles can be traced back to the use of a marked-up drawing on the sheet metal shop floor, the details of which were not incorporated in the filed project drawings. The use of marked-up drawings is generally to be deplored, but we have to be realistic about this problem and accept that there will be occasions when they are unavoidable, when there is simply no time in which to update the master drawings or computer file and issue new copies of the drawing. Under these circumstances, some sort of temporary documentation must suffice, but *only* where safeguards are in place to ensure that the original drawings do get changed to show the true 'as-built' condition of the project.

Safeguards

One way in which the updating of final drawings can be safeguarded in the event of emergency changes relies on a streamlined version of the formal modification procedure, without bypassing any of the essential control points. The originator of the emergency modification must write out an engineering change request and get it registered by the change coordinator. After seeking the immediate approval of the chief engineer (or the nominated deputy), the originator must pass one copy to the design office so that the change will eventually be incorporated in the drawings. Another copy of the change request is kept by the coordinating clerk, who must make certain that it is seen at the next change committee meeting. The original change request form is passed to the production department for action, where it becomes part of the issued manufacturing instructions.

If a working copy of a drawing does have to be marked-up, which may be inevitable if there is insufficient space on the change request form, an identical marked up copy must be deposited in the design office, together with their copy of the change request. The original change request must accompany the job right through all its production stages, particularly until it reaches final inspection and testing.

Chapter 24

Managing project risk

Everything we do, from getting out of bed in the morning to returning there at night, carries risk. Come to think of it, even lying in bed can be risky. It is not surprising that projects, which metaphorically (and sometimes literally) break new ground, attract many risks. Project risks can be predictable, or completely unforeseeable. They might be caused by the physical elements, or they could be political, economic, commercial, technical, or operational in origin. Freak events have been known to disrupt projects, such as the unexpected discovery of important archaeological remains, or the decision by a few members of a rare protected species to establish their family home on what should be the site of a new project.

The potential effects of risks range from trivial inconvenience to project disaster. Project risk management (and much of mainstream project management) is concerned with attempting to identify all the reasonably foreseeable risks, assessing the probability and severity of those risks, and then deciding what might be done to reduce their possible impact or avoid them altogether.

Some risks can occur at any stage in a project, whilst others are associated with particular tasks. Generally speaking, a risk event that occurs late in a project will be more costly in terms of time and money than a similar event nearer the start of the project. That is because, as time passes, there will be a greater value of work in progress and higher sunk costs at risk of loss or damage. Risk management must therefore be considered early, along with the initial project planning, so that a risk strategy can be developed to identify the risks and decide how to pre-empt them as far as is economically practicable through tactical measures. The strategy should be reviewed from time to time throughout the project to ensure that it remains comprehensive and valid.

Project risk management is a particularly complex subject. Even the classification of risks is not straightforward, and can be approached in different ways. There are several techniques for assessing and dealing with project risks, some of which are shared with other management disciplines (particularly quality management and reliability engineering). This chapter will outline a few of the methods commonly used.

Identifying and assessing risks

Risks can be foreseeable or totally unpredictable. For example, it is almost certain that some tasks will not be completed in line with their duration estimates and budgets. Some might exceed their estimates, while others could be finished early and cost less than expected. Indeed, statistical tools can be used to attempt an assessment of the probability of the project finishing by its target completion date. Earned-value analysis can keep final cost forecasts under review. But the razing of project headquarters to the ground through a gas explosion could hardly be predicted – although, of course, if it did happen, the effects of predictable departures from estimates would pale into insignificance.

Identifying and listing the possible risks

Checklists, which grow in size and value as companies gain more project experience, are a good starting point for listing the foreseeable risks. Studying the history of similar projects can also highlight possible problems and help the project manager to learn from the mistakes and experiences of others.

Brainstorming is an effective technique for considering many aspects of risks. A brainstorming meeting of key staff is a particularly productive method for identifying all the possible risks, along with many of the improbable ones. Much depends on how the brainstorming session is conducted. The leader should encourage an atmosphere of 'anything goes', so that participants feel free to propose even the most bizarre risks without fear of ridicule.

It is desirable, even at the early listing stage, to attempt some form of risk classification. Perhaps the most practicable initial approach is to divide the list according to the stage in the project life cycle where each risk is most likely to occur. So, to give an example, risks might be grouped initially under the following headings:

1   risks most likely to occur at the start of the project

2   risks most likely to occur during the execution of the project

3   risks that can affect the final stages of a project, particularly during commissioning

4   risks occurring during the initial period of project operation, after hand over to the customer

5   risks that can occur at any time in the project.

Once identified, risks can be ranked according to the probability of their occurrence and the severity of the impact if they should occur. For this, it is necessary to start by considering the possible causes and effects of every risk.

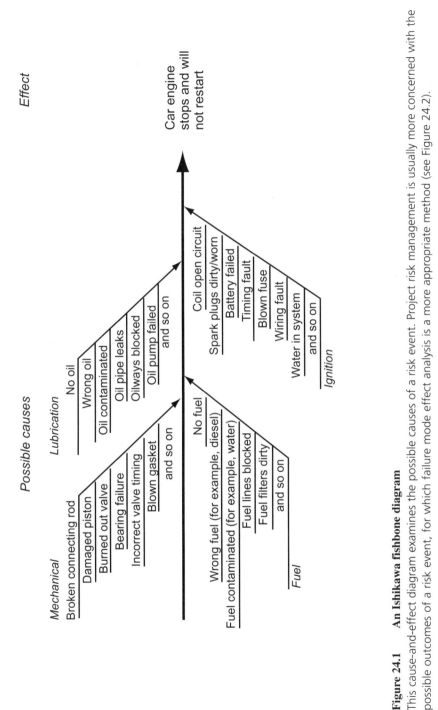

Figure 24.1   An Ishikawa fishbone diagram

This cause-and-effect diagram examines the possible causes of a risk event. Project risk management is usually more concerned with the possible outcomes of a risk event, for which failure mode effect analysis is a more appropriate method (see Figure 24.2).

Qualitative cause-and-effect analysis

Fault trees and fishbones

Fault-tree analysis (not described here) and Ishikawa fishbone diagrams are methods commonly used by reliability and safety engineers to analyse faults in design and construction. Figure 24.1, for instance, shows how an Ishikawa fishbone diagram might be compiled to analyse the numerous reasons why a car engine fails to start. Many items in this car engine example could be broken down into greater detail, leading to quite a complex diagram, with many branches to the 'fish skeleton'.

Fishbone diagrams can easily be used without adaptation to examine failures or poor performance in organizations. Wherever they are used, the process generally starts by thinking about the effect, and then looking for the possible causes. Project risk management, however, is more often conducted from the opposite viewpoint, which means first listing all the possible causes (risks), and then assessing their probable effects. So, although often mentioned in connection with project risk management, these particular cause-and-effect diagrams really approach the problem from the wrong direction.

Failure mode and effect analysis (FMEA)

Failure mode and effect analysis has also been imported into project risk management from reliability and quality engineering, but this method is more helpful because it starts by considering possible risk items (failure modes), and then proceeds to predict all their possible effects. Figure 24.2 shows a simple FMEA chart.

Item 1 in this example is related to the car engine problem in the fishbone diagram (Figure 24.1) but looks beyond the simple fact of failure to examine the possible effects of the engine failing to start. A final column allows space for pre-emptive actions to be recommended that might mitigate or prevent damage from the risk.

Only three items are shown in Figure 24.2, but there might be hundreds of items in a large, complex project. Another column is sometimes added to show when in the project life cycle the risk is most likely to occur.

The chart in Figure 24.2 illustrates a qualitative process. The characteristics of each risk are examined. But there is no attempt to give each risk a priority ranking number or to quantify the effects if the risk should occur.

Risk classification matrices

Figure 24.3 shows a risk classification matrix. This matrix comprises nine sections. Although labelled 'very simple', an even simpler four-section version is

	Item	Failure mode	Cause of failure	Effect	Remedy: recommended action
1	Project manager s car	Engine refuses to start	Poor maintenance	Project manager marooned at remote site with no other means of transport	Ensure good vehicle maintenance and keep back up car at project site
2	Main building	Building collapses during installation of heavy machinery	Errors in floor loading calculations	Personal injuries Project delays Loss of reputation	Triple-check key structural calculations
3		Building collapses during installation of heavy machinery	Floor slabs incorrectly poured	Personal injuries Project delays Loss of reputation	Ensure operatives get good training and instruction. Employ competent site engineering manager.

Figure 24.2   Part of a simple failure mode and effect matrix (FMEA)

often used, containing the following quadrants:

● high chance – high impact

● high chance – low impact

● low chance – high impact

● low chance – low impact.

As with failure mode and effect analysis, this again is a qualitative method, in which no attempt is made to evaluate any risk numerically. Each risk item is considered for its likelihood of occurrence (chance), and for the relative scale of the impact on the project should it occur.

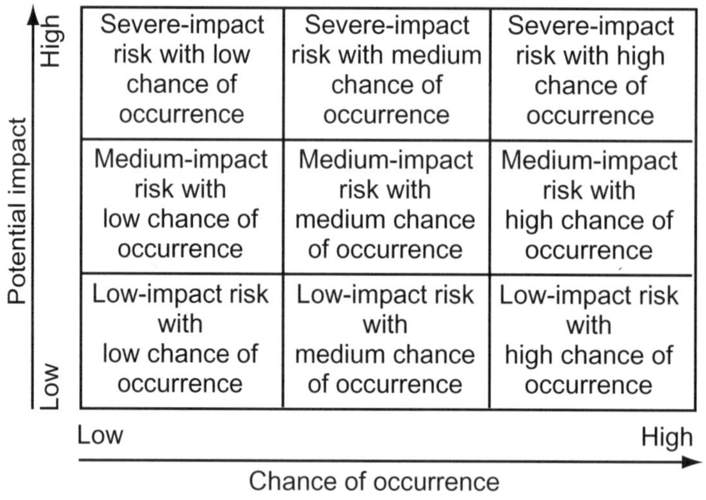

	Low		High
High	Severe-impact risk with low chance of occurrence	Severe-impact risk with medium chance of occurrence	Severe-impact risk with high chance of occurrence
Potential impact	Medium-impact risk with low chance of occurrence	Medium-impact risk with medium chance of occurrence	Medium-impact risk with high chance of occurrence
Low	Low-impact risk with low chance of occurrence	Low-impact risk with medium chance of occurrence	Low-impact risk with high chance of occurrence

Chance of occurrence

Figure 24.3   A very simple risk classification matrix

Suppose, for instance, that a project is being planned to move a large company headquarters from a central city location to a country town. The possibility of some office equipment being lost, damaged or stolen in transit might be high, but the impact could be considered medium. The chance that some key staff might decide not to relocate with the company could be thought to have a medium chance, and the effect could have a medium impact on the company's performance when starting up in the new location. The collapse of the new premises just before occupation date through an earthquake in Swindon would be very low-chance, but the impact would be devastatingly high. The chance of moving day being made thoroughly miserable for all concerned through rain would be high, but with low practical impact. Figure 24.4 portrays a simple qualitative risk assessment matrix showing how the principles illustrated in Figure 24.3 might be applied in practice.

Risk event	Chance of happening	Potential harm to project	Difficulty of detection	Comment
Action by environmentalists	High	High	Low	We shall be building in a nature reserve.
Strikes or other industrial action	Low	High	Low	Loyal workforce with no previous problems.
Project manager struck by lightning	Low	Medium	Low	But she is a keen golfer.
Hairline cracks in structural steel	Low	High	High	Suppliers have high-quality reputation.
Software bugs	Medium	High	High	Process safety depends on computer controls.
Exchange rate changes	Medium	Medium	Low	Not difficult to detect but impossible to predict.
Materials shortages	Medium	Medium	Low	

Figure 24.4   A simple qualitative risk matrix

Quantitative analysis

Quantitative analysis methods attempt to assign numerical values to risks and their possible effects. They often examine the probable impact on project time and costs. Alternatively, the evaluation process can produce a ranking number for every identified risk. Ranking numbers denote the priority that a risk should claim for management attention and expenditure on preventive measures.

Although all quantitative methods produce 'actual' numbers, they can give a false sense of precision. It must be remembered that the results are based on estimates, assumptions and human judgement. Those contributing assessments might be fundamentally flawed, mistaken, or simply too difficult for any person to make with any degree of certainty.

Failure mode effect criticality analysis (FMECA)

The qualitative failure, mode and effect analysis method illustrated in Figure 24.2 can be adapted and extended to attempt risk quantification. The method then becomes failure mode effect and criticality analysis (FMECA). Figure 24.5 shows one version. In this example three assessment columns are provided, in each of which the risk analyst is expected to enter a number expressing the degree of significance. Every item is ranked on a scale of one to five, with the highest numbers indicating the greatest degree of seriousness. The entries might be those of the risk analyst or, preferably, the collective opinions of a risk committee or brainstorming group.

Item 2 in Figure 24.5, for example, considers the possibility and potential seriousness of a building collapse. This is for a building created as part of the project, and the collapse in question might happen during the installation of heavy machinery on upper-level floors. If the floors have been incorrectly designed, they might not be sufficiently strong to carry the weight of the machinery. The assessor clearly thinks this is unlikely to happen because she has ranked chance at the bottom end of the 1-5 scale. There is no doubt, however, that if this event did occur it would be extremely serious, so the severity has been marked as 5.

Detection difficulty means the perceived difficulty of noticing the cause of this risk (design error in this case) in time to prevent the risk event. Here there is a considerable element of judgement, but the assessor thinks that although the chance of a design error is very low, the difficulty of spotting a mistake if it did occur would be higher (3 on the scale of 1-5).

The product of these three parameters, 1 x 5 x 3, gives a total ranking number of 15. Theoretically, when this exercise has been performed on every item in the list, the list can be sorted in descending sequence of these ranking numbers, so that risks with the highest priority for management attention come at the top of the list.

Some assessors use weighted parameters. For example, it might be considered that the severity of the risk should play a higher part in deciding ranking priority. So the severity column could be marked on a higher scale, say from 1-10. Item 2 in Figure 24.5 might then be marked 9 on this extended scale, which would increase the ranking factor for this item from 15 to 27.

Although not usual practice, a case might be argued for allowing zero scores in the 'Chance' and 'Severity' columns. That could, of course, result in a total ranking factor of zero. That would be one way in which to dispose of some of the more outlandish risk events identified during an 'anything goes' brainstorming session.

Sensitivity analysis

Sensitivity analysis is particularly useful in considering the effects of risks arising through incorrect forecasting of parameter values during project financial appraisal. The process involves repeating the appraisal calculations several times for stepped variations in the values of one chosen parameter, to test the effect on the outcome. Suppose, for example, that the revenues (cash inflows) from a project in future years cannot be forecast reliably. After calculating the net present value of the project using the best estimates, the calculation can be repeated using a range of lower and higher cash inflows to test the sensitivity of net present value (or internal rate of return) to variations in revenue. This subject was explained in more detail in the tollbridge case study in Chapter 6 (see page 139).

	Item	Failure mode	Cause of failure	Effect	Chance	Severity	Detection difficulty	Total ranking
1	**Project manager's car**	Engine refuses to start	Poor maintenance	Project manager marooned at remote site with no other means of transport	2	1	3	6
2	**Main building**	Building collapses during installation of heavy machinery	Errors in floor loading calculations	Personal injuries Project delays Loss of reputation	1	5	3	15
3		Building collapses during installation of heavy machinery	Floor slabs incorrectly poured	Personal injuries Project delays Loss of reputation	1	5	2	10

Figure 24.5   Part of a failure mode effect and criticality analysis matrix (FMECA)

PERT and Monte Carlo analysis

PERT (program evaluation and review technique), a method for dealing with uncertainty in project task duration estimates, was described in Chapter 8 (see page 208). The section 'Programs for probability and risk analysis' in Chapter 14 included an example showing how, using Monte Carlo analysis, many calculations of critical path analysis can be conducted with randomly selected values of pessimistic, most likely and optimistic task durations. *Pertmaster* and *OPERA* are two of the many software applications that can perform this function. There is no reason why the method cannot be extended to consider cost estimates rather than duration estimates.

Methods for dealing with risks

When all the known risks have been listed, assessed and ranked it is time to consider what might be done about them. The manager has a range of options:

1 **Avoid the risk** – The only way to avoid a risk is to abandon the possible causes, which could even mean deciding not to undertake a project at all.

2 **Take precautions to prevent or mitigate risk impact** – This is a most important part of risk management, requiring the active participation of all managers and staff. It needs a high-level risk prevention strategy combined with executive determination to ensure that all preventive measures are always followed throughout all parts of the organization. It requires the creation of a risk prevention culture, covering all aspects of project tasks, health and safety, and consideration for the environment. Here are a few examples of the many possible practical measures, listed in random sequence:
    - high security fencing to reduce the chance of gatecrashers at an open air pop festival
    - provision of marquees at a garden party in case of rain
    - regular inspection and testing of electrical equipment to ensure safe operation
    - double-checking to detect errors in design calculations for vital project components or structures
    - provision of backup electrical power supplies for vital operations, essential services and computers
    - frequent backup and secure offline storage of business data
    - avoidance of trailing electric cables in offices
    - ensuring that means of escape routes in buildings are always clear of obstructions and that smoke screen doors are kept closed
    - regular fire drills, testing of fire alarms and emergency lighting
    - on-the-job training of back-up staff to understudy key roles in the organization

- regular inspection and maintenance of lifts and hoists
- provision of safety clothing and equipment to protect workers, and enforcement of their use
- restricted access to hazardous areas
- provision of secure handrails to all stairways
- choosing the time of year most likely to provide fair weather for outdoor projects
- adequate training of all those operating potentially hazardous machinery
- regular financial audits and the installation of procedures to identify or deter fraud
- and so on, and so on: this list could be very long.

3   **Accept the risk** – Rain might make the day chosen for office relocation miserable for all concerned, but the risk would have to be accepted. There are numerous small things than can go wrong during the course of any project, and most of these risks can be accepted in the knowledge that their effect is not likely to be serious, and that they can be overcome by corrective measures or re-planning.

4   **Share the risk** – If a project, or a substantial part of it, appears to carry very high risk, the contractor might seek one or more partners to undertake the work as a joint venture. Then the impact of any failure would be shared among the partners. Sharing a risk big enough to ruin one company might reduce its impact to little more than a temporary inconvenience.

5   **Limit the risk** – There are occasions when project risks should only be accepted with safeguards in place to limit their potential effect. A good example is an internal project, perhaps for pure research, that cannot be adequately defined at the outset. No one can tell how much the project will eventually cost or what its outcome might be. Yet the opportunities are too great to consider avoiding the risk altogether.

  The usual solution to starting an ill-defined project is to limit the risk by authorizing work step by step. It may be possible to divide the project into a number of stages for this purpose: indeed, the process is sometimes called *stage gating*. The stages might be determined by:
- the occurrence of significant events in the project that can easily be recognized when they happen
- the imposition of a time limit for each stage
- a budgetary limit for each stage
  or
- a combination of any two or all of these.

Funding or authorization of expenditure on each new stage of the project would depend on a critical review of the work carried out up to the review date, coupled with a fresh appraisal of the value of continuing with the project.

This approach has the advantage of limiting the committed risk. Although it is not possible to define the entire project in advance, it should be possible to look the short way ahead necessary to define each new step. Each limited step so defined may then be amenable to project management procedures that cannot be used for the whole project.

In the step-by-step or stage gate approach, it must always be borne in mind that it might become necessary to abandon the project at any stage and write off the expenditure already incurred.

6   **Transfer the risk** – Some risks, or substantial parts of them, can be transferred to another party on payment of a fee or premium. This leads to the important subject of insurance, which is discussed in the next section.

Insurance

The financial impact of many risks can be offset by insuring against them. The client pays the insurance company a premium for this service, and the insurer might itself choose to spread the risk by sharing it with one or more other insurance companies. Figure 24.6 shows that managers do not enjoy complete freedom of choice when deciding which risks should be included in their insurance portfolio.

Categories of insurance

There are four main classes of insurance:

1   legal liabilities (payments to others as a result of statutory, contractual or professional commitments, compensation awarded by the courts, legal expenses, but not fines imposed by the courts)

2   protection against loss or damage to property, including work in progress

3   cover relating to personnel

4   pecuniary loss.

A policy may combine cover for two or more of the above classes of risk.

Obligatory insurances

Legal requirements oblige companies to obtain adequate insurance cover against some risks. These obligations arise either from various government laws and regulations, or from conditions contained in a binding commercial contract.

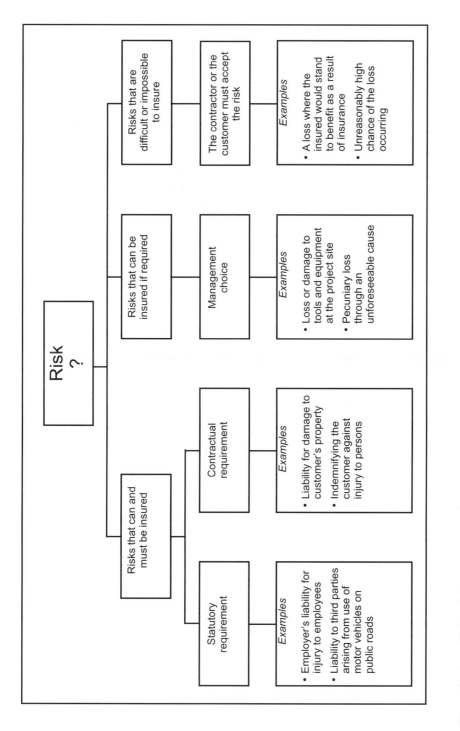

Figure 24.6   Risk and insurance in project management

Statutory requirements

At the top of the insurance shopping list are those items which must be insured in order to comply with laws and regulations. Third-party insurance for motor vehicles used on public roads is a familiar example. Employers are obliged to insure their employees against injury or illness arising from their employment (Employers' Liability Insurance) and every employer has to display a valid certificate on its noticeboards to show that such insurance exists.

Statutory regulations of particular interest to the manager of construction and engineering projects cover the periodic inspection and certification of lifting equipment, pressure systems and local-exhaust ventilation plant. No project which includes the installation of such equipment should be handed over to a client without the relevant written (or other) scheme of examination and the accompanying inspection certificates. If the correct documentation is not supplied, the client will not legally be able to operate the equipment.

In the UK, these regulations form part of the Health and Safety at Work Act 1974. Much of this legislation resulted from European Directives, and similar legislation has been enacted in other EU member countries. The relevant inspection work is usually performed by engineer-surveyors employed by an engineering insurance company. The insurance company is sometimes engaged by the contract principal, but more usually by the main contractor. The larger of these insurance companies, with many years' experience of such work, are able to advise on compliance with national and local legislation covering equipment and construction materials.

The project or site manager must check that inspection certificates required by the regulations are current and valid for plant hired for use on a construction site. This will help to protect the project manager's organization from any liability that might arise from the use of a plant hire fleet that has been poorly managed by the plant hire company.

Contractual requirements and other legal liabilities

In commercial and industrial projects, whether for construction or manufacturing, it is certain that some onus will be placed upon the parties (usually the contractor) to insure against several risks. All the model terms of contract for engineering, civil and construction contracts embody such requirements. The project contractor will also wish to make certain that subcontractors are bound, in turn, by similar conditions.

Liability insurances are most likely to feature prominently in project contracts. The project purchaser will want to know, for example, that the contractor has adequate cover for legal liability in the event of personal injury, illness or death caused to anyone as a result of the project.

In summary, liability insurances may be required for:

- compensation to persons for bodily harm (employees of either party, others working on site, visitors and members of the public)

- property loss or damage, including work-in-progress

- financial loss

- infringement of property rights

- accidents

- product liability (arising from use of a product)

- professional negligence

- nuisance caused by the works

- environmental damage.

Every organization or professional person with project responsibility (including architects, consultants, surveyors, designers and project management organizations) must make certain that they have adequate professional liability insurance to cover any liability that they might incur in the course of their work.

Other risks that can be covered by insurance

In addition to the statutory and contractual requirements, there is a range of other risks against which a contractor might be required to insure, or for which a contractor might decide that insurance is prudent. Some of these are listed below.

Contractors' all-risks insurance for construction and engineering projects

All-risks insurance cover provides protection during the works, until the project is complete and handed over to the customer. Thereafter, insurance becomes the customer's responsibility.

All-risks policies typically protect work in progress against fire, storm damage, theft and malicious damage but any new policy proposal should be studied with care, as it is likely to list exceptions. In addition to work in progress, the cover should include loss or damage to:

- construction plant and machinery

- hired plant

- construction materials in transit to site

- temporary buildings and site huts

- employees' tools and effects.

Reinstatement costs after an accident will also be covered, including the costs of removing debris, and the fees of architects, surveyors and consulting engineers. The insurer might also agree to pay additional expenses (such as overtime costs and express carriage rates) incurred as a result of expediting reinstatement work.

Contract all-risks (CAR) policies usually apply to civil engineering and construction projects, while the less common engineering all-risks (EAR) policies are for contracts that relate specifically to the construction and installation of machinery.

Decennial (latent defects) insurance

Decennial insurance, which can cover a period of up to ten years, is designed to insure against damage to premises caused specifically by an inherent defect in the design, materials or construction of a project. In the event of a successful claim, decennial insurance removes the need for the project owner to suffer the expense of taking legal action for recompense against the contractor.

Accident and sickness insurance

Provisions for personal accident, sickness and medical expenses insurance will need particular consideration when employees are required to travel, whether at home or abroad. Those working on projects in foreign countries will expect to be adequately covered for the higher risks involved, and such cover will have to be extended to spouses and children if they are also allowed to travel.

Key person insurance

Key person insurance offers various kinds of protection to an employer against expenses or loss of profits which result when illness, injury or death prevents one or more named key persons from performing the duties expected of them. Arrangements are flexible, and policies can be tailored to suit particular circumstances.

Pecuniary insurance

Pecuniary insurances are designed to protect a company against financial losses from a variety of causes. Risks that can be covered include embezzlement, loss through interruption of business, and legal expenses. Advance profits insurance may be possible in some limited circumstances to provide cover for delay in receiving planned return on project investment caused by late completion of the project.

Of particular interest to contractors where business with foreign customers is involved is export credit insurance. In the UK, the Government's Export Credits Guarantee Department (ECGD) provides guarantees that can provide security against bank loans for large capital goods and long term projects. Most industrialized companies have similar schemes. The contractor will be expected to bear some of the risk, although its proportion will usually be small. The security offered by credit insurance can be an important factor in obtaining finance for a project.

Risks which cannot be covered by insurance

There are risks which an underwriter will either refuse to insure, or for which the premium demanded would be prohibitive. Such cases arise in the following circumstances:

- where the chances against a loss occurring are too high or, in other words, where the risk is seen as more of a certainty than reasonable chance – examples are losses made through speculative trading or because of disadvantageous changes in foreign exchange rates

- where the insurer is not able to spread its risk over a sufficient number of similar risks

- where the insurer does not have access to sufficient data from the past to be able to quantify the future risk

- where the insured would stand to gain as a result of a claim. Except in some forms of personal insurance, the principle of insurance is to attempt to reinstate the insured's position to that which existed before the loss event. A person cannot, for example, expect to benefit personally from a claim for loss or damage to property not belonging to him or her (property in which he or she has no *insurable interest*).

These items must therefore be excluded from the insurance portfolio. In some cases, other commercial remedies might exist for offsetting the risks.

Obtaining insurance

Insurance can be sought directly from an underwriter, or through a broker – preferably one with a good reputation and experienced in the insured's type of project activity. The insurer will need to be supplied with sufficient information for the risk to be adequately defined, and the contractor will be expected to inform the insurer of any change of circumstances likely to affect the risks insured. The insurer may wish to make investigations or even follow up the project work using its own experts.

Professional advice from insurers can often be of great benefit in reducing risks, especially in the areas of health and safety and crime prevention.

Two events in 2001 had a severe impact on insurers and will affect reinsurance and capacity for many years to come. One of these events was the insolvency and collapse of Independent Insurance plc, a company that insured a large number of contractors and construction trade clients for very low premiums. This caused every insurance company and broker to conduct internal audits, critically re-examining the risks to their own businesses. The other 2001 event was, of course, the 11 September terrorist atrocities in the USA, which highlighted to insurance and reinsurance companies the potential for such enormous claims to be repeated in the future, whether from terrorist attacks or other causes. Insurers have since sought to limit their exposure to such risks, and they have instituted a regime of stricter underwriting controls and lower risk acceptance thresholds.

Liability insurance is becoming expensive. Employer's liability cover, even though a legal requirement, is becoming difficult to obtain. Some insurance companies have had to close because they were unable to effect such insurance.

It is therefore now more important than ever for a project manager to involve an insurance specialist at a very early planning stage, lest he or she should find that no insurance cover is available at short notice.

Planning for a crisis

Some risk events can have such a potential impact on a project that special crisis management contingency plans must be made. Such contingency plans can extend to projects that would need to be set up specially and rapidly to deal with a sudden crisis, for example in areas that are particularly liable to epidemic diseases, famine, flooding, hurricanes, earthquakes or other natural disasters. Crisis contingency plans should also be put in place by process industries and other companies that carry out operations which, if they should go wrong, could be hazardous for people and the environment beyond the factory gates. One cannot always say when or where a disaster will strike, but at least plans can be put in place to be implemented immediately if the need arises.

Once the possibility of a crisis has been established, the first step in devising a contingency plan is to identify the key people who will take charge of the crisis management project. These people will constitute a sleeping organization, ready to awake at a moment's notice in case of need. The core organization might include senior representatives of local and national government, the emergency services, particular charities and relief organizations, and so on. Each person should have the authority to instruct others within his or her home organization, and the permission to identify the relevant resources that could be made available should the crisis happen. A team leader or steering committee must be appointed that will manage the project should it become live. This group of key people might be called the Crisis Action Committee.

Once the key people have been elected or selected to serve on the Action Committee, they must meet to design appropriate contingency plans, and then meet again at regular intervals to ensure that the plans are kept up to date. The committee might have to arrange for emergency funds, stores and special equipment to be stockpiled or at least located against the time when they might suddenly be needed. Lists of secondary organizations and other helpers must be established, which, although not part of the action committee, could be called upon to give urgent and immediate assistance. These secondary associations might include, for example, specialist engineering or chemical contractors, explosives or decontamination experts, building and demolition contractors, caterers, and a wide range of charitable organizations that could offer relief services. There might also be a need to plan for immediate advertising in the appropriate media to make public appeals for funds.

One thing that the action committee will need to do as early as possible is to assess what might happen should the crisis arise, and use their collective imagination to consider and be prepared in advance for as many of the problems as possible. A table-top exercise can contribute to this process, where the members of the Action Committee carry out a role-playing exercise to consider as precisely as possible what might happen and what they themselves and their subordinates might do should the crisis happen. Many crisis contingency plans can be tested by field exercises, in which some or all of the services act out their parts as if the crisis had actually happened. Field exercises can reveal shortcomings in the contingency plans and test vital aspects such as mobility, response speeds and how to communicate and coordinate the various participants under emergency conditions, when power, water and telephones might all be out of action.

When the plans have been made and tested, they must be documented, incorporating all the lessons learned from table-top and field exercises so that they are ready to put into action effectively and with minimum delay. This is, in effect, creating a project handbook or project manual for a project that might never happen. When a crisis does cross from imagination to reality, however, contingency planning can save time, and many lives.

Chapter 25

Managing project closure

Project management activities do not usually end abruptly when all the tasks on the plan have been performed successfully. A number of loose but important ends need to be tied up in a process which some (with inadequate respect for the English language) call 'closeout'.

Reasons for closing a project

Projects do not always end successfully, and there are a number of reasons why projects are occasionally closed before their intended finish date. Here are a few of the many possible reasons for stopping work on a project:

1   The project has been completed and handed over to the project owner, with or without complete success.

2   The project contractor has run out of funds, leaving the owner to find a new contractor.

3   The project owner has permanently run out of funds, killing the project.

4   The project owner wishes to make fundamental changes, causing the project to be scrapped and restarted.

5   Changed economic or political conditions mean that the project will no longer be financially viable for the owner in the foreseeable future (for example, a fall in the price or demand for a commodity that removes financial justification for building new plant to increase production capacity).

6   The customer asks for the project to be 'put on hold' (delayed indefinitely) pending a possible improvement in market conditions, or to await the results of a reappraisal.

7   Government policy changes (possible for many reasons) resulting in termination of some government contracts. Defence contracts for weapons systems, ships and aircraft are always subject to such risks.

8   An Act of God (flood, tempest and so on) has intervened, causing further work on the project to be suspended or abandoned.

9   Hostile activities have broken out in an internal or international conflict.

Premature project closure can affect the closedown procedures, but all sections in this chapter (except for 'Final product definition') assume successful completion and handover to the project owner.

Formal project closure

Just as it was necessary to issue a formal document of authority to open a project and allow expenditure to begin, so the end or significant interruption of a project must be marked by a formal announcement that stops further expenditure and sets the closedown procedures in motion.

Cost cut-off

The most significant reason for issuing a formal project closure statement is to forbid further expenditure against the main project cost codes. This is particularly important if hard-won profits are not to be eroded by an insidious continuation of timesheet bookings to the project simply because the account still happens to be open. It is well known that the recording of hours on timesheets is open to abuse: there is always a tendency for the less scrupulous staff to try and 'lose' unaccountable or wasted time by booking it to large projects where, it is hoped, it will go unnoticed. Obviously, good supervision will minimize this risk, but an instruction to the computer to reject all further timesheet entries against the project number is more effective.

Company accountants may wish to hold a project account open for their own use beyond the official project closure date, to collect a few 'tail-end' costs. Although further man-hour time bookings are banned after the closure date, there are usually items such as late invoices from suppliers and subcontractors. On a large project these can continue to arrive for several months after project completion. They represent considerable sums, but they should not affect the calculated profit significantly, because (unless there has been loose control of subcontracts and dayworks) these costs should have been known and accrued in the accounts when they were committed (that is, when the orders were issued).

Project closure document

The formal closure notice need only be a very simple form, but it should contain the following information:

- project title
- project number
- the effective closure date
- reason for closure
- any special instructions
- signature authorizing the closure
- distribution, which should at least include all those who received the authorization notice when the project was opened.

An example of a fairly comprehensive closure notice is given in Figure 25.1.

Authorizing post-project expenditure

Although a guillotine must be imposed on time bookings at project closure, it must be recognized that large projects often leave a backwash of documentation work in their wake. Some of these activities are summarized in this chapter. They may require considerable effort, although much of this can be assigned to clerical and fairly junior engineering staff. Just how well such tasks are performed depends to a large extent upon how much money the contractor is prepared to spend on them.

In some firms, final documentation will be treated as an overhead expense, while others may be more fortunate in having budgets and funding contractually agreed with their clients for this purpose. Whether treated as an overhead cost or as a directly recoverable expense, post-project work should be regarded as a work package, separately identifiable from the main project, which should be allocated its own, separate, strictly budgeted account number. This work, all in-house and under local supervision, should be relatively easy to monitor and control. It is often prudent to limit authorization to a few named individuals, so that only timesheets bearing the staff or roll numbers of these people will be accepted by the computer for bookings against the closure account.

The form illustrated in Figure 25.1 not only announces project closure, but also acts as an authorization document for a limited amount of expenditure on the post-project work package. By no means typical, this example would obviously need modification in practice to suit each contractor's own project circumstances and management systems. It does, however, demonstrate a method that can help to ensure the orderly closedown of a project. The version in Figure 25.1 states the budgets allowed. It also includes a checklist of all the final project activities, together with some management directives regarding the disposal of documents.

Notice of project closure

The following project will be closed to time bookings and all expenses with effect from the date given below

Client: Lox Chemicals Limited   Project number: LX 5150

Project title: Loxylene Plant (Huddersfield)   Closure date: 20 Apr 04

The following budgets are hereby authorized for the closedown activities marked in the checklist below

| Department | hours by standard cost staff grade | | | | | | £ |
	1	2	3	4	5	6	
Project engineering	10			20	40		960
Planning				10			140
Purchasing			15				240
Installation and commissioning							
Construction management	5						100
Computing				1			14
Records and archives			10	200			2560
TOTALS	15		25	31	240		4014

Special instructions:
> Take special care with filing. A follow-up project is expected. All files to be destroyed after five years unless otherwise directed below.

CHECKLIST OF PROJECT CLOSURE ACTIVITIES

Project case history	PM to write, keep it brief
Project specification	Has been kept up to date but needs checking
Project variations	List and check that the file is complete
Drawing schedules	Keep 10 years in engineering files
Design calculations	Keep indefinitely in engineering files
Our drawings	Check they are as-built and keep indefinitely
Client's drawings	Return to client
Purchase control schedules	Keep 10 years in engineering files
Vendors' drawings	Keep 10 years
Purchase orders	
Expediting/inspection reports	
Test certificates	Keep 10 years
Operating/maintenance instructions	Keep 15 years
Spares lists	
Maintenance contracts	
Subcontract documents	Keep 10 years
Correspondence files	
Final cost records	Keep 10 years in general reference files
Photographs	Edit. Discuss with publicity dept and client
Critical path networks	Destroy after 1 year and erase computer files
Management information system	Delete project from MIS at year end

Prepared by: A.Scribe   Project manager: I.Diddit   Authorized by: *B J G Whitechief*

Figure 25.1   Project closure notice with checklist

Final project cost records

Final cost accounting information provides an important databank from which comparative cost estimates can be made for future projects. This is especially true of the man-hour records. Costs for materials and purchased equipment, and the monetary conversion of man-hours into wages plus overheads, are not quite so useful because these records become invalidated by cost inflation as time passes. Those needing to retrieve information from any of these records will find their task made immeasurably easier if all the data have been filed under a logical and standard cost-coding system which has been rigidly applied across all projects.

Disposal of surplus material stocks

Surplus materials and components will probably remain upon completion of a project. Sensible consideration must be given to the most cost-effective method for their disposal.

Some specialized components may be saleable to the customer as part of a recommended holding of spare parts. Other items may be returned to common stock, sold, or (if necessary) scrapped.

Redundant stocks must not be allowed to accumulate, because they represent a useless investment in money and space. It might be argued that quantities of very tiny, low-cost items take up little space and represent insignificant investment ('worth keeping because they might come in useful one day'), but even these can cost time and money to store and count at each annual stocktaking.

If project materials and components are never going to be used, their value can be expected to dwindle steadily towards zero as they deteriorate or become obsolete.

Final project definition: The end of a continuous process

Chapter 3 described the project-definition process, and Figure 3.1 showed how this can be continuous throughout the project life cycle. In any substantial project, definition does not end until after the project has finished, when the last document has been updated, registered and filed or archived.

Formal project variation, modification and concession procedures are all part of this process (see Chapter 23). The project manager or engineers must ensure that any deviations from drawings are fed back for incorporation. This can be a particularly significant problem where work has taken place at a site remote from the contractor's home office.

The remainder of this chapter is concerned with documenting the project 'as built', and with the safe retention of documents.

As-built condition of a manufacturing or capital engineering project

Whether a project is for new design and manufacture of equipment or for a mining, civil engineering, petrochemical or other capital project, it is important that the 'as-built' condition on completion is adequately recorded. This is vital if the contractor is to be able to fulfil post-contract obligations to the client. In theory, all that is necessary is to list every drawing, specification and other document describing the project design, configuration and content (not forgetting to include the serial and correct revision numbers of all these documents). All engineering changes should have been incorporated, so that every document is in its final condition.

Records should also include spare copies of operating and maintenance instructions, including those written by the contractor for the whole project, as well as those received from the suppliers of bought-out equipment built into the project.

Provided that all this material is stored in a properly indexed, secure system, there should be no serious information problems in store for people concerned with operating, maintaining, repairing or modifying the project in the future.

Engineering design records

For engineering design records, the first need is to keep a set of project drawings. Sometimes clients will, having paid for the engineering design of a project, consider all project drawings to be their own property. The client's own drawing sheets may even have been used. The contractor will still want to keep a set of drawings on file (probably in digital form).

Drawing schedules

The key to indexing and defining all the drawings at the end of a project is either the central drawing register or, preferably, a specific project drawing schedule. For manufacturing projects, bills of materials or parts lists will identify all the project drawings.

A guide to the contents and format of a drawing schedule is given in Figure 25.2. This example contains some brief progress information, but that is not the principal purpose of the schedule, and is only advisable when a database allows schedule information to be added and updated automatically in line with the main project planning process.

Drawing schedules, bills of materials or parts lists will need to be prepared in sub-sets, corresponding to the work breakdown structure of the project. This breakdown arrangement is similar to that described in Chapter 18 for purchase schedules (see Figure 18.4).

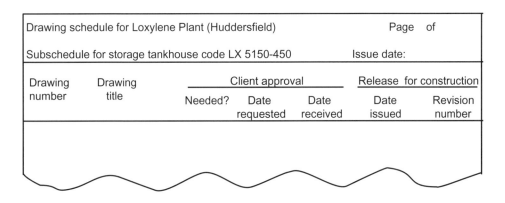

Figure 25.2   Column headings for a drawing schedule

The final set of drawing schedules should list every drawing used in the project, and give its drawing number and correct revision number.

Documenting purchased equipment

For the purposes of illustration, suppose that a client has formally accepted the handover of a complex manufacturing plant, the result of a very large turnkey project. Everything has been managed for the client, including the construction of the buildings, purchasing and installation of all the plant, cranes and other equipment, and final commissioning. Quite obviously, the contractor retains a follow-up responsibility to the client for arranging service under guarantee, assisting with operating problems, and in being able (if required) to carry out future modifications or extensions to the plant.

To provide such a service, the contractor needs adequate technical records of the equipment purchased from external suppliers. These records must be obtained from the vendors during the course of the project in the form of layout drawings, technical specifications, operating and maintenance instructions, lists of recommended spares, lubrication charts, test certificates, and so on.

In most cases, at least one copy of all such documents would be sent to the client, but every prudent contractor will retain a set. Whilst it should theoretically always be possible to go back to the relevant vendor for information in the event of a subsequent problem, vendor companies have a distressing habit of going out of business, or of losing their former identities in mergers and takeovers.

There may also be a considerable benefit to the contractor in keeping detailed records of equipment purchases, because these can often be of use to engineers when specifying equipment for future, non-related projects.

Purchase schedules

On large capital projects, the purchase schedules are the main index of purchasing documentation. The relevant purchase specification numbers (with their correct revision status), supplier and purchase order details should all be traceable through this route. Purchase schedules were described in Chapter 18, and are illustrated in Figures 18.3 and 18.4.

Other documentation

Design calculations

Design calculations are a vital part of project records. It is essential that these are numbered, indexed and stored with at least as much care as that given to the main drawing files. They may be called for in the unfortunate event of subsequent malfunction or structural failure, especially if personal injury results.

Change documents and inspection certificates

All contract variations, modifications, engineering change requests, concessions, production permits, final inspection reports, test certificates and similar documents helping to define the final design status and quality of the project should be filed and indexed.

Correspondence and internal memoranda

Letters to and from vendors can be filed with the relevant purchase order files, where they form part of the technical and contractual record. Other correspondence, not least that with the client, can be filed by date order.

An embarrassing problem sometimes arises because files have been built up in at least two places: in the central filing registry and in the project engineering department. One way to turn this difficulty into an advantage is to have all the project correspondence filed in two different ways. Files held in the project engineering department can be filed by subject according to the project work breakdown structure. Provided the project files are properly managed, they can be added to the central files when the project ends. The central registry files can be kept in simple date order. This dual approach ensures that any document should be retrievable if either its subject or its date is known.

Internal correspondence between departments is usually of less importance, but can be kept along with the relevant subject files if required.

Case history or project diary

If sufficient time and money can be spared for the purpose, it is sometimes useful for the project manager to write a brief case history or diary of the project. This document does not have to be a literary masterpiece, but it should record every significant event, and list all serious problems together with their solutions. When filed with the project specification, minutes of meetings and other key documents, a case history becomes a valuable asset in the future if legal or other questions arise about the project. Reference to past case histories may also help when formulating the strategy for new projects, and reading about past mistakes can help new managers to avoid repeating them in the future. 'Lessons learned' should therefore feature as a main heading.

As-built condition of a multiple manufacturing project

Many manufacturing ventures, although starting from one initial design project, result in the manufacture of more than one final product. Although these final products all started from the same design, if they are not all made in one identical batch it is highly possible that modifications will be introduced between batches. It is even possible for changes to be allowed during the production of one batch. Similar problems exist when the final product is made in continuous manufacture and assembly. The individual build state of every part of the project or every product must be known for reasons of maintenance, interchangeability of parts, and to allow recall or investigation in the event of any failure in service. After listing three case examples, this section will set out the principles of documentation necessary to define the build status of individual products.

Examples

1   A customer ordered seven trailer-mounted, towable automatic testing units for checking out military aircraft. The first of these was a fully serviceable prototype. The final six performed the same functions, but were built slightly differently in the light of experience with the prototype. There were further slight differences between all six units, but all were built to the same drawings (although at various revision numbers). Each complete tester contained a large number of plug-in units, which could be interchanged between all seven sets of test equipment. For maintenance and servicing purposes, it was essential to know the exact build status of each tester, including the build status of every plug-in unit.

2   A defence subcontractor was building electronic equipment for a guided missile. There were prototype and pre-production versions, both built in small

quantities and with drawing changes introduced at various points in the overall programme. There were therefore small changes in build status from one unit to the next. It was essential to know the exact content of every unit built.

3   A more familiar example is the automobile manufacturer, who will introduce modifications throughout the production life of the vehicle. When any owner takes a car for repair or servicing, the garage will need to know the actual build status of that particular car (typically with reference to the year of manufacture and the chassis or engine serial number).

Identifying individual units

The first requirement is that each unit built should be identifiable by some mark or number which distinguishes it from its fellows. This objective is usually achieved by the allocation of batch or serial numbers. These, together with a type or part number, enable any unit to be identified positively, with no possible fear of misinterpretation.

A diesel-engined a.c. generator type 10256, serial number 1023, leaves no room for doubt. If this unit is received back at the factory for servicing, repair or modification, there is no question regarding its origin, and its design status should be known. It should be possible to look at the general assembly drawing and parts list or bills of material for the generator and so discover the numbers of all the drawings and process specifications that went into its making.

Document revision numbers

Document serial numbers, by themselves, are not a sufficient description. It must always be possible to find out the relevant revision numbers and modification status of drawings and specifications that relate to a particular serial numbered unit or production batch.

Suppose that several diesel a.c. generators of the type just described have been supplied for a large project at different times. All are called 'a.c. generator type 10256', but they are *not* all identical. A number of modifications have been introduced over the period, so that different production batches contain small but significant design differences. How now can anyone tell exactly what went into the making of one of these generators, knowing only its type number and serial number?

The most common method of circumventing this problem is to compile a build schedule for each batch. This is tedious, but possibly unavoidable.

Build schedules

A build schedule comprises a list of all the drawings and specifications used in the manufacture of every unit, with the correct revision number of every drawing shown. If there is any drawing which has more than one sheet, the revision number of every sheet must be given. A separate build schedule must be compiled for every project item that is made and assembled as a single unit, but one build schedule can be used to cover a number of items where these are made as an identical batch.

Formats such as that shown in Figure 25.3 allow all the essential details to be recorded. Build schedules might be single-page affairs or, for larger projects, many pages long. Build schedule data were originally compiled on paper sheets, then microfiche or microfilm became popular, but build schedules are now ideally suited to computer-based systems.

Note that there is little point in maintaining build schedules of units with differing build standards if all the drawing information cannot be retrieved. It follows that reference files must be kept of all relevant revisions of each drawing in such cases.

Also, the comfortable premise that the latest issue of a drawing must be the correct issue is destroyed. Indeed, it can happen that different revisions of the same drawing are in use at the same time when a factory is dealing with assemblies or batches of different modification status.

Product labelling

The build schedule procedure should be supported by labelling the actual products or project hardware. Each label should be durable, and should show the part number and the batch or serial number. Small engraved or stamped metal plates are often used. Some companies also provide spaces on the labels to allow modification numbers to be added as each modification is carried out (which includes modifications made in the field).

As-built condition of a project that is interrupted before completion

This chapter started by listing a few reasons why a project might be closed or put on hold before its successful completion. An as-built record will be particularly important, yet most difficult to achieve, if there is any expectation that the customer will resurrect a cancelled project at a later date. Interrupted projects pose great difficulties, especially if work-in-progress has reached the stage when materials have been bought or some components are in various stages of manufacture.

Build schedule				Product number:			
Product or assembly:				Issue date:			
Batch/serial numbers covered:				Sheet of sheets			

Drawing or spec. number	Sheet	Rev.	Drawing or spec. number	Sheet	Rev.

The following modification numbers are incorporated in this build schedule issue

HONEYCOMBE PRODUCTS LIMITED   LUTON   BEDFORDSHIRE

Figure 25.3   A build schedule sheet

A build schedule specifies the content and modification status of a manufactured product or project. It is particularly useful in defining the content of project hardware items that can co-exist in different versions. Definition is achieved by listing all drawings and associated documents, together with the revision numbers that apply to the unit.

I remember one large project for a copper mining company that was suspended late in its engineering design phase because of a fall in the price of copper. Closing and archiving the project took many months. Although the actual costs of recording the as-built condition of this project were recovered from the customer on a cost-plus basis, the contractor incurred considerable subsequent cost and space problems in storing the vast quantities of drawings and other engineering data. That project was never restarted.

Project interruptions usually prove very expensive for the contractor. Even if all the sunk costs are recovered from the customer, it is not easy to estimate the considerable costs of 'mothballing' the project against the day when it might be restarted. Questions might arise about where responsibility lies for storage of partially completed drawings and hardware. Some very difficult contractual negotiations might be needed before a solution is found that is fair to both parties.

Managing files and archives

The amount of work needed at the end of a project to close down all the files and store the information safely will be indirectly proportional to the care and attention given to files during the active life of the project.

Storage

It is very easy to build up substantial numbers of files in a very short space of time. These can occupy large areas of expensive office floor. I used to assert that no company could hope to have an infinite life, because as time tends to infinity the company will choke to death on its own files. In recent years, various technologies have helped to overcome this problem, first through the use of microfilm and, later, through digital storage on a range of media. It seems, however, that paper will never be absent from the office.

If bulky documents are a problem, the following options can be considered:

1   Hire off-site space for the storage of non-active files, possibly in a secure repository managed by one of the specialist archive companies – this method has the drawback that the files can easily be forgotten, the only reminder of their existence being the regular invoices for space rental.

2   Label each file prominently with a review date, at which time the file must be considered for microfilming or scanning before being destroyed.

3   Invest in space-saving filing equipment – lateral filing cabinets use less space than drawer-type filing cabinets. Motorized rotary files can be purchased which extend upwards into ceiling voids.

If any method other than hard copy is used (which really means either microfilm or digital storage), adequate safeguards need to be taken to ensure compatibility with existing and future equipment

Indexing and retrieval

Finding any document in a large file repository, regardless of the storage medium used, demands that all records are carefully indexed. It should be possible, for instance, to be able to search for an individual letter from a client either by reference to its subject, or by its date, or by both of these. If the storage medium is digital, searching to retrieve information should be easier using keywords.

Security

Records are usually at risk from fire, flood or loss, and it is always good sense to consider maintaining a security copy (on the basis that tragedy is unlikely to strike in two places simultaneously). However, if there should be a fire which consumes the original files, the backup copy will be of less practical use without an index of its contents. An up-to-date copy of the index for the main files must therefore form part of the security files.

The security of computer files is obviously important, but this is a subject that should be familiar to any competent person responsible for computing activities in a company. This person will ensure that regular backup copies are made and held offline in data safes or other secure areas.

Information held in computer files must be remembered at project closure time. Unwanted files should be erased. Whilst a few unwanted items left on floppy disks may not present a problem, a forgotten set of project management files held on a hard disk (possibly including a large network analysis exercise, drawing schedules and purchase schedules) is a needless waste of storage space. Any such files that are not required as part of an online database should be erased or transferred to some more suitable offline storage as part of the project closure procedure.

References and further reading for Part VI

Bentley, T. (1976), *Information, Communication and the Paperwork Explosion*, Maidenhead, McGraw-Hill

Burke, Rory (1999), *Project Management: Planning and Control*, 3rd edn, Chichester, Wiley

Chapman, C.B. and Ward, S.A. (1997), *Project Risk Management: Processes, Techniques and Insights*, Chichester, Wiley

Chapman, C.B. and Ward, S.A. (2002), *Managing Project Risk and Uncertainty*, Chichester, Wiley

Chicken, J.C. (1998), *The Philosophy of Risk*, London, Thomas Telford

Dorfman, M.S. (2001), *Introduction to Risk Management and Insurance,* Hemel Hempstead, Prentice-Hall

Duffy, P. (1993), *Kluwer Handbook of Insurance,* 4th edn, Kingston-upon-Thames, Kluwer (loose-leaf)

Freeman, P.K. (1997), *Managing Environmental Risk Through Insurance,* Kingston-upon-Thames, Kluwer

Grey, S. (1995), *Practical Risk Assessments for Project Management,* Chichester, Wiley

Hodgin, R.W. (1996), *Professional Liability: Law and Insurance*, London, Lloyd's Commercial Law Library

Institution of Civil Engineers and the Institute of Actuaries (1998), *Risk Analysis and Management for Projects,* London, Thomas Telford

Jeynes, J. (2001), *Risk Management: 10 Principles,* Oxford, Butterworth-Heinemann

Kliem, R.L. and Ludin, I.S. (1997), *Reducing Project Risk*, Aldershot, Gower

Raftery, J. (1993), *Risk Analysis in Project Management*, London, Spon

Regester, M. and Larkin, J. (2001), *Risk Issues and Crisis Management*, London, Kogan Page

RICS (1995), *Introductory Guidance to Insurance under Building Contracts,* Coventry, RICS Books

Ridley, J. (1999), *Risk Management for Occupational Health and Safety,* Oxford, Butterworth-Heinemann

Simon, P. et al. (Eds) (1997), *Project Risk Analysis and Management Guide: PRAM,* High Wycombe, Association for Project Management

Vaughan, E.J. and Vaughan, T.M. (2002), *Fundamentals of Risk and Insurance,* Chichester, Wiley

A general project management bibliography

Andersen, E.S., Grude, K.V. and Haug. T. (1998), *Goal Directed Project Management: Effective Techniques and Strategies*, 2nd edn, London, Kogan Page

Backhouse, C.J. and Brookes, N.J. (Eds) (1996), *Concurrent Engineering*, Aldershot, Gower (in association with The Design Council)

Baguley, P. (1999), *Project Management*, London, Teach Yourself Books

Bartlett. J. (2000), *Managing Programmes of Business Change*, 3rd edn, Hook, Hampshire, Project Manager Today

Burke, R. (1999), *Project Management: Planning and Control*, 3rd edn, Chichester, Wiley

Chapman, C.B., Cooper, D.F. and Page, M.J. (1987), *Management for Engineers*, Chichester, Wiley

Churchouse, C. (1999), *Managing Projects: A Gower Workbook*, Aldershot, Gower

Cleland, D.I. (Ed) (1998), *Field Guide to Project Management*, New York, Van Nostrand Reinhold

Cleland, D.I. and King, W.R. (1998) *Project Management Handbook*, New York, Van Nostrand Reinhold

Devaux, S.A. (1999), *Total Project Control: A Manager's Guide to Integrated Planning, Measuring and Tracking*, New York, Wiley

Frigenti, E. and Comninos, D. (2002), *The Practice of Project Management: A Guide to the Business-focused Approach*, London, Kogan Page

Gray, F.G. and Larson, E.W. (2002), *Project Management: the Managerial Process*, 2nd edn, Singapore, McGraw-Hill

Hamilton, A. (1997), *Management by Projects*, London, Thomas Telford

Harrison, F.L. (1992), *Advanced Project Management: A Structured Approach*, 3rd edn, Aldershot, Gower

Hartman, F.T. (2000), *Don't Park Your Brain Outside*, Pennsylvania, Project Management Institute

Healey, P.L. (1997), *Project Management: Getting the Job Done on Time and in Budget*, Oxford, Butterworth-Heinemann

Holroyd, T. (1999), *Site Management for Engineers*, London, Thomas Telford

Kerzner, H. (2000), *Applied Project Management: Best Practices on Implementation*, New York, Wiley

Kerzner, H. (2001), *Project Management: A Systems Approach to Planning, Scheduling and Controlling*, 7th edn, New York, Wiley

Kliem, R.L. and Ludin, I.S. (1992), *The People Side of Project Management*, Gower, Aldershot

Kor, R. and Wijnen, G. (2000), *50 Checklists for Project and Programme Managers*, Aldershot, Gower

Lester, A. (1991), *Project Planning and Control*, 2nd edn, Oxford, Butterworth-Heinemann

Lewis, J.P. (2001), *Project Planning and Scheduling and Control: A Hands-on Guide to Bringing Projects in on Time and on Budget*, New York, McGraw-Hill

Lock, D. (Ed.) (1993), *Handbook of Engineering Management*, 2nd edn, Oxford, Butterworth-Heinemann

Lockyer, K.G. and Gordon, J. (1996), *Critical Path Analysis and Other Project Management Techniques*, 6th edn, London, Pitman

Loftus, J. (Ed.) (1999), *Project Management of Multiple Projects and Contracts*, London, Thomas Telford

Mantel, S.J., Meredith, J.R., Shafer, S.M. and Sutton, M.M. (2001), *Project Management in Practice*, New York, Wiley

Maylor, H. (2002), *Project Management*, 3rd edn, London, Financial Times/Pitman

Meredith, J.R. and Mantel, S.J. Jnr (2003), *Project Management: A Managerial Approach*, 5th edn, New York, Wiley

O'Neill, J.J. (1989), *Management of Industrial Construction Projects*, Oxford, Heinemann Newnes

Randolph, W.A. (1991), *Getting the Job Done: Managing Project Teams and Task Forces for Success*, Hemel Hempstead, Prentice-Hall

Reiss, G. (1995), *Project Management Demystified: Today's Tools and Techniques*, 2nd edn, London, Spon

Reiss, G. (1996), *Programme Management Demystified: Managing Multiple Projects Successfully*, London, Spon

Rosenau, M.D. Jr (1998), *Successful Project Management*, 3rd edn, New York, Wiley

Shtub, A. and Bard, J.F. (1994), *Project Management: Engineering, Technology and Implementation*, Englewood Cliffs, Prentice-Hall

Simon, P. et al. (Eds) (1997), *Project Risk Analysis and Management Guide: PRAM*, High Wycombe, APM Group

Stevens, M. (Ed.) (2002), *Project Management Pathways*, High Wycombe, Association for Project Management

Teale, D. (2001), *Project Risk Assessment*, London, Hodder & Stoughton

Turner, J.R. (1998) *Handbook of Project-based Management: Improving the Process for Achieving Strategic Objectives*, 2nd edn, Maidenhead, McGraw-Hill

Turner, J.R. and Simister, S.J. (2000), *Gower Handbook of Project Management*, 3rd edn, Aldershot, Gower

Watson, M. (1998), *Managing Smaller Projects*, Hook (Hampshire), Project Manager Today

Wearne, S.H. (1989), *Control of Engineering Projects*, London, Thomas Telford

Webb, A. (2000), *Project Management for Successful Product Innovation*, Aldershot, Gower

Webster, G. (1999), *Managing Projects at Work*, Aldershot, Gower

Woodward, J.F. (1997), *Construction Project Management: Getting it Right First Time*, London, Thomas Telford

Index